Bedford Cultural Editions

CHARLES W. CHESNUTT
The Marrow of Tradition

EDITED BY

Nancy Bentley
University of Pennsylvania

AND

Sandra Gunning
University of Michigan

D0038353

BEDFORD/ST. MARTIN'S   BOSTON ♦ NEW YORK

For Bedford/St. Martin's

Developmental Editors: Katherine A. Retan, Joanne Diaz
Editorial Assistant: Emily Goodall
Editorial Assistant, Publishing Services: Maria Teresa Burwell
Production Supervisor: Tina Cameron
Marketing Manager: Richard Cadman
Project Management: Stratford Publishing Services, Inc.
Cover Design: Claire Jarvis
Cover Art: Race Riots in Wilmington, North Carolina, 1898. © Bettman/Corbis.
Composition: Stratford Publishing Services, Inc.
Printing and Binding: Haddon Craftsmen, an RR Donnelley & Sons Company

President: Charles H. Christensen
Editorial Director: Joan E. Feinberg
Editor in Chief: Karen S. Henry
Director of Marketing: Karen R. Melton
Director of Editing, Design, and Production: Marcia Cohen
Manager, Publishing Services: Emily Berleth

Library of Congress Control Number: 2001094352

12   11   10
f

For information, write: Bedford/St. Martin's, 75 Arlington Street,
Boston, MA 02116   (617-399-4000)

ISBN-10: 0-312-19406-4 (paperback)
       0-312-29434-4 (hardcover)
ISBN-13: 978-0-312-19406-2 (paperback)
       978-0-312-29434-2 (hardcover)

About the Series

The need to "historicize" literary texts — and even more to analyze the historical and cultural issues all texts embody — is now embraced by almost all teachers, scholars, critics, and theoreticians. But the question of how to teach such issues in the undergraduate classroom is still a difficult one. Teachers do not always have the historical information they need for a given text, and contextual documents and sources are not always readily available in the library — even if the teacher has the expertise (and students have the energy) to ferret them out. The Bedford Cultural Editions represent an effort to make available for the classroom the kinds of facts and documents that will enable teachers to use the latest historical approaches to textual analysis and cultural criticism. The best scholarly and theoretical work has for many years gone well beyond the "new critical" practices of formalist analysis and close reading, and we offer here a practical classroom model of the ways that many different kinds of issues can be engaged when texts are not thought of as islands unto themselves.

The impetus for the recent cultural and historical emphasis has come from many directions: the so-called new historicism of the late 1980s, the dominant historical versions of both feminism and Marxism, the cultural studies movement, and a sharply changed focus in older movements such as reader response, structuralism, deconstruction, and psychoanalytic theory. Emphases differ, of course, among schools and individuals, but what these movements and approaches have in common is a commitment to explore — and to have students in the classroom study interactively — texts in their full historical and cultural dimensions. The aim is to discover how older texts (and those from other traditions) differ from our own assumptions and expectations, and thus the focus in teaching falls on cultural and historical difference rather than on similarity or continuity.

The most striking feature of the Bedford Cultural Editions — and the one most likely to promote creative classroom discussion — is the inclusion of a generous selection of historical documents that contextualize the main text in a variety of ways. Each volume contains works (or passages from works) that are contemporary with the main text: legal and social documents, journalistic and autobiographical accounts, histories, sections from conduct books, travel books, poems, novels, and other historical sources. These materials have several uses. Often they provide information beyond what the main text offers. They provide, too, different perspectives on a particular theme, issue, or event central to the text, suggesting the range of opinions contemporary readers would have brought to their reading and allowing students to experience for themselves the details of cultural disagreement and debate. The documents are organized in thematic units — each with an introduction by the volume editor that historicizes a particular issue and suggests the ways in which individual selections work to contextualize the main text.

Each volume also contains a general introduction that provides students with information concerning the political, social, and intellectual context for the work as well as information concerning the material aspects of the text's creation, production, and distribution. There are also relevant illustrations, a chronology of important events, and, when helpful, an account of the reception history of the text. Finally, both the main work and its accompanying documents are carefully annotated in order to enable students to grasp the significance of historical references, literary allusions, and unfamiliar terms. Everywhere we have tried to keep the special needs of the modern student — especially the culturally conscious student of the turn of the millennium — in mind.

For each title, the volume editor has chosen the best teaching text of the main work and explained his or her choice. Old spellings and capitalizations have been preserved (except that the long "s" has been regularized to the modern "s") — the overwhelming preference of the two hundred teacher-scholars we surveyed in preparing the series. Original habits of punctuation have also been kept, except for occasional places where the unusual usage would obscure the syntax for modern readers. Whenever possible, the supplementary texts and documents are reprinted from the first edition or the one most relevant to the issue at hand. We have thus meant to preserve — rather than counter — for modern students the sense of "strangeness" in older texts, expecting that the oddness will help students to see where older texts are *not* like modern ones, and expecting too that today's historically informed teachers will find their own creative ways to make something of such historical and cultural differences.

In developing this series, our goal has been to foreground the kinds of issues that typically engage teachers and students of literature and history now. We have not tried to move readers toward a particular ideological, political, or social position or to be exhaustive in our choice of contextual materials. Rather, our aim has been to be provocative — to enable teachers and students of literature to raise the most pressing political, economic, social, religious, intellectual, and artistic issues on a larger field than any single text can offer.

J. Paul Hunter, University of Chicago
William E. Cain, Wellesley College
Series Editors

About This Volume

With remarkable swiftness, Charles W. Chesnutt has become a major figure in American literary history. A recent survey of the scholarship on U.S. literature noted that a decade ago this African American novelist had rated only one reference in that year's annual overview of scholarly criticism (Oggel 259–60). In 1999, however, Chesnutt followed only Mark Twain and Henry James as the writer receiving the most critical study for the literature of the late nineteenth-century period. *The Marrow of Tradition*, Chesnutt's most important novel, has reached an increasingly large audience in recent years. Yet most readers take up the book knowing nothing about the 1898 race riot on which the novel is based. They tend to know little more about the white supremacy movement that fueled the riot. A chief aim of this edition, then, is to help readers learn about the historical and cultural context of the violence that occurred in Wilmington, North Carolina, two days after the November 1898 election.

To appreciate the important relations between *The Marrow of Tradition* and its historical moment, however, it is not enough merely to learn about relevant events and politics. The substantiated facts of what happened in Wilmington matter, of course. But just as history helps us understand the novel, Chesnutt's novel is likewise a sophisticated lens for understanding the facts of this difficult history. The resources available to Chesnutt as a novelist — narrative conventions for analyzing complexities of feeling and motive, the fiction writer's license to pose connections between what might appear unrelated events — these features allow Chesnutt to make a powerful literary study of post-Reconstruction history. When Chesnutt invents a white criminal who disguises himself as a minstrel-like performer in blackface, for instance, he prompts his readers to ask provocative questions of the events in Wilmington. Were the crimes against black people in Wilmington made possible by a manipulation of stereotypes? Does the southern history of racial violence have anything to do with race-based popular entertainment? Similarly, when Chesnutt's novel addresses the southern epidemic of lynching in this era, his story directs our attention in purposeful ways. What could it mean that Chesnutt holds back from narrating for us the act of lynching itself while underscoring the behavior of the white people who charter special railway cars and erect bleachers at the site of a lynching? Directing readers to ask questions of southern history, *The Marrow of Tradition* is not only a landmark literary achievement but also a kind of historical tutor that insists on a critical examination of events and materials through literary means.

The historical materials in this edition are intended to help readers understand the debates, practices, and political events that formed the context for *The Marrow of Tradition*. The documents are simultaneously meant to encourage readers to follow Chesnutt's lead in using literary tools for the task of interpreting history. We include part of the landmark *Plessy v. Ferguson* case, for instance, not only because it institutionalized racial segregation but also because Chesnutt (who was trained in the law) offers in Chapter 5 of *Marrow* a brilliant analysis of the lived implications of the Plessy case and its legal language.

There are four groupings of documents in this edition. The first set presents a number of influential or telling writings on race and its relevance to matters of class and gender. The second offers important documents illuminating the troubled relationship between law and lawlessness in the post-Reconstruction era. A third group pertains to the Wilmington riot itself as an event that crystallized the racial and legal conflicts set forth in the previous two sections. Finally, a fourth section offers a number of wide-ranging artifacts, from photographs to an excerpt of a World's Fair program, selected to focus on the cultural practices that made segregation not just a regime of law but a pervasive way of life.

ACKNOWLEDGMENTS

We are grateful for the assistance we have received from many colleagues, friends, and institutions. Our thanks to Kathy Retan at Bedford/St. Martin's for proposing the project and supplying incisive suggestions. Her consistent support kept the work going forward. Joanne Diaz at Bedford/St. Martin's offered expert guidance in the last stages of writing when her patience and alacrity were much needed and even more appreciated. Emily Berleth expertly guided the book through production, and Emily Goodall assisted with numerous details.

We are also pleased to thank the referees who gave cogent advice and welcome encouragement at a number of junctures. Our gratitude goes to Stephen Best, Dana Nelson, Donald Gibson, Robert S. Levine, and Richard Yarborough. We owe a special debt to the additional friends and colleagues who shared wisdom of all kinds during the several years that we worked on the project. We wish to thank Frances Foster, Elaine Freedgood, Jonathan Freedman, John González, Nellie McKay, Michele Mitchell, Chris Looby, Stephanie Smith, and Julie Vandivere.

Our research assistants made an invaluable contribution to the creation of this book. Jeff Allred, Valarie Moses, and Martha Schoolman demonstrated their savvy and impressive judgment as scholarly sleuths. Cyrus Mulready deserves special thanks for his help with writing the headnotes in Chapters 3 and 4. The volume could not have been completed without the help of librarians at several institutions. We wish to thank Beth Howse at Fisk University Library, Elizabeth Dunn at the Special Collections Library of Duke University, and Mary Ellen Brooks at the Hargrett Library of the University of Georgia. Fred Romanski at the National Archives was extraordinarily helpful in securing an elusive document. We are also grateful to the librarians and expert staff at the University of North Carolina, the University of Pennsylvania, Emory University, the University of Michigan, Ann Arbor, and the Library of Congress. James Allen very graciously gave us permission to use several photographs for the volume.

Keith L. T. Alexander earns special thanks for his unfailing support. Karl Ulrich along with James Bentley Ulrich and Nathan Bentley Ulrich helped in countless ways and deserve special gratitude as well.

Nancy Bentley
University of Pennsylvania
Sandra Gunning
University of Michigan

About the Text

This volume reprints the text of *The Marrow of Tradition* published in 1901 by Houghton, Mifflin and Company, the novel's original publishing house. Readers should be aware that this reprinted text preserves most of the peculiarities in spelling and punctuation in the original edition, though a few punctuation conventions have been modernized.

For the documents in Part Two we have used the original edition of the text whenever possible. We have retained the archaic spellings, idioms, and punctuation conventions in most cases, though our annotations offer explanations for many words, phrases, and allusions that may be unfamiliar.

Contents

Illustrations

Part One

The Marrow of Tradition
The Complete Text

Introduction:
Cultural and
Historical Background

If I do write, I shall write for a purpose, a high, holy purpose, and this will inspire me to greater effort. The object of my writings would be not so much the elevation of the colored people as the elevation of the whites, — for I consider the unjust spirit of caste which is so insidious as to pervade a whole nation, and so powerful as to subject a whole race and all connected with it to scorn and social ostracism — I consider this to be the barrier to the moral progress of the American people.

> — Charles W. Chesnutt, May 29, 1880

Every time I read a good novel, I want to write one. It is the dream of my life — to be an author!

> — Charles W. Chesnutt, March 26, 1881

Though only a twenty-three-year-old African American school principal in Fayetteville, North Carolina, when he made these journal entries, Charles Waddell Chesnutt was indeed destined to claim for himself the title of "author." By 1905 he had published two short story collections, countless essays, three novels, and a biography of the great nineteenth-century civil rights activist, writer, and orator Frederick Douglass. At a time when many white Americans still believed that a black author was an oxymoron, Chesnutt would enter into an exclusively white literary world, associating with powerful publishers, editors, and writers such as Walter Hines Page, William Dean Howells, Albion W. Tourgée, George Washington Cable, and Mark Twain. As his early journal meditations demonstrate, Chesnutt understood keenly the relationship between ambition, artistic achievement, and social responsibility. This lifelong dedication to effecting social change through writing conditioned much of his literary efforts, and emerges most powerfully in what modern scholars now consider to be Chesnutt's best, most daring, and — for its time — most controversial novel, *The Marrow of Tradition.*

Published in 1901, *The Marrow of Tradition* is the fictionalized retelling of an infamous race riot that broke out in Wilmington, North Carolina, just after Election Day on November 10, 1898. In *Marrow* Chesnutt renamed the town Wellington, but in writing an exposé of white racism and political corruption, he suggests that Wellington was not just Wilmington, North Carolina, but indeed that it epitomized many racially divided American cities. The importance of the novel and the boldness of Chesnutt's views on the racial status quo of the South becomes clearer once we grasp the significance of the riot. On the morning of November 10, an armed white mob led by some of Wilmington's prominent citizens launched a premeditated, organized attack on the city's over 11,000 black residents. The riot was not some freak event; rather, it had deep roots in the politically fraught years after the Civil War, and widespread implications for the effectiveness of federal laws to protect the rights of African Americans.

For roughly a decade after the Civil War northern Republicans had worked to "reconstruct" the political life of the nation in order to accommodate newly freed slaves as citizens. By the 1890s, the North exhibited a growing apathy toward what many dubbed the "Negro Problem," and in many southern states, white supremacist Democratic politicians had a free reign in excluding blacks from the political process. Still, in the election of 1896 North Carolina's black Republicans had managed to forge a coalition with whites of the Populist Party, who had felt that their interests were not adequately represented under the Democrats. The result was a slate of "fusionist" candidates who were elected to state and congressional office, including the white Republican Daniel Russell as the state's governor, and George H. White as the nation's only black member of the U.S. House of Representatives. Alarmed at what seemed to be growing black political power in the state, white supremacists in Wilmington saw the upcoming elections for city council in November 1898 as crucial for determining which political faction — a Democratic, white supremacist contingent, or an interracial coalition of Republicans and Populists — would govern North Carolina's foremost city. Even after Democrats won the local seats that had been up for election (largely through fraud and voter intimidation), white supremacists acted to overthrow the remaining Republican office holders by staging a bloody riot.

This political power struggle was influenced by additional factors that were even more inflammatory. On August 18, 1898, Alexander Manly, the black editor of Wilmington's *Daily Record,* published an angry rebuttal to claims of white middle-class Georgia feminist Rebecca Latimer Felton, who had argued that black rapists were the scourge of the rural South. As Felton summarized: "if it takes lynching to protect woman's dearest possession from drunken, ravening human beasts — then I say lynch a thousand a week if it becomes necessary" (p. 411 in this volume). In response, Manly argued that "our experience among poor white people in the country teaches us that the women of that race are not any more particular in the matter of clandestine meetings with colored men than are the white men with colored women. Meetings of this kind go on for some time, until the woman's infatuation or the man's boldness bring attention to them and the man is lynched for rape" (pp. 407–08). As scholars such as Richard Yarborough have stressed, the uproar over Manly's editorial "encouraged white[s] . . . to link what they saw as black impudence, presumption, and disrespect, on the one hand, with an allegedly pervasive black male sexual threat, on the other" ("Violence, Manhood, and Black Heroism" 228). In this climate, white supremacists interpreted the political battle over Wilmington's city government as also a racial battle over who would dominate the social and moral life of the South. For weeks before the November 8, 1898, election, white supremacists staged rallies and demonstrations aimed at intimidating black voters, and white-owned papers such as Josephus Daniels' *Raleigh News and Observer* and Thomas Clawson's *Wilmington Messenger* published overtly racist editorials and cartoons. By the morning after the election, the hysteria over "black domination" had reached its peak when a committee of twenty-five white citizens leading an armed white mob of 2,000 marched on Manly's *Record* office.

Fortunately, Manly had already left Wilmington, but his offices were razed, and his printing press destroyed. According to historian H. Leon Prather Sr., a variety of conflicting accounts of the violence emerged from all sides: from horrified blacks who had lived through the event, from triumphant white rioters, and from both local and national newspapers and magazines. Some stories suggested that anywhere from nine to over one hundred African Americans were killed, while there were claims that the nearby "Cape Fear [river was] clotted with black bodies" (Prather 35). Fearing for their lives, hundreds of black Wilmington residents fled to the nearby woods during the riot, hiding for two days without food, proper clothes, or adequate shelter, in near freezing conditions. When they returned to the city, many found that their homes and businesses had been destroyed. Prior to the November massacre, Wilmington had had a black-majority population. But in the wake of the riot, so many African Americans moved or were forced out of town that Wilmington soon had a white majority.

The day after the riot, Chesnutt described himself to the white publisher Walter Hines Page as "deeply concerned and very much depressed at the condition of affairs in North Carolina." He called the riot "an outbreak of pure, malignant and altogether indefensible race prejudice, which makes me feel personally humiliated, and ashamed for the country and the state" (*"To Be an Author"* 116). The grandson of a white farmer and the child of free mulatto parents, Chesnutt had never experienced slavery, but according to his daughter Helen, he came to an early understanding of the violence underlying American racial division. As a young boy in Fayetteville, Chesnutt had come upon the dead body of a black man who moments before had been shot by a white man in full view of townspeople. According to Helen Chesnutt, the murder was for "the alleged 'nameless crime,'" (6) that is, rape. But as countless opponents of white racial violence argued, as the Wilmington Riot demonstrated, and as Chesnutt himself was to show in *The Marrow of Tradition*, the fear of black male sexuality was linked more often than not to white fears of blacks as a *political* force in the struggle for sectional rule. In fact, antiblack violence persisted from the 1870s to the so-called red summer of 1919 and beyond, with the rise of white supremacist organizations such as the Ku Klux Klan and the Knights of the White Camelia, and the outbreak of race riots in southern towns such as Colfax and Coushatta, Louisiana; in Vicksburg, Clinton, and Carrollton, Mississippi; Charleston, South Carolina; Atlanta, Georgia; and in major U.S. cities such as Washington, D.C., and Chicago. Also, by 1900 the lynching of black men for the alleged crime of rape was institutionalized as a particularly gruesome, extralegal means used by white supremacists to wage war on black communities.

In *The Marrow of Tradition*, Chesnutt re-created the impact of the Wilmington race riot by dramatizing its effect on a broadly inclusive, interracial cast of characters. His goal was to offer his readers, in the words of John Edgar Wideman, "a panoramic view of Southern society" at the start of the twentieth century, one that included "all classes, both races, and a variety of perspectives — social, economic and political" (64). True to his twofold vision of the responsibilities of the novelist, Chesnutt stressed in a 1901 Cleveland *World* article that though its "primary object" was "to entertain," *The Marrow of Tradition* resided squarely "in the category of purpose novels." Drawing not only on the 1898 Wilmington riot, but also a July 24, 1900, race riot in New Orleans, Chesnutt had deliberately written a novel "to throw light upon the vexed moral and sociological problems which grow out of the presence, in our southern states, of two diverse races, in nearly equal numbers" (169). Chesnutt knew that these "vexed moral and sociological problems" were at the root of antiblack violence, that their histories stretched back before the abolition of slavery, and that they inextricably linked ex-masters, ex-slaves, and their descendants. In *The Marrow of Tradition,* Chesnutt would not only have to tell an engaging story, but would also have to dramatize effectively for his readers the weight of history and established custom — that is, the very nature and origins of the tradition of race privilege "bred in the bone," as the novel's title implies. This tradition, according to Chesnutt in the *World* article, had "made the white people masters, rulers, who absorbed all the power, the wealth, the honors of the community, and jealously guarded this monopoly, with which they claimed to be divinely endowed, by denying to those who were not of their caste the opportunity to acquire any of these desirable things" (169). By creating characters whose past and present histories tied them directly to the social upheavals created by the end of the Civil War, Chesnutt offered his readers a complex analysis of the social and political pressures that had made such violence possible.

THE HOPE AND FAILURE OF RECONSTRUCTION

Though the plot of *The Marrow of Tradition* is set in the contemporary moment of Chesnutt's turn-of-the-century world, the inextricably linked worlds of black and white in the novel go back to the formative years of slavery and the period that officially came to be known as Reconstruction. Indeed, Chesnutt's early life encompasses this very period: to escape southern racism, Chesnutt's free black parents had moved from Fayetteville, North Carolina, to Cleveland, Ohio, in

1856, where their son Charles was born two years later. In 1866, a year after Confederate general Robert E. Lee surrendered to his Union counterpart Ulysses S. Grant at the Appomattox courthouse in Virginia, the Chesnutt family moved back to Fayetteville, where Charles was to spend the formative years of his life until he returned to Cleveland for good in 1884. Having spent his childhood in a southern state, Chesnutt was among the first generation of African Americans to witness firsthand the often tense negotiation between North and South (and between blacks and whites) of the enormous social, economic, and political transitions that came about with the demise of slavery. Certainly, there were several daunting challenges. What would be the status of the newly freed slaves — indeed of all blacks — now that slavery was abolished? How would southern communities built on chattel slavery make the economic and political transition to a slave-free society? Could the ex-slave and ex-master now suddenly stand on equal footing, when just a few years earlier the former was legally a nonperson and subject to any and all forms of physical abuse and exploitation under southern law? After the Republican president Abraham Lincoln was assassinated in 1865, these questions were passed on to Vice President Andrew Johnson and to a Republican-led Congress that was determined to make the newly defeated Confederate states pay for the devastation of the Civil War.

Lasting from 1867 to 1877, Reconstruction framed not just the regional struggle between the victorious North and the defeated South, but also a national struggle to reimagine the concept of a U.S. citizenship open to both races. Determined to build on the dramatic changes ushered in by emancipation, a Republican-dominated Congress ratified in quick succession three significant amendments to the U.S. Constitution: the Thirteenth Amendment (1865) abolishing slavery; the Fourteenth Amendment (1868) declaring "[a]ll persons born or naturalized in the United States" to be citizens, and therefore entitled to "life, liberty," and "property"; and the Fifteenth Amendment (1870), which guaranteed "[t]he right of [male] citizens of the United States to vote," without regard to "race, color, or previous condition of servitude" (pp. 338–40). Congress also passed a series of Civil Rights Acts between 1866 and 1870 in an effort to ensure the enforcement of the recently added constitutional amendments. And on March 3, 1865, the federal government also established the temporary Freedman's Bureau to regulate black-white relations under new, wage-labor agreements, to settle disputes, and to assist in the reunion of black families disrupted by slavery.

As Eric Foner and other historians have rightly stressed, in this period blacks were not merely "passive victims of the actions of others, or simply a 'problem' confronting white society." Rather, they were "active agents in the making of Reconstruction whose quest for individual and community autonomy did much to establish the era's political and economic agenda" (xv). Indeed, at every opportunity ex-slaves and freeborn blacks took advantage of their newfound political freedom. Spurred by Congress's initial barring of those whites who had fought against the Union during the war, and by conventions held throughout the former Confederate states to draft new, postslavery state constitutions, African American men entered politics at the state and national levels in greater numbers than were ever possible before. Working side by side with white Republicans, they rewrote laws to allow blacks to testify in court and to travel freely from town to town, established hospitals and agencies for the relief of the poor, and effected road and sanitary improvements. Education for the freedmen and their families was a special priority: thus school boards were organized, and free blacks north and south joined with white philanthropic organizations such as the American Missionary Association to provide schooling for ex-slaves and their children. Eventually, African Americans would work with white philanthropists to establish historically black colleges and universities such as: Fisk University in Nashville, Tennessee (1866); Howard University in Washington, D.C. (1867); the Hampton Institute in Virginia (1868); and Alabama's Tuskegee Institute (1881). A student of the postslavery Howard School (named after the Union General O. O. Howard, the founder of Howard University), and then later the young principal of the State Colored Normal School, Chesnutt was shaped by this imperative toward African American education, and in *The Marrow of Tradition* he has the mulatto Dr. Miller establish a nursing school in turn-of-the-century Wellington.

Though much was attempted, the reforms of Reconstruction were doomed from the start. For one thing, among white Republicans and northern abolitionists, supporting the eradication of slavery rarely meant acknowledging the racial equality of blacks. Southern-born Republican president Andrew Johnson was typical of a growing faction in his party: while Johnson had supported the eradication of slavery, "freedmen had no role in his vision of a reconstructed South" (Foner 84). Unlike radical Republicans, Johnson did not support black enfranchisement; instead, he sought to achieve a *rapprochement* with the white South by limiting black opportunities whenever possible, while on the other hand supporting former slaveholders in their struggles to thwart the changes wrought by emancipation. The president was soon outmaneuvered by the radical Republicans: by 1867 they had almost achieved his impeachment, passed the Reconstruction Act over his veto, and instituted military rule over the former Confederate states. However, the battle of wills between the president and members of his own party mirrored the growing split in white American popular opinion about whether blacks were in fact equal to whites, and whether they were fit to exercise the franchise. Even among those white Americans who opted for "a New South" (as did the *Atlanta Constitution* editor Henry Grady, who helped popularize the phrase), the goal increasingly became the maintenance of white supremacy in all aspects of political, social, and economic life.

Not surprisingly, the enforcement of the Thirteenth, Fourteenth, and Fifteenth Amendments grew more difficult, as Southerners argued successfully for privileging a state government's right to interpret the law. Blacks who were involved in pro-Republican union leagues or who exercised their right to vote or run for public office now found that newly won social and political gains were slowly diminishing. For instance, through the system of sharecropping, ex-masters attempted to enforce labor contracts on black wage workers that restricted their freedom of movement and hampered their ability to receive fair compensation for work performed. Also, by the 1870s black conduct was regulated by any number of criminal codes that allowed stiff jail terms for minor infractions. In areas where white supremacy reigned, blacks failed consistently to obtain fair court trials or to win lawsuits against the perpetrators of white-on-black terrorism. Imprisoned at a much higher rate than whites, many blacks were virtually reenslaved by a method of contract labor that involved leasing prisoners out to local businesses. For those African Americans not formally incarcerated, daily life was quickly regulated with the institution of racial segregation on trains, on streetcars, in theaters, and in restaurants.

The inglorious end of Reconstruction finally came in 1877 as a result of the close presidential election between the Republican candidate Rutherford B. Hayes and his Democratic counterpart Samuel Tilden, when the party that had freed the slaves officially turned its back on the freedmen. In a negotiated compromise with the Democratic party, white Republicans gained the presidency for Hayes in exchange for the withdrawal of federal troops posted at the South Carolina and Louisiana state houses. Republicans also gave the general assurance that southern states would be allowed to conduct their

Anti-Reconstruction political cartoon (1871) by A. Zenneck. Courtesy of the Library of Congress.

affairs without interference from the federal government. With Washington essentially turning a blind eye to race relations in the New South, white supremacists were now free to use both violence and chicanery to disempower ex-slaves and their descendants.

LYNCHING, RAPE, AND THE CONCEPTION OF RACE IN AN (INTER)NATIONAL CONTEXT

Even at the height of radical Republican support for Reconstruction, there had been violent clashes between blacks and their white allies on the one hand, and those southern whites who sought to resist the enfranchisement of African Americans on the other. Indeed, many a "carpetbagger" (as white southerners dismissively called the white northerners who moved South after the Civil War) lost his life at the hands of white supremacist vigilante groups. By 1867, the Ku Klux Klan had been inaugurated, establishing the most infamous white supremacist group in American history. Though in five years federal authorities were able to suppress the Klan, they were unable to eradicate white mob violence in general. Indeed, white racial aggression remained such an ever-present problem throughout the late nineteenth and early twentieth centuries that by the 1920s the Klan reemerged, this time with an even wider membership.

Within this context of mob rule and vigilantism, by the end of the nineteenth century white supremacists had "modernized and perfected [antiblack] violence" to produce what historian Grace Elizabeth Hale has termed "the spectator lynching" (203). Lynching had always been a problem from the first days of Reconstruction, but Hale dates "the founding event in the history of spectacle lynching of a southern black by a large crowd of southern whites" to the 1893 lynching of Henry Smith in Paris, Texas (207). Accused of raping and murdering three-year-old Myrtle Vance, Smith was hunted down by a posse of some 2,000 white men, tied to a chair, and paraded through the streets of Paris before cheering white onlookers. Some 10,000 white men, women, and children arrived on specially chartered trains to witness an elaborate execution ritual, where Smith was transported to a high platform, tortured with red-hot irons, and then burned alive. According to some reports, while photographers took pictures from one vantage point, from another lynchers set up a gramophone to record "the whole proceeding — including the cries of the victim" (Williamson 186). Reportedly, after Smith's death members of the crowd scrambled to collect pieces of the charred body to serve as souvenirs. In the years following Smith's execution, there were other lynchings that were just as brutal: the murder of Sam Hose in Newnan, Georgia (1899); of nineteen-year-old Jesse Washington in Waco, Texas (1916); and of Claude Neale in Marianna, Florida (1934).

White supremacists justified these acts by claiming that only extraordinary measures could combat the black barbarity (namely the allegedly widespread rape of white women) unleashed after slavery. Yet in almost all cases, not only were the lynching victims never convicted of the accused crime, but the constant cry of black rape obscured the fact that many lynching victims were also black women and children. (Ironically, many rape victims in the South were black women who had been attacked by white men.) Still, the promotion of the "black rapist" by white supremacist propaganda was so effective that, as conservative black leader and educator Booker T. Washington

Lynch mob for Myrtle Vance murder, Paris, Texas, 1893. Courtesy of the Library of Congress.

would experience firsthand, the white public nationwide accepted the myth that every black man was potentially a racial threat. Visiting New York in 1911 and in poor health at the time, Washington was simply standing in the foyer of a white-occupied apartment building when he was attacked by a white man who accused him of burglary. Later, white women on the scene claimed that Washington had made sexual advances toward them (Harlan 379–82). All charges were dropped when Washington was finally able to convince police of his identity, but the episode demonstrates the threatening atmosphere in which all African Americans lived in the period, regardless of their geographical location or their station in life.

African American women as well as men saw it as their duty to challenge white public misperceptions about racial violence. Indeed, black women activists and journalists such as Mary Church Terrell and Ida B. Wells launched broad investigations of lynching, demonstrating that rape was rarely a factor behind white retaliation: as Terrell argued, "everybody . . . knows that many a negro who has been accused of assault or murder, or other violation of the law, and has been tortured to death by a mob, has afterward been proven innocent of the crime with which he was charged" (858). The work of Terrell and Wells also proved that there were countless underreported incidents where black women and children were murdered by lynch mobs, proving that there was no direct link between racial violence and alleged black rape.

In the face of such evidence, and despite the very real dangers faced by African Americans, some leaders such as Booker T. Washington urged blacks to take the proverbial high road and meet white aggression with good will and hard work. Washington's strategy was to show the white South it had nothing to fear, that it would benefit from valuing and protecting black labor (see pp. 277–78). However, other African Americans such as Ida B. Wells demanded a more militant stance, urging blacks to fight fire with fire. In an 1889, speech journalist John Edward Bruce told his fellow blacks that "if they [whites] burn your houses, burn theirs. If they kill your wives and children, kill theirs. Pursue them relentlessly. Meet force with force, everywhere it is offered. . . . By a vigorous adherence to this course, the shedding of human blood by white men will soon become a thing of the past" ("The Application of Force" 32). Others, such as AME Bishop Henry McNeal Turner and New Orleans resident Robert Charles, advocated black repatriation to Africa. (Though he was an agent for a repatriation organization, Charles himself would lose his life to a white mob in the July 24, 1900, race riot that, along with the Wilmington massacre, served as an inspiration for Chesnutt's *Marrow*.) The protest against white violence went on uninterrupted into the twentieth century when the National Association for the Advancement of Colored People (NAACP), founded in 1909 and working under the impetus of black and white figures such as W. E. B. Du Bois, Walter White, and Mary White Ovington, launched full-scale investigations of lynching and lobbied Congress repeatedly to pass antilynching bills.

It is hard to say whether such activism actually reduced violence against African Americans. However, it is clear that blacks were not content to simply suffer in silence, and their rigorous and often militant protests did much to challenge the white supremacist hold on the American public's imagination. At a time when no American women possessed the right to vote, antilynching activism also allowed black women a unique national arena for public participation. Like black men, their lives and the lives of their children were at stake in the issue of lynching, and black women could logically claim that their participation in all political, economic, and social spheres was proper for reasons of self-defense.

The Marrow of Tradition dramatizes the hallmark strategy of American white supremacy during and after Reconstruction, namely the rhetorical collapse of black political power with black male sexuality. But Chesnutt makes clear that the problem of racial antagonism was not simply the squaring off of homogeneous white and black populations one against the other. For Chesnutt, readers needed to understand the complex heterogeneity that characterized both black and white communities, a heterogeneity that shaped and textured each community's response to white supremacist violence. As with *The Marrow of Tradition,* the world inhabited by black characters in African American novels such as Frances Ellen Watkins Harper's *Iola Leroy: Or, Shadows Uplifted* (1892), Pauline E. Hopkins's *Contending Forces: A Romance Illustrative of Negro Life North and South* (1900), Paul Laurence Dunbar's *The Sport of the Gods* (1903), and James Weldon Johnson's *The Autobiography of an Ex-Colored Man* (1912) was inspired by real life. Like the characters in these novels, real African Americans generally worked together for the benefit of racial progress, but the role of class, skin color, educational level, and place of birth (that is, rural or urban, North or South) structured all community interactions. Gender division, too, had a particular impact. As historian Elsa Barkeley Brown has shown in her research on gender and race in postemancipation Richmond, Virginia, though they did not have the vote, African American women wielded a great deal of influence over their men at the voting booth during Reconstruction. According to Brown, however, black women's influence over the political leanings of black men was challenged over time, as black men sought to create for themselves an image of virtuous masculinity that had as its foil the opposing vision of genteel, domesticated (and therefore nonpoliticized) black womanhood. But at no point did African American women ever relinquish their role as agents of social and political change. Indeed self-help organizations such as the National Association of Colored Women (NACW) organized groups of black women at both the local and national levels to combat racial prejudice, promote educational and employment opportunities, provide relief for the sick and the poor, and maintain a vibrant black cultural life despite the reality of white racial aggression.

For Americans in general, issues of class and gender have always been intricately intertwined, and this was certainly true for blacks at the turn of the century. As historian Willard B. Gatewood explains, "black class structure resembled a pyramid with the overwhelming majority belonging to the lower class at the bottom, and a tiny majority constituting the 'aristocracy' at the top," while "[b]etween the two was an emerging middle class, relatively small in size, but steadily growing" (26). These class divisions were felt throughout all black communities and organizations. For instance, the NACW's motto "Lifting as We Climb" suggested not only that the progress of black women was synonymous with the progress of all African Americans, but also that the greater one's achievements and social standing, the more urgent one's duty was to race and community. Not surprisingly, this uplift ideology fostered the idea among many African Americans that black racial progress was automatically tied to the notion of black class progress. However, as *The Marrow of Tradition* demonstrates, the inevitable gap between those few blacks who were able to achieve economic stability and the much larger number who were trapped in the working class meant that the strategy of class "uplift" was a vexed and sometimes divisive goal for the African American population as a whole.

Many blacks were also keenly aware of how the politics of skin color could spark a great deal of internal community tension around this topic of "racial progress." Exasperated by intraracial squabbling about color, black journalist John Edward Bruce railed against "[m]ulattoes . . . who are obsessed with the idea that their fair complexions, straight hair and patrician blood necessarily make them superior to black people" ("Color Prejudice Among Negroes" 128). Some modern readers have suggested that Chesnutt (who was himself light enough to pass for white) was guilty of this charge. Certainly Chesnutt's light-skinned characters in *Marrow* are central to the novel's plot and, by the end of the story, to the future of the nation. Also, in a series of articles published in the *Boston Evening Transcript* in 1900, he argued for the superiority of mulattoes as the group that would dominate American life into the twentieth century (see Part Two, Chapter 1). Chesnutt's use of the mulatto figure needs to be examined carefully. Did he employ the mulatto in his writing as a rhetorical device, as a metaphor to dramatize the unreality of the color line? Did he in fact believe that mulattoes were uniquely equipped as race leaders? Why were mulattoes assumed to be the blacks most likely to attain financial and professional success? However one chooses to answer these questions, it is clear that Chesnutt's analysis of the racial antagonism dividing the United States at the turn of the century was deeply entangled in the debates and prejudices of that antagonism.

As was the case with blacks, American whites' understanding of race emerged in conjunction with other realities of social difference. For instance, the well-meaning but misguided white antilynching commentators Ray Stannard Baker (see Part Two, Chapter 2) and Andrew Sledd argued that the brutality exercised by a white mob could only mean that rioters were from the working classes. But as Chesnutt's *The Marrow of Tradition* dramatizes, lynching was a group event implicating white men (and women) of all social standings. As the public declaration issued by the Wilmington rioters makes clear, the mob that had terrorized black neighborhoods that day included wealthy and prominent middle-class men. Moreover, many historians believe that it was the accumulation of property and civic influence by Wilmington's African Americans that sparked the greatest anger in the white rioters. A good many black residents saw it that way as well. However, no matter the evidence before them, or their own commitment to social reform, Sledd and Baker were middle-class urbanites who could not escape their distrust of the white working classes: indeed, given the expanding gulf between rich and poor, and the rise in working class agitation through union activity, socialism, and the Populist party in the 1890s, whites as a group were more divided than ever before along economic lines.

White Americans' conception of their identity was also shaped by their understanding of ethnicity and gender roles. There was a clear sense for instance that being an Irish or an Italian immigrant did not automatically mean that one was "white." Indeed, in the 1880s and 1890s, anxiety over miscegenation ran parallel with the anxiety of "native born" white Americans over the question posed by many eugenicists: were long-established white communities reproducing fast enough to match the birth rate of either African Americans or newly arrived European immigrants? Indeed, many white American academics and public figures feared that the "original" U.S. white population would eventually die off from lack of reproductive vigor, and with them would disappear the "best" American traits. Eugenicists were hardly comforted by the nationwide rise of the "New Woman" in the later half of the nineteenth century, when many white women agitated for educational and employment opportunities outside the home, for female suffrage, and — especially with the advent of feminist activists such as Margaret Sanger — for birth control. This state of affairs prompted the white academic E. D. Cope to lament in 1890 that there were in fact "*two* perils" facing the United States, namely both the presence of African Americans, and the white New Woman, since both were irresponsible and unfit for sharing power with middle-class white men.

As inhabitants of the United States, blacks and whites were unmistakably affected by events beyond national shores, especially the Spanish-American War of 1898, which eventually allowed the nation to build an empire that included Cuba, Puerto Rico, and the Philippines. The year 1898 also saw the annexation of Hawaii, when American marines marched through the streets of Honolulu to overthrow a legitimate Hawaiian monarchy in order to give American businessmen full control over the islands' lucrative agricultural industry. As W. E. B. Du Bois observed in *The Souls of Black Folk* (1903), "[t]he problem of the twentieth century is the problem of the color-line, — the relation of the darker to the lighter races of men in Asia and Africa, in America and the islands of the sea" (221). For Du Bois and many other African Americans, local struggles over race and power could not be divorced from their global equivalents. In *The Marrow of Tradition* Chesnutt had this connection in mind when, in a thinly veiled reference to the Spanish-American War, he sketched the broader links between white supremacist violence at home and imperial warfare overseas:

> the nation was rushing onward with great strides towards colossal wealth and world-domination, before the exigencies of which mere abstract ethical theories must not be permitted to stand. The same argument that justified the conquest of an inferior nation could not be denied to those who sought the suppression of an inferior race. In the South, an obscure jealousy of the negro's progress, an obscure fear of the very equality so contemptuously denied, furnished a rich soil for successful agitation. (p. 190)

As the last black congressman until 1928, George H. White would argue in 1900: "Should not a nation be just to all of her citizens, protect them alike in all their rights, on every foot of her soil — in a word, show herself capable of governing all within her domain before she undertakes to exercise sovereign authority over those of a foreign land. . . ?" (p. 396).

PLANTATION FICTION AND NATIONAL MARKETS

As observers such as Wells, Du Bois, and Congressman White presented it, the "problem of the color-line" involved matters of class, ethnic identity, the power struggles between men and women, and the interplay of national and international politics. In American fiction and culture, however, race and all its attendant complexities were most often reduced to a framework of sectional differences between North and South. Beginning in the 1870s and 1880s, at the moment when Reconstruction reforms were all but dismantled, a body of fiction depicting the antebellum South in idyllic terms became enormously popular. This romanticized "plantation fiction," such as Thomas Nelson Page's short story collection *In Ole Virginia* (1887) and Joel Chandler Harris's *Uncle Remus: His Songs and Sayings* (1881), looked back to the era of slavery with a keen nostalgia. Coming at a moment when the North no longer felt any urgency to champion black civil rights, readers embraced a genre of fiction that looked back on the plantation as a world of pastoral beneficence. In this world masters and mistresses were kind aristocrats and slaves were contented dependents who served their white protectors out of a sense of familial devotion. In the post–Civil War era, as this fiction depicted it, white landowners and their former slaves retained relations of mutual fondness from this shared legacy of the plantation.

Both black and white authors in this period used dialect speech to signify local authenticity, but in plantation fiction the stylized vernacular of black dialect was frequently deployed to make slaves themselves the defenders of southern slaveholding culture. Sam, a former slave who narrates one of Page's stories, speaks longingly of the lost world before the war. "Dem wuz good ole times, marster — de bes' Sam ever see," he proclaims. "Dyar warn' no trouble nor nothin" (10). That this fiction managed to remember the plantation as a world of "no trouble"— with former slaves themselves made to voice the memories — tells us something of the powerful idealizing force of this literary nostalgia. Clearly this way of remembering was also a willful forgetting. Readers in the white South could look back and see an affectionate plantation family rather than ugly cruelties or deprivations. Northern readers, for their part, could smooth over any inconsistencies between the North's earlier attack on slavery and its current abandonment of Reconstructionist goals for racial equity.

All of Charles Chesnutt's creative work, including *The Marrow of Tradition,* challenged this body of fiction that had mythologized the Old South. Interestingly, Chesnutt made his entry into professional fiction writing by imitating and slyly revising the conventions of plantation fiction. A number of his early short stories feature an ex-slave, Uncle Julius, who recounts tales of bygone plantation life and slave lore in black dialect. Julius's "conjure tales," usually turning on an episode of conjuring or the magical transformation of a slave into an object or animal, retained the air of quaint enchantment that characterized popular plantation fiction. Julius never overtly challenges the mythology of the plantation "family" that depicted master-slave relations of mutual warmth. But in a number of his tales, the effects of conjure magic on enslaved men and women reveal the underlying horrors of the slave system. In "Po' Sandy," for instance, a man who agrees to be transformed into a pine tree in order to avoid separation from his beloved wife is later cut down and sent to a sawmill, while his wife is forced to listen to the gruesome moans emitted as the pine is sawed into planks. Disguised as folklore, these tales of the dehumanizing treatment of black men and women under slavery uncover the essential brutality at the heart of plantation life while still maintaining picturesque details of local color that characterized the genre.

A number of Chesnutt's plantation stories appeared in leading national magazines and were later gathered in a collection called *The Conjure Woman* (1899), published by the prestigious Boston firm of Houghton Mifflin. But even as he established himself as an author of Old South fiction, Chesnutt recognized risks. As he was writing his first major novels, Chesnutt had a deepening understanding of the way the colorful customs of the antebellum plantation world, recreated and avidly consumed as mass entertainment, could have devastating consequences for African Americans in the postbellum United States.

Chesnutt develops this insight about entertainment in an especially incisive passage of *The Marrow of Tradition*. At the beginning of Chapter XIII, Chesnutt's narrator describes a "party of Northern visitors" arrived in Wellington to see for themselves what the narrator dryly terms "the negro problem" (p. 116). As the visitors explore Wellington, the town's white citizens go to elaborate lengths to control what the Northerners see and hear; the resulting picture of "social conditions" in the South is stage-managed to the smallest detail. Like everything else the visitors observe, the culminating spectacle is an arranged performance: the Northerners are invited to watch a "genuine negro cakewalk," or type of dance competition, sponsored by the white managers of the hotel. But Chesnutt makes it clear that even this black folk performance has been appropriated by hostile whites. The history and meaning of the cakewalk was complex and included both a celebration of black cultural roots and a satiric mimicry of white masters. But the white citizens invite the Northerners to read the performance as proof of "the joyous, happy-go-lucky disposition of the Southern darky and his entire contentment with existing conditions" (p. 117).

With this scene Chesnutt exposes the way staging "pleasing impression[s] of Southern customs" (p. 117) as innocuous entertainment could serve as a damaging political weapon. Framed by white sponsors, the cakewalk is transformed from a complex cultural practice into the kind of patronizing spectacle that was the centerpiece of blackface minstrel shows. After framing the spectacle in this way, the white sponsors hold up the performance as self-evident proof of black people's political contentment.

This kind of political manipulation was an especially potent threat, Chesnutt knew, in the new era of mass-market capitalism. By underscoring the way the South and its traditions could be deliberately staged for an audience of curious observers, Chesnutt asks readers to recognize a crucial link between entertainment and post-Reconstruction politics, a link forged in a commercial world that produced an enormous volume of racist stories and shows for mass consumption. The myth of the Old South was, ironically, produced and distributed by a highly modernized national economy. Fiction writers continued to produce plantation romances that tapped the vastly expanded national markets of this period. Chesnutt's era saw an explosion of minstrel shows that traveled by rail to perform on a wide-ranging circuit of vaudeville theaters, private parties, and large musical revues. Fairs and large national expositions featured re-creations of antebellum plantation life, sometimes with ex-slaves singing or performing on elaborate sets. In this way, new mass markets and popular spectacles made Old South nostalgia a national phenomenon. Commercial and political profits were not the only motives for the white producers of these various reproductions; America's postwar absorption in Southern culture included a genuine interest in discovering and preserving black folk life. But serious ethnological interest tended to be submerged in the flood of mass entertainment.

Chesnutt's novel challenges that array of images and stories by insisting that readers look at "pleasing" customs with profound skepticism. Significantly, the white Northerners who visit Wellington are fooled. They never realize that the supposedly objective picture of southern conditions has been fixed, just as they fail to observe that among the "genuine" black performers is a white person, Tom Delamere, a dissolute young man who is indulging his penchant for dressing in blackface and blaming his mischief on innocent black people. Tom's later appearance in the same blackface disguise turns out to be a cover for thievery and a vicious murder. Chesnutt's point is clear: staging "pleasing" racial types and customs (pleasing to whom and why?) might very well shield — indeed, could encourage — acts of greed and racial hatred. In this way Chesnutt's plot asks us to recognize that white people's nostalgia for antebellum tradition and their pleasure in postbellum forms of entertainment were finally of a piece with the fierce racial and political struggles of the era.

By pointing to connections between entertainment and exploitation, *The Marrow of Tradition* insists that segregation was not simply a set of laws. It was more fundamentally a total culture, a way of life. Stories and spectacles of a mythic Old South, gentle as they were in tone, were just as important as Jim Crow laws in fostering a sense of white entitlement and supremacy. Segregation relied upon not just structures of power but sources of pleasure. W. E. B. Du Bois commented on the role of pleasure in a culture of white supremacy. The "effort to keep the white group solid," Du Bois writes, encouraged a degree of pleasure in cruelty. "Every white man [and woman] became a recognized official to keep Negroes 'in their places.' Negro baiting and even lynching became a form of amusement" (qtd. in Hale 199). Like Du Bois, Chesnutt also points to lynching as the ultimate extension of other forms of amusement, a merging of race-based pleasure into racial violence. As with the case of the lynching of Sam Hose, the near-lynching of Sandy in Chesnutt's novel is both a moment of extreme public anger — a "white heat"— and a moment of perverse public entertainment. The preparations for Sandy's violent death include the chartering of special railroad cars to "bring spectators to the scene," the erection of special seats in order that "the spectacle might be the more easily and comfortably viewed," and even plans by some young men for seizing body parts after the lynching as "souvenirs" (p. 178). As the ultimate spectacle, the lynched body exposes the role of visual pleasure and mass spectatorship in white techniques of racial control.

CONTEXTS OF REALISM AND REFORM

Chesnutt's effort to unveil plantation myths is one factor that links his novel to the movement of literary realism. Influenced by European novelists, white American realist writers such as William Dean Howells, Henry James, Sarah Orne Jewett, and Mark Twain wrote novels that self-consciously rejected historical romances like Sir Walter Scott's Waverly novels and sentimental marriage novels like Susan Warner's *The Wide, Wide World,* two genres that still dominated the market for fiction. As its advocates saw it, realism turned away from fanciful or romantic plots and examined closely the details of everyday life and real human speech. Howells, remarking on Chesnutt's two published collections of short stories about black life in the South, announced that Chesnutt "has won the ear of the more intelligent public" for his "thorough mastery" and "unerring knowledge of the life he had chosen in its peculiar racial characteristics."

> As these stories are of our own time and country, and as there is not a swashbuckler of the seventeenth century, or a sentimentalist of this, or a princess of an imaginary kingdom, in any of them, they will probably not reach half a million readers in six months, but in twelve months possibly more readers will remember them than if they had reached the half million. They are new and fresh and strong, as life always is, and fable never is. ("Mr. Charles Chesnutt's Stories" 700)

On the basis of his short stories Chesnutt won admittance to the ranks of realists for the "passionless handling of a phase of our common life" in the real social relations of the day. Howells and other realists thought that the extravagance and emotional excess of most popular fiction not only failed to make those stories true to life but warped readers' abilities to see social life clearly. Like Twain (whose 1894 novel *Pudd'nhead Wilson* Chesnutt drew upon for *The Marrow of Tradition* and his later novel *Paul Marchand, F.M.C.*), Chesnutt uses irony in his fiction to expose the discrepancy between the South's refined ideals and its engrained forms of racial and sexual exploitation.

But if Chesnutt shared the realists' impulse to dismantle fictional formulas, *The Marrow of Tradition* also points up a blind spot in certain realist precepts. The racial discord Chesnutt revealed did not lend itself to the "passionless handling" Howells had earlier praised in Chesnutt's short stories. Although *The Marrow of Tradition* refrains from any overt moralizing, the novel's urgency reflects the influence of a different literary tradition Chesnutt calls a "literature of necessity"— fiction written with the express purpose of effecting social change. In conceiving a career as a writer, Chesnutt was inspired by two novels that lodged passionate protests against white oppression, Harriet Beecher Stowe's antislavery novel *Uncle Tom's Cabin* (1852) and Albion Tourgée's *A Fool's Errand* (1879), a story of the abusive treatment of freedmen during Reconstruction. Both were massive bestsellers, and the profits they earned were certainly part of their attraction for the young Chesnutt. But their success was also proof for him that the "province of literature" could include the work of promoting racial equality. By effecting a profound transformation of conscious-ness, Chesnutt believed, literature could lead readers to a "desired state of feeling." "The object of my writings would not be so much the elevation of the colored people," Chesnutt recorded in his journal, "as the elevation of the whites" (*Journals* 139).

But even though *Uncle Tom's Cabin* and *A Fool's Errand* convinced Chesnutt that the novel could be an agent of "moral revolution," he found Stowe and Tourgée — white authors who saw African Ameri-can life from the outside — finally lacking in their understanding of black America. Chesnutt was irritated by Tourgée's depiction of bi-racial characters, figures "always bewailing their fate," as Chesnutt put it, "and cursing the drop of black blood which 'taints'. . . their otherwise pure race" (*"To Be An Author"* 65–66). Chesnutt was also impatient with the narrow range of social roles and occupations that white editors and readers were prepared to accept for black charac-ters. Writers from Europe, he noted with frustration, enjoyed a greater freedom than did any American author to portray black people in all walks of life. To make the most of fiction's transformative powers, Chesnutt felt, a writer needed both a mastery of literary technique and an immersion in the history, habits of mind, and intricate social codes of the South, black as well as white. Why could not someone like him-self, Chesnutt asked, "who has lived among colored people all his life," who has closely observed white Southerners and knows "all the phases of the slavery question" from avid study, "why could not such a man, if he possessed the same ability, write a far better book about the South than Judge Tourgee or Mrs. Stowe has written? Answer who can!" (*Journals* 125).

Chesnutt's own "answer," *The Marrow of Tradition,* also advanced a tradition of black antislavery writing and protest fiction. African American authors such Frederick Douglass, William Wells Brown, and Martin Delany, for instance, had forged a tradition of forceful, even militant, black fictional characters, a type largely absent from the fic-tion written by white authors. Chesnutt's laborer Josh Green, filled with rage at the murder of his father by KKK terrorists, re-creates for a postbellum world the fierce black heroes of antislavery narratives such as Douglass's *The Heroic Slave* (1853), Brown's *Clotel* (1853), and Delany's *Blake* (1862). Yet in portraying heroic black manhood, these writers had to surmount a dilemma — critic Richard Yarborough describes it as a "conceptual briar patch"— that found the black bondsman unmanly because a captive slave, yet branded him a beast if he rebelled in violence ("Race, Violence, and Manhood" 174).

Chesnutt's novel suggests that a similar double bind was in place even half a century later. Josh Green's willingness to use violence to defend himself and others clearly counts as a form of valor in *Marrow*. Yet the novel also seems uneasy with his militancy: Josh's working-class position links his defiance with a certain coarseness, while his self-sacrificing courage is qualified when it is seen through the eyes of the more refined and educated Dr. Miller, who draws back from endorsing what he also clearly admires, even envies.

Like his examination of black manhood, Chesnutt's meditations in *Marrow* on the legacy of women's sexual abuse under slavery advances another traditional concern of nineteenth-century black protest fiction. The sexual vulnerability of women who were the personal property of white men was a stark theme for the authors of slave narratives, and a number of black women writers continued to explore the implications of slaves' dilemmas for the postwar black family. Authors such as Frances Harper and Pauline Hopkins offered wrenching stories of disorder erupting in postbellum society, the legacy of the rape and interracial liaisons that had been the open secrets of the plantation world. Similarly in *The Marrow of Tradition* Chesnutt's story of half-sisters Janet Miller and Olivia Carteret supplies a domestic plot whose revelations about their interracial family match the outbreak of interracial violence.

The novel's meditation on the quandaries of black manhood and interracial melodrama reflects the transitional nature of the book, its place in between traditions of nineteenth-century reform fiction and twentieth-century modernism. Chesnutt, along with contemporaries such as Harper and Hopkins, Sutton Griggs, Paul Laurence Dunbar, and journalist David Bryant Fulton, set out to revise both the protest fiction of white writers as well as the mythologies of the southern romancers like Joel Chandler Harris and Thomas Nelson Page. Chesnutt's attempts at remaking narrative conventions would combine social analysis with self-reflexiveness about literary form, two hallmarks of the high achievement in black creativity associated with the Harlem Renaissance of the 1930s.

In 1928 Chesnutt was awarded the Springarn Medal in recognition of innovations important to later black writers. At the time of its publication, however, it was precisely *The Marrow of Tradition*'s innovative wedding of literary protest with sophisticated ironies and self-reflection that prompted resistance. Despite his earlier praise of Chesnutt's truth-telling, William Dean Howells received *The Marrow of Tradition* with a revealing ambivalence: he lamented the novel's

implicit "judgment" on American race relations in the same breath
that he conceded the validity of that judgment. "It cannot be said that
either his aesthetics or his ethics are false," Howells writes, but the editor nevertheless called *Marrow* a "bitter, bitter" book. "One cannot
blame him for that," Howells admits:

> If the tables could once be turned, and it could be that it was the black
> race which violently and lastingly triumphed in the bloody revolution at
> Wilmington, North Carolina, a few years ago, what would not we
> excuse to the white man who made the atrocity the argument of his fic-
> tion? (p. 456)

Though Howells affirms the accuracy of Chesnutt's portrait, a violent
coup was simply not amenable to the kind of "passionless handling"
Howells wished to encourage in American fiction writers. The atrocity
Chesnutt depicts strains the limits of Howells's brand of realism. Chesnutt's unsparing picture could not but embody a moral and political
judgment, but for Howells any resemblance to political advocacy
threatened to violate the role of fine art. At the same time, with the
popular audiences in both the North and South enchanted with stories
of an idyllic Old South, Chesnutt's sophisticated critique of the power
of custom was largely ignored.

The Marrow of Tradition earned tepid sales and largely disappoint-
ing reviews, and Chesnutt essentially abandoned his career as a full-
time fiction writer. But from its publication, *The Marrow of Tradition*
has stood as one of the most penetrating analyses we have of the culture of segregation. The recognition Chesnutt won by the end of the
twentieth century is a testament to how acutely he explored the racial
dynamics at the century's beginning.

Chronology of
Chesnutt's Life and Times

1856

Charles Chesnutt's freeborn parents, Andrew Jackson Chesnutt and Ann Maria Sampson, leave Fayetteville, North Carolina, for Cleveland, Ohio.

1857

Andrew Chesnutt marries Ann Maria Sampson in Cleveland.

Founding of *Atlantic Monthly* under the editorship of James Russell Lowell (1819–1891).

March: In the case of *Dred Scott v. Sandford,* the slave Scott sues for his freedom on the grounds that his master had transported him from a slave to a free state. The U.S. Supreme Court upholds his enslavement, declaring that blacks are not American citizens, and therefore have no rights.

Herman Melville (1819–1891), *The Confidence-Man.*

1858

Williams Wells Brown (1814?–1884) pens the *The Escape; Or, A Leap for Freedom,* the first play by an African American.

June 20: Birth of Charles Waddell Chesnutt in Cleveland. Chesnutt's father works as a horse-car conductor, while his mother teaches slave children, in defiance of the law. After Charles, they have two other sons, Lewis and Andrew Jr.

1859

October: John Brown's raid at Harper's Ferry.

Harriet Wilson (1828?–1863?), *Our Nig; or, Sketches From the Life of a Free Black;* Harriet Beecher Stowe (1811–1896), *The Minister's Wooing.*

1860

Abraham Lincoln elected president of the United States; South Carolina secedes from the Union.

Rebecca Harding Davis (1831–1910), *Life in the Iron-Mills;* Nathaniel Hawthorne (1804–1864), *The Marble Faun.*

1861

April 12–13: Confederates bombard Fort Sumter, South Carolina, firing the first shots of the Civil War.

Harriet Jacobs (1813?–1897), *Incidents in the Life of a Slave Girl;* Martin Robison Delany (1812–1885), *Blake; or, the Huts of America* serialized between 1861 and 1862 in the *Weekly Anglo-African.*

1863

January 1: Emancipation Proclamation issued by President Lincoln, freeing southern slaves in all states controlled by the Confederacy.

January 26: Recruitment begins for the Fifty-Fourth Massachusetts Volunteers, the first northern black regiment. In July the regiment suffers great losses at the battle for Fort Wagner, in Charleston, North Carolina.

July 1–3: Despite heavy casualties, the Union victory at Battle of Gettysburg marks a turning point in the Civil War.

July 4: Union general Ulysses S. Grant captures the town of Vicksburg, thereby gaining control of the Mississippi River and severely handicapping Confederate forces.

July 13–17: White mobs attack African Americans during the bloody New York draft riots.

November 19: Lincoln delivers the Gettysburg Address.

1865

March 3: Freedman's Bureau established.

April 9: Civil War ends with the surrender of Confederate general Robert E. Lee to Union general Ulysses S. Grant at the courthouse in Appomattox, Virginia.

April 14: Fatal shooting of President Lincoln by the actor John Wilkes Booth at the Ford Theatre, Washington, D.C.

December 18: Thirteenth Amendment to the Constitution adopted, abolishing slavery in states formerly controlled by the Confederacy.

Walt Whitman (1819–1892), *Drum Taps*.

1866

Chesnutt's family moves back to Fayetteville, where, aided financially by his white father, Andrew Chesnutt opens a grocery store.

January 9: Fisk University founded in Nashville, Tennessee.

April 9: despite President Johnson's veto, Congress passes a Civil Rights Bill.

Melville, *Battle-Pieces*.

1867

Nine-year-old Charles Chesnutt attends the newly founded Howard School in Fayetteville.

March: Guided by radical Republicans, Congress passes the Reconstruction Acts against President Johnson's veto; Howard University and Talladega College founded.

May: The white supremacist Knights of the White Camelia founded in Louisiana.

1868

February 23: Birth of W. E. B. Du Bois in Great Barrington, Massachusetts.

April 1: Founding of Hampton Institute.

May 16: Republican bid to impeach President Johnson fails by one vote in the Senate.

July 21: Fourteenth Amendment to the Constitution ratified, granting citizenship and equal protection under the law to all those born or naturalized in the United States.

September 22: Race riot in New Orleans.

November 3: Ulysses S. Grant elected president.

1869

Central Pacific and Union Pacific railroads meet at Promontory Point, Utah, establishing first U.S. transcontinental railway.

Frances Harper (1825–1911), *Minnie's Sacrifice* and *Moses: A Story of the Nile*; Stowe, *Old Town Folks*.

1870

March 30: Fifteenth Amendment to the Constitution ratified, guaranteeing black men the vote.

May 31: First Enforcement Act passed to bolster civil rights constitutional amendments.

Whitman, *Democratic Vistas*.

1871

Death of Ann Maria Chesnutt.

April: Congress passes the Ku Klux Klan Act; leading into the following year, federal prosecution of Ku Klux Klan organizations in the South.

William Dean Howells (1837–1920) becomes the editor of the *Atlantic Monthly*.

1872

Chesnutt's father, Andrew, marries Mary Ochiltree; this second marriage results in six more children.

1873

Supreme Court ruling on the *Benevolent Association of New Orleans v. The Crescent City Livestock Land and Slaughter-House Company*, better know as the Slaughterhouse case.

April 13: Over sixty blacks murdered in Colfax, Louisiana, race riot.

1874

Chesnutt begins a journal that he keeps sporadically until 1882.

Antiblack, anti-Republican riot in Coushatta, Louisiana, and later in Vicksburg, Mississippi.

1875

Chesnutt relocates to Charlotte, North Carolina, for a teaching appointment. Race riot in Clinton, Mississippi.

March 1: Congressional Civil Rights Bill guaranteeing blacks equal access to public places.

1876

U.S. Supreme Court rules on *United States v. Cruikshank*.

In Montana, General George Armstrong Custer and his men are killed at the Battle of Little Bighorn by the Sioux and Cheyenne under Sitting Bull and Crazy Horse respectively.

Mark Twain (1835–1910), *The Adventures of Tom Sawyer;* Harper, *Sowing and Reaping: A Temperance Story.*

1877

Chesnutt begins teaching at Fayetteville's State Colored Normal School.

November: Reconstruction effectively comes to an end with the election of Republican Rutherford B. Hayes to the presidency; federal troops withdrawn from state capitals in South Carolina and Louisiana.

1878

Chesnutt marries Susan Perry, a teacher at the Howard School. In all they have four children: Ethel, Helen, Edwin, and Dorothy.

U.S. Supreme Court rules on *Hall v. DeCuir.*

1879

Restless for other opportunities, Chesnutt travels to Washington, D.C., looking unsuccessfully for work.

Death of William Lloyd Garrison, leading abolitionist of the antebellum era, and editor of *The Liberator.*

Albion W. Tourgée (1838–1905), *A Fool's Errand;* Henry James (1843–1916), *Daisy Miller;* George Washington Cable (1844–1925), *Old Creole Days.*

1880

Chesnutt takes the position of principal of the Normal School in Fayetteville.

November 2: James Garfield elected president.

Cable, *The Grandissimes.*

1881

Tuskegee Institute founded by Lewis Adams and George Campbell, Booker T. Washington appointed principal; President Garfield assassinated, and succeeded by Vice President Chester Arthur.

Frederick Douglass (1818–1895), *The Life and Times of Frederick Douglass;* Joel Chandler Harris (1848–1908), *Uncle Remus: His Songs and Sayings;* Whitman, sixth edition of *Leaves of Grass,* originally published in 1855; James, *The Portrait of a Lady.*

Howells resigns from the *Atlantic Monthly.*

1883

Still restless, Chesnutt resigns from teaching and establishes himself as a stenographer and reporter in New York City. Later this year he moves to Cleveland, finding employment as a clerk and then stenographer at the Nickel Plate Railroad Company. The U.S. Supreme Court declares the 1875 Civil Rights Bill unconstitutional. Death of legendary black feminist and abolitionist Sojourner Truth in Battle Creek, Michigan.

1884

Chesnutt moves his family from Fayetteville to Cleveland. Race riot in Danville, Virginia; reports suggest that at least fifty blacks are lynched for the year.

Grover Cleveland elected president.

Helen Hunt Jackson (1830–1885), *Ramona*.

1885

Chesnutt pursues law studies with Judge Samuel E. Williams, of the Nickel Plate Railroad Company.

Howells becomes editor at *Harper's*.

Howells, *The Rise of Silas Lapham;* Twain, *The Adventures of Huckleberry Finn;* Cable, *The Silent South*.

1886

Chesnutt passes the Ohio bar examination; publishes "The Goophered Grapevine" in the *Atlantic Monthly*.

May: During Chicago's Haymarket Square Riot over seventy people are killed when a bomb explodes during a clash between police and prolabor union demonstrators; death of poet Emily Dickinson.

James, *The Princess Casamassima* and *The Bostonians*.

1887

Reformers Jane Addams and Ellen Gates Starr found Hull House in Chicago.

Thomas Nelson Page (1853–1922), *In Ole Virginia*.

1888

Chesnutt sets up his own office as a court reporter; publishes "Po' Sandy" in the *Atlantic Monthly*.

Harper, *Trial and Triumph*.

1889

Chesnutt publishes the short story "The Sheriff's Children" and the essay "What Is a White Man?" in the *New York Independent;* declines an offer to become George Washington Cable's secretary. White historian Philip A. Bruce (1856–1933) publishes *The Plantation Negro as a Freeman.*

1890

National American Woman Suffrage Association founded.

Howells, *A Hazard of New Fortunes;* Cable, *The Negro Question.*

1891

Number of reported lynchings of black Americans rises to one hundred and thirteen for the year.

William Dean Howells's *An Imperative Duty* serialized in *Harper's Monthly.*

1892

Ellis Island in New York City's harbor opens as a processing center for immigrants to the United States.

June: Homer Adolph Plessy attempts to ride in a first-class car in Louisiana and is ordered to a segregated coach. He refuses to obey and is later arrested.

Anna Julia Cooper (1858–1964), *A Voice from the South;* Charlotte Perkins Gilman (1860–1935), *The Yellow Wallpaper;* Harper, *Iola Leroy: or Shadows Uplifted.*

1893

Columbian Exposition held in Chicago; black feminist Fannie Barrier Williams speaks before the World Congress of Representative Women on "The Intellectual Progress of the Colored Woman."

Historian Frederick Jackson Turner (1861–1932) addresses the American Historical Association on "The Significance of the Frontier in American History."

Stephen Crane (1871–1900), *Maggie, A Girl of the Streets.*

1894

Members of the American Railroad Union go on strike to protest wage cuts for Pullman car workers in Chicago.

Twain, *Pudd'nhead Wilson;* Kate Chopin (1851–1904), *Bayou Folk;* Crane, *The Red Badge of Courage.*

1895

Booker T. Washington speaks at the Cotton States and International Exhibition in Atlanta; death of Frederick Douglass.

Ida B. Wells publishes her second antilynching pamphlet, "A Red Record," to protest spreading epidemic of lynching. By this year reports suggest that up to one hundred blacks a year are being lynched across the South.

Paul Laurence Dunbar (1872–1906), *Majors and Minors.*

1896

Chesnutt travels to Europe.

National Association of Colored Women founded.

May 18: After hearing the arguments prepared by lawyer Albion Tourgée and his associates, the U.S. Supreme Court rules against the plaintiff in *Plessy v. Ferguson.*

November 3: White Republican Daniel Russell elected governor of North Carolina; U.S. representative George H. White only black politician elected to Congress; William McKinley elected president.

W. E. B. Du Bois (1868–1963), *The Suppression of the African Slave-Trade to the United States;* Dunbar, *Lyrics of Lowly Life.*

1897

American Negro Academy founded by Alexander Crummell, W. E. B. Du Bois and others; Du Bois delivers "The Conservation of Races" before the Academy.

August 12: Rebecca Latimer Felton delivers a speech before the Georgia State Agricultural Society urging her fellow whites to lynch black men.

Chopin, *A Night in Acadie.*

1898

Chesnutt publishes "The Wife of His Youth" in the *Atlantic Monthly.*

United States declares war on Spain and annexes Hawaii.

August 18: Alexander Manly's editorial.

November 8: Election Day.

November 10: Race riot in Wilmington, North Carolina.

1899

Chesnutt publishes short story collections *The Conjure Woman* and *The Wife of His Youth and Other Stories of the Color Line,* as well as the biography *Frederick Douglass;* closes stenography office so that he can turn to writing full time.

Sam Hose lynched in Newnan, Georgia.

Frank Norris (1870–1902), *McTeague;* Sutton E. Griggs (1872–1933), *Imperium in Imperio;* Chopin, *The Awakening;* Gilman, *Women and Economics.*

1900

Chesnutt meets William Dean Howells; publishes the three-part essay "The Future American" in the *Boston Evening Transcript,* as well as his first novel, *The House Behind the Cedars.*

Frances Benjamin Johnston (1864–1852) commissioned to photograph the Hampton Normal and Agricultural Institute in Hampton, Virginia, for exhibition at the Paris Exposition.

July 24–27: Race riot breaks out in New Orleans; Ida B. Wells publishes "Mob Rule in New Orleans"; along with the 1898 Wilmington riot, the violence in New Orleans inspires Chesnutt to write *The Marrow of Tradition.*

August 2: North Carolina voters accept a voter eligibility amendment to the state constitution that institutes the "grandfather clause," a literacy test, and a poll tax, effectively disenfranchising African Americans.

November 8: Birth of white Georgia writer Margaret Mitchell, future author of *Gone With the Wind.*

David Bryant Fulton (1863–1941), *Hanover: or the Persecution of the Lowly: A Story of the Wilmington Massacre,* published in response to the 1898 Wilmington, North Carolina, riot; Pauline Elizabeth Hopkins (1859–1930), *Contending Forces: A Romance Illustrative of Negro Life North and South;* Theodore Dreiser (1871–1945), *Sister Carrie.*

1901

Chesnutt lectures throughout the South, and visits Wilmington, North Carolina, where he researches the 1898 race riot; publishes *The Marrow of Tradition* with Houghton Mifflin, and "Charles W. Chesnutt's Own View of His New Story 'The Marrow of Tradition'" in the Cleveland *World;* William Dean Howells reviews the novel in *North American Review,* calling it "a bitter, bitter book"; Chesnutt reopens his stenography business.

After the assassination of President William McKinley, Vice President Theodore Roosevelt takes over the White House. The sole remaining black congressman, George H. White, completes his term in the House of Representatives.

Norris, *The Octopus;* Washington, *Up From Slavery;* Griggs, *Overshadowed.*

1902

White feminist leader and suffragist Elizabeth Cady Stanton dies.

Thomas Dixon Jr. (1864–1946), *The Leopard's Spots;* Griggs, *Unfettered.*

1903

Chesnutt publishes "The Disfranchisement of the Negro" in *The Negro Problems: A Series of Articles by Representative American Negroes of To-day,* edited by Booker T. Washington.

Du Bois, *The Souls of Black Folk;* Dunbar, *The Sport of the Gods;* Gilman, *The Home: Its Work and Influence.*

1904

Chesnutt named to Booker T. Washington's advisory Committee of Twelve; publishes "Baxter's Procrustes" in the *Atlantic Monthly.*

President Theodore Roosevelt wins a second term.

1905

Chesnutt publishes *The Colonel's Dream* with Doubleday, Page. Ceases professional publications.

Industrial Workers of the World (IWW) founded.

First meeting of the Niagara Movement.

Edith Wharton (1862–1937), *The House of Mirth;* Dixon, *The Clansman;* Griggs, *The Hindered Hand; Or, the Reign of the Repressionist;* Gertrude Stein (1874–1946), *Three Lives.*

1906

August 13: Three companies of the all-black Twenty-Fifth Regiment were involved in a riot in Brownville, Texas. With no formal investigation of the cause of the disturbance, President Theodore Roosevelt orders a dishonorable discharge of all the soldiers.

September 22–24: Race riot in Atlanta.

1908

Birth of African American author Richard Wright; race riot in Springfield, Illinois.

November 3: William H. Taft elected president.

Ray Stannard Baker (1870–1946), *Following the Color Line: American Negro Citizenship in the Progressive Era;* Stein, *The Making of Americans.*

1907
James, *The American Scene.*

1909
Black and white activists, including W. E. B. Du Bois and Jane Addams, join in forming the National Association for the Advancement of Colored People (NAACP).

White feminist and woman suffragist Susan B. Anthony dies.

William Howard Taft assumes the presidency.

1910
Chesnutt invited to address the early NAACP, and serves on the organization's General Committee; suffers a stroke.

Du Bois founds the NAACP journal *The Crisis.*

More and more southern blacks begin to move north for better opportunities, in what would later be known as the Great Migration.

1911
Founding of the National Urban League to help southern blacks relocating north during the Great Migration.

1912
Chesnutt tours Europe with daughter Helen; named to Cleveland's Chamber of Commerce.

James Weldon Johnson (1871–1938), *The Autobiography of an Ex-Colored Man.*

1913
Woodrow Wilson begins term as president.

Death of Harriet Tubman, escaped slave, Union scout, and spy who rescued hundreds on the Underground Railroad before emancipation.

Pauline Johnson (1861–1913), *The Moccasin Maker;* Willa Cather (1873–1947), *O Pioneers!*

1914
Jamaican-born pan-African leader Marcus Garvey (1887–1940) establishes the Universal Negro Improvement Association.

White nurse and birth control advocate Margaret Sanger (1883–1966) starts publishing the feminist journal *The Woman Rebel*.

World War I breaks out in Europe.

1915

Opening of *Birth of a Nation*, W. D. Griffith's screen version of the racist novel *The Clansman*; screenings are met with protests from the NAACP and other problack organizations.

December: the reorganization of the Ku Klux Klan in the twentieth century.

Cather, *Song of the Lark*.

1916

May 15: The lynching of nineteen-year-old Jesse Washington, Waco, Texas.

1917

The United States enters World War I; race riots in East St. Louis, Illinois, and Houston, Texas.

July 28: Thousands of blacks participate in a silent protest march in New York City to protest racial violence.

1918

Race riots in Chester, Pennsylvania, and in Philadelphia; Garvey founds *Negro World* newspaper.

November: Treaty of Versailles ends World War I.

Cather, *My Ántonia*.

1919

Meeting of Du Bois's Pan-African Congress in Paris.

During the "Red Summer" of 1919, a total of twenty-six race riots break out through the country, including Washington, D.C., and Chicago.

Ratification of the Nineteenth Amendment to the U. S. Constitution, guaranteeing American women the right to vote.

Claude McKay (1889–1948), "If We Must Die"; Sherwood Anderson (1876–1941), *Winesburg, Ohio*.

1920

Black filmmaker Oscar Micheaux makes *Within Our Gates* in answer to *Birth of a Nation*.

November 2: Warren G. Harding elected president.

Wharton, *The Age of Innocence.*

1922

Dyer lynching bill passes the House, but falls to pass the Senate.

McKay, *Harlem Shadows;* Sinclair Lewis (1885–1951), *Babbitt.*

1921

Sanger founds the American Birth Control League; Felton appointed for one day to the U.S. Senate.

1923

June 21: Garvey sentenced to five years in prison for mail fraud.

Jean Toomer (1894–1967), *Cane.*

1924

Sensational trial of the Rhinelander case, where the marriage of mixed-race Alice Jones to white New York socialite Leonard Rhinelander is contested on the grounds that the groom was unaware of Jones's racial identity.

November 4: Calvin Coolidge elected president.

Jessie Redmon Fauset (1882–1961), *There Is Confusion;* Micheaux, *Body and Soul,* starring Paul Robeson.

1925

May 19: Birth of Malcolm Little — later known as Malcolm X — in Omaha, Nebraska.

Marita Bonner (1899–1971), "On Being Young — a Woman — and Colored" in *The Crisis;* Alain Locke, (1886–1954), ed., *The New Negro;* Countee Cullen (1903–1946), *Color.*

1926

Langston Hughes (1902–1967), *The Weary Blues* and "The Negro Artist and the Racial Mountain"; Eric Walrond (1898–1966), *Tropic Death;* Ernest Hemingway (1899–1961), *The Sun Also Rises.*

1927

Houghton Mifflin issues a new edition of *The Conjure Woman.*

Hemingway, *A Farewell to Arms;* Bonner, *The Pot Maker.*

1928

July 3: Chesnutt is awarded the NAACP's Springarn Medal.

November 6: Oscar DePriest of Illinois first black representative to serve in Congress since George H. White of North Carolina finished his term in 1901.

Nella Larson (1893–1964), *Quicksand;* Rudolph Fisher (1897–1934), *The Walls of Jericho;* McKay, *Home to Harlem;* Bonner, *The Purple Flower.*

1929

January 15: Birth of civil rights leader Martin Luther King Jr. in Atlanta.

October: Infamous Wall Street crash initiates the Great Depression, lasting until 1934.

William Faulkner (1897–1962), *The Sound and the Fury;* Larsen, *Passing;* Bonner, *Exit: An Illusion;* Fauset, *Plum Bun.*

1931

Jane Addams is the first American woman to win the Nobel Peace Prize.

March 25: Ida B. Wells-Barnett dies in Chicago.

April: Trial of the nine black youths in Scottsboro, Alabama, for allegedly raping two white women. Later the Supreme Court overthrew eight of the convictions, because the accused had never been granted adequate legal representation. By 1937 Alabama's continued attempts at retrial result in the conviction of four of the "Scottsboro Boys."

Fauset, *The Chinaberry Tree.*

1932

November 8: Election of Franklin D. Roosevelt to the presidency.

November 15: Surrounded by his family, Chesnutt dies at home at the age of seventy-four. At the time of his death his unpublished papers include six novels and numerous short stories. Much of this material, including the novels *Mandy Oxendine* (1997), *Paul Marchand, F.M.C.* (1998), and *The Quarry* (1999), have been recently published, and many of his speeches, essays, and letters newly anthologized.

George Schuyler (1895–1977), *Black No More;* Wallace Thurman (1902–1934), *Infants of the Spring;* Fisher, *The Conjure Man Dies;* Faulker, *Light in August.*

THE MARROW OF
TRADITION

[1901 Houghton Mifflin Edition]

I like you and your book, ingenious Hone!
In whose capacious all-embracing leaves
The very marrow of tradition's shown.

CHARLES LAMB,
To the Editor of the Every-Day Book.

Charles Chesnutt in 1899. Courtesy of Special Collections, Fisk University Library.

CONTENTS

I. AT BREAK OF DAY

"Stay here beside her, major. I shall not be needed for an hour yet. Meanwhile I'll go downstairs and snatch a bit of sleep, or talk to old Jane."

The night was hot and sultry. Though the windows of the chamber were wide open, and the muslin curtains looped back, not a breath of air was stirring. Only the shrill chirp of the cicada and the muffled croaking of the frogs in some distant marsh broke the night silence. The heavy scent of magnolias, overpowering even the strong smell of drugs in the sickroom, suggested death and funeral wreaths, sorrow and tears, the long home, the last sleep. The major shivered with apprehension as the slender hand which he held in his own contracted nervously and in a spasm of pain clutched his fingers with a viselike grip.

Major Carteret, though dressed in brown linen, had thrown off his coat for greater comfort. The stifling heat, in spite of the palm-leaf fan which he plied mechanically, was scarcely less oppressive than his own thoughts. Long ago, while yet a mere boy in years, he had come back from Appomattox[1] to find his family, one of the oldest and proudest in the state, hopelessly impoverished by the war, — even their ancestral home swallowed up in the common ruin. His elder brother had sacrificed his life on the bloody altar of the lost cause, and his father, broken and chagrined, died not many years later, leaving the major the last of his line. He had tried in various pursuits to gain a foothold in the new life, but with indifferent success until he won the hand of Olivia Merkell, whom he had seen grow from a small girl to glorious womanhood. With her money he had founded the Morning Chronicle, which he had made the leading organ of his party and the most influential paper in the State. The fine old house in which they lived was hers. In this very room she had first drawn the breath of life; it had been their nuptial chamber; and here, too, within a few hours, she might die, for it seemed impossible that one could long endure such frightful agony and live.

One cloud alone had marred the otherwise perfect serenity of their happiness. Olivia was childless. To have children to perpetuate the name of which he was so proud, to write it still higher on the roll of

---

[1] *Appomattox:* Appomattox County Courthouse in Virginia was the location of Confederate general Robert E. Lee's surrender to Union general Ulysses S. Grant on April 9, 1865, marking the end of the Civil War.

honor, had been his dearest hope. His disappointment had been proportionately keen. A few months ago this dead hope had revived, and
altered the whole aspect of their lives. But as time went on, his wife's
age had begun to tell upon her, until even Dr. Price, the most cheerful
and optimistic of physicians, had warned him, while hoping for the
best, to be prepared for the worst. To add to the danger, Mrs. Carteret
had only this day suffered from a nervous shock, which, it was feared,
had hastened by several weeks the expected event.

Dr. Price went downstairs to the library, where a dim light was
burning. An old black woman, dressed in a gingham frock, with a red
bandana handkerchief coiled around her head by way of turban, was
seated by an open window. She rose and curtsied as the doctor entered
and dropped into a willow rocking-chair near her own.

"How did this happen, Jane?" he asked in a subdued voice, adding,
with assumed severity, "You ought to have taken better care of your
mistress."

"Now look a-hyuh, Doctuh Price," returned the old woman in an
unctuous whisper, "you don' wanter come talkin' none er yo' foolishness 'bout my not takin' keer er Mis' 'Livy. *She* never would 'a' said
sech a thing! Seven er eight mont's ago, w'en she sent fer me, I says ter
her, says I: —

"'Lawd, Lawd, honey! You don' tell me dat after all dese long
w'ary years er waitin' de good Lawd is done heared yo' prayer an' is
gwine ter sen' you de chile you be'n wantin' so long an' so bad? Bless
his holy name! Will I come an' nuss yo' baby? Why, honey, I nussed
you, an' nussed yo' mammy thoo her las' sickness, an' laid her out
w'en she died. I would n' *let* nobody e'se nuss yo' baby; an' mo'over,
I'm gwine ter come an' nuss you too. You 're young side er me, Mis'
'Livy, but you 're ove'ly ole ter be havin' yo' fus' baby, an' you 'll need
somebody roun', honey, w'at knows all 'bout de fam'ly, an' deir ways
an' deir weaknesses, an' I don' know who dat'd be ef it wa'n't me.'

"'Deed, Mammy Jane,' says she, 'dere ain' nobody e'se I'd have
but you. You kin come ez soon ez you wanter an' stay ez long ez you
mineter.'

"An hyuh I is, an' hyuh I'm gwine ter stay. Fer Mis 'Livy is my ole
mist'ess's daughter, an' my ole mist'ess wuz good ter me, an' dey ain'
none er her folks gwine ter suffer ef ole Jane kin he'p it."

"Your loyalty does you credit, Jane," observed the doctor; "but you
have n't told me yet what happened to Mrs. Carteret to-day. Did the
horse run away, or did she see something that frightened her?"

"No, suh, de hoss did n' git skeered at nothin', but Mis' 'Livy did see somethin', er somebody; an' it wa'n't no fault er mine ner her'n neither, — it goes fu'ther back, suh, fu'ther dan dis day er dis year. Does you 'member de time w'en my ole mist'ess, Mis' 'Livy upstairs's mammy, died? No? Well, you wuz prob'ly 'way ter school den, studyin' ter be a doctuh. But I'll tell you all erbout it.

"W'en my ole mist'ess, Mis' 'Liz'beth Merkell, — an' a good mist'ess she wuz, — tuck sick fer de las' time, her sister Polly — ole Mis' Polly Ochiltree w'at is now — come ter de house ter he'p nuss her. Mis' 'Livy upstairs yander wuz erbout six years ole den, de sweetes' little angel you ever laid eyes on; an' on her dyin' bed Mis' 'Liz'beth ax' Mis' Polly fer ter stay hyuh an' take keer er her chile, an' Mis' Polly she promise'. She wuz a widder fer de secon' time, an' did n' have no child'en, an' could jes' as well come as not.

"But dere wuz trouble after de fune'al, an' it happen' right hyuh in dis lib'ary. Mars Sam wuz settin' by de table, w'en Mis' Polly come downstairs, slow an' solemn, an' stood dere in de middle er de flo', all in black, till Mars Sam sot a cheer fer her.

" 'Well, Samuel,' says she, 'now dat we 've done all we can fer po' 'Liz'beth, it only 'mains fer us ter consider Olivia's future.'

"Mars Sam nodded his head, but did n' say nothin'.

" 'I don' need ter tell you,' says she, 'dat I am willin' ter carry out de wishes er my dead sister, an' sac'ifice my own comfo't, an' make myse'f yo' housekeeper an' yo' child's nuss, fer my dear sister's sake. It wuz her dyin' wish, an' on it I will ac', ef it is also yo'n.'

"Mars Sam did n' want Mis' Polly ter come, suh; fur he did n' like Mis' Polly. He wuz skeered er Miss Polly."

"I don't wonder," yawned the doctor, "if she was anything like she is now."

"Wuss, suh, fer she wuz younger, an' stronger. She always would have her say, no matter 'bout what, an' her own way, no matter who 'posed her. She had already be'n in de house fer a week, an' Mars Sam knowed ef she once come ter stay, she 'd be de mist'ess of eve'ybody in it an' him too. But w'at could he do but say yas?

" 'Den it is unde'stood, is it,' says Mis' Polly, w'en he had spoke, 'dat I am ter take cha'ge er de house?'

" 'All right, Polly,' says Mars Sam, wid a deep sigh.

"Mis' Polly 'lowed he wuz sighin' fer my po' dead mist'ess, fer she did n' have no idee er his feelin's to'ds her, — she alluz did 'low dat all de gent'emen wuz in love wid 'er.

" 'You won' fin' much ter do,' Mars Sam went on, 'fer Julia is a good housekeeper, an' kin ten' ter mos' eve'ything, under yo' d'rections.'

"Mis' Polly stiffen' up like a ramrod. 'It mus' be unde'stood, Samuel,' says she, 'dat w'en I 'sumes cha'ge er yo' house, dere ain' gwine ter be no 'vided 'sponsibility; an' as fer dis Julia, me an' her could n' git 'long tergether nohow. Ef I stays, Julia goes.'

"W'en Mars Sam heared dat, he felt better, an' 'mence' ter pick up his courage. Mis' Polly had showed her han' too plain. My mist'ess had n' got col' yit, an' Mis' Polly, who 'd be'n a widder fer two years dis las' time, wuz already fig'rin' on takin' her place fer good, an' she did n' want no other woman roun' de house dat Mars Sam might take a' intrus' in.

" 'My dear Polly,' says Mars Sam, quite determine', 'I could n' possibly sen' Julia 'way. Fac' is, I could n' git 'long widout Julia. She 'd be'n runnin' dis house like clockwo'k befo' you come, an' I likes her ways. My dear, dead 'Liz'beth sot a heap er sto' by Julia, an' I'm gwine ter keep her here fer 'Liz'beth's sake.'

"Mis' Polly's eyes flash' fire.

" 'Ah,' says she, 'I see — I see! You perfers her housekeepin' ter mine, indeed! Dat is a fine way ter talk ter a lady! An' a heap er rispec' you is got fer de mem'ry er my po' dead sister!'

"Mars Sam knowed w'at she 'lowed she seed wa'n't so; but he did n' let on, fer it only made him de safer. He wuz willin' fer her ter 'magine w'at she please', jes' so long ez she kep' out er his house an' let him alone.

" 'No, Polly,' says he, gittin' bolder ez she got madder, 'dere ain' no use talkin'. Nothin' in de worl' would make me part wid Julia.'

"Mis' Polly she r'ared an' she pitch', but Mars Sam helt on like grim death. Mis' Polly would n' give in neither, an' so she fin'lly went away. Dey made some kind er 'rangement afterwa'ds, an' Miss Polly tuck Mis' 'Livy ter her own house. Mars Sam paid her bo'd an' 'lowed Mis' Polly somethin' fer takin' keer er her."

"And Julia stayed?"

"Julia stayed, suh, an' a couple er years later her chile wuz bawn, right here in dis house."

"But you said," observed the doctor, "that Mrs. Ochiltree was in error about Julia."

"Yas, suh, so she wuz, w'en my ole mist'ess died. But dis wuz two years after, — an' w'at has ter be has ter be. Julia had a easy time; she had a black gal ter wait on her, a buggy to ride in, an' eve'ything she wanted. Eve'ybody s'posed Mars Sam would give her a house an' lot, er leave her somethin' in his will. But he died suddenly, and did n' leave no will, an' Mis' Polly got herse'f 'pinted gyardeen ter young Mis' 'Livy, an' driv Julia an' her young un out er de house, an' lived here in dis house wid Mis' 'Livy till Mis' 'Livy ma'ied Majah Carteret."

"And what became of Julia?" asked Dr. Price.

Such relations, the doctor knew very well, had been all too common in the old slavery days, and not a few of them had been projected into the new era. Sins, like snakes, die hard. The habits and customs of a people were not to be changed in a day, nor by the stroke of a pen. As family physician, and father confessor by brevet, Dr. Price had looked upon more than one hidden skeleton; and no one in town had had better opportunities than old Jane for learning the undercurrents in the lives of the old families.

"Well," resumed Jane, "eve'ybody s'posed, after w'at had happen', dat Julia 'd keep on livin' easy, fer she wuz young an' good-lookin'. But she did n'. She tried ter make a livin' sewin', but Mis' Polly would n' let de bes' w'ite folks hire her. Den she tuck up washin', but did n' do no better at dat; an' bimeby she got so discourage' dat she ma'ied a shif'less yaller man, an' died er consumption soon after, — an' wuz 'bout ez well off, fer dis man could n' hardly feed her nohow."

"And the child?"

"One er de No'the'n w'ite lady teachers at de mission school tuck a likin' ter little Janet, an' put her thoo school, an' den sent her off ter de No'th fer ter study ter be a school teacher. W'en she come back, 'stead er teachin' she ma'ied ole Adam Miller's son."

"The rich stevedore's son, Dr. Miller?"

"Yas, suh, dat 's de man, — you knows 'im. Dis yer boy wuz jes' gwine 'way fer ter study ter be a doctuh, an' he ma'ied dis Janet, an' tuck her 'way wid 'im. Dey went off ter Europe, er Irope, er Orope, er somewhere er 'nother, 'way off yander, an' come back here las' year an' sta'ted dis yer horspital an' school fer ter train de black gals fer nusses."

"He 's a very good doctor, Jane, and is doing a useful work. Your chapter of family history is quite interesting, — I knew part of it before, in a general way; but you have n't yet told me what brought on Mrs. Carteret's trouble."

"I 'm jes' comin' ter dat dis minute, suh, — w'at I be'n tellin' you is all a part of it. Dis yer Janet, w'at 's Mis' 'Livy's half-sister, is ez much like her ez ef dey wuz twins. Folks sometimes takes 'em fer one er-nudder, — I s'pose it tickles Janet mos' ter death, but it do make Mis' 'Livy rippin'. An' den 'way back yander jes' after de wah, w'en de ole Carteret mansion had ter be sol', Adam Miller bought it, an' dis yer Janet an' her husban' is be'n livin' in it ever sence ole Adam died, 'bout a year ago; an' dat makes de majah mad, 'ca'se he don' wanter see cullud folks livin' in de ole fam'ly mansion w'at he wuz bawn in. An' mo'over, an' dat 's de wust of all, w'iles Mis' 'Livy ain' had no child'en befo', dis yer sister er her'n is got a fine-lookin' little yaller boy, w'at favors de fam'ly so dat ef Mis' 'Livy 'd see de chile anywhere, it 'd mos' break her heart fer ter think 'bout her not havin' no child'en herse'f. So ter-day, w'en Mis' 'Livy wuz out ridin' an' met dis yer Janet wid her boy, an' w'en Mis' 'Livy got ter studyin' 'bout her own chances, an' how she mought not come thoo safe, she jes' had a fit er hysterics right dere in de buggy. She wuz mos' home, an' William got her here, an' you knows de res'."

Major Carteret, from the head of the stairs, called the doctor anxiously.

"You had better come along up now, Jane," said the doctor.

For two long hours they fought back the grim spectre that stood by the bedside. The child was born at dawn. Both mother and child, the doctor said, would live.

"Bless its 'ittle hea't!" exclaimed Mammy Jane, as she held up the tiny mite, which bore as much resemblance to mature humanity as might be expected of an infant which had for only a few minutes drawn the breath of life. "Bless its 'ittle hea't! it 's de ve'y spit an' image er its pappy!"

The doctor smiled. The major laughed aloud. Jane's unconscious witticism, or conscious flattery, whichever it might be, was a welcome diversion from the tense strain of the last few hours.

"Be that as it may," said Dr. Price cheerfully, "and I'll not dispute it, the child is a very fine boy, — a very fine boy, indeed! Take care of it, major," he added with a touch of solemnity, "for your wife can never bear another."

With the child's first cry a refreshing breeze from the distant ocean cooled the hot air of the chamber; the heavy odor of the magnolias, with its mortuary suggestiveness, gave place to the scent of rose and lilac and honeysuckle. The birds in the garden were singing lustily.

All these sweet and pleasant things found an echo in the major's heart. He stood by the window, and looking toward the rising sun, breathed a silent prayer of thanksgiving. All nature seemed to rejoice in sympathy with his happiness at the fruition of this long-deferred hope, and to predict for this wonderful child a bright and glorious future.

Old Mammy Jane, however, was not entirely at ease concerning the child. She had discovered, under its left ear, a small mole, which led her to fear that the child was born for bad luck. Had the baby been black, or yellow, or poor-white, Jane would unhesitatingly have named, as his ultimate fate, a not uncommon form of taking off, usually resultant upon the infraction of certain laws, or, in these swift modern days, upon too violent a departure from established social customs. It was manifestly impossible that a child of such high quality as the grandson of her old mistress should die by judicial strangulation; but nevertheless the warning was a serious thing, and not to be lightly disregarded.

Not wishing to be considered as a prophet of evil omen, Jane kept her own counsel in regard to this significant discovery. But later, after the child was several days old, she filled a small vial with water in which the infant had been washed, and took it to a certain wise old black woman, who lived on the farther edge of the town and was well known to be versed in witchcraft and conjuration. The conjure woman added to the contents of the bottle a bit of calamus root, and one of the cervical vertebræ from the skeleton of a black cat, with several other mysterious ingredients, the nature of which she did not disclose. Following instructions given her, Aunt Jane buried the bottle in Carteret's back yard, one night during the full moon, as a good-luck charm to ward off evil from the little grandson of her dear mistress, so long since dead and gone to heaven.

II. THE CHRISTENING PARTY

They named the Carteret baby Theodore Felix. Theodore was a family name, and had been borne by the eldest son for several generations, the major himself being a second son. Having thus given the child two beautiful names, replete with religious and sentimental significance, they called him — "Dodie."

The baby was christened some six weeks after its birth, by which time Mrs. Carteret was able to be out. Old Mammy Jane, who had been brought up in the church, but who, like some better informed people in all ages, found religion not inconsistent with a strong vein of superstition, felt her fears for the baby's future much relieved when the rector had made the sign of the cross and sprinkled little Dodie with the water from the carved marble font, which had come from England in the reign of King Charles the Martyr, as the ill-fated son of James I.[1] was known to St. Andrew's. Upon this special occasion Mammy Jane had been provided with a seat downstairs among the white people, to her own intense satisfaction, and to the secret envy of a small colored attendance in the gallery, to whom she was ostentatiously pointed out by her grandson Jerry, porter at the Morning Chronicle office, who sat among them in the front row.

On the following Monday evening the major gave a christening party in honor of this important event. Owing to Mrs. Carteret's still delicate health, only a small number of intimate friends and family connections were invited to attend. These were the rector of St. Andrew's; old Mrs. Polly Ochiltree, the godmother; old Mr. Delamere, a distant relative and also one of the sponsors; and his grandson, Tom Delamere. The major had also invited Lee Ellis, his young city editor, for whom he had a great liking apart from his business value, and who was a frequent visitor at the house. These, with the family itself, which consisted of the major, his wife, and his half-sister, Clara Pemberton, a young woman of about eighteen, made up the eight persons for whom covers were laid.

Ellis was the first to arrive, a tall, loose-limbed young man, with a slightly freckled face, hair verging on auburn, a firm chin, and honest gray eyes. He had come half an hour early, and was left alone for a few minutes in the parlor, a spacious, high-ceilinged room, with large windows, and fitted up in excellent taste, with stately reminiscences of a past generation. The walls were hung with figured paper. The ceiling was whitewashed, and decorated in the middle with a plaster centre-piece, from which hung a massive chandelier sparkling with prismatic rays from a hundred crystal pendants. There was a handsome mantel, set with terra-cotta tiles, on which fauns and satyrs, nymphs and dryads, disported themselves in idyllic abandon. The furniture was old, and in keeping with the room.

At seven o'clock a carriage drove up, from which alighted an elderly gentleman, with white hair and mustache, and bowed somewhat with years. Short of breath and painfully weak in the legs, he was assisted from the carriage by a colored man, apparently about forty years old, to whom short side-whiskers and spectacles imparted an air of sobriety. This attendant gave his arm respectfully to the old

---

[1] *in the reign of King Charles the martyr, as the ill-fated son of James I:* Charles I ruled Great Britain during a tumultuous period from 1625 to 1649. His reign ended violently when he was found guilty of treason and beheaded.

gentleman, who leaned upon it heavily, but with as little appearance of dependence as possible. The servant, assuming a similar unconsciousness of the weight resting upon his arm, assisted the old gentleman carefully up the steps.

"I'm all right now, Sandy," whispered the gentleman as soon as his feet were planted firmly on the piazza. "You may come back for me at nine o'clock."

Having taken his hand from his servant's arm, he advanced to meet a lady who stood in the door awaiting him, a tall, elderly woman, gaunt and angular of frame, with a mottled face, and high cheekbones partially covered by bands of hair entirely too black and abundant for a person of her age, if one might judge from the lines of her mouth, which are rarely deceptive in such matters.

"Perhaps you 'd better not send your man away, Mr. Delamere," observed the lady, in a high shrill voice, which grated upon the old gentleman's ears. He was slightly hard of hearing, but, like most deaf people, resented being screamed at. "You might need him before nine o'clock. One never knows what may happen after one has had the second stroke. And moreover, our butler has fallen down the back steps — negroes are so careless! — and sprained his ankle so that he can't stand. I 'd like to have Sandy stay and wait on the table in Peter's place, if you don't mind."

"I thank you, Mrs. Ochiltree, for your solicitude," replied Mr. Delamere, with a shade of annoyance in his voice, "but my health is very good just at present, and I do not anticipate any catastrophe which will require my servant's presence before I am ready to go home. But I have no doubt, madam," he continued, with a courteous inclination, "that Sandy will be pleased to serve you, if you desire it, to the best of his poor knowledge."

"I shall be honored, ma'am," assented Sandy, with a bow even deeper than his master's, "only I 'm 'feared I ain't rightly dressed fer ter wait on table. I wuz only goin' ter pra'r-meetin', an' so I did n' put on my bes' clo's. Ef Mis' Ochiltree ain' gwine ter need me fer de nex' fifteen minutes, I kin ride back home in de ca'ige an' dress myse'f suitable fer de occasion, suh."

"If you think you 'll wait on the table any better," said Mrs. Ochiltree, "you may go along and change your clothes; but hurry back, for it is seven now, and dinner will soon be served."

Sandy retired with a bow. While descending the steps to the carriage, which had waited for him, he came face to face with a young man just entering the house.

"Am I in time for dinner, Sandy?" asked the newcomer.

"Yas, Mistuh Tom, you're in plenty or time. Dinner won't be ready till *I* git back, which won' be fer fifteen minutes er so yit."

Throwing away the cigarette which he held between his fingers, the young man crossed the piazza with a light step, and after a preliminary knock, for an answer to which he did not wait, entered the house with the air of one thoroughly at home. The lights in the parlor had been lit, and Ellis, who sat talking to Major Carteret when the newcomer entered, covered him with a jealous glance.

Slender and of medium height, with a small head of almost perfect contour, a symmetrical face, dark almost to swarthiness, black eyes, which moved somewhat restlessly, curly hair of raven tint, a slight mustache, small hands and feet, and fashionable attire, Tom Delamere, the grandson of the old gentleman who had already arrived, was easily the handsomest young man in Wellington. But no discriminating observer would have characterized his beauty as manly. It conveyed no impression of strength, but did possess a certain element, feline rather than feminine, which subtly negatived the idea of manliness.

He gave his hand to the major, nodded curtly to Ellis, saluted his grandfather respectfully, and inquired for the ladies.

"Olivia is dressing for dinner," replied the major; "Mrs. Ochiltree is in the kitchen, struggling with the servants. Clara — Ah, here she comes now!"

Ellis, whose senses were preternaturally acute where Clara was concerned, was already looking toward the hall and was the first to see her. Clad in an evening gown of simple white, to the close-fitting corsage of which she had fastened a bunch of pink roses, she was to Ellis a dazzling apparition. To him her erect and well-moulded form was the embodiment of symmetry, her voice sweet music, her movements the perfection of grace; and it scarcely needed a lover's imagination to read in her fair countenance a pure heart and a high spirit, — the truthfulness that scorns a lie, the pride which is not haughtiness. There were suggestive depths of tenderness, too, in the curl of her lip, the droop of her long lashes, the glance of her blue eyes, — depths that Ellis had long since divined, though he had never yet explored them. She gave Ellis a friendly nod as she came in, but for the smile with which she greeted Delamere, Ellis would have given all that he possessed, — not a great deal, it is true, but what could a man do more?

"You are the last one, Tom," she said reproachfully. "Mr. Ellis has been here half an hour."

Delamere threw a glance at Ellis which was not exactly friendly.

Why should this fellow always be on hand to emphasize his own shortcomings?

"The rector is not here," answered Tom triumphantly. "You see I am not the last."

"The rector," replied Clara, "was called out of town at six o'clock this evening, to visit a dying man, and so cannot be here. You are the last, Tom, and Mr. Ellis was the first."

Ellis was ruefully aware that this comparison in his favor was the only visible advantage that he had gained from his early arrival. He had not seen Miss Pemberton a moment sooner by reason of it. There had been a certain satisfaction in being in the same house with her, but Delamere had arrived in time to share or, more correctly, to monopolize, the sunshine of her presence.

Delamere gave a plausible excuse which won Clara's pardon and another enchanting smile, which pierced Ellis like a dagger. He knew very well that Delamere's excuse was a lie. Ellis himself had been ready as early as six o'clock, but judging this to be too early, had stopped in at the Clarendon Club for half an hour, to look over the magazines. While coming out he had glanced into the card-room, where he had seen his rival deep in a game of cards, from which Delamere had evidently not been able to tear himself until the last moment. He had accounted for his lateness by a story quite inconsistent with these facts.

The two young people walked over to a window on the opposite side of the large room, where they stood talking to one another in low tones. The major had left the room for a moment. Old Mr. Delamere, who was watching his grandson and Clara with an indulgent smile, proceeded to rub salt into Ellis's wounds.

"They make a handsome couple," he observed. "I remember well when her mother, in her youth an ideally beautiful woman, of an excellent family, married Daniel Pemberton, who was not of so good a family, but had made money. The major, who was only a very young man then, disapproved of the match; he considered that his mother, although a widow and nearly forty, was marrying beneath her. But he has been a good brother to Clara, and a careful guardian of her estate. Ah, young gentleman, you cannot appreciate, except in imagination, what it means, to one standing on the brink of eternity, to feel sure that he will live on in his children and his children's children!"

Ellis was appreciating at that moment what it meant, in cold blood, with no effort of the imagination, to see the girl whom he loved absorbed completely in another man. She had looked at him only once since Tom Delamere had entered the room, and then merely to use him as a spur with which to prick his favored rival.

"Yes, sir," he returned mechanically, "Miss Clara is a beautiful young lady."

"And Tom is a good boy — a fine boy," returned the old gentleman. "I am very well pleased with Tom, and shall be entirely happy when I see them married."

Ellis could not echo this sentiment. The very thought of this marriage made him miserable. He had always understood that the engagement was merely tentative, a sort of family understanding, subject to confirmation after Delamere should have attained his majority, which was still a year off, and when the major should think Clara old enough to marry. Ellis saw Delamere with the eye of a jealous rival, and judged him mercilessly, — whether correctly or not the sequel will show. He did not at all believe that Tom Delamere would make a fit husband for Clara Pemberton; but his opinion would have had no weight, — he could hardly have expressed it without showing his own interest. Moreover, there was no element of the sneak in Lee Ellis's make-up. The very fact that he might profit by the other's discomfiture left Delamere secure, so far as he could be affected by anything that Ellis might say. But Ellis did not shrink from a fair fight, and though in this one the odds were heavily against him, yet so long as this engagement remained indefinite, so long, indeed, as the object of his love was still unwed, he would not cease to hope. Such a sacrifice as this marriage clearly belonged in the catalogue of impossibilities. Ellis had not lived long enough to learn that impossibilities are merely things of which we have not learned, or which we do not wish to happen.

Sandy returned at the end of a quarter of an hour, and dinner was announced. Mr. Delamere led the way to the dining-room with Mrs. Ochiltree. Tom followed with Clara. The major went to the head of the stairs and came down with Mrs. Carteret upon his arm, her beauty rendered more delicate by the pallor of her countenance and more complete by the happiness with which it glowed. Ellis went in alone. In the rector's absence it was practically a family party which sat down, with the exception of Ellis, who, as we have seen, would willingly have placed himself in the same category.

The table was tastefully decorated with flowers, which grew about the house in lavish profusion. In warm climates nature adorns herself with true feminine vanity.

"What a beautiful table!" exclaimed Tom, before they were seated.

"The decorations are mine," said Clara proudly. "I cut the flowers and arranged them all myself."

"Which accounts for the admirable effect," rejoined Tom with a bow, before Ellis, to whom the same thought had occurred, was able to express himself. He had always counted himself the least envious of men, but for this occasion he coveted Tom Delamere's readiness.

"The beauty of the flowers," observed old Mr. Delamere, with sententious gallantry, "is reflected upon all around them. It is a handsome company."

Mrs. Ochiltree beamed upon the table with a dry smile.

"I don't perceive any effect that it has upon you or me," she said. "And as for the young people, 'Handsome is as handsome does.' If Tom here, for instance, were as good as he looks" —

"You flatter me, Aunt Polly," Tom broke in hastily, anticipating the crack of the whip; he was familiar with his aunt's conversational idiosyncrasies.

"If you are as good as you look," continued the old lady, with a cunning but indulgent smile, "some one has been slandering you."

"Thanks, Aunt Polly! Now you don't flatter me."

"There is Mr. Ellis," Mrs. Ochiltree went on, "who is not half so good-looking, but is steady as a clock, I dare say."

"Now, Aunt Polly," interposed Mrs. Carteret, "let the gentlemen alone."

"She does n't mean half what she says," continued Mrs. Carteret apologetically, "and only talks that way to people whom she likes."

Tom threw Mrs. Carteret a grateful glance. He had been apprehensive, with the sensitiveness of youth, lest his old great-aunt should make a fool of him before Clara's family. Nor had he relished the comparison with Ellis, who was out of place, anyway, in this family party. He had never liked the fellow, who was too much of a plodder and a prig to make a suitable associate for a whole-souled, generous-hearted young gentleman. He tolerated him as a visitor at Carteret's and as a member of the Clarendon Club, but that was all.

"Mrs. Ochiltree has a characteristic way of disguising her feelings," observed old Mr. Delamere, with a touch of sarcasm.

Ellis had merely flushed and felt uncomfortable at the reference to himself. The compliment to his character hardly offset the reflection upon his looks. He knew he was not exactly handsome, but it was not pleasant to have the fact emphasized in the presence of the girl he loved; he would like at least fair play, and judgment upon the subject left to the young lady.

Mrs. Ochiltree was quietly enjoying herself. In early life she had been accustomed to impale fools on epigrams, like flies on pins, to see them wriggle. But with advancing years she had lost in some measure the faculty of nice discrimination — it was pleasant to see her victims squirm, whether they were fools or friends. Even one's friends, she argued, were not always wise, and were sometimes the better for being told the truth. At her niece's table she felt at liberty to speak her mind, which she invariably did, with a frankness that sometimes bordered on brutality. She had long ago outgrown the period where ambition or passion, or its partners, envy and hatred, were springs of action in her life, and simply retained a mild enjoyment in the exercise of an old habit, with no active malice whatever. The ruling passion merely grew stronger as the restraining faculties decreased in vigor.

A diversion was created at this point by the appearance of old Mammy Jane, dressed in a calico frock, with clean white neckerchief and apron, carrying the wonderful baby in honor of whose naming this feast had been given. Though only six weeks old, the little Theodore had grown rapidly, and Mammy Jane declared was already quite large for his age, and displayed signs of an unusually precocious intelligence. He was passed around the table and duly admired. Clara thought his hair was fine. Ellis inquired about his teeth. Tom put his finger in the baby's fist to test his grip. Old Mr. Delamere was unable to decide as yet whether he favored most his father or his mother. The object of these attentions endured them patiently for several minutes, and then protested with a vocal vigor which led to his being taken promptly back upstairs. Whatever fate might be in store for him, he manifested no sign of weak lungs.

"Sandy," said Mrs. Carteret when the baby had retired, "pass that tray standing upon the side table, so that we may all see the presents."

Mr. Delamere had brought a silver spoon, and Tom a napkin ring. Ellis had sent a silver watch; it was a little premature, he admitted, but the boy would grow to it, and could use it to play with in the mean time. It had a glass back, so that he might see the wheels go round. Mrs. Ochiltree's present was an old and yellow ivory rattle, with a handle which the child could bite while teething, and a knob screwed on at the end to prevent the handle from slipping through the baby's hand.

"I saw that in your cedar chest, Aunt Polly," said Clara, "when I was a little girl, and you used to pull the chest out from under your bed to get me a dime."

"You kept the rattle in the right-hand corner of the chest," said

Tom, "in the box with the red silk purse, from which you took the gold piece you gave me every Christmas."

A smile shone on Mrs. Ochiltree's severe features at this appreciation, like a ray of sunlight on a snow-bank.

"Aunt Polly's chest is like the widow's cruse,"[2] said Mrs. Carteret, "which was never empty."

"Or Fortunatus's purse,[3] which was always full," added old Mr. Delamere, who read the Latin poets, and whose allusions were apt to be classical rather than scriptural.

"It will last me while I live," said Mrs. Ochiltree, adding cautiously, "but there 'll not be a great deal left. It won't take much to support an old woman for twenty years."

Mr. Delamere's man Sandy had been waiting upon the table with the decorum of a trained butler, and a gravity all his own. He had changed his suit of plain gray for a long blue coat with brass buttons, which dated back to the fashion of a former generation, with which he wore a pair of plaid trousers of strikingly modern cut and pattern. With his whiskers, his spectacles, and his solemn air of responsibility, he would have presented, to one unfamiliar with the negro type, an amusingly impressive appearance. But there was nothing incongruous about Sandy to this company, except perhaps to Tom Delamere, who possessed a keen eye for contrasts and always regarded Sandy, in that particular rig, as a very comical darkey.

"Is it quite prudent, Mrs. Ochiltree," suggested the major at a moment when Sandy, having set down the tray, had left the room for a little while, "to mention, in the presence of the servants, that you keep money in the house?"

"I beg your pardon, major," observed old Mr. Delamere, with a touch of stiffness. "The only servant in hearing of the conversation has been my own; and Sandy is as honest as any man in Wellington."

"You mean, sir," replied Carteret, with a smile, "as honest as any *negro* in Wellington."

"I make no exceptions, major," returned the old gentleman, with emphasis. "I would trust Sandy with my life, — he saved it once at the risk of his own."

---

[2] *widow's cruse:* In the biblical story from 1 Kings 17, the widow who aids Elijah finds that her cruse, or holder for cooking oil, is miraculously replenished.

[3] *Fortunatus's purse:* In the medieval romance, the begger old Fortunatus receives a purse with a limitless supply of gold from the goddess Fortune. The purse proves to be a curse, leading to the death of Fortunatus and his son.

"No doubt," mused the major, "the negro is capable of a certain doglike fidelity, — I make the comparison in a kindly sense, — a certain personal devotion which is admirable in itself, and fits him eminently for a servile career. I should imagine, however, that one could more safely trust his life with a negro than his portable property."

"Very clever, major! I read your paper, and know that your feeling is hostile toward the negro, but" —

The major made a gesture of dissent, but remained courteously silent until Mr. Delamere had finished.

"For my part," the old gentleman went on, "I think they have done very well, considering what they started from, and their limited opportunities. There was Adam Miller, for instance, who left a comfortable estate. His son George carries on the business, and the younger boy, William, is a good doctor and stands well with his profession. His hospital is a good thing, and if my estate were clear, I should like to do something for it."

"You are mistaken, sir, in imagining me hostile to the negro," explained Carteret. "On the contrary, I am friendly to his best interests. I give him employment; I pay taxes for schools to educate him, and for court-houses and jails to keep him in order. I merely object to being governed by an inferior and servile race."

Mrs. Carteret's face wore a tired expression. This question was her husband's hobby, and therefore her own nightmare. Moreover, she had her personal grievance against the negro race, and the names mentioned by old Mr. Delamere had brought it vividly before her mind. She had no desire to mar the harmony of the occasion by the discussion of a distasteful subject.

Mr. Delamere, glancing at his hostess, read something of this thought, and refused the challenge to further argument.

"I do not believe, major," he said, "that Olivia relishes the topic. I merely wish to say that Sandy is an exception to any rule which you may formulate in derogation of the negro. Sandy is a gentleman in ebony!"

Tom could scarcely preserve his gravity at this characterization of old Sandy, with his ridiculous air of importance, his long blue coat, and his loud plaid trousers. That suit would make a great costume for a masquerade. He would borrow it some time, — there was nothing in the world like it.

"Well, Mr. Delamere," returned the major good-humoredly, "no doubt Sandy is an exceptionally good negro, — he might well be, for he has had the benefit of your example all his life, — and we know that he is a faithful servant. But nevertheless, if I were Mrs. Ochiltree, I should put my money in the bank. Not all negroes are as honest as Sandy, and an elderly lady might not prove a match for a burly black burglar."

"Thank you, major," retorted Mrs. Ochiltree, with spirit, "I 'm not yet too old to take care of myself. That cedar chest has been my bank for forty years, and I shall not change my habits at my age."

At this moment Sandy reëntered the room. Carteret made a warning gesture, which Mrs. Ochiltree chose not to notice.

"I 've proved a match for two husbands, and am not afraid of any man that walks the earth, black or white, by day or night. I have a revolver, and know how to use it. Whoever attempts to rob me will do so at his peril."

After dinner Clara played the piano and sang duets with Tom Delamere. At nine o'clock Mr. Delamere's carriage came for him, and he went away accompanied by Sandy. Under cover of the darkness the old gentleman leaned on his servant's arm with frank dependence, and Sandy lifted him into the carriage with every mark of devotion.

Ellis had already excused himself to go to the office and look over the late proofs for the morning paper. Tom remained a few minutes longer than his grandfather, and upon taking his leave went round to the Clarendon Club, where he spent an hour or two in the card-room with a couple of congenial friends. Luck seemed to favor him, and he went home at midnight with a comfortable balance of winnings. He was fond of excitement, and found a great deal of it in cards. To lose was only less exciting than to win. Of late he had developed into a very successful player, — so successful, indeed, that several members of the club generally found excuses to avoid participating in a game where he made one.

III. THE EDITOR AT WORK

To go back a little, for several days after his child's birth Major Carteret's chief interest in life had been confined to the four walls of the chamber where his pale wife lay upon her bed of pain, and those of the adjoining room where an old black woman crooned lovingly over a little white infant. A new element had been added to the major's consciousness, broadening the scope and deepening the strength of his affections. He did not love Olivia the less, for maternity had crowned her wifehood with an added glory; but side by side with this old and tried attachment was a new passion, stirring up dormant hopes and kindling new desires. His regret had been more than personal at the thought that with himself an old name should be lost to the State; and now all the old pride of race, class, and family welled up anew, and swelled and quickened the current of his life.

Upon the major's first appearance at the office, which took place the second day after the child's birth, he opened a box of cigars in honor of the event. The word had been passed around by Ellis, and the whole office force, including reporters, compositors, and pressmen, came in to congratulate the major and smoke at his expense. Even Jerry, the colored porter, — Mammy Jane's grandson and therefore a protégé of the family, — presented himself among the rest, or rather, after the rest. The major shook hands with them all except Jerry, though he acknowledged the porter's congratulations with a kind nod and put a good cigar into his outstretched palm, for which Jerry thanked him without manifesting any consciousness of the omission. He was quite aware that under ordinary circumstances the major would not have shaken hands with white workingmen, to say nothing of negroes; and he had merely hoped that in the pleasurable distraction of the moment the major might also overlook the distinction of color. Jerry's hope had been shattered, though not rudely; for the major had spoken pleasantly and the cigar was a good one. Mr. Ellis had once shaken hands with Jerry, — but Mr. Ellis was a young man, whose Quaker[1] father had never owned any slaves, and he could not be expected to have as much pride as one of the best "quality," whose families had possessed land and negroes for time out of mind. On the whole, Jerry preferred the careless nod of the editor-in-chief to the more familiar greeting of the subaltern.

Having finished this pleasant ceremony, which left him with a comfortable sense of his new dignity, the major turned to his desk. It had been much neglected during the week, and more than one matter claimed his attention; but as typical of the new trend of his thoughts, the first subject he took up was one bearing upon the future of his son. Quite obviously the career of a Carteret must not be left to chance, — it must be planned and worked out with a due sense of the value of good blood.

There lay upon his desk a letter from a well-known promoter, offering the major an investment which promised large returns, though

---

[1] *Quaker:* Quakers were outspoken opponents of slavery and advocates for civil rights in the period before the Civil War.

several years must elapse before the enterprise could be put upon a paying basis. The element of time, however, was not immediately important. The Morning Chronicle provided him an ample income. The money available for this investment was part of his wife's patrimony. It was invested in a local cotton mill, which was paying ten per cent, but this was a beggarly return compared with the immense profits promised by the offered investment, — profits which would enable his son, upon reaching manhood, to take a place in the world commensurate with the dignity of his ancestors, one of whom, only a few generations removed, had owned an estate of ninety thousand acres of land and six thousand slaves.

This letter having been disposed of by an answer accepting the offer, the major took up his pen to write an editorial. Public affairs in the state were not going to his satisfaction. At the last state election his own party, after an almost unbroken rule of twenty years, had been defeated by the so-called "Fusion" ticket, a combination of Republicans and Populists. A clean sweep had been made of the offices in the state, which were now filled by new men. Many of the smaller places had gone to colored men, their people having voted almost solidly for the Fusion ticket. In spite of the fact that the population of Wellington was two thirds colored, this state of things was gall and wormwood to the defeated party, of which the Morning Chronicle was the acknowledged organ. Major Carteret shared this feeling. Only this very morning, while passing the city hall, on his way to the office, he had seen the steps of that noble building disfigured by a fringe of job-hunting negroes, for all the world — to use a local simile — like a string of buzzards sitting on a rail, awaiting their opportunity to batten upon the helpless corpse of a moribund city.

Taking for his theme the unfitness of the negro to participate in government, — an unfitness due to his limited education, his lack of experience, his criminal tendencies, and more especially to his hopeless mental and physical inferiority to the white race, — the major had demonstrated, it seemed to him clearly enough, that the ballot in the hands of the negro was a menace to the commonwealth. He had argued, with entire conviction, that the white and black races could never attain social and political harmony by commingling their blood; he had proved by several historical parallels that no two unassimilable races could ever live together except in the relation of superior and inferior; and he was just dipping his gold pen into the ink to indite his conclusions from the premises thus established, when Jerry, the porter, announced two visitors.

"Gin'l Belmont an' Cap'n McBane would like ter see you, suh."

"Show them in, Jerry."

The man who entered first upon this invitation was a dapper little gentleman with light-blue eyes and a Vandyke beard. He wore a frock coat, patent leather shoes, and a Panama hat. There were crow's-feet about his eyes, which twinkled with a hard and, at times, humorous shrewdness. He had sloping shoulders, small hands and feet, and walked with the leisurely step characteristic of those who have been reared under hot suns.

Carteret gave his hand cordially to the gentleman thus described.

"How do you do, Captain McBane," he said, turning to the second visitor.

The individual thus addressed was strikingly different in appearance from his companion. His broad shoulders, burly form, square jaw, and heavy chin betokened strength, energy, and unscrupulousness. With the exception of a small, bristling mustache, his face was clean shaven, with here and there a speck of dried blood due to a carelessly or unskillfully handled razor. A single deep-set gray eye was shadowed by a beetling brow, over which a crop of coarse black hair, slightly streaked with gray, fell almost low enough to mingle with his black, bushy eyebrows. His coat had not been brushed for several days, if one might judge from the accumulation of dandruff upon the collar, and his shirt-front, in the middle of which blazed a showy diamond, was plentifully stained with tobacco juice. He wore a large slouch hat, which, upon entering the office, he removed and held in his hand.

Having greeted this person with an unconscious but quite perceptible diminution of the warmth with which he had welcomed the other, the major looked around the room for seats for his visitors, and perceiving only one chair, piled with exchanges, and a broken stool propped against the wall, pushed a button, which rang a bell in the ball, summoning the colored porter to his presence.

"Jerry," said the editor when his servant appeared, "bring a couple of chairs for these gentlemen."

While they stood waiting, the visitors congratulated the major on the birth of his child, which had been announced in the Morning Chronicle, and which the prominence of the family made in some degree a matter of public interest.

"And now that you have a son, major," remarked the gentleman first described, as he lit one of the major's cigars, "you 'll be all the more interested in doing something to make this town fit to live in, which is what we came up to talk about. Things are in an awful condition! A negro justice of the peace has opened an office on Market Street, and only yesterday summoned a white man to appear before him. Negro lawyers get most of the business in the criminal court. Last evening a group of young white ladies, going quietly along the street arm-in-arm, were forced off the sidewalk by a crowd of negro girls. Coming down the street just now, I saw a spectacle of social equality and negro domination that made my blood boil with indignation, — a white and a black convict, chained together, crossing the city in charge of a negro officer! We cannot stand that sort of thing, Carteret, — it is the last straw! Something must be done, and that quickly!"

The major thrilled with responsive emotion. There was something prophetic in this opportune visit. The matter was not only in his own thoughts, but in the air; it was the spontaneous revulsion of white men against the rule of an inferior race. These were the very men, above all others in the town, to join him in a movement to change these degrading conditions.

General Belmont, the smaller of the two, was a man of good family, a lawyer by profession, and took an active part in state and local politics. Aristocratic by birth and instinct, and a former owner of slaves, his conception of the obligations and rights of his caste was nevertheless somewhat lower than that of the narrower but more sincere Carteret. In serious affairs Carteret desired the approval of his conscience, even if he had to trick that docile organ into acquiescence. This was not difficult to do in politics, for he believed in the divine right of white men and gentlemen, as his ancestors had believed in and died for the divine right of kings. General Belmont was not without a gentleman's distaste for meanness, but he permitted no fine scruples to stand in the way of success. He had once been minister, under a Democratic administration, to a small Central American state. Political rivals had characterized him as a tricky demagogue, which may of course have been a libel. He had an amiable disposition, possessed the gift of eloquence, and was a prime social favorite.

Captain George McBane had sprung from the poor-white class, to which, even more than to the slaves, the abolition of slavery had opened the door of opportunity. No longer overshadowed by a slave-holding caste, some of this class had rapidly pushed themselves forward. Some had made honorable records. Others, foremost in negro-baiting and election frauds, had done the dirty work of politics, as their fathers had done that of slavery, seeking their reward at first in minor offices, — for which men of gentler breeding did not care, — until their ambition began to reach out for higher honors.

Of this class McBane — whose captaincy, by the way, was merely a polite fiction — had been one of the most successful. He had held, until recently, as the reward of questionable political services, a contract with the State for its convict labor,[2] from which in a few years he had realized a fortune. But the methods which made his contract profitable had not commended themselves to humane people, and charges of cruelty and worse had been preferred against him. He was rich enough to escape serious consequences from the investigation which followed, but when the Fusion ticket carried the state he lost his contract, and the system of convict labor was abolished. Since then McBane had devoted himself to politics: he was ambitious for greater wealth, for office, and for social recognition. A man of few words and self-engrossed, he seldom spoke of his aspirations except where speech might favor them, preferring to seek his ends by secret "deals" and combinations rather than to challenge criticism and provoke rivalry by more open methods.

At sight, therefore, of these two men, with whose careers and characters he was entirely familiar, Carteret felt sweep over his mind the conviction that now was the time and these the instruments with which to undertake the redemption of the state from the evil fate which had befallen it.

Jerry, the porter, who had gone downstairs to the counting-room to find two whole chairs, now entered with one in each hand. He set a chair for the general, who gave him an amiable nod, to which Jerry responded with a bow and a scrape. Captain McBane made no acknowledgment, but fixed Jerry so fiercely with his single eye that upon placing the chair Jerry made his escape from the room as rapidly as possible.

"I don' like dat Cap'n McBane," he muttered, upon reaching the hall. "Dey says he got dat eye knock' out tryin' ter whip a cullud 'oman, when he wuz a boy, an' dat he ain' never had no use fer niggers sence, — 'cep'n' fer what he could make onten 'em wid his convic'

---

[2] *a contract with the State for its convict labor:* From the 1870s onward, southern states sought to generate additional income by leasing convict laborers to private individuals and businesses. The resulting labor force was largely African American, since blacks were imprisoned at a much higher rate than whites, often for petty offenses. Since there were few regulations governing the fair treatment of convict laborers, the lease system was tantamount to the reinstitution of the most brutal forms of slavery.

labor contrac's. His daddy wuz a' overseer befo' 'im, an' it come nachul fer him ter be a nigger-driver. I don' want dat one eye er his'n restin' on me no longer'n I kin he'p, an' I don' know how I 'm gwine ter like dis job ef he 's gwine ter be comin' roun' here. He ain' nothin' but po' w'ite trash nohow; but Lawd! Lawd! look at de money he 's got, — livin' at de hotel, wearin' di'mon's, an' colloguin' wid de bes' quality er dis town! 'Pears ter me de bottom rail is gittin' mighty close ter de top. Well, I s'pose it all comes f'm bein' w'ite. I wush ter Gawd I wuz w'ite!"

After this fervent aspiration, having nothing else to do for the time being, except to remain within call, and having caught a few words of the conversation as he went in with the chairs, Jerry, who possessed a certain amount of curiosity, placed close to the wall the broken stool upon which he sat while waiting in the hall, and applied his ear to a hole in the plastering of the hallway. There was a similar defect in the inner wall, between the same two pieces of studding, and while this inner opening was not exactly opposite the outer, Jerry was enabled, through the two, to catch in a more or less fragmentary way what was going on within.

He could hear the major, now and then, use the word "negro," and McBane's deep voice was quite audible when he referred, it seemed to Jerry with alarming frequency, to "the damned niggers," while the general's suave tones now and then pronounced the word "niggro," — a sort of compromise between ethnology and the vernacular. That the gentlemen were talking politics seemed quite likely, for gentlemen generally talked politics when they met at the Chronicle office. Jerry could hear the words "vote," "franchise," "eliminate," "constitution," and other expressions which marked the general tenor of the talk, though he could not follow it all, — partly because he could not hear everything distinctly, and partly because of certain limitations which nature had placed in the way of Jerry's understanding anything very difficult or abstruse.

He had gathered enough, however, to realize, in a vague way, that something serious was on foot, involving his own race, when a bell sounded over his head, at which he sprang up hastily and entered the room where the gentlemen were talking.

"Jerry," said the major, "wait on Captain McBane."

"Yas, suh," responded Jerry, turning toward the captain, whose eye he carefully avoided meeting directly.

"Take that half a dollar, boy," ordered McBane, "an' go 'cross the street to Mr. Sykes's, and tell him to send me three whiskies. Bring back the change, and make has'e."

The captain tossed the half dollar at Jerry, who, looking to one side, of course missed it. He picked the money up, however, and backed out of the room. Jerry did not like Captain McBane, to begin with, and it was clear that the captain was no gentleman, or he would not have thrown the money at him. Considering the source, Jerry might have overlooked this discourtesy had it not been coupled with the remark about the change, which seemed to him in very poor taste.

Returning in a few minutes with three glasses on a tray, he passed them round, handed Captain McBane his change, and retired to the hall.

"Gentlemen," exclaimed the captain, lifting his glass, "I propose a toast: 'No nigger domination.'"

"Amen!" said the others, and three glasses were solemnly drained.

"Major," observed the general, smacking his lips, "*I* should like to use Jerry for a moment, if you will permit me."

Jerry appeared promptly at the sound of the bell. He had remained conveniently near, — calls of this sort were apt to come in sequence.

"Jerry," said the general, handing Jerry half a dollar, "go over to Mr. Brown's, — I get my liquor there, — and tell them to send me three glasses of my special mixture. And, Jerry, — you may keep the change!"

"Thank y', gin'l, thank y', marster," replied Jerry, with unctuous gratitude, bending almost double as he backed out of the room.

"Dat 's a gent'eman, a rale ole-time gent'eman," he said to himself when he had closed the door. "But dere 's somethin' gwine on in dere, — dere sho' is! 'No nigger damnation!' Dat soun's all right, — I 'm sho' dere ain' no nigger I knows w'at wants damnation, do' dere 's lots of 'em w'at deserves it; but ef dat one-eyed Cap'n McBane got anything ter do wid it, w'atever it is, it don' mean no good fer de niggers, — damnation 'd be better fer 'em dan dat Cap'n McBane! He looks at a nigger lack he could jes' eat 'im alive."

"This mixture, gentlemen," observed the general when Jerry had returned with the glasses, "was originally compounded by no less a person than the great John C. Calhoun[3] himself, who confided the recipe to my father over the convivial board. In this nectar of the gods, gentlemen, I drink with you to 'White Supremacy!'"

---

[3] *John C. Calhoun:* John C. Calhoun (1782–1850) was elected vice president under John Quincy Adams in 1824 and then under Andrew Jackson in 1828. He resigned as Jackson's vice president after the two split over Calhoun's support of nullification and states' rights. After leaving office, Calhoun joined the U.S. Senate as a representative of South Carolina.

"White Supremacy everywhere!" added McBane with fervor.

"Now and forever!" concluded Carteret solemnly.

When the visitors, half an hour later, had taken their departure, Carteret, inspired by the theme, and in less degree by the famous mixture of the immortal Calhoun, turned to his desk and finished, at a white heat, his famous editorial in which he sounded the tocsin[4] of a new crusade.

At noon, when the editor, having laid down his pen, was leaving the office, he passed Jerry in the hall without a word or a nod. The major wore a rapt look, which Jerry observed with a vague uneasiness.

"He looks jes' lack be wuz walkin' in his sleep," muttered Jerry uneasily. "Dere 's somethin' up, sho 's you bawn! 'No nigger damnation!' Anybody 'd 'low dey wuz all gwine ter heaven; but I knows better! W'en a passel er w'ite folks gits ter talkin' 'bout de niggers lack dem in yander, it 's mo' lackly dey 're gwine ter ketch somethin' e'se dan heaven! I got ter keep my eyes open an' keep up wid w'at's happenin'. Ef dere 's gwine ter be anudder flood 'roun' here, I wants ter git in de ark wid de w'ite folks, — I may haf ter be anudder Ham,[5] an' sta't de cullud race all over ag'in."

IV. THEODORE FELIX

THE young heir of the Carterets had thriven apace, and at six months old was, according to Mammy Jane, whose experience qualified her to speak with authority, the largest, finest, smartest, and altogether most remarkable baby that had ever lived in Wellington. Mammy Jane had recently suffered from an attack of inflammatory rheumatism, as the result of which she had returned to her own home. She nevertheless came now and then to see Mrs. Carteret. A younger nurse had been procured to take her place, but it was understood that Jane would come whenever she might be needed.

"You really mean that about Dodie, do you, Mammy Jane?" asked the delighted mother, who never tired of hearing her own opinion confirmed concerning this wonderful child, which had come to her like an angel from heaven.

---

[4] *tocsin:* An alarm signal.

[5] *Ham:* In Gen. 9, Noah's son Ham looks at his father's naked body, and in anger Noah curses Ham and his descendants the Canaanites to a life of servitude to Ham's brothers. Justifications for the enslaving of African Americans were often founded on spurious interpretations of this story.

"Does I mean it!" exclaimed Mammy Jane, with a tone and an expression which spoke volumes of reproach. "Now, Mis' 'Livy, what is I ever uttered er said er spoke er done dat would make you s'pose I could tell you a lie 'bout yo' own chile?"

"No, Mammy Jane, I 'm sure you would n't."

" 'Deed, ma'am, I'm tellin' you de Lawd's truf. I don' haf ter tell no lies ner strain no p'ints 'bout my ole mist'ess's gran'chile. Dis yer boy is de ve'y spit an' image er yo' brother, young Mars Alick, w'at died w'en he wuz 'bout eight mont's ole, w'iles I wuz laid off havin' a baby er my own, an' could n' be roun' ter look after 'im. An' dis chile is a rale quality chile, he is, — I never seed a baby wid sech fine hair fer his age, ner sech blue eyes, ner sech a grip, ner sech a heft. W'y, dat chile mus' weigh 'bout twenty-fo' poun's, an' he not but six mont's ole. Does dat gal w'at does de nussin' w'iles I 'm gone ten' ter dis chile right, Mis' 'Livy?"

"She does fairly well, Mammy Jane, but I could hardly expect her to love the baby as you do. There 's no one like you, Mammy Jane."

" 'Deed dere ain't, honey; you is talkin' de gospel truf now! None er dese yer young folks ain' got de trainin' my ole mist'ess give me. Dese yer newfangle' schools don' l'rn 'em nothin' ter compare wid it. I 'm jes' gwine ter give dat gal a piece er my min', befo' I go, so she 'll ten' ter dis chile right."

The nurse came in shortly afterwards, a neat-looking brown girl, dressed in a clean calico gown, with a nurse's cap and apron.

"Look a-here, gal," said Mammy Jane sternly, "I wants you ter understan' dat you got ter take good keer er dis chile; fer I nussed his mammy dere, an' his gran'mammy befo' 'im, an' you is got a priv'lege dat mos' lackly you don' 'preciate. I wants you to 'member, in yo' incomin's an' outgoin's, dat I got my eye on you, an' am gwine ter see dat you does yo' wo'k right."

"Do you need me for anything, ma'am?" asked the young nurse, who had stood before Mrs. Carteret, giving Mammy Jane a mere passing glance, and listening impassively to her harangue. The nurse belonged to the younger generation of colored people. She had graduated from the mission school,[1] and had received some instruction in Dr. Miller's class for nurses. Standing, like most young people of her race, on the border line between two irreconcilable states of life, she had neither the picturesqueness of the slave, nor the unconscious

---

[1] *mission school*: During Reconstruction, a number of religious organizations, including the American Missionary Association, established schools in the South for the education of freedmen and their children.

dignity of those of whom freedom has been the immemorial birthright; she was in what might be called the chip-on-the-shoulder stage, through which races as well as individuals must pass in climbing the ladder of life, — not an interesting, at least not an agreeable stage, but an inevitable one, and for that reason entitled to a paragraph in a story of Southern life, which, with its as yet imperfect blending of old with new, of race with race, of slavery with freedom, is like no other life under the sun.

Had this old woman, who had no authority over her, been a little more polite, or a little less offensive, the nurse might have returned her a pleasant answer. These old-time negroes, she said to herself, made her sick with their slavering over the white folks, who, she supposed, favored them and made much of them because they had once belonged to them, — much the same reason why they fondled their cats and dogs. For her own part, they gave her nothing but her wages, and small wages at that, and she owed them nothing more than equivalent service. It was purely a matter of business; she sold her time for their money. There was no question of love between them.

Receiving a negative answer from Mrs. Carteret, she left the room without a word, ignoring Mammy Jane completely, and leaving that venerable relic of ante-bellum times gasping in helpless astonishment.

"Well, I nevuh!" she ejaculated, as soon as she could get her breath, "ef dat ain' de beatinis' pe'fo'mance I ever seed er heared of! Dese yer young niggers ain' got de manners dey waz bawned wid! I don' know w'at dey 're comin' to, w'en dey ain' got no mo' rispec' fer ole age — I don' know — I don' know!"

"Now what are you croaking about, Jane?" asked Major Carteret, who came into the room and took the child into his arms.

Mammy Jane hobbled to her feet and bobbed a curtsy. She was never lacking in respect to white people of proper quality; but Major Carteret, the quintessence of aristocracy, called out all her reserves of deference. The major was always kind and considerate to these old family retainers, brought up in the feudal atmosphere now so rapidly passing away. Mammy Jane loved Mrs. Carteret; toward the major she entertained a feeling bordering upon awe.

"Well, Jane," returned the major sadly, when the old nurse had related her grievance, "the old times have vanished, the old ties have been ruptured. The old relations of dependence and loyal obedience on the part of the colored people, the responsibility of protection and kindness upon that of the whites, have passed away forever. The young negroes are too self-assertive. Education is spoiling them, Jane;

they have been badly taught. They are not content with their station in life. Some time they will overstep the mark. The white people are patient, but there is a limit to their endurance.

"Dat 's w'at I tells dese young niggers," groaned Mammy Jane, with a portentous shake of her turbaned head, "w'en I hears 'em gwine on wid deir foolishniss; but dey don' min' me. Dey 'lows dey knows mo' d'n I does, 'ca'se dey be'n l'arnt ter look in a book. But, pshuh! my ole mist'ess showed me mo' d'n dem niggers 'll l'arn in a thousan' years! I 's fetch' my gran'son' Jerry up ter be 'umble, an' keep in 'is place. An' I tells dese other niggers dat ef dey'd do de same, an' not crowd de w'ite folks, dey'd git ernuff ter eat, an' live out deir days in peace an' comfo't. But dey don' min' me — dey don' min' me!"

"If all the colored people were like you and Jerry, Jane," rejoined the major kindly, "there would never be any trouble. You have friends upon whom, in time of need, you can rely implicitly for protection and succor. You served your mistress faithfully before the war; you remained by her when the other negroes were running hither and thither like sheep without a shepherd; and you have transferred your allegiance to my wife and her child. We think a great deal of you, Jane."

"Yes, indeed, Mammy Jane," assented Mrs. Carteret, with sincere affection, glancing with moist eyes from the child in her husband's arms to the old nurse, whose dark face was glowing with happiness at these expressions of appreciation, "you shall never want so long as we have anything. We would share our last crust with you."

"Thank y', Mis' 'Livy," said Jane with reciprocal emotion. "I knows who my frien's is, an' I ain' gwine ter let nothin' worry me. But fer de Lawd's sake, Mars Philip, gimme dat chile, an' lemme pat 'im on de back, er he 'll choke hisse'f ter death!"

The old nurse had been the first to observe that little Dodie, for some reason, was gasping for breath. Catching the child from the major's arms, she patted it on the back, and shook it gently. After a moment of this treatment, the child ceased to gasp, but still breathed heavily, with a strange, whistling noise.

"Oh, my child!" exclaimed the mother, in great alarm, taking the baby in her own arms, "what can be the matter with him, Mammy Jane?"

"Fer de Lawd's sake, ma'am, I don' know, 'less he 's swallered somethin'; an' he ain' had nothin' in his han's but de rattle Mis' Polly give 'im."

Mrs. Carteret caught up the ivory rattle, which hung suspended by a ribbon from the baby's neck.

"He has swallowed the little piece off the end of the handle," she cried, turning pale with fear, "and it has lodged in his throat. Telephone Dr. Price to come immediately, Philip, before my baby chokes to death! Oh, my baby, my precious baby!"

An anxious half hour passed, during which the child lay quiet, except for its labored breathing. The suspense was relieved by the arrival of Dr. Price, who examined the child carefully.

"It 's a curious accident," he announced at the close of his inspection. "So far as I can discover, the piece of ivory has been drawn into the trachea, or windpipe, and has lodged in the mouth of the right bronchus. I 'll try to get it out without an operation, but I can't guarantee the result."

At the end of another half hour Dr. Price announced his inability to remove the obstruction without resorting to more serious measures.

"I do not see," he declared, "how an operation can be avoided."

"Will it be dangerous?" inquired the major anxiously, while Mrs. Carteret shivered at the thought.

"It will be necessary to cut into his throat from the outside. All such operations are more or less dangerous, especially on small children. If this were some other child, I might undertake the operation unassisted; but I know how you value this one, major, and I should prefer to share the responsibility with a specialist."

"Is there one in town?" asked the major.

"No, but we can get one from out of town."

"Send for the best one in the country," said the major, "who can be got here in time. Spare no expense, Dr. Price. We value this child above any earthly thing."

"The best is the safest," replied Dr. Price. "I will send for Dr. Burns, of Philadelphia, the best surgeon in that line in America. If he can start at once, he can reach here in sixteen or eighteen hours, and the case can wait even longer, if inflammation does not set in."

The message was dispatched forthwith. By rare good fortune the eminent specialist was able to start within an hour or two after the receipt of Dr. Price's telegram. Meanwhile the baby remained restless and uneasy, the doctor spending most of his time by its side. Mrs. Carteret, who had never been quite strong since the child's birth, was a prey to the most agonizing apprehensions.

Mammy Jane, while not presuming to question the opinion of Dr. Price, and not wishing to add to her mistress's distress, was secretly oppressed by forebodings which she was unable to shake off. The child was born for bad luck. The mole under its ear, just at the point

where the hangman's knot would strike, had foreshadowed dire misfortune. She had already observed several little things which had rendered her vaguely anxious.

For instance, upon one occasion, on entering the room where the baby had been left alone, asleep in his crib, she had met a strange cat hurrying from the nursery, and, upon examining closely the pillow upon which the child lay, had found a depression which had undoubtedly been due to the weight of the cat's body. The child was restless and uneasy, and Jane had ever since believed that the cat had been sucking little Dodie's breath, with what might have been fatal results had she not appeared just in the nick of time.

This untimely accident of the rattle, a fatality for which no one could be held responsible, had confirmed the unlucky omen. Jane's duties in the nursery did not permit her to visit her friend the conjure woman; but she did find time to go out in the back yard at dusk, and to dig up the charm which she had planted there. It had protected the child so far; but perhaps its potency had become exhausted. She picked up the bottle, shook it vigorously, and then laid it back, with the other side up. Refilling the hole, she made a cross over the top with the thumb of her left hand, and walked three times around it.

What this strange symbolism meant, or whence it derived its origin, Aunt Jane did not know. The cross was there, and the Trinity, though Jane was scarcely conscious of these, at this moment, as religious emblems. But she hoped, on general principles, that this performance would strengthen the charm and restore little Dodie's luck. It certainly had its moral effect upon Jane's own mind, for she was able to sleep better, and contrived to impress Mrs. Carteret with her own hopefulness.

V. A JOURNEY SOUTHWARD

As the south-bound train was leaving the station at Philadelphia, a gentleman took his seat in the single sleeping-car attached to the train, and proceeded to make himself comfortable. He hung up his hat and opened his newspaper, in which he remained absorbed for a quarter of an hour. When the train had left the city behind, he threw the paper aside, and looked around at the other occupants of the car. One of these, who had been on the car since it had left New York, rose from his seat upon perceiving the other's glance, and came down the aisle.

"How do you do, Dr. Burns?" he said, stopping beside the seat of the Philadelphia passenger.

The gentleman looked up at the speaker with an air of surprise, which, after the first keen, incisive glance, gave place to an expression of cordial recognition.

"Why, it 's Miller!" he exclaimed, rising and giving the other his hand, "William Miller — Dr. Miller, of course. Sit down, Miller, and tell me all about yourself, — what you 're doing, where you 've been, and where you 're going. I 'm delighted to meet you, and to see you looking so well — and so prosperous."

"I deserve no credit for either, sir," returned the other, as he took the proffered seat, "for I inherited both health and prosperity. It is a fortunate chance that permits me to meet you."

The two acquaintances, thus opportunely thrown together so that they might while away in conversation the tedium of their journey, represented very different and yet very similar types of manhood. A celebrated traveler, after many years spent in barbarous or savage lands, has said that among all varieties of mankind the similarities are vastly more important and fundamental than the differences. Looking at these two men with the American eye, the differences would perhaps be the more striking, or at least the more immediately apparent, for the first was white and the second black, or, more correctly speaking, brown; it was even a light brown, but both his swarthy complexion and his curly hair revealed what has been described in the laws of some of our states as a "visible admixture" of African blood.

Having disposed of this difference, and having observed that the white man was perhaps fifty years of age and the other not more than thirty, it may be said that they were both tall and sturdy, both well dressed, the white man with perhaps a little more distinction; both seemed from their faces and their manners to be men of culture and accustomed to the society of cultivated people. They were both handsome men, the elder representing a fine type of Anglo-Saxon, as the term is used in speaking of our composite white population; while the mulatto's erect form, broad shoulders, clear eyes, fine teeth, and pleasingly moulded features showed nowhere any sign of that degeneration which the pessimist so sadly maintains is the inevitable heritage of mixed races.

As to their personal relations, it has already appeared that they were members of the same profession. In past years they had been teacher and pupil. Dr. Alvin Burns was professor in the famous medical college where Miller had attended lectures. The professor had taken an interest in his only colored pupil, to whom he had been attracted by his earnestness of purpose, his evident talent, and his

excellent manners and fine physique. It was in part due to Dr. Burns's friendship that Miller had won a scholarship which had enabled him, without drawing too heavily upon his father's resources, to spend in Europe, studying in the hospitals of Paris and Vienna, the two most delightful years of his life. The same influence had strengthened his natural inclination toward operative surgery, in which Dr. Burns was a distinguished specialist of national reputation.

Miller's father, Adam Miller, had been a thrifty colored man, the son of a slave, who, in the olden time, had bought himself with money which he had earned and saved, over and above what he had paid his master for his time. Adam Miller had inherited his father's thrift, as well as his trade, which was that of a stevedore, or contractor for the loading and unloading of vessels at the port of Wellington. In the flush turpentine days following a few years after the civil war, he had made money. His savings, shrewdly invested, had by constant accessions become a competence. He had brought up his eldest son to the trade; the other he had given a professional education, in the proud hope that his children or his grandchildren might be gentlemen in the town where their ancestors had once been slaves.

Upon his father's death, shortly after Dr. Miller's return from Europe, and a year or two before the date at which this story opens, he had promptly spent part of his inheritance in founding a hospital, to which was to be added a training school for nurses, and in time perhaps a medical college and a school of pharmacy. He had been strongly tempted to leave the South, and seek a home for his family and a career for himself in the freer North, where race antagonism was less keen, or at least less oppressive, or in Europe, where he had never found his color work to his disadvantage. But his people had needed him, and he had wished to help them, and had sought by means of this institution to contribute to their uplifting. As he now informed Dr. Burns, he was returning from New York, where he had been in order to purchase equipment for his new hospital, which would soon be ready for reception of patients.

"How much I can accomplish I do not know," said Miller, "but I'll do what I can. There are eight or nine million of us, and it will take a great deal of learning of all kinds to leaven that lump."

"It is a great problem, Miller, the future of your race," returned the other, "a tremendously interesting problem. It is a serial story which we are all reading, and which grows in vital interest with each successive installment. It is not only your problem, but ours. Your race must come up or drag ours down."

"We shall come up," declared Miller; "slowly and painfully, perhaps, but we shall win our way. If our race had made as much progress everywhere as they have made in Wellington, the problem would be well on the way toward solution."

"Wellington?" exclaimed Dr. Burns. "That 's where I 'm going. A Dr. Price, of Wellington, has sent for me to perform an operation on a child's throat. Do you know Dr. Price?"

"Quite well," replied Miller, "he is a friend of mine."

"So much the better. I shall want you to assist me. I read in the Medical Gazette, the other day, an account of a very interesting operation of yours. I felt proud to number you among my pupils. It was a remarkable case — a rare case. I must certainly have you with me in this one."

"I shall be delighted, sir," returned Miller, "if it is agreeable to all concerned."

Several hours were passed in pleasant conversation while the train sped rapidly southward. They were already far down in Virginia, and had stopped at a station beyond Richmond, when the conductor entered the car.

"All passengers," he announced, "will please transfer to the day coaches ahead. The sleeper has a hot box, and must be switched off here."

Dr. Burns and Miller obeyed the order, the former leading the way into the coach immediately in front of the sleeping-car.

"Let 's sit here, Miller," he said, having selected a seat near the rear of the car and deposited his suitcase in a rack. "It 's on the shady side."

Miller stood a moment hesitatingly, but finally took the seat indicated, and a few minutes later the journey was again resumed.

When the train conductor made his round after leaving the station, he paused at the seat occupied by the two doctors, glanced interrogatively at Miller, and then spoke to Dr. Burns, who sat in the end of the seat nearest the aisle.

"This man is with you?" he asked, indicating Miller with a slight side movement of his head, and a keen glance in his direction.

"Certainly," replied Dr. Burns curtly, and with some surprise. "Don't you see that he is?"

The conductor passed on. Miller paid no apparent attention to this little interlude, though no syllable had escaped him. He resumed the conversation where it had been broken off, but nevertheless followed with his eyes the conductor, who stopped at a seat near the forward end of the car, and engaged in conversation with a man whom Miller had not hitherto noticed.

As this passenger turned his head and looked back toward Miller, the latter saw a broad-shouldered, burly white man, and recognized in his square-cut jaw, his coarse, firm mouth, and the single gray eye with which he swept Miller for an instant with a scornful glance, a well-known character of Wellington, with whom the reader has already made acquaintance in these pages. Captain McBane wore a frock coat and a slouch hat; several buttons of his vest were unbuttoned, and his solitaire diamond blazed in his soiled shirt-front like the headlight of a locomotive.

The conductor in his turn looked back at Miller, and retraced his steps. Miller braced himself for what he feared was coming, though he had hoped, on account of his friend's presence, that it might be avoided.

"Excuse me, sir," said the conductor, addressing Dr. Burns, "but did I understand you to say that this man was your servant?"

"No, indeed!" replied Dr. Burns indignantly. "The gentleman is not my servant, nor anybody's servant, but is my friend. But, by the way, since we are on the subject, may I ask what affair it is of yours?"

"It's very much my affair," returned the conductor, somewhat nettled at this questioning of his authority. "I'm sorry to part *friends*, but the law of Virginia does not permit colored passengers to ride in the white cars. You'll have to go forward to the next coach," he added, addressing Miller this time.

"I have paid my fare on the sleeping-car, where the separate-car law[1] does not apply," remonstrated Miller.

"I can't help that. You can doubtless get your money back from the sleeping-car company. But this is a day coach, and is distinctly marked 'White,' as you must have seen before you sat down here. The sign is put there for that purpose."

He indicated a large card neatly framed and hung at the end of the car, containing the legend, "White," in letters about a foot long, painted in white upon a dark background, typical, one might suppose, of the distinction thereby indicated.

---

[1] *the separate-car law:* Following the Civil War, a series of segregation laws were passed in the South designed to counteract civil rights initiatives. *Plessy v. Ferguson,* a landmark Supreme Court decision, declared these state and local laws constitutional in 1896. The 1954 and 1956 cases *Brown v. Board of Education* and *Gayle v. Browder* specifically overturned the *Plessy* ruling.

"You shall not stir a step, Miller," exclaimed Dr. Burns wrathfully. "This is an outrage upon a citizen of a free country. You shall stay right here."

"I'm sorry to discommode you," returned the conductor, "but there's no use kicking. It's the law of Virginia, and I am bound by it as well as you. I have already come near losing my place because of not enforcing it, and I can take no more such chances, since I have a family to support."

"And my friend has his rights to maintain," returned Dr. Burns with determination. "There is a vital principle at stake in the matter."

"Really, sir," argued the conductor, who was a man of peace and not fond of controversy, "there's no use talking — he absolutely cannot ride in this car."

"How can you prevent it?" asked Dr. Burns, lapsing into the argumentative stage.

"The law gives me the right to remove him by force. I can call on the train crew to assist me, or on the other passengers. If I should choose to put him off the train entirely, in the middle of a swamp, he would have no redress — the law so provides. If I did not wish to use force, I could simply switch this car off at the next siding, transfer the white passengers to another, and leave you and your friend in possession until you were arrested and fined or imprisoned."

"What he says is absolutely true, doctor," interposed Miller at this point. "It is the law, and we are powerless to resist it. If we made any trouble, it would merely delay your journey and imperil a life at the other end. I'll go into the other car."

"You shall not go alone," said Dr. Burns stoutly, rising in his turn. "A place that is too good for you is not good enough for me. I will sit wherever you do."

"I'm sorry again," said the conductor, who had quite recovered his equanimity, and calmly conscious of his power, could scarcely restrain an amused smile; "I dislike to interfere, but white passengers are not permitted to ride in the colored car."

"This is an outrage," declared Dr. Burns, "a d——d outrage! You are curtailing the rights, not only of colored people, but of white men as well. I shall sit where I please!"

"I warn you, sir," rejoined the conductor, hardening again, "that the law will be enforced. The beauty of the system lies in its strict impartiality — it applies to both races alike."

"And is equally infamous in both cases," declared Dr. Burns. "I shall immediately take steps — "

"Never mind, doctor," interrupted Miller, soothingly, "it's only for a little while. I'll reach my destination just as surely in the other car, and we can't help it, anyway. I'll see you again at Wellington."

Dr. Burns, finding resistance futile, at length acquiesced and made way for Miller to pass him.

The colored doctor took up his valise and crossed the platform to the car ahead. It was an old car, with faded upholstery, from which the stuffing projected here and there through torn places. Apparently the floor had not been swept for several days. The dust lay thick upon the window sills, and the water-cooler, from which he essayed to get a drink, was filled with stale water which had made no recent acquaintance with ice. There was no other passenger in the car, and Miller occupied himself in making a rough calculation of what it would cost the Southern railroads to haul a whole car for every colored passenger. It was expensive, to say the least; it would be cheaper, and quite as considerate of their feelings, to make the negroes walk.

The car was conspicuously labeled at either end with large cards, similar to those in the other car, except that they bore the word "Colored" in black letters upon a white background. The author of this piece of legislation had contrived, with an ingenuity worthy of a better cause, that not merely should the passengers be separated by the color line, but that the reason for this division should be kept constantly in mind. Lest a white man should forget that he was white, — not a very likely contingency, — these cards would keep him constantly admonished of the fact; should a colored person endeavor, for a moment, to lose sight of his disability, these staring signs would remind him continually that between him and the rest of mankind not of his own color, there was by law a great gulf fixed.

Having composed himself, Miller had opened a newspaper, and was deep in an editorial which set forth in glowing language the inestimable advantages which would follow to certain recently acquired islands[2] by the introduction of American liberty, when the rear door of the car opened to give entrance to Captain George McBane, who took a seat near the door and lit a cigar. Miller knew him quite well by sight and by reputation, and detested him as heartily. He represented the aggressive, offensive element among the white people of the New South, who made it hard for a negro to maintain his self-respect or to enjoy even the rights conceded to colored men by Southern laws.

----

[2] *recently acquired islands:* The U.S. government assumed control of Cuba and the Philippines after defeating the Spanish military during the 1898 Spanish-American War.

McBane had undoubtedly identified him to the conductor in the other car. Miller had no desire to thrust himself upon the society of white people, which, indeed, to one who had traveled so much and so far, was no novelty; but he very naturally resented being at this late day — the law had been in operation only a few months — branded and tagged and set apart from the rest of mankind upon the public highways, like an unclean thing. Nevertheless, he preferred even this to the exclusive society of Captain George McBane.

"Porter," he demanded of the colored train attaché who passed through the car a moment later, "is this a smoking car for white men?"

"No, suh," replied the porter, "but they comes in here sometimes, when they ain' no cullud ladies on the kyar."

"Well, I have paid first-class fare, and I object to that man's smoking in here. You tell him to go out."

"I 'll tell the conductor, suh," returned the porter in a low tone. "I 'd jus' as soon talk ter the devil as ter that man."

The white man had spread himself over two seats, and was smoking vigorously, from time to time spitting carelessly in the aisle, when the conductor entered the compartment.

"Captain," said Miller, "this car is plainly marked 'Colored.' I have paid first-class fare, and I object to riding in a smoking car."

"All right," returned the conductor, frowning irritably. "I 'll speak to him."

He walked over to the white passenger, with whom he was evidently acquainted, since he addressed him by name.

"Captain McBane," he said, "it 's against the law for you to ride in the nigger car."

"Who are you talkin' to?" returned the other. "I 'll ride where I damn please."

"Yes, sir, but the colored passenger objects. I 'm afraid I 'll have to ask you to go into the smoking-car."

"The hell you say!" rejoined McBane. "I 'll leave this car when I get good and ready, and that won't be till I 've finished this cigar. See?"

He was as good as his word. The conductor escaped from the car before Miller had time for further expostulation. Finally McBane, having thrown the stump of his cigar into the aisle and added to the floor a finishing touch in the way of expectoration, rose and went back into the white car.

Left alone in his questionable glory, Miller buried himself again in his newspaper, from which he did not look up until the engine stopped at a tank station to take water.

As the train came to a standstill, a huge negro, covered thickly with dust, crawled off one of the rear trucks unobserved, and ran round the rear end of the car to a watering-trough by a neighboring well. Moved either by extreme thirst or by the fear that his time might be too short to permit him to draw a bucket of water, he threw himself down by the trough, drank long and deep, and plunging his head into the water, shook himself like a wet dog, and crept furtively back to his dangerous perch.

Miller, who had seen this man from the car window, had noticed a very singular thing. As the dusty tramp passed the rear coach, he cast toward it a glance of intense ferocity. Up to that moment the man's face, which Miller had recognized under its grimy coating, had been that of an ordinarily good-natured, somewhat reckless, pleasure-loving negro, at present rather the worse for wear. The change that now came over it suggested a concentrated hatred almost uncanny in its murderousness. With awakened curiosity Miller followed the direction of the negro's glance, and saw that it rested upon a window where Captain McBane sat looking out. When Miller looked back, the negro had disappeared.

At the next station a Chinaman, of the ordinary laundry type, boarded the train, and took his seat in the white car without objection. At another point a colored nurse found a place with her mistress.

"White people," said Miller to himself, who had seen these passengers from the window, "do not object to the negro as a servant. As the traditional negro, — the servant, — he is welcomed; as an equal, he is repudiated."

Miller was something of a philosopher. He had long ago had the conclusion forced upon him that an educated man of his race, in order to live comfortably in the United States, must be either a philosopher or a fool; and since he wished to be happy, and was not exactly a fool, he had cultivated philosophy. By and by he saw a white man, with a dog, enter the rear coach. Miller wondered whether the dog would be allowed to ride with his master, and if not, what disposition would be made of him. He was a handsome dog, and Miller, who was fond of animals, would not have objected to the company of a dog, as a dog. He was nevertheless conscious of a queer sensation when he saw the porter take the dog by the collar and start in his own direction, and felt consciously relieved when the canine passenger was taken on past him into the baggage-car ahead. Miller's hand was hanging over the arm of his seat, and the dog, an intelligent shepherd, licked it as he passed. Miller was not entirely sure that he would not have liked the porter to leave the dog there; he was a friendly dog, and seemed inclined to be sociable.

Toward evening the train drew up at a station where quite a party of farm laborers, fresh from their daily toil, swarmed out from the conspicuously labeled colored waiting-room, and into the car with Miller. They were a jolly, good-natured crowd, and, free from the embarrassing presence of white people, proceeded to enjoy themselves after their own fashion. Here an amorous fellow sat with his arm around a buxom girl's waist. A musically inclined individual — his talents did not go far beyond inclination — produced a mouth-organ and struck up a tune, to which a limber-legged boy danced in the aisle. They were noisy, loquacious, happy, dirty, and malodorous. For a while Miller was amused and pleased. They were his people, and he felt a certain expansive warmth toward them in spite of their obvious shortcomings. By and by, however, the air became too close, and he went out upon the platform. For the sake of the democratic ideal, which meant so much to his race, he might have endured the affliction. He could easily imagine that people of refinement, with the power in their hands, might be tempted to strain the democratic ideal in order to avoid such contact; but personally, and apart from the mere matter of racial sympathy, these people were just as offensive to him as to the whites in the other end of the train. Surely, if a classification of passengers on trains was at all desirable, it might be made upon some more logical and considerate basis than a mere arbitrary, tactless, and, by the very nature of things, brutal drawing of a color line. It was a veritable bed of Procrustes,[3] this standard which the whites had set for the negroes. Those who grew above it must have their heads cut off, figuratively speaking, — must be forced back to the level assigned to their race; those who fell beneath the standard set had their necks stretched, literally enough, as the ghastly record in the daily papers gave conclusive evidence.

Miller breathed more freely when the lively crowd got off at the next station, after a short ride. Moreover, he had a light heart, a conscience void of offense, and was only thirty years old. His philosophy had become somewhat jaded on this journey, but he pulled it together for a final effort. Was it not, after all, a wise provision of nature that had given to a race, destined to a long servitude and a slow emergence

---

[3] *bed of Procrustes:* According to Greek myth, Procrustes adjusted the bodies of his guests to fit his beds, cutting off limbs or stretching out bodies when necessary. Thus, a bed of Procrustes is anything — in this case, a law — that is overly rigid or unforgiving.

therefrom, a cheerfulness of spirit which enabled them to catch pleasure on the wing, and endure with equanimity the ills that seemed inevitable? The ability to live and thrive under adverse circumstances is the surest guaranty of the future. The race which at the last shall inherit the earth — the residuary legatee of civilization — will be the race which remains longest upon it. The negro was here before the Anglo-Saxon was evolved, and his thick lips and heavy-lidded eyes looked out from the inscrutable face of the Sphinx across the sands of Egypt while yet the ancestors of those who now oppress him were living in caves, practicing human sacrifice, and painting themselves with woad[4] — and the negro is here yet.

" 'Blessed are the meek,' "[5] quoted Miller at the end of these consoling reflections, " 'for they shall inherit the earth.' If this be true, the negro may yet come into his estate, for meekness seems to be set apart as his portion."

The journey came to an end just as the sun had sunk into the west.

Simultaneously with Miller's exit from the train, a great black figure crawled off the trucks of the rear car, on the side opposite the station platform. Stretching and shaking himself with a free gesture, the black man, seeing himself unobserved, moved somewhat stiffly round the end of the car to the station platform.

" 'Fo de Lawd!" he muttered, "ef I had n' had a cha'm' life, I 'd 'a' never got here on dat ticket, an' dat's a fac' — it sho' am! I kind er 'lowed I wuz gone a dozen times, ez it wuz. But I got my job ter do in dis worl', an' I knows I ain' gwine ter die 'tel I 've 'complished it. I jes' want one mo' look at dat man, an' den I 'll haf ter git somethin' ter eat; fer two raw turnips in twelve hours is slim pickin's fer a man er my size!"

VI. JANET

As the train drew up at the station platform, Dr. Price came forward from the white waiting-room, and stood expectantly by the door of the white coach. Miller, having left his car, came down the platform in time to intercept Burns as he left the train, and to introduce him to Dr. Price.

---

[4] *woad*: A blue dye prepared from leaves.
[5] *Blessed are the meek*: Matt. 5.5. "Blessed are the meek, for they shall inherit the earth."

"My carriage is in waiting," said Dr. Price. "I should have liked to have you at my own house, but my wife is out of town. We have a good hotel, however, and you will doubtless find it more convenient."

"You are very kind, Dr. Price. Miller, won't you come up and dine with me?"

"Thank you, no," said Miller, "I am expected at home. My wife and child are waiting for me in the buggy yonder by the platform."

"Oh, very well; of course you must go; but don't forget our appointment. Let's see, Dr. Price, I can eat and get ready in half an hour — that will make it" —

"I have asked several of the local physicians to be present at eight o'clock," said Dr. Price. "The case can safely wait until then."

"Very well, Miller, be on hand at eight. I shall expect you without fail. Where shall he come, Dr. Price?"

"To the residence of Major Philip Carteret, on Vine Street."

"I have invited Dr. Miller to be present and assist in the operation," Dr. Burns continued, as they drove toward the hotel. "He was a favorite pupil of mine, and is a credit to the profession. I presume you saw his article in the Medical Gazette?"

"Yes, and I assisted him in the case," returned Dr. Price. "It was a colored lad, one of his patients, and he called me in to help him. He is a capable man, and very much liked by the white physicians."

Miller's wife and child were waiting for him in fluttering anticipation. He kissed them both as he climbed into the buggy.

"We came at four o'clock," said Mrs. Miller, a handsome young woman, who might be anywhere between twenty-five and thirty, and whose complexion, in the twilight, was not distinguishable from that of a white person, "but the train was late two hours, they said. We came back at six, and have been waiting ever since."

"Yes, papa," piped the child, a little boy of six or seven, who sat between them, "and I am very hungry."

Miller felt very much elated as he drove homeward through the twilight. By his side sat the two persons whom he loved best in all the world. His affairs were prosperous. Upon opening his office in the city, he had been received by the members of his own profession with a cordiality generally frank, and in no case much reserved. The colored population of the city was large, but in the main poor, and the white physicians were not unwilling to share this unprofitable practice with a colored doctor worthy of confidence. In the intervals of the work upon his hospital, he had built up a considerable practice among his own people; but except in the case of some poor unfortunate whose pride had been lost in poverty or sin, no white patient had ever called upon him for treatment. He knew very well the measure of his powers, — a liberal education had given him opportunity to compare himself with other men, — and was secretly conscious that in point of skill and knowledge he did not suffer by comparison with any other physician in the town. He liked to believe that the race antagonism which hampered his progress and that of his people was a mere temporary thing, the outcome of former conditions, and bound to disappear in time, and that when a colored man should demonstrate to the community in which he lived that he possessed character and power, that community would find a way in which to enlist his services for the public good.

He had already made himself useful, and had received many kind words and other marks of appreciation. He was now offered a further confirmation of his theory: having recognized his skill, the white people were now ready to take advantage of it. Any lurking doubt he may have felt when first invited by Dr. Burns to participate in the operation, had been dispelled by Dr. Price's prompt acquiescence.

On the way homeward Miller told his wife of this appointment. She was greatly interested; she was herself a mother, with an only child. Moreover, there was a stronger impulse than mere humanity to draw her toward the stricken mother. Janet had a tender heart, and could have loved this white sister, her sole living relative of whom she knew. All her life long she had yearned for a kind word, a nod, a smile, the least thing that imagination might have twisted into a recognition of the tie between them. But it had never come.

And yet Janet was not angry. She was of a forgiving temper; she could never bear malice. She was educated, had read many books, and appreciated to the full the social forces arrayed against any such recognition as she had dreamed of. Of the two barriers between them a man might have forgiven the one; a woman would not be likely to overlook either the bar sinister or the difference of race, even to the slight extent of a silent recognition. Blood is thicker than water, but, if it flows too far from conventional channels, may turn to gall and wormwood. Nevertheless, when the heart speaks, reason falls into the background, and Janet would have worshipped this sister, even afar off, had she received even the slightest encouragement. So strong was this weakness that she had been angry with herself for her lack of pride, or even of a decent self-respect. It was, she sometimes thought, the heritage of her mother's race, and she was ashamed of it as part of the taint of slavery. She had never acknowledged, even to her husband, from whom she concealed nothing else, her secret thoughts upon this life-long sorrow. This silent grief was nature's penalty, or society's revenge, for whatever heritage of beauty or intellect or personal charm had come to her with her father's blood. For she had received no other inheritance. Her sister was rich by right of her birth; if Janet had been fortunate, her good fortune had not been due to any provision made for her by her white father.

She knew quite well how passionately, for many years, her proud sister had longed and prayed in vain for the child which had at length brought joy into her household, and she could feel, by sympathy, all the sickening suspense with which the child's parents must await the result of this dangerous operation.

"O Will," she adjured her husband anxiously, when he had told her of the engagement, "you must be very careful. Think of the child's poor mother! Think of our own dear child, and what it would mean to lose him!"

VII. THE OPERATION

DR. PRICE was not entirely at ease in his mind as the two doctors drove rapidly from the hotel to Major Carteret's. Himself a liberal man, from his point of view, he saw no reason why a colored doctor might not operate upon a white male child, — there are fine distinctions in the application of the color line, — but several other physicians had been invited, some of whom were men of old-fashioned notions, who might not relish such an innovation.

This, however, was but a small difficulty compared with what might be feared from Major Carteret himself. For he knew Carteret's unrelenting hostility to anything that savored of recognition of the negro as the equal of white men. It was traditional in Wellington that no colored person had ever entered the front door of the Carteret residence, and that the luckless individual who once presented himself there upon alleged business and resented being ordered to the back door had been unceremoniously thrown over the piazza railing into a rather thorny clump of rose-bushes below. If Miller were going as a servant, to hold a basin or a sponge, there would be no difficulty; but as a surgeon — well, he would n't borrow trouble. Under the circumstances the major might yield a point.

But as they neared the house the major's unyielding disposition loomed up formidably. Perhaps if the matter were properly presented to Dr. Burns, he might consent to withdraw the invitation. It was not yet too late to send Miller a note.

"By the way, Dr. Burns," he said, "I 'm very friendly to Dr. Miller, and should personally like to have him with us to-night. But — I ought to have told you this before, but I could n't very well do so, on such short notice, in Miller's presence — we are a conservative people, and our local customs are not very flexible. We jog along in much the same old way our fathers did. I 'm not at all sure that Major Carteret or the other gentlemen would consent to the presence of a negro doctor."

"I think you misjudge your own people," returned Dr. Burns, "they are broader than you think. We have our prejudices against the negro at the North, but we do not let them stand in the way of anything that *we* want. At any rate, it is too late now, and I will accept the responsibility. If the question is raised, I will attend to it. When I am performing an operation I must be *aut Cæsar, aut nullus.*"[1]

Dr. Price was not reassured, but he had done his duty and felt the reward of virtue. If there should be trouble, he would not be responsible. Moreover, there was a large fee at stake, and Dr. Burns was not likely to prove too obdurate.

They were soon at Carteret's, where they found assembled the several physicians invited by Dr. Price. These were successively introduced as Drs. Dudley, Hooper, and Ashe, all of whom were gentlemen of good standing, socially and in their profession, and considered it a high privilege to witness so delicate an operation at the hands of so eminent a member of their profession.

Major Carteret entered the room and was duly presented to the famous specialist. Carteret's anxious look lightened somewhat at sight of the array of talent present. It suggested, of course, the gravity of the impending event, but gave assurance of all the skill and care which science could afford.

Dr. Burns was shown to the nursery, from which he returned in five minutes.

"The case is ready," he announced. "Are the gentlemen all present?"

"I believe so," answered Dr. Price quickly.

Miller had not yet arrived. Perhaps, thought Dr. Price, a happy accident, or some imperative call, had detained him. This would be fortunate indeed. Dr. Burns's square jaw had a very determined look. It would be a pity if any acrimonious discussion should arise on the eve

---

[1] *aut Cæsar, aut nullus:* "Either Caesar or no one." Dr. Burns suggests that absolute power is the only acceptable position.

of a delicate operation. If the clock on the mantel would only move faster, the question might never come up.

"I don't see Dr. Miller," observed Dr. Burns, looking around the room. "I asked him to come at eight. There are ten minutes yet."

Major Carteret looked up with a sudden frown.

"May I ask to whom you refer?" he inquired, in an ominous tone.

The other gentlemen showed signs of interest, not to say emotion. Dr. Price smiled quizzically.

"Dr. Miller, of your city. He was one of my favorite pupils. He is also a graduate of the Vienna hospitals, and a surgeon of unusual skill. I have asked him to assist in the operation."

Every eye was turned toward Carteret, whose crimsoned face had set in a look of grim determination.

"The person to whom you refer is a negro, I believe?" he said.

"He is a colored man, certainly," returned Dr. Burns, "though one would never think of his color after knowing him well."

"I do not know, sir," returned Carteret, with an effort at self-control, "what the customs of Philadelphia or Vienna may be; but in the South we do not call negro doctors to attend white patients. I could not permit a negro to enter my house upon such an errand."

"I am here, sir," replied Dr. Burns with spirit, "to perform a certain operation. Since I assume the responsibility, the case must be under my entire control. Otherwise I cannot operate."

"Gentlemen," interposed Dr. Price, smoothly, "I beg of you both — this is a matter for calm discussion, and any asperity is to be deplored. The life at stake here should not be imperiled by any consideration of minor importance."

"Your humanity does you credit, sir," retorted Dr. Burns. "But other matters, too, are important. I have invited this gentleman here. My professional honor is involved, and I merely invoke my rights to maintain it. It is a matter of principle, which ought not to give way to a mere prejudice."

"That also states the case for Major Carteret," rejoined Dr. Price, suavely. "He has certain principles, — call them prejudices, if you like, — certain inflexible rules of conduct by which he regulates his life. One of these, which he shares with us all in some degree, forbids the recognition of the negro as a social equal."

"I do not know what Miller's social value may be," replied Dr. Burns, stoutly, "or whether you gain or lose by your attitude toward him. I have invited him here in a strictly professional capacity, with which his color is not at all concerned."

"Dr. Burns does not quite appreciate Major Carteret's point of view," said Dr. Price. "This is not with him an unimportant matter, or a mere question of prejudice, or even of personal taste. It is a sacred principle, lying at the very root of our social order, involving the purity and prestige of our race. You Northern gentlemen do not quite appreciate our situation; if you lived here a year or two you would act as we do. Of course," he added, diplomatically, "if there were no alternative — if Dr. Burns were willing to put Dr. Miller's presence on the ground of imperative necessity" —

"I do nothing of the kind, sir," retorted Dr. Burns with some heat. "I have not come all the way from Philadelphia to undertake an operation which I cannot perform without the aid of some particular physician. I merely stand upon my professional rights."

Carteret was deeply agitated. The operation must not be deferred; his child's life might be endangered by delay. If the negro's presence were indispensable he would even submit to it, though in order to avoid so painful a necessity, he would rather humble himself to the Northern doctor. The latter course involved merely a personal sacrifice — the former a vital principle. Perhaps there was another way of escape. Miller's presence could not but be distasteful to Mrs. Carteret for other reasons. Miller's wife was the living evidence of a painful episode in Mrs. Carteret's family, which the doctor's presence would inevitably recall. Once before, Mrs. Carteret's life had been endangered by encountering, at a time of great nervous strain, this ill-born sister and her child. She was even now upon the verge of collapse at the prospect of her child's suffering, and should be protected from the intrusion of any idea which might add to her distress.

"Dr. Burns," he said, with the suave courtesy which was part of his inheritance, "I beg your pardon for my heat, and throw myself upon your magnanimity, as between white men" —

"I am a gentleman, sir, before I am a white man," interposed Dr. Burns, slightly mollified, however, by Cateret's change of manner.

"The terms should be synonymous," Carteret could not refrain from saying. "As between white men, and gentlemen, I say to you, frankly, that there are vital, personal reasons, apart from Dr. Miller's color, why his presence in this house would be distasteful. With this statement, sir, I throw myself upon your mercy. My child's life is worth more to me than any earthly thing, and I must be governed by your decision."

Dr. Burns was plainly wavering. The clock moved with provoking slowness. Miller would be there in five minutes.

"May I speak with you privately a moment, doctor?" asked Dr. Price.

They withdrew from the room and were engaged in conversation for a few moments. Dr. Burns finally yielded.

"I shall nevertheless feel humiliated when I meet Miller again," he said, "but of course if there is a personal question involved, that alters the situation. Had it been merely a matter of color, I should have maintained my position. As things stand, I wash my hands of the whole affair, so far as Miller is concerned, like Pontius Pilate[2] — yes, indeed, sir, I feel very much like that individual."

"I 'll explain the matter to Miller," returned Dr. Price, amiably, "and make it all right with him. We Southern people understand the negroes better than you do, sir. Why should we not? They have been constantly under our interested observation for several hundred years. You feel this vastly more than Miller will. He knows the feeling of the white people, and is accustomed to it. He wishes to live and do business here, and is quite too shrewd to antagonize his neighbors or come where he is not wanted. He is in fact too much of a gentleman to do so."

"I shall leave the explanation to you entirely," rejoined Dr. Burns, as they reëntered the other room.

Carteret led the way to the nursery, where the operation was to take place. Dr. Price lingered for a moment. Miller was not likely to be behind the hour, if he came at all, and it would be well to head him off before the operation began.

Scarcely had the rest left the room when the door-bell sounded, and a servant announced Dr. Miller.

Dr. Price stepped into the hall and met Miller face to face.

He had meant to state the situation to Miller frankly, but now that the moment had come he wavered. He was a fine physician, but he shrank from strenuous responsibilities. It had been easy to theorize about the negro; it was more difficult to look this man in the eyes — whom at this moment he felt to be as essentially a gentleman as himself — and tell him the humiliating truth.

As a physician his method was to ease pain — he would rather take the risk of losing a patient from the use of an anæsthetic than from the shock of an operation. He liked Miller, wished him well, and

---

[2] *Pontius Pilate*: Matt. 27.19–25 tells of the Pilate, the Roman governor of Judea who conceded to the demands of Jerusalem and ordered Jesus to be crucified, claiming he had "washed his hands" of the deed: "I am innocent of the blood of this just person: see ye to it."

would not wittingly wound his feelings. He really thought him too much of a gentleman for the town, in view of the restrictions with which he must inevitably be hampered. There was something melancholy, to a cultivated mind, about a sensitive, educated man who happened to be off color. Such a person was a sort of social misfit, an odd quantity, educated out of his own class, with no possible hope of entrance into that above it. He felt quite sure that if he had been in Miller's place, he would never have settled in the South — he would have moved to Europe, or to the West Indies, or some Central or South American state where questions of color were not regarded as vitally important.

Dr. Price did not like to lie, even to a negro. To a man of his own caste, his word was his bond. If it were painful to lie, it would be humiliating to be found out. The principle of *noblesse oblige*[3] was also involved in the matter. His claim of superiority to the colored doctor rested fundamentally upon the fact that he was white and Miller was not; and yet this superiority, for which he could claim no credit, since he had not made himself, was the very breath of his nostrils, — he would not have changed places with the other for wealth untold; and as a gentleman, he would not care to have another gentleman, even a colored man, catch him in a lie. Of this, however, there was scarcely any danger. A word to the other surgeons would insure their corroboration of whatever he might tell Miller. No one of them would willingly wound Dr. Miller or embarrass Dr. Price; indeed, they need not know that Miller had come in time for the operation.

"I 'm sorry, Miller," he said with apparent regret, "but we were here ahead of time, and the case took a turn which would admit of no delay, so the gentlemen went in. Dr. Burns is with the patient now, and asked me to explain why we did not wait for you."

"I 'm sorry too," returned Miller, regretfully, but nothing doubting. He was well aware that in such cases danger might attend upon delay. He had lost his chance, through no fault of his own or of any one else.

"I hope that all is well?" he said, hesitatingly, not sure whether he would be asked to remain.

"All is well, so far. Step round to my office in the morning, Miller, or come in when you 're passing, and I 'll tell you the details."

This was tantamount to a dismissal, so Miller took his leave. Descending the doorsteps, he stood for a moment, undecided whether to

---

[3] *noblesse oblige:* French for "nobility obligates"; the idea that charitable and honorable behavior is required of those of high social status or noble birth.

return home or to go to the hotel and await the return of Dr. Burns, when he heard his name called from the house in a low tone.

"Oh, doctuh!"

He stepped back toward the door, outside of which stood the colored servant who had just let him out.

"Dat 's all a lie, doctuh," he whispered, " 'bout de operation bein' already pe'fo'med. Dey-all had jes' gone in de minute befo' you come — Doctuh Price had n' even got out 'n de room. Dey be'n quollin' 'bout you fer de las' ha'f hour. Majah Ca'te'et say he would n' have you, an' de No'then doctuh say he would n't do nothin' widout you, an' Doctuh Price he j'ined in on bofe sides, an' dey had it hot an' heavy, nip an' tuck, till bimeby Majah Ca'te'et up an' say it wa'n't altogether yo' color he objected to, an' wid dat de No'then doctuh give in. He 's a fine man, suh, but dey wuz too much fer 'im!"

"Thank you, Sam, I 'm much obliged," returned Miller mechanically. "One likes to know the truth."

Truth, it has been said, is mighty, and must prevail; but it sometimes leaves a bad taste in the mouth. In the ordinary course of events Miller would not have anticipated such an invitation, and for that reason had appreciated it all the more. The rebuff came with a corresponding shock. He had the heart of a man, the sensibilities of a cultivated gentleman; the one was sore, the other deeply wounded. He was not altogether sure, upon reflection, whether he blamed Dr. Price very much for the amiable lie, which had been meant to spare his feelings, or thanked Sam a great deal for the unpalatable truth.

Janet met him at the door. "How is the baby?" she asked excitedly.

"Dr. Price says he is doing well."

"What is the matter, Will, and why are you back so soon?"

He would have spared her the story, but she was a woman, and would have it. He was wounded, too, and wanted sympathy, of which Janet was an exhaustless fountain. So he told her what had happened. She comforted him after the manner of a loving woman, and felt righteously indignant toward her sister's husband, who had thus been instrumental in the humiliation of her own. Her anger did not embrace her sister, and yet she felt obscurely that their unacknowledged relationship had been the malignant force which had given her husband pain, and defeated his honorable ambition.

When Dr. Price entered the nursery, Dr. Burns was leaning attentively over the operating table. The implements needed for the operation were all in readiness — the knives, the basin, the sponge, the materials for dressing the wound — all the ghastly paraphernalia of vivisection.

Mrs. Carteret had been banished to another room, where Clara vainly attempted to soothe her. Old Mammy Jane, still burdened by her fears, fervently prayed the good Lord to spare the life of the sweet little grandson of her dear old mistress.

Dr. Burns had placed his ear to the child's chest, which had been bared for the incision. Dr. Price stood ready to administer the anæsthetic. Little Dodie looked up with a faint expression of wonder, as if dimly conscious of some unusual event. The major shivered at the thought of what the child must undergo.

"There 's a change in his breathing," said Dr. Burns, lifting his head. "The whistling noise is less pronounced, and he breathes easier. The obstruction seems to have shifted."

Applying his ear again to the child's throat, he listened for a moment intently, and then picking the baby up from the table, gave it a couple of sharp claps between the shoulders. Simultaneously a small object shot out from the child's mouth, struck Dr. Price in the neighborhood of his waistband, and then rattled lightly against the floor. Whereupon the baby, as though conscious of his narrow escape, smiled and gurgled, and reaching upward clutched the doctor's whiskers with his little hand, which, according to old Jane, had a stronger grip than any other infant's in Wellington.

VIII. THE CAMPAIGN DRAGS

THE campaign for white supremacy was dragging. Carteret had set out, in the columns of the Morning Chronicle, all the reasons why this movement, inaugurated by the three men who had met, six months before, at the office of the Chronicle, should be supported by the white public. Negro citizenship was a grotesque farce — Sambo and Dinah[1] raised from the kitchen to the cabinet were a spectacle to make the gods laugh. The laws by which it had been sought to put the negroes on a level with the whites must be swept away in theory, as they had failed in fact. If it were impossible, without a further education of public opinion, to secure the repeal of the fifteenth amendment,[2] it was at

---

[1] *Sambo and Dinah:* Names for disparaging stereotypes of African Americans that circulated widely in minstrel shows.

[2] *fifteenth amendment:* Passed in 1869, the Fifteenth Amendment sought to ensure voting rights for all U.S. citizens, regardless of "race, color, or previous servitude."

least the solemn duty of the state to endeavor, through its own constitution,[3] to escape from the domination of a weak and incompetent
electorate and confine the negro to that inferior condition for which
nature had evidently designed him.

In spite of the force and intelligence with which Carteret had
expressed these and similar views, they had not met the immediate
response anticipated. There were thoughtful men, willing to let well
enough alone, who saw no necessity for such a movement. They
believed that peace, prosperity, and popular education offered a surer
remedy for social ills than the reopening of issues supposed to have
been settled. There were timid men who shrank from civic strife. There
were busy men, who had something else to do. There were a few fair
men, prepared to admit, privately, that a class constituting half to two
thirds of the population were fairly entitled to some representation in
the law-making bodies. Perhaps there might have been found, somewhere in the state, a single white man ready to concede that all men
were entitled to equal rights before the law.

That there were some white men who had learned little and forgotten nothing goes without saying, for knowledge and wisdom are not
impartially distributed among even the most favored race. There were
ignorant and vicious negroes, and they had a monopoly of neither
ignorance nor crime, for there were prosperous negroes and poverty-
stricken whites. Until Carteret and his committee began their baleful
campaign the people of the state were living in peace and harmony.
The anti-negro legislation in more southern states, with large negro
majorities, had awakened scarcely an echo in this state, with a population two thirds white. Even the triumph of the Fusion party had
not been regarded as a race issue. It remained for Carteret and his
friends to discover, with inspiration from whatever supernatural
source the discriminating reader may elect, that the darker race, docile
by instinct, humble by training, patiently waiting upon its as yet uncertain destiny, was an incubus, a corpse chained to the body politic, and
that the negro vote was a source of danger to the state, no matter how
cast or by whom directed.

To discuss means for counteracting this apathy, a meeting of the
"Big Three," as they had begun to designate themselves jocularly, was

[3] *through its own constitution:* After Reconstruction U.S. Supreme Court rulings on
civil rights were increasingly in favor of states' rights. In turn, under the control of
Democrats, many southern states, including North Carolina, rewrote the voter eligibility clauses in their state constitutions to deliberately disenfranchise black voters.

held at the office of the "Morning Chronicle," on the next day but one after little Dodie's fortunate escape from the knife.

"It seems," said General Belmont, opening the discussion, "as though we had undertaken more than we can carry through. It is clear that we must reckon on opposition, both at home and abroad. If we are to hope for success, we must extend the lines of our campaign. The North, as well as our own people, must be convinced that we have right upon our side. We are conscious of the purity of our motives, but we should avoid even the appearance of evil."

McBane was tapping the floor impatiently with his foot during this harangue.

"I don't see the use," he interrupted, "of so much beating about the bush. We may as well be honest about this thing. We are going to put the niggers down because we want to, and think we can; so why waste our time in mere pretense? I 'm no hypocrite myself, — if I want a thing I take it, provided I 'm strong enough."

"My dear captain," resumed the general, with biting suavity, "your frankness does you credit, — 'an honest man's the noblest work of God,' — but we cannot carry on politics in these degenerate times without a certain amount of diplomacy. In the good old days when your father was alive, and perhaps nowadays in the discipline of convicts, direct and simple methods might be safely resorted to; but this is a modern age, and in dealing with so fundamental a right as the suffrage we must profess a decent regard for the opinions of even that misguided portion of mankind which may not agree with us. This is the age of crowds, and we must have the crowd with us."

The captain flushed at the allusion to his father's calling, at which he took more offense than at the mention of his own. He knew perfectly well that these old aristocrats, while reaping the profits of slavery, had despised the instruments by which they were attained — the poor-white overseer only less than the black slave. McBane was rich; he lived in Wellington, but he had never been invited to the home of either General Belmont or Major Carteret, nor asked to join the club of which they were members. His face, therefore, wore a distinct scowl, and his single eye glowed ominously. He would help these fellows carry the state for white supremacy, and then he would have his innings, — he would have more to say than they dreamed, as to who should fill the offices under the new deal. Men of no better birth or breeding than he had represented Southern states in Congress since the war. Why should he not run for governor, representative, whatever he chose? He had money enough to buy out half a dozen of these broken-down aristocrats, and money was all-powerful.

"You see, captain," the general went on, looking McBane smilingly and unflinchingly in the eye, "we need white immigration — we need Northern capital. 'A good name is better than great riches,' and we must prove our cause a righteous one."

"We must be armed at all points," added Carteret, "and prepared for defense as well as for attack, — we must make our campaign a national one."

"For instance," resumed the general, "you, Carteret, represent the Associated Press. Through your hands passes all the news of the state. What more powerful medium for the propagation of an idea? The man who would govern a nation by writing its songs was a blethering idiot beside the fellow who can edit its news dispatches. The negroes are playing into our hands, — every crime that one of them commits is reported by us. With the latitude they have had in this state they are growing more impudent and self-assertive every day. A yellow demagogue in New York made a speech only a few days ago, in which he deliberately, and in cold blood, advised negroes to defend themselves to the death when attacked by white people! I remember well the time when it was death for a negro to strike a white man."

"It 's death now, if he strikes the right one," interjected McBane, restored to better humor by this mention of a congenial subject.

The general smiled a fine smile. He had heard the story of how McBane had lost his other eye.

"The local negro paper is quite outspoken, too," continued the general, "if not impudent. We must keep track of that; it may furnish us some good campaign material."

"Yes," returned Carteret, "we must see to that. I threw a copy into the waste-basket this morning, without looking at it. Here it is now!"

IX. A WHITE MAN'S "NIGGER"

CARTERET fished from the depths of the waste-basket and handed to the general an eighteen by twenty-four sheet, poorly printed on cheap paper, with a "patent" inside, a number of advertisements of proprietary medicines, quack doctors, and fortune-tellers, and two or three columns of editorial and local news. Candor compels the admission that it was not an impressive sheet in any respect, except when regarded as the first local effort of a struggling people to make public expression of their life and aspirations. From this point of view it did not speak at all badly for a class to whom, a generation before, newspapers, books, and learning had been forbidden fruit.

"It 's an elegant specimen of journalism, is n't it?" laughed the general, airily. "Listen to this 'ad': —

" 'Kinky, curly hair made straight by one application of our specific. Our face bleach will turn the skin of a black or brown person four or five shades lighter, and of a mulatto perfectly white. When you get the color you wish, stop using the preparation.'

"Just look at those heads! — 'Before using' and 'After using.' We 'd better hurry, or there 'll be no negroes to disfranchise! If they don't stop till they get the color they desire, and the stuff works according to contract, they 'll all be white. Ah! what have we here? This looks as though it might be serious."

Opening the sheet the general read aloud an editorial article, to which Carteret listened intently, his indignation increasing in strength from the first word to the last, while McBane's face grew darkly purple with anger.

The article was a frank and somewhat bold discussion of lynching and its causes.[1] It denied that most lynchings were for the offense most generally charged as their justification, and declared that, even of those seemingly traced to this cause, many were not for crimes at all, but for voluntary acts which might naturally be expected to follow from the miscegenation laws by which it was sought, in all the Southern States, to destroy liberty of contract, and, for the purpose of maintaining a fanciful purity of race, to make crimes of marriages to which neither nature nor religion nor the laws of other states interposed any insurmountable barrier. Such an article in a Northern newspaper would have attracted no special attention, and might merely have furnished food to an occasional reader for serious thought upon a subject not exactly agreeable; but coming from a colored man, in a Southern city, it was an indictment of the laws and social system of the South that could not fail of creating a profound sensation.

"Infamous — infamous!" exclaimed Carteret, his voice trembling with emotion. "The paper should be suppressed immediately."

"The impudent nigger ought to be horsewhipped and run out of town," growled McBane.

---

[1] *The article was a frank and somewhat bold discussion of lynching and its causes:* This "article" is based loosely on a piece black newspaper editor Alex Manly wrote for his newspaper, the *Wilmington Record*. Manly's editorial is republished in this volume (see Part Two, Chapter 3).

"Gentlemen," said the general soothingly, after the first burst of indignation had subsided, "I believe we can find a more effective use for this article, which, by the way, will not bear too close analysis, — there 's some truth in it, at least there 's an argument."

"That is not the point," interrupted Carteret.

"No," interjected McBane with an oath, "that ain't at all the point. Truth or not, no damn nigger has any right to say it."

"This article," said Carteret, "violates an unwritten law of the South. If we are to tolerate this race of weaklings among us, until they are eliminated by the stress of competition, it must be upon terms which we lay down. One of our conditions is violated by this article, in which our wisdom is assailed, and our women made the subject of offensive comment. We must make known our disapproval."

"I say lynch the nigger, break up the press, and burn down the newspaper office," McBane responded promptly.

"Gentlemen," interposed the general, "would you mind suspending the discussion for a moment, while I send Jerry across the street? I think I can then suggest a better plan."

Carteret rang the bell for Jerry, who answered promptly. He had been expecting such a call ever since the gentlemen had gone in.

"Jerry," said the general, "step across to Brown's and tell him to send me three Calhoun cocktails. Wait for them, — here 's the money."

"Yas, suh," replied Jerry, taking the proffered coin.

"And make has'e, charcoal," added McBane, "for we 're gettin' damn dry."

A momentary cloud of annoyance darkened Carteret's brow. McBane had always grated upon his aristocratic susceptibilities. The captain was an upstart, a product of the democratic idea operating upon the poor white man, the descendant of the indentured bondservant and the socially unfit. He had wealth and energy, however, and it was necessary to make use of him; but the example of such men was a strong incentive to Carteret in his campaign against the negro. It was distasteful enough to rub elbows with an illiterate and vulgar white man of no ancestry, — the risk of similar contact with negroes was to be avoided at any cost. He could hardly expect McBane to be a gentleman, but when among men of that class he might at least try to imitate their manners. A gentleman did not order his own servants around offensively, to say nothing of another's.

The general had observed Carteret's annoyance, and remarked pleasantly while they waited for the servant's return: —

"Jerry, now, is a very good negro. He's not one of your new negroes, who think themselves as good as white men, and want to run the government. Jerry knows his place, — he is respectful, humble, obedient, and content with the face and place assigned to him by nature."

"Yes, he's one of the best of 'em," sneered McBane. "He'll call any man 'master' for a quarter, or 'God' for half a dollar; for a dollar he'll grovel at your feet, and for a cast-off coat you can buy an option on his immortal soul, — if he has one! I've handled niggers for ten years, and I know 'em from the ground up. They're all alike, — they're a scrub race, an affliction to the country, and the quicker we're rid of 'em all the better."

Carteret had nothing to say by way of dissent. McBane's sentiments, in their last analysis, were much the same as his, though he would have expressed them less brutally.

"The negro," observed the general, daintily flicking the ash from his cigar, "is all right in his place and very useful to the community. We lived on his labor for quite a long time, and lived very well. Nevertheless we are better off without slavery, for we can get more out of the free negro, and with less responsibility. I really do not see how we could get along without the negroes. If they were all like Jerry, we'd have no trouble with them."

Having procured the drinks, Jerry, the momentary subject of the race discussion which goes on eternally in the South, was making his way back across the street, somewhat disturbed in mind.

"O Lawd!" he groaned, "I never troubles trouble till trouble troubles me; but w'en I got dem drinks befo', Gin'l Belmont gimme half a dollar an' tol' me ter keep de change. Dis time he did n' say nothin' 'bout de change. I s'pose he jes' fergot erbout it, but w'at is a po' nigger gwine ter do w'en he has ter conten' wid w'ite folks's fergitfulniss? I don' see no way but ter do some fergittin' myse'f. I'll jes' stan' outside de do' here till dey gits so wrop' up in deir talk dat dey won' 'member nothin' e'se, an' den at de right minute I'll han' de glasses 'roun, an' mos' lackly de gin'l 'll fergit all 'bout de change."

While Jerry stood outside, the conversation within was plainly audible, and some inkling of its purport filtered through his mind.

"Now, gentlemen," the general was saying, "here's my plan. That editorial in the negro newspaper is good campaign matter, but we should reserve it until it will be most effective. Suppose we just stick it in a pigeon-hole, and let the editor, — what's his name?"

"The nigger's name is Barber," replied McBane. "I 'd like to have him under me for a month or two; he 'd write no more editorials."

"Let Barber have all the rope he wants," resumed the general, "and he 'll be sure to hang himself. In the mean time we will continue to work up public opinion, — we can use this letter privately for that purpose, — and when the state campaign opens we 'll print the editorial, with suitable comment, scatter it broadcast throughout the state, fire the Southern heart, organize the white people on the color line, have a little demonstration with red shirts and shotguns, scare the negroes into fits, win the state for white supremacy, and teach our colored fellow citizens that we are tired of negro domination and have put an end to it forever. The Afro-American Banner will doubtless die about the same time."

"And so will the editor!" exclaimed McBane ferociously; "I 'll see to that. But I wonder where that nigger is with them cocktails? I 'm so thirsty I could swallow blue blazes."

"Here 's yo' drinks, gin'l," announced Jerry, entering with the glasses on a tray.

The gentlemen exchanged compliments and imbibed — McBane at a gulp, Carteret with more deliberation, leaving about half the contents of his glass.

The general drank slowly, with every sign of appreciation. "If the illustrious statesman," he observed, "whose name this mixture bears, had done nothing more than invent it, his fame would still deserve to go thundering down the endless ages."

"It ain't bad liquor," assented McBane, smacking his lips.

Jerry received the empty glasses on the tray and left the room. He had scarcely gained the hall when the general called him back.

"O Lawd!" groaned Jerry, "he 's gwine ter ax me fer de change. Yas, suh, yas, suh; comin', gin'l, comin', suh!"

"You may keep the change, Jerry," said the general.

Jerry's face grew radiant at this announcement. "Yas, suh, gin'l; thank y', suh; much obleedzed, suh. I wuz jus' gwine ter fetch it in, suh, w'en I had put de tray down. Thank y', suh, truly, suh!"

Jerry backed and bowed himself out into the hall.

"Dat wuz a close shave," he muttered, as he swallowed the remaining contents of Major Carteret's glass. "I 'lowed dem twenty cents wuz gone dat time, — an' whar I wuz gwine ter git de money ter take my gal ter de chu'ch festibal ter-night, de Lawd only knows! — 'less'n I borried it off'n Mr. Ellis, an' I owes him sixty cents a'ready. But I wonduh w'at dem w'ite folks in dere is up ter? Dere 's one thing sho', —

dey 're gwine ter git after de niggers some way er 'nuther, an' w'en dey does, whar is Jerry gwine ter be? Dat 's de mos' impo'tantes' question. I 'm gwine ter look at dat newspaper dey be'n talkin' 'bout, an' 'less'n my min' changes might'ly, I 'm gwine ter keep my mouf shet an' stan' in wid de Angry-Saxon race, — ez dey calls deyse'ves nowadays, — an' keep on de right side er my bread an' meat. W'at nigger ever give me twenty cents in all my bawn days?"

"By the way, major," said the general, who lingered behind McBane as they were leaving, "is Miss Clara's marriage definitely settled upon?"

"Well, general, not exactly; but it 's the understanding that they will marry when they are old enough."

"I was merely thinking," the general went on, "that if I were you I 'd speak to Tom about cards and liquor. He gives more time to both than a young man can afford. I 'm speaking in his interest and in Miss Clara's, — we of the old families ought to stand together."

"Thank you, general, for the hint. I 'll act upon it."

This political conference was fruitful in results. Acting upon the plans there laid out, McBane traveled extensively through the state, working up sentiment in favor of the new movement. He possessed a certain forceful eloquence; and white supremacy was so obviously the divine intention that he had merely to affirm the doctrine in order to secure adherents.

General Belmont, whose business required him to spend much of the winter in Washington and New York, lost no opportunity to get the ear of lawmakers, editors, and other leaders of national opinion, and to impress upon them, with persuasive eloquence, the impossibility of maintaining existing conditions, and the tremendous blunder which had been made in conferring the franchise upon the emancipated race.

Carteret conducted the press campaign, and held out to the Republicans of the North the glittering hope that, with the elimination of the negro vote, and a proper deference to Southern feeling, a strong white Republican party might be built up in the New South. How well the bait took is a matter of history, — but the promised result is still in the future. The disfranchisement of the negro has merely changed the form of the same old problem. The negro had no vote before the rebellion, and few other rights, and yet the negro question was, for a century, the pivot of American politics. It plunged the nation into a bloody war, and it will trouble the American government and the American conscience until a sustained attempt is made to settle it upon principles of justice and equity.

The personal ambitions entertained by the leaders of this movement are but slightly involved in this story. McBane's aims have been touched upon elsewhere. The general would have accepted the nomination for governor of the state, with a vision of a senatorship in the future. Carteret hoped to vindicate the supremacy of his race, and make the state fit for his son to live in, and, incidentally, he would not refuse any office, worthy of his dignity, which a grateful people might thrust upon him.

So powerful a combination of bigot, self-seeking demagogue, and astute politician was fraught with grave menace to the peace of the state and the liberties of the people, — by which is meant the whole people, and not any one class, sought to be built up at the expense of another.

X. DELAMERE PLAYS A TRUMP

Carteret did not forget what General Belmont had said in regard to Tom. The major himself had been young, not so very long ago, and was inclined toward indulgence for the foibles of youth. A young gentleman should have a certain knowledge of life, — but there were limits. Clara's future happiness must not be imperiled.

The opportunity to carry out this purpose was not long delayed. Old Mr. Delamere wished to sell some timber which had been cut at Belleview, and sent Tom down to the Chronicle office to leave an advertisement. The major saw him at the desk, invited him into his sanctum, and delivered him a mild lecture. The major was kind, and talked in a fatherly way about the danger of extremes, the beauty of moderation, and the value of discretion as a rule of conduct. He mentioned collaterally the unblemished honor of a fine old family, its contemplated alliance with his own, and dwelt upon the sweet simplicity of Clara's character. The major was a man of feeling and of tact, and could not have put the subject in a way less calculated to wound the *amour propre* of a very young man.

Delamere had turned red with anger while the major was speaking. He was impulsive, and an effort was required to keep back the retort that sprang once or twice to his lips; but his conscience was not clear, and he could not afford hard words with Clara's guardian and his grandfather's friend. Clara was rich, and the most beautiful girl in town; they were engaged; he loved her as well as he could love anything of which he seemed sure; and he did not mean that any one else should have her. The major's mild censure disturbed slightly his sense of security; and while the major's manner did not indicate that he knew anything definite against him, it would be best to let well enough alone.

"Thank you, major," he said, with well-simulated frankness. "I realize that I may have been a little careless, more from thoughtlessness than anything else; but my heart is all right, sir, and I am glad that my conduct has been brought to your attention, for what you have said enables me to see it in a different light. I will be more careful of my company hereafter; for I love Clara, and mean to try to be worthy of her. Do you know whether she will be at home this evening?"

"I have heard nothing to the contrary," replied the major warmly. "Call her up by telephone and ask — or come up and see. You 're always welcome, my boy."

Upon leaving the office, which was on the second floor, Tom met Ellis coming up the stairs. It had several times of late occurred to Tom that Ellis had a sneaking fondness for Clara. Panoplied in his own engagement, Tom had heretofore rather enjoyed the idea of a hopeless rival. Ellis was such a solemn prig, and took life so seriously, that it was a pleasure to see him sit around sighing for the unattainable. That he should be giving pain to Ellis added a certain zest to his own enjoyment.

But this interview with the major had so disquieted him that upon meeting Ellis upon the stairs he was struck by a sudden suspicion. He knew that Major Carteret seldom went to the Clarendon Club, and that he must have got his information from some one else. Ellis was a member of the club, and a frequent visitor. Who more likely than he to try to poison Clara's mind, or the minds of her friends, against her accepted lover? Tom did not think that the world was using him well of late; bad luck had pursued him, in cards and other things, and despite his assumption of humility, Carteret's lecture had left him in an ugly mood. He nodded curtly to Ellis without relaxing the scowl that disfigured his handsome features.

"That 's the damned sneak who 's been giving me away," he muttered. "I 'll get even with him yet for this."

Delamere's suspicions with regard to Ellis's feelings were not, as we have seen, entirely without foundation. Indeed, he had underestimated the strength of this rivalry and its chances of success. Ellis had been watching Delamere for a year. There had been nothing surreptitious about it, but his interest in Clara had led him to note things about his favored rival which might have escaped the attention of others less concerned.

Ellis was an excellent judge of character, and had formed a very decided opinion of Tom Delamere. To Ellis, unbiased by ancestral traditions, biased perhaps by jealousy, Tom Delamere was a type of the degenerate aristocrat. If, as he had often heard, it took three or four generations to make a gentleman, and as many more to complete the curve and return to the base from which it started, Tom Delamere belonged somewhere on the downward slant, with large possibilities of further decline. Old Mr. Delamere, who might be taken as the apex of an ideal aristocratic development, had been distinguished, during his active life, as Ellis had learned, for courage and strength of will, courtliness of bearing, deference to his superiors, of whom there had been few, courtesy to his equals, kindness and consideration for those less highly favored, and above all, a scrupulous sense of honor; his grandson Tom was merely the shadow without the substance, the empty husk without the grain. Of grace he had plenty. In manners he could be perfect, when he so chose. Courage and strength he had none. Ellis had seen this fellow, who boasted of his descent from a line of cavaliers, turn pale with fright and spring from a buggy to which was harnessed a fractious horse, which a negro stable-boy drove fearlessly. A valiant carpet-knight, skilled in all parlor exercises, great at whist or euchre, a dream of a dancer, unexcelled in cakewalk or "coon" impersonations,[1] for which he was in large social demand, Ellis had seen him kick an inoffensive negro out of his path and treat a poor-white man with scant courtesy. He suspected Delamere of cheating at cards, and knew that others entertained the same suspicion. For while regular in his own habits, — his poverty would not have permitted him any considerable extravagance, — Ellis's position as a newspaper man kept him in touch with what was going on about town. He was a member, proposed by Carteret, of the Clarendon Club, where cards were indulged in within reasonable limits, and a certain set were known to bet dollars in terms of dimes.

Delamere was careless, too, about money matters. He had a habit of borrowing, right and left, small sums which might be conveniently forgotten by the borrower, and for which the lender would dislike to ask. Ellis had a strain of thrift, derived from a Scotch ancestry, and a tenacious memory for financial details. Indeed, he had never had so

---

[1] *cakewalk or "coon" impersonations:* The cakewalk was an African American dance competition that became popular with white audiences. White stage performers often performed cakewalks and stereotyped "coon" songs in blackface makeup. For a description of the cakewalk tradition, see the introduction to Part Two, Chapter 4 in this volume.

much money that he could lose track of it. He never saw Delamere without being distinctly conscious that Delamere owed him four dollars, which he had lent at a time when he could ill afford to spare it. It was a prerogative of aristocracy, Ellis reflected, to live upon others, and the last privilege which aristocracy in decay would willingly relinquish. Neither did the aristocratic memory seem able to retain the sordid details of a small pecuniary transaction.

No doubt the knowledge that Delamere was the favored lover of Miss Pemberton lent a touch of bitterness to Ellis's reflections upon his rival. Ellis had no grievance against the "aristocracy" of Wellington. The "best people" had received him cordially, though his father had not been of their caste; but Ellis hated a hypocrite, and despised a coward, and he felt sure that Delamere was both. Otherwise he would have struggled against his love for Clara Pemberton. His passion for her had grown with his appreciation of Delamere's unworthiness. As a friend of the family, he knew the nature and terms of the engagement, and that if the marriage took place at all, it would not be for at least a year. This was a long time, — many things might happen in a year, especially to a man like Tom Delamere. If for any reason Delamere lost his chance, Ellis meant to be next in the field. He had not made love to Clara, but he had missed no opportunity of meeting her and making himself quietly and unobtrusively agreeable.

On the day after this encounter with Delamere on the stairs of the Chronicle office, Ellis, while walking down Vine Street, met old Mrs. Ochiltree. She was seated in her own buggy, which was of ancient build and pattern, driven by her colored coachman and man of all work.

"Mr. Ellis," she called in a shrill voice, having directed her coachman to draw up at the curb as she saw the young man approaching, "come here. I want to speak to you."

Ellis came up to the buggy and stood uncovered beside it.

"People are saying," said Mrs. Ochiltree, "that Tom Delamere is drinking hard, and has to be carried home intoxicated, two or three times a week, by old Mr. Delamere's man Sandy. Is there any truth in the story?"

"My dear Mrs. Ochiltree, I am not Tom Delamere's keeper. Sandy could tell you better than I."

"You are dodging my question, Mr. Ellis. Sandy would n't tell me the truth, and I know that you would n't lie, — you don't look like a liar. They say Tom is gambling scandalously. What do you know about that?"

"You must excuse me, Mrs. Ochiltree. A great deal of what we hear is mere idle gossip, and the truth is often grossly exaggerated. I 'm a member of the same club with Delamere, and gentlemen who belong to the same club are not in the habit of talking about one another. As long as a man retains his club membership, he 's presumed to be a gentleman. I would n't say anything against Delamere if I could."

"You don't need to," replied the old lady, shaking her finger at him with a cunning smile. "You are a very open young man, Mr. Ellis, and I can read you like a book. You are much smarter than you look, but you can't fool me. Good-morning."

Mrs. Ochiltree drove immediately to her niece's, where she found Mrs. Carteret and Clara at home. Clara was very fond of the baby, and was holding him in her arms. He was a fine baby, and bade fair to realize the bright hopes built upon him.

"You hold a baby very naturally, Clara," chuckled the old lady. "I suppose you are in training. But you ought to talk to Tom. I have just learned from Mr. Ellis that Tom is carried home drunk two or three times a week, and that he is gambling in the most reckless manner imaginable."

Clara's eyes flashed indignantly. Ere she could speak, Mrs. Carteret exclaimed: —

"Why, Aunt Polly! did Mr. Ellis say that?"

"I got it from Dinah," she replied, "who heard it from her husband, who learned it from a waiter at the club. And" —

"Pshaw!" said Mrs. Carteret, "mere servants' gossip."

"No, it is n't, Olivia. I met Mr. Ellis on the street, and asked him point blank, and he did n't deny it. He 's a member of the club, and ought to know."

"Well, Aunt Polly, it can't be true. Tom is here every other night, and how could he carry on so without showing the signs of it? and where would he get the money? You know he has only a moderate allowance."

"He may win it at cards, — it 's better to be born lucky than rich," returned Mrs. Ochiltree. "Then he has expectations, and can get credit. There 's no doubt that Tom is going on shamefully."

Clara's indignation had not yet found vent in speech; Olivia had said all that was necessary, but she had been thinking rapidly. Even if all this had been true, why should Mr. Ellis have said it? Or, if he had not stated it directly, he had left the inference to be drawn. It seemed a most unfair and ungentlemanly thing. What motive could Ellis have for such an act?

She was not long in reaching a conclusion which was not flattering to Ellis. Mr. Ellis came often to the house, and she had enjoyed his society in a friendly way. That he had found her pleasant company had been very evident. She had never taken his attentions seriously, however, or regarded his visits as made especially to her, nor had the rest of the family treated them from that point of view. Her engagement to Tom Delamere, though not yet formally ratified, was so well understood by the world of Wellington that Mr. Ellis would scarcely have presumed to think of her as anything more than a friend.

This revelation of her aunt's, however, put a different face upon his conduct. Certain looks and sighs and enigmatical remarks of Ellis, to which she had paid but casual attention and attached no particular significance, now recurred to her memory with a new meaning. He had now evidently tried, in a roundabout way, to besmirch Tom's character and undermine him in her regard. While loving Tom, she had liked Ellis well enough, as a friend; but he had abused the privileges of friendship, and she would teach him a needed lesson.

Nevertheless, Mrs. Ochiltree's story had given Clara food for thought. She was uneasily conscious, after all, that there might be a grain of truth in what had been said, enough, at least, to justify her in warning Tom to be careful, lest his enemies should distort some amiable weakness into a serious crime.

She put this view of the case to Tom at their next meeting, assuring him, at the same time, of her unbounded faith and confidence. She did not mention Ellis's name, lest Tom, in righteous indignation, might do something rash, which he might thereafter regret. If any subtler or more obscure motive kept her silent as to Ellis, she was not aware of it; for Clara's views of life were still in the objective stage, and she had not yet fathomed the deepest recesses of her own consciousness.

Delamere had the cunning of weakness. He knew, too, better than any one else could know, how much truth there was in the rumors concerning him, and whether or not they could be verified too easily for him to make an indignant denial. After a little rapid reflection, he decided upon a different course.

"Clara," he said with a sigh, taking the hand which she generously yielded to soften any suggestion of reproach which he may have read into her solicitude, "you are my guardian angel. I do not know, of course, who has told you this pack of lies, — for I can see that you have heard more than you have told me, — but I think I could guess the man they came from. I am not perfect, Clara, though I have done nothing of which a gentleman should be ashamed. There is one sure way to stop the tongue of calumny. My home life is not ideal, — grandfather is an old, weak man, and the house needs the refining and softening influence of a lady's presence. I do not love club life; its ideals are not elevating. With you by my side, dearest, I should be preserved from every influence except the purest and the best. Don't you think, dearest, that the major might be induced to shorten our weary term of waiting?"

"Oh, Tom," she demurred blushingly, "I shall be young enough at eighteen; and you are barely twenty-one."

But Tom proved an eloquent pleader, and love a still more persuasive advocate. Clara spoke to the major the same evening, who looked grave at the suggestion, and said he would think about it. They were both very young; but where both parties were of good family, in good health and good circumstances, an early marriage might not be undesirable. Tom was perhaps a little unsettled, but blood would tell in the long run, and marriage always exercised a steadying influence.

The only return, therefore, which Ellis received for his well-meant effort to ward off Mrs. Ochiltree's embarrassing inquiries was that he did not see Clara upon his next visit, which was made one afternoon while he was on night duty at the office. In conversation with Mrs. Carteret he learned that Clara's marriage had been definitely agreed upon, and the date fixed, — it was to take place in about six months. Meeting Miss Pemberton on the street the following day, he received the slightest of nods. When he called again at the house, after a week of misery, she treated him with a sarcastic coolness which chilled his heart.

"How have I offended you, Miss Clara?" he demanded desperately, when they were left alone for a moment.

"Offended me?" she replied, lifting her eyebrows with an air of puzzled surprise. "Why, Mr. Ellis! What could have put such a notion into your head? Oh dear, I think I hear Dodie, — I know you'll excuse me, Mr. Ellis, won't you? Sister Olivia will be back in a moment; and we're expecting Aunt Polly this afternoon, — if you'll stay awhile she 'll be glad to talk to you! You can tell her all the interesting news about your friends!"

XI. THE BABY AND THE BIRD

WHEN Ellis, after this rebuff, had disconsolately taken his leave, Clara, much elated at the righteous punishment she had inflicted upon the slanderer, ran upstairs to the nursery, and, snatching Dodie from Mammy Jane's arms, began dancing gayly with him round the room.

"Look a-hyuh, honey," said Mammy Jane, "you better be keerful wid dat chile, an' don' drap 'im on de flo'. You might let him fall on his head an' break his neck. My, my! but you two does make a pretty pic-tur'! You 'll be wantin' ole Jane ter come an' nuss yo' child'en some er dese days," she chuckled unctuously.

Mammy Jane had been very much disturbed by the recent dangers through which little Dodie had passed; and his escape from strangu-lation, in the first place, and then from the knife had impressed her as little less than miraculous. She was not certain whether this result had been brought about by her manipulation of the buried charm, or by the prayers which had been offered for the child, but was inclined to believe that both had coöperated to avert the threatened calamity. The favorable outcome of this particular incident had not, however, altered the general situation. Prayers and charms, after all, were merely temporary things, which must be constantly renewed, and might be forgotten or overlooked; while the mole, on the contrary, neither faded nor went away. If its malign influence might for a time seem to disappear, it was merely lying dormant, like the germs of some deadly disease, awaiting its opportunity to strike at an unguarded spot.

Clara and the baby were laughing in great glee, when a mocking-bird, perched on the topmost bough of a small tree opposite the nurs-ery window, burst suddenly into song, with many a trill and quaver. Clara, with the child in her arms, sprang to the open window.

"Sister Olivia," she cried, turning her face toward Mrs. Carteret, who at that moment entered the room, "come and look at Dodie."

The baby was listening intently to the music, meanwhile gurgling with delight, and reaching his chubby hands toward the source of this pleasing sound. It seemed as though the mockingbird were aware of his appreciative audience, for he ran through the songs of a dozen dif-ferent birds, selecting, with the discrimination of a connoisseur and entire confidence in his own powers, those which were most difficult and most alluring.

Mrs. Carteret approached the window, followed by Mammy Jane, who waddled over to join the admiring party. So absorbed were the three women in the baby and the bird that neither one of them observed a neat top buggy, drawn by a sleek sorrel pony, passing slowly along the street before the house. In the buggy was seated a lady, and beside her a little boy, dressed in a child's sailor suit and a straw hat. The lady, with a wistful expression, was looking toward the party grouped in the open window.

Mrs. Carteret, chancing to lower her eyes for an instant, caught the other woman's look directed toward her and her child. With a glance of cold aversion she turned away from the window.

Old Mammy Jane had observed this movement, and had divined the reason for it. She stood beside Clara, watching the retreating buggy.

"Uhhuh!" she said to herself, "it 's huh sister Janet! She ma'ied a doctuh, an' all dat, an' she lives in a big house, an' she 's be'n roun' de worl' an de Lawd knows where e'se; but Mis' 'Livy don' like de sight er her, an' never will, ez long ez de sun rises an' sets. Dey ce't'nly does favor one anudder, — anybody mought 'low dey wuz twins, ef dey did n' know better. Well, well! Fo'ty yeahs ago who 'd 'a' ever expected ter see a nigger gal ridin' in her own buggy? My, my! but I don' know, — I don' know! It don' look right, an' it ain' gwine ter las'! — you can't make me b'lieve!"

Meantime Janet, stung by Mrs. Carteret's look, — the nearest approach she had ever made to a recognition of her sister's existence, — had turned away with hardening face. She had struck her pony sharply with the whip, much to the gentle creature's surprise, when the little boy, who was still looking back, caught his mother's sleeve and exclaimed excitedly: —

"Look, look, mamma! The baby, — the baby!"

Janet turned instantly, and with a mother's instinct gave an involuntary cry of alarm.

At the moment when Mrs. Carteret had turned away from the window, and while Mammy Jane was watching Janet, Clara had taken a step forward, and was leaning against the window-sill. The baby, convulsed with delight, had given a spasmodic spring and slipped from Clara's arms. Instinctively the young woman gripped the long skirt as it slipped through her hands, and held it tenaciously, though too frightened for an instant to do more. Mammy Jane, ashen with sudden dread, uttered an inarticulate scream, but retained self-possession enough to reach down and draw up the child, which hung dangerously suspended, head downward, over the brick pavement below.

"Oh, Clara, Clara, how could you!" exclaimed Mrs. Carteret reproachfully; "you might have killed my child!"

She had snatched the child from Jane's arms, and was holding him closely to her own breast. Struck by a sudden thought, she drew near the window and looked out. Twice within a few weeks her child had been in serious danger, and upon each occasion a member of the Miller family had been involved, for she had heard of Dr. Miller's presumption in trying to force himself where he must have known he would be unwelcome.

Janet was just turning her head away as the buggy moved slowly off. Olivia felt a violent wave of antipathy sweep over her toward this baseborn sister who had thus thrust herself beneath her eyes. If she had not cast her brazen glance toward the window, she herself would not have turned away and lost sight of her child. To this shameless intrusion, linked with Clara's carelessness, had been due the catastrophe, so narrowly averted, which might have darkened her own life forever. She took to her bed for several days, and for a long time was cold toward Clara, and did not permit her to touch the child.

Mammy Jane entertained a theory of her own about the accident, by which the blame was placed, in another way, exactly where Mrs. Carteret had laid it. Julia's daughter, Janet, had been looking intently toward the window just before little Dodie had sprung from Clara's arms. Might she not have cast the evil eye upon the baby, and sought thereby to draw him out of the window? One would not ordinarily expect so young a woman to possess such a power, but she might have acquired it, for this very purpose, from some more experienced person. By the same reasoning, the mockingbird might have been a familiar of the witch, and the two might have conspired to lure the infant to destruction. Whether this were so or not, the transaction at least wore a peculiar look. There was no use telling Mis' 'Livy about it, for she did n't believe, or pretended not to believe, in witchcraft and conjuration. But one could not be too careful. The child was certainly born to be exposed to great dangers, — the mole behind the left ear was an unfailing sign, — and no precaution should be omitted to counteract its baleful influence.

While adjusting the baby's crib, a few days later, Mrs. Carteret found fastened under one of the slats a small bag of cotton cloth, about half an inch long and tied with a black thread, upon opening which she found a few small roots or fibres and a pinch of dried and crumpled herbs. It was a good-luck charm which Mammy Jane had placed there to ward off the threatened evil from the grandchild of her dear old mistress. Mrs. Carteret's first impulse was to throw the bag into the fire, but on second thoughts she let it remain. To remove it would give unnecessary pain to the old nurse. Of course these old negro superstitions were absurd, — but if the charm did no good, it at least would do no harm.

XII. ANOTHER SOUTHERN PRODUCT

ONE morning shortly after the opening of the hospital, while Dr. Miller was making his early rounds, a new patient walked in with a smile on his face and a broken arm hanging limply by his side. Miller recognized in him a black giant by the name of Josh Green, who for many years had worked on the docks for Miller's father, — and simultaneously identified him as the dust-begrimed negro who had stolen a ride to Wellington on the trucks of a passenger car.

"Well, Josh," asked the doctor, as he examined the fracture, "how did you get this? Been fighting again?"

"No, suh, I don' s'pose you could ha'dly call it a fight. One er dem dagoes off'n a Souf American boat gimme some er his jaw, an' I give 'im a back answer, an' here I is wid a broken arm. He got holt er a belayin'-pin befo' I could hit 'im."

"What became of the other man?" demanded Miller suspiciously. He perceived, from the indifference with which Josh bore the manipulation of the fractured limb, that such an accident need not have interfered seriously with the use of the remaining arm, and he knew that Josh had a reputation for absolute fearlessness.

"Lemme see," said Josh reflectively, "ef I kin 'member w'at *did* become er him! Oh, yes, I 'member now! Dey tuck him ter de Marine Horspittle in de amberlance, 'cause his leg wuz broke, an' I reckon somethin' must 'a' accident'ly hit 'im in de jaw, fer he wuz scatt'rin' teeth all de way 'long de street. I did n' wan' ter kill de man, fer he might have somebody dependin' on 'im, an' I knows how dat 'd be ter dem. But no man kin call me a damn' low-down nigger and keep on enjoyin' good health right along."

"It was considerate of you to spare his life," said Miller dryly, "but you 'll hit the wrong man some day. These are bad times for bad negroes. You 'll get into a quarrel with a white man, and at the end of it there 'll be a lynching, or a funeral. You 'd better be peaceable and endure a little injustice, rather than run the risk of a sudden and violent death."

"I expec's ter die a vi'lent death in a quarrel wid a w'ite man," replied Josh, in a matter-of-fact tone, "an' fu'thermo', he 's gwine ter die at the same time, er a little befo'. I be'n takin' my own time 'bout killin' 'im; I ain' be'n crowdin' de man, but I 'll be ready after a w'ile, an' den he kin look out!"

"And I suppose you 're merely keeping in practice on these other fellows who come your way. When I get your arm dressed, you 'd better leave town till that fellow's boat sails; it may save you the expense of a trial and three months in the chain-gang. But this talk about killing a man is all nonsense. What has any man in this town done to you, that you should thirst for his blood?"

"No, suh, it ain' nonsense, — it 's straight, solem' fac'. I 'm gwine ter kill dat man as sho' as I 'm settin' in dis cheer; an' dey ain' nobody kin say I ain' got a right ter kill 'im. Does you 'member de Ku-Klux?"[1]

"Yes, but I was a child at the time, and recollect very little about them. It is a page of history which most people are glad to forget."

"Yas, suh; I was a chile, too, but I wuz right in it, an' so I 'members mo' erbout it 'n you does. My mammy an' daddy lived 'bout ten miles f'm here, up de river. One night a crowd er w'ite men come ter ou' house an' tuck my daddy out an' shot 'im ter death, an' skeered my mammy so she ain' be'n herse'f f'm dat day ter dis. I wa'n't mo' 'n ten years ole at de time, an' w'en my mammy seed de w'ite men comin', she tol' me ter run. I hid in de bushes an' seen de whole thing, an' it wuz branded on my mem'ry, suh, like a red-hot iron bran's de skin. De w'ite folks had masks on, but one of 'em fell off — he wuz de boss, he wuz de head man, an' tol' de res w'at ter do, — an' I seen his face. It wuz a easy face ter 'member; an' I swo' den, 'way down deep in my hea't, little ez I wuz, dat some day er 'nother I 'd kill dat man. I ain't never had no doubt erbout it; it 's jus' w'at I 'm livin' fer, an' I know I ain' gwine ter die till I 've done it. Some lives fer one thing an' some fer another, but dat 's my job. I ain' be'n in no has'e, fer I 'm not ole yit, an' dat man is in good health. I 'd like ter see a little er de worl' befo' I takes chances on leavin' it sudden; an', mo'over, somebody's got ter take keer er de ole 'oman. But her time 'll come some er dese days, an den *his* time 'll be come — an prob'ly mine. But I ain' keerin' 'bout myse'f; w'en I git thoo wid him, it won' make no dif-f'ence 'bout me."

Josh was evidently in dead earnest. Miller recalled, very vividly, the expression he had seen twice on his patient's face, during the journey to Wellington. He had often seen Josh's mother, old Aunt Milly, — "Silly Milly," the children called her, — wandering aimlessly about the street, muttering to herself incoherently. He had felt a certain childish

---

[1] *Does you 'member de Ku-Klux?:* The Ku Klux Klan was formed in Tennessee in 1866 as a secret society designed to oppose Republican state governments and civil rights advocates in the South. Members included former Confederate soldiers and other white Southerners who advanced their platform by terrorizing African Americans and white Republicans. The original Klan was suppressed by the federal government in the 1870s, but has seen resurgences throughout the twentieth century.

awe at the sight of one of God's creatures who had lost the light of reason, and he had always vaguely understood that she was the victim of human cruelty, though he had dated it farther back into the past. This was his first knowledge of the real facts of the case.

He realized, too, for a moment, the continuity of life, how inseparably the present is woven with the past, how certainly the future will be but the outcome of the present. He had supposed this old wound healed. The negroes were not a vindictive people. If, swayed by passion or emotion, they sometimes gave way to gusts of rage, these were of brief duration. Absorbed in the contemplation of their doubtful present and their uncertain future, they gave little thought to the past, — it was a dark story, which they would willingly forget. He knew the timeworn explanation that the Ku-Klux movement, in the main, was merely an ebullition of boyish spirits, begun to amuse young white men by playing upon the fears and superstitions of ignorant negroes. Here, however, was its tragic side, — the old wound still bleeding, the fruit of one tragedy, the seed of another. He could not approve of Josh's application of the Mosaic law of revenge,[2] and yet the incident was not without significance. Here was a negro who could remember an injury, who could shape his life to a definite purpose, if not a high or holy one. When his race reached the point where they would resent a wrong, there was hope that they might soon attain the stage where they would try, and, if need be, die, to defend a right. This man, too, had a purpose in life, and was willing to die that he might accomplish it. Miller was willing to give up his life to a cause. Would he be equally willing, he asked himself, to die for it? Miller had no prophetic instinct to tell him how soon he would have the opportunity to answer his own question. But he could not encourage Josh to carry out this dark and revengeful purpose. Every worthy consideration required him to dissuade his patient from such a desperate course.

"You had better put away these murderous fancies, Josh," he said seriously. "The Bible says that we should 'forgive our enemies, bless them that curse us, and do good to them that despitefully use us.'"

"Yas, suh, I 've l'arnt all dat in Sunday-school, an' I 've heared de preachers say it time an' time ag'in. But it 'pears ter me dat dis fergitfulniss an' fergivniss is mighty one-sided. De w'ite folks don' fergive nothin' de niggers does. Dey got up de Ku-Klux, dey said, on 'count er

---

[2] *Josh's application of the Mosaic law of revenge:* According to the law of Moses, the code that governed the ancient Hebrews, justice required punishment equal to the crime committed. See Exod. 21–23.

de kyarpit-baggers.[3] Dey be'n talkin' 'bout de kyarpit-baggers ever sence, an' dey 'pears ter fergot all 'bout de Ku-Klux. But I ain ' fergot. De niggers is be'n train' ter fergiveniss; an' fer fear dey might fergit how ter fergive, de w'ite folks gives 'em somethin' new ev'y now an' den, ter practice on. A w'ite man kin do w'at he wants ter a nigger, but de minute de nigger gits back at 'im, up goes de nigger, an' don' come down tell somebody cuts 'im down. If a nigger gits a' office, er de race 'pears ter be prosperin' too much, de w'ite folks up an' kills a few, so dat de res' kin keep on fergivin' an' bein' thankful dat dey 're lef' alive. Don' talk ter me 'bout dese w'ite folks, — I knows 'em, I does! Ef a nigger wants ter git down on his marrow-bones, an' eat dirt, an' call 'em 'marster,' he 's a good nigger, dere 's room fer *him*. But I ain' no w'ite folks' nigger, I ain'. I don' call no man 'marster.' I don' wan' nothin' but w'at I wo'k fer, but I wants all er dat. I never moles's no w'ite man, 'less 'n he moles's me fus'. But w'en de ole 'oman dies, doc-tuh, an' I gits a good chance at dat w'ite man, — dere ain' no use talkin', suh! — dere 's gwine ter be a mix-up, an' a fune'al, er two fune'als — er may be mo', ef anybody is keerliss enough to git in de way."

"Josh," said the doctor, laying a cool hand on the other's brow, "you 're feverish, and don't know what you 're talking about. I should n't let my mind dwell on such things, and you must keep quiet until this arm is well, or you may never be able to hit any one with it again."

Miller determined that when Josh got better he would talk to him seriously and dissuade him from this dangerous design. He had not asked the name of Josh's enemy, but the look of murderous hate which the dust-begrimed tramp of the railway journey had cast at Captain George McBane rendered any such question superfluous. McBane was probably deserving of any evil fate which might befall him; but such a revenge would do no good, would right no wrong; while every such crime, committed by a colored man, would be imputed to the race, which was already staggering under a load of obloquy because, in the eyes of a prejudiced and undiscriminating public, it must answer as a whole for the offenses of each separate individual. To die in defense of the right was heroic. To kill another for revenge was pitifully human and weak: "Vengeance is mine, I will repay," saith the Lord.[4]

---

[3] *de kyarpit-baggers:* Named for the satchels or suitcases made of cloth, "carpetbag-ger" was a derisive term for white Northerners who took up residence in the South after the Civil War in order to participate in business or politics.

[4] *"Vengeance is mine, I will repay," saith the Lord.* Rom. 12.19.

XIII. THE CAKEWALK

OLD Mr. Delamere's servant, Sandy Campbell, was in deep trouble.
A party of Northern visitors had been staying for several days at the
St. James Hotel. The gentlemen of the party were concerned in a projected cotton mill, while the ladies were much interested in the study of
social conditions, and especially in the negro problem. As soon as their
desire for information became known, they were taken courteously
under the wing of prominent citizens and their wives, who gave them,
at elaborate luncheons, the Southern white man's views of the negro,
sighing sentimentally over the disappearance of the good old negro of
before the war, and gravely deploring the degeneracy of his descendants. They enlarged upon the amount of money the Southern whites
had spent for the education of the negro, and shook their heads over
the inadequate results accruing from this unexampled generosity. It
was sad, they said, to witness this spectacle of a dying race, unable to
withstand the competition of a superior type. The severe reprisals
taken by white people for certain crimes committed by negroes were of
course not the acts of the best people, who deplored them; but still a
certain charity should be extended towards those who in the intense
and righteous anger of the moment should take the law into their own
hands and deal out rough but still substantial justice; for no negro was
ever lynched without incontestable proof of his guilt. In order to be
perfectly fair, and give their visitors an opportunity to see both sides of
the question, they accompanied the Northern visitors to a colored
church where they might hear a colored preacher, who had won a joc-
ular popularity throughout the whole country by an oft-repeated sermon intended to demonstrate that the earth was flat like a pancake.
This celebrated divine could always draw a white audience, except on
the days when his no less distinguished white rival in the field of sensa-
tionalism preached his equally famous sermon to prove that hell was
exactly one half mile, linear measure, from the city limits of Wellington. Whether accidentally or not, the Northern visitors had no opportunity to meet or talk alone with any colored person in the city except
the servants at the hotel. When one of the party suggested a visit to the
colored mission school, a Southern friend kindly volunteered to
accompany them.

The visitors were naturally much impressed by what they learned
from their courteous hosts, and felt inclined to sympathize with the
Southern people, for the negro is not counted as a Southerner, except
to fix the basis of congressional representation. There might of course

be things to criticise here and there, certain customs for which they did not exactly see the necessity, and which seemed in conflict with the highest ideals of liberty, but surely these courteous, soft-spoken ladies and gentlemen, entirely familiar with local conditions, who descanted so earnestly and at times pathetically upon the grave problems confronting them, must know more about it than people in the distant North, without their means of information. The negroes who waited on them at the hotel seemed happy enough, and the teachers whom they had met at the mission school had been well-dressed, well-mannered, and apparently content with their position in life. Surely a people who made no complaints could not be very much oppressed.

In order to give the visitors, ere they left Wellington, a pleasing impression of Southern customs, and particularly of the joyous, happy-go-lucky disposition of the Southern darky and his entire contentment with existing conditions, it was decided by the hotel management to treat them, on the last night of their visit, to a little diversion, in the shape of a genuine negro cakewalk.

On the afternoon of this same day Tom Delamere strolled into the hotel, and soon gravitated to the bar, where he was a frequent visitor. Young men of leisure spent much of their time around the hotel, and no small part of it in the bar. Delamere had been to the club, but had avoided the card-room. Time hanging heavy on his hands, he had sought the hotel in the hope that some form of distraction might present itself.

"Have you heard the latest, Mr. Delamere?" asked the bartender, as he mixed a cocktail for his customer.

"No, Billy; what is it?"

"There's to be a big cakewalk upstairs to-night. The No'the'n gentlemen an' ladies who are down here to see about the new cotton fact'ry want to study the nigger some more, and the boss has got up a cakewalk for 'em, 'mongst the waiters and chambermaids, with a little outside talent."

"Is it to be public?" asked Delamere.

"Oh, no, not generally, but friends of the house won't be barred out. The clerk 'll fix it for you. Ransom, the head waiter, will be floor manager."

Delamere was struck with a brilliant idea. The more he considered it, the brighter it seemed. Another cocktail imparted additional brilliancy to the conception. He had been trying, after a feeble fashion, to keep his promise to Clara, and was really suffering from lack of excitement.

He left the bar-room, found the head waiter, held with him a short conversation, and left in his intelligent and itching palm a piece of money.

The cakewalk was a great success. The most brilliant performer was a late arrival, who made his appearance just as the performance was about to commence. The newcomer was dressed strikingly, the conspicuous features of his attire being a long blue coat with brass buttons and a pair of plaid trousers. He was older, too, than the other participants, which made his agility the more remarkable. His partner was a new chambermaid, who had just come to town, and whom the head waiter introduced to the newcomer upon his arrival. The cake was awarded to this couple by a unanimous vote. The man presented it to his partner with a grandiloquent flourish, and returned thanks in a speech which sent the Northern visitors into spasms of delight at the quaintness of the darky dialect and the darky wit. To cap the climax, the winner danced a buck dance with a skill and agility that brought a shower of complimentary silver, which he gathered up and passed to the head waiter.

Ellis was off duty for the evening. Not having ventured to put in an appearance at Carteret's since his last rebuff, he found himself burdened with a superfluity of leisure, from which he essayed to find relief by dropping into the hotel office at about nine o'clock. He was invited up to see the cakewalk, which he rather enjoyed, for there was some graceful dancing and posturing. But the grotesque contortions of one participant had struck him as somewhat overdone, even for the comical type of negro. He recognized the fellow, after a few minutes' scrutiny, as the body-servant of old Mr. Delamere. The man's present occupation, or choice of diversion, seemed out of keeping with his employment as attendant upon an invalid old gentleman, and strangely inconsistent with the gravity and decorum which had been so noticeable when this agile cakewalker had served as butler at Major Carteret's table, upon the occasion of the christening dinner. There was a vague suggestion of unreality about this performance, too, which Ellis did not attempt to analyze, but which recurred vividly to his memory upon a subsequent occasion.

Ellis had never pretended to that intimate knowledge of negro thought and character by which some of his acquaintances claimed the ability to fathom every motive of a negro's conduct, and predict in advance what any one of the darker race would do under a given set of circumstances. He would not have believed that a white man could possess two so widely varying phases of character; but as to negroes, they were as yet a crude and undeveloped race, and it was not safe to make predictions concerning them. No one could tell at what moment the thin veneer of civilization might peel off and reveal the underlying savage.

The champion cakewalker, much to the surprise of his sable companions, who were about equally swayed by admiration and jealousy, disappeared immediately after the close of the performance. Any one watching him on his way home through the quiet streets to old Mr. Delamere's would have seen him now and then shaking with laughter. It had been excellent fun. Nevertheless, as he neared home, a certain aspect of the affair, hitherto unconsidered, occurred to him, and it was in a rather serious frame of mind that he cautiously entered the house and sought his own room.

The cakewalk had results which to Sandy were very serious. The following week he was summoned before the disciplinary committee of his church and charged with unchristian conduct, in the following particulars, to wit: dancing, and participating in a sinful diversion called a cakewalk, which was calculated to bring the church into disrepute and make it the mockery of sinners.

Sandy protested his innocence vehemently, but in vain. The proof was overwhelming. He was positively identified by Sister 'Manda Patterson, the hotel cook, who had watched the whole performance from the hotel corridor for the sole, single, solitary, and only purpose, she averred, of seeing how far human wickedness could be carried by a professing Christian. The whole thing had been shocking and offensive to her, and only a stern sense of duty had sustained her in looking on, that she might be qualified to bear witness against the offender. She had recognized his face, his clothes, his voice, his walk — there could be no shadow of doubt that it was Brother Sandy. This testimony was confirmed by one of the deacons, whose son, a waiter at the hotel, had also seen Sandy at the cakewalk.

Sandy stoutly insisted that he was at home the whole evening; that he had not been near the hotel for three months; that he had never in his life taken part in a cakewalk, and that he did not know how to dance. It was replied that wickedness, like everything else, must have a beginning; that dancing was an art that could be acquired in secret, and came natural to some people. In the face of positive proof, Sandy's protestations were of no avail; he was found guilty, and suspended from church fellowship until he should have repented and made full confession.

Sturdily refusing to confess a fault of which he claimed to be innocent, Sandy remained in contumacy, thereby falling somewhat into
disrepute among the members of his church, the largest in the city. The
effect of a bad reputation being subjective as well as objective, and
poor human nature arguing that one may as well have the game as the
name, Sandy insensibly glided into habits of which the church would
not have approved, though he took care that they should not interfere
with his duties to Mr. Delamere. The consolation thus afforded, however, followed as it was by remorse of conscience, did not compensate
him for the loss of standing in the church, which to him was a social
club as well as a religious temple. At times, in conversation with young
Delamere, he would lament his hard fate.

Tom laughed until he cried at the comical idea which Sandy's plaint
always brought up, of half-a-dozen negro preachers sitting in solemn
judgment upon that cakewalk, — it had certainly been a good cakewalk! — and sending poor Sandy to spiritual Coventry.

"Cheer up, Sandy, cheer up! he would say when Sandy seemed most
depressed. "Go into my room and get yourself a good drink of liquor.
The devil's church has a bigger congregation than theirs, and we have
the consolation of knowing that when we die, we 'll meet all our
friends on the other side. Brace up, Sandy, and be a man, or, if you
can't be a man, be as near a man as you can!"

Hoping to revive his drooping spirits, Sandy too often accepted the
proffered remedy.

XIV. THE MAUNDERINGS OF OLD MRS. OCHILTREE

WHEN Mrs. Carteret had fully recovered from the shock attendant
upon the accident at the window, where little Dodie had so narrowly
escaped death or serious injury, she ordered her carriage one afternoon
and directed the coachman to drive her to Mrs. Ochiltree's.

Mrs. Carteret had discharged her young nurse only the day before,
and had sent for Mammy Jane, who was now recovered from her
rheumatism, to stay until she could find another girl. The nurse had
been ordered not to take the child to negroes' houses. Yesterday, in
driving past the old homestead of her husband's family, now occupied
by Dr. Miller and his family, Mrs. Carteret had seen her own baby's
carriage standing in the yard.

When the nurse returned home, she was immediately discharged.
She offered some sort of explanation, to the effect that her sister

worked for Mrs. Miller, and that some family matter had rendered it necessary for her to see her sister. The explanation only aggravated the offense; if Mrs. Carteret could have overlooked the disobedience, she would by no means have retained in her employment a servant whose sister worked for the Miller woman.

Old Mrs. Ochiltree had within a few months begun to show signs of breaking up. She was over seventy years old, and had been of late, by various afflictions, confined to the house much of the time. More than once within the year, Mrs. Carteret had asked her aunt to come and live with her; but Mrs. Ochiltree, who would have regarded such a step as an acknowledgment of weakness, preferred her lonely independence. She resided in a small, old-fashioned house, standing back in the middle of a garden on a quiet street. Two old servants made up her modest household.

This refusal to live with her niece had been lightly borne, for Mrs. Ochiltree was a woman of strong individuality, whose comments upon her acquaintance, present or absent, were marked by a frankness at times no less than startling. This characteristic caused her to be more or less avoided. Mrs. Ochiltree was aware of this sentiment on the part of her acquaintance, and rather exulted in it. She hated fools. Only fools ran away from her, and that because they were afraid she would expose their folly. If most people were fools, it was no fault of hers, and she was not obliged to indulge them by pretending to believe that they knew anything. She had once owned considerable property, but was reticent about her affairs, and told no one how much she was worth, though it was supposed that she had considerable ready money, besides her house and some other real estate. Mrs. Carteret was her nearest living relative, though her grand-nephew Tom Delamere had been a great favorite with her. If she did not spare him her tongue-lashings, it was nevertheless expected in the family that she would leave him something handsome in her will.

Mrs. Ochiltree had shared in the general rejoicing upon the advent of the Carteret baby. She had been one of his godmothers, and had hinted at certain intentions held by her concerning him. During Mammy Jane's administration she had tried the old nurse's patience more or less by her dictatorial interference. Since her partial confinement to the house, she had gone, when her health and the weather would permit, to see the child, and at other times had insisted that it be sent to her in charge of the nurse at least every other day.

Mrs. Ochiltree's faculties had shared insensibly in the decline of her health. This weakness manifested itself by fits of absent-mindedness, in which she would seemingly lose connection with the present, and live over again, in imagination, the earlier years of her life. She had buried two husbands, had tried in vain to secure a third, and had never borne any children. Long ago she had petrified into a character which nothing under heaven could change, and which, if death is to take us as it finds us, and the future life to keep us as it takes us, promised anything but eternal felicity to those with whom she might associate after this life. Tom Delamere had been heard to say, profanely, that if his Aunt Polly went to heaven, he would let his mansion in the skies on a long lease, at a low figure.

When the carriage drove up with Mrs. Carteret, her aunt was seated on the little front piazza, with her wrinkled hands folded in her lap, dozing the afternoon away in fitful slumber.

"Tie the horse, William," said Mrs. Carteret, "and then go in and wake Aunt Polly, and tell her I want her to come and drive with me."

Mrs. Ochiltree had not observed her niece's approach, nor did she look up when William drew near. Her eyes were closed, and she would let her head sink slowly forward, recovering it now and then with a spasmodic jerk.

"Colonel Ochiltree," she muttered, "was shot at the battle of Culpepper Court House, and left me a widow for the second time. But I would not have married any man on earth after him."

"Mis' Ochiltree!" cried William, raising his voice, "oh, Mis' Ochiltree!"

"If I had found a man, — a real man, — I might have married again. I did not care for weaklings. I could have married John Delamere if I had wanted him. But pshaw! I could have wound him round" —

"Go round to the kitchen, William," interrupted Mrs. Carteret impatiently, "and tell Aunt Dinah to come and wake her up."

William returned in a few moments with a fat, comfortable looking black woman, who curtsied to Mrs. Carteret at the gate, and then going up to her mistress seized her by the shoulder and shook her vigorously.

"Wake up dere, Mis' Polly," she screamed, as harshly as her mellow voice would permit. "Mis' 'Livy wants you ter go drivin' wid 'er!"

"Dinah," exclaimed the old lady, sitting suddenly upright with a defiant assumption of wakefulness, "why do you take so long to come when I call? Bring me my bonnet and shawl. Don't you see my niece waiting for me at the gate?"

"Hyuh dey is, hyuh dey is!" returned Dinah, producing the bonnet and shawl, and assisting Mrs. Ochiltree to put them on.

Leaning on William's arm, the old lady went slowly down the walk, and was handed to the rear seat with Mrs. Carteret.

"How 's the baby to-day, Olivia, and why did n't you bring him?"

"He has a cold to-day, and is a little hoarse," replied Mrs. Carteret, "so I thought it best not to bring him out. Drive out the Weldon road, William, and back by Pine Street."

The drive led past an eminence crowned by a handsome brick building of modern construction, evidently an institution of some kind, surrounded on three sides by a grove of venerable oaks.

"Hugh Poindexter," Mrs. Ochiltree exclaimed explosively, after a considerable silence, "has been building a new house, in place of the old family mansion burned during the war."

"It is n't Mr. Poindexter's house, Aunt Polly. That is the new colored hospital built by the colored doctor."

"The new colored hospital, indeed, and the colored doctor! Before the war the negroes were all healthy, and when they got sick we took care of them ourselves! Hugh Poindexter has sold the graves of his ancestors to a negro, — I should have starved first!"

"He had his grandfather's grave opened, and there was nothing to remove, except a few bits of heart-pine from the coffin. All the rest had crumbled into dust."

"And he sold the dust to a negro! The world is upside down."

"He had the tombstone transferred to the white cemetery, Aunt Polly, and he has moved away."

"Esau[1] sold his birthright for a mess of pottage. When I die, if you outlive me, Olivia, which is not likely, I shall leave my house and land to this child! He is a Carteret, — he would never sell them to a negro. I can't trust Tom Delamere, I 'm afraid."

The carriage had skirted the hill, passing to the rear of the new building.

"Turn to the right, William," ordered Mrs. Carteret, addressing the coachman, "and come back past the other side of the hospital."

A turn to the right into another road soon brought them to the front of the building, which stood slightly back from the street, with no intervening fence or inclosure. A sorrel pony in a light buggy was fastened to a hitching-post near the entrance. As they drove past, a lady came out of the front door and descended the steps, holding by the hand a very pretty child about six years old.

---

[1] *Esau:* Gen. 25.27–34 tells the story of Isaac's twin sons, Jacob and Esau. Taken in by Jacob's deception, Esau traded his right of inheritance as the older son for food, or a "mess of pottage."

"Who is that woman, Olivia?" asked Mrs. Ochiltree abruptly, with signs of agitation.

The lady coming down the steps darted at the approaching carriage a look which lingered involuntarily.

Mrs. Carteret, perceiving this glance, turned away coldly.

With a sudden hardening of her own features the other woman lifted the little boy into the buggy and drove sharply away in the direction opposite to that taken by Mrs. Carteret's carriage.

"Who is that woman, Olivia?" repeated Mrs. Ochiltree, with marked emotion.

"I have not the honor of her acquaintance," returned Mrs. Carteret sharply. "Drive faster, William."

"I want to know who that woman is," persisted Mrs. Ochiltree querulously. "William," she cried shrilly, poking the coachman in the back with the end of her cane, "who is that woman?"

"Dat 's Mis' Miller, ma'am," returned the coachman, touching his hat; "Doctuh Miller's wife."

"What was her mother's name?"

"Her mother's name wus Julia Brown. She's be'n dead dese twenty years er mo'. Why, you knowed Julia, Mis' Polly! — she used ter b'long ter yo' own father befo' de wah; an' after de wah she kep' house fer" —

"Look to your horses, William!" exclaimed Mrs. Carteret sharply.

"It's that hussy's child," said Mrs. Ochiltree, turning to her niece with great excitement. "When your father died, I turned the mother and the child out into the street. The mother died and went to — the place provided for such as she. If I had n't been just in time, Olivia, they would have turned you out. I saved the property for you and your son! You can thank me for it all!"

"Hush, Aunt Polly, for goodness' sake! William will hear you. Tell me about it when you get home."

Mrs. Ochiltree was silent, except for a few incoherent mumblings. What she might say, what distressing family secret she might repeat in William's hearing, should she take another talkative turn, was beyond conjecture.

Olivia looked anxiously around for something to distract her aunt's attention, and caught sight of a colored man, dressed in sober gray, who was coming toward the carriage.

"There 's Mr. Delamere's Sandy!" exclaimed Mrs. Carteret, touching her aunt on the arm. "I wonder how his master is? Sandy, oh, Sandy!"

Sandy approached the carriage, lifting his hat with a slight exaggeration of Chesterfieldian elegance. Sandy, no less than his master, was a survival of an interesting type. He had inherited the feudal deference for his superiors in position, joined to a certain self-respect which saved him from sycophancy. His manners had been formed upon those of old Mr. Delamere, and were not a bad imitation; for in the man, as in the master, they were the harmonious reflection of a mental state.

"How is Mr. Delamere, Sandy?" asked Mrs. Carteret, acknowledging Sandy's salutation with a nod and a smile.

"He ain't ez peart ez he has be'n, ma'am," replied Sandy, "but he 's doin' tol'able well. De doctuh say he 's good fer a dozen years yit, ef he 'll jes' take good keer of hisse'f an' keep f'm gittin' excited; fer sence dat secon' stroke, excitement is dange'ous fer 'im."

"I 'm sure you take the best care of him," returned Mrs. Carteret kindly.

"You can't do anything for him, Sandy," interposed old Mrs. Ochiltree, shaking her head slowly to emphasize her dissent. "All the doctors in creation could n't keep him alive another year. I shall outlive him by twenty years, though we are not far from the same age."

"Lawd, ma'am!" exclaimed Sandy, lifting his hands in affected amazement, — his study of gentle manners had been more than superficial, — "whoever would 'a' s'picion' dat you an' Mars John wuz nigh de same age? I 'd 'a' 'lowed you wuz ten years younger 'n him, easy, ef you wuz a day!"

"Give my compliments to the poor old gentleman," returned Mrs. Ochiltree, with a simper of senile vanity, though her back was weakening under the strain of the effort to sit erect that she might maintain this illusion of comparative youthfulness. "Bring him to see me some day when he is able to walk."

"Yas'm, I will," rejoined Sandy. "He 's gwine out ter Belleview nex' week, fer ter stay a mont' er so, but I 'll fetch him 'roun' w'en he comes back. I 'll tell 'im dat you ladies 'quired fer 'im."

Sandy made another deep bow, and held his hat in his hand until the carriage had moved away. He had not condescended to notice the coachman at all, who was one of the young negroes of the new generation; while Sandy regarded himself as belonging to the quality, and seldom stooped to notice those beneath him. It would not have been becoming in him, either, while conversing with white ladies, to have noticed a colored servant. Moreover, the coachman was a Baptist, while Sandy was a Methodist, though under a cloud, and considered a Methodist in poor standing was better than a Baptist of any degree of sanctity.

"Lawd, Lawd!" chuckled Sandy, after the carriage had departed, "I never seed nothin' lack de way dat ole lady do keep up her temper! Wid one foot in de grave, an' de other hov'rin' on de edge, she talks 'bout my ole marster lack he wuz in his secon' chil'hood. But I 'm jes' willin' ter bet dat he 'll outlas' her! She ain't half de woman she wuz dat night I waited on de table at de christenin' pa'ty, w'en she 'lowed she wuz n' feared er no man livin'."

XV. MRS. CARTERET SEEKS AN EXPLANATION

As a stone dropped into a pool of water sets in motion a series of concentric circles which disturb the whole mass in varying degree, so Mrs. Ochiltree's enigmatical remark had started in her niece's mind a disturbing train of thought. Had her words, Mrs. Carteret asked herself, any serious meaning, or were they the mere empty babblings of a clouded intellect?

"William," she said to the coachman when they reached Mrs. Ochiltree's house, "you may tie the horse and help us out. I shall be here a little while."

William helped the ladies down, assisted Mrs. Ochiltree into the house, and then went round to the kitchen. Dinah was an excellent hand at potato-pone and other culinary delicacies dear to the Southern heart, and William was a welcome visitor in her domain.

"Now, Aunt Polly," said Mrs. Carteret resolutely, as soon as they were alone, "I want to know what you meant by what you said about my father and Julia, and this — this child of hers?"

The old woman smiled cunningly, but her expression soon changed to one more grave.

"Why do you want to know?" she asked suspiciously. "You 've got the land, the houses, and the money. You 've nothing to complain of. Enjoy yourself, and be thankful!"

"I 'm thankful to God," returned Olivia, "for all his good gifts, — and He has blessed me abundantly, — but why should I be thankful to *you* for the property my father left me?"

"Why should you be thankful to me?" rejoined Mrs. Ochiltree with querulous indignation. "You 'd better ask why *should n't* you be thankful to me. What have I not done for you?"

"Yes, Aunt Polly, I know you 've done a great deal. You reared me in your own house when I had been cast out of my father's; you have been a second mother to me, and I am very grateful, — you can never say that I have not shown my gratitude. But if you have done anything else for me, I wish to know it. Why should I thank you for my inheritance?"

"Why should you thank me? Well, because I drove that woman and her brat away."

"But she had no right to stay, Aunt Polly, after father died. Of course she had no moral right before, but it was his house, and he could keep her there if he chose. But after his death she surely had no right."

"Perhaps not so surely as you think, — if she had not been a negro. Had she been white, there might have been a difference. When I told her to go, she said" —

"What did she say, Aunt Polly," demanded Olivia eagerly.

It seemed for a moment as though Mrs. Ochiltree would speak no further: but her once strong will, now weakened by her bodily infirmities, yielded to the influence of her niece's imperious demand.

"I 'll tell you the whole story," she said, "and then you 'll know what I did for you and yours."

Mrs. Ochiltree's eyes assumed an introspective expression, and her story, as it advanced, became as keenly dramatic as though memory had thrown aside the veil of intervening years and carried her back directly to the events which she now described.

"Your father," she said, "while living with that woman, left home one morning the picture of health. Five minutes later he tottered into the house groaning with pain, stricken unto death by the hand of a just God, as a punishment for his sins."

Olivia gave a start of indignation, but restrained herself.

"I was at once informed of what had happened, for I had means of knowing all that took place in the household. Old Jane — she was younger then — had come with you to my house; but her daughter remained, and through her I learned all that went on.

"I hastened immediately to the house, entered without knocking, and approached Mr. Merkell's bedroom, which was on the lower floor and opened into the hall. The door was ajar, and as I stood there for a moment I heard your father's voice.

"'Listen, Julia,' he was saying. 'I shall not live until the doctor comes. But I wish you to know, *dear* Julia!' — he called her 'dear Julia!' — 'before I die, that I have kept my promise. You did me one great service, Julia, — you saved me from Polly Ochiltree!' Yes, Olivia, that is what he said! 'You have served me faithfully and well, and I owe you a great deal, which I have tried to pay.'

" 'Oh, Mr. Merkell, dear Mr. Merkell,' cried the hypocritical hussy, falling to her knees by his bedside, and shedding her crocodile tears, 'you owe me nothing. You have done more for me than I could ever repay. You will not die and leave me, — no, no, it cannot be!'

" 'Yes, I am going to die, — I am dying now, Julia. But listen, — compose yourself and listen, for this is a more important matter. Take the keys from under my pillow, open the desk in the next room, look in the second drawer on the right, and you will find an envelope containing three papers: one of them is yours, one is the paper I promised to make, and the third is a letter which I wrote last night. As soon as the breath has left my body, deliver the envelope to the address endorsed upon it. Do not delay one moment, or you may live to regret it. Say nothing until you have delivered the package, and then be guided by the advice which you receive, — it will come from a friend of mine who will not see you wronged.'

"I slipped away from the door without making my presence known and entered, by a door from the hall, the room adjoining the one where Mr. Merkell lay. A moment later there was a loud scream. Returning quickly to the hall, I entered Mr. Merkell's room as though just arrived.

" 'How is Mr. Merkell?' I demanded, as I crossed the threshold.

" 'He is dead,' sobbed the woman, without lifting her head, — she had fallen on her knees by the bedside. She had good cause to weep, for my time had come.

" 'Get up,' I said. 'You have no right here. You pollute Mr. Merkell's dead body by your touch. Leave the house immediately, — your day is over!'

" 'I will not!' she cried, rising to her feet and facing me with brazen-faced impudence. 'I have a right to stay, — he has given me the right!'

" 'Ha, ha!' I laughed. 'Mr. Merkell is dead, and I am mistress here henceforth. Go, and go at once, — do you hear?'

" 'I hear, but I shall not heed. I can prove my rights! I shall not leave!'

" 'Very well,' I replied, 'we shall see. The law will decide.'

"I left the room, but did not leave the house. On the contrary, I concealed myself where I could see what took place in the room adjoining the death-chamber.

"She entered the room a moment later, with her child on one arm and the keys in the other hand. Placing the child on the floor, she put the key in the lock, and seemed surprised to find the desk already unfastened. She opened the desk, picked up a roll of money and a ladies' watch, which first caught her eye, and was reaching toward the drawer upon the right, when I interrupted her: —

" 'Well, thief, are you trying to strip the house before you leave it?'

"She gave an involuntary cry, clasped one hand to her bosom and with the other caught up her child, and stood like a wild beast at bay.

" 'I am not a thief,' she panted. 'The things are mine!'

" 'You lie,' I replied. 'You have no right to them, — no more right than you have to remain in this house!'

" 'I have a right,' she persisted, 'and I can prove it!'

"She turned toward the desk, seized the drawer, and drew it open. Never shall I forget her look, — never shall I forget that moment; it was the happiest of my life. The drawer was empty!

"Pale as death she turned and faced me.

" 'The papers!' she shrieked, 'the papers! *You* have stolen them!'

" 'Papers?' I laughed, 'what papers? Do you take me for a thief, like yourself?'

" 'There were papers here,' she cried, 'only a minute since. They are mine, — give them back to me!'

" 'Listen, woman,' I said sternly, 'you are lying — or dreaming. My brother-in-law's papers are doubtless in his safe at his office, where they ought to be. As for the rest, — you are a thief.'

" 'I am not,' she screamed; "I am his wife. He married me, and the papers that were in the desk will prove it.'

" 'Listen,' I exclaimed, when she had finished, — 'listen carefully, and take heed to what I say. You are a liar. You have no proofs, — there never were any proofs of what you say, because it never happened, — it is absurd upon the face of it. Not one person in Wellington would believe it. Why should he marry you? He did not need to! You are merely lying, — you are not even self-deceived. If he had really married you, you would have made it known long ago. That you did not is proof that your story is false.'

"She was hit so hard that she trembled and sank into a chair. But I had no mercy — she had saved your father from *me* — 'dear Julia,' indeed!

" 'Stand up,' I ordered. 'Do not dare to sit down in my presence. I have you on the hip, my lady, and will teach you your place.'

"She struggled to her feet, and stood supporting herself with one hand on the chair. I could have killed her, Olivia! She had been my father's slave; if it had been before the war, I would have had her whipped to death.

" 'You are a thief,' I said, 'and of that there *are* proofs. I have caught you in the act. The watch in your bosom is my own, the money belongs to Mr. Merkell's estate, which belongs to my niece, his daughter Olivia. I saw you steal them. My word is worth yours a hundred times over, for I am a lady, and you are — what? And now hear me: if ever you breathe to a living soul one word of this preposterous story, I will charge you with the theft, and have you sent to the penitentiary. Your child will be taken from you, and you shall never see it again. I will give you now just ten minutes to take your brat and your rags out of this house forever. But before you go, put down your plunder there upon the desk!'

"She laid down the money and the watch, and a few minutes later left the house with the child in her arms.

"And now, Olivia, you know how I saved your estate, and why you should be grateful to me."

Olivia had listened to her aunt's story with intense interest. Having perceived the old woman's mood, and fearful lest any interruption might break the flow of her narrative, she had with an effort kept back the one question which had been hovering upon her lips, but which could now no longer be withheld.

"What became of the papers, Aunt Polly?"

"Ha, ha!" chuckled Mrs. Ochiltree with a cunning look, "did I not tell you that she found no papers?"

A change had come over Mrs. Ochiltree's face, marking the reaction from her burst of energy. Her eyes were half closed, and she was muttering incoherently. Olivia made some slight effort to arouse her, but in vain, and realizing the futility of any further attempt to extract information from her aunt at this time, she called William and drove homeward.

XVI. ELLIS TAKES A TRICK

LATE one afternoon a handsome trap, drawn by two spirited bays, drove up to Carteret's gate. Three places were taken by Mrs. Carteret, Clara, and the major, leaving the fourth seat vacant.

"I 've asked Ellis to drive out with us," said the major, as he took the lines from the colored man who had the trap in charge. "We 'll go by the office and pick him up."

Clara frowned, but perceiving Mrs. Carteret's eye fixed upon her, restrained any further expression of annoyance.

The major's liking for Ellis had increased within the year. The young man was not only a good journalist, but possessed sufficient cleverness and tact to make him excellent company. The major was fond of argument, but extremely tenacious of his own opinions. Ellis handled the foils of discussion with just the requisite skill to draw out the major, permitting himself to be vanquished, not too easily, but, as it were, inevitably, by the major's incontrovertible arguments.

Olivia had long suspected Ellis of feeling a more than friendly interest in Clara. Herself partial to Tom, she had more than once thought it hardly fair to Delamere, or even to Clara, who was young and impressionable, to have another young man constantly about the house. True, there had seemed to be no great danger, for Ellis had neither the family nor the means to make him a suitable match for the major's sister; nor had Clara made any secret of her dislike for Ellis, or of her resentment for his supposed depreciation of Delamere. Mrs. Carteret was inclined to a more just and reasonable view of Ellis's conduct in this matter, but nevertheless did not deem it wise to undeceive Clara. Dislike was a stout barrier, which remorse might have broken down. The major, absorbed in schemes of empire and dreams of his child's future, had not become cognizant of the affair. His wife, out of friendship for Tom, had refrained from mentioning it; while the major, with a delicate regard for Clara's feelings, had said nothing at home in regard to his interview with her lover.

At the Chronicle office Ellis took the front seat beside the major. After leaving the city pavements, they bowled along merrily over an excellent toll-road, built of oyster shells from the neighboring sound, stopping at intervals to pay toll to the gate-keepers, most of whom were white women with tallow complexions and snuff-stained lips, — the traditional "poor-white." For part of the way the road was bordered with a growth of scrub oak and pine, interspersed with stretches of cleared land, white with the opening cotton or yellow with ripening corn. To the right, along the distant river-bank, were visible here and there groups of turpentine pines, though most of this growth had for some years been exhausted. Twenty years before, Wellington had been the world's greatest shipping port for naval stores. But as the turpentine industry had moved southward, leaving a trail of devastated forests in its rear, the city had fallen to a poor fifth or sixth place in this trade, relying now almost entirely upon cotton for its export business.

Occasionally our party passed a person, or a group of persons, — mostly negroes approximating the pure type, for those of lighter color grew noticeably scarcer as the town was left behind. Now and then one of these would salute the party respectfully, while others glanced at them indifferently or turned away. There would have seemed, to a stranger, a lack of spontaneous friendliness between the people of these two races, as though each felt that it had no part or lot in the other's life. At one point the carriage drew near a party of colored folks who were laughing and jesting among themselves with great glee. Paying no attention to the white people, they continued to laugh and shout boisterously as the carriage swept by.

Major Carteret's countenance wore an angry look.

"The negroes around this town are becoming absolutely insufferable," he averred. "They are sadly in need of a lesson in manners."

Half an hour later they neared another group, who were also making merry. As the carriage approached, they became mute and silent as the grave until the major's party had passed.

"The negroes are a sullen race," remarked the major thoughtfully. "They will learn their lesson in a rude school, and perhaps much sooner than they dream. By the way," he added, turning to the ladies, "What was the arrangement with Tom? Was he to come out this evening?"

"He came out early in the afternoon," replied Clara, "to go a-fishing. He is to join us at the hotel."

After an hour's drive they reached the hotel, in front of which stretched the beach, white and inviting, along the shallow sound. Mrs. Carteret and Clara found seats on the veranda. Having turned the trap over to a hostler, the major joined a group of gentlemen, among whom was General Belmont, and was soon deep in the discussion of the standing problem of how best to keep the negroes down.

Ellis remained by the ladies. Clara seemed restless and ill at ease. Half an hour elapsed and Delamere had not appeared.

"I wonder where Tom is," said Mrs. Carteret.

"I guess he has n't come in yet from fishing," said Clara. "I wish he would come. It 's lonesome here. Mr. Ellis, would you mind looking about the hotel and seeing if there 's any one here that we know?"

For Ellis the party was already one too large. He had accepted this invitation eagerly, hoping to make friends with Clara during the evening. He had never been able to learn definitely the reason of her coldness, but had dated it from his meeting with old Mrs. Ochiltree, with which he felt it was obscurely connected. He had noticed Delamere's scowling look, too, at their last meeting. Clara's injustice, whatever its cause, he felt keenly. To Delamere's scowl he had paid little attention, — he despised Tom so much that, but for his engagement to Clara, he would have held his opinions in utter contempt.

He had even wished that Clara might make some charge against him, — he would have preferred that to her attitude of studied indifference, the only redeeming feature about which was that it *was* studied, showing that she, at least, had him in mind. The next best thing, he reasoned, to having a woman love you, is to have her dislike you violently, — the main point is that you should be kept in mind, and made the subject of strong emotions. He thought of the story of Hall Caine's,[1] where the woman, after years of persecution at the hands of an unwelcome suitor, is on the point of yielding, out of sheer irresistible admiration for the man's strength and persistency, when the lover, unaware of his victory and despairing of success, seizes her in his arms and, springing into the sea, finds a watery grave for both. The analogy of this case with his own was, of course, not strong. He did not anticipate any tragedy in their relations; but he was glad to be thought of upon almost any terms. He would not have done a mean thing to make her think of him; but if she did so because of a misconception, which he was given no opportunity to clear up, while at the same time his conscience absolved him from evil and gave him the compensating glow of martyrdom, it was at least better than nothing.

He would, of course, have preferred to be upon a different footing. It had been a pleasure to have her speak to him during the drive, — they had exchanged a few trivial remarks in the general conversation. It was a greater pleasure to have her ask a favor of him, — a pleasure which, in this instance, was partly offset when he interpreted her request to mean that he was to look for Tom Delamere. He accepted the situation gracefully, however, and left the ladies alone.

Knowing Delamere's habits, he first went directly to the barroom, — the atmosphere would be congenial, even if he were not drinking. Delamere was not there. Stepping next into the office, he asked the clerk if young Mr. Delamere had been at the hotel.

"Yes, sir," returned the man at the desk, "he was here at luncheon, and then went out fishing in a boat with several other gentlemen. I think they came back about three o'clock. I 'll find out for you."

He rang the bell, to which a colored boy responded.

---

[1] *Hall Caine's:* English writer Hall Caine (1853–1931) was known for his widely popular novels at the turn of the century.

"Front," said the clerk, "see if young Mr. Delamere 's upstairs. Look in 255 or 256, and let me know at once."

The bell-boy returned in a moment.

"Yas, suh," he reported, with a suppressed grin, "he 's in 256, suh. De do' was open, an' I seed 'im from de hall, suh."

"I wish you 'd go up and tell him," said Ellis, "that — What are you grinning about?" he asked suddenly, noticing the waiter's expression.

"Nothin', suh, nothin' at all, suh," responded the negro, lapsing into the stolidity of a wooden Indian. "What shall I tell Mr. Delamere, suh?"

"Tell him," resumed Ellis, still watching the boy suspiciously, — "no, I 'll tell him myself."

He ascended the broad stair to the second floor. There was an upper balcony and a parlor, with a piano for the musically inclined. To reach these one had to pass along the hall upon which the room mentioned by the bell-boy opened. Ellis was quite familiar with the hotel. He could imagine circumstances under which he would not care to speak to Delamere; he would merely pass through the hall and glance into the room casually, as any one else might do, and see what the darky downstairs might have meant by his impudence.

It required but a moment to reach the room. The door was not wide open, but far enough ajar for him to see what was going on within.

Two young men, members of the fast set at the Clarendon Club, were playing cards at a small table, near which stood another, decorated with an array of empty bottles and glasses. Sprawling on a lounge, with flushed face and disheveled hair, his collar unfastened, his vest buttoned awry, lay Tom Delamere, breathing stertorously, in what seemed a drunken sleep. Lest there should be any doubt of the cause of his condition, the fingers of his right hand had remained clasped mechanically around the neck of a bottle which lay across his bosom.

Ellis turned away in disgust, and went slowly back to the ladies.

"There seems to be no one here yet," he reported. "We came a little early for the evening crowd. The clerk says Tom Delamere was here to luncheon, but he has n't seen him for several hours."

"He 's not a very gallant cavalier," said Mrs. Carteret severely. "He ought to have been waiting for us."

Clara was clearly disappointed, and made no effort to conceal her displeasure, leaving Ellis in doubt as to whether or not he were its object. Perhaps she suspected him of not having made a very thorough search. Her next remark might have borne such a construction.

"Sister Olivia," she said pettishly, "let 's go up to the parlor. I can play the piano anyway, if there 's no one to talk to."

"I find it very comfortable here, Clara," replied her sister placidly. "Mr. Ellis will go with you. You 'll probably find some one in the parlor, or they 'll come when you begin to play."

Clara's expression was not cordial, but she rose as if to go. Ellis was in a quandary. If she went through the hall, the chances were at least even that she would see Delamere. He did not care a rap for Delamere, — if he chose to make a public exhibition of himself, it was his own affair; but to see him would surely spoil Miss Pemberton's evening, and, in her frame of mind, might lead to the suspicion that Ellis had prearranged the exposure. Even if she should not harbor this unjust thought, she would not love the witness of her discomfiture. We had rather not meet the persons who have seen, even though they never mention, the skeletons in our closets. Delamere had disposed of himself for the evening. Ellis would have a fairer field with Delamere out of sight and unaccounted for, than with Delamere in evidence in his present condition.

"Would n't you rather take a stroll on the beach, Miss Clara?" he asked, in the hope of creating a diversion.

"No, I 'm going to the parlor. *You* need n't come, Mr. Ellis, if you 'd rather go down to the beach. I can quite as well go alone."

"I 'd rather go with you," he said meekly.

They were moving toward the door opening into the hall, from which the broad staircase ascended. Ellis, whose thoughts did not always respond quickly to a sudden emergency, was puzzling his brain as to how he should save her from any risk of seeing Delamere. Through the side door leading from the hall into the office, he saw the bell-boy to whom he had spoken seated on the bench provided for the servants.

"Won't you wait for me just a moment, Miss Clara, while I step into the office? I 'll be with you in an instant."

Clara hesitated.

"Oh, certainly," she replied nonchalantly.

Ellis went direct to the bell-boy. "Sit right where you are," he said, "and don't move a hair. What is the lady in the hall doing?"

"She 's got her back tu'ned this way, suh. I 'spec' she 's lookin' at the picture on the opposite wall, suh."

"All right," whispered Ellis, pressing a coin into the servant's hand. "I 'm going up to the parlor with the lady. You go up ahead of us, and keep in front of us along the hall. Don't dare to look back. I shall keep on talking to the lady, so that you can tell by my voice where we are. When you get to room 256, go in and shut the door behind you: pretend that you were called, — ask the gentlemen what they want, — tell any kind of a lie you like, — but keep the door shut until you 're sure we 've got by. Do you hear?"

"Yes, suh," replied the negro intelligently.

The plan worked without a hitch. Ellis talked steadily, about the hotel, the furnishings, all sorts of irrelevant subjects, to which Miss Pemberton paid little attention. She was angry with Delamere, and took no pains to conceal her feelings. The bell-boy entered room 256 just before they reached the door. Ellis had heard loud talking as they approached, and as they were passing there was a crash of broken glass, as though some object had been thrown at the door.

"What is the matter there?" exclaimed Clara, quickening her footsteps and instinctively drawing closer to Ellis.

"Some one dropped a glass, I presume," replied Ellis calmly.

Miss Pemberton glanced at him suspiciously. She was in a decidedly perverse mood. Seating herself at the piano, she played brilliantly for a quarter of an hour. Quite a number of couples strolled up to the parlor, but Delamere was not among them.

"Oh dear!' exclaimed Miss Pemberton, as she let her fingers fall upon the keys with a discordant crash, after the last note, "I don't see why we came out here to-night. Let 's go back downstairs."

Ellis felt despondent. He had done his utmost to serve and to please Miss Pemberton, but was not likely, he foresaw, to derive much benefit from his opportunity. Delamere was evidently as much or more in her thoughts by reason of his absence than if he had been present. If the door should have been opened, and she should see him from the hall upon their return, Ellis could not help it. He took the side next to the door, however, meaning to hurry past the room so that she might not recognize Delamere.

Fortunately the door was closed and all quiet within the room. On the stairway they met the bell-boy, rubbing his head with one hand and holding a bottle of seltzer upon a tray in the other. The boy was well enough trained to give no sign of recognition, though Ellis guessed the destination of the bottle.

Ellis hardly knew whether to feel pleased or disappointed at the success of his manœuvres. He had spared Miss Pemberton some mortification, but he had saved Tom Delamere from merited exposure. Clara ought to know the truth, for her own sake.

On the beach, a few rods away, fires were burning, around which several merry groups had gathered. The smoke went mostly to one side, but a slight whiff came now and then to where Mrs. Carteret sat awaiting them.

"They 're roasting oysters," said Mrs. Carteret. "I wish you 'd bring me some, Mr. Ellis."

Ellis strolled down to the beach. A large iron plate, with a turned-up rim like a great baking-pan, supported by legs which held it off the ground, was set over a fire built upon the sand. This primitive oven was heaped with small oysters in the shell, taken from the neighboring sound, and hauled up to the hotel by a negro whose pony cart stood near by. A wet coffee-sack of burlaps was spread over the oysters, which, when steamed sufficiently, were opened by a colored man and served gratis to all who cared for them.

Ellis secured a couple of plates of oysters, which he brought to Mrs. Carteret and Clara; they were small, but finely flavored.

Meanwhile Delamere, who possessed a remarkable faculty of recuperation from the effects of drink, had waked from his sleep, and remembering his engagement, had exerted himself to overcome the ravages of the afternoon's debauch. A dash of cold water braced him up somewhat. A bottle of seltzer and a big cup of strong coffee still further strengthened his nerves.

When Ellis returned to the veranda, after having taken away the plates, Delamere had joined the ladies and was explaining the cause of his absence.

He had been overcome by the heat, he said, while out fishing, and had been lying down ever since. Perhaps he ought to have sent for a doctor, but the fellows had looked after him. He had n't sent word to his friends because he had n't wished to spoil their evening.

"That was very considerate of you, Tom," said Mrs. Carteret dryly, "but you ought to have let us know. We have been worrying about you very much. Clara has found the evening dreadfully dull."

"Indeed, no, sister Olivia," said the young lady cheerfully, "I 've been having a lovely time. Mr. Ellis and I have been up in the parlor; I played the piano; and we 've been eating oysters and having a most delightful time. Won't you take me down there to the beach, Mr. Ellis? I want to see the fires. Come on."

"Can't I go?" asked Tom jealously.

"No, indeed, you must n't stir a foot! You must not overtax yourself so soon; it might do you serious injury. Stay here with sister Olivia."

She took Ellis's arm with exaggerated cordiality. Delamere glared after them angrily. Ellis did not stop to question her motives, but took the goods the gods provided. With no very great apparent effort, Miss Pemberton became quite friendly, and they strolled along the beach, in sight of the hotel, for nearly half an hour. As they were coming up she asked him abruptly, —

"Mr. Ellis, did you know Tom was in the hotel?"

Ellis was looking across the sound, at the lights of a distant steamer which was making her way toward the harbor.

"I wonder," he said musingly, as though he had not heard her question, "if that is the Ocean Belle?"

"And was he really sick?" she demanded.

"She's later than usual this trip," continued Ellis, pursuing his thought. "She was due about five o'clock."

Miss Pemberton, under cover of the darkness, smiled a fine smile, which foreboded ill for some one. When they joined the party on the piazza, the major had come up and was saying that it was time to go. He had been engaged in conversation, for most of the evening, with General Belmont and several other gentlemen.

"Here comes the general now. Let me see. There are five of us. The general has offered me a seat in his buggy, and Tom can go with you-all."

The general came up and spoke to the ladies. Tom murmured his thanks; it would enable him to make up a part of the delightful evening he had missed.

When Mrs. Carteret had taken the rear seat, Clara promptly took the place beside her. Ellis and Delamere sat in front. When Delamere, who had offered to drive, took the reins, Ellis saw that his hands were shaking.

"Give me the lines," he whispered. "Your nerves are unsteady and the road is not well lighted."

Delamere prudently yielded the reins. He did not like Ellis's tone, which seemed sneering rather than expressive of sympathy with one who had been suffering. He wondered if the beggar knew anything about his illness. Clara had been acting strangely. It would have been just like Ellis to have slandered him. The upstart had no business with Clara anyway. He would cheerfully have strangled Ellis, if he could have done so with safety to himself and no chance of discovery.

The drive homeward through the night was almost a silent journey. Mrs. Carteret was anxious about her baby. Clara did not speak, except now and then to Ellis with reference to some object in or near the road. Occasionally they passed a vehicle in the darkness, sometimes barely avoiding a collision. Far to the north the sky was lit up with the glow of a forest fire. The breeze from the Sound was deliciously cool. Soon the last toll-gate was passed and the lights of the town appeared.

Ellis threw the lines to William, who was waiting, and hastened to help the ladies out.

"Good-night, Mr. Ellis," said Clara sweetly, as she gave Ellis her hand. "Thank you for a very pleasant evening. Come up and see us soon."

She ran into the house without a word to Tom.

XVII. THE SOCIAL ASPIRATIONS OF CAPTAIN McBANE

It was only eleven o'clock, and Delamere, not being at all sleepy, and feeling somewhat out of sorts as the combined results of his afternoon's debauch and the snubbing he had received at Clara's hands, directed the major's coachman, who had taken charge of the trap upon its arrival, to drive him to the St. James Hotel before returning the horses to the stable. First, however, the coachman left Ellis at his boarding-house, which was near by. The two young men parted with as scant courtesy as was possible without an open rupture.

Delamere hoped to find at the hotel some form of distraction to fill in an hour or two before going home. Ill fortune favored him by placing in his way the burly form of Captain George McBane, who was sitting in an armchair alone, smoking a midnight cigar, under the hotel balcony. Upon Delamere's making known his desire for amusement, the captain proposed a small game of poker in his own room.

McBane had been waiting for some such convenient opportunity. We have already seen that the captain was desirous of social recognition, which he had not yet obtained beyond the superficial acquaintance acquired by association with men about town. He had determined to assault society in its citadel by seeking membership in the Clarendon Club, of which most gentlemen of the best families of the city were members.

The Clarendon Club was a historic institution, and its membership a social cult, the temple of which was located just off the main street of the city, in a dignified old colonial mansion which had housed it for the nearly one hundred years during which it had maintained its existence unbroken. There had grown up around it many traditions and special usages. Membership in the Clarendon was the *sine qua non* of high social standing, and was conditional upon two of three things, — birth, wealth, and breeding. Breeding was the prime essential, but, with rare exceptions, must be backed by either birth or money.

Having decided, therefore, to seek admission into this social arcanum, the captain, who had either not quite appreciated the standard of the Clarendon's membership, or had failed to see that he fell beneath it, looked about for an intermediary through whom to approach the object of his desire. He had already thought of Tom Delamere in this connection, having with him such an acquaintance as one forms around a hotel, and having long ago discovered that Delamere was a young man of superficially amiable disposition, vicious instincts, lax principles, and a weak will, and, which was quite as much to the purpose, a member of the Clarendon Club. Possessing mental characteristics almost entirely opposite, Delamere and the captain had certain tastes in common, and had smoked, drunk, and played cards together more than once.

Still more to his purpose, McBane had detected Delamere trying to cheat him at cards. He had said nothing about this discovery, but had merely noted it as something which at some future time might prove useful. The captain had not suffered by Delamere's deviation from the straight line of honor, for while Tom was as clever with the cards as might be expected of a young man who had devoted most of his leisure for several years to handling them, McBane was past master in their manipulation. During a stormy career he had touched more or less pitch, and had escaped few sorts of defilement.

The appearance of Delamere at a late hour, unaccompanied, and wearing upon his countenance an expression in which the captain read aright the craving for mental and physical excitement, gave him the opportunity for which he had been looking. McBane was not the man to lose an opportunity, nor did Delamere require a second invitation. Neither was it necessary, during the progress of the game, for the captain to press upon his guest the contents of the decanter which stood upon the table within convenient reach.

The captain permitted Delamere to win from him several small amounts, after which he gradually increased the stakes and turned the tables.

Delamere, with every instinct of a gamester, was no more a match for McBane in self-control than in skill. When the young man had lost all his money, the captain expressed his entire willingness to accept notes of hand, for which he happened to have convenient blanks in his apartment.

When Delamere, flushed with excitement and wine, rose from the gaming table at two o'clock, he was vaguely conscious that he owed McBane a considerable sum, but could not have stated how much. His opponent, who was entirely cool and collected, ran his eye carelessly over the bits of paper to which Delamere had attached his signature.

"Just one thousand dollars even," he remarked.

The announcement of this total had as sobering an effect upon Delamere as though he had been suddenly deluged with a shower of cold water. For a moment he caught his breath. He had not a dollar in the world with which to pay this sum. His only source of income was an allowance from his grandfather, the monthly installment of which, drawn that very day, he had just lost to McBane, before starting in upon the notes of hand.

"I 'll give you your revenge another time," said McBane, as they rose. "Luck is against you to-night, and I 'm unwilling to take advantage of a clever young fellow like you. Meantime," he added, tossing the notes of hand carelessly on a bureau, "don't worry about these bits of paper. Such small matters should n't cut any figure between friends; but if you are around the hotel to-morrow, I should like to speak to you upon another subject."

"Very well, captain," returned Tom somewhat ungraciously.

Delamere had been completely beaten with his own weapons. He had tried desperately to cheat McBane. He knew perfectly well that McBane had discovered his efforts and had cheated him in turn, for the captain's play had clearly been gauged to meet his own. The biter had been bit, and could not complain of the outcome.

The following afternoon McBane met Delamere at the hotel, and bluntly requested the latter to propose him for membership in the Clarendon Club.

Delamere was annoyed at this request. His aristocratic gorge rose at the presumption of this son of an overseer and ex-driver of convicts. McBane was good enough to win money from, or even to lose money to, but not good enough to be recognized as a social equal. He would instinctively have blackballed McBane had he been proposed by some one else; with what grace could he put himself forward as the sponsor for this impossible social aspirant? Moreover, it was clearly a vulgar, cold-blooded attempt on McBane's part to use his power over him for a personal advantage.

"Well, now, Captain McBane," returned Delamere diplomatically, "I 've never put any one up yet, and it 's not regarded as good form for so young a member as myself to propose candidates. I 'd much rather you 'd ask some older man."

"Oh, well," replied McBane, "just as you say, only I thought you had cut your eye teeth."

Delamere was not pleased with McBane's tone. His remark was not acquiescent, though couched in terms of assent. There was a sneering savagery about it, too, that left Delamere uneasy. He was, in a measure, in McBane's power. He could not pay the thousand dollars, unless it fell from heaven, or he could win it from some one else. He would not dare go to his grandfather for help. Mr. Delamere did not even know that his grandson gambled. He might not have objected, perhaps, to a gentleman's game, with moderate stakes, but he would certainly, Tom knew very well, have looked upon a thousand dollars as a preposterous sum to be lost at cards by a man who had nothing with which to pay it. It was part of Mr. Delamere's creed that a gentleman should not make debts that he was not reasonably able to pay.

There was still another difficulty. If he had lost the money to a gentleman, and it had been his first serious departure from Mr. Delamere's perfectly well understood standard of honor, Tom might have risked a confession and thrown himself on his grandfather's mercy; but he owed other sums here and there, which, to his just now much disturbed imagination, loomed up in alarming number and amount. He had recently observed signs of coldness, too, on the part of certain members of the club. Moreover, like most men with one commanding vice, he was addicted to several subsidiary forms of iniquity, which in case of a scandal were more than likely to come to light. He was clearly and most disagreeably caught in the net of his own hypocrisy. His grandfather believed him a model of integrity, a pattern of honor; he could not afford to have his grandfather undeceived.

He thought of old Mrs. Ochiltree. If she were a liberal soul, she could give him a thousand dollars now, when he needed it, instead of making him wait until she died, which might not be for ten years or more, for a legacy which was steadily growing less and might be entirely exhausted if she lived long enough, — some old people were very tenacious of life! She was a careless old woman, too, he reflected, and very foolishly kept her money in the house. Latterly she had been growing weak and childish. Some day she might be robbed, and then his prospective inheritance from that source would vanish into thin air!

With regard to this debt to McBane, if he could not pay it, he could at least gain a long respite by proposing the captain at the club. True, he would undoubtedly be blackballed, but before this inevitable event his name must remain posted for several weeks, during which interval McBane would be conciliatory. On the other hand, to propose McBane would arouse suspicion of his own motives; it might reach his grandfather's ears, and lead to a demand for an explanation, which it would be difficult to make. Clearly, the better plan would be to temporize with McBane, with the hope that something might intervene to remove this cursed obligation.

"Suppose, captain," he said affably, "we leave the matter open for a few days. This is a thing that can't be rushed. I 'll feel the pulse of my friends and yours, and when we get the lay of the land, the affair can be accomplished much more easily."

"Well, that 's better," returned McBane, somewhat mollified, — "*if* you 'll do that."

"To be sure I will," replied Tom easily, too much relieved to resent, if not too preoccupied to perceive, the implied doubt of his veracity.

McBane ordered and paid for more drinks, and they parted on amicable terms.

"We 'll let these notes stand for the time being, Tom," said McBane, with significant emphasis, when they separated.

Delamere winced at the familiarity. He had reached that degree of moral deterioration where, while principles were of little moment, the externals of social intercourse possessed an exaggerated importance. McBane had never before been so personal. He had addressed the young aristocrat first as "Mr. Delamere," then, as their acquaintance advanced, as "Delamere." He had now reached the abbreviated Christian name stage of familiarity. There was no lower depth to which Tom could sink, unless McBane should invent a nickname by which to address him.

He did not like McBane's manner, — it was characterized by a veiled insolence which was exceedingly offensive. He would go over to the club and try his luck with some honest player, — perhaps something might turn up to relieve him from his embarrassment.

He put his hand in his pocket mechanically, — and found it empty! In the present state of his credit, he could hardly play without money.

A thought struck him. Leaving the hotel, he hastened home, where he found Sandy dusting his famous suit of clothes on the back piazza. Mr. Delamere was not at home, having departed for Belleview about two o'clock, leaving Sandy to follow him in the morning.

"Hello, Sandy," exclaimed Tom, with an assumed jocularity which he was very far from feeling, "what are you doing with those gorgeous garments?"

"I 'm a-dustin' of 'em, Mistuh Tom, dat 's w'at I 'm a-doin'. Dere 's somethin' wrong 'bout dese clo's er mine — I don' never seem ter be able ter keep 'em clean no mo'. Ef I b'lieved in dem ole-timey sayin's, I 'd 'low dere wuz a witch come here eve'y night an' tuk 'em out an' wo' 'em, er tuk me out an' rid me in 'em. Dere wuz somethin' wrong 'bout dat cakewalk business, too, dat I ain' never unde'stood an' don' know how ter 'count fer, 'less dere wuz some kin' er dev'lishness goin' on dat don' show on de su'face."

"Sandy," asked Tom irrelevantly, "have you any money in the house?"

"Yas, suh, I got de money Mars John give me ter git dem things ter take out ter Belleview in de mawnin'."

"I mean money of your own."

"I got a qua'ter ter buy terbacker wid," returned Sandy cautiously.

"Is that all? Have n't you some saved up?"

"Well, yas, Mistuh Tom," returned Sandy, with evident reluctance, "dere 's a few dollahs put away in my bureau drawer fer a rainy day, — not much, suh."

"I 'm a little short this afternoon, Sandy, and need some money right away. Grandfather is n't here, so I can't get any from him. Let me take what you have for a day or two, Sandy, and I 'll return it with good interest."

"Now, Mistuh Tom," said Sandy seriously, "I don' min' lettin' you take my money, but I hopes you ain' gwine ter use it fer none er dem rakehelly gwines-on er yo'n, — gamblin' an' bettin' an' so fo'th. Yo' grandaddy 'll fin out 'bout you yit, ef you don' min' yo' P's an' Q's. I does my bes' ter keep yo' misdoin's f'm 'im, an' sense I b'en tu'ned out er de chu'ch — thoo no fault er my own, God knows! — I 've tol' lies 'nuff 'bout you ter sink a ship. But it ain't right, Mistuh Tom, it ain't right! an' I only does it fer de sake er de fam'ly honuh, dat Mars John sets so much sto' by, an' ter save his feelin's; fer de doctuh says he mus' n' git ixcited 'bout nothin', er it mought bring on another stroke."

"That 's right, Sandy," replied Tom approvingly; "but the family honor is as safe in my hands as in grandfather's own, and I 'm going to use the money for an excellent purpose, in fact to relieve a case of genuine distress; and I 'll hand it back to you in a day or two, — perhaps to-morrow. Fetch me the money, Sandy, — that 's a good darky!"

"All right, Mistuh Tom, you shill have de money; but I wants ter tell you, suh, dat in all de yeahs I has wo'ked fer yo' gran'daddy, he has never called me, a 'darky' ter my face, suh. Co'se I knows dere 's w'ite folks an' black folks, — but dere 's manners, suh, dere 's manners, an' gent'emen oughter be de ones ter use 'em, suh, ef dey ain't ter be fergot enti'ely!"

"There, there, Sandy," returned Tom in a conciliatory tone, "I beg your pardon! I 've been associating with some Northern white folks at the hotel, and picked up the word from them. You 're a high-toned colored gentleman, Sandy, — the finest one on the footstool."

Still muttering to himself, Sandy retired to his own room, which was in the house, so that he might be always near his master. He soon returned with a time-stained leather pocket-book and a coarse-knit cotton sock, from which two receptacles he painfully extracted a number of bills and coins.

"You count dat, Mistuh Tom, so I 'll know how much I 'm lettin' you have."

"This is n't worth anything," said Tom, pushing aside one roll of bills. "It 's Confederate money."

"So it is, suh. It ain't wuth nothin' now; but it has be'n money, an' who kin tell but what it mought be money agin? De rest er dem bills is greenbacks, — dey 'll pass all right, I reckon."

The good money amounted to about fifty dollars, which Delamere thrust eagerly into his pocket.

"You won't say anything to grandfather about this, will you, Sandy," he said, as he turned away.

"No, suh, co'se I won't! Does I ever tell 'im 'bout yo' gwines-on? Ef I did," he added to himself, as the young man disappeared down the street, "I would n' have time ter do nothin' e'se ha'dly. I don' know whether I 'll ever see dat money agin er no, do' I 'magine de ole gent'e-man would n' lemme lose it ef he knowed. But I ain' gwine ter tell him, whether I git my money back er no, fer he is jes' so wrop' up in dat boy dat I b'lieve it 'd jes' break his hea't ter fin' out how he 's be'n gwine on. Doctuh Price has tol' me not ter let de ole gent'eman git ixcited, er e'se dere 's no tellin' w'at mought happen. He 's be'n good ter me, he

has, an' I 'm gwine ter take keer er him, — dat 's w'at I is, ez long ez I
has de chance."

Delamere went directly to the club, and soon lounged into the card-
room, where several of the members were engaged in play. He saun-
tered here and there, too much absorbed in his own thoughts to notice
that the greetings he received were less cordial than those usually
exchanged between the members of a small and select social club.
Finally, when Augustus, commonly and more appropriately called
"Gus," Davidson came into the room, Tom stepped toward him.

"Will you take a hand in a game, Gus?"

"Don't care if I do," said the other. "Let 's sit over here."

Davidson led the way to a table near the fireplace, near which stood
a tall screen, which at times occupied various places in the room.
Davidson took the seat opposite the fireplace, leaving Delamere with
his back to the screen.

Delamere staked half of Sandy's money, and lost. He staked the
rest, and determined to win, because he could not afford to lose. He
had just reached out his hand to gather in the stakes, when he was
charged with cheating at cards, of which two members, who had quietly entered the room and posted themselves behind the screen, had
secured specific proof.

A meeting of the membership committee was hastily summoned, it
being an hour at which most of them might be found at the club. To
avoid a scandal, and to save the feelings of a prominent family,
Delamere was given an opportunity to resign quietly from the club, on
condition that he paid all his gambling debts within three days, and
took an oath never to play cards again for money. This latter condition
was made at the suggestion of an elderly member, who apparently
believed that a man who would cheat at cards would stick at perjury.

Delamere acquiesced very promptly. The taking of the oath was
easy. The payment of some fifteen hundred dollars of debts was a different matter. He went away from the club thoughtfully, and it may be
said, in full justice to a past which was far from immaculate, that in his
present thoughts he touched a depth of scoundrelism far beyond anything of which he had as yet deemed himself capable. When a man of
good position, of whom much is expected, takes to evil courses, his
progress is apt to resemble that of a well-bred woman who has started
on the downward path, — the pace is all the swifter because of the distance which must be traversed to reach the bottom. Delamere had

made rapid headway; having hitherto played with sin, his servant had now become his master, and held him in an iron grip.

XVIII. SANDY SEES HIS OWN HA'NT[1]

HAVING finished cleaning his clothes, Sandy went out to the kitchen for supper, after which he found himself with nothing to do. Mr. Delamere's absence relieved him from attendance at the house during the evening. He might have smoked his pipe tranquilly in the kitchen until bedtime, had not the cook intimated, rather pointedly, that she expected other company. To a man of Sandy's tact a word was sufficient, and he resigned himself to seeking companionship elsewhere.

Under normal circumstances, Sandy would have attended prayer-meeting on this particular evening of the week; but being still in contumacy, and cherishing what he considered the just resentment of a man falsely accused, he stifled the inclination which by long habit led him toward the church, and set out for the house of a friend with whom it occurred to him that he might spend the evening pleasantly. Unfortunately, his friend proved to be not at home, so Sandy turned his footsteps toward the lower part of the town, where the streets were well lighted, and on pleasant evenings quite animated. On the way he met Josh Green, whom he had known for many years, though their paths did not often cross. In his loneliness Sandy accepted an invitation to go with Josh and have a drink, — a single drink.

When Sandy was going home about eleven o'clock, three sheets in the wind, such was the potent effect of the single drink and those which had followed it, he was scared almost into soberness by a remarkable apparition. As it seemed to Sandy, he saw himself hurrying along in front of himself toward the house. Possibly the muddled condition of Sandy's intellect had so affected his judgment as to vitiate any conclusion he might draw, but Sandy was quite sober enough to perceive that the figure ahead of him wore his best clothes and looked exactly like him, but seemed to be in something more of a hurry, a discrepancy which Sandy at once corrected by quickening his own pace so as to maintain as nearly as possible an equal distance between himself and his double. The situation was certainly an incomprehensible one, and savored of the supernatural.

[1] *ha'nt:* A dialect word for "haunt," meaning a spirit or ghost.

"Ef dat 's me gwine 'long in front," mused Sandy, in vinous perplex-ity, "den who is dis behin' here? Dere ain' but one er me, an' my ha'nt would n' leave my body 'tel I wuz dead. Ef dat 's me in front, den I mus' be my own ha'nt; an' whichever one of us is de ha'nt, de yuther must be dead an' don' know it. I don' know what ter make er no sech gwines-on, I don't. Maybe it ain' me after all, but it certainly do look lack me."

When the apparition disappeared in the house by the side door, Sandy stood in the yard for several minutes, under the shade of an elm-tree, before he could make up his mind to enter the house. He took courage, however, upon the reflection that perhaps, after all, it was only the bad liquor he had drunk. Bad liquor often made people see double.

He entered the house. It was dark, except for a light in Tom Delamere's room. Sandy tapped softly at the door.

"Who 's there?" came Delamere's voice, in a somewhat startled tone, after a momentary silence.

"It 's me, suh; Sandy."

They both spoke softly. It was the rule of the house when Mr. Delamere had retired, and though he was not at home, habit held its wonted sway.

"Just a moment, Sandy."

Sandy waited patiently in the hall until the door was opened. If the room showed any signs of haste or disorder, Sandy was too full of his own thoughts — and other things — to notice them.

"What do you want, Sandy," asked Tom.

"Mistuh Tom," asked Sandy solemnly, "ef I wuz in yo' place, an' you wuz in my place, an' we wuz bofe in de same place, whar would I be?"

Tom looked at Sandy keenly, with a touch of apprehension. Did Sandy mean anything in particular by this enigmatical inquiry, and if so, what? But Sandy's face clearly indicated a state of mind in which consecutive thought was improbable; and after a brief glance Delamere breathed more freely.

"I give it up, Sandy," he responded lightly. "That 's too deep for me."

" 'Scuse me, Mistuh Tom, but is you heared er seed anybody er any-thing come in de house fer de las' ten minutes?"

"Why, no, Sandy, I have n't heard any one. I came from the club an hour ago. I had forgotten my key, and Sally got up and let me in, and then went back to bed. I 've been sitting here reading ever since. I should have heard any one who came in."

"Mistuh Tom," inquired Sandy anxiously, "would you 'low dat I 'd be'n drinkin' too much?"

"No, Sandy, I should say you were sober enough, though of course you may have had a few drinks. Perhaps you 'd like another? I 've got something good here."

"No, suh, Mistuh Tom, no, suh! No mo' liquor fer me, suh, never! When liquor kin make a man see his own ha'nt, it 's 'bout time fer dat man ter quit drinkin', it sho' is! Good-night, Mistuh Tom."

As Sandy turned to go, Delamere was struck by a sudden and daring thought. The creature of impulse, he acted upon it immediately.

"By the way, Sandy," he exclaimed carelessly, "I can pay you back that money you were good enough to lend me this afternoon. I think I 'll sleep better if I have the debt off my mind, and I should n't wonder if you would. You don't mind having it in gold, do you?"

"No, indeed, suh," replied Sandy. "I ain' seen no gol' fer so long dat de sight er it 'd be good fer my eyes."

Tom counted out ten five-dollar gold pieces upon the table at his elbow.

"'And here 's another, Sandy," he said, adding an eleventh, "as interest for the use of it."

"Thank y', Mistuh Tom. I did n't spec' no intrus', but I don' never 'fuse gol' w'en I kin git it."

"And here," added Delamere, reaching carelessly into a bureau drawer, "is a little old silk purse that I 've had since I was a boy. I 'll put the gold in it, Sandy; it will hold it very nicely."

"Thank y', Mistuh Tom. You 're a gentleman, suh, an' wo'thy er de fam'ly name. Good-night, suh, an' I hope yo' dreams 'll be pleasanter 'n' mine. Ef it wa'n't fer dis gol' kinder takin' my min' off'n dat ha'nt, I don' s'pose I 'd be able to do much sleepin' ter-night. Good-night, suh."

"Good-night, Sandy."

Whether or not Delamere slept soundly, or was troubled by dreams, pleasant or unpleasant, it is nevertheless true that he locked his door, and sat up an hour later, looking through the drawers of his bureau, and burning several articles in the little iron stove which constituted part of the bedroom furniture.

It is also true that he rose very early, before the household was stirring. The cook slept in a room off the kitchen, which was in an outhouse in the back yard. She was just stretching herself, preparatory to getting up, when Tom came to her window and said that he was going off fishing, to be gone all day, and that he would not wait for breakfast.

XIX. A MIDNIGHT WALK

ELLIS left the office of the Morning Chronicle about eleven o'clock the same evening and set out to walk home. His boarding-house was only a short distance beyond old Mr. Delamere's residence, and while he might have saved time and labor by a slightly shorter route, he generally selected this one because it led also by Major Carteret's house. Sometimes there would be a ray of light from Clara's room, which was on one of the front corners; and at any rate he would have the pleasure of gazing at the outside of the casket that enshrined the jewel of his heart. It was true that this purely sentimental pleasure was sometimes dashed with bitterness at the thought of his rival; but one in love must take the bitter with the sweet, and who would say that a spice of jealousy does not add a certain zest to love? On this particular evening, however, he was in a hopeful mood. At the Clarendon Club, where he had gone, a couple of hours before, to verify a certain news item for the morning paper, he had heard a story about Tom Delamere which, he imagined, would spike that gentleman's guns for all time, so far as Miss Pemberton was concerned. So grave an affair as cheating at cards could never be kept secret, — it was certain to reach her ears; and Ellis was morally certain that Clara would never marry a man who had been proved dishonorable. In all probability there would be no great sensation about the matter. Delamere was too well connected; too many prominent people would be involved, — even Clara, and the editor himself, of whom Delamere was a distant cousin. The reputation of the club was also to be considered. Ellis was not the man to feel a malicious delight in the misfortunes of another, nor was he a pessimist who welcomed scandal and disgrace with open arms, as confirming a gloomy theory of human life. But, with the best intentions in the world, it was no more than human nature that he should feel a certain elation in the thought that his rival had been practically disposed of, and the field left clear; especially since this good situation had been brought about merely by the unmasking of a hypocrite, who had held him at an unfair disadvantage in the race for Clara's favor.

The night was quiet, except for the faint sound of distant music now and then, or the mellow laughter of some group of revelers. Ellis met but few pedestrians, but as he neared old Mr. Delamere's, he saw two men walking in the same direction as his own, on the opposite side of the street. He had observed that they kept at about an equal distance apart, and that the second, from the stealthy manner in which he was making his way, was anxious to keep the first in sight, without disclosing his own presence. This aroused Ellis's curiosity, which was satisfied in some degree when the man in advance stopped beneath a lamp-post and stood for a moment looking across the street, with his face plainly visible in the yellow circle of light. It was a dark face, and Ellis recognized it instantly as that of old Mr. Delamere's body servant, whose personal appearance had been very vividly impressed upon Ellis at the christening dinner at Major Carteret's. He had seen Sandy once since, too, at the hotel cakewalk. The negro had a small bundle in his hand, the nature of which Ellis could not make out.

When Sandy had stopped beneath the lamp-post, the man who was following him had dodged behind a tree-trunk. When Sandy moved on, Ellis, who had stopped in turn, saw the man in hiding come out and follow Sandy. When this second man came in range of the light, Ellis wondered that there should be two men so much alike. The first of the two had undoubtedly been Sandy. Ellis had recognized the peculiar, old-fashioned coat that Sandy had worn upon the two occasions when he had noticed him. Barring this difference, and the somewhat unsteady gait of the second man, the two were as much alike as twin brothers.

When they had entered Mr. Delamere's house, one after the other, — in the stillness of the night Ellis could perceive that each of them tried to make as little noise as possible, — Ellis supposed that they were probably relatives, both employed as servants, or that some younger negro, taking Sandy for a model, was trying to pattern himself after his superior. Why all this mystery, of course he could not imagine, unless the younger man had been out without permission and was trying to avoid the accusing eye of Sandy. Ellis was vaguely conscious that he had seen the other negro somewhere, but he could not for the moment place him, — there were so many negroes, nearly three negroes to one white man in the city of Wellington!

The subject, however, while curious, was not important as compared with the thoughts of his sweetheart which drove it from his mind. Clara had been kind to him the night before, — whatever her motive, she had been kind, and could not consistently return to her attitude of coldness. With Delamere hopelessly discredited, Ellis hoped to have at least fair play, — with fair play, he would take his chances of the outcome.

XX. A SHOCKING CRIME

On Friday morning, when old Mrs. Ochiltree's cook Dinah went to wake her mistress, she was confronted with a sight that well-nigh blanched her ebony cheek and caused her eyes almost to start from her head with horror. As soon as she could command her trembling limbs sufficiently to make them carry her, she rushed out of the house and down the street, bareheaded, covering in an incredibly short time the few blocks that separated Mrs. Ochiltree's residence from that of her niece.

She hastened around the house, and finding the back door open and the servants stirring, ran into the house and up the stairs with the familiarity of an old servant, not stopping until she reached the door of Mrs. Carteret's chamber, at which she knocked in great agitation.

Entering in response to Mrs. Carteret's invitation, she found the lady, dressed in a simple wrapper, superintending the morning toilet of little Dodie, who was a wakeful child, and insisted upon rising with the birds, for whose music he still showed a great fondness, in spite of his narrow escape while listening to the mockingbird.

"What is it, Dinah?" asked Mrs. Carteret, alarmed at the frightened face of her aunt's old servitor.

"O my Lawd, Mis' 'Livy, my Lawd, my Lawd! My legs is trim'lin' so dat I can't ha'dly hol' my han's stiddy 'nough ter say w'at I got ter say! O Lawd have mussy on us po' sinners! W'atever is gwine ter happen in dis worl' er sin an' sorrer!"

"What in the world is the matter, Dinah?" demanded Mrs. Carteret, whose own excitement had increased with the length of this preamble. "Has anything happened to Aunt Polly?"

"Somebody done broke in de house las' night, Mis' 'Livy, an' kill' Mis' Polly, an' lef' her layin' dead on de flo', in her own blood, wid her cedar chis' broke' open, an' eve'thing scattered roun' de flo'! O my Lawd, my Lawd, my Lawd, my Lawd!"

Mrs. Carteret was shocked beyond expression. Perhaps the spectacle of Dinah's unrestrained terror aided her to retain a greater measure of self-control than she might otherwise have been capable of. Giving the nurse some directions in regard to the child, she hastily descended the stairs, and seizing a hat and jacket from the rack in the hall, ran immediately with Dinah to the scene of the tragedy. Before the thought of this violent death all her aunt's faults faded into insignificance, and only her good qualities were remembered. She had reared Olivia; she had stood up for the memory of Olivia's mother when others had seemed to forget what was due to it. To her niece she had been a second mother, and had never been lacking in affection.

More than one motive, however, lent wings to Mrs. Carteret's feet. Her aunt's incomplete disclosures on the day of the drive past the hospital had been weighing upon Mrs. Carteret's mind, and she had intended to make another effort this very day, to get an answer to her question about the papers which the woman had claimed were in existence. Suppose her aunt had really found such papers, — papers which would seem to prove the preposterous claim made by her father's mulatto mistress? Suppose that, with the fatuity which generally leads human beings to keep compromising documents, her aunt had preserved these papers? If they should be found there in the house, there might be a scandal, if nothing worse, and this was to be avoided at all hazards.

Guided by some fortunate instinct, Dinah had as yet informed no one but Mrs. Carteret of her discovery. If they could reach the house before the murder became known to any third person, she might be the first to secure access to the remaining contents of the cedar chest, which would be likely to be held as evidence in case the officers of the law forestalled her own arrival.

They found the house wrapped in the silence of death. Mrs. Carteret entered the chamber of the dead woman. Upon the floor, where it had fallen, lay the body in a pool of blood, the strongly marked countenance scarcely more grim in the rigidity of death than it had been in life. A gaping wound in the head accounted easily for the death. The cedar chest stood open, its strong fastenings having been broken by a steel bar which still lay beside it. Near it were scattered pieces of old lace, antiquated jewelry, tarnished silverware, — the various mute souvenirs of the joys and sorrows of a long and active life.

Kneeling by the open chest, Mrs. Carteret glanced hurriedly through its contents. There were no papers there except a few old deeds and letters. She had risen with a sigh of relief, when she perceived the end of a paper projecting from beneath the edge of a rug which had been carelessly rumpled, probably by the burglar in his hasty search for plunder. This paper, or sealed envelope as it proved to be, which evidently contained some inclosure, she seized, and at the sound of approaching footsteps thrust hastily into her own bosom.

The sight of two agitated women rushing through the quiet streets at so early an hour in the morning had attracted attention and aroused curiosity, and the story of the murder, having once become known, spread with the customary rapidity of bad news. Very soon a policeman, and a little later a sheriff's officer, arrived at the house and took charge of the remains to await the arrival of the coroner.

By nine o'clock a coroner's jury had been summoned, who, after brief deliberation, returned a verdict of willful murder at the hands of some person or persons unknown, while engaged in the commission of a burglary.

No sooner was the verdict announced than the community, or at least the white third of it, resolved itself spontaneously into a committee of the whole to discover the perpetrator of this dastardly crime, which, at this stage of the affair, seemed merely one of robbery and murder.

Suspicion was at once directed toward the negroes, as it always is when an unexplained crime is committed in a Southern community. The suspicion was not entirely an illogical one. Having been, for generations, trained up to thriftlessness, theft, and immorality, against which only thirty years of very limited opportunity can be offset, during which brief period they have been denied in large measure the healthful social stimulus and sympathy which holds most men in the path of rectitude, colored people might reasonably be expected to commit at least a share of crime proportionate to their numbers. The population of the town was at least two thirds colored. The chances were, therefore, in the absence of evidence, at least two to one that a man of color had committed the crime. The Southern tendency to charge the negroes with all the crime and immorality of that region, unjust and exaggerated as the claim may be, was therefore not without a logical basis to the extent above indicated.

It must not be imagined that any logic was needed, or any reasoning consciously worked out. The mere suggestion that the crime had been committed by a negro was equivalent to proof against any negro that might be suspected and could not prove his innocence. A committee of white men was hastily formed. Acting independently of the police force, which was practically ignored as likely to favor the negroes, this committee set to work to discover the murderer.

The spontaneous activity of the whites was accompanied by a visible shrinkage of the colored population. This could not be taken as any indication of guilt, but was merely a recognition of the palpable fact that the American habit of lynching had so whetted the thirst for black blood that a negro suspected of crime had to face at least the possibility of a short shrift and a long rope, not to mention more gruesome horrors, without the intervention of judge or jury. Since to have a black face at such a time was to challenge suspicion, and since there was neither the martyr's glory nor the saint's renown in being killed for some one else's crime, and very little hope of successful resistance in case of an attempt at lynching, it was obviously the part of prudence for those thus marked to seek immunity in a temporary disappearance from public view.

XXI. THE NECESSITY OF AN EXAMPLE

ABOUT ten o'clock on the morning of the discovery of the murder, Captain McBane and General Belmont, as though moved by a common impulse, found themselves at the office of the Morning Chronicle. Carteret was expecting them, though there had been no appointment made. These three resourceful and energetic minds, representing no organized body, and clothed with no legal authority, had so completely arrogated to themselves the leadership of white public sentiment as to come together instinctively when an event happened which concerned the public, and, as this murder presumably did, involved the matter of race.

"Well, gentlemen," demanded McBane impatiently, "what are we going to do with the scoundrel when we catch him?"

"They 've got the murderer," announced the reporter, entering the room.

"Who is he?" they demanded in a breath.

"A nigger by the name of Sandy Campbell, a servant of old Mr. Delamere."

"How did they catch him?"

"Our Jerry saw him last night, going toward Mrs. Ochiltree's house, and a white man saw him coming away half an hour later."

"Has he confessed?"

"No, but he might as well. When the posse went to arrest him, they found him cleaning the clothes he had worn last night, and discovered in his room a part of the plunder. He denies it strenuously, but it seems a clear case."

"There can be no doubt," said Ellis, who had come into the room behind the reporter. "I saw the negro last night, at twelve o'clock, going into Mr. Delamere's yard, with a bundle in his hand."

"He is the last negro I should have suspected," said Carteret. "Mr. Delamere had implicit confidence in him."

"All niggers are alike," remarked McBane sententiously. "The only way to keep them from stealing is not to give them the chance. A nigger will steal a cent off a dead man's eye. He has assaulted and murdered a white woman, — an example should be made of him."

Carteret recalled very distinctly the presence of this negro at his own residence on the occasion of little Theodore's christening dinner. He remembered having questioned the prudence of letting a servant know that Mrs. Ochiltree kept money in the house. Mr. Delamere had insisted strenuously upon the honesty of this particular negro. The whole race, in the major's opinion, was morally undeveloped, and only held within the bounds by the restraining influence of the white people. Under Mr. Delamere's thumb this Sandy had been a model servant, — faithful, docile, respectful, and self-respecting; but Mr. Delamere had grown old, and had probably lost in a measure his moral influence over his servant. Left to his own degraded ancestral instincts, Sandy had begun to deteriorate, and a rapid decline had culminated in this robbery and murder, — and who knew what other horror? The criminal was a negro, the victim a white woman; — it was only reasonable to expect the worst.

"He 'll swing for it," observed the general.

Ellis went into another room, where his duty called him.

"He should burn for it," averred McBane. "I say, burn the nigger."

"This," said Carteret, "is something more than an ordinary crime, to be dealt with by the ordinary processes of law. It is a murderous and fatal assault upon a woman of our race, — upon our race in the person of its womanhood, its crown and flower. If such crimes are not punished with swift and terrible directness, the whole white womanhood of the South is in danger."

"Burn the nigger," repeated McBane automatically.

"Neither is this a mere sporadic crime," Carteret went on. "It is symptomatic; it is the logical and inevitable result of the conditions which have prevailed in this town for the past year. It is the last straw."

"Burn the nigger," reiterated McBane. "We seem to have the right nigger, but whether we have or not, burn *a* nigger. It is an assault upon the white race, in the person of old Mrs. Ochiltree, committed by the black race, in the person of some nigger. It would justify the white people in burning *any* nigger. The example would be all the more powerful if we got the wrong one. It would serve notice on the niggers that we shall hold the whole race responsible for the misdeeds of each individual."

"In ancient Rome," said the general, "when a master was killed by a slave, all his slaves were put to the sword."

"We could n't afford that before the war," said McBane, "but the niggers don't belong to anybody now, and there 's nothing to prevent our doing as we please with them. A dead nigger is no loss to any white man. I say, burn the nigger."

"I do not believe," said Carteret, who had gone to the window and was looking out, — "I do not believe that we need trouble ourselves personally about his punishment. I should judge, from the commotion in the street, that the public will take the matter into its own hands. I, for one, would prefer that any violence, however justifiable, should take place without my active intervention."

"It won't take place without mine, if I know it," exclaimed McBane, starting for the door.

"Hold on a minute, captain," exclaimed Carteret. "There's more at stake in this matter than the life of a black scoundrel. Wellington is in the hands of negroes and scalawags.[1] What better time to rescue it?"

"It's a trifle premature," replied the general. "I should have preferred to have this take place, if it was to happen, say three months hence, on the eve of the election, — but discussion always provokes thirst with me; I wonder if I could get Jerry to bring us some drinks?"

Carteret summoned the porter. Jerry's usual manner had taken on an element of self-importance, resulting in what one might describe as a sort of condescending obsequiousness. Though still a porter, he was also a hero, and wore his aureole.

"Jerry," said the general kindly, "the white people are very much pleased with the assistance you have given them in apprehending this scoundrel Campbell. You have rendered a great public service, Jerry, and we wish you to know that it is appreciated."

"Thank y', gin'l, thank y', suh! I alluz tries ter do my duty, suh, an' stan' by dem dat stan's by me. Dat low-down nigger oughter be lynch', suh, don't you think, er e'se bu'nt? Dere ain' nothin' too bad ter happen ter 'im."

"No doubt he will be punished as he deserves, Jerry," returned the general, "and we will see that you are suitably rewarded. Go across the street and get me three Calhoun cocktails. I seem to have nothing less than a two-dollar bill, but you may keep the change, Jerry, — all the change."

Jerry was very happy. He had distinguished himself in the public view, for to Jerry, as to the white people themselves, the white people were the public. He had won the goodwill of the best people, and had already begun to reap a tangible reward. It is true that several strange white men looked at him with lowering brows as he crossed the street, which was curiously empty of colored people; but he nevertheless went firmly forward, panoplied in the consciousness of his own rectitude, and serenely confident of the protection of the major and the major's friends.

"Jerry is about the only negro I have seen since nine o'clock," observed the general when the porter had gone. "If this were election day, where would the negro vote be?"

"In hiding, where most of the negro population is to-day," answered

---

[1] *scalawags:* A derogatory name for Southerners who sympathized with northern Republicans during Reconstruction.

McBane. "It's a pity, if old Mrs. Ochiltree had to go this way, that it could n't have been deferred a month or six weeks."

Carteret frowned at this remark, which, coming from McBane, seemed lacking in human feeling, as well as in respect to his wife's dead relative.

"But," resumed the general, "if this negro is lynched, as he well deserves to be, it will not be without its effect. We still have in reserve for the election a weapon which this affair will only render more effective. What became of the piece in the negro paper?"

"I have it here," answered Carteret. "I was just about to use it as the text for an editorial."

"Save it awhile longer," responded the general. "This crime itself will give you text enough for a four-volume work."

When this conference ended, Carteret immediately put into press an extra edition of the Morning Chronicle, which was soon upon the streets, giving details of the crime, which was characterized as an atrocious assault upon a defenseless old lady, whose age and sex would have protected her from harm at the hands of any one but a brute in the lowest human form. This event, the Chronicle suggested, had only confirmed the opinion, which had been of late growing upon the white people, that drastic efforts were necessary to protect the white women of the South against brutal, lascivious, and murderous assaults at the hands of negro men. It was only another significant example of the results which might have been foreseen from the application of a false and pernicious political theory, by which ignorance, clothed in a little brief authority, was sought to be exalted over knowledge, vice over virtue, an inferior and degraded race above the heaven-crowned Anglo-Saxon. If an outraged people, justly infuriated, and impatient of the slow processes of the courts, should assert their inherent sovereignty, which the law after all was merely intended to embody, and should choose, in obedience to the higher law, to set aside, temporarily, the ordinary judicial procedure, it would serve as a warning and an example to the vicious elements of the community, of the swift and terrible punishment which would fall, like the judgment of God, upon any one who laid sacrilegious hands upon white womanhood.

XXII. HOW NOT TO PREVENT A LYNCHING

DR. MILLER, who had sat up late the night before with a difficult case at the hospital, was roused, about eleven o'clock, from a deep and dreamless sleep. Struggling back into consciousness, he was informed by his wife, who stood by his bedside, that Mr. Watson, the colored lawyer, wished to see him upon a matter of great importance.

"Nothing but a matter of life and death would make me get up just now," he said with a portentous yawn.

"This *is* a matter of life and death," replied Janet. "Old Mrs. Polly Ochiltree was robbed and murdered last night, and Sandy Campbell has been arrested for the crime, — and they are going to lynch him!"

"Tell Watson to come right up," exclaimed Miller, springing out of bed. "We can talk while I'm dressing."

While Miller made a hasty toilet Watson explained the situation. Campbell had been arrested on the charge of murder. He had been seen, during the night, in the neighborhood of the scene of the crime, by two different persons, a negro and a white man, and had been identified later while entering Mr. Delamere's house, where he lived, and where damning proofs of his guilt had been discovered; the most important item of which was an old-fashioned knit silk purse, recognized as Mrs. Ochiltree's, and several gold pieces of early coinage, of which the murdered woman was known to have a number. Watson brought with him one of the first copies procurable of the extra edition of the Chronicle, which contained these facts and further information.

They were still talking when Mrs. Miller, knocking at the door, announced that big Josh Green wished to see the doctor about Sandy Campbell. Miller took his collar and necktie in his hand and went downstairs, where Josh sat waiting.

"Doctuh," said Green, "de w'ite folks is talkin' 'bout lynchin' Sandy Campbell fer killin' ole Mis' Ochiltree. He never done it, an' dey ought n' ter be 'lowed ter lynch 'im."

"They ought not to lynch him, even if he committed the crime," returned Miller, "but still less if he did n't. What do you know about it?"

"I know he was wid me, suh, las' night, at de time when dey say ole Mis' Ochiltree wuz killed. We wuz down ter Sam Taylor's place, havin' a little game of kyards an' a little liquor. Den we lef dere an' went up ez fur ez de corner er Main an' Vine Streets, where we pa'ted, an' Sandy went 'long to'ds home. Mo'over, dey say he had on check' britches an' a blue coat. When Sandy wuz wid me he had on gray clo's, an' when we sep'rated he wa'n't in no shape ter be changin' his clo's, let 'lone robbin' er killin' anybody."

"Your testimony ought to prove an alibi for him," declared Miller.

"Dere ain' gwine ter be no chance ter prove nothin', 'less'n we kin do it mighty quick! Dey say dey 're gwine ter lynch 'im ter-night, — some on 'em is talkin' 'bout burnin' 'im. My idee is ter hunt up de niggers an' git 'em ter stan' tergether an' gyard de jail."

"Why should n't we go to the principal white people of the town and tell them Josh's story, and appeal to them to stop this thing until Campbell can have a hearing?"

"It would n't do any good," said Watson despondently; "their blood is up. It seems that some colored man attacked Mrs. Ochiltree, — and he was a murderous villain, whoever he may be. To quote Josh would destroy the effect of his story, — we know he never harmed any one but himself" —

"An' a few keerliss people w'at got in my way," corrected Josh.

"He has been in court several times for fighting, — and that's against him. To have been at Sam Taylor's place is against Sandy, too, rather than in his favor. No, Josh, the white people would believe that you were trying to shield Sandy, and you would probably be arrested as an accomplice."

"But look a-here, Mr. Watson, — Dr. Miller, is we-all jes' got ter set down here, widout openin' ou' mouths, an' let dese w'ite folks hang er bu'n a man w'at we *know* ain't guilty? Dat ain't no law, ner jestice, ner nothin'! Ef you-all won't he'p, I 'll do somethin' myse'f! Dere 's two niggers ter one white man in dis town, an' I 'm sho' I kin fin' fifty of 'em w'at 'll fight, ef dey kin fin' anybody ter lead 'em."

"Now hold on, Josh," argued Miller; "what is to be gained by fighting? Suppose you got your crowd together and surrounded the jail, — what then?"

"There 'd be a clash," declared Watson, "and instead of one dead negro there 'd be fifty. The white people are claiming now that Campbell did n't stop with robbery and murder. A special edition of the Morning Chronicle, just out, suggests a further purpose, and has all the old shopworn cant about race purity and supremacy and imperative necessity, which always comes to the front whenever it is sought to justify some outrage on the colored folks. The blood of the whites is up I tell you!"

"Is there anything to that suggestion?" asked Miller incredulously.

"It does n't matter whether there is or not," returned Watson. "Merely to suggest it proves it. Nothing was said about this feature until the paper came out, — and even its statement is vague and indefinite, — but now the claim is in every mouth. I met only black looks as I came down the street. White men with whom I have long been on friendly terms passed me without a word. A negro has been arrested on suspicion, — the entire race is condemned on general principles."

"The whole thing is profoundly discouraging," said Miller sadly. "Try as we may to build up the race in the essentials of good citizenship and win the good opinion of the best people, some black scoundrel comes along, and by a single criminal act, committed in the twinkling of an eye, neutralizes the effect of a whole year's work."

"It 's mighty easy neut'alize', er whatever you call it," said Josh sullenly. "De w'ite folks don' want too good an opinion er de niggers, — ef dey had a good opinion of 'em, dey would n' have no excuse fer 'busin' an' hangin' an' burnin' 'em. But ef dey can't keep from doin' it, let 'em git de right man! Dis way er pickin' up de fus' nigger dey comes across, an' stringin' 'im up rega'dliss, ought ter be stop', an' stop' right now!"

"Yes that 's the worst of lynch law," said Watson; "but we are wasting valuable time, — it 's hardly worth while for us to discuss a subject we are all agreed upon. One of our race, accused of certain acts, is about to be put to death without judge or jury, ostensibly because he committed a crime, — really because he is a negro, for if he were white he would not be lynched. It is thus made a race issue, on the one side as well as on the other. What can we do to protect him?"

"We kin fight, ef we haf ter," replied Josh resolutely.

"Well, now, let us see. Suppose the colored people armed themselves? Messages would at once be sent to every town and county in the neighborhood. White men from all over the state, armed to the teeth, would at the slightest word pour into town on every railroad train, and extras would be run for their benefit."

"They 're already coming in," said Watson.

"We might go to the sheriff," suggested Miller, "and demand that he telegraph the governor to call out the militia."

"I spoke to the sheriff an hour ago," replied Watson. "He has a white face and a whiter liver. He does not dare call out the militia to protect a negro charged with such a brutal crime; — and if he did, the militia are white men, and who can say that their efforts would not be directed to keeping the negroes out of the way, in order that the white devils might do their worst? The whole machinery of the state is in the hands of white men, elected partly by our votes. When the color line is drawn, if they choose to stand together with the rest of their race against us, or to remain passive and let the others work their will, we are helpless, — our cause is hopeless."

"We might call on the general government," said Miller. "Surely the President would intervene."

"Such a demand would be of no avail," returned Watson. "The government can only intervene under certain conditions, of which it must be informed through designated channels. It never sees anything that is not officially called to its attention. The whole negro population of the South might be slaughtered before the necessary red tape could be spun out to inform the President that a state of anarchy prevailed. There 's no hope there."

"Den w'at we gwine ter do?" demanded Josh indignantly; "jes' set here an' let 'em hang Sandy, er bu'n 'im?"

"God knows!" exclaimed Miller. "The outlook is dark, but we should at least try to do something. There must be *some* white men in the town who would stand for law and order, — there 's no possible chance for Sandy to escape hanging by due process of law, if he is guilty. We might at least try half a dozen gentlemen."

"We 'd better leave Josh here," said Watson, "He 's too truculent. If we went on the street he 'd make trouble, and if he accompanied us he 'd do more harm than good. Wait for us here, Josh, until we 've seen what we can do. We 'll be back in half an hour."

In half an hour they had both returned.

"It 's no use," reported Watson gloomily. "I called at the mayor's office and found it locked. He is doubtless afraid on his own account, and would not dream of asserting his authority. I then looked up Judge Everton, who has always seemed to be fair. My reception was cold. He admitted that lynching was, as a rule, unjustifiable, but maintained that there were exceptions to all rules, — that laws were made, after all, to express the will of the people in regard to the ordinary administration of justice, but that in an emergency the sovereign people might assert itself and take the law into its own hands, — the creature was not greater than the creator. He laughed at my suggestion that Sandy was innocent. 'If he is innocent,' he said, 'then produce the real criminal. You negroes are standing in your own light when you try to protect such dastardly scoundrels as this Campbell, who is an enemy of society and not fit to live. I shall not move in the matter. If a negro wants the protection of the law, let him obey the law.' A wise judge, — a second Daniel come to judgment! If this were the law, there would be no need of judges or juries."

"I called on Dr. Price," said Miller, "my good friend Dr. Price, who would rather lie than hurt my feelings. 'Miller,' he declared, 'this is no affair of mine, or yours. I have too much respect for myself and my profession to interfere in such a matter, and you will accomplish nothing, and only lessen your own influence, by having anything to say.' 'But the man may be innocent,' I replied; 'there is every reason to believe that he is.' He shook his head pityingly. 'You are self-deceived, Miller; your prejudice has warped your judgment. The proof is overwhelming that he robbed this old lady, laid violent hands upon her, and left her dead. If he did no more, he has violated the written and unwritten law of the Southern States. I could not save him if I would, Miller, and frankly, I would not if I could. If he is innocent, his people can console themselves with the reflection that Mrs. Ochiltree was also innocent, and balance one crime against the other, the white against the black. Of course I shall take no part in whatever may be done, — but it is not my affair, nor yours. Take my advice, Miller, and keep out of it.'

"That is the situation," added Miller, summing up. "Their friend-ship for us, a slender stream at the best, dries up entirely when it strikes their prejudices. There is seemingly not one white man in Wellington who will speak a word for law, order, decency, or human-ity. Those who do not participate will stand idly by and see an untried man deliberately and brutally murdered. Race prejudice is the devil unchained."

"Well, den, suh," said Josh, "where does we stan' now? W'at is we gwine ter do? I would n' min' fightin', fer my time ain't come yit, — I feels dat in my bones. W'at we gwine ter do, dat 's w'at I wanter know."

"What does old Mr. Delamere have to say about the matter?" asked Miller suddenly. "Why have n't we thought of him before? Has he been seen?"

"No," replied Watson gloomily, "and for a good reason, — he is not in town. I came by the house just now, and learned that he went out to his country place yesterday afternoon, to remain a week. Sandy was to have followed him out there this morning, — it 's a pity he did n't go yesterday. The old gentleman has probably heard nothing about the matter."

"How about young Delamere?"

"He went away early this morning, down the river, to fish. He 'll probably not hear of it before night, and he 's only a boy anyway, and could very likely do nothing," said Watson.

Miller looked at his watch.

"Belleview is ten miles away," he said. "It is now eleven o'clock. I can drive out there in an hour and a half at the farthest. I 'll go and see Mr. Delamere, — he can do more than any living man, if he is able to do anything at all. There 's never been a lynching here, and one good white man, if he choose, may stem the flood long enough to give jus-tice a chance. Keep track of the white people while I 'm gone, Watson; and you, Josh, learn what the colored folks are saying, and do nothing rash until I return. In the meantime, do all that you can to find out who did commit this most atrocious murder."

XXIII. BELLEVIEW

MILLER did not reach his destination without interruption. At one point a considerable stretch of the road was under repair, which made it necessary for him to travel slowly. His horse cast a shoe, and threatened to go lame; but in the course of time he arrived at the entrance gate of Belleview, entering which he struck into a private road, bordered by massive oaks, whose multitudinous branches, hung with long streamers of trailing moss, formed for much of the way a thick canopy above his head. It took him only a few minutes to traverse the quarter of a mile that lay between the entrance gate and the house itself.

This old colonial plantation, rich in legendary lore and replete with historic distinction, had been in the Delamere family for nearly two hundred years. Along the bank of the river which skirted its domain the famous pirate Blackbeard had held high carnival, and was reputed to have buried much treasure, vague traditions of which still lingered among the negroes and poor-whites of the country roundabout. The beautiful residence, rising white and stately in a grove of ancient oaks, dated from 1750, and was built of brick which had been brought from England. Enlarged and improved from generation to generation, it stood, like a baronial castle, upon a slight eminence from which could be surveyed the large demesne[1] still belonging to the estate, which had shrunk greatly from its colonial dimensions. While still embracing several thousand acres, part forest and part cleared land, it had not of late years been profitable; in spite of which Mr. Delamere, with the conservatism of his age and caste, had never been able to make up his mind to part with any considerable portion of it. His grandson, he imagined, could make the estate pay and yet preserve it in its integrity. Here, in pleasant weather, surrounded by the scenes which he loved, old Mr. Delamere spent much of the time during his declining years.

Dr. Miller had once passed a day at Belleview, upon Mr. Delamere's invitation. For this old-fashioned gentleman, whose ideals not even slavery had been able to spoil, regarded himself as a trustee for the great public, which ought, in his opinion, to take as much pride as he in the contemplation of this historic landmark. In earlier years Mr.

---

[1] *demesne:* The land immediately adjacent to a mansion.

Delamere had been a practicing lawyer, and had numbered Miller's father among his clients. He had always been regarded as friendly to the colored people, and, until age and ill health had driven him from active life, had taken a lively interest in their advancement since the abolition of slavery. Upon the public opening of Miller's new hospital, he had made an effort to be present, and had made a little speech of approval and encouragement which had manifested his kindliness and given Miller much pleasure.

It was with the consciousness, therefore, that he was approaching a friend, as well as Sandy's master, that Miller's mind was chiefly occupied as his tired horse, scenting the end of his efforts, bore him with a final burst of speed along the last few rods of the journey; for the urgency of Miller's errand, involving as it did the issues of life and death, did not permit him to enjoy the charm of mossy oak or forest reaches, or even to appreciate the noble front of Belleview House when it at last loomed up before him.

"Well, William," said Mr. Delamere, as he gave his hand to Miller from the armchair in which he was seated under the broad and stately portico, "I did n't expect to see you out here. You 'll excuse my not rising, — I 'm none too firm on my legs. Did you see anything of my man Sandy back there on the road? He ought to have been here by nine o'clock, and it 's now one. Sandy is punctuality itself, and I don't know how to account for his delay."

Clearly there need be no time wasted in preliminaries. Mr. Delamere had gone directly to the subject at hand.

"He will not be here to-day, sir," replied Miller. "I have come to you on his account."

In a few words Miller stated the situation.

"Preposterous!" exclaimed the old gentlemen, with more vigor than Miller had supposed him to possess. "Sandy is absolutely incapable of such a crime as robbery, to say nothing of murder; and as for the rest, that is absurd upon the face of it! And so the poor old woman is dead! Well, well, well! she could not have lived much longer anyway; but Sandy did not kill her, — it 's simply impossible! Why, *I* raised that boy! He was born on my place. I 'd as soon believe such a thing of my own grandson as of Sandy! No negro raised by a Delamere would ever commit such a crime. I really believe, William, that Sandy has the family honor of the Delameres quite as much at heart as I have. Just tell them I say Sandy is innocent, and it will be all right."

"I 'm afraid, sir," rejoined Miller, who kept his voice up so that the old gentleman could understand without having it suggested that

Miller knew he was hard of hearing, "that you don't quite appreciate the situation. *I* believe Sandy innocent; *you* believe him innocent; but there are suspicious circumstances which do not explain themselves, and the white people of the city believe him guilty, and are going to lynch him before he has a chance to clear himself."

"Why does n't he explain the suspicious circumstances?" asked Mr. Delamere. "Sandy is truthful and can be believed. I would take Sandy's word as quickly as another man's oath."

"He has no chance to explain," said Miller. "The case is prejudged. A crime has been committed. Sandy is charged with it. He is black, and therefore he is guilty. No colored lawyer would be allowed in the jail, if one should dare to go there. No white lawyer will intervene. He 'll be lynched to-night, without judge, jury, or preacher, unless we can stave the thing off for a day or two."

"Have you seen my grandson?" asked the old gentleman. "Is he not looking after Sandy?"

"No, sir. It seems he went down the river this morning to fish, before the murder was discovered; no one knows just where he has gone, or at what hour he will return."

"Well, then," said Mr. Delamere, rising from his chair with surprising vigor, "I shall have to go myself. No faithful servant of mine shall be hanged for a crime he did n't commit, so long as I have a voice to speak or a dollar to spend. There 'll be no trouble after I get there, William. The people are naturally wrought up at such a crime. A fine old woman, — she had some detestable traits, and I was always afraid she wanted to marry me, but she was of an excellent family and had many good points, — an old woman of one of the best families, struck down by the hand of a murderer! You must remember, William, that blood is thicker than water, and that the provocation is extreme, and that a few hotheads might easily lose sight of the great principles involved and seek immediate vengeance, without too much discrimination. But they are good people, William, and when I have spoken, and they have an opportunity for the sober second thought, they will do nothing rashly, but will wait for the operation of the law, which will, of course, clear Sandy."

"I 'm sure I hope so," returned Miller. "Shall I try to drive you back, sir, or will you order your own carriage?"

"My horses are fresher, William, and I 'll have them brought around. You can take the reins, if you will, — I 'm rather old to drive, — and my man will come behind with your buggy."

In a few minutes they set out along the sandy road. Having two fresh horses, they made better headway than Miller had made coming out, and reached Wellington easily by three o'clock.

"I think, William," said Mr. Delamere, as they drove into the town, "that I had better talk with Sandy. He may be able to explain away the things that seem to connect him with this atrocious affair; and that will put me in a better position to talk to other people about it."

Miller drove directly to the county jail. Thirty or forty white men, who seemed to be casually gathered near the door, closed up when the carriage approached. The sheriff, who had seen them from the inside, came to the outer door and spoke to the visitor through a grated wicket.

"Mr. Wemyss," said Mr. Delamere, when he had made his way to the entrance with the aid of his cane, "I wish to see my servant, Sandy Campbell, who is said to be in your custody."

The sheriff hesitated. Meantime there was some parleying in low tones among the crowd outside. No one interfered, however, and in a moment the door opened sufficiently to give entrance to the old gentleman, after which it closed quickly and clangorously behind him.

Feeling no desire to linger in the locality, Miller, having seen his companion enter the jail, drove the carriage round to Mr. Delamere's house, and leaving it in charge of a servant with instructions to return for his master in a quarter of an hour, hastened to his own home to meet Watson and Josh and report the result of his efforts.

XXIV. TWO SOUTHERN GENTLEMEN

THE iron bolt rattled in the lock, the door of a cell swung open, and when Mr. Delamere had entered was quickly closed again.

"Well, Sandy!"

"Oh, Mars John! Is you fell from hebben ter he'p me out er here? I prayed de Lawd ter sen' you, an' He answered my prayer, an' here you is, Mars John, — here you is! Oh, Mars John, git me out er dis place!"

"Tut, tut, Sandy!" answered his master; "of course I'll get you out. That's what I've come for. How in the world did such a mistake ever happen? You would no more commit such a crime than I would!"

"No, suh, 'deed I would n', an' you know I would n'! I would n' want ter bring no disgrace on de fam'ly dat raise' me, ner ter make no trouble fer you, suh; but here I is, suh, lock' up in jail, an' folks talkin'

'bout hangin' me fer somethin' dat never entered my min', suh. I swea'
ter God I never thought er sech a thing!"

"Of course you did n't, Sandy," returned Mr. Delamere soothingly;
"and now the next thing, and the simplest thing, is to get you out of
this. I 'll speak to the officers, and at the preliminary hearing to-morrow
I 'll tell them all about you, and they will let you go. You won't mind
spending one night in jail for your sins."

"No, suh, ef I wuz sho' I 'd be 'lowed ter spen' it here. But dey say
dey 're gwine ter lynch me ter-night, — I kin hear 'em talkin' f'm de
winders er de cell, suh."

"Well, I say, Sandy, that they shall do no such thing! Lynch a man
brought up by a Delamere, for a crime of which he is innocent? Preposterous! I 'll speak to the authorities and see that you are properly
protected until this mystery is unraveled. If Tom had been here, he
would have had you out before now, Sandy. My grandson is a genuine
Delamere, is he not, Sandy?"

"Yas, suh, yas, suh," returned Sandy, with a lack of enthusiasm
which he tried to conceal from his master. "An' I s'pose ef he had n'
gone fishin' so soon dis mawnin', he 'd 'a' be'n lookin' after me, suh."

"It has been my love for him and your care of me, Sandy," said the
old gentleman tremulously, "that have kept me alive so long; but now
explain to me everything concerning this distressing matter, and I shall
then be able to state your case to better advantage."

"Well, suh," returned Sandy, "I mought 's well tell de whole tale an'
not hol' nothin' back. I wuz kind er lonesome las' night, an' sence I
be'n tu'ned outen de chu'ch on account er dat cakewalk I did n' go ter,
so he'p me God! I did n' feel like gwine ter prayer-meetin', so I went
roun' ter see Solomon Williams, an' he wa'n't home, an' den I walk'
down street an' met Josh Green, an' he ax' me inter Sam Taylor's place,
an' I sot roun' dere wid Josh till 'bout 'leven o'clock, w'en I sta'ted
back home. I went straight ter de house, suh, an' went ter bed an' ter
sleep widout sayin' a wo'd ter a single soul excep' Mistuh Tom, who
wuz settin' up readin' a book w'en I come in. I wish I may drap dead in
my tracks, suh, ef dat ain't de God's truf, suh, eve'y wo'd of it!"

"I believe every word of it, Sandy; now tell me about the clothes
that you are said to have been found cleaning, and the suspicious articles that were found in your room?"

"Dat 's w'at beats me, Mars John," replied Sandy, shaking his head
mournfully. "W'en I lef' home las' night after supper, my clo's wuz all
put erway in de closet in my room, folded up on de she'f ter keep de
moths out. Dey wuz my good clo's, — de blue coat dat you wo' ter de

weddin' fo'ty years ago, an' dem dere plaid pants I gun Mistuh Cohen fo' dollars fer three years ago; an' w'en I looked in my closet dis mawnin', suh, befo' I got ready ter sta't fer Belleview, dere wuz my clo's layin' on de flo', all muddy an' crumple' up, des lack somebody had wo' 'em in a fight! Somebody e'se had wo' my clo's, — er e'se dere 'd be'n some witchcraf', er some sort er devilment gwine on dat I can't make out, suh, ter save my soul!"

"There was no witchcraft, Sandy, but that there was some deviltry might well be. Now, what other negro, who might have been mistaken for you, could have taken your clothes? Surely no one about the house?"

"No, suh, no, suh. It could n't 'a' be'n Jeff, fer he wuz at Belleview wid you; an' it could n't 'a' be'n Billy, fer he wuz too little ter wear my clo's; an' it could n't 'a' be'n Sally, fer she 's a 'omen. It 's a myst'ry ter me, suh!"

"Have you no enemies? Is there any one in Wellington whom you imagine would like to do you an injury?"

"Not a livin' soul dat I knows of, suh. I 've be'n tu'ned out'n de chu'ch, but I don' know who my enemy is dere, er ef it wuz all a mistake, like dis yer jailin' is; but de Debbil is in dis somewhar, Mars John, — an' I got my reasons fer sayin' so."

"What do you mean, Sandy?"

Sandy related his experience of the proceeding evening; how he had seen the apparition preceding him to the house, and how he had questioned Tom upon the subject.

"There 's some mystery here, Sandy," said Mr. Delamere reflectively. "Have you told me all, now, upon your honor? I am trying to save your life, Sandy, and I must be able to trust your word implicitly. You must tell me every circumstance; a very little and seemingly unimportant bit of evidence may sometimes determine the issue of a great lawsuit. There is one thing especially, Sandy: where did you get the gold which was found in your trunk?"

Sandy's face lit up with hopefulness.

"Why, Mars John, I kin 'splain dat part easy. Dat wuz money I had lent out, an' I got back f'm — But no, suh, I promise' not ter tell."

"Circumstances absolve you from your promise, Sandy. Your life is of more value to you than any other thing. If you will explain where you got the gold, and the silk purse that contained it, which is said to be Mrs. Ochiltree's, you will be back home before night."

Old Mr. Delamere's faculties, which had been waning somewhat in sympathy with his health, were stirred to unusual acuteness by his servant's danger. He was watching Sandy with all the awakened instincts of the trial lawyer. He could see clearly enough that, in beginning to account for the possession of the gold, Sandy had started off with his explanation in all sincerity. At the mention of the silk purse, however, his face had blanched to an ashen gray, and the words had frozen upon his lips.

A less discerning observer might have taken these things as signs of guilt, but not so Mr. Delamere.

"Well, Sandy," said his master encouragingly, "go on. You got the gold from" —

Sandy remained silent. He had had a great shock, and had taken a great resolution.

"Mars John," he asked dreamily, "you don' b'lieve dat I done dis thing?"

"Certainly not, Sandy, else why should I be here?"

"An' nothin' would n' make you b'lieve it, suh?"

"No, Sandy, — I could not believe it of you. I 've known you too long and too well."

"An' you would n' b'lieve it, not even ef I would n' say one wo'd mo' about it?"

"No, Sandy, I believe you no more capable of this crime than I would be, — or my grandson, Tom. I wish Tom were here, that he might help me overcome your stubbornness; but you 'll not be so foolish, so absurdly foolish, Sandy, as to keep silent and risk your life merely to shield some one else, when by speaking you might clear up this mystery and be restored at once to liberty. Just tell me where you got the gold," added the old gentleman persuasively. "Come, now, Sandy, that 's a good fellow!"

"Mars John," asked Sandy softly, "w'en my daddy, 'way back yander befo' de wah, wuz about ter be sol' away f'm his wife an' child'en, you bought him an' dem, an' kep' us all on yo' place tergether, did n't you suh?"

"Yes, Sandy, and he was a faithful servant, and proved worthy of all I did for him."

"And w'en he had wo'ked fer you ten years, suh, you sot 'im free?"

"Yes, Sandy, he had earned his freedom."

"An' w'en de wah broke out, an' my folks wuz scattered, an' I did n' have nothin' ter do ner nowhar ter go, you kep' me on yo' place, and tuck me ter wait on you, suh, did n't you?"

"Yes, Sandy, and you have been a good servant and a good friend; but tell me now about this gold, and I 'll go and get you out of this, right away, for I need you, Sandy, and you 'll not be of any use to me shut up here!"

"Jes' hol' on a minute befo' you go, Mars John; fer ef dem people outside should git holt er me befo' you *does* git me out er here, I may never see you no mo', suh, in dis worl'. W'en Mars Billy McLean shot me by mistake, w'ile we wuz out huntin' dat day, who wuz it boun' up my woun's an' kep' me from bleedin' ter def, an' kyar'ed me two miles on his own shoulders ter a doctuh?"

"Yes, Sandy, and when black Sally ran away with your young mistress and Tom, when Tom was a baby, who stopped the runaway, and saved their lives at the risk of his own?"

"Dat wa'n't nothin', suh'; anybody could 'a' done dat, w'at wuz strong ernuff an' swif' ernuff. You is be'n good ter me, suh, all dese years, an' I 've tried ter do my duty by you, suh, an' by Mistuh Tom, who wuz yo' own gran'son, an' de las' one er de fam'ly."

"Yes, you have, Sandy, and when I am gone, which will not be very long, Tom will take care of you, and see that you never want. But we are wasting valuable time, Sandy, in these old reminiscences. Let us get back to the present. Tell me about the gold, now, so that I may at once look after your safety. It may not even be necessary for you to remain here all night."

"Jes' one wo'd mo', Mars John, befo' you go! I know you 're gwine ter do de bes' you kin fer me, an' I 'm sorry I can't he'p you no mo' wid it; but ef dere should be any accident, er ef you *can't* git me out er here, don' bother yo' min' 'bout it no mo', suh, an' don' git yo'se'f ixcited, fer you know de doctuh says, suh, dat you can't stan' ixcitement; but jes' leave me in de han's er de Lawd, suh, — *He 'll* look after me, here er hereafter. I know I 've fell f'm grace mo' d'n once, but I 've done made my peace wid Him in dis here jail-house, suh, an' I ain't 'feared ter die — ef I haf ter. I ain' got no wife ner child'n ter mo'n fer me, an' I 'll die knowin' dat I 've done my duty ter dem dat hi'ed me, an' trusted me, an' had claims on me. Fer I wuz raise' by a Delamere, suh, an' all de ole Delameres wuz gent'emen, an' deir principles spread ter de niggers 'round 'em, suh; an' ef I has ter die fer somethin' I did n' do, — I kin die, suh, like a gent'emen! But ez fer dat gol', suh, I ain' gwine ter say one wo'd mo' 'bout it ter nobody in dis worl'!"

Nothing could shake Sandy's determination. Mr. Delamere argued, expostulated, but all in vain. Sandy would not speak.

More and more confident of some mystery, which would come out in time, if properly investigated, Mr. Delamere, strangely beset by a vague sense of discomfort over and beyond that occasioned by his servant's danger, hurried away upon his errand of mercy. He felt less confident of the outcome than when he had entered the jail, but was quite as resolved that no effort should be spared to secure protection of Sandy until there had been full opportunity for the truth to become known.

"Take good care of your prisoner, sheriff," he said sternly, as he was conducted to the door. "He will not be long in your custody, and I shall see that you are held strictly accountable for his safety."

"I 'll do what I can, sir," replied the sheriff in an even tone and seemingly not greatly impressed by this warning. "If the prisoner is taken from me, it will be because the force that comes for him is too strong for resistance."

"There should be no force too strong for an honest man in your position to resist, — whether successfully or not is beyond the question. The officer who is intimidated by threats, or by his own fears, is recreant to his duty, and no better than the mob which threatens him. But you will have no such test, Mr. Wemyss! I shall see to it myself that there is no violence!"

XXV. THE HONOR OF A FAMILY

Mr. Delamere's coachman, who, in accordance with instructions left by Miller, had brought the carriage around to the jail and was waiting anxiously at the nearest corner, drove up with some trepidation as he saw his master emerge from the prison. The old gentleman entered the carriage and gave the order to be driven to the office of the Morning Chronicle. According to Jerry, the porter, whom he encountered at the door, Carteret was in his office, and Mr. Delamere, with the aid of his servant, climbed the stairs painfully and found the editor at his desk.

"Carteret," exclaimed Mr. Delamere, "what is all this talk about lynching my man for murder and robbery and criminal assault? It 's perfectly absurd! The man was raised by me; he has lived in my house forty years. He has been honest, faithful, and trustworthy. He would no more be capable of this crime than you would, or my grandson Tom. Sandy has too much respect for the family to do anything that would reflect disgrace upon it."

"My dear Mr. Delamere," asked Carteret, with an indulgent smile, "how could a negro possibly reflect discredit upon a white family? I should really like to know."

"How, sir? A white family raised him. Like all the negroes, he has been clay in the hands of the white people. They are what we have made them, or permitted them to become."

"We are not God, Mr. Delamere! We do not claim to have created these — masterpieces."

"No; but we thought to overrule God's laws, and we enslaved these people for our greed, and sought to escape the manstealer's curse by laying to our souls the flattering unction that we were making of barbarous negroes civilized and Christian men. If we did not, if instead of making them Christians we have made some of them brutes, we have only ourselves to blame, and if these prey upon society, it is our just punishment! But my negroes, Carteret, were well raised and well behaved. This man is innocent of this offense, I solemnly affirm, and I want your aid to secure his safety until a fair trial can be had."

"On your bare word, sir?" asked Carteret, not at all moved by this outburst.

Old Mr. Delamere trembled with anger, and his withered cheek flushed darkly, but he restrained his feelings, and answered with an attempt at calmness: —

"Time was, sir, when the word of a Delamere was held as good as his bond, and those who questioned it were forced to maintain their skepticism upon the field of honor. Time was, sir, when the law was enforced in this state in a manner to command the respect of the world! Our lawyers, our judges, our courts, were a credit to humanity and civilization. I fear I have outlasted my epoch, — I have lived to hear of white men, the most favored of races, the heirs of civilization, the conservators of liberty, howling like red Indians around a human being slowly roasting at the stake."

"My dear sir," said Carteret soothingly, "you should undeceive yourself. This man is no longer your property. The negroes are no longer under our control, and with their emancipation ceased our responsibility. Their insolence and disregard for law have reached a point where they must be sternly rebuked."

"The law," retorted Mr. Delamere, "furnishes a sufficient penalty for any crime, however heinous, and our code is by no means lenient. To my old-fashioned notions, death would seem an adequate punishment for any crime, and torture has been abolished in civilized countries for a hundred years. It would be better to let a crime go entirely unpunished, than to use it as a pretext for turning the whole white population into a mob of primitive savages, dancing in hellish glee around the mangled body of a man who has never been tried for a crime. All this, however, is apart from my errand, which is to secure your assistance in heading off this mob until Sandy can have a fair hearing and an opportunity to prove his innocence."

"How can I do that, Mr. Delamere?"

"You are editor of the Morning Chronicle. The Chronicle is the leading newspaper of the city. This morning's issue practically suggested the mob; the same means will stop it. I will pay the expense of an extra edition, calling off the mob, on the ground that newly discovered evidence has shown the prisoner's innocence."

"But where is the evidence?" asked Carteret.

Again Mr. Delamere flushed and trembled. "*My* evidence, sir! I say the negro was morally incapable of the crime. A man of forty-five does not change his nature over-night. He is no more capable of a disgraceful deed than my grandson would be!"

Carteret smiled sadly.

"I am sorry, Mr. Delamere," he said, "that you should permit yourself to be so exercised about a worthless scoundrel who has forfeited his right to live. The proof against him is overwhelming. As to his capability of crime, we will apply your own test. You have been kept in the dark too long, Mr. Delamere, — indeed, we all have, — about others as well as this negro. Listen sir: last night, at the Clarendon Club, Tom Delamere was caught cheating outrageously at cards. He had been suspected for some time; a trap was laid for him, and he fell into it. Out of regard for you and for my family, he has been permitted to resign quietly, with the understanding that he first pay off his debts, which are considerable."

Mr. Delamere's face, which had taken on some color in the excitement of the interview, had gradually paled to a chalky white while Carteret was speaking. His head sunk forward; already an old man, he seemed to have aged ten years in but little more than as many seconds.

"Can this be true?" he demanded in a hoarse whisper. "Is it — entirely authentic?"

"True as gospel; true as it is that Mrs. Ochiltree has been murdered, and that this negro killed her. Ellis was at the club a few minutes after the affair happened, and learned the facts from one of the participants. Tom made no attempt at denial. We have kept the matter out of the other papers, and I would have spared your feelings, — I surely would not wish to wound them, — but the temptation proved too strong for me, and it seemed the only way to convince you: it was your own test. If a gentleman of a distinguished name and an honorable ancestry,

with all the restraining forces of social position surrounding him, to
hold him in check, can stoop to dishonor, what is the improbability of
an illiterate negro's being at least *capable* of crime?"

"Enough sir," said the old gentleman. "You have proved enough.
My grandson may be a scoundrel, — I can see, in the light of this revelation, how he might be; and he seems not to have denied it. I maintain, nevertheless, that my man Sandy is innocent of the charge against
him. He *has* denied it, and it has not been proved. Carteret, I owe that
negro my life; he, and his father before him, have served me and mine
faithfully and well. I cannot see him killed like a dog, without judge or
jury, — no, not even if he were guilty, which I do not believe!"

Carteret felt a twinge of remorse for the pain he had inflicted upon
this fine old man, this ideal gentleman of the ideal past, — the past
which he himself so much admired and regretted. He would like to
spare his old friend any further agitation; he was in a state of health
where too great excitement might prove fatal. But how could he? The
negro was guilty, and sure to die sooner or later. He had not meant to
interfere, and his intervention might be fruitless.

"Mr. Delamere," he said gently, "there is but one way to gain time.
You say the negro is innocent. Appearances are against him. The only
way to clear him is to produce the real criminal, or prove an alibi. If
you, or some other white man of equal standing, could swear that the
negro was in your presence last night at any hour when this crime
could have taken place, it might be barely possible to prevent the
lynching for the present; and when he is tried, which will probably be
not later than next week, he will have every opportunity to defend
himself, with you to see that he gets no less than justice. I think it can
be managed, though there is still a doubt. I will do my best, for your
sake, Mr. Delamere, — solely for your sake, be it understood, and not
for that of the negro, in whom you are entirely deceived."

"I shall not examine your motives, Carteret," replied the other, "if
you can bring about what I desire."

"Whatever is done," added Carteret, "must be done quickly. It is
now four o'clock; no one can answer for what may happen after
seven. If he can prove an alibi, there may yet be time to save him.
White men might lynch a negro on suspicion; they would not kill
a man who was proven, by the word of white men, to be entirely
innocent."

"I do not know," returned Mr. Delamere, shaking his head sadly.
"After what you have told me, it is no longer safe to assume what

white men will or will not do; — what I have learned here has shaken my faith in humanity. I am going away, but shall return in a short time. Shall I find you here?"

"I will await your return," said Carteret.

He watched Mr. Delamere pityingly as the old man moved away on the arm of the coachman waiting in the hall. He did not believe that Mr. Delamere could prove an alibi for his servant, and without some positive proof the negro would surely die, — as he well deserved to die.

XXVI. THE DISCOMFORT OF ELLIS

MR. ELLIS was vaguely uncomfortable. In the first excitement following the discovery of the crime, he had given his bit of evidence, and had shared the universal indignation against the murderer. When public feeling took definite shape in the intention to lynch the prisoner, Ellis felt a sudden sense of responsibility growing upon himself. When he learned, an hour later, that it was proposed to burn the negro, his part in the affair assumed a still graver aspect; for his had been the final word to fix the prisoner's guilt.

Ellis did not believe in lynch law. He had argued against it, more than once, in private conversation, and had written several editorials against the practice, while in charge of the Morning Chronicle during Major Carteret's absence. A young man, however, and merely representing another, he had not set up as a reformer, taking rather the view that this summary method of punishing crime, with all its possibilities of error, to say nothing of the resulting disrespect of the law and contempt for the time-honored methods of establishing guilt, was a mere temporary symptom of the unrest caused by the unsettled relations of the two races at the South. There had never before been any special need for any vigorous opposition to lynch law, so far as the community was concerned, for there had not been a lynching in Wellington since Ellis had come there, eight years before, from a smaller town, to seek a place for himself in the world of action. Twenty years before, indeed, there had been wild doings, during the brief Ku-Klux outbreak, but that was before Ellis's time, — or at least when he was but a child. He had come of a Quaker family, — the modified Quakers of the South, — and while sharing in a general way the Southern prejudice against the negro, his prejudices had been tempered by the peaceful tenets of his father's sect. His father had been a Whig, and a non-slaveholder; and while he had gone with the South in the civil war so far as a man of peace could go, he had not done so for love of slavery.

As the day wore on, Ellis's personal responsibility for the intended *auto-da-fé* bore more heavily upon him. Suppose he had been wrong? He had seen the accused negro; he had recognized him by his clothes, his whiskers, his spectacles, and his walk; but he had also seen another man, who resembled Sandy so closely that but for the difference in their clothes, he was forced to acknowledge, he could not have told them apart. Had he not seen the first man, he would have sworn with even greater confidence that the second was Sandy. There had been, he recalled, about one of the men — he had not been then nor was he now able to tell which — something vaguely familiar, and yet seemingly discordant to whichever of the two it was, or, as it seemed to him now, to any man of that race. His mind reverted to the place where he had last seen Sandy, and then a sudden wave of illumination swept over him, and filled him with a thrill of horror. The cakewalk, — the dancing, — the speech, — they were not Sandy's at all, nor any negro's! It was a white man who had stood in the light of the street lamp, so that the casual passer-by might see and recognize in him old Mr. Delamere's servant. The scheme was a dastardly one, and worthy of a heart that was something worse than weak and vicious.

Ellis resolved that the negro should not, if he could prevent it, die for another's crime; but what proof had he himself to offer in support of his theory? Then again, if he denounced Tom Delamere as the murderer, it would involve, in all probability, the destruction of his own hopes with regard to Clara. Of course she could not marry Delamere after the disclosure, — the disgraceful episode at the club would have been enough to make that reasonably certain; it had put a nail in Delamere's coffin, but this crime had driven it in to the head and clinched it. On the other hand, would Miss Pemberton ever speak again to the man who had been the instrument of bringing disgrace upon the family? Spies, detectives, police officers, may be useful citizens, but they are rarely pleasant company for other people. We fee the executioner, but we do not touch his bloody hand. We might feel a certain tragic admiration for Brutus condemning his sons to death, but we would scarcely invite Brutus to dinner after the event. It would harrow our feelings too much.

Perhaps, thought Ellis, there might be a way out of the dilemma. It might be possible to save this innocent negro without, for the time being, involving Delamere. He believed that murder will out, but it need not be through his initiative. He determined to go to the jail and interview the prisoner, who might give such an account of himself as would establish his innocence beyond a doubt. If so, Ellis would exert himself to stem the tide of popular fury. If, as a last resort, he could save Sandy only by denouncing Delamere, he would do his duty, let it cost him what it might.

The gravity of his errand was not lessened by what he saw and heard on the way to the jail. The anger of the people was at a white heat. A white woman had been assaulted and murdered by a brutal negro. Neither advanced age, nor high social standing, had been able to protect her from the ferocity of a black savage. Her sex, which should have been her shield and buckler, had made her an easy mark for the villainy of a black brute. To take the time to try him would be a criminal waste of public money. To hang him would be too slight a punishment for so dastardly a crime. An example must be made.

Already the preparations were under way for the impending execution. A T-rail from the railroad yard had been procured, and men were burying it in the square before the jail. Others were bringing chains, and a load of pine wood was piled in convenient proximity. Some enterprising individual had begun the erection of seats from which, for a pecuniary consideration, the spectacle might be the more easily and comfortably viewed.

Ellis was stopped once or twice by persons of his acquaintance. From one he learned that the railroads would run excursions from the neighboring towns in order to bring spectators to the scene; from another that the burning was to take place early in the evening, so that the children might not be kept up beyond their usual bedtime. In one group that he passed he heard several young men discussing the question of which portions of the negro's body they would prefer for souvenirs. Ellis shuddered and hastened forward. Whatever was to be done must be done quickly, or it would be too late. He saw that already it would require a strong case in favor of the accused to overcome the popular verdict.

Going up the steps of the jail, he met Mr. Delamere, who was just coming out, after a fruitless interview with Sandy.

"Mr. Ellis," said the old gentleman, who seemed greatly agitated, "this is monstrous!"

"It is indeed, sir!" returned the younger man. "I mean to stop it if I can. The negro did not kill Mrs. Ochiltree."

Mr. Delamere looked at Ellis keenly, and, as Ellis recalled afterwards, there was death in his eyes. Unable to draw a syllable from

Sandy, he had found his servant's silence more eloquent than words. Ellis felt a presentiment that this affair, however it might terminate, would be fatal to this fine old man, whom the city could ill spare, in spite of his age and infirmities.

"Mr. Ellis," asked Mr. Delamere, in a voice which trembled with ill-suppressed emotion, "do you know who killed her?"

Ellis felt a surging pity for his old friend; but every step that he had taken toward the jail had confirmed and strengthened his own resolution that this contemplated crime, which he dimly felt to be far more atrocious than that of which Sandy was accused, in that it involved a whole community rather than one vicious man, should be stopped at any cost. Deplorable enough had the negro been guilty, it became, in view of his certain innocence, an unspeakable horror, which for all time would cover the city with infamy.

"Mr. Delamere," he replied, looking the elder man squarely in the eyes, " I think I do, — and I am very sorry."

"And who was it, Mr. Ellis?"

He put the question hopelessly, as though the answer were a foregone conclusion.

"I do not wish to say at present," replied Ellis, with a remorseful pang, "unless it becomes absolutely necessary, to save the negro's life. Accusations are dangerous, — as this case proves, — unless the proof be certain."

For a moment it seemed as though Mr. Delamere would collapse upon the spot. Rallying almost instantly, however, he took the arm which Ellis involuntarily offered, and said with an effort: —

"Mr. Ellis, you are a gentleman whom it is an honor to know. If you have time, I wish you would go with me to my house, — I can hardly trust myself alone, — and thence to the Chronicle office. This thing shall be stopped, and you will help me stop it."

It required but a few minutes to cover the half mile that lay between the prison and Mr. Delamere's residence.

XXVII. THE VAGARIES OF THE HIGHER LAW

Mr. Delamere went immediately to his grandson's room, which he entered alone, closing and locking the door behind him. He had requested Ellis to wait in the carriage.

The bed had been made, and the room was apparently in perfect order. There was a bureau in the room, through which Mr. Delamere proceeded to look thoroughly. Finding one of the drawers locked, he tried it with a key of his own, and being unable to unlock it, took a poker from beside the stove and broke it ruthlessly open.

The contents served to confirm what he had heard concerning his grandson's character. Thrown together in disorderly confusion were bottles of wine and whiskey; soiled packs of cards; a dice-box with dice; a box of poker chips, several revolvers, and a number of photographs and paper-covered books at which the old gentleman merely glanced to ascertain their nature.

So far, while his suspicion had been strengthened, he had found nothing to confirm it. He searched the room more carefully, and found, in the wood-box by the small heating-stove which stood in the room, a torn and crumpled bit of paper. Stooping to pick this up, his eye caught a gleam of something yellow beneath the bureau, which lay directly in his line of vision.

First he smoothed out the paper. It was apparently the lower half of a label, or part of the cover of a small box, torn diagonally from corner to corner. From the business card at the bottom, which gave the name of a firm of manufacturers of theatrical supplies in a Northern city, and from the letters remaining upon the upper and narrower half, the bit of paper had plainly formed part of the wrapper of a package of burnt cork.

Closing his fingers spasmodically over this damning piece of evidence, Mr. Delamere knelt painfully, and with the aid of his cane drew out from under the bureau the yellow object which had attracted his attention. It was a five-dollar gold piece of a date back toward the beginning of the century.

To make assurance doubly sure, Mr. Delamere summoned the cook from the kitchen in the back yard. In answer to her master's questions, Sally averred that Mr. Tom had got up very early, had knocked at her window, — she slept in a room off the kitchen in the yard, — and had told her that she need not bother about breakfast for him, as he had had a cold bite from the pantry; that he was going hunting and fishing, and would be gone all day. According to Sally, Mr. Tom had come in about ten o'clock the night before. He had forgotten his night-key, Sandy was out, and she had admitted him with her own key. He had said that he was very tired and was going immediately to bed.

Mr. Delamere seemed perplexed; the crime had been committed later in the evening than ten o'clock. The cook cleared up the mystery.

"I reckon he must 'a' be'n dead ti'ed, suh, fer I went back ter his room fifteen er twenty minutes after he come in fer ter fin' out w'at he

wanted fer breakfus'; an' I knock' two or three times, rale ha'd, an'
Mistuh Tom did n' wake up no mo' d'n de dead. He sho'ly had a good
sleep, er he 'd never a' got up so ea'ly."

"Thank you, Sally," said Mr. Delamere, when the woman had finished, "that will do."

"Yes."

It was a matter of the supremest indifference to Mr. Delamere
whether he should ever eat again, but he would not betray his feelings
to a servant. In a few minutes he was driving rapidly with Ellis toward
the office of the Morning Chronicle. Ellis could see that Mr. Delamere
had discovered something of tragic import. Neither spoke. Ellis gave
all his attention to the horses, and Mr. Delamere remained wrapped in
his own sombre reflections.

When they reached the office, they were informed by Jerry that
Major Carteret was engaged with General Belmont and Captain
McBane. Mr. Delamere knocked peremptorily at the door of the inner
office, which was opened by Carteret in person.

"Oh, it is you, Mr. Delamere."

"Carteret," exclaimed Mr. Delamere, "I must speak to you immediately, and alone."

"Excuse me a moment, gentlemen," said Carteret, turning to those
within the room. "I 'll be back in a moment — don't go away."

Ellis had left the room, closing the door behind him. Mr. Delamere
and Carteret were quite alone.

"Carteret," declared the old gentleman, "this murder must not take
place."

" 'Murder' is a hard word," replied the editor, frowning slightly.

"It is the right word," rejoined Mr. Delamere, decidedly. "It would
be a foul and most unnatural murder, for Sandy did not kill Mrs.
Ochiltree."

Carteret with difficulty restrained a smile of pity. His old friend was
very much excited, as the tremor in his voice gave proof. The criminal
was his trusted servant, who had proved unworthy of confidence. No
one could question Mr. Delamere's motives; but he was old, his judgment was no longer to be relied upon. It was a great pity that he
should so excite and overstrain himself about a worthless negro, who
had forfeited his life for a dastardly crime. Mr. Delamere had had two
paralytic strokes, and a third might prove fatal. He must be dealt with
gently.

"Mr. Delamere," he said, with patient tolerance, "I think you are
deceived. There is but one sure way to stop this execution. If your

servant is innocent, you must produce the real criminal. If the negro, with such overwhelming proofs against him, is not guilty, who is?"

"I will tell you who is," replied Mr. Delamere. "The murderer is," — the words came with a note of anguish, as though torn from his very heart, — "the murderer is Tom Delamere, my own grandson!"

"Impossible, sir!" exclaimed Carteret, starting back involuntarily. "That could not be! The man was seen leaving the house, and he was black!"

"All cats are gray in the dark, Carteret; and, moreover, nothing is easier than for a white man to black his face. God alone knows how many crimes have been done in this guise! Tom Delamere, to get the money to pay his gambling debts, committed this foul murder, and then tried to fasten it upon as honest and faithful a soul as ever trod the earth."

Carteret, though at first overwhelmed by this announcement, perceived with quick intuition that it might easily be true. It was but a step from fraud to crime, and in Delamere's need of money there lay a palpable motive for robbery, — the murder may have been an afterthought. Delamere knew as much about the cedar chest as the negro could have known, and more.

But a white man must not be condemned without proof positive.

"What foundation is there, sir," he asked, "for this astounding charge?"

Mr. Delamere related all that had taken place since he had left Belleview a couple of hours before, and as he proceeded, step by step, every word carried conviction to Carteret. Tom Delamere's skill as a mimic and a negro impersonator was well known; he had himself laughed at more than one of his performances. There had been a powerful motive, and Mr. Delamere's discoveries had made clear the means. Tom's unusual departure, before breakfast, on a fishing expedition was a suspicious circumstance. There was a certain devilish ingenuity about the affair which he would hardly have expected of Tom Delamere, but for which the reason was clear enough. One might have thought that Tom would have been satisfied with merely blacking his face, and leaving to chance the identification of the negro who might be apprehended. He would hardly have implicated, out of pure malignity, his grandfather's old servant, who had been his own care-taker for many years. Here, however, Carteret could see where Tom's own desperate position operated to furnish a probable motive for the crime. The surest way to head off suspicion from himself was to direct it strongly toward some particular person, and this he had been able to do conclusively by his access to Sandy's clothes, his skill in making up to resemble him, and by the episode of the silk purse. By placing himself beyond reach during the next day, he would not be called upon to corroborate or deny any inculpating statements which Sandy might make, and in the very probable case that the crime should be summarily avenged, any such statements on Sandy's part would be regarded as mere desperate subterfuges of the murderer to save his own life. It was a bad affair.

"The case seems clear," said Carteret reluctantly but conclusively. "And now, what shall we do about it?"

"I want you to print a handbill," said Mr. Delamere, "and circulate it through the town, stating that Sandy Campbell is innocent and Tom Delamere guilty of this crime. If this is not done, I will go myself and declare it to all who will listen, and I will publicly disown the villain who is no more grandson of mine. There is no deeper sink of iniquity into which he could fall."

Carteret's thoughts were chasing one another tumultuously. There could be no doubt that the negro was innocent, from the present aspect of affairs, and he must not be lynched; but in what sort of position would the white people be placed, if Mr. Delamere carried out his Spartan purpose of making the true facts known? The white people of the city had raised the issue of their own superior morality, and had themselves made this crime a race question. The success of the impending "revolution," for which he and his *confrères* had labored so long, depended in large measure upon the maintenance of their race prestige, which would be injured in the eyes of the world by such a fiasco. While they might yet win by sheer force, their cause would suffer in the court of morals, where they might stand convicted as pirates, instead of being applauded as patriots. Even the negroes would have the laugh on them, — the people whom they hoped to make approve and justify their own despoilment. To be laughed at by the negroes was a calamity only less terrible than failure or death.

Such an outcome of an event which had already been heralded to the four corners of the earth would throw a cloud of suspicion upon the stories of outrage which had gone up from the South for so many years, and had done so much to win the sympathy of the North for the white South and to alienate it from the colored people. The reputation of the race was threatened. They must not lynch the negro, and yet, for the credit of the town, its aristocracy, and the race, the truth of this ghastly story must not see the light, — at least not yet.

"Mr. Delamere," he exclaimed, "I am shocked and humiliated. The negro must be saved, of course, but — consider the family honor."

"Tom is no longer a member of my family. I disown him. He has covered the family name — my name, sir — with infamy. We have no longer a family honor. I wish never to hear his name spoken again!"

For several minutes Carteret argued with his old friend. Then he went into the other room and consulted with General Belmont.

As a result of these conferences, and of certain urgent messages sent out, within half an hour thirty or forty of the leading citizens of Wellington were gathered in the Morning Chronicle office. Several other curious persons, observing that there was something in the wind, and supposing correctly that it referred to the projected event of the evening, crowded in with those who had been invited.

Carteret was in another room, still arguing with Mr. Delamere. "It 's a mere formality, sir," he was saying suavely, "accompanied by a mental reservation. We know the facts; but this must be done to justify us, in the eyes of the mob, in calling them off before they accomplish their purpose."

"Carteret," said the old man, in a voice eloquent of the struggle through which he had passed, "I would not perjure myself to prolong my own miserable existence another day, but God will forgive a sin committed to save another's life. Upon your head be it, Carteret, and not on mine!"

"Gentlemen," said Carteret, entering with Mr. Delamere the room where the men were gathered, and raising his hand for silence, "the people of Wellington were on the point of wreaking vengeance upon a negro who was supposed to have been guilty of a terrible crime. The white men of this city, impelled by the highest and holiest sentiments, were about to take steps to defend their hearthstones and maintain the purity and ascendancy of their race. Your purpose sprung from hearts wounded in their tenderest susceptibilities."

"'Rah, 'rah!" shouted a tipsy sailor, who had edged in with the crowd.

"But this same sense of justice," continued Carteret oratorically, "which would lead you to visit swift and terrible punishment upon the guilty, would not permit you to slay an innocent man. Even a negro, as long as he behaves himself and keeps in his place, is entitled to the protection of the law. We may be stern and unbending in the punishment of crime, as befits our masterful race, but we hold the scales of justice with even and impartial hand."

"'Rah f' 'mpa'tial han'!" cried the tipsy sailor, who was immediately ejected with slight ceremony.

"We have discovered, beyond a doubt, that the negro Sandy

Campbell, now in custody, did not commit this robbery and murder, but that it was perpetrated by some unknown man, who has fled from the city. Our venerable and distinguished fellow townsman, Mr. Delamere, in whose employment this Campbell has been for many years, will vouch for his character, and states, furthermore, that Campbell was with him all last night, covering any hour at which this crime could have been committed."

"If Mr. Delamere will swear to that," said some one in the crowd, "the negro should not be lynched."

There were murmurs of dissent. The preparations had all been made. There would be great disappointment if the lynching did not occur.

"Let Mr. Delamere swear, if he wants to save the nigger," came again from the crowd.

"Certainly," assented Carteret. "Mr. Delamere can have no possible objection to taking the oath. Is there a notary public present, or a justice of the peace?"

A man stepped forward. "I am a justice of the peace," he announced.

"Very well, Mr. Smith," said Carteret, recognizing the speaker. "With your permission, I will formulate the oath, and Mr. Delamere may repeat it after me, if he will. I solemnly swear," —

"I solemnly swear," —

Mr. Delamere's voice might have come from the tomb, so hollow and unnatural did it sound.

"So help me God," —

"So help me God," —

"That the negro Sandy Campbell, now in jail on the charge of murder, robbery, and assault, was in my presence last night between the hours of eight and two o'clock."

Mr. Delamere repeated this statement in a firm voice; but to Ellis, who was in the secret, his words fell upon the ear like clods dropping upon the coffin in an open grave.

"I wish to add," said General Belmont, stepping forward, "that it is not our intention to interfere, by anything which may be done at this meeting, with the orderly process of the law, or to advise the prisoner's immediate release. The prisoner will remain in custody, Mr. Delamere, Major Carteret, and I guaranteeing that he will be proved entirely innocent at the preliminary hearing to-morrow morning."

Several of those present looked relieved; others were plainly disappointed; but when the meeting ended, the news went out that the lynching had been given up. Carteret immediately wrote and had struck off a handbill giving a brief statement of the proceedings, and sent out a dozen boys to distribute copies among the people on the streets. That no precaution might be omitted, a call was issued to the Wellington Grays, the crack independent military company of the city, who in an incredibly short time were on guard at the jail.

Thus a slight change in the point of view had demonstrated the entire ability of the leading citizens to maintain the dignified and orderly processes of the law whenever they saw fit to do so.

The night passed without disorder, beyond the somewhat rough handling of two or three careless negroes that came in the way of small parties of the disappointed who had sought alcoholic consolation.

At ten o'clock the next morning, a preliminary hearing of the charge against Campbell was had before a magistrate. Mr. Delamere, perceptibly older and more wizened than he had seemed the day before, and leaning heavily on the arm of a servant, repeated his statement of the evening before. Only one or two witnesses were called, among whom was Mr. Ellis, who swore positively that in his opinion the prisoner was not the man whom he had seen and at first supposed to be Campbell. The most sensational piece of testimony was that of Dr. Price, who had examined the body, and who swore that the wound in the head was not necessarily fatal, and might have been due to a fall, — that she had more than likely died of shock attendant upon the robbery, she being of advanced age and feeble health. There was no evidence, he said, of any other personal violence.

Sandy was not even bound over to the grand jury, but was discharged upon the ground that there was not sufficient evidence upon which to hold him. Upon his release he received the congratulations of many present, some of whom would cheerfully have done him to death a few hours before. With the childish fickleness of a mob, they now experienced a satisfaction almost as great as, though less exciting than, that attendant upon taking life. We speak of the mysteries of inanimate nature. The workings of the human heart are the profoundest mystery of the universe. One moment they make us despair of our kind, and the next we see in them the reflection of the divine image. Sandy, having thus escaped from the Mr. Hyde of the mob, now received the benediction of its Dr. Jekyll. Being no cynical philosopher, and realizing how nearly the jaws of death had closed upon him, he was profoundly grateful for his escape, and felt not the slightest desire to investigate or criticise any man's motives.

With the testimony of Dr. Price, the worst feature of the affair came to an end. The murder eliminated or rendered doubtful, the crime became a mere vulgar robbery, the extent of which no one could estimate, since no living soul knew how much money Mrs. Ochiltree had had in the cedar chest. The absurdity of the remaining charge became more fully apparent in the light of the reaction from the excitement of the day before.

Nothing further was ever done about the case; but though the crime went unpunished, it carried evil in its train. As we have seen, the charge against Campbell had been made against the whole colored race. All over the United States the Associated Press had flashed the report of another dastardly outrage by a burly black brute, — all black brutes it seems are burly, — and of the impending lynching with its prospective horrors. This news, being highly sensational in its character, had been displayed in large black type on the front pages of the daily papers. The dispatch that followed, to the effect that the accused had been found innocent and the lynching frustrated, received slight attention, if any, in a fine-print paragraph on an inside page. The facts of the case never came out at all. The family honor of the Delameres was preserved, and the prestige of the white race in Wellington was not seriously impaired.

Upon leaving the preliminary hearing, old Mr. Delamere had requested General Belmont to call at his house during the day upon professional business. This the general did in the course of the afternoon.

"Belmont," said Mr. Delamere, "I wish to make my will. I should have drawn it with my own hand; but you know my motives, and can testify to my soundness of mind and memory."

He thereupon dictated a will, by the terms of which he left to his servant, Sandy Campbell, three thousand dollars, as a mark of the testator's appreciation of services rendered and sufferings endured by Sandy on behalf of his master. After some minor dispositions, the whole remainder of the estate was devised to Dr. William Miller, in trust for the uses of his hospital and training-school for nurses, on condition that the institution be incorporated and placed under the management of competent trustees. Tom Delamere was not mentioned in the will.

"There, Belmont," he said, "that load is off my mind. Now, if you will call in some witnesses, — most of my people can write, — I shall feel entirely at ease."

The will was signed by Mr. Delamere, and witnessed by Jeff and Billy, two servants in the house, neither of whom received any information as to its contents, beyond the statement that they were witnessing their master's will.

"I wish to leave that with you for safe keeping, Belmont," said Mr. Delamere, after the witnesses had retired. "Lock it up in your safe until I die, which will not be very long, since I have no further desire to live."

An hour later Mr. Delamere suffered a third paralytic stroke, from which he died two days afterwards, without having in the meantime recovered the power of speech.

The will was never produced. The servants stated, and General Belmont admitted, that Mr. Delamere had made a will a few days before his death; but since it was not discoverable, it seemed probably that the testator had destroyed it. This was all the more likely, the general was inclined to think, because the will had been of a most unusual character. What the contents of the will were, he of course did not state, it having been made under the seal of professional secrecy.

This suppression was justified by the usual race argument: Miller's hospital was already well established, and, like most negro institutions, could no doubt rely upon Northern philanthropy for any further support it might need. Mr. Delamere's property belonged of right to the white race, and by the higher law should remain in the possession of white people. Loyalty to one's race was a more sacred principle than deference to a weak old man's whims.

Having reached this conclusion, General Belmont's first impulse was to destroy the will; on second thoughts he locked it carefully away in his safe. He would hold it awhile. It might some time be advisable to talk the matter over with young Delamere, who was of a fickle disposition and might wish to change his legal adviser.

XXVIII. IN SEASON AND OUT

Wellington soon resumed its wonted calm, and in a few weeks the intended lynching was only a memory. The robbery and assault, however, still remained a mystery to all but a chosen few. The affair had been dropped as absolutely as though it had never occurred. No colored man ever learned the reason of this sudden change of front, and Sandy Campbell's loyalty to his old employer's memory kept him silent. Tom Delamere did not offer to retain Sandy in his service, though he presented him with most of the old gentleman's wardrobe. It is only justice to Tom to state that up to this time he had not been informed of the contents of his grandfather's latest will. Major Carteret gave Sandy employment as butler, thus making a sort of vicarious atonement, on the part of the white race, of which the major felt himself in a way the embodiment, for the risk to which Sandy had been subjected.

Shortly after these events Sandy was restored to the bosom of the church, and, enfolded by its sheltering arms, was no longer tempted to stray from the path of rectitude, but became even a more rigid Methodist than before his recent troubles.

Tom Delamere did not call upon Clara again in the character of a lover. Of course they could not help meeting, from time to time, but he never dared presume upon their former relations. Indeed, the social atmosphere of Wellington remained so frigid toward Delamere that he left town, and did not return for several months.

Ellis was aware that Delamere had been thrown over, but a certain delicacy restrained him from following up immediately the advantage which the absence of his former rival gave him. It seemed to him, with the quixotry of a clean, pure mind, that Clara would pass through a period of mourning for her lost illusion, and that it would be indelicate, for the time being, to approach her with a lover's attentions. The work of the office had been unusually heavy of late. The major, deeply absorbed in politics, left the detail work of the paper to Ellis. Into the intimate counsels of the revolutionary committee Ellis had not been admitted, nor would he have desired to be. He knew, of course, in a general way, the results that it was sought to achieve; and while he did not see their necessity, he deferred to the views of older men, and was satisfied to remain in ignorance of anything which he might disapprove. Moreover, his own personal affairs occupied his mind to an extent that made politics or any other subject a matter of minor importance.

As for Dr. Miller, he never learned of Mr. Delamere's good intentions toward his institution, but regretted the old gentleman's death as the loss of a sincere friend and well-wisher of his race in their unequal struggle.

Despite the untiring zeal of Carteret and his associates, the campaign for the restriction of the suffrage, which was to form the basis of a permanent white supremacy, had seemed to languish for a while after the Ochiltree affair. The lull, however, was only temporary, and more apparent than real, for the forces adverse to the negro were merely gathering strength for a more vigorous assault. While little was said in Wellington, public sentiment all over the country became every day more favorable to the views of the conspirators. The nation was rushing forward with giant strides toward colossal wealth and world-domination, before the exigencies of which mere abstract ethical theories must not be permitted to stand. The same argument that justified the conquest of an inferior nation[1] could not be denied to those who sought the suppression of an inferior race. In the South, an obscure jealousy of the negro's progress, an obscure fear of the very equality so contemptuously denied, furnished a rich soil for successful agitation. Statistics of crime, ingeniously manipulated, were made to present a fearful showing against the negro. Vital statistics were made to prove that he had degenerated from an imaginary standard of physical excellence which had existed under the benign influence of slavery. Constant lynchings emphasized his impotence, and bred everywhere a growing contempt for his rights.

At the North, a new Pharaoh[2] had risen, who knew not Israel, — a new generation, who knew little of the fierce passions which had played around the negro in a past epoch, and derived their opinions of him from the "coon song" and the police reports. Those of his old friends who survived were disappointed that he had not flown with clipped wings; that he had not in one generation of limited opportunity attained the level of the whites. The whole race question seemed to have reached a sort of *impasse,* a blind alley, of which no one could see the outlet. The negro had become a target at which any one might try a shot. Schoolboys gravely debated the question as to whether or not the negro should exercise the franchise. The pessimist gave him up in despair; while the optimist, smilingly confident that everything would come out all right in the end, also turned aside and went his buoyant way to more pleasing themes.

For a time there were white men in the state who opposed any reactionary step unless it were of general application. They were conscientious men, who had learned the ten commandments and wished to do right; but this class was a small minority, and their objections were

---

[1] *the conquest of an inferior nation:* As a result of the defeat of the Spanish in the Spanish-American War of 1898, the United States took control of Cuba and the Philippine Islands.

[2] *Pharaoh:* Pharaoh was an honorific title for kings of ancient Egypt. In the Book of Exodus, the prophet Moses delivers the Hebrews from their enslavement under Pharaoh. Chesnutt's allusion indicts the North for imposing a new kind of bondage on African Americans in the wake of Reconstruction. To conciliate white Southerners, lawmakers in the North let the southern states erode or ignore black civil rights.

soon silenced by the all-powerful race argument. Selfishness is the most constant of human motives. Patriotism, humanity, or the love of God may lead to sporadic outbursts which sweep away the heaped-up wrongs of centuries; but they languish at times, while the love of self works on ceaselessly, unwearyingly, burrowing always at the very roots of life, and heaping up fresh wrongs for other centuries to sweep away. The state was at the mercy of venal and self-seeking politicians, bent upon regaining their ascendency at any cost, stultifying their own minds by vague sophistries and high-sounding phrases, which deceived none but those who wished to be deceived, and these but imperfectly; and dulling the public conscience by a loud clamor in which the calm voice of truth was for the moment silenced. So the cause went on.

Carteret, as spokesman of the campaign, and sincerest of all its leaders, performed prodigies of labor. The Morning Chronicle proclaimed, in season and out, the doctrine of "White Supremacy." Leaving the paper in charge of Ellis, the major made a tour of the state, rousing the white people of the better class to an appreciation of the terrible danger which confronted them in the possibility that a few negroes might hold a few offices or dictate the terms upon which white men should fill them. Difficulties were explained away. The provisions of the Federal Constitution, it was maintained, must yield to the "higher law," and if the Constitution could neither be altered nor bent to this end, means must be found to circumvent it.

The device finally hit upon for disfranchising the colored people in this particular state was the notorious "grandfather clause."[3] After providing various restrictions of the suffrage, based upon education, character, and property, which it deemed would in effect disfranchise the colored race, an exception was made in favor of all citizens whose fathers or grandfathers had been entitled to vote prior to 1867. Since none but white men could vote prior to 1867, this exception obviously took in the poor and ignorant whites, while the same class of negroes were excluded.

It was ingenious, but it was not fair. In due time a constitutional convention was called, in which the above scheme was adopted and submitted to a vote of the people for ratification. The campaign was fought on the color line. Many white Republicans, deluded with the hope that by the elimination of the negro vote their party might receive

---

[3] *grandfather clause:* To circumvent federal laws designed to grant former slaves the right to vote, southern state governments instituted "grandfather clauses" that stipulated only those whose grandparents had the right to vote were themselves eligible to vote.

accessions from the Democratic ranks, went over to the white party.
By fraud in once place, by terrorism in another, and everywhere by the
resistless moral force of the united whites, the negroes were reduced to
the apathy of despair, their few white allies demoralized, and the
amendment adopted by a large majority. The negroes were taught that
this is a white man's country, and that the sooner they made up their
minds to this fact, the better for all concerned. The white people
would be good to them so long as they behaved themselves and kept
their place. As theoretical equals, — practical equality being forever
out of the question, either by nature or by law, — there could have
been nothing but strife between them, in which the weaker party
would invariably have suffered most.

Some colored men accepted the situation thus outlined, if not as
desirable, at least as inevitable. Most of them, however, had little faith
in this condescending friendliness which was to take the place of constitutional rights. They knew they had been treated unfairly; that their
enemies had prevailed against them; that their whilom friends had
stood passively by and seen them undone. Many of the most enterprising and progressive left the state, and those who remain still labor
under a sense of wrong and outrage which renders them distinctly less
valuable as citizens.

The great steal was made, but the thieves did not turn honest, —
the scheme still shows the mark of the burglar's tools. Sins, like chickens, come home to roost. The South paid a fearful price for the wrong
of negro slavery; in some form or other it will doubtless reap the fruits
of this later iniquity.

Drastic as were these "reforms," the results of which we have anticipated somewhat, since the new Constitution was not to take effect
immediately, they moved all too slowly for the little coterie of Wellington conspirators, whose ambitions and needs urged them to prompt
action. Under the new Constitution it would be two full years before the
"nigger amendment" became effective, and meanwhile the Wellington
district would remain hopelessly Republican. The committee decided,
about two months before the fall election, that an active local campaign must be carried on, with a view to discourage the negroes from
attending the polls on election day.

The question came up for discussion one forenoon in a meeting at
the office of the Morning Chronicle, at which all of the "Big Three"
were present.

"Something must be done," declared McBane, "and that damn quick. Too many white people are saying that it will be better to wait until the amendment goes into effect. That would mean to leave the niggers in charge of this town for two years after the state has declared white supremacy! I 'm opposed to leaving it in their hands one hour, — them 's my sentiments!"

This proved to be the general opinion, and the discussion turned to the subject of ways and means.

"What became of that editorial in the nigger paper?" inquired the general in his blandest tones, cleverly directing a smoke ring toward the ceiling. "It lost some of its point back there, when we came near lynching that nigger; but now that that has blown over, why would n't it be a good thing to bring into play at the present juncture? Let 's read it over again."

Carteret extracted the paper from the pigeon-hole where he had placed it some months before. The article was read aloud with emphasis and discussed phrase by phrase. Of its wording there could be little criticism, — it was temperately and even cautiously phrased. As suggested by the general, the Ochiltree affair had proved that it was not devoid of truth. Its great offensiveness lay in its boldness: that a negro should publish in a newspaper what white people would scarcely acknowledge to themselves in secret was much as though a Russian *moujik* or a German peasant should rush into print to question the divine right of the Lord's Anointed. The article was racial *lèse-majesté*[4] in the most aggravated form. A peg was needed upon which to hang a *coup d'état*, and this editorial offered the requisite opportunity. It was unanimously decided to republish the obnoxious article, with comment adapted to fire the inflammable Southern heart and rouse it against any further self-assertion of the negroes in politics or elsewhere.

"The time is ripe!" exclaimed McBane. "In a month we can have the niggers so scared that they won't dare stick their heads out of doors on 'lection day."

"I wonder," observed the general thoughtfully, after this conclusion had been reached, "if we could n't have Jerry fetch us some liquor?"

Jerry appeared in response to the usual summons. The general gave him the money, and ordered three Calhoun cocktails. When Jerry returned with the glasses on a tray, the general observed him with pointed curiosity.

[4] *lèse-majesté:* An offense against one's dignity.

"What in h—ll is the matter with you, Jerry? Your black face is splotched with brown and yellow patches, and your hair shines as though you had fallen head-foremost into a firkin of butter. What 's the matter with you?"

Jerry seemed much embarrassed by this inquiry.

"Nothin', suh, nothin'," he stammered. "It 's — it 's jes' somethin' I be'n puttin' on my hair, suh, ter improve de quality, suh."

"Jerry," returned the general, bending a solemn look upon the porter, "you have been playing with edged tools, and your days are numbered. You have been reading the Afro-American Banner."

He shook open the paper, which he had retained in his hand, and read from one of the advertisements: —

" 'Kinky, curly hair made straight in two applications. Dark skins lightened two shades; mulattoes turned perfectly white.'

"This stuff is rank poison, Jerry," continued the general with a mock solemnity which did not impose upon Jerry, who nevertheless listened with an air of great alarm. He suspected that the general was making fun of him; but he also knew that the general would like to think that Jerry believed him in earnest; and to please the white folks was Jerry's consistent aim in life. "I can see the signs of decay in your face, and your hair will all fall out in a week or two at the latest, — mark my words!"

McBane had listened to this pleasantry with a sardonic sneer. It was a waste of valuable time. To Carteret it seemed in doubtful taste. These grotesque advertisements had their tragic side. They were proof that the negroes had read the handwriting on the wall. These pitiful attempts to change their physical characteristics were an acknowledgment, on their own part, that the negro was doomed, and that the white man was to inherit the earth and hold all other races under his heel. For, as the months had passed, Carteret's thoughts, centring more and more upon the negro, had led him farther and farther, until now he was firmly convinced that there was no permanent place for the negro in the United States, if indeed anywhere in the world, except under the ground. More pathetic even than Jerry's efforts to escape from the universal doom of his race was his ignorance that even if he could, by some strange alchemy, bleach his skin and straighten his hair, there would still remain, underneath it all, only the unbleached darky, — the ass in the lion's skin.

When the general had finished his facetious lecture, Jerry backed out of the room shamefacedly, though affecting a greater confusion than he really felt. Jerry had not reasoned so closely as Carteret, but he had realized that it was a distinct advantage to be white, — an advantage which white people had utilized to secure all the best things in the world; and he had entertained the vague hope that by changing his complexion he might share this prerogative. While he suspected the general's sincerity, he nevertheless felt a little apprehensive lest the general's prediction about the effects of the face-bleach and other preparations might prove true, — the general was a white gentleman and ought to know, — and decided to abandon their use.

This purpose was strengthened by his next interview with the major. When Carteret summoned him, an hour later, after the other gentlemen had taken their leave, Jerry had washed his head thoroughly and there remained no trace of the pomade. An attempt to darken the lighter spots in his cuticle by the application of printer's ink had not proved equally successful, — the retouching left the spots as much too dark as they had formerly been too light.

"Jerry," said Carteret sternly, "when I hired you to work for the Chronicle, you were black. The word 'negro' means 'black.' The best negro is a black negro, of the pure type, as it came from the hand of God. If you wish to get along well with the white people, the blacker you are the better, — white people do not like negroes who want to be white. A man should be content to remain as God made him and where God placed him. So no more of this nonsense. Are you going to vote at the next election?"

"What would you 'vise me ter do, suh?" asked Jerry cautiously.

"I do not advise you. You ought to have sense enough to see where your own interests lie. I put it to you whether you cannot trust yourself more safely in the hands of white gentlemen, who are your true friends, than in the hands of ignorant and purchasable negroes and unscrupulous white scoundrels?"

"Dere 's no doubt about it, suh," assented Jerry, with a vehemence proportioned to his desire to get back into favor. "I ain' gwine ter have nothin' ter do wid de 'lection, suh! Ef I don' vote, I kin keep my job, can't I, suh?"

The major eyed Jerry with an air of supreme disgust. What could be expected of a race so utterly devoid of tact? It seemed as though this negro thought a white gentleman might want to bribe him to remain away from the polls; and the negro's willingness to accept the imaginary bribe demonstrated the venal nature of the colored race, — its entire lack of moral principle!

"You will retain your place, Jerry," he said severely, "so long as you perform your duties to my satisfaction and behave yourself properly."

With this grandiloquent subterfuge Carteret turned to his next article on white supremacy. Jerry did not delude himself with any fine-spun sophistry. He knew perfectly well that he held his job upon the condition that he stayed away from the polls at the approaching election. Jerry was a fool —

> "The world of fools hath such a store,
>   That he who would not see an ass,
> Must stay at home and shut his door
>   And break his looking-glass."

But while no one may be entirely wise, there are degrees of folly, and Jerry was not all kinds of a fool.

XXIX. MUTTERINGS OF THE STORM

EVENTS moved rapidly during the next few days. The reproduction, in the Chronicle, of the article from the Afro-American Banner, with Carteret's inflammatory comment, took immediate effect. It touched the Southern white man in his most sensitive spot. To him such an article was an insult to white womanhood, and must be resented by some active steps, — mere words would be no answer at all. To meet words with words upon such a subject would be to acknowledge the equality of the negro and his right to discuss or criticise the conduct of the white people.

The colored people became alarmed at the murmurings of the whites, which seemed to presage a coming storm. A number of them sought to arm themselves, but ascertained, upon inquiring at the stores, that no white merchant would sell a negro firearms. Since all the dealers in this sort of merchandise were white men, the negroes had to be satisfied with oiling up the old army muskets which some of them possessed, and the few revolvers with which a small rowdy element generally managed to keep themselves supplied. Upon an effort being made to purchase firearms from a Northern city, the express company, controlled by local men, refused to accept the consignment. The white people, on the other hand, procured both arms and ammunition in large quantities, and the Wellington Grays drilled with great assiduity at their armory.

All this went on without any public disturbance of the town's tranquillity. A stranger would have seen nothing to excite his curiosity. The white people did their talking among themselves, and merely grew more distant in their manner toward the colored folks, who instinctively closed their ranks as the whites drew away. With each day that passed the feeling grew more tense. The editor of the Afro-American Banner, whose office had been quietly garrisoned for several nights by armed negroes, became frightened, and disappeared from the town between two suns.

The conspirators were jubilant at the complete success of their plans. It only remained for them to so direct this aroused public feeling that it might completely accomplish the desired end, — to change the political complexion of the city government and assure the ascendency of the whites until the amendment should go into effect. A revolution, and not a riot, was contemplated.

With this end in view, another meeting was called at Carteret's office.

"We are now ready," announced General Belmont, "for the final act of this drama. We must decide promptly, or events may run away from us."

"What do you suggest?" asked Carteret.

"Down in the American tropics," continued the general, "they have a way of doing things. I was in Nicaragua, ten years ago, when Paterno's revolution drove out Igorroto's government.[1] It was as easy as falling off a log. Paterno had the arms and the best men. Igorroto was not looking for trouble, and the guns were at his breast before he knew it. We have the guns. The negroes are not expecting trouble, and are easy to manage compared with the fiery mixture that flourishes in the tropics."

"I should not advocate murder," returned Carteret. "We are animated by high and holy principles. We wish to right a wrong, to remedy an abuse, to save our state from anarchy and our race from humiliation. I don't object to frightening the negroes, but I am opposed to unnecessary bloodshed."

"I 'm not quite so particular," struck in McBane. "They need to be taught a lesson, and a nigger more or less would n't be missed. There 's too many of 'em now."

"Of course," continued Carteret, "if we should decide upon a certain mode of procedure, and the negroes should resist, a different reasoning might apply; but I will have no premeditated murder."

---

[1] *Nicaragua . . . Paterno's revolution . . . Igorroto's government:* This is likely a fictitious account, as "Paterno" and "Igorroto" are invented names. The allusion to Nicaragua is nonetheless apt, as a coup d'état brought Jose Santos Zelaya to power in 1893.

"In Central and South America," observed the general reflectively, "none are hurt except those who get in the way."

"There 'll be no niggers hurt," said McBane contemptuously, "unless they strain themselves running. One white man can chase a hundred of 'em. I 've managed five hundred at a time. I 'll pay for burying all the niggers that are killed."

The conference resulted in a well-defined plan, to be put into operation the following day, by which the city government was to be wrested from the Republicans and their negro allies.

"And now," said General Belmont, "while we are cleansing the Augean stables,[2] we may as well remove the cause as the effect. There are several negroes too many in this town, which will be much the better without them. There 's that yellow lawyer, Watson. He 's altogether too mouthy, and has too much business. Every nigger that gets into trouble sends for Watson, and white lawyers, with families to support and social positions to keep up, are deprived of their legitimate source of income."

"There 's that damn nigger real estate agent," blurted out McBane. "Billy Kitchen used to get most of the nigger business, but this darky has almost driven him to the poorhouse. A white business man is entitled to a living in his own profession and his own home. That nigger don't belong here nohow. He came from the North a year or two ago, and is hand in glove with Barber, the nigger editor, which is enough of itself to damn him. *He 'll* have to go!"

"How about the collector of the port?"

"We 'd better not touch him. It would bring the government down upon us, which we want to avoid. We don't need to worry about the nigger preachers either. They want to stay here, where the loaves and the fishes are. We can make 'em write letters to the newspapers justifying our course, as a condition of their remaining."

"What about Billings?" asked McBane. Billings was the white Republican mayor. "Is that skunk to be allowed to stay in town?"

"No," returned the general, "every white Republican office-holder ought to be made to go. This town is only big enough for Democrats, and negroes who can be taught to keep their place."

"What about the colored doctor," queried McBane, "with the hospital, and the diamond ring, and the carriage, and the other fallals?"

---

[2] *Augean stables:* In Greek mythology, the fifth labor of Hercules was to clean the stables of King Augeas, who was said to have more horses and livestock than anyone in Greece. Hercules accomplishes the seemingly impossible task by diverting two rivers through the stables to wash them out.

"I should n't interfere with Miller," replied the general decisively. "He 's a very good sort of a negro, does n't meddle with politics, nor tread on any one else's toes. His father was a good citizen, which counts in his favor. He 's spending money in the community too, and contributes to its prosperity."

"That sort of nigger, though, sets a bad example," retorted McBane. "They make it all the harder to keep the rest of 'em down."

" 'One swallow does not make a summer,' " quoted the general. "When we get things arranged, there 'll be no trouble. A stream cannot rise higher than its fountain, and a smart nigger without a constituency will no longer be an object of fear. I say, let the doctor alone."

"He 'll have to keep mighty quiet, though," muttered McBane discontentedly. "I don't like smart niggers. I 've had to shoot several of them, in the course of my life."

"Personally, I dislike the man," interposed Carteret, "and if I consulted my own inclinations, would say expel him with the rest; but my grievance is a personal one, and to gratify it in that way would be a loss to the community. I wish to be strictly impartial in this matter, and to take no step which cannot be entirely justified by a wise regard for the public welfare."

"What 's the use of all this hypocrisy, gentlemen?" sneered McBane. "Every last one of us has an axe to grind! The major may as well put an edge on his. We 'll never get a better chance to have things our way. If this nigger doctor annoys the major, we 'll run him out with the rest. This is a white man's country, and a white man's city, and no nigger has any business here when a white man wants him gone!"

Carteret frowned darkly at this brutal characterization of their motives. It robbed the enterprise of all its poetry, and put a solemn act of revolution upon the plane of a mere vulgar theft of power. Even the general winced.

"I would not consent," he said irritably, "to Miller's being disturbed."

McBane made no further objection.

There was a discreet knock at the door.

"Come in," said Carteret.

Jerry entered. "Mistuh Ellis wants ter speak ter you a minute, suh," he said.

Carteret excused himself and left the room.

"Jerry," said the general, "you lump of ebony, the sight of you reminds me! If your master does n't want you for a minute, step across to Mr. Brown's and tell him to send me three cocktails."

"Yas, suh," responded Jerry, hesitating. The general had said nothing about paying.

"And tell him, Jerry, to charge them. I 'm short of change to-day."

"Yas, suh; yas, suh," replied Jerry, as he backed out of the presence, adding, when he had reached the hall: "Dere ain' no change fer Jerry dis time, sho': I 'll jes' make dat *fo'* cocktails, an' de gin'l won't never know de diffe'nce. I ain' gwine 'cross de road fer nothin', not ef I knows it."

Half an hour later, the conspirators dispersed. They had fixed the hour of the proposed revolution, the course to be pursued, the results to be obtained; but in stating their equation they had overlooked one factor, — God, or Fate, or whatever one may choose to call the Power that holds the destinies of man in the hollow of his hand.

XXX. THE MISSING PAPERS

MRS. CARTERET was very much disturbed. It was supposed that the shock of her aunt's death had affected her health, for since that event she had fallen into a nervous condition which gave the major grave concern. Much to the general surprise, Mrs. Ochiltree had left no will, and no property of any considerable value except her homestead, which descended to Mrs. Carteret as the natural heir. Whatever she may have had on hand in the way of ready money had undoubtedly been abstracted from the cedar chest by the midnight marauder, to whose visit her death was immediately due. Her niece's grief was held to mark a deep-seated affection for the grim old woman who had reared her.

Mrs. Carteret's present state of mind, of which her nervousness was a sufficiently accurate reflection, did in truth date from her aunt's death, and also in part from the time of the conversation with Mrs. Ochiltree, one afternoon, during and after the drive past Miller's new hospital. Mrs. Ochiltree had grown steadily more and more childish after that time, and her niece had never succeeded in making her pick up the thread of thought where it had been dropped. At any rate, Mrs. Ochiltree had made no further disclosure upon the subject.

An examination, not long after her aunt's death, of the papers found near the cedar chest on the morning after the murder had contributed to Mrs. Carteret's enlightenment, but had not promoted her peace of mind.

When Mrs. Carteret reached home, after her hurried exploration of the cedar chest, she thrust into a bureau drawer the envelope she had found. So fully was her mind occupied, for several days, with the funeral, and with the excitement attending the arrest of Sandy Campbell, that she deferred the examination of the contents of the envelope until near the end of the week.

One morning, while alone in her chamber, she drew the envelope from the drawer, and was holding it in her hand, hesitating as to whether or not she should open it, when the baby in the next room began to cry.

The child's cry seemed like a warning, and yielding to a vague uneasiness, she put the paper back.

"Phil," she said to her husband at luncheon, "Aunt Polly said some strange things to me one day before she died, — I don't know whether she was quite in her right mind or not; but suppose that my father had left a will by which it was provided that half his property should go to that woman and her child?"

"It would never have gone by such a will," replied the major easily. "Your Aunt Polly was in her dotage, and merely dreaming. Your father would never have been such a fool; but even if he had, no such will could have stood the test of the courts. It would clearly have been due to the improper influence of a designing woman."

"So that legally, as well as morally," said Mrs. Carteret, "the will would have been of no effect?"

"Not the slightest. A jury would soon have broken down the legal claim. As for any moral obligation, there would have been nothing moral about the affair. The only possible consideration for such a gift was an immoral one. I don't wish to speak harshly of your father, my dear, but his conduct was gravely reprehensible. The woman herself had no right or claim whatever; she would have been whipped and expelled from the town, if justice — blind, bleeding justice, then prostrate at the feet of slaves and aliens — could have had her way!"

"But the child" —

"The child was in the same category. Who was she, to have inherited the estate of your ancestors, of which, a few years before, she would herself have formed a part? The child of shame, it was hers to pay the penalty. But the discussion is all in the air, Olivia. Your father never did and never would have left such a will."

This conversation relieved Mrs. Carteret's uneasiness. Going to her room shortly afterwards, she took the envelope from her bureau drawer and drew out a bulky paper. The haunting fear that it might be such a will as her aunt had suggested was now removed; for such an instrument, in the light of what her husband had said confirming her own intuitions, would be of no valid effect. It might be just as well, she thought, to throw the paper in the fire without looking at it. She wished to think as well as might be of her father, and she felt that her respect for his memory would not be strengthened by the knowledge that he had meant to leave his estate away from her; for her aunt's words had been open to the construction that she was to have been left destitute. Curiosity strongly prompted her to read the paper. Perhaps the will contained no such provision as she had feared, and it might convey some request or direction which ought properly to be complied with.

She had been standing in front of the bureau while these thoughts passed through her mind, and now, dropping the envelope back into the drawer mechanically, she unfolded the document. It was written on legal paper, in her father's own hand.

Mrs. Carteret was not familiar with legal verbiage, and there were several expressions of which she did not perhaps appreciate the full effect; but a very hasty glance enabled her to ascertain the purport of the paper. It was a will, by which, in one item, her father devised to his daughter Janet, the child of the woman known as Julia Brown, the sum of ten thousand dollars, and a certain plantation or tract of land a short distance from the town of Wellington. The rest and residue of his estate, after deducting all legal charges and expenses, was bequeathed to his beloved daughter, Olivia Merkell.

Mrs. Carteret breathed a sigh of relief. Her father had not preferred another to her, but had left to his lawful daughter the bulk of his estate. She felt at the same time a growing indignation at the thought that that woman should so have wrought upon her father's weakness as to induce him to think of leaving so much valuable property to her bastard — property which by right should go, and now would go, to her own son, to whom by every rule of law and decency it ought to descend.

A fire was burning in the next room, on account of the baby, — there had been a light frost the night before, and the air was somewhat chilly. For the moment the room was empty. Mrs. Carteret came out from her chamber and threw the offending paper into the fire, and watched it slowly burn. When it had been consumed, the carbon residue of one sheet still retained its form, and she could read the words on the charred portion. A sentence, which had escaped her eye in her rapid reading, stood out in ghostly black upon the gray background: —

"All the rest and residue of my estate I devise and bequeath to my daughter Olivia Merkell, the child of my beloved first wife."

Mrs. Carteret had not before observed the word "first." Instinctively she stretched toward the fire the poker which she held in her hand, and at its touch the shadowy remnant fell to pieces, and nothing but ashes remained upon the hearth.

Not until the next morning did she think again of the envelope which had contained the paper she had burned. Opening the drawer where it lay, the oblong blue envelope confronted her. The sight of it was distasteful. The indorsed side lay uppermost, and the words seemed like a mute reproach: —

"The Last Will and Testament of Samuel Merkell."

Snatching up the envelope, she glanced into it mechanically as she moved toward the next room, and perceived a thin folded paper which had heretofore escaped her notice. When opened, it proved to be a certificate of marriage, in due form, between Samuel Merkell and Julia Brown. It was dated from a county in South Carolina, about two years before her father's death.

For a moment Mrs. Carteret stood gazing blankly at this faded slip of paper. Her father *had* married this woman! — at least he had gone through the form of marriage with her, for to him it had surely been no more than an empty formality. The marriage of white and colored persons was forbidden by law. Only recently she had read of a case where both the parties to such a crime, a colored man and a white woman, had been sentenced to long terms in the penitentiary. She even recalled the circumstances. The couple had been living together unlawfully, — they were very low people, whose private lives were beneath the public notice, — but influenced by a religious movement pervading the community, had sought, they said at the trial, to secure the blessing of God upon their union. The higher law, which imperiously demanded that the purity and prestige of the white race be preserved at any cost, had intervened at this point.

Mechanically she moved toward the fireplace, so dazed by this discovery as to be scarcely conscious of her own actions. She surely had not formed any definite intention of destroying this piece of paper when her fingers relaxed unconsciously and let go their hold upon it. The draught swept it toward the fireplace. Ere scarcely touching the flames it caught, blazed fiercely, and shot upward with the current of air. A moment later the record of poor Julia's marriage was scattered to the four winds of heaven, as her poor body had long since mingled with the dust of the earth.

The letter remained unread. In her agitation at the discovery of the marriage certificate, Olivia had almost forgotten the existence of the letter. It was addressed to "John Delamere, Esq., as Executor of my Last Will and Testament," while the lower left-hand corner bore the direction: "To be delivered only after my death, with seal unbroken."

The seal was broken already; Mr. Delamere was dead; the letter could never be delivered. Mrs. Carteret unfolded it and read: —

MY DEAR DELAMERE, — I have taken the liberty of naming you as executor of my last will, because you are my friend, and the only man of my acquaintance whom I feel that I can trust to carry out my wishes, appreciate my motives, and preserve the silence I desire.

I have, first, a confession to make. Inclosed in this letter you will find a certificate of marriage between my child Janet's mother and myself. While I have never exactly repented of this marriage, I have never had the courage to acknowledge it openly. If I had not married Julia, I fear Polly Ochiltree would have married me by main force, — as she would marry you or any other gentleman unfortunate enough to fall in the way of this twice-widowed man-hunter. When my wife died, three years ago, her sister Polly offered to keep house for me and the child. I would sooner have had the devil in the house, and yet I trembled with alarm, — there seemed no way of escape, — it was so clearly and obviously the proper thing.

But she herself gave me my opportunity. I was on the point of consenting, when she demanded, as a condition of her coming, that I discharge Julia, my late wife's maid. She was laboring under a misapprehension in regard to the girl, but I grasped at the straw, and did everything to foster her delusion. I declared solemnly that nothing under heaven would induce me to part with Julia. The controversy resulted in my permitting Polly to take the child, while I retained the maid.

Before Polly put this idea into my head, I had scarcely looked at Julia, but this outbreak turned my attention toward her. She was a handsome girl, and, as I soon found out, a good girl. My wife, who raised her, was a Christian woman, and had taught her modesty and virtue. She was free. The air was full of liberty, and equal rights, and all the abolition claptrap, and she made marriage a condition of her remaining longer in the house. In a moment of weakness I took her away to a place where we were not known, and married her. If she had left me, I should have fallen a victim to Polly Ochiltree, — to which any fate was preferable.

And then, old friend, my weakness kept to the fore. I was ashamed of this marriage, and my new wife saw it. Moreover, she loved me, — too well, indeed, to wish to make me unhappy. The ceremony had satisfied her conscience, had set her right, she said, with God; for the opinions of men she did not care, since I loved her, — she only wanted to compensate me, as best she could, for the great honor I had done my handmaiden, — for she had read her Bible, and I was the Abraham to her Hagar,[1] compared with whom she considered herself at a great advantage. It was her own proposition that nothing be said of this marriage. If any shame should fall on her, it would fall lightly, for it would be undeserved. When the child came, she still kept silence. No one, she argued, could blame an innocent child for the accident of birth, and in the sight of God this child had every right to exist; while among her own people illegitimacy would involve but little stigma.

I need not say that I was easily persuaded to accept this sacrifice; but touched by her fidelity, I swore to provide handsomely for them both. This I have tried to do by the will of which I ask you to act as executor. Had I left the child more, it might serve as a ground for attacking the will; my acknowledgment of the tie of blood is sufficient to justify a reasonable bequest.

I have taken this course for the sake of my daughter Olivia, who is dear to me, and whom I would not wish to make ashamed; and in deference to public opinion, which it is not easy to defy. If, after my death, Julia should choose to make our secret known, I shall of course be beyond the reach of hard words; but loyalty to my memory will probably keep her silent. A strong man would long since have acknowledged her before the world and taken the consequences; but, alas! I am only myself, and the atmosphere I live in does not encourage moral heroism. I should like to be different, but it is God who hath made us, and not we ourselves!

Nevertheless, old friend, I will ask of you one favor. If in the future this child of Julia's and of mine should grow to womanhood; if she should prove to have her mother's gentleness and love of virtue; if, in the new era which is opening up for her mother's race, to which,

---

[1] *I was the Abraham to her Hagar:* In Gen. 16–17, the prophet Abraham takes Hagar as a second wife when his first wife Sarah is unable to produce any children. Hagar was Sarah's Egyptian maid.

unfortunately, she must belong, she should become, in time, an educated woman; and if the time should ever come when, by virtue of her
education or the development of her people, it would be to her a
source of shame or unhappiness that she was an illegitimate child, —
if you are still alive, old friend, and have the means of knowing or
divining this thing, go to her and tell her, for me, that she is my lawful
child, and ask her to forgive her father's weakness.

When this letter comes to you, I shall have passed to — the Beyond;
but I am confident that you will accept this trust, for which I thank
you now, in advance, most heartily.

The letter was signed with her father's name, the same signature
which had been attached to the will.

Having firmly convinced herself of the illegality of the papers, and
of her own right to destroy them, Mrs. Carteret ought to have felt
relieved that she had thus removed all traces of her dead father's folly.
True, the other daughter remained, — she had seen her on the street
only the day before. The sight of this person she had always found
offensive, and now, she felt, in view of what she had just learned, it
must be even more so. Never, while this woman lived in the town,
would she be able to throw the veil of forgetfulness over this blot upon
her father's memory.

As the day wore on, Mrs. Carteret grew still less at ease. To herself,
marriage was a serious thing, — to a right-thinking woman the most
serious concern of life. A marriage certificate, rightfully procured, was
scarcely less solemn, so far as it went, than the Bible itself. Her own
she cherished as the apple of her eye. It was the evidence of her wifehood, the seal of her child's legitimacy, her patent of nobility, — the
token of her own and her child's claim to social place and consideration. She had burned this pretended marriage certificate because it
meant nothing. Nevertheless, she could not ignore the knowledge of
another such marriage, of which every one in the town knew, — a celebrated case, indeed, where a white man, of a family quite as prominent as her father's, had married a colored woman during the military
occupation of the state just after the civil war. The legality of the marriage had never been questioned. It had been fully consummated by
twenty years of subsequent cohabitation. No amount of social persecution had ever shaken the position of the husband. With an iron will
he had stayed on in the town, a living protest against the established
customs of the South, so rudely interrupted for a few short years; and,

though his children were negroes, though he had never appeared in public with his wife, no one had ever questioned the validity of his marriage or the legitimacy of his offspring.

The marriage certificate which Mrs. Carteret had burned dated from the period of the military occupation. Hence Mrs. Carteret, who was a good woman, and would not have done a dishonest thing, felt decidedly uncomfortable. She had destroyed the marriage certificate, but its ghost still haunted her.

Major Carteret, having just eaten a good dinner, was in a very agreeable humor when, that same evening, his wife brought up again the subject of their previous discussion.

"Phil," she asked, "Aunt Polly told me that once, long before my father died, when she went to remonstrate with him for keeping that woman in the house, he threatened to marry Julia if Aunt Polly ever said another word to him about the matter. Suppose he *had* married her, and had *then* left a will, — would the marriage have made any difference, so far as the will was concerned?"

Major Carteret laughed. "Your Aunt Polly," he said, "was a remarkable woman, with a wonderful imagination, which seems to have grown more vivid as her memory and judgment weakened. Why should your father marry his negro housemaid? Mr. Merkell was never rated as a fool, — he had one of the clearest heads in Wellington. I saw him only a day or two before he died, and I could swear before any court in Christendom that he was of sound mind and memory to the last. These notions of your aunt were mere delusions. Your father was never capable of such a folly."

"Of course I am only supposing a case," returned Olivia. "Imagining such a case, just for the argument, would the marriage have been legal?"

"That would depend. If he had married her during the military occupation, or over in South Carolina, the marriage would have been legally valid, though morally and socially outrageous."

"And if he had died afterwards, leaving a will?"

"The will would have controlled the disposition of his estate, in all probability."

"Suppose he had left no will?"

"You are getting the matter down pretty fine, my dear! The woman would have taken one third of the real estate for life, and could have lived in the homestead until she died. She would also have had half the other property, — the money and goods and furniture, everything except the land, — and the negro child would have shared with you the balance of the estate. That, I believe, is according to the law of descent and distribution."

Mrs. Carteret lapsed into a troubled silence. Her father *had* married the woman. In her heart she had no doubt of the validity of the marriage, so far as the law was concerned; if one marriage of such a kind would stand, another contracted under similar conditions was equally as good. If the marriage had been valid, Julia's child had been legitimate. The will she had burned gave this sister of hers — she shuddered at the word — but a small part of the estate. Under the law, which intervened now that there was no will, the property should have been equally divided. If the woman had been white, — but the woman had *not* been white, and the same rule of moral conduct did not, *could* not, in the very nature of things, apply, as between white people! For, if this were not so, slavery had been, not merely an economic mistake, but a great crime against humanity. If it had been such a crime, as for a moment she dimly perceived it might have been, then through the long centuries there had been piled up a catalogue of wrong and outrage which, if the law of compensation be a law of nature, must some time, somewhere, in some way, be atoned for. She herself had not escaped the penalty, of which, she realized, this burden placed upon her conscience was but another installment.

If she should make known the facts she had learned, it would mean what? — a division of her father's estate, a recognition of the legality of her father's relations with Julia. Such a stain upon her father's memory would be infinitely worse than if he had not married her. To have lived with her without marriage was a social misdemeanor, at which society in the old days had winked, or at most had frowned. To have married her was to have committed the unpardonable social sin. Such a scandal Mrs. Carteret could not have endured. Should she seek to make restitution, it would necessarily involve the disclosure of at least some of the facts. Had she not destroyed the will, she might have compromised with her conscience by producing it and acting upon its terms, which had been so stated as not to disclose the marriage. This was now rendered impossible by her own impulsive act; she could not mention the will at all, without admitting that she had destroyed it.

Mrs. Carteret found herself in what might be called, vulgarly, a moral "pocket." She could, of course, remain silent. Mrs. Carteret was a good woman, according to her lights, with a cultivated conscience, to which she had always looked as her mentor and infallible guide.

Hence Mrs. Carteret, after this painful discovery, remained for a long time ill at ease, — so disturbed, indeed, that her mind reacted upon her nerves, which had never been strong; and her nervousness affected her strength, which had never been great, until Carteret, whose love for her had been deepened and strengthened by the advent of his son, became alarmed for her health, and spoke very seriously to Dr. Price concerning it.

XXXI. THE SHADOW OF A DREAM[1]

Mrs. Carteret awoke, with a start, from a troubled dream. She had been sailing across a sunlit sea, in a beautiful boat, her child lying on a bright-colored cushion at her feet. Overhead the swelling sail served as an awning to keep off the sun's rays, which far ahead were reflected with dazzling brilliancy from the shores of a golden island. Her son, she dreamed, was a fairy prince, and yonder lay his kingdom, to which he was being borne, lying there at her feet, in this beautiful boat, across the sunlit sea.

Suddenly and without warning the sky was overcast. A squall struck the boat and tore away the sail. In the distance a huge billow — a great white wall of water — came sweeping toward their frail craft, threatening it with instant destruction. She clasped her child to her bosom, and a moment later found herself struggling in the sea, holding the child's head above the water. As she floated there, as though sustained by some unseen force, she saw in the distance a small boat approaching over the storm-tossed waves. Straight toward her it came, and she had reached out her hand to grasp its side, when the rower looked back, and she saw that it was her sister. The recognition had been mutual. With a sharp movement of one oar the boat glided by, leaving her clutching at the empty air.

She felt her strength begin to fail. Despairingly she signaled with her disengaged hand; but the rower, after one mute, reproachful glance, rowed on. Mrs. Carteret's strength grew less and less. The child became heavy as lead. Herself floating in the water, as though it were her native element, she could no longer support the child. Lower and lower it sank, — she was powerless to save it or to accompany it, — until, gasping wildly for breath, it threw up its little hands and sank,

---

[1] *The Shadow of a Dream:* Shakespeare, *Ham.* 2.2. 259–61.

the cruel water gurgling over its head, — when she awoke with a start and a chill, and lay there trembling for several minutes before she heard little Dodie in his crib, breathing heavily.

She rose softly, went to the crib, and changed the child's position to an easier one. He breathed more freely, and she went back to bed, but not to sleep.

She had tried to put aside the distressing questions raised by the discovery of her father's will and the papers accompanying it. Why should she be burdened with such a responsibility, at this late day, when the touch of time had well-nigh healed these old sores? Surely, God had put his curse not alone upon the slave, but upon the stealer of men! With other good people she had thanked Him that slavery was no more, and that those who once had borne its burden upon their consciences could stand erect and feel that they themselves were free. The weed had been cut down, but its roots remained, deeply imbedded in the soil, to spring up and trouble a new generation. Upon her weak shoulders was placed the burden of her father's weakness, her father's folly. It was left to her to acknowledge or not this shameful marriage and her sister's rights in their father's estate.

Balancing one consideration against another, she had almost decided that she might ignore this tie. To herself, Olivia Merkell, — Olivia Carteret, — the stigma of base birth would have meant social ostracism, social ruin, the averted face, the finger of pity or of scorn. All the traditional weight of public disapproval would have fallen upon her as the unhappy fruit of an unblessed union. To this other woman it could have had no such significance, — it had been the lot of her race. To them, twenty-five years before, sexual sin had never been imputed as more than a fault. She had lost nothing by her supposed illegitimacy; she would gain nothing by the acknowledgment of her mother's marriage.

On the other hand, what would be the effect of this revelation upon Mrs. Carteret herself? To have it known that her father had married a negress would only be less dreadful than to have it appear that he had committed some terrible crime. It was a crime now, by the laws of every Southern State, for white and colored persons to intermarry. She shuddered before the possibility that at some time in the future some person, none too well informed, might learn that her father had married a colored woman, and might assume that she, Olivia Carteret, or her child, had sprung from this shocking *mésalliance*, — a fate to which she would willingly have preferred death. No, this marriage must never be made known; the secret should remain buried forever in her own heart!

But there still remained the question of her father's property and her father's will. This woman was her father's child, — of that there could be no doubt, it was written in her features no less than in her father's will. As his lawful child, — of which, alas! there could also be no question, — she was entitled by law to half his estate. Mrs. Carteret's problem had sunk from the realm of sentiment to that of material things, which, curiously enough, she found much more difficult. For, while the negro, by the traditions of her people, was barred from the world of sentiment, his rights of property were recognized. The question had become, with Mrs. Carteret, a question of *meum* and *tuum*. Had the girl Janet been poor, ignorant, or degraded, as might well have been her fate, Mrs. Carteret might have felt a vicarious remorse for her aunt's suppression of the papers; but fate had compensated Janet for the loss; she had been educated, she had married well; she had not suffered for lack of the money of which she had been defrauded, and did not need it now. She had a child, it is true, but this child's career would be so circumscribed by the accident of color that too much wealth would only be a source of unhappiness; to her own child, on the contrary, it would open every door of life.

It would be too lengthy a task to follow the mind and conscience of this much-tried lady in their intricate workings upon this difficult problem; for she had a mind as logical as any woman's, and a conscience which she wished to keep void of offense. She had to confront a situation involving the element of race, upon which the moral standards of her people were hopelessly confused. Mrs. Carteret reached the conclusion, ere daylight dawned, that she would be silent upon the subject of her father's second marriage. Neither party had wished it known, — neither Julia nor her father, — and she would respect her father's wishes. To act otherwise would be to defeat his will, to make known what he had carefully concealed, and to give Janet a claim of title to one half her father's estate, while he had only meant her to have the ten thousand dollars named in the will.

By the same reasoning, she must carry out her father's will in respect to this bequest. Here there was another difficulty. The mining investment into which they had entered shortly after the birth of little Dodie had tied up so much of her property that it would have been difficult to procure ten thousand dollars immediately; while a demand for half the property at once would mean bankruptcy and ruin. Moreover, upon what ground could she offer her sister any sum of money whatever? So sudden a change of heart, after so many years of silence, would raise the presumption of some right on the part of Janet in her father's estate. Suspicion once aroused, it might be possible to trace this hidden marriage, and establish it by legal proof. The marriage once verified, the claim for half the estate could not be denied. She could not plead her father's will to the contrary, for this would be to acknowledge the suppression of the will, in itself a criminal act.

There was, however, a way of escape. This hospital which had recently been opened was the personal property of her sister's husband. Some time in the future, when their investments matured, she would present to the hospital a sum of money equal to the amount her father had meant his colored daughter to have. Thus indirectly both her father's will and her own conscience would be satisfied.

Mrs. Carteret had reached this comfortable conclusion, and was falling asleep, when her attention was again drawn by her child's breathing. She took it in her own arms and soon fell asleep.

"By the way, Olivia," said the major, when leaving the house next morning for the office, "if you have any business down town to-day, transact it this forenoon. Under no circumstances must you or Clara or the baby leave the house after midday."

"Why, what's the matter, Phil?"

"Nothing to alarm you, except that there may be a little political demonstration which may render the streets unsafe. You are not to say anything about it where the servants might hear."

"Will there be any danger for you, Phil?" she demanded with alarm.

"Not the slightest, Olivia dear. No one will be harmed; but it is best for ladies and children to stay indoors."

Mrs. Carteret's nerves were still more or less unstrung from her mental struggles of the night, and the memory of her dream came to her like a dim foreboding of misfortune. As though in sympathy with its mother's feelings, the baby did not seem as well as usual. The new nurse was by no means an ideal nurse, — Mammy Jane understood the child much better. If there should be any trouble with the negroes, toward which her husband's remark seemed to point, — she knew the general political situation, though not informed in regard to her husband's plans, — she would like to have Mammy Jane near her, where the old nurse might be protected from danger or alarm.

With this end in view she dispatched the nurse, shortly after breakfast, to Mammy Jane's house in the negro settlement on the other side of the town, with a message asking the old woman to come immediately to Mrs. Carteret's. Unfortunately, Mammy Jane had gone to visit a sick woman in the country, and was not expected to return for several hours.

XXXII. THE STORM BREAKS

THE Wellington riot began at three o'clock in the afternoon of a day as fair as ever was selected for a deed of darkness. The sky was clear, except for a few light clouds that floated, white and feathery, high in air, like distant islands in a sapphire sea. A salt-laden breeze from the ocean a few miles away lent a crisp sparkle to the air.

At three o'clock sharp the streets were filled, as if by magic, with armed white men. The negroes, going about, had noted, with uneasy curiosity, that the stores and places of business, many of which closed at noon, were unduly late in opening for the afternoon, though no one suspected the reason for the delay; but at three o'clock every passing colored man was ordered, by the first white man he met, to throw up his hands. If he complied, he was searched, more or less roughly, for firearms, and then warned to get off the street. When he met another group of white men the scene was repeated. The man thus summarily held up seldom encountered more than two groups before disappearing across lots to his own home or some convenient hiding-place. If he resisted any demand of those who halted him — But the records of the day are historical; they may be found in the newspapers of the following date, but they are more firmly engraved upon the hearts and memories of the people of Wellington. For many months there were negro families in the town whose children screamed with fear and ran to their mothers for protection at the mere sight of a white man.

Dr. Miller had received a call, about one o'clock, to attend a case at the house of a well-to-do colored farmer, who lived some three or four miles from the town, upon the very road, by the way, along which Miller had driven so furiously a few weeks before, in the few hours that intervened before Sandy Campbell would probably have been burned at the stake. The drive to his patient's home, the necessary inquiries, the filling of the prescription from his own medicine-case, which he carried along with him, the little friendly conversation about the weather and the crops, and, the farmer being an intelligent and thinking man, the inevitable subject of the future of their race, — these, added to the return journey, occupied at least two hours of Miller's time.

As he neared the town on his way back, he saw ahead of him half a dozen men and women approaching, with fear written in their faces, in every degree from apprehension to terror. Women were weeping and children crying, and all were going as fast as seemingly lay in their power, looking behind now and then as if pursued by some deadly enemy. At sight of Miller's buggy they made a dash for cover, disappearing, like a covey of frightened partridges, in the underbrush along the road.

Miller pulled up his horse and looked after them in startled wonder. "What on earth can be the matter?" he muttered, struck with a vague feeling of alarm. A psychologist, seeking to trace the effects of slavery upon the human mind, might find in the South many a curious illustration of this curse, abiding long after the actual physical bondage had terminated. In the olden time the white South labored under the constant fear of negro insurrections. Knowing that they themselves, if in the negroes' place, would have risen in the effort to throw off the yoke, all their reiterated theories of negro subordination and inferiority could not remove that lurking fear, founded upon the obscure consciousness that the slaves ought to have risen. Conscience, it has been said, makes cowards of us all. There was never, on the continent of America, a successful slave revolt, nor one which lasted more than a few hours, or resulted in the loss of more than a few white lives; yet never was the planter quite free from the fear that there might be one.

On the other hand, the slave had before his eyes always the fear of the master. There were good white men, according to their lights, — according to their training and environment, — among the Southern slaveholders, who treated their slaves kindly, as slaves, from principle, because they recognized the claims of humanity, even under the dark skin of a human chattel. There was many a one who protected or pampered his negroes, as the case might be, just as a man fondles his dog, — because they were his; they were a part of his estate, an integral part of the entity of property and person which made up the aristocrat; but with all this kindness, there was always present, in the consciousness of the lowest slave, the knowledge that he was in his master's power, and that he could make no effectual protest against the abuse of that authority. There was also the knowledge, among those who could think at all, that the best of masters was himself a slave to a system, which hampered his movements but scarcely less than those of his bondmen.

When, therefore, Miller saw these men and women scampering into the bushes, he divined, with this slumbering race consciousness which

years of culture had not obliterated, that there was some race trouble
on foot. His intuition did not long remain unsupported. A black head
was cautiously protruded from the shrubbery, and a black voice — if
such a description be allowable — addressed him: —

"Is dat you, Doctuh Miller?"

"Yes. Who are you, and what 's the trouble?"

"What 's de trouble, suh? Why, all hell 's broke loose in town yon-
duh. De w'ite folks is riz 'gins' de niggers, an' say dey 're gwine ter kill
eve'y nigger dey kin lay han's on."

Miller's heart leaped to his throat, as he thought of his wife and
child. This story was preposterous; it could not be true, and yet there
must be something in it. He tried to question his informant, but the
man was so overcome with excitement and fear that Miller saw clearly
that he must go farther for information. He had read in the Morning
Chronicle, a few days before, the obnoxious editorial quoted from the
Afro-American Banner, and had noted the comment upon it by the
white editor. He had felt, as at the time of its first publication, that
the editorial was ill-advised. It could do no good, and was calculated
to arouse the animosity of those whose friendship, whose tolerance, at
least, was necessary and almost indispensable to the colored people.
They were living, at the best, in a sort of armed neutrality with the
whites; such a publication, however serviceable elsewhere, could have
no other effect in Wellington than to endanger this truce and defeat the
hope of a possible future friendship. The right of free speech entitled
Barber to publish it; a larger measure of common-sense would have
made him withhold it. Whether it was the republication of this article
that had stirred up anew the sleeping dogs of race prejudice and whetted their thirst for blood, he could not yet tell; but at any rate, there
was mischief on foot.

"Fer God's sake, doctuh, don' go no closeter ter dat town," pleaded
his informant, "er you 'll be killt sho'. Come on wid us, suh, an' tek
keer er yo'se'f. We 're gwine ter hide in de swamps till dis thing
is over!"

"God, man!" exclaimed Miller, urging his horse forward, "my wife
and child are in the town!"

Fortunately, he reflected, there were no patients confined in the hospital, — if there should be anything in this preposterous story. To one
unfamiliar with Southern life, it might have seemed impossible that
these good Christian people, who thronged the churches on Sunday, and
wept over the sufferings of the lowly Nazarene,[1] and sent missionaries

---

[1] *lowly Nazarene:* The phrase is an allusion to Jesus of Nazareth.

to the heathen, could be hungering and thirsting for the blood of their fellow men; but Miller cherished no such delusion. He knew the history of his country; he had the threatened lynching of Sandy Campbell vividly in mind; and he was fully persuaded that to race prejudice, once aroused, any horror was possible. That women or children would be molested of set purpose he did not believe, but that they might suffer by accident was more than likely.

As he neared the town, dashing forward at the top of his horse's speed, he heard his voice called in a loud and agitated tone, and, glancing around him, saw a familiar form standing by the roadside, gesticulating vehemently.

He drew up the horse with a suddenness that threw the faithful and obedient animal back upon its haunches. The colored lawyer, Watson, came up to the buggy. That he was laboring under great and unusual excitement was quite apparent from his pale face and frightened air.

"What's the matter, Watson?" demanded Miller, hoping now to obtain some reliable information.

"Matter!" exclaimed the other. "Everything 's the matter! The white people are up in arms. They have disarmed the colored people, killing half a dozen in the process, and wounding as many more. They have forced the mayor and aldermen to resign, have formed a provisional city government *à la française,* and have ordered me and half a dozen other fellows to leave town in forty-eight hours, under pain of sudden death. As they seem to mean it, I shall not stay so long. Fortunately my wife and children are away. I knew you were out here, however, and I thought I 'd come out and wait for you, so that we might talk the matter over. I don't imagine they mean you any harm, personally, because you tread on nobody's toes; but you 're too valuable a man for the race to lose, so I thought I 'd give you warning. I shall want to sell you my property, too, at a bargain. For I 'm worth too much to my family to dream of ever attempting to live here again."

"Have you seen anything of my wife and child?" asked Miller, intent upon the danger to which they might be exposed.

"No; I did n't go to the house. I inquired at the drugstore and found out where you had gone. You need n't fear for them, — it is not a war on women and children."

"War of any kind is always hardest on the women and children," returned Miller; "I must hurry on and see that mine are safe."

"They 'll not carry the war so far into Africa as that," returned Watson; "but I never saw anything like it. Yesterday I had a hundred white friends in the town, or thought I had, — men who spoke pleasantly to me on the street, and sometimes gave me their hands to shake.

Not one of them said to me to-day: 'Watson, stay at home this afternoon.' I might have been killed, like any one of half a dozen others who have bit the dust, for any word that one of my 'friends' had said to warn me. When the race cry is started in this neck of the woods, friendship, religion, humanity, reason, all shrivel up like dry leaves in a raging furnace."

The buggy, into which Watson had climbed, was meanwhile rapidly nearing the town.

"I think I 'll leave you here, Miller," said Watson, as they approached the outskirts, "and make my way home by a roundabout path, as I should like to get there unmolested. Home! — a beautiful word that, is n't it, for an exiled wanderer? It might not be well, either, for us to be seen together. If you put the hood of your buggy down, and sit well back in the shadow, you may be able to reach home without interruption; but avoid the main streets. I 'll see you again this evening, if we 're both alive, and I can reach you; for my time is short. A committee are to call in the morning to escort me to the train. I am to be dismissed from the community with public honors."

Watson was climbing down from the buggy, when a small party of men were seen approaching, and big Josh Green, followed by several other resolute-looking colored men, came up and addressed them.

"Dr. Miller," cried Green, "Mr. Watson, — we 're lookin' fer a leader. De w'ite folks are killin' de niggers, an' we ain' gwine ter stan' up an' be shot down like dogs. We 're gwine ter defen' ou' lives, an' we ain' gwine ter run away f'm no place where we 've got a right ter be; an' woe be ter de w'ite man w'at lays han's on us! Dere 's two niggers in dis town ter eve'y w'ite man, an' ef we 've got ter be killt, we 'll take some w'ite folks 'long wid us, ez sho' ez dere 's a God in heaven, — ez I s'pose dere is, dough He mus' be 'sleep, er busy somewhar e'se ter-day. Will you-all come an' lead us?"

"Gentlemen," said Watson, "what is the use? The negroes will not back you up. They have n't the arms, nor the moral courage, nor the leadership."

"We 'll git de arms, an' we 'll git de courage, ef you 'll come an' lead us! We wants leaders, — dat 's w'y we come ter you!"

"What 's the use?" returned Watson despairingly. "The odds are too heavy. I 've been ordered out of town; if I stayed, I 'd be shot on sight, unless I had a body-guard around me."

"We 'll be yo' body-guard!" shouted half a dozen voices.

"And when my body-guard was shot, what then? I have a wife and children. It is my duty to live for them. If I died, I should get no glory and no reward, and my family would be reduced to beggary, — to which they 'll soon be near enough as it is. This affair will blow over in a day or two. The white people will be ashamed of themselves to-morrow, and apprehensive of the consequences for some time to come. Keep quiet, boys, and trust in God. You won't gain anything by resistance."

"'God he'ps dem dat he'ps demselves,'" returned Josh stoutly. "Ef Mr. Watson won't lead us, will you, Dr. Miller?" said the spokesman, turning to the doctor.

For Miller it was an agonizing moment. He was no coward, morally or physically. Every manly instinct urged him to go forward and take up the cause of these leaderless people, and, if need be, to defend their lives and their rights with his own, — but to what end?

"Listen, men," he said. "We would only be throwing our lives away. Suppose we made a determined stand and won a temporary victory. By morning every train, every boat, every road leading into Wellington, would be crowded with white men, — as they probably will be any way, — with arms in their hands, curses on their lips, and vengeance in their hearts. In the minds of those who make and administer the laws, we have no standing in the court of conscience. They would kill us in the fight, or they would hang us afterwards, — one way or another, we should be doomed. I should like to lead you; I should like to arm every colored man in this town, and have them stand firmly in line, not for attack, but for defense; but if I attempted it, and they should stand by me, which is questionable, — for I have met them fleeing from the town, — my life would pay the forfeit. Alive, I may be of some use to you, and you are welcome to my life in that way, — I am giving it freely. Dead, I should be a mere lump of carrion. Who remembers even the names of those who have been done to death in the Southern States for the past twenty years?"

"I 'members de name er one of 'em," said Josh, "an' I 'members de name er de man dat killt 'im, an' I s'pec' his time is mighty nigh come."

"My advice is not heroic, but I think it is wise. In this riot we are placed as we should be in a war: we have no territory, no base of supplies, no organization, no outside sympathy, — we stand in the position of a race, in a case like this, without money and without friends. Our time will come, — the time when we can command respect for our rights; but it is not yet in sight. Give it up, boys, and wait. Good may come of this, after all."

Several of the men wavered, and looked irresolute.

"I reckon that 's all so, doctuh," returned Josh, "an', de way you put it, I don' blame you ner Mr. Watson; but all dem reasons ain' got no weight wid me. I 'm gwine in dat town, an' ef any w'ite man 'sturbs me, dere 'll be trouble, — dere 'll be double trouble, — I feels it in my bones!"

"Remember your old mother, Josh," said Miller.

"Yas, suh, I 'll 'member her; dat 's all I kin do now. I don' need ter wait fer her no mo', fer she died dis mo'nin. I 'd lack ter see her buried, suh, but I may not have de chance. Ef I gits killt, will you do me a favor?"

"Yes, Josh; what is it?"

"Ef I should git laid out in dis commotion dat 's gwine on, will you collec' my wages f'm yo' brother, and see dat de ole 'oman is put away right?"

"Yes, of course."

"Wid a nice coffin, an' a nice fune'al, an' a head-bo'd an' a foot-bo'd?"

"Yes."

"All right, suh! Ef I don' live ter do it, I 'll know it'll be 'tended ter right. Now we 're gwine out ter de cotton compress, an' git a lot er colored men tergether, an' ef de w'ite folks 'sturbs me, I should n't be s'prise' ef dere 'd be a mix-up; — an' ef dere is, me an *one* w'ite man 'll stan' befo' de jedgment th'one er God dis day; an' it won't be me w'at 'll be 'feared er de jedgment. Come along, boys! Dese gentlemen may have somethin' ter live fer; but ez fer my pa't, I 'd ruther be a dead nigger any day dan a live dog!"

XXXIII. INTO THE LION'S JAWS

THE party under Josh's leadership moved off down the road. Miller, while entirely convinced that he had acted wisely in declining to accompany them, was yet conscious of a distinct feeling of shame and envy that he, too, did not feel impelled to throw away his life in a hopeless struggle.

Watson left the buggy and disappeared by a path at the roadside. Miller drove rapidly forward. After entering the town, he passed several small parties of white men, but escaped scrutiny by sitting well back in his buggy, the presumption being that a well-dressed man with a good horse and buggy was white. Torn with anxiety, he reached home at about four o'clock. Driving the horse into the yard, he sprang down from the buggy and hastened to the house, which he found locked, front and rear.

A repeated rapping brought no response. At length he broke a window, and entered the house like a thief.

"Janet, Janet!" he called in alarm, "where are you? It is only I, — Will!"

There was no reply. He ran from room to room, only to find them all empty. Again he called his wife's name, and was about rushing from the house, when a muffled voice came faintly to his ear, —

"Is dat you, Doctuh Miller?"

"Yes. Who are you and where are my wife and child?"

He was looking around in perplexity, when the door of a low closet under the kitchen sink was opened from within, and a woolly head was cautiously protruded.

"Are you *sho'* dat 's you, doctuh?"

"Yes, Sally; where are" —

"An' not some w'ite man come ter bu'n down de house an' kill all de niggers?"

"No, Sally, it 's me all right. Where is my wife? Where is my child?"

"Dey went over ter see Mis' Butler 'long 'bout two o'clock, befo' dis fuss broke out, suh. Oh, Lawdy, Lawdy, suh! Is all de cullud folks be'n killt 'cep'n' me an' you, suh? Fer de Lawd's sake, suh, you won' let 'em kill me, will you, suh? I 'll wuk fer you fer nuthin', suh, all my bawn days, ef you 'll save my life, suh!"

"Calm yourself, Sally. You 'll be safe enough if you stay right here, I 've no doubt. They 'll not harm women, — of that I 'm sure enough, although I have n't yet got the bearings of this deplorable affair. Stay here and look after the house. I must find my wife and child!"

The distance across the city to the home of the Mrs. Butler whom his wife had gone to visit was exactly one mile. Though Miller had a good horse in front of him, he was two hours in reaching his destination. Never will the picture of that ride fade from his memory. In his dreams he repeats it night after night, and sees the sights that wounded his eyes, and feels the thoughts — the haunting spirits of the thoughts — that tore his heart as he rode through hell to find those whom he was seeking.

For a short distance he saw nothing, and made rapid progress. As he turned the first corner, his horse shied at the dead body of a negro, lying huddled up in the collapse which marks sudden death. What Miller shuddered at was not so much the thought of death, to the sight of which his profession had accustomed him, as the suggestion of what it signified. He had taken with allowance the wild statement of the fleeing fugitives. Watson, too, had been greatly excited, and Josh

Green's group were desperate men, as much liable to be misled by their courage as the others by their fears; but here was proof that murder had been done, — and his wife and children were in the town. Distant shouts, and the sound of firearms, increased his alarm. He struck his horse with the whip, and dashed on toward the heart of the city, which he must traverse in order to reach Janet and the child.

At the next corner lay the body of another man, with the red blood oozing from a ghastly wound in the forehead. The negroes seemed to have been killed, as the band plays in circus parades, at the street intersections, where the example would be most effective. Miller, with a wild leap of the heart, had barely passed this gruesome spectacle, when a sharp voice commanded him to halt, and emphasized the order by covering him with a revolver. Forgetting the prudence he had preached to others, he had raised his whip to strike the horse, when several hands seized the bridle.

"Come down, you damn fool," growled an authoritative voice. "Don't you see we 're in earnest? Do you want to get killed?"

"Why should I come down?" asked Miller.

"Because we 've ordered you to come down! This is the white people's day, and when they order, a nigger must obey. We 're going to search you for weapons."

"Search away. You 'll find nothing but a case of surgeon's tools, which I 'm more than likely to need before this day is over, from all indications."

"No matter; we 'll make sure of it! That 's what we 're here for. Come down, if you don't want to be pulled down!"

Miller stepped down from his buggy. His interlocutor, who made no effort at disguise, was a clerk in a dry-goods store where Miller bought most of his family and hospital supplies. He made no sign of recognition, however, and Miller claimed no acquaintance. This man, who had for several years emptied Miller's pockets in the course of more or less legitimate trade, now went through them, aided by another man, more rapidly than ever before, the searchers convincing themselves that Miller carried no deadly weapon upon his person. Meanwhile, a third ransacked the buggy with like result. Miller recognized several others of the party, who made not the slightest attempt at disguise, though no names were called by any one.

"Where are you going?" demanded the leader.

"I am looking for my wife and child," replied Miller.

"Well, run along, and keep them out of the streets when you find them; and keep your hands out of this affair, if you wish to live in this town, which from now on will be a white man's town, as you niggers will be pretty firmly convinced before night."

Miller drove on as swiftly as might be.

At the next corner he was stopped again. In the white man who held him up, Miller recognized a neighbor of his own. After a short detention and a perfunctory search, the white man remarked apologetically: —

"Sorry to have had to trouble you, doctuh, but them 's the o'ders. It ain't men like you that we 're after, but the vicious and criminal class of niggers."

Miller smiled bitterly as he urged his horse forward. He was quite well aware that the virtuous citizen who had stopped him had only a few weeks before finished a term in the penitentiary, to which he had been sentenced for stealing. Miller knew that he could have bought all the man owned for fifty dollars, and his soul for as much more.

A few rods farther on, he came near running over the body of a wounded man who lay groaning by the wayside. Every professional instinct urged him to stop and offer aid to the sufferer; but the uncertainty concerning his wife and child proved a stronger motive and urged him resistlessly forward. Here and there the ominous sound of firearms was audible. He might have thought this merely a part of the show, like the "powder play" of the Arabs, but for the bloody confirmation of its earnestness which had already assailed his vision. Somewhere in this seething cauldron of unrestrained passions were his wife and child, and he must hurry on.

His progress was painfully slow. Three times he was stopped and searched. More than once his way was barred, and he was ordered to turn back, each such occasion requiring a detour which consumed many minutes. The man who last stopped him was a well-known Jewish merchant. A Jew — God of Moses! — had so far forgotten twenty centuries of history as to join in the persecution of another oppressed race! When almost reduced to despair by these innumerable delays, he perceived, coming toward him, Mr. Ellis, the sub-editor of the Morning Chronicle. Miller had just been stopped and questioned again, and Ellis came up as he was starting once more upon his endless ride.

"Dr. Miller," said Ellis kindly, "it is dangerous for you on the streets. Why tempt the danger?"

"I am looking for my wife and child," returned Miller in desperation. "They are somewhere in this town, — I don't know where, — and I must find them."

Ellis had been horror-stricken by the tragedy of the afternoon, the wholly superfluous slaughter of a harmless people, whom a show of force would have been quite sufficient to overawe. Elaborate explanations were afterwards given for these murders, which were said, perhaps truthfully, not to have been premeditated, and many regrets were expressed. The young man had been surprised, quite as much as the negroes themselves, at the ferocity displayed. His own thoughts and feelings were attuned to anything but slaughter. Only that morning he had received a perfumed note, calling his attention to what the writer described as a very noble deed of his, and requesting him to call that evening and receive the writer's thanks. Had he known that Miss Pemberton, several weeks after their visit to the Sound, had driven out again to the hotel and made some inquiries among the servants, he might have understood better the meaning of this missive. When Miller spoke of his wife and child, some subtle thread of suggestion coupled the note with Miller's plight.

"I 'll go with you, Dr. Miller," he said, "if you 'll permit me. In my company you will not be disturbed."

He took a seat in Miller's buggy, after which it was not molested.

Neither of them spoke. Miller was sick at heart; he could have wept with grief, even had the welfare of his own dear ones not been involved in this regrettable affair. With prophetic instinct he foresaw the hatreds to which this day would give birth; the long years of constraint and distrust which would still further widen the breach between two peoples whom fate had thrown together in one community.

There was nothing for Ellis to say. In his heart he could not defend the deeds of this day. The petty annoyances which the whites had felt at the spectacle of a few negroes in office; the not unnatural resentment of a proud people at what had seemed to them a presumptuous freedom of speech and lack of deference on the part of their inferiors, — these things, which he knew were to be made the excuse for overturning the city government, he realized full well were no sort of justification for the wholesale murder or other horrors which might well ensue before the day was done. He could not approve the acts of his own people; neither could he, to a negro, condemn them. Hence he was silent.

"Thank you, Mr. Ellis," exclaimed Miller, when they had reached the house where he expected to find his wife. "This is the place where I was going. I am — under a great obligation to you."

"Not at all, Dr. Miller. I need not tell you how much I regret this deplorable affair."

Ellis went back down the street. Fastening his horse to the fence, Miller sprang forward to find his wife and child. They would certainly be there, for no colored woman would be foolhardy enough to venture on the streets after the riot had broken out.

As he drew nearer, he felt a sudden apprehension. The house seemed strangely silent and deserted. The doors were closed, and the venetian blinds shut tightly. Even a dog which had appeared slunk timidly back under the house, instead of barking vociferously according to the usual habit of his kind.

XXXIV. THE VALLEY OF THE SHADOW [1]

MILLER knocked at the door. There was no response. He went round to the rear of the house. The dog had slunk behind the wood-pile. Miller knocked again, at the back door, and, receiving no reply, called aloud.

"Mrs. Butler! It is I, Dr. Miller. Is my wife here?"

The slates of a near-by blind opened cautiously.

"Is it really you, Dr. Miller?"

"Yes, Mrs. Butler. I am looking for my wife and child, — are they here?"

"No, sir; she became alarmed about you, soon after the shooting commenced, and I could not keep her. She left for home half an hour ago. It is coming on dusk, and she and the child are so near white that she did not expect to be molested."

"Which way did she go?"

"She meant to go by the main street. She thought it would be less dangerous than the back streets. I tried to get her to stay here, but she was frantic about you, and nothing I could say would keep her. Is the riot almost over, Dr. Miller? Do you think they will murder us all, and burn down our houses?"

"God knows," replied Miller, with a groan. "But I must find her, if I lose my own life in the attempt."

Surely, he thought, Janet would be safe. The white people of Wellington were not savages; or at least their temporary reversion to savagery would not go as far as to include violence to delicate women and children. Then there flashed into his mind Josh Green's story of his "silly" mother, who for twenty years had walked the earth as a child, as the result of one night's terror, and his heart sank within him.

---

[1] *The Valley of the Shadow:* From Psalms 23.4. "Yea, though I walk through the valley of the shadow of death, I will fear no evil: for thou art with me; thy rod and thy staff they comfort me."

Miller realized that his buggy, by attracting attention, had been a hindrance rather than a help in his progress across the city. In order to follow his wife, he must practically retrace his steps over the very route he had come. Night was falling. It would be easier to cross the town on foot. In the dusk his own color, slight in the daytime, would not attract attention, and by dodging in the shadows he might avoid those who might wish to intercept him. But he must reach Janet and the boy at any risk. He had not been willing to throw his life away hopelessly, but he would cheerfully have sacrificed it for those whom he loved.

He had gone but a short distance, and had not yet reached the centre of mob activity, when he intercepted a band of negro laborers from the cotton compress, with big Josh Green at their head.

"Hello, doctuh!" cried Josh, "does you wan' ter jine us?"

"I 'm looking for my wife and child, Josh. They 're somewhere in this den of murderers. Have any of you seen them?"

No one had seen them.

"You men are running a great risk," said Miller. "You are rushing on to certain death."

"Well, suh, maybe we is; but we 're gwine ter die fightin'. Dey say de w'ite folks is gwine ter bu'n all de cullud schools an' chu'ches, an' kill all de niggers dey kin ketch. Dey 're gwine ter bu'n yo' new hospittle, ef somebody don' stop 'em."

"Josh — men — you are throwing your lives away. It is a fever; it will wear off to-morrow, or to-night. They 'll not burn the schoolhouses, nor the hospital — they are not such fools, for they benefit the community; and they 'll only kill the colored people who resist them. Every one of you with a gun or a pistol carries his death warrant in his own hand. I 'd rather see the hospital burn than have one of you lose his life. Resistance only makes the matter worse, — the odds against you are too long."

"Things can't be any wuss, doctuh," replied one of the crowd sturdily. "A gun is mo' dange'ous ter de man in front of it dan ter de man behin' it. Dey 're gwine ter kill us anyhow; an' we 're tired, — we read de newspapers, — an' we 're tired er bein' shot down like dogs, widout jedge er jury. We 'd ruther die fightin' dan be stuck like pigs in a pen!"

"God help you!" said Miller. "As for me, I must find my wife and child."

"Good-by, doctuh," cried Josh, brandishing a huge knife. "'Member 'bout de ole 'oman, ef you lives thoo dis. Don' fergit de headbo'd an' de footbo'd, an' a silver plate on de coffin, ef dere 's money ernuff."

They went their way, and Miller hurried on. They might resist attack; he thought it extremely unlikely that they would begin it; but he knew perfectly well that the mere knowledge that some of the negroes contemplated resistance would only further inflame the infuriated whites. The colored men might win a momentary victory, though it was extremely doubtful; and they would as surely reap the harvest later on. The qualities which in a white man would win the applause of the world would in a negro be taken as the marks of savagery. So thoroughly diseased was public opinion in matters of race that the negro who died for the common rights of humanity might look for no meed of admiration or glory. At such a time, in the white man's eyes, a negro's courage would be mere desperation; his love of liberty, a mere animal dislike of restraint. Every finer human instinct would be interpreted in terms of savagery. Or, if forced to admire, they would none the less repress. They would applaud his courage while they stretched his neck, or carried off the fragments of his mangled body as souvenirs, in much the same way that savages preserve the scalps or eat the hearts of their enemies.

But concern for the fate of Josh and his friends occupied only a secondary place in Miller's mind for the moment. His wife and child were somewhere ahead of him. He pushed on. He had covered about a quarter of a mile more, and far down the street could see the signs of greater animation, when he came upon the body of a woman lying upon the sidewalk. In the dusk he had almost stumbled over it, and his heart came up in his mouth. A second glance revealed that it could not be his wife. It was a fearful portent, however, of what her fate might be. The "war" had reached the women and children. Yielding to a professional instinct, he stooped, and saw that the prostrate form was that of old Aunt Jane Letlow. She was not yet quite dead, and as Miller, with a tender touch, placed her head in a more comfortable position, her lips moved with a last lingering flicker of consciousness: —

"Comin', missis, comin'!"

Mammy Jane had gone to join the old mistress upon whose memory her heart was fixed; and yet not all her reverence for her old mistress, nor all her deference to the whites, nor all their friendship for her, had been able to save her from this raging devil of race hatred which momentarily possessed the town.

Perceiving that he could do no good, Miller hastened onward, sick at heart. Whenever he saw a party of white men approaching, — these brave reformers never went singly, — he sought concealment in the shadow of a tree or the shrubbery in some yard until they had passed.

He had covered about two thirds of the distance homeward, when his eyes fell upon a group beneath a lamp-post, at sight of which he turned pale with horror, and rushed forward with a terrible cry.

XXXV. "MINE ENEMY, O MINE ENEMY!"[1]

THE proceedings of the day — planned originally as a "demonstration," dignified subsequently as a "revolution," under any name the culmination of the conspiracy formed by Carteret and his colleagues — had by seven o'clock in the afternoon developed into a murderous riot. Crowds of white men and half-grown boys, drunk with whiskey or with license, raged through the streets, beating, chasing, or killing any negro so unfortunate as to fall into their hands. Why any particular negro was assailed, no one stopped to inquire; it was merely a white mob thirsting for black blood, with no more conscience or discrimination than would be exercised by a wolf in a sheepfold. It was race against race, the whites against the negroes; and it was a one-sided affair, for until Josh Green got together his body of armed men, no effective resistance had been made by any colored person, and the individuals who had been killed had so far left no marks upon the enemy by which they might be remembered.

"Kill the niggers!" rang out now and then through the dusk, and far down the street and along the intersecting thoroughfares distant voices took up the ominous refrain, — "Kill the niggers! Kill the damned niggers!"

Now, not a dark face had been seen on the street for half an hour, until the group of men headed by Josh made their appearance in the negro quarter. Armed with guns and axes, they presented quite a formidable appearance as they made their way toward the new hospital, near which stood a schoolhouse and a large church, both used by the colored people. They did not reach their destination without having met a number of white men, singly or in twos or threes; and the rumor spread with incredible swiftness that the negroes in turn were up in arms, determined to massacre all the whites and burn the town. Some of the whites became alarmed, and recognizing the power of the negroes, if armed and conscious of their strength, were impressed by the immediate necessity of overpowering and overawing them. Others,

---

[1] "*Mine Enemy, O Mine Enemy!*": From an exchange in 1 Kings 21.20. Ahab addresses the prophet Elijah: "Hast thou found me, O mine enemy?" Elijah replies, "I have found thee: because thou hast sold thyself to work evil in the sight of the Lord."

with appetites already whetted by slaughter, saw a chance, welcome rather than not, of shedding more black blood. Spontaneously the white mob flocked toward the hospital, where rumor had it that a large body of desperate negroes, breathing threats of blood and fire, had taken a determined stand.

It had been Josh's plan merely to remain quietly and peaceably in the neighborhood of the little group of public institutions, molesting no one, unless first attacked, and merely letting the white people see that they meant to protect their own; but so rapidly did the rumor spread, and so promptly did the white people act, that by the time Josh and his supporters had reached the top of the rising ground where the hospital stood, a crowd of white men much more numerous than their own party were following them at a short distance.

Josh, with the eye of a general, perceived that some of his party were becoming a little nervous, and decided that they would feel safer behind shelter.

"I reckon we better go inside de hospittle, boys," he exclaimed. "Den we 'll be behind brick walls, an' dem other fellows 'll be outside, an' ef dere 's any fightin' we 'll have de bes' show. We ain' gwine ter do no shootin' till we 're pestered, an' dey 'll be less likely ter pester us ef dey can't git at us widout runnin' some resk. Come along in! Be men! De gov'ner er de President is gwine ter sen' soldiers ter stop dese gwines-on, an' meantime we kin keep dem white devils f'm bu'nin' down our hospittles an' chu'ch-houses. W'en dey comes an' fin's out dat we jes' means ter pertect ou' prope'ty, dey 'll go 'long 'bout deir own business. Er, ef dey wants a scrap, dey kin have it! Come erlong, boys!"

Jerry Letlow, who had kept out of sight during the day, had started out, after night had set in, to find Major Carteret. Jerry was very much afraid. The events of the day had filled him with terror. Whatever the limitations of Jerry's mind or character may have been, Jerry had a keen appreciation of the danger to the negroes when they came in conflict with the whites, and he had no desire to imperil his own skin. He valued his life for his own sake, and not for any altruistic theory that it might be of service to others. In other words, Jerry was something of a coward. He had kept in hiding all day, but finding, toward evening, that the riot did not abate, and fearing, from the rumors which came to his ears, that all the negroes would be exterminated, he had set out, somewhat desperately, to try to find his white patron and protector.

He had been cautious to avoid meeting any white men, and, anticipating no danger from those of his own race, went toward the party which he saw approaching, whose path would cross his own. When they were only a few yards apart, Josh took a step forward and caught Jerry by the arm.

"Come along, Jerry, we need you! Here 's another man, boys. Come on now, and fight fer yo' race!"

In vain Jerry protested. "I don' wan' ter fight," he howled. "De w'ite folks ain' gwine ter pester me; dey 're my frien's. Tu'n me loose, — tu'n me loose, er we all gwine ter git killed!"

The party paid no attention to Jerry's protestations. Indeed, with the crowd of whites following behind, they were simply considering the question of a position from which they could most effectively defend themselves and the building which they imagined to be threatened. If Josh had released his grip of Jerry, that worthy could easily have escaped from the crowd; but Josh maintained his hold almost mechanically, and, in the confusion, Jerry found himself swept with the rest into the hospital, the doors of which were promptly barricaded with the heavier pieces of furniture, and the windows manned by several men each, Josh, with the instinct of a born commander, posting his forces so that they could cover with their guns all the approaches to the building. Jerry still continuing to make himself troublesome, Josh, in a moment of impatience, gave him a terrific box on the ear, which stretched him out upon the floor unconscious.

"Shet up," he said; "ef you can't stan' up like a man, keep still, and don't interfere wid men w'at will fight!"

The hospital, when Josh and his men took possession, had been found deserted. Fortunately there were no patients for that day, except one or two convalescents, and these, with the attendants, had joined the exodus of the colored people from the town.

A white man advanced from the crowd without toward the main entrance to the hospital. Big Josh, looking out from a window, grasped his gun more firmly, as his eyes fell upon the man who had murdered his father and darkened his mother's life. Mechanically he raised his rifle, but lowered it as the white man lifted up his hand as a sign that he wished to speak.

"You niggers," called Captain McBane loudly, — it was that worthy, — "you niggers are courtin' death, an' you won't have to court her but a minute er two mo' befo' she 'll have you. If you surrender and give up your arms, you 'll be dealt with leniently, — you may get off with the chain-gang or the penitentiary. If you resist, you 'll be shot like dogs."

"Dat 's no news, Mr. White Man," replied Josh, appearing boldly at the window. "We 're use' ter bein' treated like dogs by men like you. If you w'ite people will go 'long an' ten' ter yo' own business an' let us alone, we 'll ten' ter ou'n. You 've got guns, an' we 've got jest as much right ter carry 'em as you have. Lay down yo'n, an' we 'll lay down ou'n, — we did n' take 'em up fust; but we ain' gwine ter let you bu'n down ou' chu'ches an' school'ouses, er dis hospittle, an' we ain' comin' out er dis house, where we ain' disturbin' nobody, fer you ter shoot us down er sen' us ter jail. You hear me!"

"All right," responded McBane. "You 've had fair warning. Your blood be on your" —

His speech was interrupted by a shot from the crowd, which splintered the window-casing close to Josh's head. This was followed by half a dozen other shots, which were replied to, almost simultaneously, by a volley from within, by which one of the attacking party was killed and another wounded.

This roused the mob to frenzy.

"Vengeance! vengeance!" they yelled. "Kill the niggers!"

A negro had killed a white man, — the unpardonable sin, admitting neither excuse, justification, nor extenuation. From time immemorial it had been bred in the Southern white consciousness, and in the negro consciousness also, for that matter, that the person of a white man was sacred from the touch of a negro, no matter what the provocation. A dozen colored men lay dead in the streets of Wellington, inoffensive people, slain in cold blood because they had been bold enough to question the authority of those who had assailed them, or frightened enough to flee when they had been ordered to stand still; but their lives counted nothing against that of a riotous white man, who had courted death by attacking a body of armed men.

The crowd, too, surrounding the hospital, had changed somewhat in character. The men who had acted as leaders in the early afternoon, having accomplished their purpose of overturning the local administration and establishing a provisional government of their own, had withdrawn from active participation in the rioting, deeming the negroes already sufficiently overawed to render unlikely any further trouble from that source. Several of the ringleaders had indeed begun to exert themselves to prevent further disorder, or any loss of property, the possibility of which had become apparent; but those who set in motion the forces of evil cannot always control them afterwards. The baser element of the white population, recruited from the wharves and the saloons, was now predominant.

Captain McBane was the only one of the revolutionary committee who had remained with the mob, not with any purpose to restore or preserve order, but because he found the company and the occasion entirely congenial. He had had no opportunity, at least no tenable excuse, to kill or maim a negro since the termination of his contract with the state for convicts, and this occasion had awakened a dormant appetite for these diversions. We are all puppets in the hands of Fate, and seldom see the strings that move us. McBane had lived a life of violence and cruelty. As a man sows, so shall he reap. In works of fiction, such men are sometimes converted. More often, in real life, they do not change their natures until they are converted into dust. One does well to distrust a tamed tiger.

On the outskirts of the crowd a few of the better class, or at least of the better clad, were looking on. The double volley described had already been fired, when the number of these was augmented by the arrival of Major Carteret and Mr. Ellis, who had just come from the Chronicle office, where the next day's paper had been in hasty preparation. They pushed their way towards the front of the crowd.

"This must be stopped, Ellis," said Carteret. "They are burning houses and killing women and children. Old Jane, good old Mammy Jane, who nursed my wife at her bosom, and has waited on her and my child within a few weeks, was killed only a few rods from my house, to which she was evidently fleeing for protection. It must have been by accident, — I cannot believe that any white man in town would be dastard enough to commit such a deed intentionally! I would have defended her with my own life! We must try to stop this thing!"

"Easier said than done," returned Ellis. "It is in the fever stage, and must burn itself out. We shall be lucky if it does not burn the town out. Suppose the negroes should also take a hand at the burning? We have advised the people to put the negroes down, and they are doing the job thoroughly."

"My God!" replied the other, with a gesture of impatience, as he continued to elbow his way through the crowd; "I meant to keep them in their places, — I did not intend wholesale murder and arson."

Carteret, having reached the front of the mob, made an effort to gain their attention.

"Gentlemen!" he cried in his loudest tones. His voice, unfortunately, was neither loud nor piercing.

"Kill the niggers!" clamored the mob.

"Gentlemen, I implore you" —

The crash of a dozen windows, broken by stones and pistol shots, drowned his voice.

"Gentlemen!" he shouted; "this is murder, it is madness; it is a disgrace to our city, to our state, to our civilization!"

"That's right!" replied several voices. The mob had recognized the speaker. "It *is* a disgrace, and we'll not put up with it a moment longer. Burn 'em out! Hurrah for Major Carteret, the champion of 'white supremacy'! Three cheers for the Morning Chronicle and 'no nigger domination'!"

"Hurrah, hurrah, hurrah!" yelled the crowd.

In vain the baffled orator gesticulated and shrieked in the effort to correct the misapprehension. Their oracle had spoken; not hearing what he said, they assumed it to mean encouragement and coöperation. Their present course was but the logical outcome of the crusade which the Morning Chronicle had preached, in season and out of season, for many months. When Carteret had spoken, and the crowd had cheered him, they felt that they had done all that courtesy required, and he was good-naturedly elbowed aside while they proceeded with the work in hand, which was now to drive out the negroes from the hospital and avenge the killing of their comrade.

Some brought hay, some kerosene, and others wood from a pile which had been thrown into a vacant lot nearby. Several safe ways of approach to the building were discovered, and the combustibles placed and fired. The flames, soon gaining a foothold, leaped upward, catching here and there at the exposed woodwork, and licking the walls hungrily with long tongues of flame.

Meanwhile a desultory firing was kept up from the outside, which was replied to scatteringly from within the hospital. Those inside were either not good marksmen, or excitement had spoiled their aim. If a face appeared at a window, a dozen pistol shots from the crowd sought the spot immediately.

Higher and higher leaped the flames. Suddenly from one of the windows sprang a black figure, waving a white handkerchief. It was Jerry Letlow. Regaining consciousness after the effect of Josh's blow had subsided, Jerry had kept quiet and watched his opportunity. From a safe vantage-ground he had scanned the crowd without, in search of some white friend. When he saw Major Carteret moving disconsolately away after his futile effort to stem the torrent, Jerry made a dash for the window. He sprang forth, and, waving his handkerchief as a flag of truce, ran toward Major Carteret, shouting frantically: —

"Majah Carteret — O majah! It 's me, suh, Jerry, suh! I did n' go in dere myse'f, suh, — I wuz drag' in dere! I would n' do nothin' 'g'inst de w'ite folks, suh, — no, 'ndeed, I would n', suh!"

Jerry's cries were drowned in a roar of rage and a volley of shots from the mob. Carteret, who had turned away with Ellis, did not even hear his servant's voice. Jerry's poor flag of truce, his explanations, his reliance upon his white friends, all failed him in the moment of supreme need. In that hour, as in any hour when the depths of race hatred are stirred, a negro was no more than a brute beast, set upon by other brute beasts whose only instinct was to kill and destroy.

"Let us leave this inferno, Ellis," said Carteret, sick with anger and disgust. He had just become aware that a negro was being killed, though he did not know whom. "We can do nothing. The negroes have themselves to blame, — they tempted us beyond endurance. I counseled firmness, and firm measures were taken, and our purpose was accomplished. I am not responsible for these subsequent horrors, — I wash my hands of them. Let us go!"

The flames gained headway and gradually enveloped the burning building, until it became evident to those within as well as those without that the position of the defenders was no longer tenable. Would they die in the flames, or would they be driven out? The uncertainty soon came to an end.

The besieged had been willing to fight, so long as there seemed a hope of successfully defending themselves and their property; for their purpose was purely one of defense. When they saw the case was hopeless, inspired by Josh Green's reckless courage, they were still willing to sell their lives dearly. One or two of them had already been killed, and as many more disabled. The fate of Jerry Letlow had struck terror to the hearts of several others, who could scarcely hide their fear. After the building had been fired, Josh's exhortations were no longer able to keep them in the hospital. They preferred to fight and be killed in the open, rather than to be smothered like rats in a hole.

"Boys!" exclaimed Josh, — "men! — fer nobody but men would do w'at you have done, — the day has gone 'g'inst us. We kin see ou' finish; but fer my part, I ain' gwine ter leave dis worl' widout takin' a w'ite man 'long wid me, an' I sees my man right out yonder waitin', — I be'n waitin' fer him twenty years, but he won' have ter wait fer me mo' 'n 'bout twenty seconds. Eve'y one er you pick yo' man! We 'll open de do', an' we 'll give some w'ite men a chance ter be sorry dey ever started dis fuss!"

The door was thrown open suddenly, and through it rushed a dozen or more black figures, armed with knives, pistols, or clubbed muskets. Taken by sudden surprise, the white people stood motionless for a moment, but the approaching negroes had scarcely covered half the distance to which the heat of the flames had driven back the mob, before they were greeted with a volley that laid them all low but two. One of these, dazed by the fate of his companions, turned instinctively to flee, but had scarcely faced around before he fell, pierced in the back by a dozen bullets.

Josh Green, the tallest and biggest of them all, had not apparently been touched. Some of the crowd paused in involuntary admiration of this black giant, famed on the wharves for his strength, sweeping down upon them, a smile upon his face, his eyes lit up with a rapt expression which seemed to take him out of mortal ken. This impression was heightened by his apparent immunity from the shower of lead which less susceptible persons had continued to pour at him.

Armed with a huge bowie-knife, a relic of the civil war, which he had carried on his person for many years for a definite purpose, and which he had kept sharpened to a razor edge, he reached the line of the crowd. All but the bravest shrank back. Like a wedge he dashed through the mob, which parted instinctively before him, and all oblivious of the rain of lead which fell around him, reached the point where Captain McBane, the bravest man in the party, stood waiting to meet him. A pistol-flame flashed in his face, but he went on, and raising his powerful right arm, buried his knife to the hilt in the heart of his enemy. When the crowd dashed forward to wreak vengeance on his dead body, they found him with a smile still upon his face.

One of the two died as the fool dieth.[2] Which was it, or was it both? "Vengeance is mine," saith the Lord, and it had not been left to Him. But they that do violence must expect to suffer violence. McBane's death was merciful, compared with the nameless horrors he had heaped upon the hundreds of helpless mortals who had fallen into his hands during his career as a contractor of convict labor.

Sobered by this culminating tragedy, the mob shortly afterwards dispersed. The flames soon completed their work, and this handsome structure, the fruit of old Adam Miller's industry, the monument of his son's philanthropy, a promise of good things for the future of the city, lay smouldering in ruins, a melancholy witness to the fact that our boasted civilization is but a thin veneer, which cracks and scales off at the first impact of primal passions.

---

[2] *the fool dieth:* Eccles. 2.16. "And how dieth the wise man? as the fool."

XXXVI. FIAT JUSTITIA[1]

By the light of the burning building, which illuminated the street for several blocks, Major Carteret and Ellis made their way rapidly until they reached into the street where the major lived. Reaching the house, Carteret tried the door and found it locked. A vigorous ring at the bell brought no immediate response. Carteret had begun to pound impatiently upon the door, when it was cautiously opened by Miss Pemberton, who was pale, and trembled with excitement.

"Where is Olivia?" asked the major.

"She is upstairs, with Dodie and Mrs. Albright's hospital nurse. Dodie has the croup. Virgie ran away after the riot broke out. Sister Olivia had sent for Mammy Jane, but she did not come. Mrs. Albright let her white nurse come over."

"I 'll go up at once," said the major anxiously. "Wait for me, Ellis, — I 'll be down in a few minutes.

"Oh, Mr. Ellis," exclaimed Clara, coming toward him with both hands extended, "can nothing be done to stop this terrible affair?"

"I wish I could do something," he murmured fervently, taking both her trembling hands in his own broad palms, where they rested with a surrendering trustfulness which he has never since had occasion to doubt. "It has gone too far, already, and the end, I fear, is not yet; but it cannot grow much worse."

The editor hurried upstairs. Mrs. Carteret, wearing a worried and haggard look, met him at the threshold of the nursery.

"Dodie is ill," she said. "At three o'clock, when the trouble began, I was over at Mrs. Albright's, — I had left Virgie with the baby. When I came back, she and all the other servants had gone. They had heard that the white people were going to kill all the negroes, and fled to seek safety. I found Dodie lying in a draught, before an open window, gasping for breath. I ran back to Mrs. Albright's — I had found her much better to-day, — and she let her nurse come over. The nurse says that Dodie is threatened with membranous croup."

"Have you sent for Dr. Price?"

"There was no one to send, — the servants were gone, and the nurse was afraid to venture out into the street. I telephoned for Dr. Price, and found that he was out of town; that he had gone up the river this morning to attend a patient, and would not be back until to-morrow. Mrs. Price thought that he had anticipated some kind of

---

[1] *Fiat Justitia:* "Let justice be done."

trouble in the town to-day, and had preferred to be where he could not be called upon to assume any responsibility."

"I suppose you tried Dr. Ashe?"

"I could not get him, nor any one else, after that first call. The telephone service is disorganized on account of the riot. We need medicine and ice. The drugstores are all closed on account of the riot, and for the same reason we could n't get any ice."

Major Carteret stood beside the brass bedstead upon which his child was lying, — his only child, around whose curly head clustered all his hopes; upon whom all his life for the past year had been centred. He stooped over the bed, beside which the nurse had stationed herself. She was wiping the child's face, which was red and swollen and covered with moisture, the nostrils working rapidly, and the little patient vainly endeavoring at intervals to cough up the obstruction to his breathing.

"Is it serious?" he inquired anxiously. He had always thought of the croup as a childish ailment, that yielded readily to proper treatment; but the child's evident distress impressed him with sudden fear.

"Dangerous," replied the young woman laconically. "You came none too soon. If a doctor is n't got at once, the child will die, — and it must be a good doctor."

"Whom can I call?" he asked. "You know them all, I suppose. Dr. Price, our family physician, is out of town."

"Dr. Ashe has charge of his cases when he is away," replied the nurse. "If you can't find him, try Dr. Hooper. The child is growing worse every minute. On your way back you 'd better get some ice, if possible."

The major hastened downstairs.

"Don't wait for me, Ellis," he said. "I shall be needed here for a while. I 'll get to the office as soon as possible. Make up the paper, and leave another stick out for me to the last minute, but fill it up in case I 'm not on hand by twelve. We must get the paper out early in the morning."

Nothing but a matter of the most vital importance would have kept Major Carteret away from his office this night. Upon the presentation to the outer world of the story of this riot would depend the attitude of the great civilized public toward the events of the last ten hours. The Chronicle was the source from which the first word would be expected; it would give the people of Wellington their cue as to the position which they must take in regard to this distressful affair, which had so far transcended in ferocity the most extreme measures which the conspirators had anticipated. The burden of his own responsibility weighed heavily upon him, and could not be shaken off; but he must do first the duty nearest to him, — he must first attend to his child.

Carteret hastened from the house, and traversed rapidly the short distance to Dr. Ashe's office. Far down the street he could see the glow of the burning hospital, and he had scarcely left his own house when the fusillade of shots, fired when the colored men emerged from the burning building, was audible. Carteret would have hastened back to the scene of the riot, to see what was now going on, and to make another effort to stem the tide of bloodshed; but before the dread of losing his child, all other interests fell into the background. Not all the negroes in Wellington could weigh in the balance for one instant against the life of the feeble child now gasping for breath in the house behind him.

Reaching the house, a vigorous ring brought the doctor's wife to the door.

"Good-evening, Mrs. Ashe. Is the doctor at home?"

"No, Major Carteret. He was called to attend Mrs. Wells, who was taken suddenly ill, as a result of the trouble this afternoon. He will be there all night, no doubt."

"My child is very ill, and I must find some one."

"Try Dr. Yates. His house is only four doors away."

A ring at Dr. Yates's door brought out a young man.

"Is Dr. Yates in?"

"Yes, sir."

"Can I see him?"

"You might see him, sir, but that would be all. His horse was frightened by the shooting on the streets, and ran away and threw the doctor, and broke his right arm. I have just set it; he will not be able to attend any patients for several weeks. He is old and nervous, and the shock was great."

"Are you not a physician?" asked Carteret, looking at the young man keenly. He was a serious, gentlemanly looking young fellow, whose word might probably be trusted.

"Yes, I am Dr. Evans, Dr. Yates's assistant. I 'm really little more than a student, but I 'll do what I can."

"My only child is sick with the croup, and requires immediate attention."

"I ought to be able to handle a case of the croup," answered Dr. Evans, "at least in the first stages. I 'll go with you, and stay by the child, and if the case is beyond me, I may keep it in check until another physician comes."

He stepped back into another room, and returning immediately with his hat, accompanied Carteret homeward. The riot had subsided; even the glow from the smouldering hospital was no longer visible. It seemed that the city, appalled at the tragedy, had suddenly awakened to a sense of its own crime. Here and there a dark face, emerging cautiously from some hiding-place, peered from behind fence or tree, but shrank hastily away at the sight of a white face. The negroes of Wellington, with the exception of Josh Green and his party, had not behaved bravely on this critical day in their history; but those who had fought were dead, to the last man; those who had sought safety in flight or concealment were alive to tell the tale.

"We pass right by Dr. Thompson's," said Dr. Evans. "If you have n't spoken to him, it might be well to call him for consultation, in case the child should be very bad."

"Go on ahead," said Carteret, "and I 'll get him."

Evans hastened on, while Carteret sounded the old-fashioned knocker upon the doctor's door. A gray-haired negro servant, clad in a dress suit and wearing a white tie, came to the door.

"De doctuh, suh," he replied politely to Carteret's question, "has gone ter ampitate de ahm er a gent'eman who got one er his bones smashed wid a pistol bullet in de — fightin' dis atternoon, suh. He's jes' gone, suh, an' lef' wo'd dat he 'd be gone a' hour er mo', suh."

Carteret hastened homeward. He could think of no other available physician. Perhaps no other would be needed, but if so, he could find out from Evans whom it was best to call.

When he reached the child's room, the young doctor was bending anxiously over the little frame. The little lips had become livid, the little nails, lying against the white sheet, were blue. The child's efforts to breathe were most distressing, and each gasp cut the father like a knife. Mrs. Carteret was weeping hysterically.

"How is he, doctor?" asked the major.

"He is very low," replied the young man. "Nothing short of tracheotomy — an operation to open the windpipe — will relieve him. Without it, in half or three quarters of an hour he will be unable to breathe. It is a delicate operation, a mistake in which would be as fatal as the disease. I have neither the knowledge nor the experience to attempt it, and your child's life is too valuable for a student to practice upon. Neither have I the instruments here."

"What shall we do?" demanded Carteret. "We have called all the best doctors, and none are available."

The young doctor's brow was wrinkled with thought. He knew a doctor who could perform the operation. He had heard, also, of a certain event at Carteret's house some months before, when an unwelcome physician had been excluded from a consultation, — but it was the last chance.

"There is but one other doctor in town who has performed the operation, so far as I know," he declared, "and that is Dr. Miller. If you can get him, he can save your child's life."

Carteret hesitated involuntarily. All the incidents, all the arguments, of the occasion when he had refused to admit the colored doctor to his house, came up vividly before his memory. He had acted in accordance with his lifelong beliefs, and had carried his point; but the present situation was different, — this was a case of imperative necessity, and every other interest or consideration must give way before the imminence of his child's peril. That the doctor would refuse the call, he did not imagine: it would be too great an honor for a negro to decline, — unless some bitterness might have grown out of the proceedings of the afternoon. That this doctor was a man of some education he knew; and he had been told that he was a man of fine feeling, — for a negro, — and might easily have taken to heart the day's events. Nevertheless, he could hardly refuse a professional call, — professional ethics would require him to respond. Carteret had no reason to suppose that Miller had ever learned of what had occurred at the house during Dr. Burns's visit to Wellington. The major himself had never mentioned the controversy, and no doubt the other gentlemen had been equally silent.

"I 'll go for him myself," said Dr. Evans, noting Carteret's hesitation and suspecting its cause. "I can do nothing here alone, for a little while, and I may be able to bring the doctor back with me. He likes a difficult operation."

It seemed an age ere the young doctor returned, though it was really only a few minutes. The nurse did what she could to relieve the child's sufferings, which grew visibly more and more acute. The mother, upon the other side of the bed, held one of the baby's hands in her own, and controlled her feelings as best she might. Carteret paced the floor anxiously, going every few seconds to the head of the stairs to listen for Evans's footsteps on the piazza without. At last the welcome sound was audible, and a few strides took him to the door.

"Dr. Miller is at home, sir," reported Evans, as he came in. "He says that he was called to your house once before, by a third person who claimed authority to act, and that he was refused admittance. He declares that he will not consider such a call unless it come from you personally."

"That is true, quite true," replied Carteret. "His position is a just one. I will go at once. Will — will — my child live until I can get Miller here?"

"He can live for half an hour without an operation. Beyond that I could give you little hope."

Seizing his hat, Carteret dashed out of the yard and ran rapidly to Miller's house; ordinarily a walk of six or seven minutes, Carteret covered it in three, and was almost out of breath when he rang the bell of Miller's front door.

The ring was answered by the doctor in person.

"Dr. Miller, I believe?" asked Carteret.

"Yes, sir."

"I am Major Carteret. My child is seriously ill, and you are the only available doctor who can perform the necessary operation."

"Ah! You have tried all the others, — and then you come to me!"

"Yes, I do not deny it," admitted the major, biting his lip. He had not counted on professional jealousy as an obstacle to be met. "But I *have* come to you, as a physician, to engage your professional services for my child, — my only child. I have confidence in your skill, or I should not have come to you. I request — nay, I implore you to lose no more time, but come with me at once! My child's life is hanging by a thread, and you can save it!"

"Ah!" replied the other, "as a father whose only child's life is in danger, you implore *me,* of all men in the world, to come and save it!"

There was a strained intensity in the doctor's low voice that struck Carteret, in spite of his own preoccupation. He thought he heard, too, from the adjoining room, the sound of some one sobbing softly. There was some mystery here which he could not fathom unaided.

Miller turned to the door behind him and threw it open. On the white cover of a low cot lay a childish form in the rigidity of death, and by it knelt, with her back to the door, a woman whose shoulders were shaken by the violence of her sobs. Absorbed in her grief, she did not turn, or give any sign that she had recognized the intrusion.

"There, Major Carteret!" exclaimed Miller, with the tragic eloquence of despair, "there lies a specimen of your handiwork! There lies *my* only child, laid low by a stray bullet in this riot which you and your paper have fomented; struck down as much by your hand as though you had held the weapon with which his life was taken!"

"My God!" exclaimed Carteret, struck with horror. "Is the child dead?"

"There he lies," continued the other, "an innocent child, — there he lies dead, his little life snuffed out like a candle, because you and a handful of your friends thought you must override the laws and run this town at any cost! — and there kneels his mother, overcome by grief. We are alone in the house. It is not safe to leave her unattended. My duty calls me here, by the side of my dead child and my suffering wife! I cannot go with you. There is a just God in heaven! — as you have sown, so may you reap!"[2]

Carteret possessed a narrow, but a logical mind, and except when confused or blinded by his prejudices, had always tried to be a just man. In the agony of his own predicament, — in the horror of the situation at Miller's house, — for a moment the veil of race prejudice was rent in twain, and he saw things as they were, in their correct proportions and relations, — saw clearly and convincingly that he had no standing here, in the presence of death, in the home of this stricken family. Miller's refusal to go with him was pure, elemental justice; he could not blame the doctor for his stand. He was indeed conscious of a certain involuntary admiration for a man who held in his hands the power of life and death, and could use it, with strict justice, to avenge his own wrongs. In Dr. Miller's place he would have done the same thing. Miller had spoken the truth, — as he had sown, so must he reap! He could not expect, could not ask, this father to leave his own household at such a moment.

Pressing his lips together with grim courage, and bowing mechanically, as though to Fate rather than the physician, Carteret turned and left the house. At a rapid pace he soon reached home. There was yet a chance for his child: perhaps some one of the other doctors had come; perhaps, after all, the disease had taken a favorable turn, — Evans was but a young doctor, and might have been mistaken. Surely, with doctors all around him, his child would not be permitted to die for lack of medical attention! He found the mother, the doctor, and the nurse still grouped, as he had left them, around the suffering child.

"How is he now?" he asked, in a voice that sounded like a groan.

"No better," replied the doctor; "steadily growing worse. He can go on probably for twenty minutes longer without an operation."

---

[2] *as you have sown, so may you reap!*: Gal. 6.7. "Be not deceived; God is not mocked: for whatsoever a man soweth, that shall he also reap."

"Where is the doctor?" demanded Mrs. Carteret, looking eagerly toward the door. "You should have brought him right upstairs. There 's not a minute to spare! Phil, Phil, our child will die!"

Carteret's heart swelled almost to bursting with an intense pity. Even his own great sorrow became of secondary importance beside the grief which his wife must soon feel at the inevitable loss of her only child. And it was his fault! Would that he could risk his own life to spare her and to save the child!

Briefly, and as gently as might be, he stated the result of his errand. The doctor had refused to come, for a good reason. He could not ask him again.

Young Evans felt the logic of the situation, which Carteret had explained sufficiently. To the nurse it was even clearer. If she or any other woman had been in the doctor's place, she would have given the same answer.

Mrs. Carteret did not stop to reason. In such a crisis a mother's heart usurps the place of intellect. For her, at that moment, there were but two facts in all the world. Her child lay dying. There was within the town, and within reach, a man who could save him. With an agonized cry she rushed wildly from the room.

Carteret sought to follow her, but she flew down the long stairs like a wild thing. The least misstep might have precipitated her to the bottom; but ere Carteret, with a remonstrance on his lips, had scarcely reached the uppermost step, she had thrown open the front door and fled precipitately out into the night.

XXXVII. THE SISTERS

Miller's doorbell rang loudly, insistently, as though demanding a response. Absorbed in his own grief, into which he had relapsed upon Carteret's departure, the sound was an unwelcome intrusion. Surely the man could not be coming back! If it were some one else — What else might happen to the doomed town concerned him not. His child was dead, — his distracted wife could not be left alone.

The doorbell rang — clamorously — appealingly. Through the long hall and the closed door of the room where he sat, he could hear some one knocking, and a faint voice calling.

"Open, for God's sake, open!"

It was a woman's voice, — the voice of a woman in distress. Slowly Miller rose and went to the door, which he opened mechanically.

A lady stood there, so near the image of his own wife, whom he had just left, that for a moment he was well-nigh startled. A little older, perhaps, a little fairer of complexion, but with the same form, the same features, marked by the same wild grief. She wore a loose wrapper, which clothed her like the drapery of a statue. Her long dark hair, the counterpart of his wife's, had fallen down, and hung disheveled about her shoulders. There was blood upon her knuckles, where she had beaten with them upon the door.

"Dr. Miller," she panted, breathless from her flight and laying her hand upon his arm appealingly, — when he shrank from the contact she still held it there, — "Dr. Miller, you will come and save my child? You know what it is to lose a child! I am so sorry about your little boy! You will come to mine!"

"Your sorrow comes too late, madam," he said harshly. "My child is dead. I charged your husband with his murder, and he could not deny it. Why should I save your husband's child?"

"Ah, Dr. Miller!" she cried, with his wife's voice, — she never knew how much, in that dark hour, she owed to that resemblance — "it is *my* child, and I have never injured you. It is my child, Dr. Miller, my only child. I brought it into the world at the risk of my own life! I have nursed it, I have watched over it, I have prayed for it, — and it now lies dying! Oh, Dr. Miller, dear Dr. Miller, if you have a heart, come and save my child!"

"Madam," he answered more gently, moved in spite of himself, "my heart is broken. My people lie dead upon the streets, at the hands of yours. The work of my life is in ashes, — and, yonder, stretched out in death, lies my own child! God! woman, you ask too much of human nature! Love, duty, sorrow, *justice,* call me here. I cannot go!"

She rose to her full height. "Then you are a murderer," she cried wildly. "His blood be on your head, and a mother's curse beside!"

The next moment, with a sudden revulsion of feeling, she had thrown herself at his feet, — at the feet of a negro, this proud white woman, — and was clasping his knees wildly.

"O God!" she prayed, in tones which quivered with anguish, "pardon my husband's sins, and my own, and move this man's hard heart, by the blood of thy Son, who died to save us all!"

It was the last appeal of poor humanity. When the pride of intellect and caste is broken; when we grovel in the dust of humiliation; when sickness and sorrow come, and the shadow of death falls upon us, and there is no hope elsewhere, — we turn to God, who sometimes swallows the insult, and answers the appeal.

Miller raised the lady to her feet. He had been deeply moved, — but he had been more deeply injured. This was his wife's sister, — ah, yes! but a sister who had scorned and slighted and ignored the existence of his wife for all her life. Only Miller, of all the world, could have guessed what this had meant to Janet, and he had merely divined it through the clairvoyant sympathy of love. This woman could have no claim upon him because of this unacknowledged relationship. Yet, after all, she *was* his wife's sister, his child's kinswoman. She was a fellow creature, too, and in distress.

"Rise, madam," he said, with a sudden inspiration, lifting her gently. "I will listen to you on one condition. My child lies dead in the adjoining room, his mother by his side. Go in there, and make your request of her. I will abide by her decision."

The two women stood confronting each other across the body of the dead child, mute witness of this first meeting between two children of the same father. Standing thus face to face, each under the stress of the deepest emotions, the resemblance between them was even more striking than it had seemed to Miller when he had admitted Mr. Carteret to the house. But Death, the great leveler, striking upon the one hand and threatening upon the other, had wrought a marvelous transformation in the bearing of the two women. The sad-eyed Janet towered erect, with menacing aspect, like an avenging goddess. The other, whose pride had been her life, stood in the attitude of a trembling supplicant.

"*You* have come here," cried Janet, pointing with a tragic gesture to the dead child, — "*you*, to gloat over your husband's work. All my life you have hated and scorned and despised me. Your presence here insults me and my dead. What are you doing here?"

"Mrs. Miller," returned Mrs. Carteret tremulously, dazed for a moment by this outburst, and clasping her hands with an imploring gesture, "my child, my only child, is dying, and your husband alone can save his life. Ah, let me have my child," she moaned, heart-rendingly. "It is my only one — my sweet child — my ewe lamb!"

"This was *my* only child!" replied the other mother; "and yours is no better to die than mine!"

"You are young," said Mrs. Carteret, "and may yet have many children, — this is my only hope! If you have a human heart, tell your husband to come with me. He leaves it to you; he will do as you command."

"Ah," cried Janet, "I have a human heart, and therefore I will not let him go. *My* child is dead — O God, my child, my child!"

She threw herself down by the bedside, sobbing hysterically. The other woman knelt beside her, and put her arm about her neck. For a moment Janet, absorbed in her grief, did not repulse her.

"Listen," pleaded Mrs. Carteret. "You will not let my baby die! You are my sister; — the child is your own near kin!"

"My child was nearer," returned Janet, rising again to her feet and shaking off the other woman's arm. "He was my son, and I have seen him die. I have been your sister for twenty-five years, and you have only now, for the first time, called me so!"

"Listen — sister," returned Mrs. Carteret. Was there no way to move this woman? Her child lay dying, if he were not dead already. She would tell everything, and leave the rest to God. If it would save her child, she would shrink at no sacrifice. Whether the truth would still further incense Janet, or move her to mercy, she could not tell; she would leave the issue to God.

"Listen, sister!" she said. "I have a confession to make. You *are* my lawful sister. My father was married to your mother. You are entitled to his name, and to half his estate."

Janet's eyes flashed with bitter scorn.

"And you have robbed me all these years, and now tell me that as a reason why I should forgive the murder of my child?"

"No, no," cried the other wildly, fearing the worst. "I have known of it only a few weeks, — since my Aunt Polly's death. I had not meant to rob you, — I had meant to make restitution. Sister! for our father's sake, who did you no wrong, give me my child's life!"

Janet's eyes slowly filled with tears — bitter tears — burning tears. For a moment even her grief at her child's loss dropped to second place in her thoughts. This, then, was the recognition for which, all her life, she had longed in secret. It had come, after many days, and in larger measure than she had dreamed; but it had come, not with frank kindliness and sisterly love, but in a storm of blood and tears; not freely given, from an open heart, but extorted from a reluctant conscience by the agony of a mother's fears. Janet had obtained her heart's desire, and now that it was at her lips, found it but apples of Sodom, filled with dust and ashes!

"Listen!" she cried, dashing her tears aside. "I have but one word for you, — one last word, — and then I hope never to see your face again! My mother died of want, and I was brought up by the hand of charity. Now, when I have married a man who can supply my needs, you offer me back the money which you and your friends have robbed me of! You imagined that the shame of being a negro swallowed up every other ignominy, — and in your eyes I am a negro, though I am your sister, and you are white, and people have taken me for you on the streets, — and you, therefore, left me nameless all my life! Now, when an honest man has given me a name of which I can be proud, you offer me the one of which you robbed me, and of which I can make no use. For twenty-five years I, poor, despicable fool, would have kissed your feet for a word, a nod, a smile. Now, when this tardy recognition comes, for which I have waited so long, it is tainted with fraud and crime and blood, and I must pay for it with my child's life!"

"And I must forfeit that of mine, it seems, for withholding it so long," sobbed the other, as, tottering, she turned to go. "It is but just."

"Stay — do not go yet!" commanded Janet imperiously, her pride still keeping back her tears. "I have not done. I throw you back your father's name, your father's wealth, your sisterly recognition. I want none of them, — they are bought too dear! ah, God, they are bought too dear! But that you may know that a woman may be foully wronged, and yet may have a heart to feel, even for one who has injured her, you may have your child's life, if my husband can save it! Will," she said, throwing open the door into the next room, "go with her!"

"God will bless you for a noble woman!" exclaimed Mrs. Carteret. "You do not mean all the cruel things you have said, — ah no! I will see you again, and make you take them back; I cannot thank you now! Oh, doctor, let us go! I pray God we may not be too late!"

Together they went out into the night. Mrs. Carteret tottered under the stress of her emotions, and would have fallen, had not Miller caught and sustained her with his arm until they reached the house, where he turned over her fainting form to Carteret at the door.

"Is the child still alive?" asked Miller.

"Yes, thank God," answered the father, "but nearly gone."

"Come on up, Dr. Miller," called Evans from the head of the stairs. "There 's time enough, but none to spare."

Part Two

The Marrow of Tradition
Cultural Contexts

1

Caste, Race, and Gender
after Reconstruction

In newspaper accounts and personal statements describing the Wilmington race riot of 1898, white supremacists repeatedly claimed that they were fighting a race "war" for white freedom against black "domination." This interpretation of events appeared to pit a homogeneous white community united in the protection of home and hearth against an equally homogeneous group of barbaric blacks. In direct contrast to this reading of the southern state of affairs, Chesnutt's *The Marrow of Tradition* presents a cast of characters that are anything but unified on either side of the color line. While McBane and Ellis are privileged because of their racial status as white men, their class origins mark them as inferior in the eyes of the novel's blue-blooded Carterets and Delameres. And even among the members of these two southern aristocratic white families, the variety of opinions about race, honor, and morality makes it impossible to classify them as a solid social group. The same is true of the novel's black characters. Though all are equally vulnerable to white violence, Sandy, Mammy Jane, Jerry, Josh Green, Janet, and Dr. Miller mirror the array of class and color divisions that defined turn-of-the-century black America.

Chesnutt's *The Marrow of Tradition* challenges readers to think in complicated ways about the densely structured social relations behind popular terms such as "white men" or the southern "black belt" or "the Negro problem." As represented by Chesnutt, the deep rifts in turn-of-the-century U.S. society ensured that questions of race intersected with conditions of classed and gendered experience, and that one's place of birth (North or South? The United States or Europe?) was almost as important as one's skin color. Certainly, by the end of the nineteenth century the hysteria about race had created massive support for the eugenics movement. Numerous books, tracts, treatises, and organizations devoted to eugenics revealed a white obsession with racial "purity," as Americans fretted about preserving the "best" racial traits the nation had to offer. However, this seeming centrality of "race" belies a number of other issues that existed beyond the presumed threat of African Americans. If white supremacists were complaining of alleged negro domination, most white Americans were hotly debating the question of whether or not white women should raise large families in order to preserve the "future" of the race. If white supremacists were fearful of blacks invading their social space, white Americans in general were equally fearful that recently arrived European immigrants, with their various languages, religious practices, foods, and social customs, would destroy any hope of a "characteristic" American identity. While there were concerns about the safety of white women around black men, there were just as many concerns about the restless urban white working class, as well as rural farmers, many of whom turned to political agitation and even open violence to protest the sharp divide between rich and poor. If these issues generated powerful social anxieties similar and related to the anxiety over race, then by 1900 race itself was merely one of many factors shaping national attitudes. By the turn of the century, discussions of race had contributed a vocabulary for — and were also shaped by — other discussions of difference emerging from class, gender, and white ethnic antagonism. As represented in the following selections, this vocabulary suggests that even though white supremacists argued that race marked an unbridgeable biological gulf between all blacks and all whites, the American public's actual understanding of race was fluid and flexible enough to accommodate other perceptions of difference within their experience of daily life.

The excerpt from Philip A. Bruce's 1889 *The Plantation Negro as a Freeman* typifies the openly hostile opinions on black family life, morality, and masculinity that formed the basis of white supremacist philosophy at the end of the nineteenth century. Claiming that "the sphere in which the negroes move socially is as wide apart from that . . . of the whites . . . as if the two races inhabited different countries," Bruce celebrates what he sees as a natural white "instinct" for racial separation, suggesting that any other attitude would "be considered as heinous as defending incest and rape" (see p. 257 in this volume). His characterization is particularly instructive: the white supremacists' metaphoric use of sexual assault to refer to what were essentially social and political relations shaped a public image of African American men as ultra-aggressive and out of control, driven by wild passions to brutalize law-abiding whites who only wanted to protect their domestic interests. Ironically, the rise of white supremacist violence meant that black men were the ones more likely to be struggling to protect their women and children from barbaric mobs. The work of scholars such as Bruce allowed violent whites to convince themselves that they were not victimizing innocent black citizens.

Still, some Anglo-Americans did argue for a different reading of the dangers and pressures within American society. In the 1890s the southern lawyer Thomas E. Watson emerged as a charismatic leader of Populism, a short-lived political faction made up of economically dispossessed whites. It was the Populist Party's "fusion" with black and white Republicans in the 1896 election in North Carolina that enabled the appointment of both a Republican governor in the state and black congressmen in Washington. (This "fusion" also aided blacks in gaining a measure of political power in the city of Wilmington, thereby provoking the white supremacist backlash that eventually resulted in the 1898 race riot.) The excerpt included from Watson's 1892 "The Negro Question in the South" argues that the divisive cry of "Negro domination" pit poor farmers of both races against one another. The Populist Party, according to Watson, urged black and white farmers to see that " '[y]ou are kept apart that you may be separately fleeced of your earnings' " and " '[y]ou are deceived and blinded that you may not see how this race antagonism perpetuates a monetary system which beggars both' " (p. 267). As historian Michael Honey describes it, once whites refocused on class differences, race ceased to be "a biological phenomenon" and instead emerged "as a historical creation rooted in the division of labor and wealth" (179).

A sense of commonality, one that implied familiarity rather than racial separation, is evident as well in the selection from William Dean Howells's 1892 novel *An Imperative Duty*. Originally serialized in the magazine *Harper's Monthly*, the novel tells the story of a white man who marries a black woman. What is useful for our purposes is the way Howells articulates a problack stance by making a third entity, Irish immigrants, the real pariahs of American society. In the serialized version of the novel the white hero Olney is revolted by what Howells describes as the "simian" or apelike features of the newly arrived Irish.

Olney observes that immigrants can achieve whiteness after "purification" over several generations. This intertwined language of racial stereotype and eugenics bears out historian David Roediger's observation that even among Americans of European descent "ethnicity . . . [was] one thing . . . and whiteness quite another" (183). Howells's language reveals clearly how rhetoric usually associated with race relations could also effortlessly be pressed into service to describe other "alien" groups when the need arose.

The simultaneous existence and infusion of white supremacist beliefs into broader nineteenth-century analyses of social difference generated contradictory moments in many of the statements on race, class, and gender uttered by politicians, writers, and activists of the period. This is why in his article Tom Watson can make an argument for interracial class solidarity on the one hand, while on the other adding the caveat that class unity has nothing to do with social equality between the races. In assuring his readers that "[e]ach citizen regulates his own visiting list — and always will" (p. 268), Watson uncannily echoes the majority opinion in *Plessy v. Ferguson* (see Chapter Two, p. 353), which sanctioned segregation by claiming in part that the law had no right to interfere with a white person's assumed preference for a whites-only social setting. Among other reasons, Populism failed by the end of the nineteenth century because the arguments for white racial superiority proved too strong for many working-class whites to resist. In comparison to Watson, Howells's novel represents an alternate kind of white consciousness that appears able to overcome racial prejudices. But just as Philip Bruce uses the metaphors of sexual taboos to describe the "threat" of racial equality, so too does Howells utilize the metaphor of a repulsive brute animalism to fix the distinctions between white ethnic groups in the mind of his readers. Bruce and Howells might have different views on whether or not African Americans are inferior to whites, but they structure their opinions in similar, even overlapping, rhetorical frames.

The next three selections demonstrate that blacks had a range of responses to the ebb and flow of white debates on race, ethnicity, and class. One strategy was Booker T. Washington's policy of "accommodation," best exemplified in his 1895 address at the Atlanta Exposition. Here Washington argues that blacks were content with economic security and would not demand social and political equality. In his series of articles published in 1900 entitled "The Future American," Charles W. Chesnutt evokes the white supremacist's worst nightmare by claiming that mulattoes were the strongest racial element in

American society, and that they alone would survive into the future. While it is not entirely clear how much Chesnutt actually believed that the population of the United States would be transformed by miscegenation, his claims about the "future American" might be read as a veiled warning to whites: under the current system of widespread discrimination, white supremacists were creating the conditions for mass black resentment, so that miscegenation might actually be pursued by blacks as a way to achieve their long delayed freedom. W. E. B. Du Bois's 1897 essay "The Conservation of Races" presents yet another perspective, an important statement on African American nationalism and African diasporic consciousness. Scholars of African American intellectual history have traditionally placed Washington and Du Bois on opposite ends of the political spectrum, suggesting that the conservative Washington stood in the way of black self-improvement, while Du Bois exemplified a progressive vision of black self-determination that was more characteristic of the twentieth century. However, we need to recognize that Washington and Du Bois offered black Americans a range of stances designed to challenge weaknesses in the rhetoric of white supremacy. Indeed, what if we saw Washington as an astute racial politician who understood the complex anxieties dividing white Americans of his day? While his speech seems to promise no political agitation, it also makes a sly reference to the Anglo-American antipathy toward "those of foreign birth and strange tongue"— that is, European immigrants — as a way of suggesting, in a fashion similar to Watson and Howells, that the logical ally of white America was the African American (p. 276). Though Washington appears to be as much of a "nativist" as Howells's character Olney, his view demonstrates a grasp of the contradictions inherent in white debates about group identity, and he exploits these contradictions to create some potential space of safety for blacks.

As the excerpts from the writings of Theodore Roosevelt and Charlotte Perkins Gilman reveal, white Americans saw women as central to the future of U.S. society, though not in the ways presented by white supremacist theorists such as Philip Bruce. Roosevelt's essay on "birth reform" addresses white survival not in the context of race war, but from the point of view of what sociologists of his day called white "race suicide": that is, the tendency of native-born whites to reproduce in lower numbers than "alien" groups such European immigrants and African Americans. For Roosevelt, the decline of the white birth rate could only be hastened by the interest in female independence emerging among middle- and upper-class white women. On the other hand, for the early white feminist theorist Gilman, a woman had to have the possibility of a life beyond what she called the "sex-function" if she was ever to become a responsible mother. Though neither Roosevelt nor Gilman make reference to race riots, the myth of the black rapist, immigration, class antagonism, or "the Negro Problem," the telltale language of eugenics is central to their arguments, and for both of them gender roles are inseparable from the question of class, race, and ethnicity.

The role of women in the shaping of community life was just as central to black Americans as to white, though with a different resonance. Facing their own unique challenges, African American feminists were as active as their white counterparts in agitating for a radically revised role for black women within and outside of the home. As the excerpt from Fannie Barrier Williams's 1893 speech "The Intellectual Progress of the Colored Women" reveals, black women's affirmation of their virtue, their dedication to community "uplift," social morality, and education were direct challenges to stereotypes of black female licentiousness and laziness that white Americans such as Bruce had accepted readily throughout the eighteenth and nineteenth centuries. Indeed, black female activists worked hard to improve life for themselves and their communities, and sought to articulate a concept of uplift that could be embraced by black men as well.

Echoing the motto of the National Association of Colored Women, "Lifting as We Climb," in his 1903 commencement address at the single black high school in Washington, D.C., African American educator Roscoe Conkling Bruce calls upon African American teachers, merchants, and doctors to reach out to those blacks lower down on the economic ladder. (Countless black self-help groups throughout the nation shared Bruce's philosophy, and the example of Dr. Miller and his hospital in *The Marrow of Tradition* evoke this community uplift tradition.) But imbedded in Bruce's calls for uplift is the assumption that the achievement of middle-class status should be the ultimate goal of all African Americans.

Ever sensitive to the variety of tensions that structure any community, *Marrow* explores the consequences of class differences among blacks in the confrontation between the middle-class African Americans led by Miller, and their working-class counterparts led by Josh Green. In his presentation of Dr. Miller, Chesnutt implies that while the nation's small African American middle-class (that is, Roscoe Bruce's doctors, teachers, and merchants) appear to be at the forefront of black progress, their own investment in social stability makes it difficult for them to provide aggressive and radical leadership in the face of racial violence. In making Josh the working-class leader that the middle-class Miller fails to be, Chesnutt implies that "uplift" should not obscure the fact that often it is those on the bottom of the black social ladder who make the most important race leaders.

PHILIP A. BRUCE

From *The Plantation Negro as a Freeman*

After 1865, as the historical facts of slavery and the Civil War retreated from national memory, many white Americans turned to writers and scholars to help them reevaluate both the true nature of the antebellum South and the future possibilities of the national post-Reconstruction moment. After 1877, with Republicans retreating from their initial pledge to uphold radical political reform and black suffrage, the "plantation fiction" of popular white writers such as Thomas Nelson Page vindicated the South by portraying the preemancipation relationship between master and slave as mutually affectionate. But the portrayal of blacks outside of slavery was another matter: by the turn of the century, as southern state legislatures rewrote their constitutions to disenfranchise African American voters, the Ku Klux Klan novels of Thomas Dixon Jr. confirmed the rightness of such actions by representing the post–Civil War generation of blacks as violent and lawless. As the work of lawyer, editor, and historian Philip Alexander Bruce (1856–1933) makes clear, white scholarship on the "New South" did not necessarily provide a corrective to white supremacist fiction. Born into a wealthy Virginia family, and the recipient of degrees from the University of Virginia and Harvard Law School, Bruce devoted a great deal of time to writing southern history that directly aided and abetted the post-Reconstruction backlash against African Americans, arguing, like Dixon, that as they moved beyond slavery, blacks were inevitably devolving into barbarism. Published in 1889, his first treatise *The Plantation Negro as a Freeman: Observations on His Character, Condition, and Prospects in Virginia* (New York: Putnam, 1889) confirmed white Americans' worst racial fears by giving a "thorough" analysis of the depravity of black life both public and private.

HUSBAND AND WIFE.

. . . Marriage, however solemnly contracted and however public the religious ceremony sanctioning it, does not wholly hamper the sexual liberty of either of the parties. The wife, as a rule, is as innocently unconscious as the husband that both have entered into a mutual pledge to be faithful to the vows that they have pronounced. To them, the ceremony is a form which sentimentally means little, and practically signifies only that the woman shall attend to all household duties and the man shall work and support the family. Very unfortunately, this view is even held by those who are regarded as the spiritual leaders and exemplars of their race. Many of the plantation preachers frequently offend against the sacredness of their own marriages and the marriages of members of their flocks, and instead of following that course of propriety which their position requires that they shall follow, they too often employ their commanding influence to corrupt and lead astray. . . .

All those qualities that signify a concentration of sinister feeling are found more fully developed in the wives than in the husbands, and their manner of giving expression to these, whether in word or deed, is much more forcible and reckless of consequences, but at the same time they are more dissimulative and secretive when it is necessary to be so to attain some object which they have in view. Their moral influence over their husbands is often pernicious; much of the crime which the latter commit is secretly or openly instigated by the wives, who frequently go so far as to be active accomplices themselves, in gross as well as petty violations of law. Unhappily, many are inclined, too, to stimulate their husbands to be insolent to the whites, and to rebel against the authority which employers have the right to exercise under contract. Their bearing when thrown with members of the white race is often presumptuous, when there is no reason why it should be, apart from the spirit of antagonism which seems to have been engendered in their own hearts; and the consequence is that the whites avoid all intercourse with them, unless domestic servants, all communication being generally held indirectly. Although shrewder and more intelligent than their husbands, yet they are, on the whole, more superstitious, and for this reason they are the principal supporters of the notorious trick doctors, their faith in the occult powers of these rank impostors being implicit. As their controversies among themselves are carried on with so much violence and bitterness, when their animosity is thoroughly aroused, they are eager to turn to whatever will ensure gratification for their vehement spite and resentment, and they are sunk low enough in credulity to believe that supernatural agencies can be compelled to intervene in their behalf. . . .

BLACKS AND WHITES.

. . . This divergence between the social life of the one race and that of the other in those scenes where it would be supposed a common humanity and similar material interests would bring the members of both together, leaves a strong impression upon the observer. Omit the domestic servants from consideration, who constitute only a few in the general multitude, and it is found that the sphere in which the negroes move socially is as wide apart from that in which the social existence of the whites is passed, as if the two races inhabited different countries, and were, therefore, locally cut off from each other. Individuals representing both are constantly thrown with each other, it is true; negroes and white men meet as employers and employés, or as common laborers; but their association stops there, and it is of a formal character as far as it goes. The two distinct societies do not join, when they come together at all, in such a way as to result in a complete blending, however brief, of their separate systems. The remotest anticipation of such union, without reserve, even in the most insignificant and superficial social affairs, touches the sensibilities of the white people with as lively repugnance and abhorrence as if it signified a descent into an unmeasurable depth of degradation. To acknowledge social equality in small things is to give up the general principle which is applicable equally to small and great; and to do so in either is to relinquish their grasp upon every thing that they value and every thing that they love. It is to strike a blow at the integrity of their social life; it is to revolutionize their natures, and to enfeeble their appreciation of existence itself. Until all the traditions and emotions which their superiority of mental and moral character, and differences of race and condition, have created have been destroyed, they will continue to feel as they do now. Until then, even to discuss the probability of a change of sentiment, will be accounted as an insult; to justify such a change will be considered as heinous as defending incest and rape; and to predict it with confidence, will be taken as a proof that the speaker, if white, is an enemy of his people, who should, therefore, be condemned and avoided. The present strength of this sentiment in the breasts of the white people, is largely ascribable, and upon the most reasonable and natural grounds, to the ignorance and licentiousness of the typical negro of the present age that would make him highly objectionable to refined sensibilities and cultivated minds, even if his skin were that of a Caucasian. . . .

THE NEGRO AND THE COMMONWEALTH.

The presence of the negro even as a slave put the safety of every community in which he lived in jeopardy, but that presence at once assumed a far more alarming significance when the fetters were suddenly struck from his limbs and all the rights of citizenship were conferred upon him. To endow him with privileges so important in themselves, and so momentous in their possible consequences, was only justifiable as a measure that was necessary for the protection of the liberty of the beneficiary. As to whether it was really necessary or not, it would now be idle to discuss. There can be no difference of opinion, however, as to the total insufficiency of the preparation which he had received for exercise of responsibilities so grave and far-reaching as those that are incident to suffrage. Illiterate, credulous, feeble in judgment, weak in discrimination, a child in his habits of dependence and self-indulgence, accessible to every temptation and with little ability to resist, without a hope or aspiration above his physical pleasures, he was raised on the instant from the level of a beast of burden to the full enjoyment of the noblest prerogative of freedom — the right to vote. It was virtually the admission to the franchise of a man who, from the degradation of his previous condition, was as incapable as a savage out of the bush of understanding the duties of that new situation in which the force of circumstances, which he had neither directed nor anticipated, had placed him. The moral and mental disposition of each individual, as well as the great numerical strength of his race, might have been expected with absolute confidence to invest its members as a body with such a sinister political power as had never been paralleled before. To confer the right of suffrage upon them, even for the purpose of educating and sobering them, was an experiment that was certain to inflict the most serious injury on every social and political institution before the process of instruction and improvement could be finished satisfactorily. Consummated in the period of indescribable anarchy and bewilderment that succeeded the close of the war, its inevitable tendency was to prolong, if not to perpetuate, the state of general confusion that then prevailed.

Under its operation it seemed to be impossible that any thing that remained of the social and political polity that had been valued and revered in the past could survive even for a decade or generation, and it would not have done so but for the impotence of the negro and the firmness of the Anglo-Saxon. The momentousness of the issue raised rather than lowered the courage of the whites, and the stress of that struggle to retain what was very dear to them as men and citizens, which followed, touched the sensibilities and strengthened the resolution of the lowest and highest among them alike, consolidating them by the influence of a common sympathy, and stimulating them by the force of a common motive. . . .

The negroes have produced no leaders of uncommon ability among themselves; indeed, no individual of their race has appeared who has shown any talent for organization, or any capacity for grasping the most enlightened ideas of policy, or disinterestedness enough to be inspired by the highest motives of patriotism. The typical black politician has been as destructive in his ambitions, and as unscrupulous in his methods, as the worst of his white associates, and far more venal. As a public speaker, he has developed great power of verbal expression, which very frequently rises to a phenomenal verbosity. If he is ever at a loss for one word, he quickly substitutes for it the first that enters his mind, whether it is apt or not; the longer it is, and the more difficult to pronounce, the more appropriate it seems to himself and his audience. As a rule, his harangues are without any relevancy or coherence; mere sound without sense and violence without force; strange imitations of the model which he is aiming to copy; a gross travesty, indeed, that would be ludicrous but for the number of voters whom the speaker represents. . . .

THE NEGRO AND CRIMINAL LAW.

Rape is the most frightful crime which the negroes commit against the white people, and their disposition to perpetrate it has increased in spite of the quick and summary punishment that always follows; and it will be seen that this disposition will grow in proportion as that vague respect which the blacks still entertain for a white skin declines. There is something strangely alluring and seductive to them in the appearance of a white woman; they are aroused and stimulated by its foreignness to their experience of sexual pleasures, and it moves them to gratify their lust at any cost and in spite of every obstacle. This proneness of the negro is so well understood that the white women of every class, from the highest to the lowest, are afraid to venture to any distance alone, or even to wander unprotected in the immediate vicinity of their homes; their appreciation of the danger being as keen, and their apprehension of corporal injury as vivid, as if the country were in arms. If it were not for this prudence and caution on their part, as well as the capital punishment that ensues so swiftly, this crime would be far more frequent than it is. It occurs often enough, however, to inflame the aversion of the white people to the race to a heat that leaves a permanent impression upon their general relations with its members; and not unnaturally, for rape, indescribably beastly and loathsome always, is marked, in the instance of its perpetration by a negro, by a diabolical persistence and a malignant atrocity of detail that have no reflection in the whole extent of the natural history of the most bestial and ferocious animals. He is not content merely with the consummation of his purpose, but takes that fiendish delight in the degradation of his victim which he always shows when he can reek[1] his vengeance upon one whom he has hitherto been compelled to fear; and, here, the white woman in his power is, for the time being, the representative of that race which has always overawed him. That this feeling enters largely into the motive of this crime is proven by the fact that he is guilty of it as often against women who are very much advanced in years as against those who have not passed the period of their youth. His invariable impulse after the accomplishment of his purpose is to murder his victim, that being the only means suggested to his mind of escaping the consequence of the act, and this impulse is carried into effect with the utmost barbarity, unless he is accidently interrupted and frightened off. . . .

GENERAL CHARACTERISTICS — MENTAL.

. . . A transfusion of Caucasian blood . . . seems to quicken the African mind, and as the volume of that transfusion is increased, there is a nearer approach in many important particulars, to the intellectual traits of the white people. The mass of the mulattoes, however, although brighter and livelier in understanding than the blacks, are not, on the whole, distinguished for a notable superiority in mental

---

[1] *reek:* Either a misspelling for *wreak* ("to give vent") or an older usage for *reek,* meaning "to pile up."

grasp and comprehension. While the average mulatto pupil in the public schools learns more readily and rapidly than his darker companions, and while too, a much larger number of scholars of his color may show proficiency as compared with the same number of young negroes of unmixed blood, yet the most intelligent representatives of the two respective shades, stand on the same footing, substantially, the pure black reaching this position of equality by greater toil and steadier plodding.

I shall omit the mulattoes from view, as a class that is likely in a few generations to revert almost wholly to the original type in all rural districts where even now, they are not numerous and influential enough to constitute a circle of their own, which they can continue indefinitely by intermarriage, and where, in fact, their rapid decline in numbers, is due not only to the growing reserve of the white men, but also to the marked preference which the blacks themselves have for women of the lightest complexion. . . .

FUTURE OF THE NEGRO.

. . . The reversion to the original type is apt to make the negro a more dangerous political factor, because it will increase his inability to grasp enlightened ideas of public policy. He will probably sink to a lower plane of political ignorance, and grow still more out of sympathy with the institutions under which he lives. As the social and intellectual gulf between himself and the white people widens, he is likely to fall more completely under the influence of his antipathy to the dominant class; and this, in general, will shape his political action. Bribery, perhaps, will be the only effective means of inducing a large number of his fellows to cast their votes with the whites on important issues, and, in consequence, bribery in one form or another will play a very conspicuous part in all communities where many members of his race are found. The social aspect of negro suffrage is certain to grow more threatening as the blacks increase, inasmuch as this implies their more thorough subjection to those evil influences that emanate from themselves when dwelling together in a mass. The motives that have led the great body of whites to vote together in this age, must augment in force in the age to follow. As a people, there is strong reason to believe that they will not consent to be governed by a horde of ignorant black voters, and in this they will be influenced not so much by sentimental feeling, as by a determination to maintain a stable administration that will fulfil all the needs of society. A reunion will be the final result of every important division in the ranks of the white voters, because the fact that the ballots of the negroes are cast in favor of one side or another, will in the end produce a revulsion of sentiment throughout white society. While many of the whites will always seek to use negro suffrage for the attainment of their own purposes, the triumph of any faction composed of a small minority of white voters and a large majority of the blacks cannot be lasting, inasmuch as that triumph, if prolonged for a considerable length of time, will introduce such disastrous elements of confusion, and foster such embittered antagonism of race, as to be destructive of the coalition. The special bearing of public questions is certain to sink into insignificance as compared with the general bearing of the continued success of the negroes at the polls. The acknowledged issues of all the most important elections will be overshadowed to a great extent by the silent issues raised by the direct conflict of the masses of blacks and whites. It is not improbable that such occasions will be attended with much disorder, arising less from heated political opposition than from passions inflamed by antipathies of race.

THOMAS E. WATSON

From *The Negro Question in the South*

Despite what seemed to be the increasing ubiquity of antiblack attitudes after the Civil War, American whites were not a homogeneous group. Though he was by no means problack, the white Georgia-born Thomas E. Watson (1856–1922) was more interested in saving the South from northern industrialists than he was in demonizing freedmen and their descendants. As an early agrarian activist Watson worked with Georgia's Farmers' Alliance in the 1880s and then with the Populist Party in the 1890s, both of which pragmatically argued for the unity of economic interests among blacks and whites when such tactics were necessary for advancing the interests of poor whites. Thus at least for a time Watson was at odds with white supremacist agendas as they were expressed among southern Democrats. (In his commitment to a third party option Watson even ran as the Populist Party's presidential candidate in 1904 and 1908.) Although he supported interracial political solidarity at some points in his career, he did not believe in racial equality. No more immune to bigotry than many of his contemporaries, by the last decade and a half of his life Watson railed bitterly against Catholics and Jews, and advocated the return of the Ku Klux Klan. Excerpted below, Watson's "The Negro Question in the South" comes from his earlier period as an advocate for agrarian reform. The article makes clear his belief in an inherent white superiority, but Watson argues for the unity of rural political and economic interests in order to empower farmers, and he understands that such empowerment would be possible only if it cut across racial lines. The article appeared in *The Arena,* vol. 6, ed. B. O. Flower (Boston: Arena Publishing Co., 1892).

The Negro Question in the South has been for nearly thirty years a source of danger, discord, and bloodshed. It is an ever-present irritant and menace.

Several millions of slaves were told that they were the prime cause of the civil war; that their emancipation was the result of the triumph of the North over the South; that the ballot was placed in their hands as a weapon of defence against their former masters; that the war-won political equality of the black man with the white must be asserted promptly and aggressively, under the leadership of adventurers who had swooped down upon the conquered section in the wake of the Union armies. . . .

In brief, the end of the war brought changed relations and changed feelings. Heated antagonisms produced mutual distrust and dislike — ready, at any accident of unusual provocation on either side, to break out into passionate and bloody conflict.

Quick to take advantage of this deplorable situation, the politicians have based the fortunes of the old parties upon it. Northern leaders have felt that at the cry of "Southern outrage" they could not only "fire the Northern heart," but also win a unanimous vote from the colored people. Southern politicians have felt that at the cry of "Negro domination" they could drive into solid phalanx every white man in all the Southern states.

Both the old parties have done this thing until they have constructed as perfect a "slot machine" as the world ever saw. Drop the old, worn nickel of the "party slogan" into the slot, and the machine does the rest. You might beseech a Southern white tenant to listen to you upon questions of finance, taxation, and transportation; you might demonstrate with mathematical precision that herein lay his way out of poverty into comfort; you might have him "almost per-suaded" to the truth, but if the merchant who furnished his farm supplies (at tremendous usury) or the town politician (who never spoke to him excepting at election times) came along and cried "Negro rule!" the entire fabric of reason and common sense which you had patiently constructed would fall, and the poor tenant would joyously hug the chains of an actual wretchedness rather than do any experi-menting on a question of mere sentiment.

Thus the Northern Democrats have ruled the South with a rod of iron for twenty years. We have had to acquiesce when the time-honored principles we loved were sent to the rear and new doctrines and policies we despised were engrafted on our platform. All this we have had to do to obtain the assistance of Northern Democrats to pre-vent what was called "Negro supremacy." In other words, the Negro has been as valuable a portion of the stock in trade of a Democrat as he was of a Republican. Let the South ask relief from Wall Street; let it plead for equal and just laws on finance; let it beg for mercy against crushing taxation, and Northern Democracy, with all the coldness, cruelty, and subtlety of Mephistopheles,[1] would hint "Negro rule!" and the white farmer and laborer of the South had to choke down his grievance and march under Tammany's orders.[2]

Reverse the statement, and we have the method by which the black man was managed by the Republicans. . . .

If we were dealing with a few tribes of red men or a few sporadic Chinese, the question would be easily disposed of. The Anglo-Saxon would probably do just as he pleased, whether right or wrong, and the weaker man would go under.

But the Negroes number 8,000,000. They are interwoven with our business, political, and labor systems. They assimilate with our cus-toms, our religion, our civilization. They meet us at every turn, — in the fields, the shops, the mines. They are a part of our system, and they are here to stay.

Those writers who tediously wade through census reports to prove that the Negro is disappearing, are the most absurd mortals extant. The Negro is not disappearing. A Southern man who looks about him

---

[1] *Mephistopheles:* In the sixteenth-century German legend of Dr. Faust, the demonic spirit Mephistopheles convinces the alchemist and astrologer to forfeit his soul in exchange for power and knowledge.

[2] *Tammany's orders:* Originally founded as a New York City club in 1789, by the twentieth century the Society of Tammany had a well-earned reputation as a notoriously corrupt political machine of the Democratic party.

and who sees how rapidly the colored people increase, how cheaply they can live, and how readily they learn, has no patience whatever with those statistical lunatics who figure out the final disappearance of the Negro one hundred years hence. The truth is, that the "black belts" in the South are getting blacker. The race is mixing less than it ever did. Mulattoes are less common (in proportion) than during the times of slavery. Miscegenation is further off (thank God) than ever. Neither the blacks nor the whites have any relish for it. Both have a pride of race which is commendable, and which, properly directed, will lead to the best results for both. The home of the colored man is chiefly with us in the South, and there he will remain. It is there he is founding churches, opening schools, maintaining newspapers, entering the professions, serving on juries, deciding doubtful elections, drilling as a volunteer soldier, and piling up a cotton crop which amazes the world.

. . . It is safe to say that the present status of hostility between the races can only be sustained at the most imminent risk to both. It is leading by logical necessity to results which the imagination shrinks from contemplating. And the horrors of such a future can only be averted by honest attempts at a solution of the question which will be just to both races and beneficial to both. . . .

The white people of the South will never support the Republican Party. This much is certain. The black people of the South will never support the Democratic Party. This is equally certain. . . .

As long as there was no choice, except as between the Democrats and the Republicans, the situation of the two races was bound to be one of antagonism. The Republican Party represented everything which was hateful to the whites; the Democratic Party, everything which was hateful to the blacks.

Therefore a new party was absolutely necessary. It has come, and it is doing its work with marvellous rapidity.

Why does a Southern Democrat leave his party and come to ours?

Because his industrial condition is pitiably bad; because he struggles against a system of laws which have almost filled him with despair; because he is told that he is without clothing because he produces too much cotton, and without food because corn is too plentiful; because he sees everybody growing rich off the products of labor except the laborer; because the millionnaires who manage the Democratic Party have contemptuously ignored his plea for a redress of grievances and have nothing to say to him beyond the cheerful advice to "work harder and live closer."

Why has this man joined the People's Party? Because the same grievances have been presented to the Republicans by the farmer of the West, and the millionnaires who control that party have replied to the petition with the soothing counsel that the Republican farmer of the West should "work more and talk less."

Therefore, if he were confined to a choice between the two old parties, the question would merely be (on these issues) whether the pot were larger than the kettle — the color of both being precisely the same.

. . . The two races can never act together permanently, harmoniously, beneficially, till each race demonstrates to the other a readiness to leave old party affiliations and to form new ones, based upon the profound conviction that, in acting together, both races are seeking new laws which will benefit both. On no other basis under heaven can the "Negro Question" be solved.

Now, suppose that the colored man were educated upon these questions just as the whites have been; suppose he were shown that his poverty and distress came from the same sources as ours; suppose we should convince him that our platform principles assure him an escape from the ills he now suffers, and guarantee him the fair measure of prosperity his labor entitles him to receive, — would he not act just as the white Democrat who joined us did? Would he not abandon a party which ignores him as a farmer and laborer; which offers him no benefits of an equal and just financial system; which promises him no relief from oppressive taxation; which assures him of no legislation which will enable him to obtain a fair price for his produce?

Granting to him the same selfishness common to us all; granting him the intelligence to know what is best for him and the desire to attain it, why would he not act from that motive just as the white farmer has done?

That he would do so, is as certain as any future event can be made. Gratitude may fail; so may sympathy and friendship and generosity and patriotism; but in the long run, self-interest *always* controls. Let it once appear plainly that it is to the interest of a colored man to vote with the white man, and he will do it. Let it plainly appear that it is to the interest of the white man that the vote of the Negro should supplement his own, and the question of having that ballot freely cast and fairly counted, becomes vital to the *white man*. He will see that it is done.

Now let us illustrate: Suppose two tenants on my farm; one of them white, the other black. They cultivate their crops under precisely the same conditions. Their labors, discouragements, burdens, grievances, are the same.

The white tenant is driven by cruel necessity to examine into the causes of his continued destitution. He reaches certain conclusions which are not complimentary to either of the old parties. He leaves the Democracy in angry disgust. He joins the People's Party. Why? Simply because its platform recognizes that he is badly treated and proposes to fight his battle. Necessity drives him from the old party, and hope leads him into the new. In plain English, he joins the organization whose declaration of the principles is in accord with his conception of what he needs and justly deserves.

Now go back to the colored tenant. His surroundings being the same and his interests the same, why is it impossible for him to reach the same conclusions? Why is it unnatural for him to go into the new party at the same time and with the same motives?

Cannot these two men act together in peace when the ballot of the one is a vital benefit to the other? Will not political friendship be born of the necessity and the hope which is common to both? Will not race bitterness disappear before this common suffering and this mutual desire to escape it? Will not each of these citizens feel more kindly for the other when the vote of each defends the home of both? If the white man becomes convinced that the Democratic Party has played upon his prejudices, and has used his quiescence to the benefit of interests adverse to his own, will he not despise the leaders who seek to perpetuate the system?

. . . The white tenant lives adjoining the colored tenant. Their houses are almost equally destitute of comforts. Their living is confined to bare necessities. They are equally burdened with heavy taxes. They pay the same high rent for gullied and impoverished land.

They pay the same enormous prices for farm supplies. Christmas finds them both without any satisfactory return for a year's toil. Dull and heavy and unhappy, they both start the plows again when "New Year's" passes.

Now the People's Party says to these two men, "You are kept apart that you may be separately fleeced of your earnings. You are made to hate each other because upon that hatred is rested the keystone of the arch of financial despotism which enslaves you both. You are deceived and blinded that you may not see how this race antagonism perpetuates a monetary system which beggars both.". . .

Suppose these two men now to have become fully imbued with the idea that their material welfare depends upon the reforms we demand. Then they act together to secure them. Every white reformer finds it to the vital interest of his home, his family, his fortune, to see to it that the vote of the colored reformer is freely cast and fairly counted. . . .

Concede that in the final event, a colored man will vote where his material interests dictate that he should vote; concede that in the South the accident of color can make no possible difference in the interests of farmers, croppers, and laborers; concede that under full and fair discussion the people can be depended upon to ascertain where their interests lie — and we reach the conclusion that the Southern race question can be solved by the People's Party on the simple proposition that each race will be led by self-interest to support that which benefits it, when so presented that neither is hindered by the bitter party antagonisms of the past.

Let the colored laborer realize that our platform gives him a better guaranty for political independence; for a fair return for his work; a better chance to buy a home and keep it; a better chance to educate his children and see them profitably employed; a better chance to have public life freed from race collisions; a better chance for every citizen to be considered as a *citizen* regardless of color in the making and enforcing of laws, — let all this be fully realized, and the race question at the South will have settled itself through the evolution of a political movement in which both whites and blacks recognize their surest way out of wretchedness into comfort and independence. . . .

To the emasculated individual who cries "Negro supremacy!" there is little to be said. His cowardice shows him to be a degeneration from the race which has never yet feared any other race. Existing under such conditions as they now do in this country, there is no earthly chance for Negro domination, unless we are ready to admit that the colored man is our superior in will power, courage, and intellect.

Not being prepared to make any such admission in favor of any race the sun ever shone on, I have no words which can portray my contempt for the white men, Anglo-Saxons, who can knock their knees together, and through their chattering teeth and pale lips admit that they are afraid the Negroes will "dominate us."

The question of social equality does not enter into the calculation at all. That is a thing each citizen decides for himself. No statute ever yet drew the latch of the humblest home — or ever will. Each citizen regulates his own visiting list — and always will.

The conclusion, then, seems to me to be this: the crushing burdens which now oppress both races in the South will cause each to make an effort to cast them off. They will see a similarity of cause and a similarity of remedy. They will recognize that each should help the other in the work of repealing bad laws and enacting good ones. They will become political allies, and neither can injure the other without weakening both. It will be to the interest of both that each should have justice. And on these broad lines of mutual interest, mutual forbearance, and mutual support the present will be made the stepping-stone to future peace and prosperity.

WILLIAM DEAN HOWELLS

From *An Imperative Duty*

At the height of his career, novelist, playwright, essayist, travel writer, and magazine editor William Dean Howells (1837–1920) enjoyed the nickname "the Dean of American Letters," but he began life more humbly as the largely self-educated son of an Ohio printer. After a brief stint in his father's trade, Howells moved on to journalism, until he finally traveled to Boston in the 1850s to pursue a career in poetry. Under the patronage of *Atlantic Monthly* editor James Russell Lowell, Howells gained recognition as a serious writer, and after time spent abroad as an American consul in Venice, he won widespread fame for his travel narratives and expert knowledge of Italian literature and culture. When Howells succeeded to the editorship of the *Atlantic Monthly* by 1871, he showcased literary talents such as Edith Wharton, Mark Twain, Sarah Orne Jewett, and Henry James, and he was also supportive of the work of Chesnutt and black poet Paul Laurence Dunbar. Howells won acclaim not only as an editor, but as a novelist in his own right, pioneering what came to be known as American literary realism in such works as *The Rise of Silas Lapham* (1885) and *A Hazard of New Fortune* (1890). Notwithstanding his commitment to a Victorian sense of public morality, he was deeply moved by the turmoil shaping American society in the post-Reconstruction era, and he supported various social reform movements and organizations, including the National Association for the Advancement of Colored People. Indeed, reflecting his interest in "the Negro Problem," Howells's novel *An Imperative Duty* explicitly confronted miscegenation. The following excerpt features Chapter 1 of the novel as it was serialized in the June–November 1891 issue of *Harper's New Monthly Magazine* (vol. LXXXIII). Because of reader complaints, Howells toned down the novel's slurs against the Irish by the time the novel was published in book form in 1892.

I.

Olney got back to Boston about the middle of July, and found himself in the social solitude which the summer makes more noticeable in that city than in any other. The business, the hard work of life, was going on, galloping on, as it always does in America, but the pleasure of life, which he used to be part of as a younger man, was taking a rest, or if not a rest, then certainly an outing at the sea-shore. He met no one he knew, and he continued his foreign travels in his native place, after an absence so long that it made everything once so familiar bewilderingly strange.

He had sailed ten days before from Liverpool, but he felt as if he had been voyaging in a vicious circle when he landed, and had arrived in Liverpool again. In several humiliating little ways, Boston recalled the most commonplace of English cities. It was not like Liverpool in a certain civic grandiosity, a sort of lion-and-unicorn spectacularity which he had observed there. The resemblance appeared to him in the meanness and dulness of many of the streets in the older part of the town where he was lodged, and in the littleness of the houses. Then there was a curious similarity in the figures and faces of the crowd. He had been struck by the almost American look of the poorer class in Liverpool, and in Boston he was struck by its English look. He could half account for this by the fact that the average face and figure one meets in Boston in midsummer is hardly American; but the other half of the puzzle remained. He could only conjecture an approach from all directions to a common type among those who work with their hands for a living; what he had seen in Liverpool and now saw in Boston was not the English type or the American type, but the proletarian type. He noticed it especially in the women, and more especially in the young girls, as he met them in the street after their day's work was done, and on the first Sunday afternoon following his arrival, as he saw them in the Common. By far the greater part of those listening to the brass band which was then beginning to vex the ghost of our poor old Puritan Sabbath there, were given away by their accent for those primary and secondary Irish who abound with us. The old women were strong, ugly old peasant women, often with the simian cast of features which affords the caricaturist such an unmistakable Irish physiognomy; but the young women were thin and crooked, with pale, pasty complex- ions, and an effect of physical delicacy which might later be physical refinement. They went about in threes or fours, with their lank arms round one another's waists, or lounged upon the dry grass; and they seemed fond of wearing red jerseys, which accented every fact of their anatomy. Looking at them scientifically, Olney thought that if they survive to be mothers they might give us, with better conditions, a race as hale and handsome as the elder American race; but the transition from the Old World to the New, as represented in them, was painful, and it was not pretty in manner any more than in matter. Their voices were at once coarse and weak; their walk was uncertain, now awk- ward and now graceful, an undeveloped gait; their bearing was apt to be aggressive, and sometimes rude, as if from a wish to ascertain the full limits of their social freedom, rather than from ill-nature, or that bad-heartedness which most rudeness comes from.

But, in fact, Olney met nowhere the deference from beneath that his long sojourn in Europe had accustomed him to consider politeness. He was used in all public places with a kindness mixed with roughness, which is probably the real republican manner: the manner of Florence before the Medici; the manner of Venice when the Florentines were wounded by it after the Medici corrupted them; the manner of the French when the Terror[1] had done its work. Nobody proved unami- able, though everybody seemed so at first; not even the waiters at his hotel, where he was served by adoptive citizens who looked so much like brigands that he could not help expecting to be carried off and held somewhere for ransom when he first came into the dining-room. They wore immense black mustaches or huge whiskers, or else the American beard cut slanting from the corners of the mouth. They had a kind of short sack of alpaca, which did not support one's love of gen- tility like the conventional dress-coat of the world-wide waiter, or cheer one's heart like the white linen jacket and apron of the negro waiter. But Olney found them, upon what might be called personal acquaintance, neither uncivil nor unkind, though they were awkward and rather stupid. They could not hide their eagerness for fees, and they took an interest in his well-being so openly mercenary that he could scarcely enjoy his meals. With two of those four-winged whirli- gigs revolving on the table before him to scare away the flies, and

[1] *Florence before the Medici . . . the Terror:* Howells references here the rise and fall of civility in Renaissance Florence under the influence of the Medici family, and in late- eighteenth-century France, after the violent and bloody Reign of Terror during the French Revolution.

working him up to such a vertigo that he thought he must swoon into his soup, Olney was uncomfortably aware of the Irish waiter standing so close behind his chair that his stomach bulged against it, and he felt his breath coming and going on the bald spot on his crown. He could not put out his hand to take up a bit of bread without having a hairy paw thrust forward to anticipate his want; and he knew that his waiter considered each service of the kind worth a good deal extra, and expected to be remembered for it in our silver coinage, whose unique ugliness struck Olney afresh.

He would not have been ready to say that one of the negro waiters, whom he wished they had at his hotel instead of those Irishmen, would not have been just as greedy of money; but he would have clothed his greed in such a smiling courtesy and such a childish simple-heartedness that it would have been graceful and winning. He would have used tact in his ministrations; he would not have cumbered him with service, as from a wheelbarrow, but would have given him a touch of help here, and a little morsel of attention there; he would have kept aloof as well as alert. That is, he would have had all these charms if he were at his best, and he would have had some of them if he were at his worst.

In fact, the one aspect of our mixed humanity here which struck Olney as altogether agreeable in getting home was that of the race which vexes our social question with its servile past, and promises to keep it uncomfortable with its civic future. He had not forgotten that, so far as society in the society sense is concerned, we have always frankly simplified the matter, and no more consort with the negroes than we do with the lower animals, so that one would be quite likely to meet a cow or a horse in an American drawing-room as a person of color. But he had forgotten how entirely the colored people keep to themselves in all public places, and how, with the same civil rights as ourselves, they have their own neighborhoods, their own churches, their own amusements, their own resorts. They were just as free to come to the music on the Common that Sunday afternoon as any of the white people he saw there. They could have walked up and down, they could have lounged upon the grass, and no one would have molested them, though the whites would have kept apart from them. But he found very few of them there. It was not till he followed a group away from the Common through Charles Street, where they have their principal church, into Cambridge Street, which is their chief promenade, that he began to see many of them. In the humbler side-hill streets, and in the alleys branching upward from either thoroughfare, they have their homes, and here he encountered them of all ages and sexes. It seemed to him that they had increased since he was last in Boston beyond the ratio of nature; and the hotel clerk afterward told him there had been that summer an unusual influx of negroes from the South.

He would not have known the new arrivals by anything in their looks or bearing. Their environment had made as little impression on the older inhabitants, or the natives, as Time himself makes upon persons of their race, and Olney fancied that Boston did not characterize their manner, as it does that of almost every other sort of aliens. They all alike seemed shining with good-nature and good-will, and the desire of peace on earth. Their barbaric taste in color, when it flamed out in a crimson necktie or a scarlet jersey, or when it subdued itself to a sable that left no gleam of white about them but a point or rim of shirt collar, was invariably delightful to him; but he had to own that their younger people were often dressed with an innate feeling for style. Some of the young fellows were very effective dandies of the type we were then beginning to call dude, and were marked by an ultra correctness, if there is any such thing; they had that air of being clothed through and through, as to the immortal spirit as well as the perishable body, by their cloth gaiters, their light trousers, their neatly buttoned cutaway coats, their harmonious scarfs, and their silk hats. They carried on flirtations of the eye with the young colored girls they met, or when they were walking with them they paid them a court which was far above the behavior of the common young white fellows with the girls of their class in refinement and delicacy. The negroes, if they wished to imitate the manners of our race, wished to imitate the manners of the best among us; they wished to be like ladies and gentlemen. But the young white girls and their fellows whom Olney saw during the evening in possession of most of the benches in the Common and the Public Garden, and between the lawns of Commonwealth Avenue, apparently did not wish to be like ladies and gentlemen in their behavior. The fellow in each case had his arm about the girl's waist, and she had her head at times upon his shoulder; if the branch of a tree overhead cast the smallest rag or tatter of shadow upon them, she had her head on his shoulder most of the time. Olney was rather abashed when he passed close to one of these couples, but they seemed to suffer no embarrassment. They had apparently no concealments to make, nothing to be ashamed of; and they had really nothing to give them a sense of guilt. They were simply vulgar young people, who were publicly abusing the freedom our civilization gives their youth, without knowing any better, or meaning any worse. Olney knew this, but he could not help remarking to the advantage of the negroes, that among all these couples on the benches of the Common and the Garden and the Avenue he never found a colored couple. He thought that some of the young colored girls, as he met them walking with their decorous beaux, were very pretty in their way. They had very thin, high, piping voices that had an effect both of gentleness and gentility. With their brilliant complexions of lustrous black, or rich *café au lait*, or creamy white, they gave a vividness to the public spectacle which it would not otherwise have had, and the sight of these negroes in Boston somehow brought back to Olney's homesick heart a sense of Italy, where he had never seen one of their race.

BOOKER T. WASHINGTON

The Atlanta Exposition Address

Though many African Americans rose to the challenge of leading their communities at the local and national levels, few achieved the fame, power, and influence of Booker T. Washington (1856–1915). Born a Virginia slave in the last years before the Civil War, Washington served as the principal of the Tuskegee Institute from 1881 until his death, and became forever identified as an "accommodationist" who, in contrast to more militant figures such as W. E. B. Du Bois and Ida B. Wells, courted conservative white politicians, philanthropists, and business people. Discouraging black participation in politics and higher education, Washington urged that blacks focus on "industrial" education as farmers, builders, and craftspeople. Though he published many essays, a study of Frederick Douglass, and a variety of treatises on black self-help, Washington's landmark text was his life story *Up From Slavery* (1901). Here, skillfully presenting himself as the humble but plucky ex-slave boy who drew himself up from poverty by embracing the virtues of cleanliness, literacy, and fortitude, Washington offered readers an example of what might be accomplished through humble but honest black labor, a labor he deemed central to the growth, success, and national character of the United States. Modern biographers have stressed that there were *two* sides to Booker T. Washington: the public black leader who showed a nonthreatening face to whites, and the private activist who secretly financed lawsuits to fight racial discrimination. This sense of Washington's doubleness complicates one's reading of his most famous public address at the Atlanta Exposition. Delivered on

September 18, 1895, before a distinguished audience of white officials, the speech was published in *Up From Slavery: An Autobiography* (New York: A. L. Burt Company, 1900), and is reprinted here in its entirety.

Mr. President and Gentlemen of the Board of Directors and Citizens.

One-third of the population of the south is of the Negro race. No enterprise seeking the material, civil, or moral welfare of this section can disregard this element of our population and reach the highest success. I but convey to you, Mr. President and Directors, the sentiment of the masses of my race when I say that in no way have the value and manhood of the American Negro been more fittingly and generously recognized than by the managers of this magnificent Exposition at every stage of its progress. It is a recognition that will do more to cement the friendship of the two races than any occurrence since the dawn of our freedom.

Not only this, but the opportunity here afforded will awaken among us a new era of industrial progress. Ignorant and inexperienced, it is not strange that in the first years of our new life we began at the top instead of at the bottom; that a seat in Congress or the state legislature was more sought than real estate or industrial skill; that the political convention of stump speaking had more attractions than starting a dairy farm or truck garden.

A ship lost at sea for many days suddenly sighted a friendly vessel. From the mast of the unfortunate vessel was seen a signal, "Water, water; we die of thirst!" The answer from the friendly vessel at once came back, "Cast down your bucket where you are." A second time the signal, "Water, water; send us water!" ran up from the distressed vessel, and was answered, "Cast down your bucket where you are." And a third and fourth signal for water was answered, "Cast down your bucket where you are." The captain of the distressed vessel, at last heeding the injunction, cast down his bucket, and it came up full of fresh, sparkling water from the mouth of the Amazon River. To those of my race who depend on bettering their condition in a foreign land or who underestimate the importance of cultivating friendly relations with the Southern white man, who is their next-door neighbour, I would say: "Cast down your bucket where you are"— cast it down in making friends in every manly way of the people of all races by whom we are surrounded.

Cast it down in agriculture, mechanics, in commerce, in domestic service, and in the professions. And in this connection it is well to bear in mind that whatever other sins the South may be called to bear, when it comes to business, pure and simple, it is in the South that the Negro is given a man's chance in the commercial world, and in nothing is this Exposition more eloquent than in emphasizing this chance. Our greatest danger is that in the great leap from slavery to freedom we may overlook the fact that the masses of us are to live by the productions of our hands, and fail to keep in mind that we shall prosper in proportion as we learn to dignify and glorify common labour and put brains and skill into the common occupations of life; shall prosper in proportion as we learn to draw the line between the superficial and the substantial, the ornamental gewgaws of life and the useful. No race can prosper till it learns that there is as much dignity in tilling a field as in writing a poem. It is at the bottom of life we must begin, and not at the top. Nor should we permit our grievances to overshadow our opportunities.

To those of the white race who look to the incoming of those of foreign birth and strange tongue and habits for the prosperity of the South, were I permitted I would repeat what I say to my own race, "Cast down your bucket where you are." Cast it down among the eight millions of Negroes whose habits you know, whose fidelity and love you have tested in days when to have proved treacherous meant the ruin of your firesides. Cast down your bucket among these people who have, without strikes and labour wars, tilled your fields, cleared your forests, builded your railroads and cities, and brought forth treasures from the bowels of the earth, and helped make possible this magnificent representation of the progress of the South. Casting down your bucket among my people, helping and encouraging them as you are doing on these grounds, and to education of head, hand, and heart, you will find that they will buy your surplus land, make blossom the waste places in your fields, and run your factories. While doing this, you can be sure in the future, as in the past, that you and your families will be surrounded by the most patient, faithful, law-abiding, and unresentful people that the world has seen. As we have proved our loyalty to you in the past, in nursing your children, watching by the sick-bed of your mothers and fathers, and often following them with tear-dimmed eyes to their graves, so in the future, in our humble way, we shall stand by you with a devotion that no foreigner can approach, ready to lay down our lives, if need be, in defence of yours, interlacing our industrial, commercial, civil, and religious life with yours in a way that shall make the interests of both races one. In all things that are purely social we can be as separate as the fingers, yet one as the hand in all things essential to mutual progress.

There is no defence or security for any of us except in the highest intelligence and development of all. If anywhere there are efforts tending to curtail the fullest growth of the Negro, let these efforts be turned into stimulating, encouraging, and making him the most useful and intelligent citizen. Effort or means so invested will pay a thousand per cent interest. These efforts will be twice blessed —"blessing him that gives and him that takes."[1]

There is no escape through the law of man or God from the inevitable: —

> The laws of changeless justice bind
>   Oppressor with oppressed;
> And close as sin and suffering joined
>   We march to fate abreast.[2]

Nearly sixteen millions of hands will aid you in pulling the load upward, or they will pull against you the load downward. We shall constitute one-third and more of the ignorance and crime of the South, or one-third its intelligence and progress; we shall contribute one-third to the business and industrial prosperity of the South, or we shall prove a veritable body of death, stagnating, depressing, retarding every effort to advance the body politic.

Gentlemen of the Exposition, as we present to you our humble effort at an exhibition of our progress, you must not expect overmuch. Starting thirty years ago with ownership here and there in a few quilts and pumpkins and chickens (gathered from miscellaneous sources), remember the path that has led from these to the inventions and production of agricultural implements, buggies, steam-engines, newspapers, books, statuary, carving, paintings, the management of drug-stores and banks, has not been trodden without contact with thorns and thistles. While we take pride in what we exhibit as a result of our independent efforts, we do not for a moment forget that our part in this exhibition would fall far short of your expectations but for the constant help that has come to our educational life, not only from the Southern states, but especially from

[1] *"blessing him that gives and him that takes"*: Washington offers a slight paraphrase of Shakespeare's *The Merchant of Venice* 4.1.186.

[2] *"The laws . . . abreast"*: From the poem "Song of the Negro Boatmen" by antislavery poet John Greenleaf Whittier (1807–1892).

Northern philanthropists, who have made their gifts a constant stream of blessing and encouragement.

The wisest among my race understand that the agitation of questions of social equality is the extremest folly, and that progress in the enjoyment of all the privileges that will come to us must be the result of severe and constant struggle rather than of artificial forcing. No race that has anything to contribute to the markets of the world is long in any degree ostracized. It is important and right that all privileges of the law be ours, but it is vastly more important that we be prepared for the exercises of these privileges. The opportunity to earn a dollar in a factory just now is worth infinitely more than the opportunity to spend a dollar in an opera-house.

In conclusion, may I repeat that nothing in thirty years has given us more hope and encouragement, and drawn us so near to you of the white race, as this opportunity offered by the Exposition; and here bending, as it were, over the altar that represents the results of the struggles of your race and mine, both starting practically empty-handed three decades ago, I pledge that in your effort to work out the great and intricate problem which God has laid at the doors of the South, you shall have at all times the patient, sympathetic help of my race; only let this be constantly in mind, that, while from representations in these buildings of the product of field, of forest, of mine, of factory, letters, and art, much good will come, yet far above and beyond material benefits will be that higher good, that, let us pray God, will come, in a blotting out of sectional differences and racial animosities and suspicions, in a determination to administer absolute justice, in a willing obedience among all classes to the mandates of law. This, this, coupled with our material prosperity, will bring into our beloved South a new heaven and a new earth.

CHARLES W. CHESNUTT

From *The Future American*

Given the centrality of the mulatto in novels such as *A House Behind the Cedars* (1900) and *The Marrow of Tradition*, it is not surprising that Charles Chesnutt returned to the issue of miscegenation as his growing reputation afforded him invitations to write for newspapers and journals. Thus, in his three-part article "The Future American," published in the

Boston *Evening Transcript* in 1900, Chesnutt broached the controversial subject of race-mixing, insisting that, despite the best efforts of those whites in favor of Jim Crow segregation, the "darkening up" of the American population through the process of miscegenation was only a matter of time. While white scientists, politicians, and writers argued vigorously that outside of slavery blacks were headed for moral and physical decline, and most likely (they hoped) evolutionary extinction, Chesnutt suggested that evolutionary development in human existence in fact dictated the disappearance of American Caucasians as a racial group. Given the subtitles of each of the three parts of the article —"What the Race is Likely to Become in the Process of Time," "A Stream of Dark Blood in the Veins of Southern Whites," and, "A Complete Race-Amalgamation Likely to Occur"— Chesnutt was clearly committed to discomforting those readers who had written off African Americans as a viable, powerful sector of the U.S. population. Ironically, Chesnutt's celebration of light-skinned blackness as the final outcome of U.S. multiracialism would surely have brought criticism from fellow African Americans such as journalist John Edward Bruce (1856–1924) and others, who felt that intraracial color conflict among blacks had an extremely problematic history that was also in need of attention. The Boston *Evening Transcript* first published "The Future American" in its August 18, August 25, and September 1 issues. The excerpt below draws from the first and third installments.

IN THREE ARTICLES — ARTICLE 1

The future American race is a popular theme for essayists, and has been much discussed. Most expressions upon the subject, however, have been characterized by a conscious or unconscious evasion of some of the main elements of the problem involved in the formation of a future American race, or, to put it perhaps more correctly, a future ethnic type that shall inhabit the northern part of the western continent. Some of these obvious omissions will be touched upon in these articles; and if the writer has any preconceived opinions that would affect his judgment, they are at least not the hackneyed prejudices of the past — if they lead to false conclusions, they at least furnish a new point of view, from which, taken with other widely differing views, the judicious reader may establish a parallax that will enable him to approximate the truth.

The popular theory is that the future American race will consist of a harmonious fusion of the various European elements which now make up our heterogeneous population. The result is to be something infinitely superior to the best of the component elements. This perfection of type — for no good American could for a moment doubt that it will be as perfect as everything else American — is to be brought about by a combination of all the best characteristics of the different European races, and the elimination, by some strange alchemy, of all their undesirable traits — for even a good American will admit that European races, now and then, have some undesirable traits when they first come over. It is a beautiful, a hopeful, and to the eye of faith, a thrilling prospect. The defect of the argument, however, lies in the incompleteness of the premises, and its obliviousness of certain facts of human nature and human history.

Before putting forward any theory upon the subject, it may be well enough to remark that recent scientific research has swept away many hoary anthropological fallacies. It has been demonstrated that the shape or size of the head has little or nothing to do with the civilization or average intelligence of a race; that language, so recently lauded as an infallible test of racial origin is of absolutely no value in this connection, its distribution being dependent upon other conditions than race. Even color, upon which the social structure of the United States is so largely based, has been proved no test of race. The conception of a pure Aryan, Indo-European race has been abandoned in scientific circles, and the secret of the progress of Europe has been found in racial heterogeneity, rather than in racial purity. The theory that the Jews are a pure race has been exploded, and their peculiar type explained upon a different and much more satisfactory hypothesis. . . .

Proceeding then upon the firm basis laid down by science and the historic parallel, it ought to be quite clear that the future American race — the future American ethnic type — will be formed of a mingling, in a yet to be ascertained proportion, of the various racial varieties which make up the present population of the United States; or, to extend the area a little farther, of the various peoples of the northern hemisphere of the western continent; for, if certain recent tendencies are an index of the future, it is not safe to fix the boundaries of the future United States anywhere short of the Arctic Ocean on the north and the Isthmus of Panama on the south. But, even with the continuance of the present political divisions, conditions of trade and ease of travel are likely to gradually assimilate to one type all the countries of the hemisphere. Assuming that the country is so well settled that no great disturbance of ratios is likely to result from immigration, or any serious conflict of races, we may safely build our theory of a future

American race upon the present population of the country. I use the word "race" here in its popular sense — that of a people who look substantially alike, and are moulded by the same culture and dominated by the same ideals.

By the eleventh census, the ratios of which will probably not be changed materially by the census now under way, the total population of the United States was about 65,000,000, of which about seven million were black and colored, and something over 200,000 were of Indian blood. It is then in the three broad types — white, black and Indian — that the future American race will find the material for its formation. Any dream of a pure white race, of the Anglo-Saxon type, for the United States, may as well be abandoned as impossible, even if desirable. That such future race will be predominantly white may well be granted — unless climate in the course of time should modify existing types; that it will call itself white is reasonably sure; that it will conform closely to the white type is likely; but that it will have absorbed and assimilated the blood of the other two races mentioned is as certain as the operation of any law well can be that deals with so uncertain a quantity as the human race.

There are no natural obstacles to such an amalgamation. The unity of the race is not only conceded but demonstrated by actual crossing. Any theory of sterility due to race crossing may as well be abandoned; it is founded mainly on prejudice and cannot be proved by the facts. If it come from Northern or European sources, it is likely to be weakened by lack of knowledge; if from Southern sources, it is sure to be colored by prejudice. My own observation is that in a majority of cases people of mixed blood are very prolific and very long-lived. . . . Admitting that races may mix, and that they are thrown together under conditions which permit their admixture, the controlling motive will be not abstract considerations with regard to a remote posterity, but present interest and inclination.

The Indian element in the United States proper is so small proportionally — about one in three hundred — and the conditions for its amalgamation so favorable, that it would of itself require scarcely any consideration in this argument. There is no prejudice against the Indian blood, in solution. A half or quarter-breed, removed from the tribal environment, is freely received among white people. After the second or third remove he may even boast of his Indian descent; it gives him a sort of distinction, and involves no social disability. The distribution of the Indian race, however, tends to make the question largely a local one, and the survival of tribal relation may postpone the results for some little time. It will be, however, the fault of the United States Indian himself if he be not speedily amalgamated with the white population.

The Indian element, however, looms up larger when we include Mexico and Central America in our field of discussion. By the census of Mexico just completed, over eighty per cent of the population is composed of mixed and Indian races. The remainder is presumably of pure Spanish, or European blood, with a dash of Negro along the coast. The population is something over twelve millions, thus adding nine millions of Indians and Mestizos[1] to be taken into account. Add several millions of similar descent in Central America, a million in Porto Rico, who are said to have an aboriginal strain, and it may safely be figured that the Indian element will be quite considerable in the future American race. Its amalgamation will involve no great difficulty, however; it has been going on peacefully in the countries south of us for several centuries, and is likely to continue along similar lines. The peculiar disposition of the American to overlook mixed blood in a foreigner will simplify the gradual absorption of these Southern races.

The real problem, then, the only hard problem in connection with the future American race, lies in the Negro element of our population. As I have said before, I believe it is destined to play its part in the formation of this new type. The process by which this will take place will be no sudden and wholesale amalgamation — a thing certainly not to be expected, and hardly to be desired. If it were held desirable, and one could imagine a government sufficiently autocratic to enforce its behests, it would be no great task to mix the races mechanically, leaving to time merely the fixing of the resultant type.

Let us for curiosity outline the process. To start with, the Negroes are already considerably mixed — many of them in large proportion, and most of them in some degree — and the white people, as I shall endeavor to show later on, are many of them slightly mixed with the Negro. But we will assume, for the sake of the argument, that the two races are absolutely pure. We will assume, too, that the laws of the whole country were as favorable to this amalgamation as the laws of most Southern States are at present against it; i.e., that it were made a misdemeanor for two white or two colored persons to marry, so long as it was possible to obtain a mate of the other race — this would be

---

[1] *Mestizos:* Term used to describe mixed-race individuals of Native American and European descent in the Spanish-speaking Americas.

even more favorable than the Southern rule, which makes no such exception. Taking the population as one-eighth Negro, this eighth, married to an equal number of whites, would give in the next generation a population of which one-fourth would be mulattoes. Mating these in turn with white persons, the next generation would be composed one-half of quadroons, or persons one-fourth Negro. In the third generation, applying the same rule, the entire population would be composed of octoroons, or persons only one-eighth Negro, who would probably call themselves white, if by this time there remained any particular advantage in being so considered. Thus in three generations the pure whites would be entirely eliminated, and there would be no perceptible trace of the blacks left.

The mechanical mixture would be complete; as it would probably be put, the white race would have absorbed the black. There would be no inferior race to domineer over; there would be no superior race to oppress those who differed from them in racial externals. The inevitable social struggle, which in one form or another, seems to be one of the conditions of progress, would proceed along other lines than those of race. If now and then, for a few generations, an occasional trace of the black ancestor should crop out, no one would care, for all would be tarred with the same stick. This is already the case in South America, parts of Mexico and to a large extent in the West Indies. From a negroid nation, which ours is already, we would have become a composite and homogeneous people, and the elements of racial discord which have troubled our civil life so gravely and still threaten our free institutions, would have been entirely eliminated.

But this will never happen. The same result will be brought about slowly and obscurely, and, if the processes of nature are not too violently interrupted by the hand of man, in such a manner as to produce the best results with the least disturbance of natural laws. . . .

THIRD ARTICLE

I have endeavored in two former letters to set out the reasons why it seems likely that the future American ethnic type will be formed by a fusion of all the various races now peopling this continent, and to show that this process has been under way, slowly but surely, like all evolutionary movements, for several hundred years. I wish now to consider some of the conditions which will retard this fusion, as well as certain other facts which tend to promote it.

The Indian phase of the problem, so far at least as the United States is concerned, has been practically disposed of in what has already been said. The absorption of the Indians will be delayed so long as the tribal relations continue, and so long as the Indians are treated as wards of the Government, instead of being given their rights once for all, and placed upon the footing of other citizens. It is to be presumed that this will come about as the wilder Indians are educated and by the development of the country brought into closer contact with civilization, which must happen before a very great while. As has been stated, there is no very strong prejudice against the Indian blood; a well-stocked farm or a comfortable fortune will secure a white husband for a comely Indian girl any day, with some latitude, and there is no evidence of any such strong race instinct or organization as will make the Indians of the future wish to perpetuate themselves as a small but insignificant class in a great population, thus emphasizing distinctions which would be overlooked in the case of the individual.

The Indian will fade into the white population as soon as he chooses, and in the United States proper the slender Indian strain will ere long leave no trace discoverable by anyone but the anthopological [sic] expert. In New Mexico and Central America, on the contrary, the chances seem to be that the Indian will first absorb the nonindigenous elements, unless, which is not unlikely, European immigration shall increase the white contingent.

The Negro element remains, then, the only one which seems likely to present any difficulty of assimilation. The main obstacle that retards the absorption of the Negro into the general population is the apparently intense prejudice against color which prevails in the United States. This prejudice loses much of its importance, however, when it is borne in mind that it is almost purely local and does not exist in quite the same form anywhere else in the world, except among the Boers[2] of South Africa, where it prevails in an even more aggravated form; and, as I shall endeavor to show, this prejudice in the United States is more apparent than real, and is a caste prejudice which is merely accentuated by differences of race. At present, however, I wish to consider it merely as a deterrent to amalgamation.

This prejudice finds forcible expression in the laws which prevail in all the Southern States, without exception, forbidding the intermarriage of white persons and persons of color — these last being generally defined within certain degrees. While it is evident that such

---

[2] *the Boers:* White settlers of Dutch descent in colonial South Africa.

laws alone will not prevent the intermingling of races, which goes merrily on in spite of them, it is equally apparent that this placing of mixed marriages beyond the pale of the law is a powerful deterrent to any honest or dignified amalgamation. Add to this legal restriction, which is enforced by severe penalties, the social odium accruing to the white party to such a union, and it may safely be predicted that so long as present conditions prevail in the South, there will be little marrying or giving in marriage between persons of different race. So ferocious is this sentiment against intermarriage, that in a recent Missouri case, where a colored man ran away with and married a young white woman, the man was pursued by a "posse"— a word which is rapidly being debased from its proper meaning by its use in the attempt to dignify the character of lawless Southern mobs — and shot to death; the woman was tried and convicted of the "crime" of miscegenation" [sic] — another honest word which the South degrades along with the Negro.

Another obstacle to race fusion lies in the drastic and increasing proscriptive legislation by which the South attempts to keep the white and colored races apart in every place where their joint presence might be taken to imply equality; or, to put it more directly, the persistent effort to degrade the Negro to a distinctly and permanently inferior caste. This is undertaken by means of separate schools, separate railroad and street cars, political disfranchisement, debasing and abhorrent prison systems, and an unflagging campaign of calumny, by which the vices and shortcomings of the Negroes are grossly magnified and their virtues practically lost sight of. The popular argument that the Negro ought to develop his own civilization, and has no right to share in that of the white race, unless by favor, comes with poor grace from those who are forcing their civilization upon others at the cannon's mouth; it is, moreover, uncandid and unfair. The white people of the present generation did not make their civilization; they inherited it ready-made, and much of the wealth which is so strong a factor in their power was created by the unpaid labor of the colored people. The present generation has, however, brought to a high state of development one distinctively American institution, for which it is entitled to such credit as it may wish to claim; I refer to the custom of lynching, with its attendant horrors.

The principal deterrent to race admixture, however, is the low industrial and social efficiency of the colored race. If it be conceded that these are the result of environment, then their cause is not far to seek, and the cure is also in sight. Their poverty, their ignorance and their servile estate render them as yet largely ineligible for social fusion with a race whose pride is fed not only by the record of its achievements but by a constant comparison with a less developed and less fortunate race, which it has held so long in subjection.

The forces that tend to the future absorption of the black race are, however, vastly stronger than those arrayed against it. As experience has demonstrated, slavery was favorable to the mixing of the races. The growth, under healthy civil conditions, of a large and self-respecting colored citizenship would doubtless tend to lessen the clandestine association of the two races; but the effort to degrade the Negro may result, if successful, in a partial restoration of the old status. But, assuming that the present anti-Negro legislation is but a temporary reaction, then the steady progress of the colored race in wealth and culture and social efficiency will, in the course of time, materially soften the asperities of racial prejudice and permit them to approach the whites more closely, until, in time, the prejudice against intermarriage shall have been overcome by other considerations.

It is safe to say that the possession of a million dollars, with the ability to use it to the best advantage, would throw such a golden glow over a dark complexion as to override anything but a very obdurate prejudice. Mr. Spahr, in his well-studied and impartial book on "America's Working People," [3] states as his conclusion, after a careful study of conditions in the South, that the most advanced third of the Negroes of that section has already, in one generation of limited opportunity, passed in the race of life the least advanced third of the whites. To pass the next third will prove a more difficult task, no doubt, but the Negroes will have the impetus of their forward movement to push them ahead.

The outbreaks of race prejudice in recent years are the surest evidence of the Negro's progress. No effort is required to keep down a race which manifests no desire nor ability to rise; but with each new forward movement of the colored race it is brought into contact with the whites at some fresh point, which evokes a new manifestation of prejudice until custom has adjusted things to the new condition. When all Negroes were poor and ignorant they could be denied their rights with impunity. As they grow in knowledge and in wealth they become self-assertive, and make it correspondingly troublesome for those who

[3] *Mr. Spahr . . . on "America's Working People"*: Activist editor and economist Charles Barzillai Spahr (1860–1904) published his class study *America's Working People* in 1900.

would ignore their claims. It is much easier, by a supreme effort, as recently attempted with temporary success in North Carolina,[4] to knock the race down and rob it of its rights once for all, than to repeat the process from day to day and with each individual; it saves wear and tear on the conscience, and makes it easy to maintain a superiority which it might in the course of a short time require some little effort to keep up.

This very proscription, however, political and civil in the South, social all over the country, varying somewhat in degree, will, unless very soon relaxed, prove a powerful factor in the mixture of the races. If it is only by becoming white that colored people and their children are to enjoy the rights and dignities of citizenship, they will have every incentive to "lighten the breed," to use a current phrase, that they may claim the white man's privileges as soon as possible. That this motive is already at work may be seen in the enormous extent to which certain "face bleachers" and "hair straighteners" are advertised in the newspapers printed for circulation among the colored people. The most powerful factor in achieving any result is the wish to bring it about. The only thing that ever succeeded in keeping two races separated when living on the same soil — the only true ground of caste — is religion, and as has been alluded to in the case of the Jews, this is only superficially successful. The colored people are the same as the whites in religion; they have the same standards and mediums of culture, the same ideals, and the presence of the successful white race as a constant incentive to their ambition. The ultimate result is not difficult to forsee. The races will be quite as effectively amalgamated by lightening the Negroes as they would be by darkening the whites. It is only a social fiction, indeed, which makes of a person seven-eighths white a Negro; he is really much more a white man. . . .

The formation of this future American race is not a pressing problem. Because of the conditions under which it must take place, it is likely to be extremely slow — much slower, indeed, in our temperate climate and highly organized society, than in the American tropics and sub-tropics, where it is already well under way, if not a fait accompli. That it must come in the United States, sooner or later, seems to be a foregone conclusion, as the result of natural law — lex dura, sed tamen lex[5] — a hard pill, but one which must be swallowed. There

---

[4] *as recently attempted . . . in North Carolina:* That is, the Wilmington race riot of 1898.

[5] *lex dura, sed tamen lex:* The law is hard, but it is the law nevertheless.

can manifestly be no such thing as a peaceful and progressive civilization in a nation divided by two warring races, and homogeneity of type, at least in externals, is a necessary condition of harmonious social progress.

If this, then, must come, the development and progress of all the constituent elements of the future American race is of the utmost importance as bearing upon the quality of the resultant type. The white race is still susceptible of some improvement; and if, in time, the more objectionable Negro traits are eliminated, and his better qualities correspondingly developed, his part in the future American race may well be an important and valuable one.

W. E. B. DU BOIS

From *The Conservation of Races*

Regarded by modern historians as Booker T. Washington's chief rival for African American leadership at the end of the nineteenth century, novelist, scholar, educator, editor, and social activist William Edward Burghardt Du Bois (1868–1963) enjoyed a long and varied career that spanned not only the post-Reconstruction years but also the rise of the modern black civil rights movement and the mid-twentieth-century struggle for independence among the colonized peoples of Africa and the West Indies. Northern-born but of Haitian descent on his father's side, and equipped with degrees from Fisk and Harvard Universities, Du Bois began his professional life as a professor at Atlanta University; as such he was socially at some distance from the rural African American folk culture he celebrated in his acclaimed (and largely anti-Washingtonian) *The Souls of Black Folk* (1903). Thoroughly committed to making a difference as an activist, by 1910 he left academia to help lead the National Association for the Advancement of Colored People (NAACP), of which he was a cofounder. As the editor of the NAACP's *The Crisis,* Du Bois turned his largely black readership's attention to political and cultural events both national and international. The following excerpt from his 1897 essay "The Conservation of Races" suggests that even as a young man Du Bois cultivated a nascent black nationalist position that by his death in the early 1960s would prompt him to forsake his U.S. citizenship and settle in the African republic of Ghana. The essay was initially delivered as an address to the American Negro Academy, the first black scholarly society in the United States. It was then published in the Academy's *Occasional Papers* series (Washington, D.C.: The American Negro Academy, 1897).

The American Negro has always felt an intense personal interest in discussions as to the origins and destinies of races: primarily because back of most discussions of race with which he is familiar, have lurked certain assumptions as to his natural abilities, as to his political, intellectual and moral status, which he felt were wrong. He has, consequently, been led to deprecate and minimize race distinctions, to believe intensely that out of one blood God created all nations, and to speak of human brotherhood as though it were the possibility of an already dawning to-morrow.

Nevertheless, in our calmer moments we must acknowledge that human beings are divided into races; that in this country the two most extreme types of the world's races have met, and the resulting problem as to the future relations of these types is not only of intense and living interest to us, but forms an epoch in the history of mankind.

It is necessary, therefore, in planning our movements, in guiding our future development, that at times we rise above the pressing, but smaller questions of separate schools and cars, wage-discrimination and lynch law, to survey the whole question of race in human philosophy and to lay, on a basis of broad knowledge and careful insight, those large lines of policy and higher ideals which may form our guiding lines and boundaries in the practical difficulties of every day. For it is certain that all human striving must recognize the hard limits of natural law, and that any striving, no matter how intense and earnest, which is against the constitution of the world, is vain. The question, then, which we must seriously consider is this: What is the real meaning of Race; what has, in the past, been the law of race development, and what lessons has the past history of race development to teach the rising Negro people?

When we thus come to inquire into the essential difference of races we find it hard to come at once to any definite conclusion. Many criteria of race differences have in the past been proposed, as color, hair, cranial measurements and language. And manifestly, in each of these respects, human beings differ widely. They vary in color, for instance, from the marble-like pallor of the Scandinavian to the rich, dark brown of the Zulu, passing by the creamy Slav, the yellow Chinese, the light brown Sicilian and the brown Egyptian. Men vary, too, in the texture of hair from the obstinately straight hair of the Chinese to the obstinately tufted and frizzled hair of the Bushman. In measurement of heads, again, men vary; from the broad-headed Tartar to the medium-headed European and the narrow-headed Hottentot; or, again in language, from the highly-inflected Roman tongue to the monosyllabic Chinese. All these physical characteristics are patent enough, and if they agreed with each other it would be very easy to classify mankind. Unfortunately for scientists, however, these criteria of race are most exasperatingly intermingled. Color does not agree with texture of hair, for many of the dark races have straight hair; nor does color agree with the breadth of the head, for the yellow Tartar has a broader head than the German; nor, again, has the science of language as yet succeeded in clearing up the relative authority of these various and contradictory criteria. The final word of science, so far, is that we have at least two, perhaps three, great families of human beings — the whites and Negroes, possibly the yellow race. That other races have arisen from the intermingling of the blood of these two. This broad division of the world's races which men like Huxley and Raetzel [*sic*] have introduced as more nearly true than the old five-race scheme of Blumenbach, is nothing more than an acknowledgment that, so far as purely physical characteristics are concerned, the differences between men do not explain all the differences of their history. It declares, as Darwin[1] himself said, that great as is the physical unlikeness of the various races of men their likenesses are greater, and upon this rests the whole scientific doctrine of Human Brotherhood.

Although the wonderful developments of human history teach that the grosser physical differences of color, hair and bone go but a short way toward explaining the different roles which groups of men have played in Human Progress, yet there are differences — subtle, delicate and elusive, though they may be — which have silently but definitely separated men into groups. While these subtle forces have generally followed the natural cleavage of common blood, descent and physical peculiarities, they have at other times swept across and ignored these.

[1] *Huxley and Raetzel. . . . Darwin:* Here Du Bois cites influential European race theorists of the eighteenth and nineteenth centuries: British biologist Thomas Henry Huxley (1825–1895), a staunch defender of evolutionary theory; German journalist and geographer Friedrich Ratzel (1844–1904); German naturalist and scientist Johann Friedrich Blumenbach (1752–1840), who classified humans as Caucasian, Mongolian, Ethiopian, American, and Malay, based on appearance and geography; and Charles Darwin (1809–1882), the British naturalist who launched modern evolutionary theory with his 1859 *Origin of Species.*

At all times, however, they have divided human beings into races, which, while they perhaps transcend scientific definition, nevertheless, are clearly defined to the eye of the Historian and Sociologist.

If this be true, then the history of the world is the history, not of individuals, but of groups, not of nations, but of races, and he who ignores or seeks to override the race idea in human history ignores and overrides the central thought of all history. What, then, is a race? It is a vast family of human beings, generally of common blood and language, always of common history, traditions and impulses, who are both voluntarily and involuntarily striving together for the accomplishment of certain more or less vividly conceived ideals of life.

Turning to real history, there can be no doubt, first, as to the widespread, nay, universal, prevalence of the race idea, the race spirit, the race ideal, and as to its efficiency as the vastest and most ingenious invention for human progress. We, who have been reared and trained under the individualistic philosophy of the Declaration of Independence and the laisser-faire philosophy of Adam Smith,[2] are loath to see and loath to acknowledge this patent fact of human history. We see the Pharaohs, Caesars, Toussaints and Napoleons[3] of history and forget the vast races of which they were but epitomized expressions. We are apt to think in our American impatience, that while it may have been true in the past that closed race groups made history, that here in conglomerate America *nous avons changer tout cela*[4] — we have changed all that, and have no need of this ancient instrument of progress. This assumption of which the Negro people are especially fond, can not be established by a careful consideration of history.

We find upon the world's stage today eight distinctly differentiated races, in the sense in which History tells us the word must be used. They are, the Slavs of eastern Europe, the Teutons of middle Europe, the English of Great Britain and America, the Romance nations of Southern and Western Europe, the Negroes of Africa and America, the Semitic people of Western Asia and Northern Africa, the Hindoos of Central Asia and the Mongolians of Eastern Asia. . . .

---

[2] *Adam Smith:* Smith (1723–1790) was a highly influential Scottish economist and political philosopher.

[3] *Pharoahs, Caesars, Toussaints and Napoleons:* The Pharoahs and Caesars were powerful rulers of ancient Egypt and Rome respectively. Toussaint L'Ouverture (1743–1803) led the Haitian revolution against slavery and French rule. Napoleon Bonaparte (1769–1821) was legendary as both a powerful ruler of France and a highly successful military general.

[4] *nous avons changer tout cela:* As Du Bois himself translates, "We have changed all that."

The question now is: What is the real distinction between these nations? Is it the physical differences of blood, color and cranial measurements? Certainly we must all acknowledge that physical differences play a great part, and that, with wide exceptions and qualifications, these eight great races of to-day follow the cleavage of physical race distinctions; the English and Teuton[5] represent the white variety of mankind; the Mongolian, the yellow; the Negroes, the black. Between these are many crosses and mixtures, where Mongolian and Teuton have blended into the Slav, and other mixtures have produced the Romance nations and the Semites. But while race differences have followed mainly physical race lines, yet no mere physical distinctions would really define or explain the deeper differences — the cohesiveness and continuity of these groups. The deeper differences are spiritual, psychical, differences — undoubtedly based on the physical, but infinitely transcending them. The forces that bind together the Teuton nations are, then, first, their race identity and common blood; secondly, and more important, a common history, common laws and religion, similar habits of thought and a conscious striving together for certain ideals of life. The whole process which has brought about these race differentiations has been a growth, and the great characteristic of this growth has been the differentiation of spiritual and mental differences between great races of mankind and the integration of physical differences.

The age of nomadic tribes of closely related individuals represents the maximum of physical differences. They were practically vast families, and there were as many groups as families. As the families came together to form cities the physical differences lessened, purity of blood was replaced by the requirement of domicile, and all who lived within the city bounds became gradually to be regarded as members of the group; *i.e.,* there was a slight and slow breaking down of physical barriers. This, however, was accompanied by an increase of the spiritual and social differences between cities. This city became husbandmen, this, merchants, another warriors, and so on. The *ideals of life* for which the different cities struggled were different. When at last cities began to coalesce into nations there was another breaking down of barriers which separated groups of men. The larger and broader differences of color, hair and physical proportions were not by any means ignored, but myriads of minor differences disappeared, and the sociological and historical races of men began to approximate the present division of races as indicated by physical researches. At the

[5] *Teuton:* German.

same time the spiritual and physical differences of race groups which constituted the nations became deep and decisive. The English nation stood for constitutional liberty and commercial freedom; the German nation for science and philosophy; the Romance nations[6] stood for literature and art, and the other race groups are striving, each in its own way, to develope for civilization its particular message, its particular ideal, which shall help to guide the world nearer and nearer that perfection of human life for which we all long, that

"one far off Divine event."[7]

This has been the function of race differences up to the present time. What shall be its function in the future? Manifestly some of the great races of today — particularly the Negro race — have not as yet given to civilization the full spiritual message which they are capable of giving. . . . The question is, then: How shall this message be delivered; how shall these various ideals be realized? The answer is plain: By the development of these race groups, not as individuals, but as races. . . . For the development of Negro genius, of Negro literature and art, of Negro spirit, only Negroes bound and welded together, Negroes inspired by one vast ideal, can work out in its fullness the great message we have for humanity. We cannot reverse history; we are subject to the same natural laws as other races, and if the Negro is ever to be a factor in the world's history — if among the gaily-colored banners that deck the broad ramparts of civilization is to hang one uncompromising black, then it must be placed there by black hands, fashioned by black heads and hallowed by the travail of 200,000,000 black hearts beating in one glad song of jubilee.

For this reason, the advance guard of the Negro people — the 8,000,000 people of Negro blood in the United States of America — must soon come to realize that if they are to take their just place in the van of Pan-Negroism, then their destiny is *not* absorption by the white Americans. That if in America it is to be proven for the first time in the modern world that not only Negroes are capable of evolving individual men like Toussaint, the Saviour, but are a nation stored with wonderful possibilities of culture, then their destiny is not a servile imitation of Anglo-Saxon culture, but a stalwart originality which shall unswervingly follow Negro ideals.

---

[6] *the Romance nations:* Those countries whose languages are derived from Latin, namely, Spain, France, Portugal, and Italy.
[7] *"one far off Divine event":* From the narrative poem *Enoch Arden* by Alfred, Lord Tennyson (1809–1892).

It may, however, be objected here that the situation of our race in America renders this attitude impossible; that our sole hope of salvation lies in our being able to lose our race identity in the commingled blood of the nation; and that any other course would merely increase the friction of races which we call race prejudice, and against which we have so long and so earnestly fought.

Here, then, is the dilemma, and it is a puzzling one, I admit. No Negro who has given earnest thought to the situation of his people in America has failed, at some time in life, to find himself at these crossroads; has failed to ask himself at some time: What, after all, am I? Am I an American or am I a Negro? Can I be both? Or is it my duty to cease to be a Negro as soon as possible and be an American? If I strive as a Negro, am I not perpetuating the very cleft that threatens and separates Black and White America? Is not my only possible practical aim the subduction of all that is Negro in me to the American? Does my black blood place upon me any more obligation to assert my nationality than German, or Irish or Italian blood would?

It is such incessant self-questioning and the hesitation that arises from it, that is making the present period a time of vacillation and contradiction for the American Negro; combined race action is stifled, race responsibility is shirked, race enterprises languish, and the best blood, the best talent, the best energy of the Negro people cannot be marshalled to do the bidding of the race. They stand back to make room for every rascal and demagogue who chooses to cloak his selfish deviltry under the veil of race pride.

Is this right? Is it rational? Is it good policy? Have we in America a distinct mission as a race — a distinct sphere of action and an opportunity for race development, or is self-obliteration the highest end to which Negro blood dare aspire?

If we carefully consider what race prejudice really is, we find it, historically, to be nothing but the friction between different groups of people; it is the difference in aim, in feeling, in ideals of two different races; if, now, this difference exists touching territory, laws, language, or even religion, it is manifest that these people cannot live in the same territory without fatal collision; but if, on the other hand, there is substantial agreement in laws, language and religion; if there is a satisfactory adjustment of economic life, then there is no reason why, in the same country and on the same street, two or three great national ideals might not thrive and develop, that men of different races might not strive together for their race ideals as well, perhaps even better, than in isolation. Here, it seems to me, is the reading of the riddle that puzzles so many of us. We are Americans, not only by birth and by citizenship, but by our political ideals, our language, our religion. Farther than that, our Americanism does not go. At that point, we are Negroes, members of a vast historic race that from the very dawn of creation has slept, but half awakening in the dark forests of its African fatherland. We are the first fruits of this new nation, the harbinger of that black to-morrow which is yet destined to soften the whiteness of the Teutonic to-day. We are that people whose subtle sense of song has given America its only American music, its only American fairy tales, its only touch of pathos and humor amid its mad money-getting plutocracy. As such, it is our duty to conserve our physical powers, our intellectual endowments, our spiritual ideals; as a race we must strive by race organization, by race solidarity, by race unity to the realization of that broader humanity which freely recognizes differences in men, but sternly deprecates inequality in their opportunities of development.

For the accomplishment of these ends we need race organizations: Negro colleges, Negro newspapers, Negro business organizations, a Negro school of literature and art, and an intellectual clearing house, for all these products of the Negro mind, which we may call a Negro Academy. Not only is all this necessary for positive advance, it is absolutely imperative for negative defense. Let us not deceive ourselves at our situation in this country. Weighted with a heritage of moral iniquity from our past history, hard pressed in the economic world by foreign immigrants and native prejudice, hated here, despised there and pitied everywhere; our one haven of refuge is ourselves, and but one means of advance, our own belief in our great destiny, our own implicit trust in our ability and worth. There is no power under God's high heaven that can stop the advance of eight thousand thousand honest, earnest, inspired and united people. But — and here is the rub — they *must* be honest, fearlessly criticising their own faults, zealously correcting them; they must be *earnest*. No people that laughs at itself, and ridicules itself, and wishes to God it was anything but itself ever wrote its name in history; it *must* be inspired with the Divine faith of our black mothers, that out of the blood and dust of battle will march a victorious host, a mighty nation, a peculiar people, to speak to the nations of earth a Divine truth that shall make them free. And such a people must be united; not merely united for the organized theft of political spoils, not united to disgrace religion with whoremongers and ward-heelers,[8] not united merely to protest and pass resolutions,

---

[8] *ward-heelers:* Here Du Bois contemptuously refers to those on the payroll of a district's political machine.

but united to stop the ravages of consumption among the Negro people, united to keep black boys from loafing, gambling and crime; united to guard the purity of black women and to reduce that vast army of black prostitutes that is today marching to hell; and united in serious organizations, to determine by careful conference and thoughtful interchange of opinion the broad lines of policy and action for the American Negro.

This is the reason for being which the American Negro Academy has. It aims at once to be the epitome and expression of the intellect of the black-blooded people of America, the exponent of the race ideals of one of the world's great races. As such, the Academy must, if successful, be

- *(a)*. Representative in character.
- *(b)*. Impartial in conduct.
- *(c)*. Firm in leadership.

It must be representative in character; not in that it represents all interests or all factions, but in that it seeks to comprise something of the *best* thought, the most unselfish striving and the highest ideals. There are scattered in forgotten nooks and corners throughout the land, Negroes of some considerable training, of high minds, and high motives, who are unknown to their fellows, who exert far too little influence. These the Negro Academy should strive to bring into touch with each other and to give them a common mouthpiece.

The Academy should be impartial in conduct; while it aims to exalt the people it should aim to do so by truth — not by lies, by honesty — not by flattery. It should continually impress the fact upon the Negro people that they must not expect to have things done for them — they MUST DO FOR THEMSELVES; that they have on their hands a vast work of self-reformation to do, and that a little less complaint and whining, and a little more dogged work and manly striving would do us more credit and benefit than a thousand Force or Civil Rights bills.[9]

Finally, the American Negro Academy must point out a practical path of advance to the Negro people; there lie before every Negro today hundreds of questions of policy and right which must be settled

---

[9] *a thousand Force or Civil Rights bills:* The Civil Rights Acts of 1866 and 1875 were designed to buttress the Fourteenth and Fifteenth Amendments by stressing American citizenship as the privilege of birth or naturalization, not race, and that all citizens were entitled to equal treatment. The three Enforcement Acts of 1870 and 1871 were also meant to support the amendments, but since they stipulated fines and imprisonment for disobedient officials, they were popularly nicknamed the Force Acts.

and which each one settles now, not in accordance with any rule, but by impulse or individual preference; for instance: What should be the attitude of Negroes toward the educational qualification for voters? What should be our attitude toward separate schools? How should we meet discriminations on railways and in hotels? Such questions need not so much specific answers for each part as a general expression of policy, and nobody should be better fitted to announce such a policy than a representative honest Negro Academy. . . .

In the field of Sociology an appalling work lies before us. First, we must unflinchingly and bravely face the truth, not with apologies, but with solemn earnestness. The Negro Academy ought to sound a note of warning that would echo in every black cabin in the land: *Unless we conquer our present vices they will conquer us;* we are diseased, we are developing criminal tendencies, and an alarmingly large percentage of our men and women are sexually impure. The Negro Academy should stand and proclaim this over the housetops, crying with Garrison:[10] *I will not equivocate, I will not retreat a single inch, and I will be heard.* The Academy should seek to gather about it the talented, unselfish men, the pure and noble-minded women, to fight an army of devils that disgraces our manhood and our womanhood. There does not stand today upon God's earth a race more capable in muscle, in intellect, in morals, than the American Negro, if he will bend his energies in the right direction, if he will

> Burst his birth's invidious bar
> And grasp the skirts of happy chance,
> And breast the blows of circumstance,
> And grapple with his evil star.[11]

In science and morals, I have indicated two fields of work for the Academy. Finally, in practical policy, I wish to suggest the following *Academy Creed:*

1. We believe that the Negro people, as a race, have a contribution to make to civilization and humanity, which no other race can make.

[10] *Garrison:* The Bostonian William Lloyd Garrison (1805–1879) was the premier pre–Civil War white abolitionist in the United States. The cofounder of the American Anti-Slavery Society, and the editor of the antislavery paper the *Liberator,* Garrison's militancy earned him thousands of black and white supporters. He is reputed to have uttered these words upon founding the *Liberator* in 1831.

[11] *Burst his birth's invidious bar . . . evil star:* From Tennyson's *Enoch Arden.*

2. We believe it the duty of the Americans of Negro descent, as a body, to maintain their race identity until this mission of the Negro people is accomplished, and the ideal of human brotherhood has become a practical possibility.

3. We believe that, unless modern civilization is a failure, it is entirely feasible and practicable for two races in such essential political, economic and religious harmony as the white and colored people of America, to develop side by side in peace and mutual happiness, the peculiar contribution which each has to make to the culture of their common country.

4. As a means to this end we advocate, not such social equality between these races as would disregard human likes and dislikes, but such a social equilibrium as would, throughout all the complicated relations of life, give due and just consideration to culture, ability, and moral worth, whether they be found under white or black skins.

5. We believe that the first and greatest step toward the settlement of the present friction between the races — commonly called the Negro Problem — lies in the correction of the immorality, crime and laziness among the Negroes themselves, which still remains as a heritage from slavery. We believe that only earnest and long continued efforts on our own part can cure these social ills.

6. We believe that the second great step toward a better adjustment of the relations between the races, should be a more impartial selection of ability in the economic and intellectual world, and a greater respect for personal liberty and worth, regardless of race. We believe that only earnest efforts on the part of the white people of this country will bring much needed reform in these matters.

7. On the basis of the foregoing declaration, and firmly believing in our high destiny, we, as American Negroes, are resolved to strive in every honorable way for the realization of the best and highest aims, for the development of strong manhood and pure womanhood, and for the rearing of a race ideal in America and Africa, to the glory of God and the uplifting of the Negro people.

THEODORE ROOSEVELT

From *Birth Reform, from the Positive, Not the Negative, Side*

Long before and long after he served as the twenty-sixth president of the United States, Theodore Roosevelt (1858–1919) epitomized a patrician image of American wealth, political power, and cultural influence. Born to a prominent New York family, Roosevelt attended Harvard and started but never completed a Columbia law degree before finally turning to government service. By the time the Spanish-American War broke out in 1898, Roosevelt had already served as U.S. civil service commissioner, the police commissioner of New York, and the assistant secretary of the Navy under President William McKinley. After serving during the war as an officer with the "Rough Riders" in Cuba, Roosevelt was elected governor of New York, and then later McKinley's vice president when the latter ran again for the White House. After McKinley's assassination in 1901, Roosevelt assumed the presidency until 1904, when he was reelected for a second term. The author of extensive histories, biographies, and social commentaries, Roosevelt was at once ambitious and autocratic, a staunch nationalist who as president worked to promote the United States as an imperialistic world power. At home he displayed an enduring admiration for the courageous black soldiers who had fought in the war with Spain, and he invited Booker T. Washington to breakfast at the White House, much to the chagrin of southern white supremacists. However, his support for racial unity never went beyond such token gestures, and as his commentary "Birth Reform" suggests, he was concerned that the future of the American Anglo-Saxon "stock" was in grave danger as native-born white women in his opinion selfishly put off marriage and childbearing. The entire commentary can be found in Roosevelt's *The Foes of Our Own Household,* published in 1914. See *The Works of Theodore Roosevelt,* vol. 21 (New York: Charles Scribner's Sons, 1925).

Reforms are excellent, but if there is nobody to reform their value becomes somewhat problematical. In order to make a man into a better citizen we must first have the man. In order that there shall be a "fuller and better expressed life for the average woman," that average woman must be in actual existence. And the first necessity in "bringing up the child aright" is to produce the child.

Stated in the abstract, these propositions are of bromidic triteness. But an astonishingly large number of persons, including a lamentably large number who call themselves social reformers, either are, or act as if they were, utterly blind to them when they try to deal with life in the concrete. . . . It is true of the possibly well-meaning but certainly silly persons who fail to see that we merely enunciate a perfectly plain mathematical truth when we say that the race will die out unless the average family contains at least three children, and therefore that less than this number always means that, whether because of their fault or their misfortune, the parents are bearing less than their share of the common burdens, and are rendering less than their due proportion of patriotic service to the nation.

. . . These people see that in the "submerged tenth" of society, and even among all the very poor, excessive child-bearing is a grave evil which crushes the woman, turning her into a broken-spirited, over-worked, slatternly drudge; and which therefore crushes the family also, making it difficult for the children, on the average, to rise above a very low level. They do not see that it is the directly reverse danger against which we have to guard as soon as we rise above the class of the very poor, of those whose livelihood is so precarious that they are always on the brink of the gulf of disaster. As soon as we get above this lowest class the real danger in American families, whether of mechanics, farmers, railroad workers, railroad presidents, deep-sea fishermen, bankers, teachers, or lawyers, is not lest they have too many children, but lest they have too few. Yet it is precisely these people who are really influenced by the "birth-control" propaganda. What this nation vitally needs is not the negative preaching of birth control to the submerged tenth, and the tenth immediately adjoining, but the positive preaching of birth encouragement to the eight-tenths who make up the capable, self-respecting American stock which we wish to see perpetuate itself. . . .

The most pitiable showing is made by the graduates of the women's colleges. So far, among the older classes of the older among these colleges, the average girl is represented in the next generation by only 0.86 of a child. This means that for every five possible mothers there were two daughters. Do these colleges teach "domestic science," and if so, *what* is it that they teach? There is something radically wrong with the home-training and the school-training that produce such results. To say this, is not in the least to join with the ignorant and foolish man who denounces higher education for woman; he is usually himself a striking illustration of the need of wiser education for men. But it most certainly is a recognition of the fact, not that there should be any abandonment of, nor indeed any failure to enlarge, the scheme of higher education for women, but that for women as for men this higher education should keep a firm grip on the true perspective of life, and should refuse to sacrifice the great essentials of existence to even the easiest and pleasantest non-essentials.

The trouble in our national life, however, is far more deep-seated than anything affecting only the most highly educated classes. The same drift is visible among our people generally; most so in the East, and in the cities and big towns of the West. In Massachusetts, for the twenty-five years ending in 1911, the deaths among the native-born population exceeded the births by two hundred and seventy thousand, whereas during the same period the births in families with foreign-born parents exceeded the deaths by nearly five hundred and thirty thousand. If this process continues the work of perfecting the boasted common-school and college system for Massachusetts native Americans will prove about as useful as the labor of those worthy missionaries who on different occasions have translated the Bible into the tongues of savage races who thereupon died out.

In the West the native stock — and I use the term with elasticity to include all children of mothers and fathers who were born on this side of the water — is only just about holding its own. It is a little less than holding its own in the cities, a little more than doing so in the country districts. In the cities of Minneapolis and Cleveland, for example, such families average less than three children. In the country districts of Minnesota and Ohio they average about one child more a family, which in this case marks just the difference between increase and decrease. In the South the native white stock is still increasing, although with diminishing rapidity.

. . . When the health conditions become such that child mortality is reduced still lower than at present, and when marriages become more universal and the having and rearing of a sufficient number of children is recognized for both man and woman as the highest duty and the greatest and most extraordinary pleasure of life, then an average family of three children may mean a slow increase. Under any circumstances an average of one or two children means rapid race suicide, and therefore profound moral delinquency in those wilfully responsible for it. But this is not all! At present whoever has only three children must be understood to represent a slight drag on the forward movement of the nation, a slight falling below the average necessary standard in the performance of the indispensable duty without which there will in the end be no nation; the duty, failure to perform which means that all talk of eugenics and social reform and moral uplift and self-development represents mere empty threshing of the air, as pointless as similar talk by a suicide.

. . . I hold that the average American is a decent, self-respecting man, with large capacities for good service to himself, his country, and the world if a right appeal can be made to him and the right response evoked. Therefore, I hold that it is not best that he and his kind should perish from the earth. The great problem of civilization is to secure a relative increase of the valuable as compared with the less valuable or noxious elements in the population. This problem cannot be met unless we give full consideration to the immense influence of heredity. There is far less danger of our forgetting the also very great influence of environment, which includes education. Except in a small number of cases, the state can exercise little active control against the perpetuation of the unfit. Therefore, the real and great service must be rendered by those who help put an aroused and effective public opinion on the side of the perpetuation of the stocks from which it is particularly important that the future citizenship of the nation should be drawn. . . .

. . . If our birth-rate continues to diminish we shall by the end of this century be impotent in the face of powers like Germany, Russia, or Japan; we shall have been passed by the great states of South America.

We are dealing with rules, not with exceptions. We are discussing the birth-rate in any given community, just as we discuss the ability of a community in time of war to provide soldiers for the nation's safety. In any small group of men it may happen that, for good and sufficient reasons, it is impossible for any of the members to go to war: two or three may be physically unfit, two or three may be too old or too young, and the remaining two or three may be performing civil duties of such vital consequence to the commonwealth that it would be wrong to send them to the front. In such case no blame attaches to any individual, and high praise may attach to all. But if in a group of a thousand men more than a small minority are unwilling and unfit to go to war in the hour of the nation's need, then there is something radically wrong with them, spiritually or physically, and they stand in need of drastic treatment. So it is as regards marriage and children. In a small group there may be good and sufficient explanations why the individual men and women have remained unmarried; and the fact that those that marry have no children, or only one or two children, may be cause only for sincere and respectful sympathy. But if, in a community of a thousand men and a thousand women, a large proportion of them remain unmarried, and if of the marriages so many are sterile, or with only one or two children, that the population is decreasing, then there is something radically wrong with the people of that community as a whole. The trouble may be partly physical, partly due to the strange troubles which accompany an overstrained intensity of life. But even in this case the root trouble is probably moral; and in all probability the whole trouble is moral, and is due to a complex tissue of causation in which coldness, love of ease, striving after social position, fear of pain, dislike of hard work, and sheer inability to get life values in their proper perspective all play a part.

The fundamental instincts are not only the basic but also the loftiest instincts in human nature. The qualities that make men and women eager lovers, faithful, duty-performing, hard-working husbands and wives, and wise and devoted fathers and mothers stand at the foundations of all possible social welfare, and also represent the loftiest heights of human happiness and usefulness. No other form of personal success and happiness or of individual service to the state compares with that which is represented by the love of the one man for the one woman, of their joint work as home-maker and home-keeper, and of their ability to bring up the children that are theirs.

Among human beings, as among all other living creatures, if the best specimens do not, and the poorer specimens do, propagate, the type will go down. If Americans of the old stock lead lives of celibate selfishness (whether profligate or merely frivolous or objectless, matters little), or if the married are afflicted by that base fear of living which, whether for the sake of themselves or of their children, forbids them to have more than one or two children, disaster awaits the nation. It is not well for a nation to import its art and its literature; but it is fatal for a nation to import its babies. And it is utterly futile to make believe that fussy activity for somebody else's babies atones for failure of personal parenthood. . . .

. . . In all public offices in every grade the lowest salaries should be paid the man or woman with no children, or only one or two children, and a marked discrimination made in favor of the man or woman with a family of *over* three children. In taxation, the rate should be immensely heavier on the childless and on the families with one or two children, while an equally heavy discrimination should lie in favor of the family with *over* three children. This should apply to the income tax and inheritance tax, and as far as possible to other taxes. I speak, as usual, of the average, not the exception. Only the father and mother of over three children have done their full duty by the state; and the state should emphasize this fact. No reduction should be made in a man's taxes merely because he is married. But he should be exempted on an additional five hundred dollars of income for each of his first two children, and on an additional one thousand dollars of income for every subsequent child — for we wish to put especial emphasis on the vital need of having the third and the fourth and the fifth children. The men and women with small or reasonable incomes are the ones who should be encouraged to have children; they do not represent a class which will be tempted by such exemption to thriftlessness or extravagances. I do not believe that there should be any income exemption whatever for the unmarried man or the childless married couple; let all the exemptions be for the married couples of moderate means who have children.

An aroused and enlightened public opinion can do infinitely more. There must be a sterner sense of duty and a clearer vision of the perspectives among which duty must work. That standard of living is poor, whether for mechanic or bank president, which is based on ease, comfort, luxury, and social ambition rather than on education, culture, and wide ability to shift for oneself. The oldest duty of all is that owed by the fathers and mothers of Americans to care for the future of their country and the ideals of their race. The man and the woman must be partners in love, in mutual forbearance, in gallant facing of the future, in wise choice of duty among conflicting considerations.

CHARLOTTE PERKINS GILMAN

From *Women and Economics*

New England-born Charlotte Perkins Gilman (1860–1935) is best known as an early pioneer of the white U.S. feminist movement, and as the author of two classic pieces of early feminist fiction, *The Yellow Wallpaper* (1899), about a wife trapped by her life as a useless object of male desire, and *Herland* (1915), a fantasy about an all-female society discovered by male explorers. As a lecturer, writer, and social commentator, Gilman advocated for women's rights to education and employment outside the home, and she used her considerable intellectual talents to theorize the social and economic conditions that led to the sexual division of labor, producing sociological studies such as *Women and Economics: A Study of the Economic Relation Between Men and Women as a Factor in Social Evolution* (1899); *The Home: Its Work and Influence* (1903); and *The Man-made World; or, Our Androcentric Culture* (1911). In her definition of what constituted an "American," Gilman was also very much a eugenicist and a nationalist. As such, her painstaking arguments in defense of women and in condemnation of male aggression were composed with white, native-born U.S. citizens in mind, not African Americans or European immigrants. Thus, for Gilman, there was no contradiction between her radical and original feminism, and her belief (expressed for instance in her 1908 sociological essay "A Suggestion on the Negro Problem") that African Americans were aliens and an inescapable social burden that whites had to contend with as best they could. Despite this attitude, when she spoke about the reform of *white* American gender politics and the curtailment of white female agency, Gilman's was a powerful voice, as is evidenced in the following excerpts from *Women and Economics* (Boston: Small, Maynard and Company, 1899; 2nd ed.).

The main justification for the subjection of women, which is commonly advanced, is the alleged advantage to motherhood resultant from her extreme specialization to the uses of maternity under this condition.

There are two weak points in this position. One is that the advantage to motherhood cannot be proved: the other, that it is not the uses of maternity to which she is specialized, but the uses of sex-indulgence. So far from the economic dependence of women working in the interests of motherhood, it is the steadily acting cause of a pathological maternity and a decreasing birth-rate.

In simple early times there was a period when women were economically profited by child-bearing; when, indeed, that was their sole use, and, failing it, they were entitled to no respect or profit whatever. Such a condition tended to increase the quantity of children, if not the quality. With industrial development and the increasing weight of economic cares upon the shoulders of the man, children come to be looked upon as a burden, and are dreaded instead of desired by the hard-worked father. They subtract from the family income; and the mother, absolutely dependent upon that income and also overworked in her position of unpaid house-servant, is not impelled to court maternity by any economic pressure. In the working classes — to which the great majority of people belong — the woman is by no means "segregated to the uses of maternity." Among the most intelligent and conscientious workingmen to-day there is a strong feeling against large families, and a consistent effort is made to prevent them.

Lest this be considered as not bearing directly upon the economic position of women, but rather on the general status of the working classes, let us examine the same condition among the wealthy. It is here that the economic dependence of women is carried to its extreme. The daughters and wives of the rich fail to perform even the domestic service expected of the women of poorer families. They are from birth to death absolutely non-productive in goods or labor of economic value, and consumers of such goods and labor to an extent limited only by the purchasing power of their male relatives. In this condition the economic advantage of the woman, married or unmarried, not merely in food and clothes, but in such social advantage as she desires, lies in her power to attract and hold the devotion of men; and this power is not the power of maternity. On the contrary, maternity, by lowering the personal charms and occupying the time of the mother, fails to bring her the pleasure and profit obtainable by the woman who is not a mother. It is through the sex-relation minus its natural consequence that she profits most; and, therefore, the force of economic advantage acts against maternity instead of toward it.

In the last extreme this is clear to all in the full flower of the sexuo-economic relation, — prostitution, than which nothing runs more absolutely counter to the improvement of the race through maternity. Specialization to uses of maternity, as in the queen bee, is one thing. Specialization to uses of sex without maternity is quite another. Yet this popular opinion, that we as a race are greatly benefited by having all our women saved from direct economic activity, and so allowed to concentrate all their energies on the beautiful work of motherhood, remains strong among us. . . .

. . . [I]t is necessary to show that our highly specialized motherhood is not so advantageous as believed; that it is below rather than above the efficacy of motherhood in other species; that its deficiency is due to the sexuo-economic relation; that the restoration of economic freedom to the female will improve motherhood; and, finally, to indicate in some sort the lines of social and individual development along which this improvement may be "practically" manifested. . . .

As the main agent in reproduction, the mother is most to be venerated on basic physiological grounds. As the main agent in developing love, the great human condition, she is the fountain of all our growth. As the beginner of industry, she is again a source of progress. As the first and final educator, she outwardly moulds what she has inwardly made; and, as she is the visible, tangible, lovable, living type of all this, the being in whose person is expressed the very sum of good to the individual, it is no wonder that our strongest, deepest, tenderest feelings cluster about the great word "mother."

Fully recognizing all this, it yet remains open to us to turn the light of science and the honest labor of thought upon this phase of human life as upon any other; to lay aside our feelings, and use our reason; to discover if even here we are justified in leaving the most important work of individual life to the methods of primitive instinct. Motherhood is but a process of life, and open to study as all processes of life are open. Among unconscious, early forms it fulfils its mission by a simple instinct. In the consciousness and complexity of human life it demands far more numerous and varied forces for its right fulfilment. It is with us a conscious process, — a process rife with consequences for good or evil. With this voluntary power come new responsibility and a need for new methods, — a need not merely to consider whether or not we will enter upon the duties of maternity, but how best we can fulfil them.

Motherhood, like every other natural process, is to be measured by its results. It is good or evil as it serves its purpose. Human motherhood must be judged as it serves its purpose to the human race. Primarily, its purpose is to reproduce the race by reproducing the individual; secondarily, to improve the race by improving the individual. The mere office of reproduction is as well performed by the laying of eggs to be posthumously hatched as by many years of exquisite devotion; but in the improvement of the species we come to other requirements. The functions of motherhood have been evolved as naturally as the functions of nutrition, and each stage of development has brought new duties to the mother. The mother bird must brood her young, the mother cow must suckle them, the mother cat must hunt for them; and, in every varied service which the mother gives, its value is to be measured by its effect upon the young. To perform that which is most good for the young of the species is the measure of right motherhood, and that which is most good for the young is what will help them to a better maturity than that of their parents. To leave in the world a creature better than its parent; this is the purpose of right motherhood.

In the human race this purpose is served by two processes: first, by the simple individual function of reproduction, of which all care and nursing are but an extension; and, second, by the complex social function of education. This was primarily a maternal process, and therefore individual; but it has long since become a racial rather than an individual function, and bears no relation to sex or other personal limitation. The young of the human race require for their best development not only the love and care of the mother, but the care and instruction of many besides their mother. So largely is this true that it may be said in extreme terms that it would be better for a child to-day to be left absolutely without mother or family of any sort, in the city of Boston, for instance, than to be supplied with a large and affectionate family and be planted with them in Darkest Africa.

Human functions are race-functions, social functions; and education is one of them. The duty of the human mother, and the measure of its right or wrong fulfilment, are to be judged along these two main lines, reproduction and education. As we have no species above us with which to compare our motherhood, we must measure by those below us. We must show improvement upon them in this function which we all hold in common. . . .

The more absolutely woman is segregated to sex-functions only, cut off from all economic use and made wholly dependent on the sex-relation as means of livelihood, the more pathological does her motherhood become. The over-development of sex caused by her economic dependence on the male reacts unfavorably upon her essential duties. She is too female for perfect motherhood! . . . The female segregated to the uses of sex alone naturally deteriorates in racial development, and naturally transmits that deterioration to her offspring. The human mother, in the processes of reproduction, shows no gain in efficiency over the lower animals, but rather a loss, and so far presents no evidence to prove that her specialization to sex is of any advantage to her young. The mother of a dead baby or the baby of a dead mother; the sick baby, the crooked baby, the idiot baby; the exhausted, nervous, prematurely aged mother, — these are not uncommon among us; and they do not show much progress in our motherhood. . . .

. . . Consider not the rosy ideal of motherhood you have in your mind, but the coarse, hard facts of motherhood as you see them, and hear them, in daily life.

Motherhood in its fulfilment of educational duty can be measured only by its effects. If we take for a standard the noble men and women whose fine physique and character we so fondly attribute to "a devoted mother," what are we to say of the motherhood which has filled the world with the ignoble men and women, of depraved physique and character? If the good mother makes the good man, how about the bad ones? When we see great men and women, we give credit to their mothers. When we see inferior men and women, — and that is a common circumstance, — no one presumes to question the motherhood which has produced them. When it comes to congenital criminality, we are beginning to murmur something about "heredity"; and, to meet gross national ignorance, we do demand a better system of education. But no one presumes to suggest that the mothering of mankind could be improved upon; and yet there is where the responsibility really lies. If our human method of reproduction is defective, let the mother answer. She is the main factor in reproduction. If our human method of education is defective, let the mother answer. She is the main factor in education. . . .

The duty of the mother is first to produce children as good as or better than herself; to hand down the constitution and character of those behind her the better for her stewardship; to build up and improve the human race through her enormous power as mother; to make better people. This being done, it is then the duty of the mother, the human mother, so to educate her children as to complete what bearing and nursing have only begun. She carries the child nine months in her body, two years in her arms, and as long as she lives in her heart and mind. The education of the young is a tremendous factor in human reproduction. A right motherhood should be able to fulfil this great function perfectly. It should understand with an ever-growing power the best methods of developing, strengthening, and directing the child's faculties of body and mind, so that each generation, reaching maturity, would start clear of the last, and show a finer, fuller growth, both physically and mentally, than the preceding. That humanity does slowly improve is not here denied; but, granting our gradual improvement, is it all that we could make? And is the gain due to a commensurate improvement in motherhood?

To both we must say no. When we see how some families improve, while others deteriorate, and how uncertain and irregular is such improvement as appears, we know that we could make better progress if all children had the same rich endowment and wise care that some receive. And, when we see how much of our improvement is due to gains made in hygienic knowledge, in public provision for education and sanitary regulation, none of which has been accomplished by mothers, we are forced to see that whatever advance the race has made is not exclusively attributable to motherhood. The human mother does less for her young, both absolutely and proportionately, than any kind of mother on earth. She does not obtain food for them, nor covering, nor shelter, nor protection, nor defence. She does not educate them beyond the personal habits required in the family circle and in her limited range of social life. The necessary knowledge of the world, so indispensable to every human being, she cannot give, because she does not possess it. All this provision and education are given by other hands and brains than hers. Neither does the amount of physical care and labor bestowed on the child by its mother warrant her claims to superiority in motherhood: this is but a part of our idealism of the subject. . . .

There does not appear, in the care and education of the child as given by the mother, any special superiority in human maternity. Measuring woman first in direct comparison of her reproductive processes with those of other animals, she does not fulfil this function so easily or so well as they. Measuring her educative processes by inter-personal comparison, the few admittedly able mothers with the many painfully unable ones, she seems more lacking, if possible, than in the other branch. The gain in human education thus far has not been acquired or distributed through the mother, but through men and single women; and there is nothing in the achievements of human motherhood to prove that it is for the advantage of the race to have women give all their time to it. Giving all their time to it does not improve it either in quantity or quality. The woman who works is usually a better reproducer than the woman who does not. And the woman who does not work is not proportionately a better educator.

An extra-terrestrial sociologist, studying human life and hearing for the first time of our so-called "maternal sacrifice" as a means of benefiting the species, might be touched and impressed by the idea. "How beautiful!" he would say. "How exquisitely pathetic and tender! One-half of humanity surrendering all other human interests and activities to concentrate its time, strength, and devotion upon the functions of maternity! To bear and rear the majestic race to which they can never fully belong! To live vicariously forever, through their sons, the daughters being only another vicarious link! What a supreme and magnificent martyrdom!" And he would direct his researches toward discovering what system was used to develope and perfect this sublime consecration of half the race to the perpetuation of the other half. He would view with intense and pathetic interest the endless procession of girls, born human as their brothers were, but marked down at once as "female — abortive type — only use to produce males." He would expect to see this "sex sacrificed to reproductive necessities," yet gifted with human consciousness and intelligence, rise grandly to the occasion, and strive to fit itself in every way for its high office. He would expect to find society commiserating the sacrifice, and honoring above all the glorious creature whose life was to be sunk utterly in the lives of others, and using every force properly to rear and fully to fit these functionaries for their noble office. Alas for the extra-terrestrial sociologist and his natural expectations! After exhaustive study, finding nothing of these things, he would return to Mars or Saturn or wherever he came from, marvelling within himself at the vastness of the human paradox.

If the position of woman is to be justified by the doctrine of maternal sacrifice, surely society, or the individual, or both, would make some preparation for it. No such preparation is made. Society recognizes no such function. Premiums have been sometimes paid for large numbers of children, but they were paid to the fathers of them. The elaborate social machinery which constitutes our universal marriage market has no department to assist or advance motherhood. On the contrary, it is directly inimical to it, so that in our society life motherhood means direct loss, and is avoided by the social devotee. And the individual? Surely here right provision will be made. Young women, glorying in their prospective duties, their sacred and inalienable office, their great sex-martyrdom to race-advantage, will be found solemnly preparing for this work. What do we find? We find our young women reared in an attitude which is absolutely unconscious of and often injurious to their coming motherhood, — an irresponsible, indifferent, ignorant class of beings, so far as motherhood is concerned. They are fitted to attract the other sex for economic uses or, at most, for mutual gratification, but not for motherhood. They are reared in unbroken ignorance of their supposed principal duties, knowing nothing of these duties till they enter upon them. . . .

The education of young women has no department of maternity. It is considered indelicate to give this consecrated functionary any previous knowledge of her sacred duties. This most important and wonderful of human functions is left from age to age in the hands of absolutely untaught women. It is tacitly supposed to be fulfilled by the mysterious working of what we call "the divine instinct of maternity." Maternal instinct is a very respectable and useful instinct common to most animals. It is "divine" and "holy" only as all the laws of nature are divine and holy; and it is such only when it works to the right fulfilment of its use. If the race-preservative processes are to be held more sacred than the self-preservative processes, we must admit all the functions and faculties of reproduction to the same degree of reverence, — the passion of the male for the female as well as the passion of the mother for her young. And if, still further, we are to honor the race-preservative processes most in their highest and latest development, which is the only comparison to be made on a natural basis, we should place the great, disinterested, social function of education far above the second-selfishness of individual maternal functions. Maternal instinct, merely as an instinct, is unworthy of our superstitious reverence. It should be measured only as a means to an end, and valued in proportion to its efficacy. . . .

The human female, denied the enlarged activities which have developed intelligence in man, denied the education of the will which only comes by freedom and power, has maintained the rudimentary forces of instinct to the present day. With her extreme modification to sex, this faculty of instinct runs mainly along sex-lines, and finds fullest vent in the processes of maternity, where it has held unbroken sway. So the children of humanity are born into the arms of an endless succession of untrained mothers, who bring to the care and teaching of their children neither education for that wonderful work nor experience therein: they bring merely the intense accumulated force of a brute instinct, — the blind devoted passion of the mother for the child. Maternal love is an enormous force, but force needs direction. Simply to love the child does not serve him unless specific acts of service express this love. What these acts of service are and how they are performed make or mar his life forever. . . .

Before a man enters a trade, art, or profession, he studies it. He qualifies himself for the duties he is to undertake. He would be held a presuming impostor if he engaged in work he was not fitted to do, and his failure would mark him instantly with ridicule and reproach. In the more important professions, especially in those dealing with what we call "matters of life and death," the shipmaster or pilot, doctor or druggist, is required not only to study his business, but to pass an examination under those who have already become past masters, and obtain a certificate or a diploma or some credential to show that he is fit to be intrusted with the direct responsibility for human life.

Women enter a position which gives into their hands direct responsibility for the life or death of the whole human race with neither study nor experience, with no shadow of preparation or guarantee of capability. So far as they give it a thought, they fondly imagine that this mysterious "maternal instinct" will see them through. Instruction, if needed, they will pick up when the time comes: experience they will acquire as the children appear. "I guess I know how to bring up children!" cried the resentful old lady who was being advised: "I've buried seven!" The record of untrained instinct as a maternal faculty in the human race is to be read on the rows and rows of little gravestones which crowd our cemeteries. The experience gained by practising on the child is frequently buried with it.

No, the maternal sacrifice theory will not bear examination. As a sex specialized to reproduction, giving up all personal activity, all honest independence, all useful and progressive economic service for her glorious consecration to the uses of maternity, the human female has little to show in the way of results which can justify her position. Neither the enormous percentage of children lost by death nor the low average health of those who survive, neither physical nor mental progress, give any proof of race advantage from the maternal sacrifice.

FANNIE BARRIER WILLIAMS

From *The Intellectual Progress of the Colored Women*

African American activist Fannie Barrier Williams (1855–1944) was what many of her contemporaries referred to as a "race woman." That is, she worked tirelessly for social equality and educational and employment opportunities for black women. Born to a prominent African American family in Brockport, New York, Williams taught briefly in the South before marrying L. Laing Williams in 1887. Though she moved among Chicago's black elite after her marriage, Williams challenged racial barriers and sought a larger social role for African American women. In 1895, for instance, she was the first black woman admitted to the all-white Chicago Woman's Club, and she pushed for the establishment of reform-minded clubs for black women, helping to found the National League of Colored Women in 1893, and then later in 1896 the more well-known National Association of Colored Women. She also served on the editorial board of the *Woman's Era,* the first newspaper edited by and for black women. In addition, along with fellow black activists such as Mary Church Terrell and Ida B. Wells, Williams was instrumental in getting representation for African Americans — especially African American women — at the 1893 Chicago Columbian Exposition. By 1900 she openly supported Booker T. Washington, but she still advocated a wide range of educational opportunities for blacks, beyond the practical education sanctioned by Washington's Tuskegee Institute. Delivered before the World's Congress of Representative Women at the Columbian Exposition, the selection below is the best known of Williams's public addresses. The full text can be found in *The World Congress of Representative Women: A Historical Résumé* . . . , vol. 2, ed. May Wright Sewall (Chicago: Rand, McNally and Company, 1894).

Less than thirty years ago the term progress as applied to colored women of African descent in the United States would have been an anomaly. The recognition of that term to-day as appropriate is a fact full of interesting significance. That the discussion of progressive womanhood in this great assemblage of the representative women of the world is considered incomplete without some account of the colored women's status is a most noteworthy evidence that we have not failed to impress ourselves on the higher side of American life.

Less is known of our women than of any other class of Americans.

No organization of far-reaching influence for their special advancement, no conventions of women to take note of their progress, and no special literature reciting the incidents, the events, and all things interesting and instructive concerning them are to be found among the agencies directing their career. There has been no special interest in their peculiar condition as native-born American women. Their power to affect the social life of America, either for good or for ill, has excited not even a speculative interest. . . .

The American people have always been impatient of ignorance and poverty. They believe with Emerson[1] that "America is another word for opportunity," and for that reason success is a virtue and poverty and ignorance are inexcusable. This may account for the fact that our women have excited no general sympathy in the struggle to emancipate themselves from the demoralization of slavery. This new life of freedom, with its far-reaching responsibilities, had to be learned by these children of darkness mostly without a guide, a teacher, or a friend. In the mean vocabulary of slavery there was no definition of any of the virtues of life. The meaning of such precious terms as marriage, wife, family, and home could not be learned in a school-house. The blue-back speller, the arithmetic, and the copy-book contain no magical cures for inherited inaptitudes for the moralities. Yet it must

---

[1] *Emerson:* One of the leading poets and thinkers of the antebellum American renaissance, Ralph Waldo Emerson (1803–1882) believed in the potential of an American aesthetic, and was a proponent of transcendentalism, which stressed nature as the source of spiritual nurturance.

ever be counted as one of the most wonderful things in human history how promptly and eagerly these suddenly liberated women tried to lay hold upon all that there is in human excellence. There is a touching pathos in the eagerness of these millions of new home-makers to taste the blessedness of intelligent womanhood. The path of progress in the picture is enlarged so as to bring to view these trustful and zealous students of freedom and civilization striving to overtake and keep pace with women whose emancipation has been a slow and painful process for a thousand years. The longing to be something better than they were when freedom found them has been the most notable characteristic in the development of these women. This constant striving for equality has given an upward direction to all the activities of colored women.

Freedom at once widened their vision beyond the mean cabin life of their bondage. Their native gentleness, good cheer, and hopefulness made them susceptible to those teachings that make for intelligence and righteousness. Sullenness of disposition, hatefulness, and revenge against the master class because of two centuries of ill-treatment are not in the nature of our women.

But a better view of what our women are doing and what their present status is may be had by noticing some lines of progress that are easily verifiable.

First it should be noticed that separate facts and figures relative to colored women are not easily obtainable. Among the white women of the country independence, progressive intelligence, and definite interests have done so much that nearly every fact and item illustrative of their progress and status is classified and easily accessible. Our women, on the contrary, have had no advantage of interests peculiar and distinct and separable from those of men that have yet excited public attention and kindly recognition.

In their religious life, however, our women show a progressiveness parallel in every important particular to that of white women in all Christian churches. . . .

. . . It is our young women coming out of the schools and academies that have been insisting upon a more godly and cultivated ministry. It is the young women of a new generation and new inspirations that are making tramps of the ministers who once dominated the colored church, and whose intelligence and piety were mostly in their lungs. . . .

Closely allied to this religious development is their progress in the work of education in schools and colleges. For thirty years education has been the magic word among the colored people of this country. That their greatest need was education in its broadest sense was understood by these people more strongly than it could be taught to them. It is the unvarying testimony of every teacher in the South that the mental development of the colored women as well as men has been little less than phenomenal. In twenty-five years, and under conditions discouraging in the extreme, thousands of our women have been educated as teachers. They have adapted themselves to the work of mentally lifting a whole race of people so eagerly and readily that they afford an apt illustration of the power of self-help. Not only have these women become good teachers in less than twenty-five years, but many of them are the prize teachers in the mixed schools of nearly every Northern city.

These women have also so fired the hearts of the race for education that colleges, normal schools, industrial schools, and universities have been reared by a generous public to meet the requirements of these eager students of intelligent citizenship. As American women generally are fighting against the nineteenth century narrowness that still keeps women out of the higher institutions of learning, so our women are eagerly demanding the best of education open to their race. They continually verify what President Rankin of Howard University[2] recently said, "Any theory of educating the Afro-American that does not throw open the golden gates of the highest culture will fail on the ethical and spiritual side."

It is thus seen that our women have the same spirit and mettle that characterize the best of American women. Everywhere they are following in the tracks of those women who are swiftest in the race for higher knowledge.

To-day they feel strong enough to ask for but one thing, and that is the same opportunity for the acquisition of all kinds of knowledge that may be accorded to other women. This granted, in the next generation these progressive women will be found successfully occupying every field where the highest intelligence alone is admissible. In less than another generation American literature, American art, and American music will be enriched by productions having new and peculiar features of interest and excellence.

The exceptional career of our women will yet stamp itself indelibly upon the thought of this country.

---

[2] *President Rankin of Howard University:* The white clergyman and poet Jeremiah Eames Rankin (1828–1904) served as the president of Howard University from 1889 to 1903.

American literature needs for its greater variety and its deeper soundings that which will be written into it out of the hearts of these self-emancipating women.

The great problems of social reform that are now so engaging the highest intelligence of American women will soon need for their solution the reinforcement of that new intelligence which our women are developing. In short, our women are ambitious to be contributors to all the great moral and intellectual forces that make for the greater weal of our common country.

If this hope seems too extravagant to those of you who know these women only in their humbler capacities, I would remind you that all that we hope for and will certainly achieve in authorship and practical intelligence is more than prophesied by what has already been done, and more that can be done, by hundreds of Afro-American women whose talents are now being expended in the struggle against race resistance. . . .

The hearts of Afro-American women are too warm and too large for race hatred. Long suffering has so chastened them that they are developing a special sense of sympathy for all who suffer and fail of justice. All the associated interests of church, temperance, and social reform in which American women are winning distinction can be wonderfully advanced when our women shall be welcomed as co-workers, and estimated solely by what they are worth to the moral elevation of all the people.

I regret the necessity of speaking to the question of the moral progress of our women, because the morality of our home life has been commented upon so disparagingly and meanly that we are placed in the unfortunate position of being defenders of our name.

It is proper to state, with as much emphasis as possible, that all questions relative to the moral progress of the colored women of America are impertinent and unjustly suggestive when they relate to the thousands of colored women in the North who were free from the vicious influences of slavery. They are also meanly suggestive as regards thousands of our women in the South whose force of character enabled them to escape the slavery taints of immorality. The question of the moral progress of colored women in the United States has force and meaning in this discussion only so far as it tells the story of how the once-enslaved women have been struggling for twenty-five years to emancipate themselves from the demoralization of their enslavement.

While I duly appreciate the offensiveness of all references to American slavery, it is unavoidable to charge to that system every moral imperfection that mars the character of the colored American. The whole life and power of slavery depended upon an enforced degradation of everything human in the slaves. The slave code recognized only animal distinctions between the sexes, and ruthlessly ignored those ordinary separations that belong to the social state.

It is a great wonder that two centuries of such demoralization did not work a complete extinction of all the moral instincts. But the recuperative power of these women to regain their moral instincts and to establish a respectable relationship to American womanhood is among the earlier evidences of their moral ability to rise above their conditions. In spite of a cursed heredity that bound them to the lowest social level, in spite of everything that is unfortunate and unfavorable, these women have continually shown an increasing degree of teachableness as to the meaning of woman's relationship to man.

Out of this social purification and moral uplift have come a chivalric sentiment and regard from the young men of the race that give to the young women a new sense of protection. I do not wish to disturb the serenity of this conference by suggesting why this protection is needed and the kind of men against whom it is needed.

It is sufficient for us to know that the daughters of women who thirty years ago were not allowed to be modest, not allowed to follow the instincts of moral rectitude, who could cry for protection to no living man, have so elevated the moral tone of their social life that new and purer standards of personal worth have been created, and new ideals of womanhood, instinct with grace and delicacy, are everywhere recognized and emulated.

This moral regeneration of a whole race of women is no idle sentiment — it is a serious business; and everywhere there is witnessed a feverish anxiety to be free from the mean suspicions that have so long underestimated the character strength of our women.

These women are not satisfied with the unmistakable fact that moral progress has been made, but they are fervently impatient and stirred by a sense of outrage under the vile imputations of a diseased public opinion.

Loves that are free from the dross of coarseness, affections that are unsullied, and a proper sense of all the sanctities of human intercourse felt by thousands of these women all over the land plead for the recognition of their fitness to be judged, not by the standards of slavery, but by the higher standards of freedom and of twenty-five years of education, culture, and moral contact.

The moral aptitudes of our women are just as strong and just as weak as those of any other American women with like advantages of intelligence and environment. . . .

It is almost literally true that, except teaching in colored schools and menial work, colored women can find no employment in this free America. They are the only women in the country for whom real ability, virtue, and special talents count for nothing when they become applicants for respectable employment. Taught everywhere in ethics and social economy that merit always wins, colored women carefully prepare themselves for all kinds of occupation only to meet with stern refusal, rebuff, and disappointment. . . .

Can the people of this country afford to single out the women of a whole race of people as objects of their special contempt? Do these women not belong to a race that has never faltered in its support of the country's flag in every war since Attucks[3] fell in Boston's streets?

Are they not the daughters of men who have always been true as steel against treason to everything fundamental and splendid in the republic? In short, are these women not as thoroughly American in all the circumstances of citizenship as the best citizens of our country?

If it be so, are we not justified in a feeling of desperation against that peculiar form of Americanism that shows respect for our women as servants and contempt for them when they become women of culture? We have never been taught to understand why the unwritten law of chivalry, protection, and fair play that are everywhere the conservators of women's welfare must exclude every woman of a dark complexion.

We believe that the world always needs the influence of every good and capable woman, and this rule recognizes no exceptions based on complexion. In their complaint against hindrances to their employment colored women ask for no special favors.

They are even willing to bring to every position fifty per cent more of ability than is required of any other class of women. They plead for opportunities untrammeled by prejudice. They plead for the right of the individual to be judged, not by tradition and race estimate, but by the present evidences of individual worth. We believe this country is large enough and the opportunities for all kinds of success are great

---

[3] *Attucks:* An early patriot of the American Revolution, the runaway slave Crispus Attucks (1723?–1770) was one of the first protestors against British rule killed in the Boston Massacre of 1770.

enough to afford our women a fair chance to earn a respectable living, and to win every prize within the reach of their capabilities.

Another, and perhaps more serious, hindrance to our women is that nightmare known as "social equality." The term equality is the most inspiring word in the vocabulary of citizenship. It expresses the leveling quality in all the splendid possibilities of American life. It is this idea of equality that has made room in this country for all kinds and conditions of men, and made personal merit the supreme requisite for all kinds of achievement.

When the colored people became citizens, and found it written deep in the organic law of the land that they too had the right to life, liberty, and the pursuit of happiness, they were at once suspected of wishing to interpret this maxim of equality as meaning social equality.

Everywhere the public mind has been filled with constant alarm lest in some way our women shall approach the social sphere of the dominant race in this country. Men and women, wise and perfectly sane in all things else, become instantly unwise and foolish at the remotest suggestion of social contact with colored men and women. At every turn in our lives we meet this fear, and are humiliated by its aggressiveness and meanness. If we seek the sanctities of religion, the enlightenment of the university, the honors of politics, and the natural recreations of our common country, the social equality alarm is instantly given, and our aspirations are insulted. "Beware of social equality with the colored American" is thus written on all places, sacred or profane, in this blessed land of liberty. The most discouraging and demoralizing effect of this false sentiment concerning us is that it utterly ignores individual merit and discredits the sensibilities of intelligent womanhood. The sorrows and heartaches of a whole race of women seem to be matters of no concern to the people who so dread the social possibilities of these colored women. . . .

We come before this assemblage of women feeling confident that our progress has been along high levels and rooted deeply in the essentials of intelligent humanity. We are so essentially American in speech, in instincts, in sentiments and destiny that the things that interest you equally interest us.

We believe that social evils are dangerously contagious. The fixed policy of persecution and injustice against a class of women who are weak and defenseless will be necessarily hurtful to the cause of all women. Colored women are becoming more and more a part of the social forces that must help to determine the questions that so concern women generally. In this Congress we ask to be known and recognized for what we are worth. If it be the high purpose of these deliberations to lessen the resistance to woman's progress, you can not fail to be interested in our struggles against the many oppositions that harass us.

Women who are tender enough in heart to be active in humane societies, to be foremost in all charitable activities, who are loving enough to unite Christian womanhood everywhere against the sin of intemperance, ought to be instantly concerned in the plea of colored women for justice and humane treatment. Women of the dominant race can not afford to be responsible for the wrongs we suffer, since those who do injustice can not escape a certain penalty.

But there is no wish to overstate the obstacles to colored women or to picture their status as hopeless. There is no disposition to take our place in this Congress as faultfinders or suppliants for mercy. As women of a common country, with common interests, and a destiny that will certainly bring us closer to each other, we come to this altar with our contribution of hopefulness as well as with our complaints.

When you learn that womanhood everywhere among us is blossoming out into greater fullness of everything that is sweet, beautiful, and good in woman; when you learn that the bitterness of our experience as citizen-women has not hardened our finer feelings of love and pity for our enemies; when you learn that fierce opposition to the widening spheres of our employment has not abated the aspirations of our women to enter successfully into all the professions and arts open only to intelligence, and that everywhere in the wake of enlightened womanhood our women are seen and felt for the good they diffuse, this Congress will at once see the fullness of our fellowship, and help us to avert the arrows of prejudice that pierce the soul because of the color of our bodies.

If the love of humanity more than the love of races and sex shall pulsate throughout all the grand results that shall issue to the world from this parliament of women, women of African descent in the United States will for the first time begin to feel the sweet release from the blighting thrall of prejudice.

The colored women, as well as all women, will realize that the inalienable right to life, liberty, and the pursuit of happiness is a maxim that will become more blessed in its significance when the hand of woman shall take it from its sepulture in books and make it the gospel of every-day life and the unerring guide in the relations of all men, women, and children.

ROSCOE CONKLING BRUCE

From *Service by the Educated Negro*

Though African Americans at the turn of the century were primarily a working-class population, small enclaves of middle- and upper-class blacks flourished in communities both North and South. Highly educated, often urban-dwelling, and in some cases financially and professionally success-ful, these African Americans seemed (like Dr. Miller in *The Marrow of Tra-dition*) naturally placed to become race leaders. Roscoe Conkling Bruce (1879–1950) was part of just such a society of black elites based in Wash-ington, D.C. The son of the black Reconstruction senator Blanche K. Bruce of Mississippi, Bruce attended Washington's black, academically dis-tinguished M Street School, moving on to Philips Exeter Academy, and then finally to Harvard University. Embracing a sense of racial duty, Bruce was a passionate advocate of black education, serving in turn as the aca-demic department head at Booker T. Washington's Tuskegee Institute, and as the assistant superintendent of schools in Washington, D.C. Though Bruce cherished life amidst the District's black high society, his career as a school superintendent was marred by continual and intense disagreements with the larger black community, and in 1921 he resigned his post to become the principal of a black high school in Kendall, West Virginia. His move to rural Kendall hurt his career as an influential African American educator, and after attempting careers in law, farming, and publishing, he eventually served from 1927 to 1937 as the resident manager of New York City's black Paul Laurence Dunbar Apartments. Bruce's "Service by the Educated Negro" was composed while he was still on the faculty of Tuskegee, long before these shifts in his career. It was originally delivered as the commencement address at Bruce's alma mater, the M Street High School in Washington, D.C., on June 16, 1903, and later published in ar-ticle form in *The Colored American Magazine* (December; Boston: The Colored Co-Operative Publishing Company, 1903).

When George William Curtis[1] had received from Harvard her greatest degree, he arose at the Alumni Dinner and said, "In the old

---

[1] *George William Curtis:* Born into an old New England family, George William Curtis (1824–1892) was a noted travel writer, orator, the editor of *Harper's Weekly*, and an advocate of social reform.

Italian story the nobleman turns out of the hot street crowded with eager faces into the coolness and silence of his palace. As he looks at the pictures of the long line of ancestors he hears a voice, — or is it his own heart beating? — which says to him *noblesse oblige*.[2] The youngest scion of the oldest house is pledged by all the virtues and honor of his ancestry to a life not unworthy his lineage. When I came here I was not a nobleman, but today I have been ennobled. . . ." You, my friends, are ennobled by the diploma of a school, rich in traditions of high endeavor and actual service. Shall those traditions fail to enter your hearts, and to quicken your energies, and to chasten your ambitions? This question you are not now competent to answer, and you will not be competent until you have lived your lives.

Your equipment for the business of life is not contemptible. As workers, you have some acquaintance with the natural resources of our country, and the ways in which they have been utilized in the production and distribution of commodities through the perfecting of industrial organization and the applying of science to work. More importantly, you possess in varying degrees a group of valuable industrial qualities, — that ambition without which work is drudgery and enlargement of life unsought and unattainable; that habit of earnest endeavor which, established by continuous attention to Greek or Latin, mathematics or history, may be utilized in the school room, or on the farm, or in the court room; that habit of self-control which enables men to sacrifice vagrant impulse to sober duty; that resourcefulness which discovers better methods of getting work done; that directing intelligence by which one man can effectively organize for a given purpose, many materials and many workers. In addition to the knowledge and the qualities I have mentioned, most of you have a settled disposition toward some form of self-support appropriate to an exceptional training; while you know that some men must black other men's boots, you also know that a boot-black with a high school diploma at home means waste — waste of time, waste of money, waste of education. Moreover, you appreciate the duties and value the privileges of citizenship in a democracy, and most of you have on the whole a serious intent to do what you reasonably can to promote the general welfare. Such is your equipment as citizens. Finally, as human beings, you are able to participate in the intellectual, aesthetic, and moral interests of cultivated people. How may you with such

[2] *noblesse oblige:* Responsibility that must accompany privilege.

equipment be really useful under the conditions of American life? That is our problem.

And right here let me say that nobody wishes you to make a profession of uplifting your race. In the first place, that's a pretty big job; and in the second place, your race is uplifted whenever one of you manages well a truck farm, a grocery store, a school room, or a bank. Charity begins at home; your chief business should be to uplift each himself. My present purpose, however, is to consider mainly how such individual success may contribute to the welfare of the many.

Let us consider, first of all, how you may be of direct service by work in which the chief factor is personal influence and by work in which the chief factor is directing intelligence.

Teaching is an art inseparable from the personality of the teacher — an art in which a mature person seeks by personal influence to help immature persons build their characters soundly. . . . The best way to become a good teacher is, therefore, to become a good man or a good woman, and to grow in power to interest and influence young people. Such personality and power cannot be manufactured to order, but are slowly developed by much reading and thinking and doing and no little contact with wholesome people. . . . Frederick Douglass had no university degree, but he was certainly a man of culture; his teachers were among the choicest spirits of an aroused generation — Sumner and Garrison and Wendell Phillips[3] — and they gave him breadth and balance and clear-sightedness. . . . The thing that makes one school different from another is not so much curriculum and apparatus, as teaching body. Algebra and trigonometry, Greek and Latin, history and political economy, the student will forget; but he will not forget a teacher gentle but earnest, of disinterested scholarship and life-long devotion. The specific teaching may be quite erased from the memory, but in the heart will be left a deepening respect for the teacher. . . .

Moreover the genuine teacher knows that his duty is not bounded by the four walls of the classroom. He is dealing with boys and girls to be sure, but he is dealing with more — with social conditions. The life and work of the community he must study quite as much as he must study the child. Indeed, child and man are largely products of social

[3] *Frederick Douglass . . . Wendell Phillips:* After teaching himself how to read and write, Frederick Douglass (1817–1895) escaped from slavery to become an abolitionist, writer, newspaper editor, orator, civil rights activist, and statesman, and a celebrated and influential figure in both the United States and Europe. When Douglass first arrived north he joined forces with prominent white abolitionists Charles Sumner (1811–1874), William Lloyd Garrison (1805–1879), and Wendell Phillips (1811–1884).

conditions. The educated teacher, by friendly visits to homes and by cheerful work in churches and societies, will seek to elevate community opinion and the standard of life and work. A crowded unclean home in an undrained street is almost as much an object of concern to the educated teacher as is a hopeless little dunce who can't spell "rabbit!" Let us ground child-study in community study.

This knowledge of the life and work of the community will react upon the program of study. The educated teacher, I have said, aims at raising somewhat the level of life in the community. The program of study is an instrument for that end. . . . For an unscrubbed population the school should emphasize cleanliness; for a propertyless population, foresight and thrift. Let me speak even more definitely. In this city of Washington, as in other urban communities, the death rate of the Negro population is exceedingly high. This excessive death rate is due to a variety of causes; relatively low economic position is a powerful cause. . . . In addition to the teachings of hygiene, the school may aim to remedy the conditions expressed in the high death rate, in two ways, — first, through imparting productive capacity by the training of hands; and second, through developing wants by the touching of hearts and arousing of minds.

Already you have a manual training high school and through the grades certain work in carpentry and sewing and cooking. The increasing efficiency of all such work should be welcomed and actively aided by every educated teacher. After a while, let us hope, the schools here will offer from one end to the other, such teaching of the industrial arts as will prepare students worthily to maintain themselves under severe economic stress. Do you realize that, despite the enlargement of educational opportunities in Washington and the growth of the Negro population, there are probably here today fewer Negro artisans than there were in 1870? Here is a profound need; and for the schools a rare opportunity. Moreover, the school life of most children is short, not over five or six years. If the school possessed adequate facilities for giving industrial capacity, more parents would be willing and able to let their children remain in school seven and eight and nine years. The schools and the cultivated portion of this community cannot afford to give those who ask for bread a stone. We must send the whole boy to school and not merely his head!

Not for a moment do I decry that important function of the schools, which I have called the development of wants. Human wants are social forces. Corn and cotton are grown to supply certain bodily wants: the fine arts are cultivated in response to certain aesthetic wants; philosophy and pure science are elaborated at the quiet insistence of certain intellectual wants; religion is preached to assuage certain spiritual wants. Every voluntary act is the handmaid of some want. Now, it is the fundamental business of the schools to enlarge the range of the students [sic] interests and wants, to stir up a divine discontent. The saddest thing about the Negro peasant in his windowless cabin in Georgia, the saddest thing about the Negroes in the filthy shanties of Mobile, New York, and Washington, is not so much poverty, as slovenly unconcern. What all such people need — be they white or black, red or yellow — is the development of wants — wants for better things. A man of moderately developed wants will exert himself to get a steady job under healthful conditions, to get a comfortable house to live in — three or four sunny, pleasantly furnished rooms and, if possible a garden for vegetables and flowers — yes, he will exert himself to win a wife to make that house a home. Such wants (and they are, you will note, not impossibly spiritual) every school ought to tend to develop. . . .

So much for the work in which personal influence is the determining factor. Medicine and business are types of the work in which what I have rudely called directing intelligence determines.

In the profession of medicine, I admit, personal influence and directing intelligence subtly interlace. The Negro doctor's social position makes him specially accessible to Negroes in cases of need. As a friend of the family or of the family's friends, the doctor is not dreaded as a feelingless stranger with a terrible knife. Moreover, the Negro doctor does not feel himself a man of alien blood come to tend an inferior. Social position and understanding sympathy, then, render the Negro doctor readily accessible and very useful. Moreover, the Negro's physical condition offers the doctor large opportunities for noble service. In a book upon "Ethnic Factors in the Population of Boston," Doctor Bushee says, "In Boston the mortality of the Negro is much larger than that of any other ethnic factor;" again, "A high death rate, instead of a low birth rate is causing the Negroes to disappear," and the statistics are not much more encouraging in many other urban communities North and South. That relatively low economic position is a powerful factor in producing this alarming death rate, I have already suggested; another capital factor is pitiable ignorance of the rudiments of personal hygiene and of sanitation. Negro doctors may without much trouble diffuse throughout a community these rudiments of knowledge and in so doing will prove themselves public servants. North and

South the conspicuous financial success and substantial social service of hundreds of Negro doctors eloquently establish the correctness of this view; and of practicing physicians, the Negro people today have unmistakably too few.

What of the Negro business man? In Washington public employment and the professions have captured most of the energetic and alert Negroes, to the injury of business development. Springfield, Massachusetts; Richmond, Virginia; Dayton, Ohio, — not one of these important cities has a total population as large as the Negro population of the District of Columbia. As buyers of goods, eighty-seven thousand people are important; but as sellers of goods, the eighty-seven thousand Negroes in Washington are by no means important. For example, of the total profits on the dry goods bought in a year by the Negro population of Washington, — profits amounting to thousands of dollars, for the ratio of expenditure to income is exceptionally large, — what per cent. goes to Negro merchants? Shall I say five per cent., one per cent., or one thousandth of one per cent.? Mathematical precision is, of course, not possible, but you and I know that practically none of these profits go to Negro merchants. And you and I could name a dozen white merchants who have been enriched by those profits. And in consideration of this fact how many Negro clerks have the white merchants placed in their stores? how many Negro floor walkers? how many Negro buyers? And, my friends, how many thousands of years must elapse before the Washington Negro will add to his culture enough co-operative endeavor and competitive power to change all this? I myself have never yet been convinced that the Anglo-Saxon and the Jew really need the black man's charity. Though I cannot point out, then, to the members of this graduating class openings in established business houses, I can point out that their success in business will provide opportunities for some later class, and will help to make the spending of Negroes enrich Negroes. Let me suggest two other ways in which the Negro business man may be of great service to the many. In the first place, the rents charged Negroes in cities, for example, Washington, are considerably higher for the same accommodations than the rents charged white people. By offering good houses at reasonable rents to the Negro working class, the Negro business man will find a paying investment and a means of much service. In the second place, hotels, restaurants, and theatres even in the capital of the nation are open to black men and women only on degrading terms, or not open at all. The closing of such accommodations is really the opening for black business men of the doors of opportunity.

In discussing ways of direct service I have then mentioned teaching and preaching as types of the work in which the decisive factor is personal influence. Medicine and business I have mentioned as types of the work in which the decisive factor is directing intelligence.

And now I wish to discuss two ways in which educated Negroes may be of indirect service, — first, by offering their fellows copies for imitation, and, second, by establishing the dignity of the race. In 1881, hardly a white man or a black man in the country dreamed that in twenty-two years a Negro would have achieved the building of a beautiful city in a Southern wilderness, would have organized efficiently the business of that industrial community of some 1700 people, would have won the abiding confidence of white men and black men North and South, would have worked out a solution for the central problem in American education, would have been acknowledged master of arts by the oldest university in the land, would have written one of the impressive books of the century, would have been . . . called by . . . British critics of affairs the most notable figure in the American Republic! And yet, this miracle you and I see today with our own eyes. The example of this man is being imitated in a hundred educational and industrial communities in the Southern States. And all men feel more respect for the Negro race because out of its loins has come Booker T. Washington.[4]

A constructive statesman like Washington, educators like Lewis Moore and Lucy Moten and your own Anna Cooper, theologians like Bowen and Grimke, scholars like Blyden and Scarborough and DuBois and Kelly Miller, inventors like Woods and McCoy, a novelist like Chesnutt, a poet like Dunbar, a musician like Coleridge-Taylor, a painter like Tanner — yes, and, of those who are gone, Banneker, who searched the heavens; Toussaint, soldier and statesman; Aldridge, the tragedian, with his first medal in arts and sciences from the King of Prussia; Pushkin, the poet of the Russias; Dumas, father and son; the

---

[4] *the building of a beautiful city . . . Booker T. Washington:* A former slave, Booker T. Washington (1856–1915) rose to prominence in the post-Reconstruction era as the most powerful and internationally recognizable African American leader of his time. His chief rival was W. E. B. Du Bois (1868–1963), who opposed his conservative politics. The "beautiful city" was Greenwood Village, a 200-acre settlement north of Washington's Tuskegee Institute that served as his model of an ideal black community.

saintly Crummel; and Douglass,[5] the argument for freedom, — I say, the indirect service of such people is incalculable.

Now, for you and me no such careers are probable and yet every educated Negro who is worth his salt, is in similar fashion a copy for imitation and serves to secure respect for his race. The Negro contractor and builder; the Negro who owns a well-managed truck farm; the Negro school teacher, who has saved money enough to buy municipal bonds or shares in a railway, — that person becomes in a money getting time a definite and concrete argument to white men and to black men that black men can be more than hewers of wood and drawers of water, than cooks and coachmen. Fundamentally, you and I by our thoughtfulness, our practical interest in the happiness of others, our elevation above petty prejudice, our simplicity, our decisive prudence, our enduring energy, our devotion, may indirectly count for good in a thousand ways in the life and work of our communities.

And, now, my friends, you enter the circle of educated men and women. Your personal influence will be felt in school room and in pulpit. Your directing intelligence will count in law, and medicine, and business; as able and devoted men and women, you by your examples will steady the nerves of a staggering people and make the word Negro more than a reproach. Delicate indecision, hesitant virtue, carping

---

[5] *Lewis Moore . . . Douglass:* Here Bruce enumerates, along with Douglass, Chesnutt, Washington, and Du Bois, other distinguished men and women of African descent: Lewis Baxter Moore (1866–19?), first African American to earn a PhD from the University of Pennsylvania and a dean at Howard University; innovative teacher and Howard University benefactor Lucy Ellen Moten (1851–1933); feminist, scholar, activist, and (for a time) M Street High School's principal Anna Julia Cooper (1858–1864); the Methodist clergyman John Wesley Edward Bowen (1855–1933); Frances James Grimké (1850–1937), activist pastor and husband of the black diarist and teacher Charlotte Forten Grimké; the West Indian–born educator, diplomat, journalist, and early pan-Africanist scholar Edward Wilmot Blyden (1832–1912); classics professor William Saunders Scarborough (1852–1926), who served as Wilberforce University president; Howard University sociology professor Kelly Miller (1863–1939); inventors Granville T. Woods (1856–1910) and Elijah McCoy (1843–1929), whose widely used inventions reputedly generated the phrase "the Real McCoy"; poet, lyricist, and novelist Paul Laurence Dunbar (1872–1906); British-born black composer, conductor, and educator Samuel Coleridge-Taylor (1875–1912); the painter Henry Ossawa Tanner (1859–1937); mathematician and astronomer Benjamin Banneker (1731–1806); the leader of the Haitian revolution, Toussaint L'Ouverture (1743–1803); Ira Frederick Aldridge (1807?–1867), the world-renowned Shakespearean actor; the Russian poet Alexander Pushkin (1799–1837); French father and son writers Alexandre Dumas (1802–1870), author of *The Three Musketeers* (1844), and Alexandre Dumas the younger (1824–1895); Episcopal minister, missionary, educator, and essayist Alexander Crummell (1819–1898).

discontent, bric-a-brac culture — these ill become stalwart men and robust women. By all the honorable traditions of the noble family into which you are now adopted, you are pledged not to pick your way daintily in the soft places of the earth; you are pledged to make your lives real, useful, constructive. Remember — *noblesse oblige!*

2

Law and Lawlessness

With the passage of the Thirteenth (1865), Fourteenth (1868), and Fifteenth (1870) Amendments guaranteeing black emancipation and the right of U.S. male citizens to vote in elections, African American men were suddenly free to enter local and national government during Reconstruction. Newly elected to Congress, state legislatures, and city councils, black men now worked in tandem with white Republicans to redraft laws that had originally emerged in the context of slavery. Once installed as public officials, these African Americans made every effort to ensure blacks freedom of movement, equality before the law, access to education, and protection from voter intimidation. And, according to *The Marrow of Tradition*, for a brief period in some states blacks even achieved the right to marry interracially.

At the start of Reconstruction these constitutional amendments and the growing body of state and local laws geared toward protecting black civil rights seemed to stand as unmistakable evidence of national reform on the subject of race. However, in the years following, white supremacists in the Democratic party employed the combined methods of vigilante violence and voter intimidation to influence the composition of state legislatures: eventually southern blacks and white Republicans who had once wielded considerable power at both the state and national level found themselves "voted" out of public office. In their place, more and more white politicians supporting radical white supremacist agendas appeared on the scene, determined to roll back post–Civil War legislative reforms. These politicians could not reverse the abolition of slavery, nor did they desire to do so: in fact, most argued that they were glad slavery was over, that it had been a blight on national life, a wedge that had divided white Americans North and South. But increasingly they would come to insist that the "New South" had to be defined as a white man's region, initiating even before the end of Reconstruction a series of legal reversals and restrictions that severely thwarted any useful problack interpretations of the U.S. Constitution.

As southern Democrats regained control of state houses throughout the South, they immediately targeted the sections of state constitutions that had been rewritten after the Civil War to consolidate male suffrage, regardless of color. By 1900 for instance, Democratic-controlled state legislatures in both Louisiana and North Carolina had added the infamous "grandfather" clause to their state constitutions: for both states, the right to vote was guaranteed to men who had already been eligible to vote (or who were the sons and grandsons of eligible voters) before the specific date of January 1, 1867. But the Fifteenth Amendment guaranteeing black men the right to vote had not been passed until 1870, and black men in the South were almost always either the sons or grandsons of slaves. Clearly then the details of the grandfather clause were not merely idiosyncratic: they were deliberately designed to disenfranchise African American men, while at the same time guaranteeing that white men alone would be able to fulfill the voter requirements. And because the grandfather clause did not openly use race as a determining factor for voter eligibility, it could be interpreted as not violating the Fifteenth Amendment's requirement that no man could be denied the right to vote "on account of race, color, or previous condition of servitude" (p. 340 in this volume). For good measure, some states (including North Carolina) also threw in literacy clauses and poll tax requirements, since black voters were more than likely to be among the most poorly educated and poverty-stricken members of a community.

Such challenges to black civil rights were possible because, in the words of the white Louisiana novelist George Washington Cable, northerners were "weary of strife . . . [and] eager to turn to the cure of other evils" and so had "thrown the whole matter over to the states of the South" (p. 341). Indeed, this wholesale abandonment of black civil rights became a defining feature of the national attitude toward blacks, and as such was a further blow to the spirit of reforms achieved during the early days of Reconstruction. This ambivalence surfaced especially at every level of the judicial system, when a wave of ultraconservative U.S. Supreme Court decisions in the 1870s and 1880s effectively nullified the changes wrought by Radical Republicans. In cases such as *The Butchers' Benevolent Association of New Orleans v. The Crescent City Livestock Landing and Slaughter-House Company* (1873), *Hall v. DeCuir* (1878), and a series of suits in 1883 that tested the Civil Rights Act of 1875, majority decisions in the nation's highest court construed the definition of individual rights with the narrowest interpretation possible. Of special note too was *United States v. Cruikshank* (1876): in addition to being one of the landmark cases where the Fourteenth Amendment's guarantee of the right to vote regardless of race was severely undercut, this case also demonstrated that the Supreme Court could and did find legal arguments to overturn the convictions of those who had admitted to using violence against black voters. Clearly then, as would later be the case in the Wilmington riot in 1898, during Reconstruction the very public fact that blacks were the direct target of white violence did not mean that the law would come to their aid.

Perhaps the most infamous example of how the U.S. legal system worked to buttress white supremacy was the 1896 case *Plessy v. Ferguson*. With the support and representation of writer and lawyer Albion W. Tourgée, the light-skinned black Homer Adolph Plessy sued for the right of equal access to Louisiana railroad accommodations. Clearly influenced by the white supremacist rhetoric of the moment, the U.S. Supreme Court ruled that as long as blacks were provided with equal accommodations, the railroad had discharged its duty, and that with respect to white racial feelings, "[l]egislation is powerless to eradicate racial instincts or to abolish distinctions based upon physical differences. . . . If one race be inferior to the other socially, the Constitution of the United States cannot put them upon the same plane" (p. 357). In effect *Plessy v. Ferguson* now gave official, federal sanction to the countless Jim Crow laws throughout the South that restricted blacks like Homer Plessy to separate railroad cars and public waiting rooms, and separate seating in public places such as restaurants and theaters. Thus, at every level, laws were being rewritten or reinterpreted to support the illusion that blacks and whites were so different biologically and temperamentally that they literally had to inhabit separate social spaces.

To the annoyance of white supremacists, George Washington Cable and others would point out that black accommodations were separate but hardly equal — indeed in many cases they hardly existed at all. In describing the experiences of Dr. Miller on the train trip from North to South, Chesnutt not only prompts readers to recall *Plessy v. Ferguson*, but he also falls into line with many blacks and their white sympathizers who repeatedly pointed to the segregation of passengers on southern trains as embodying the unfairness of Jim Crow laws. At the same time, as Cable argued in his commentaries and as Chesnutt made clear in his intimations about the source of Captain McBane's wealth in *The Marrow of Tradition*, the only places where blacks could find unlimited accommodation were southern prisons. According to Cable, black prison inmates outnumbered their white counterparts to an extent that far exceeded the black to white population ratios of the South: this state of affairs demonstrated that blacks had ceased to obtain fair hearings in local courts. Also, since the largely African American convict labor was regularly leased out to private contractors for construction and road-building projects, a new system of black incarceration and forced labor emerged that closely resembled the old patterns of slavery.

In order to provide a sense of white supremacists' legal maneuvers after Reconstruction, this chapter reprints in their entirety the Thirteenth, Fourteenth, and Fifteenth Amendments, as well as the 1900 voter eligibility amendment to the North Carolina state constitution. Also provided in excerpted form are the Supreme Court opinions expressed in *Plessy v. Ferguson*. While the post-Reconstruction documents demonstrate how white supremacist thought had become part and parcel of even so-called objective processes such as the U.S. judicial system, selections in this chapter — notably the dissenting opinion by Justice John Marshall Harlan in *Plessy v. Ferguson*, and Cable's brilliant, astute 1885 essay "The Freedman's Case in Equity" — reveal that some white members of the public were not deluded by the rhetoric of antiblack constituencies. As an indignant Justice Harlan wrote when he protested the outcome of *Plessy v. Ferguson*, it was common knowledge "that the statute in question" was designed "to exclude colored persons from coaches occupied by . . . white persons," and as such, it clearly restricted "the personal freedom of citizens" (pp. 358–59).

As a minority of concerned Americans realized, protest would grow increasingly necessary and even desperate, since at the same time that white supremacists were gaining political power, they were also involved in a widespread campaign of racial terror against black populations. It should be noted that while attacks took place mostly in the South, they did spread to northern and midwestern locations. From the end of the Civil War until well into the middle of the twentieth century, whether in paramilitary groups such as the Ku Klux Klan and the Knights of the White Camelia or as loosely organized mobs composed of anywhere from a few dozen men to literally hundreds of people, white supremacists regularly and systematically attacked and destroyed black businesses, homes, and churches. Throughout the South thousands of black men, women, and children were maimed or tortured, and for women in particular, rape was a special weapon of humiliation. More often than not, white attacks included the widespread use of lynching: in this ritual, African Americans might be shot, hanged, whipped, mutilated, burned alive, or all of the above, in the presence of crowds of white onlookers, including newspaper reporters and photographers. Often local law enforcement officials were either too afraid of the mob to protect the black victim, or they simply joined with the executioners. After a lynching had occurred, the lifeless black body might well be dismembered, as individuals in the crowd made off with bits of hair, bone, teeth, or skin to serve as prized keepsakes of the event.

In part, lynchings and race riots were hard to suppress because, like the growing legal and political restrictions that undermined the gains of Reconstruction, such violence became universally accepted by whites as one strategy in a more general process of safeguarding the nation from the threat of "black rule." In a sense then, white supremacists were arguing that antiblack vigilante violence was itself part of the natural law of white racial survival, and therefore could not be considered criminal activity. At the whites-only November 9, 1898, meeting in Wilmington, North Carolina, the leaders of the planned race riot confidently justified their coming actions by arguing that "the Constitution of the United States contemplated a government to be carried on by an enlightened people"; that though they "recognize[d] the authority of the United States," they believed themselves to "represent unequivocally the sentiment of the white people of this country and city" (see p. 413). The fact that they were so openly and publicly intent upon thwarting the results of a legally decided election was of little consequence: no matter the method, all actions that gave political power to blacks were automatically reprehensible to the local white community.

The argument that lynching was the only effective means of controlling the rapacious lust of black men was challenged almost immediately by both African Americans themselves, as well as by those whites who were shocked by the practice. Perhaps the most famous antilynching activist was the black journalist Ida B. Wells. Her exhaustive

investigations began with the triple lynching in 1892 of the black grocery store co-owners Thomas Moss, Calvin McDowell, and Thomas
Stewart in Memphis, Tennessee. The "crime" perpetrated by Moss,
McDowell, and Stewart was in fact their successful grocery business,
which had begun to cut into the profits of local white merchants. As
Wells later wrote in her autobiography, "this is what opened my eyes
to what lynching really was. An excuse to get rid of Negroes who were
acquiring wealth and property and thus keep the race terrorized and
'keep the nigger down'" (64). Repeatedly Wells uncovered numerous
discrepancies in white newspaper accounts of lynching: indeed, in the
case of alleged rape, some white women had not been raped at all, but
had merely been discovered with black lovers; or, the black lynching
victim had merely been in the vicinity of an alleged assault, and had
had the bad luck of being the one caught by a vengeful white mob.
Wells's findings were echoed both by black journalist Alexander
Manly of Wilmington, in his response to Georgia's Rebecca Felton (see
p. 405), and indirectly in *Marrow's* retelling of the Manly editorial
incident (see p. 97). Of particular importance to Wells were the number of cases where black women and children rather than black men
were lynched for alleged theft, defiance of white authorities, or as
retaliation against male family members: their deaths had nothing to
do with the rape of white women.

Wells publicized her findings in a series of antilynching pamphlets,
as well as through international speaking tours designed to turn world
opinion against American white supremacist violence. Included in this
chapter are excerpts from her first pamphlet *Southern Horrors: Lynch
Law in All Its Phases,* published in 1892. Included as well are three
articles from newspapers of the period recounting lynchings: these
articles demonstrate the kind of lurid descriptions that were calculated
to both titillate and terrify white readers across the country. The vast
majority of newspaper audiences would never see a lynching, but because of the community-building power of mass-circulated newspapers,
white readers' opinions of blacks in general and southern life in particular were forever transformed by these "eye-witness" accounts. Not
surprisingly, as the 1903 *New York Herald* article on an Illinois lynching demonstrates, white violence against blacks was fast becoming a
nationwide phenomenon. Clearly, Wells, Manly, Chesnutt, and other
black activists had a keen understanding of the power of the printed
word, which is why they each worked hard, and often at great personal risk, to undermine the widespread language of white supremacy.

The task ahead was difficult, however. As the selections in this chapter by the white Chicago reformer Jane Addams and the white investigative journalist Ray Stannard Baker suggest, there was a deeply intertwined network of racist and classist beliefs that had to be addressed before the reign of white supremacy could be effectively ended. For instance, though she vehemently opposed lynching, Addams saw nothing wrong with white paternalist control over blacks, and she suggested that the problem of white violence could be addressed if Southerners simply utilized a more "humane" form of racial management: "the child who is managed by a system of . . . terrorizing is almost sure to be the vicious and stupid child" (p. 384). And even though he understood the role of local white newspapers in fomenting the bloody Atlanta race riot of 1906, the journalist Baker refused to let go of stories of alleged black rapists. Like many Americans who held white supremacist sympathies but could not reconcile themselves to lynching, Baker simply accounted for racial violence as the product of "the dangerous Negro class" and their poor white counterparts whom he claimed made up the average lynching mob. But as both Wells and Chesnutt would argue in their respective fields of journalism and fiction, and as the Wilmington riot would demonstrate, antiblack violence was often supported by all members of the white community, regardless of class.

This repeated failure of many Americans either to condemn white racial violence, or at least examine their acceptance of racial stereotypes, ensured that atrocities would continue unabated. Black public figures, however, never ceased to demand the fullest analysis of the situation: thus, in a speech before Congress in 1900, the black North Carolina representative George White called on his fellow lawmakers to put racial violence and black disenfranchisement in a broader perspective. Addressing those congressmen who were now distracted from the problem of racial antagonism by the annexation of new territory after U.S. successes in the 1898 Spanish-American war, White argued for a special and urgent recognition of the victims of lynching, and especially of the suffering of Wilmington's blacks. Brutalized by acts of local white violence, they now risked becoming victims twice over, this time of national disregard.

Thirteenth, Fourteenth, and Fifteenth Amendments to the U.S. Constitution

Ratified in 1865, 1868, and 1870 respectively, the Thirteenth, Fourteenth, and Fifteenth Amendments to the U.S. Constitution represent landmark events in American legislative and social history. Emerging immediately in the wake of the northern victory over the Confederate states, the Thirteenth Amendment truly seemed to extend over the entire nation the power of Abraham Lincoln's 1863 Emancipation Proclamation. No longer subject to the whims of white masters, the fragility and contestability of manumission papers, or the risks of outright escape, blacks now appeared to have their freedom guaranteed by the highest authority in the land. Within five more years the Fourteenth and Fifteenth Amendments affirmed black citizenship and black male suffrage. (And for good measure, Congress even passed a number of Civil Rights and Enforcement Acts, to bolster these reforms.) But in spite of the seeming incontrovertibility of the guarantees provided by the Amendments, in the years after Reconstruction they were so successfully weakened by white legal challenges that at the end of the nineteenth century they had ceased to have any real power. This state of affairs, coupled with white supremacists' constant social and physical harassment of African Americans, proved that the end of legal slavery had not after all signaled full freedom for the ex-slave. Thus, the Amendments spoke as much to the loss of black opportunity, as they did to the radical nature of the era that had engendered them. The text included here is taken from *Encyclopedia of the American Constitution,* ed. Leonard W. Levy, Kenneth L. Karst, and Dennis J. Mahoney (New York: Macmillan, 1986).

AMENDMENT XIII

SECTION 1. Neither slavery nor involuntary servitude, except as a punishment for crime whereof the party shall have been duly convicted, shall exist within the United States, or any place subject to their jurisdiction.

SECTION 2. Congress shall have power to enforce this article by appropriate legislation.

AMENDMENT XIV

Section 1. All persons born or naturalized in the United States, and subject to the jurisdiction thereof, are citizens of the United States and of the State wherein they reside. No State shall make or enforce any law which shall abridge the privileges or immunities of citizens of the United States; nor shall any State deprive any person of life, liberty, or property, without due process of law; nor deny to any person within its jurisdiction the equal protection of the laws.

Section 2. Representatives shall be apportioned among the several States according to their respective numbers, counting the whole number of persons in each State, excluding Indians not taxed. But when the right to vote at any election for the choice of electors for President and Vice President of the United States, Representatives in Congress, the Executive and Judicial officers of a State, or the members of the Legislature thereof, is denied to any of the male inhabitants of such State, being twenty-one years of age, and citizens of the United States, or in any way abridged, except for participation in rebellion, or other crime, the basis of representation therein shall be reduced in the proportion which the number of such male citizens shall bear to the whole number of male citizens twenty-one years of age in such State.

Section 3. No person shall be a Senator or Representative in Congress, or elector of President and Vice President, or hold any office, civil or military, under the United States, or under any State, who, having previously taken an oath, as a member of Congress, or as an officer of the United States, or as a member of any State legislature, or as an executive or judicial officer of any State, to support the Constitution of the United States, shall have engaged in insurrection or rebellion against the same, or given aid or comfort to the enemies thereof. But Congress may by a vote of two-thirds of each House, remove such disability.

Section 4. The validity of the public debt of the United States, authorized by law, including debts incurred for payment of pensions and bounties for services in suppressing insurrection or rebellion, shall not be questioned. But neither the United States nor any State shall assume or pay any debt or obligation incurred in aid of insurrection or rebellion against the United States, or any claim for the loss or emancipation of any slave; but all such debts, obligations and claims shall be held illegal and void.

Section 5. The Congress shall have power to enforce, by appropriate legislation, the provisions of this article.

AMENDMENT XV

SECTION 1. The right of citizens of the United States to vote shall not be denied or abridged by the United States or by any State on account of race, color, or previous condition of servitude.

SECTION 2. The Congress shall have power to enforce this article by appropriate legislation.

GEORGE WASHINGTON CABLE

From *The Freedman's Case in Equity*

A Confederate veteran turned writer, and an advisor to Charles Chesnutt, George Washington Cable (1844–1925) rose to national prominence as a brilliant author of sketches, short stories, and serialized novels about life in Louisiana. Not simply a clever local colorist catering to his largely northern white readers' taste for exotic backwaters, Cable sought a rich exploration of black and white Creole history and culture in works such as *Old Creole Days* (1879) and *The Grandissimes* (1880). Later, his essay collections such as *The Silent South* (1885) and *The Negro Question* (1890) provided in-depth analyses of the origins and deep-rooted nature of racial prejudice in the South. While his point of view won him the disdain of many whites, Cable argued that he spoke for a "Silent South" composed of concerned whites in favor of civil justice for former slaves and their descendants. (And yet, broad-minded though he was, Cable was also a curious figure of contradiction, since he fought for black civil rights on the one hand, but abhorred interracial marriage on the other.) Excerpted below is "The Freedman's Case in Equity," one of Cable's best-known addresses on black civil rights, as it first appeared in 1885 in *The Century Illustrated Monthly Magazine*. Later that year it was anthologized in *The Silent South*.

The greatest social problem before the American people to-day is, as it has been for a hundred years, the presence among us of the negro.

No comparable entanglement was ever drawn round itself by any other modern nation with so serene a disregard of its ultimate issue, or with a more distinct national responsibility. The African slave was brought here by cruel force, and with everybody's consent except his own. Everywhere the practice was favored as a measure of common aggrandizement. When a few men and women protested, they were mobbed in the public interest, with the public consent. There rests, therefore, a moral responsibility on the whole nation never to lose sight of the results of African-American slavery until they cease to work mischief and injustice.

It is true these responsibilities may not fall everywhere with the same weight; but they are nowhere entirely removed. The original seed of trouble was sown with the full knowledge and consent of the nation. The nation was to blame; and so long as evils spring from it, their correction must be the nation's duty.

The late Southern slave has within two decades risen from slavery to freedom, from freedom to citizenship, passed on into political ascendency, and fallen again from that eminence. The amended Constitution holds him up in his new political rights as well as a mere constitution can. On the other hand, certain enactments of Congress, trying to reach further, have lately been made void by the highest court of the nation. And another thing has happened. The popular mind in the old free States, weary of strife at arm's length, bewildered by its complications, vexed by many a blunder, eager to turn to the cure of other evils, and even tinctured by that race feeling whose grosser excesses it would so gladly see suppressed, has retreated from its uncomfortable dictational attitude and thrown the whole matter over to the States of the South. Here it rests, no longer a main party issue, but a group of questions which are to be settled by each of these States separately in the light of simple equity and morals, and which the genius of American government does not admit of being forced upon them from beyond their borders. Thus the whole question, become secondary in party contest, has yet reached a period of supreme importance.

Before slavery ever became a grave question in the nation's politics, — when it seemed each State's private affair, developing unmolested, — it had two different fates in two different parts of the country. In one, treated as a question of public equity, it withered away. In the other, overlooked in that aspect, it petrified and became the corner-stone of the whole social structure; and when men sought its overthrow as a national evil, it first brought war upon the land, and then grafted into the citizenship of one of the most intelligent nations in the world six millions of people from one of the most debased races on the globe.

And now this painful and wearisome question, sown in the African slave-trade, reaped in our civil war, and garnered in the national adoption of millions of an inferior race, is drawing near a second seed-time. For this is what the impatient proposal to make it a dead and buried issue really means. It means to recommit it to the silence and concealment of the covered furrow. Beyond that incubative retirement no suppressed moral question can be pushed; but all such questions, ignored in the domain of private morals, spring up and expand once more into questions of public equity; neglected as matters of public equity, they blossom into questions of national interest; and, despised in that guise, presently yield the red fruits of revolution. . . .

. . . [T]he difficulties of the situation are plain. We have, first, a revision of Southern State laws which has forced into them the recognition of certain human rights discordant with the sentiments of those who have always called themselves the community; second, the removal of the entire political machinery by which this forcing process was effected; and, third, these revisions left to be interpreted and applied under the domination of these antagonistic sentiments. These being the three terms of the problem, one of three things must result. There will arise a system of vicious evasions eventually ruinous to public and private morals and liberty, or there will be a candid reconsideration of the sentiments hostile to these enactments, or else there will be a division, some taking one course and some the other.

This is what we should look for from our knowledge of men and history; and this is what we find. The revised laws, only where they could not be evaded, have met that reluctant or simulated acceptance of their narrowest letter which might have been expected — a virtual suffocation of those principles of human equity which the unwelcome decrees do little more than shadow forth. . . .

. . . We need to go back to the roots of things and study closely, analytically, the origin, the present foundation, the rationality, the rightness, of those sentiments surviving in us which prompt an attitude qualifying in any way peculiarly the black man's liberty among us. Such a treatment will be less abundant in incident, less picturesque; but it will be more thorough.

First, then, what are these sentiments? Foremost among them stands the idea that he is of necessity an alien. He was brought to our shores a naked, brutish, unclean, captive, pagan savage, to be and remain a kind of connecting link between man and the beasts of burden. . . .

Why, then, did this notion that the man of color must always remain an alien stand so unshaken? We may readily recall how, under ancient systems, he rose not only to high privileges, but often to public station and power. Singularly, with us the trouble lay in a modern principle of liberty. The whole idea of American government rested on all men's equal, inalienable right to secure their life, liberty, and the pursuit of happiness by governments founded in their own consent. Hence, our Southern forefathers, shedding their blood, or ready to shed it, for this principle, yet proposing in equal good conscience to continue holding the American black man and mulatto and quadroon in slavery, had to anchor that conscience, their conduct, and their laws in the conviction that the man of African tincture was, not by his master's arbitrary assertion merely, but by nature and unalterably, an alien. If that hold should break, one single wave of irresistible inference would lift our whole Southern social fabric and dash it upon the rocks of negro emancipation and enfranchisement. How was it made secure? Not by books, though they were written among us from every possible point of view, but, with the mass of our slave-owners, by the calm hypothesis of a positive, intuitive knowledge. To them the statement was an axiom. They abandoned the methods of moral and intellectual reasoning, and fell back upon this assumption of a God-given instinct, nobler than reason, and which it was an insult to a freeman to ask him to prove on logical grounds.

Yet it was found not enough. The slave multiplied. Slavery was a dangerous institution. Few in the South to-day have any just idea how often the slave plotted for his freedom. Our Southern ancestors were a noble, manly people, springing from some of the most highly intelligent, aspiring, upright, and refined nations of the modern world. . . . Their acts were not always right; whose are? But for their peace of mind they had to believe them so. They therefore spoke much of the negro's contentment with that servile condition for which nature had designed him. Yet there was no escaping the knowledge that we dared not trust the slave caste with any power that could be withheld from them. So the perpetual alien was made also a perpetual menial, and the belief became fixed that this, too, was nature's decree, not ours. . . .

. . . The discipline of the plantation required that the difference between master and slave be never lost sight of by either. It made our master caste a solid mass, and fixed a common masterhood and subserviency between the ruling and the serving race.[1] Every one of us grew up in the idea that he had, by birth and race, certain broad powers of police over any and every person of color.

All at once the tempest of war snapped off at the ground every one of these arbitrary relations, without removing a single one of the sentiments in which they stood rooted. Then, to fortify the freedman in the tenure of his new rights, he was given the ballot. Before this grim fact the notion of alienism, had it been standing alone, might have given way. The idea that slavery was right did begin to crumble almost at once. . . .

With like readiness might the old alien relation have given way if we could only, while letting that pass, have held fast by the other old ideas. But they were all bound together. See our embarrassment. For more than a hundred years we had made these sentiments the absolute essentials to our self-respect. And yet if we clung to them, how could we meet the freedman on equal terms in the political field? Even to lead would not compensate us; for the fundamental profession of American politics is that the leader is servant to his followers. It was too much. The ex-master and ex-slave — the quarter-deck and the fore-castle, as it were — could not come together. But neither could the American mind tolerate a continuance of martial law. The agonies of reconstruction followed.

. . . The two main questions were really these: on the freedman's side, how to establish republican State government under the same recognition of his rights that the rest of Christendom accorded him; and on the former master's side, how to get back to the old semblance of republican State government, and — allowing that the freedman was *de facto*[2] a voter — still to maintain a purely arbitrary superiority of all whites over all blacks, and a purely arbitrary equality of all blacks among themselves as an alien, menial, and dangerous class.

Exceptionally here and there some one in the master caste did throw off the old and accept the new ideas, and, if he would allow it,

---

[1] *the serving race:* The old Louisiana Black Code says, "The free people of color ought never to . . . presume to conceive themselves equal to the white; but, on the contrary, that they ought to yield to them in every occasion, and never speak or answer to them but with respect, under the penalty of imprisonment according to the nature of the offense." (Section 21, p. 164.) [Cable's note. He no doubt refers to antebellum slave codes designed to regulate the lives of both slaves and free blacks. Ironically, even after the Civil War southern states still sought to control freedmen by instituting Black Codes that bore a great similarity to the rules set down under slavery.]

[2] *de facto:* In fact.

was instantly claimed as a leader by the newly liberated thousands around him. But just as promptly the old master race branded him also an alien reprobate, and in ninety-nine cases out of a hundred, if he had not already done so, he soon began to confirm by his actions the brand on his cheek. However, we need give no history here of the dreadful episode of reconstruction. Under an experimentative truce its issues rest to-day upon the pledge of the wiser leaders of the master class: Let us but remove the hireling demagogue, and we will see to it that the freedman is accorded a practical, complete, and cordial recognition of his equality with the white man before the law. As far as there has been any understanding at all, it is not that the originally desired ends of reconstruction have been abandoned, but that the men of North and South have agreed upon a new, gentle, and peaceable method for reaching them; that, without change as to the ends in view, compulsory reconstruction has been set aside and a voluntary reconstruction is on trial. . . .

Thus we reach the ultimate question of fact. Are the freedman's liberties suffering any real abridgment? The answer is easy. The letter of the laws, with but few exceptions, recognizes him as entitled to every right of an American citizen; and to some it may seem unimportant that there is scarcely one public relation of life in the South where he is not arbitrarily and unlawfully compelled to hold toward the white man the attitude of an alien, a menial, and a probable reprobate, by reason of his race and color. One of the marvels of future history will be that it was counted a small matter, by a majority of our nation, for six millions of people within it, made by its own decree a component part of it, to be subjected to a system of oppression so rank that nothing could make it seem small except the fact that they had already been ground under it for a century and a half.

Examine it. It proffers to the freedman a certain security of life and property, and then holds the respect of the community, that dearest of earthly boons, beyond his attainment. It gives him certain guarantees against thieves and robbers, and then holds him under the unearned contumely of the mass of good men and women. It acknowledges in constitutions and statutes his title to an American's freedom and aspirations, and then in daily practice heaps upon him in every public place the most odious distinctions, without giving ear to the humblest plea concerning mental or moral character. It spurns his ambition, tramples upon his languishing self-respect, and indignantly refuses to let him either buy with money, or earn by any excellence of inner life or outward behavior, the most momentary immunity from these public indignities even for his wife and daughters. Need we cram these pages with facts in evidence, as if these were charges denied and requiring to be proven? They are simply the present avowed and defended state of affairs peeled of its exteriors.

Nothing but the habit, generations old, of enduring it could make it endurable by men not in actual slavery. Were we whites of the South to remain every way as we are, and our six million blacks to give place to any sort of whites exactly their equals, man for man, in mind, morals, and wealth, provided only that they had tasted two years of American freedom, and were this same system of tyrannies attempted upon them, there would be as bloody an uprising as this continent has ever seen. We can say this quietly. There is not a scruple's weight of present danger. These six million freedmen are dominated by nine million whites immeasurably stronger than they, backed by the virtual consent of thirty-odd millions more. Indeed, nothing but the habit of oppression could make such oppression possible to a people of the intelligence and virtue of our Southern whites, and the invitation to practice it on millions of any other than the children of their former slaves would be spurned with a noble indignation.

Suppose, for a moment, the tables turned. Suppose the courts of our Southern States, while changing no laws requiring the impaneling of jurymen without distinction as to race, etc., should suddenly begin to draw their thousands of jurymen all black, and well-nigh every one of them counting not only himself, but all his race, better than any white man. Assuming that their average of intelligence and morals should be not below that of jurymen as now drawn, would a white man, for all that, choose to be tried in one of those courts? Would he suspect nothing? Could one persuade him that his chances of even justice were all they should be, or all they would be were the court not evading the law in order to sustain an outrageous distinction against him because of the accidents of his birth? Yet only read white man for black man, and black man for white man, and that — I speak as an eye-witness — has been the practice for years, and is still to-day; an actual emasculation, in the case of six million people both as plaintiff and defendant, of the right of trial by jury.

In this and other practices the outrage falls upon the freedman. Does it stop there? Far from it. It is the first premise of American principles that whatever elevates the lower stratum of the people lifts all the rest, and whatever holds it down holds all down. For twenty years, therefore, the nation his been working to elevate the freedman. It counts this one of the great necessities of the hour. It has poured out its wealth publicly and privately for this purpose. It is confidently expected that it will soon bestow a royal gift of millions for the reduction of the illiteracy so largely shared by the blacks. Our Southern States are, and for twenty years have been, taxing themselves for the same end. The private charities alone of the other States have given twenty millions in the same good cause. Their colored seminaries, colleges, and normal schools dot our whole Southern country, and furnish our public colored schools with a large part of their teachers. All this and much more has been or is being done in order that, for the good of himself and everybody else in the land, the colored man may be elevated as quickly as possible from all the debasements of slavery and semi-slavery to the full stature and integrity of citizenship. And it is in the face of all this that the adherent of the old régime stands in the way to every public privilege and place — steamer landing, railway platform, theater, concert-hall, art display, public library, public school, court-house, church, everything — flourishing the hot branding-iron of ignominious distinctions. He forbids the freedman to go into the water until *he* is satisfied that he knows how to swim, and for fear he should learn hangs mill-stones about his neck. This is what we are told is a small matter that will settle itself. Yes, like a roosting curse, until the outraged intelligence of the South lifts its indignant protest against this stupid firing into our own ranks.

I say the outraged intelligence of the South; for there are thousands of Southern-born white men and women in the minority in all these places — in churches, courts, schools, libraries, theaters, concert-halls, and on steamers and railway carriages — who see the wrong and folly of these things, silently blush for them, and withhold their open protests only because their belief is unfortunately stronger in the futility of their counsel than in the power of a just cause. I do not justify their silence; but I affirm their sincerity and their goodly numbers. Of late years, when condemning these evils from the platform in Southern towns, I have repeatedly found that those who I had earlier been told were the men and women in whom the community placed most confidence and pride — they were the ones who, when I had spoken, came forward with warmest hand-grasps and expressions of thanks, and pointedly and cordially justified my every utterance. And were they the young South? Not by half! The gray-beards of the old times have always been among them, saying in effect, not by any means as converts, but as fellow-discoverers, "Whereas we were blind, now we see."

Another sort among our good Southern people make a similar but feebler admission, but with the time-worn proviso that expediency makes a more imperative demand than law, justice, or logic, and demands the preservation of the old order. Somebody must be outraged, it seems; and if not the freedman, then it must be a highly refined and enlightened race of people constantly offended and grossly discommoded, if not imposed upon, by a horde of tatterdemalions,[3] male and female, crowding into a participation in their reserved privileges. Now, look at this plea. It is simply saying in another way that though the Southern whites far outnumber the blacks, and though we hold every element of power in greater degree than the blacks, and though the larger part of us claim to be sealed by nature as an exclusive upper class, and though we have the courts completely in our own hands, with the police on our right and the prisons on our left, and though we justly claim to be an intrepid people, and though we have a superb military experience, with ninety-nine hundredths of all the military equipment and no scarcity of all the accessories, yet with all the facts behind us we cannot make and enforce that intelligent and approximately just assortment of persons in public places and conveyances on the merits of exterior decency that is made in all other enlightened lands. On such a plea are made a distinction and separation that not only are crude, invidious, humiliating, and tyrannous, but which do not reach their ostensible end or come near it; and all that saves such a plea from being a confession of driveling imbecility is its utter speciousness. It is advanced sincerely; and yet nothing is easier to show than that these distinctions on the line of color are really made not from any necessity, but simply for their own sake — to preserve the old arbitrary supremacy of the master class over the menial without regard to the decency or indecency of appearance or manners in either the white individual or the colored.

See its every-day working. Any colored man gains unquestioned admission into innumerable places the moment he appears as the menial attendant of some white person, where he could not cross the threshold in his own right as a well-dressed and well-behaved master of himself. The contrast is even greater in the case of colored women. There could not be a system which when put into practice would more offensively condemn itself. It does more: it actually creates the confusion it pretends to prevent. It blunts the sensibilities of the ruling class themselves. It waives all strict demand for painstaking in either manners or dress of either master or menial and, for one result, makes the

---

[3] *tatterdemalions:* Raggedly dressed people.

average Southern railway coach more uncomfortable than the average of railway coaches elsewhere. It prompts the average Southern white passenger to find less offense in the presence of a profane, boisterous, or unclean white person than in that of a quiet, well-behaved colored man or woman attempting to travel on an equal footing with him without a white master or mistress. . . . I say, as a citizen of an extreme Southern State, a native of Louisiana, an ex-Confederate soldier, and a lover of my home, my city, and my State, as well as of my country, that this is not the best sentiment in the South, nor the sentiment of her best intelligence; and that it would not ride up and down that beautiful land dominating and domineering were it not for its tremendous power as the *traditional* sentiment of a conservative people. But is not silent endurance criminal? . . .

The laws passed in the days of compulsory reconstruction requiring "equal accommodations," etc., for colored and white persons were freedmen's follies. On their face they defeated their ends; for even in theory they at once reduced to half all opportunity for those more reasonable and mutually agreeable self-assortments which public assemblages and groups of passengers find it best to make in all other enlightened countries, making them on the score of conduct, dress, and price. They also led the whites to overlook what they would have seen instantly had these invidious distinctions been made against themselves: that their offense does not vanish at the guarantee against the loss of physical comforts. But we made, and are still making, a mistake beyond even this. For years many of us have carelessly taken for granted that these laws were being carried out in some shape that removed all just ground of complaint. It is common to say, "We allow the men of color to go and come at will, only let him sit apart in a place marked off for him." But marked off how? So as to mark him instantly as a menial. Not by railings and partitions merely, which, raised against any other class in the United States with the same invidious intent, would be kicked down as fast as put up, but by giving him besides, in every instance and without recourse, the most uncomfortable, uncleanest, and unsafest place; and the unsafety, uncleanness, and discomfort of most of these places are a shame to any community pretending to practice public justice. . . .

. . . One hot night in September of last year I was traveling by rail in the State of Alabama. At rather late bed-time there came aboard the train a young mother and her little daughter of three or four years. They were neatly and tastefully dressed in cool, fresh muslins, and as the train went on its way they sat together very still and quiet. At the next station there came aboard a most melancholy and revolting company. In filthy rags, with vile odors and the clanking of shackles and chains, nine penitentiary convicts chained to one chain, and ten more chained to another, dragged laboriously into the compartment of the car where in one corner sat this mother and child, and packed it full, and the train moved on. The keeper of the convicts told me he should take them in that car two hundred miles that night. They were going to the mines. My seat was not in that car, and I staid in it but a moment. It stank insufferably. I returned to my own place in the coach behind, where there was, and had all the time been, plenty of room. But the mother and child sat on in silence in that foul hole, the conductor having distinctly refused them admission elsewhere because they were of African blood, and not because the mother was, but because she was *not,* engaged at the moment in menial service. Had the child been white, and the mother not its natural but its hired guardian, she could have sat anywhere in the train, and no one would have ventured to object, even had she been as black as the mouth of the coal-pit to which her loathsome fellow-passengers were being carried in chains.

Such is the incident as I saw it. But the illustration would be incomplete here were I not allowed to add the comments I made upon it when in June last I recounted it, and to state the two opposite tempers in which my words were received. I said: "These are the facts. And yet you know and I know we belong to communities that, after years of hoping for, are at last taking comfort in the assurance of the nation's highest courts that no law can reach and stop this shameful foul play until we choose to enact a law to that end ourselves. And now the east and north and west of our great and prosperous and happy country, and the rest of the civilized world, as far as it knows our case, are standing and waiting to see what we will write upon the white page of to-day's and to-morrow's history, now that we are simply on our honor and on the mettle of our far and peculiarly famed Southern instinct. How long, then, shall we stand off from such ringing moral questions as these on the flimsy plea that they have a political value, and, scrutinizing the Constitution, keep saying, 'Is it so nominated in the bond? I cannot find it; 'tis not in the bond.' "[4] . . .

. . . Under our present condition in the South, it is beyond possibility that the individual black should behave mischievously without

---

[4] '*Is it so nominated in the bond? I cannot find it; 'tis not in the bond*': From Shakespeare's *The Merchant of Venice* 4.1.258, 261.

offensively rearousing the old sentiments of the still dominant white man. As we have seen, too, the white man virtually monopolizes the jury-box. Add another fact: the Southern States have entered upon a new era of material development. Now, if with these conditions in force the public mind has been captivated by glowing pictures of the remunerative economy of the convict-lease system, and by the seductive spectacle of mines and railways, turnpikes and levees, that everybody wants and nobody wants to pay for, growing apace by convict labor that seems to cost nothing, we may almost assert beforehand that the popular mind will — not so maliciously as unreflectingly — yield to the tremendous temptation to hustle the misbehaving black man into the State prison under extravagant sentence, and sell his labor to the highest bidder who will use him in the construction of public works. For ignorance of the awful condition of these penitentiaries is extreme and general, and the hasty, half-conscious assumption naturally is, that the culprit will survive this term of sentence, and its fierce discipline "teach him to behave himself."

But we need not argue from cause to effect only. Nor need I repeat one of the many painful rumors that poured in upon me the moment I began to investigate this point. The official testimony of the prisons themselves is before the world to establish the conjectures that spring from our reasoning. After the erroneous takings of the census of 1880 in South Carolina had been corrected, the population was shown to consist of about twenty blacks to every thirteen whites. One would therefore look for a preponderance of blacks on the prison lists; and inasmuch as they are a people only twenty years ago released from servile captivity, one would not be surprised to see that preponderance large. Yet, when the actual numbers confront us, our speculations are stopped with a rude shock; for what is to account for the fact that in 1881 there were committed to the State prison at Columbia, South Carolina, 406 colored persons and but 25 whites? The proportion of blacks sentenced to the whole black population was one to every 1488; that of the whites to the white population was but one to every 15,644. In Georgia the white inhabitants decidedly outnumber the blacks; yet in the State penitentiary, October 20, 1880, there were 115 whites and 1071 colored; or if we reject the summary of its tables and refer to the tables themselves (for the one does not agree with the other), there were but 102 whites and 1083 colored. Yet of 52 pardons granted in the two years then closing, 22 were to whites and only 30 to blacks. If this be a dark record, what shall we say of the records of lynch law? But for them there is not room here. . . .

What need to say more? The question is answered. Is the freedman a free man? No. We have considered his position in a land whence nothing can, and no man has a shadow of right to, drive him, and where he is multiplying as only oppression can multiply a people. We have carefully analyzed his relations to the finer and prouder race, with which he shares the ownership and citizenship of a region large enough for ten times the number of both. Without accepting one word of his testimony, we have shown that the laws made for his protection against the habits of suspicion and oppression in his late master are being constantly set aside, not for their defects, but for such merit as they possess. We have shown that the very natural source of these oppressions is the surviving sentiments of an extinct and now universally execrated institution; sentiments which no intelligent or moral people should harbor a moment after the admission that slavery was a moral mistake. We have shown the outrageousness of these tyrannies in some of their workings, and how distinctly they antagonize every State and national interest involved in the elevation of the colored race. Is it not well to have done so? For, I say again, the question has reached a moment of special importance. The South stands on her honor before the clean equities of the issue. It is no longer whether constitutional amendments, but whether the eternal principles of justice, are violated. And the answer must — it shall — come from the South. And it shall be practical. It will not cost much. We have had a strange experience: the withholding of simple rights has cost us much blood; such concessions of them as we have made have never yet cost a drop. The answer is coming. Is politics in the way? Then let it clear the track or get run over, just as it prefers. But, as I have said over and over to my brethren in the South, I take upon me to say again here, that there is a moral and intellectual intelligence there which is not going to be much longer beguiled out of its moral right of way by questions of political punctilio, but will seek that plane of universal justice and equity which it is every people's duty before God to seek, not along the line of politics, — God forbid! — but across it and across it and across it as many times as it may lie across the path, until the whole people of every once slave-holding State can stand up as one man, saying, "Is the freedman a free man?" and the whole world shall answer, "Yes."

JUSTICE HENRY BILLINGS BROWN
AND JUSTICE JOHN MARSHALL HARLAN

From *Plessy v. Ferguson*

In 1892, on a train traveling from New Orleans to Covington, Louisiana, the octoroon Homer Adolph Plessy was ordered to leave the whites-only first-class coach and sit in the segregated Jim Crow car. His refusal to move landed him in jail. Plessy's act of resistance had been prearranged by a group of Louisiana blacks in order to challenge the state's 1890 segregation law as a violation of the Thirteenth and Fourteenth Amendments. Despite an appeal to the Louisiana State Supreme Court, Plessy's conviction by Judge John H. Ferguson on the grounds that he was traveling on an intrastate train and was therefore under the jurisdiction of the state, not federal government, was upheld. The next step was to appeal Judge Ferguson's ruling before the U.S. Supreme Court. When the case finally came to the Court in 1896, Albion W. Tourgée, the white, northern-born lawyer and writer who headed Plessy's defense team, used a variety of arguments in defense of the case. One tactic was to point out the extreme lightness of Plessy's complexion to show that segregation was not about the provision of "separate but equal" facilities for two races, but rather that it was a discriminatory practice kept in place by the dubious argument that race was a firmly and easily distinguishable element in the apportioning of social accommodation. In the end the Supreme Court voted seven to one with one abstention to reject Plessy's suit, establishing a landmark precedent that upheld segregation until the practice was successfully challenged by *Brown v. Board of Education of Topeka* (1954) and by *Gayle v. Browder* (1956). Excerpted below is the Court's majority opinion issued by Judge Henry Billings Brown (1836–1913), and the important dissent in support of Plessy by Justice John Marshall Harlan (1833–1911). The full text of both opinions can be found in *U.S. Supreme Court Reports*. (Rochester, NY: Lawyer's Cooperative Publishing Company, 1901), 163–66.

DECISION BY JUSTICE HENRY BILLINGS BROWN, MAY 18, 1896.

The constitutionality of this act is attacked upon the ground that it conflicts both with the Thirteenth Amendment of the Constitution, abolishing slavery, and the Fourteenth Amendment, which prohibits certain restrictive legislation on the part of the States.

1. That it does not conflict with the Thirteenth Amendment which abolished slavery and involuntary servitude, except as a punishment for crime, is too clear for argument. Slavery implies involuntary servitude — a stage of bondage; the ownership of mankind as a chattel, or at least the control of the labor and services of one man for the benefit of another, and the absence of a legal right to the disposal of his own person, property and services. . . .

A statute which implies merely a legal distinction between the white and colored races — a distinction which is founded in the color of the two races, and which must always exist as long as white men are distinguished from the other race by color — has no tendency to destroy the legal equality of the two races, or reëstablish a state of involuntary servitude. Indeed, we do not understand that the Thirteenth Amendment is strenuously relied upon by the plaintiff in error in this connection. . . .

The object of the [Fourteenth] amendment was undoubtedly to enforce the absolute equality of the two races before the law, but in the nature of things it could not have been intended to abolish distinctions based upon color, or to enforce social, as distinguished from political equality, or a commingling of the two races upon terms unsatisfactory to either. Laws permitting, and even requiring, their separation in places where they are liable to be brought into contact do not necessarily imply the inferiority of either race to the other, and have been generally, if not universally, recognized as within the competency of the state legislatures in the exercise of their police power. The most common instance of this is connected with the establishment of separate schools for white and colored children, which has been held to be a valid exercise of the legislative power even by courts of States where the political rights of the colored race have been longest and most earnestly enforced.

One of the earliest of these cases is that of *Roberts v. City of Boston*, 5 Cush. 198, in which the Supreme Judicial Court of Massachusetts held that the general school committee of Boston had power to make provision for the instruction of colored children in separate schools established exclusively for them, and to prohibit their attendance upon the other schools. "The great principle," said Chief Justice Shaw,[1] p. 206, "advanced by the learned and eloquent advocate for

---

[1] *Chief Justice Shaw:* Lemuel Shaw (1781–1861) served as chief justice of the Massachusetts Supreme Court from 1830 to 1860.

the plaintiff," (Mr. Charles Sumner,[2]) "is, that by the constitution and laws of Massachusetts, all persons without distinction of age or sex, birth or color, origin or condition, are equal before the law. . . . But, when this great principle comes to be applied to the actual and various conditions of persons in society, it will not warrant the assertion, that men and women are legally clothed with the same civil and political powers, and that children and adults are legally to have the same functions and be subject to the same treatment; but only that the rights of all, as they are settled and regulated by law, are equally entitled to the paternal consideration and protection of the law for their maintenance and security." It was held that the powers of the committee extended to the establishment of separate schools for children of different ages, sexes and colors, and that they might also establish special schools for poor and neglected children, who have become too old to attend the primary school, and yet have not acquired the rudiments of learning, to enable them to enter the ordinary schools. Similar laws have been enacted by Congress under its general power of legislation over the District of Columbia, Rev. Stat. D. C. 281, 282, 283, 310, 319, as well as by the legislatures of many of the States, and have been generally, if not uniformly, sustained by the courts. . . .

Laws forbidding the intermarriage of the two races may be said in a technical sense to interfere with the freedom of contract, and yet have been universally recognized as within the police power of the State. *State v. Gibson,* 36 Indiana, 389.

In the present case no question of interference with interstate commerce can possibly arise, since the East Louisiana Railway appears to have been purely a local line, with both its termini within the State of Louisiana. . . .

It is claimed by the plaintiff in error that, in any mixed community, the reputation of belonging to the dominant race, in this instance the white race, is *property,* in the same sense that a right of action, or of inheritance, is property. Conceding this to be so, for the purposes of this case, we are unable to see how this statute deprives him of, or in any way affects his right to, such property. If he be a white man and assigned to a colored coach, he may have his action for damages against the company for being deprived of his so called property. Upon

---

[2] *Mr. Charles Sumner:* A Massachusetts lawyer, abolitionist, and U.S. senator, Charles Sumner (1811–1874) was a proponent of southern Reconstruction and a staunch advocate for black civil rights.

the other hand, if he be a colored man and be so assigned he has been deprived of no property, since he is not lawfully entitled to the reputation of being a white man.

In this connection, it is also suggested by the learned counsel for the plaintiff in error that the same argument that will justify the state legislature in requiring railways to provide separate accommodations for the two races will also authorize them to require separate cars to be provided for people whose hair is of a certain color, or who are aliens, or who belong to certain nationalities, or to enact laws requiring colored people to walk upon one side of the street, and white people upon the other, or requiring white men's houses to be painted white, and colored men's black, or their vehicles or business signs to be of different colors, upon the theory that one side of the street is as good as the other, or that a house or vehicle of one color is as good as one of another color. The reply to all this is that every exercise of the police power must be reasonable, and extend only to such laws as are enacted in good faith for the promotion for the public good, and not for the annoyance or oppression of a particular class. . . .

So far, then, as a conflict with the Fourteenth Amendment is concerned, the case reduces itself to the question whether the statute of Louisiana is a reasonable regulation, and with respect to this there must necessarily be a large discretion on the part of the legislature. In determining the question of reasonableness it is at liberty to act with reference to the established usages, customs and traditions of the people, and with a view to the promotion of their comfort, and the preservation of the public peace and good order. Gauged by this standard, we cannot say that a law which authorizes or even requires the separation of the two races in public conveyances is unreasonable, or more obnoxious to the Fourteenth Amendment than the acts of Congress requiring separate schools for colored children in the District of Columbia, the constitutionality of which does not seem to have been questioned, or the corresponding acts of state legislatures.

We consider the underlying fallacy of the plaintiff's argument to consist in the assumption that the enforced separation of the two races stamps the colored race with a badge of inferiority. If this be so, it is not by reason of anything found in the act, but solely because the colored race chooses to put that construction upon it. The argument necessarily assumes that if, as has been more than once the case, and is not unlikely to be so again, the colored race should become the dominant power in the state legislature, and should enact a law in precisely similar terms, it would thereby relegate the white race to an inferior position. We imagine that the white race, at least, would not acquiesce in this assumption. The argument also assumes that social prejudices may be overcome by legislation, and that equal rights cannot be secured to the negro except by an enforced commingling of the two races. We cannot accept this proposition. If the two races are to meet upon terms of social equality, it must be the result of natural affinities, a mutual appreciation of each other's merits and a voluntary consent of individuals. As was said by the Court of Appeals of New York in *People v. Gallagher,* 93 N. Y. 438, 448, "this end can neither be accomplished nor promoted by laws which conflict with the general sentiment of the community upon whom they are designed to operate. When the government, therefore, has secured to each of its citizens equal rights before the law and equal opportunities for improvement and progress, it has accomplished the end for which it was organized and performed all of the functions respecting social advantages with which it is endowed." Legislation is powerless to eradicate racial instincts or to abolish distinctions based upon physical differences, and the attempt to do so can only result in accentuating the difficulties of the present situation. If the civil and political rights of both races be equal one cannot be inferior to the other civilly or politically. If one race be inferior to the other socially, the Constitution of the United States cannot put them upon the same plane.

It is true that the question of the proportion of colored blood necessary to constitute a colored person, as distinguished from a white person is one upon which there is a difference of opinion in the different States . . . but these are questions to be determined under the laws of each State and are not properly put in issue in this case. Under the allegations of his petition it may undoubtedly become a question of importance whether, under the laws of Louisiana, the petitioner belongs to the white or colored race.

The judgment of the court below is, therefore,

Affirmed.

DISSENT BY JUSTICE JOHN MARSHALL HARLAN, MAY 18, 1896.

. . . While there may be in Louisiana persons of different races who are not citizens of the United States, the words in the act, "white and colored races," necessarily include all citizens of the United States of both races residing in that State. So that we have before us a state enactment that compels, under penalties, the separation of the two races in railroad passenger coaches, and makes it a crime for a citizen of either race to enter a coach that has been assigned to citizens of the other race.

Thus the State regulates the use of a public highway by citizens of the United States solely upon the basis of race.

However apparent the injustice of such legislation may be, we have only to consider whether it is consistent with the Constitution of the United States. . . .

The Thirteenth Amendment does not permit the withholding or the deprivation of any right necessarily inhering in freedom. It not only struck down the institution of slavery as previously existing in the United States, but it prevents the imposition of any burdens or disabilities that constitute badges of slavery or servitude. It decreed universal civil freedom in this country. This court has so adjudged. But that amendment having been found inadequate to the protection of the rights of those who had been in slavery, it was followed by the Fourteenth Amendment, which added greatly to the dignity and glory of American citizenship, and to the security of personal liberty, by declaring that "all persons born or naturalized in the United States and subject to the jurisdiction thereof, are citizens of the United States and of the State wherein they reside," and that "no State shall make or enforce any law which shall abridge the privileges or immunities of citizens of the United States; nor shall any State deprive any person of life, liberty or property without due process of law, nor deny to any person within its jurisdiction the equal protection of the laws." These two amendments, if enforced according to their true intent and meaning, will protect all the civil rights that pertain to freedom and citizenship. Finally, and to the end that no citizen should be denied, on account of his race, the privilege of participating in the political control of his country, it was declared by the Fifteenth Amendment that "the right of citizens of the United States to vote shall not be denied or abridged by the United States or by any State on account of race, color or previous condition of servitude.". . .

It was said in argument that the statute of Louisiana does not discriminate against either race, but prescribes a rule applicable alike to white and colored citizens. But this argument does not meet the difficulty. Every one knows that the statute in question had its origin in the purpose, not so much to exclude white persons from railroad cars occupied by blacks, as to exclude colored people from coaches occupied by or assigned to white persons. Railroad corporations of Louisiana did not make discrimination among whites in the matter of accommodation for travellers. The thing to accomplish was, under the guise of giving equal accommodation for white and blacks, to compel the latter to keep to themselves while travelling in railroad passenger coaches. No one would be so wanting in candor as to assert the contrary. The fundamental objection, therefore, to the statute is that it interferes with the personal freedom of citizens. . . .

It is one thing for railroad carriers to furnish, or to be required by law to furnish, equal accommodations for all whom they are under a legal duty to carry. It is quite another thing for government to forbid citizens of the white and black races from travelling in the same public conveyance, and to punish officers of railroad companies for permitting persons of the two races to occupy the same passenger coach. . . .

The white race deems itself to be the dominant race in this country. And so it is, in prestige, in achievements, in education, in wealth and in power. So, I doubt not, it will continue to be for all time, if it remains true to its great heritage and holds fast to the principles of constitutional liberty. But in view of the Constitution, in the eye of the law, there is in this country no superior, dominant, ruling class of citizens. There is no caste here. Our Constitution is color-blind, and neither knows nor tolerates classes among citizens. In respect of civil rights, all citizens are equal before the law. The humblest is the peer of the most powerful. The law regards man as man, and takes no account of his surroundings or of his color when his civil rights as guaranteed by the supreme law of the land are involved. It is, therefore, to be regretted that this high tribunal, the final expositor of the fundamental law of the land, has reached the conclusion that it is competent for a State to regulate the enjoyment by citizens of their civil rights solely upon the basis of race.

In my opinion, the judgement this day rendered will, in time, prove to be quite as pernicious as the decision made by this tribunal in the *Dred Scott case*.[3] It was adjudged in that case that the descendants of Africans who were imported into this country and sold as slaves were not included nor intended to be included under the word "citizens" in

---

[3] *Dred Scott case:* In 1857 the slave Dred Scott sued for his freedom on the grounds that his master had transported him from the slaveholding South to Illinois and then what is now present-day Wisconsin, where slavery was outlawed. The case went to the U.S. Supreme Court, which ruled against Scott, with Chief Justice Roger B. Taney asserting that, as noncitizens, slaves "had no rights which a white man was bound to respect."

the Constitution, and could not claim any of the rights and privileges which that instrument provided for and secured to citizens of the United States; that at the time of the adoption of the Constitution they were "considered as a subordinate and inferior class of beings, who had been subjugated by the dominant race and, whether emancipated or not, yet remained subject to their authority, and had no rights or privileges but such as those who held the power and the government might choose to grant them." 19 How. 393, 404. The recent amendments of the Constitution, it was supposed, had eradicated these principles from our institutions. But it seems that we have yet, in some of the States, a dominant race — a superior class of citizens, which assumes to regulate the enjoyment of civil rights, common to all citizens, upon the basis of race. The present decision, it may well be apprehended, will not only stimulate aggressions, more or less brutal and irritating, upon the admitted rights of colored citizens, but will encourage the belief that it is possible, by means of state enactments, to defeat the beneficent purposes which the people of the United States had in view when they adopted the recent amendments of the Constitution, by one of which the blacks of this country were made citizens of the United States and of the States in which they respectively reside, and whose privileges and immunities, as citizens, the States are forbidden to abridge. Sixty millions of whites are in no danger from the presence here of eight millions of blacks. The destinies of the two races, in this country, are indissolubly linked together, and the interests of both require that the common government of all shall not permit the seeds of race hate to be planted under the sanction of law. What can more certainly arouse race hate, what more certainly create and perpetuate a feeling of distrust between these races, than state enactments, which, in fact, proceed on the ground that colored citizens are so inferior and degraded that they cannot be allowed to sit in public coaches occupied by white citizens? That, as all will admit, is the real meaning of such legislation as was enacted in Louisiana. . . .

There is a race so different from our own that we do not permit those belonging to it to become citizens of the United States. Persons belonging to it are, with few exceptions, absolutely excluded from our country. I allude to the Chinese race. But by the statute in question, a Chinaman can ride in the same passenger coach with white citizens of the United States, while citizens of the black race in Louisiana, many of whom, perhaps, risked their lives for the preservation of the Union, who are entitled, by law, to participate in the political control of the State and nation, who are not excluded, by law or by reason of their race, from public stations of any kind, and who have all the legal rights that belong to white citizens, are yet declared to be criminals, liable to imprisonment, if they ride in a public coach occupied by citizens of the white race. It is scarcely just to say that a colored citizen should not object to occupying a public coach assigned to his own race. He does not object, nor, perhaps, would he object to separate coaches for his race, if his rights under the law were recognized. But he objects, and ought never to cease objecting to the proposition, that citizens of the white and black races can be adjudged criminals because they sit, or claim the right to sit, in the same public coach on a public highway. . . .

If evils will result from the commingling of the two races upon public highways established for the benefit of all, they will be infinitely less than those that will surely come from state legislation regulating the enjoyment of civil rights upon the basis of race. We boast of the freedom enjoyed by our people above all other peoples. But it is difficult to reconcile that boast with a state of the law which, practically, puts the brand of servitude and degradation upon a large class of our fellow-citizens, our equals before the law. The thin disguise of "equal" accommodations for passengers in railroad coaches will not mislead any one, nor atone for the wrong this day done. . . .

I am of opinion that the statute of Louisiana is inconsistent with the personal liberty of citizens, white and black, in that State, and hostile to both the spirit and letter of the Constitution of the United States. If laws of like character should be enacted in the several States of the Union, the effect would be in the highest degree mischievous. Slavery, as an institution tolerated by law would, it is true, have disappeared from our country, but there would remain a power in the States, by sinister legislation, to interfere with the full enjoyment of the blessings of freedom; to regulate civil rights, common to all citizens, upon the basis of race; and to place in a condition of legal inferiority a large body of American citizens, now constituting a part of the political community called the People of the United States, for whom, and by whom through representatives, our government is administered. Such a system is inconsistent with the guarantee given by the Constitution to each State of a republican form of government, and may be stricken down by Congressional action, or by the courts in the discharge of their solemn duty to maintain the supreme law of the land, anything in the constitution or laws of any State to the contrary not withstanding.

For the reasons stated, I am constrained to withhold my assent for the opinion and judgment of the majority.

Suffrage and Eligibility to Office, Article VI, the North Carolina State Constitution

The voter eligibility amendment to the North Carolina constitution offers yet another example of how white supremacists thwarted the Fourteenth and Fifteenth Amendments by using a variety of clever legal tactics. Though by the 1890s many southern states had devised state constitutional loopholes to disenfranchise African American male voters, North Carolina's blacks found that they still had some room to maneuver. Indeed, in the 1896 election black Republicans benefited from a coalition with anti-Democratic white Populists, which enabled problack successes in many key congressional and state posts, including substantial black representation on the Wilmington city council. After Wilmington's white Democrats used the 1898 riot to overturn the election results in the city, party members in the state legislature proposed a voter eligibility amendment to ensure that black men would not cast ballots in future elections. (Not surprisingly, strong support for the amendment came from Josephus Daniels, the editor of the *Charlotte News and Observer* who had inflamed white Wilmington before the riot.) Inspired by amendments in other southern states, the North Carolina constitutional amendment included a literacy test, a voting or poll tax, and the infamous "grandfather" clause, which guaranteed the vote only to men who had been born free or had been the descendant of voters born free before 1867. All three qualifications disenfranchised the majority of black voters. The literacy test and the poll tax raised protest among working-class Populists, since illiterate poor whites would also be disenfranchised, but with blacks avoiding the polls for fear of their lives, and white voters convinced that "Negro domination" had to be ended at all costs, the amendment passed by a majority on August 2, 1900. The constitutional change is reprinted below from *The State Constitutions and the Federal Constitution and Organic Laws of the Territories and Other Dependencies of the United States of America,* ed. Charles Kettleborough (Indianapolis: B. F. Bowen and Company, 1918).

SECTION 1. Every male person born in the United States, and every male person who has been naturalized, twenty-one years of age, and possessing the qualifications set out in this article, shall be entitled to vote at any election by the people in the State, except as herein otherwise provided.

Sᴇᴄ. 2. He shall have resided in the State of North Carolina for two years, in the county six months, and in the precinct, ward or other election district in which he offers to vote, four months next preceding the election: Provided, that removal from one precinct, ward or other election district, to another in the same county, shall not operate to deprive any person of the right to vote in the precinct, ward or other election district from which he has removed until four months after such removal. No person who has been convicted, or who has confessed his guilt in open Court upon indictment, of any crime, the punishment of which now is or may hereafter be imprisonment in the State's Prison, shall be permitted to vote unless the said person shall be first restored to citizenship in the manner prescribed by law.

Sᴇᴄ. 3. Every person offering to vote shall be at the time a legally registered voter as herein prescribed and in the manner hereafter provided by law, and the General Assembly of North Carolina shall enact general registration laws to carry into effect the provisions of this article.

Sᴇᴄ. 4. Every person presenting himself for registration shall be able to read and write any section of the Constitution in the English language; and before he shall be entitled to vote he shall have paid, on or before the first day of May of the year in which he proposes to vote, his poll tax[1] for the previous year as prescribed by Article V, sec. 1, of the Constitution. But no male person who was on January 1, 1867, or at any time prior thereto, entitled to vote under the laws of any State in the United States wherein he then resided, and no lineal descendant of any such person, shall be denied the right to register and vote at any election in this State by reason of his failure to possess the educational qualifications herein prescribed: Provided, he shall have registered in accordance with the terms of this section prior to December 1, 1908. The General Assembly shall provide for the registration of all persons entitled to vote without the educational qualifications herein prescribed, and shall, on or before November 1, 1908, provide for the making of a permanent record of such registration, and all persons so registered shall forever thereafter have the right to vote in all elections by the people in this State, unless disqualified under section 2 of this article: Provided, such person shall have paid his poll tax as above required.

Sᴇᴄ. 5. That this amendment to the Constitution is presented and adopted as one indivisible plan for the regulation of the suffrage, with

---

[1] *poll tax:* Tax levied on eligible voters.

the intent and purpose to so connect the different parts and to make them so dependent upon each other that the whole shall stand or fall together.

SEC. 6. All elections by the people shall be by ballot, and all elections by the General Assembly shall be viva voce.[2]

SEC. 7. Every voter in North Carolina, except as in this article disqualified, shall be eligible to office, but before entering upon the duties of the office he shall take and subscribe the following oath:

"I, ————, do solemnly swear (or affirm) that I will support and maintain the Constitution and laws of the United States and the Constitution and laws of North Carolina not inconsistent therewith, and that I will faithfully discharge the duties of my office as ————. So help me, God."

SEC. 8. The following classes of persons shall be disqualified for office: First, all persons who shall deny the being of Almighty God. Second, all persons who shall have been convicted or confessed their guilt on indictment pending, and whether sentenced or not, or under judgment suspended, of any treason or felony, or of any other crime for which the punishment may be imprisonment in the penitentiary, since becoming citizens of the United States, or of corruption or malpractice in office, unless such person shall be restored to the rights of citizenship in a manner prescribed by law.

SEC. 9. That this amendment to the Constitution shall go into effect on the first day of July, nineteen hundred and two, if a majority of votes cast at the next general election shall be cast in favor of this suffrage amendment.

---

[2] *viva voce:* An oral examination.

IDA B. WELLS

From *Southern Horrors: Lynch Law in All Its Phases*

The oldest child of a Mississippi slave couple, Ida B. Wells (1862–1931) rose to prominence in the late nineteenth and early twentieth centuries as a fiery journalist, lecturer, feminist, and antilynching activist. Wells began public life as a teacher, and later became the editor and part owner of the *Memphis Free Speech and Headlight.* For Wells, a life of respectable black womanhood required that she resist racial discrimination. Consequently, in 1884 after being ejected from a Chesapeake and Ohio Railroad passenger train for refusing to sit in a segregated car, Wells sued the railroad. (Initially successful, her suit was lost when the railroad appealed to a higher court.) Wells's specific focus on lynching began when three male friends were murdered because their grocery store competed with white establishments for black business. After investigating their deaths, she wrote an editorial arguing that rather than being a response to rape, lynching was really an attempt to thwart black advancement. Angered by her rebuke, white rioters destroyed the offices of the *Free Speech* and issued death threats against Wells. Forced into exile in New York, she developed a more extensive critique of lynching, writing for other black newspapers such as T. Thomas Fortune's *New York Age,* and she delivered antilynching lectures nationally and in Great Britain. Though she married the black Chicago lawyer Ferdinand Barnett in 1895 and raised a large family, Wells continued her campaign against lynching and expanded her work to include (among other causes) woman's suffrage, the establishment and support of black women's clubs, and relief work among southern black migrants. In all, she published three antilynching pamphlets: *Southern Horrors: Lynch Law in All Its Phases* (1892), *A Red Record* (1895), and *Mob Rule in New Orleans* (1900). The excerpt below is taken from *Southern Horrors,* republished in *On Lynchings: Southern Horrors, A Red Record, Mob Rule in New Orleans* (Salem, NH: Ayer Company, 1993).

CHAPTER I. THE OFFENSE.

Wednesday evening May 24th, 1892, the city of Memphis was filled with excitement. Editorials in the daily papers of that date caused a meeting to be held in the Cotton Exchange Building; a committee was sent for the editors of the "Free Speech" an Afro-American journal published in that city, and the only reason the open threats of lynching that were made were not carried out was because they could not be found. The cause of all this commotion was the following editorial published in the "Free Speech" May 21st, 1892, the Saturday previous.

"Eight negroes lynched since last issue of the "Free Speech" one at Little Rock, Ark., last Saturday morning where the citizens broke (?) into the penitentiary and got their man; three near Anniston, Ala., one near New Orleans; and three at Clarksville, Ga., the last three for killing a white man, and five on the same old racket — the new alarm about raping white women. The same programme of hanging, then shooting bullets into the lifeless bodies was carried out to the letter.

Nobody in this section of the country believes the old thread bare lie that Negro men rape white women. If Southern white men are not careful, they will over-reach themselves and public sentiment will have a reaction; a conclusion will then be reached which will be very damaging to the moral reputation of their women."

"The Daily Commercial" of Wednesday following, May 25th, contained the following leader:

"Those negroes who are attempting to make the lynching of individuals of their race a means for arousing the worst passions of their kind are playing with a dangerous sentiment. The negroes may as well understand that there is no mercy for the negro rapist and little patience with his defenders. A negro organ printed in this city, in a recent issue publishes the following atrocious paragraph: 'Nobody in this section of the country believes the old thread-bare lie that negro men rape white women. If Southern white men are not careful they will over-reach themselves, and public sentiment will have a reaction; and a conclusion will be reached which will be very damaging to the moral reputation of their women.'

The fact that a black scoundrel is allowed to live and utter such loathsome and repulsive calumnies is a volume of evidence as to the wonderful patience of Southern whites. But we have had enough of it.

There are some things that the Southern white man will not tolerate, and the obscene intimations of the foregoing have brought the writer to the very outermost limit of public patience. We hope we have said enough."

The "Evening Scimitar" of same date, copied the "Commercial's" editorial with these words of comment: "Patience under such circumstances is not a virtue. If the negroes themselves do not apply the remedy without delay it will be the duty of those whom he has attacked to tie the wretch who utters these calumnies to a stake at the intersection of Main and Madison Sts., brand him in the forehead with a hot iron and perform upon him a surgical operation with a pair of tailor's shears."

Acting upon this advice, the leading citizens met in the Cotton Exchange Building the same evening, and threats of lynching were freely indulged, not by the lawless element upon which the deviltry of the South is usually saddled — but by the leading business men, in their leading business centre. Mr. Fleming, the business manager and owning a half interest the Free Speech, had to leave town to escape the mob, and was afterwards ordered not to return; letters and telegrams sent me in New York where I was spending my vacation advised me that bodily harm awaited my return. Creditors took possession of the office and sold the outfit, and the "Free Speech" was as if it had never been.

The editorial in question was prompted by the many inhuman and fiendish lynchings of Afro-Americans which have recently taken place and was meant as a warning. Eight lynched in one week and five of them charged with rape! The thinking public will not easily believe freedom and education more brutalizing than slavery, and the world knows that the crime of rape was unknown during four years of civil war, when the white women of the South were at the mercy of the race which is all at once charged with being a bestial one.

Since my business has been destroyed and I am an exile from home because of that editorial, the issue has been forced, and as the writer of it I feel that the race and the public generally should have a statement of the facts as they exist. They will serve at the same time as a defense for the Afro-Americans Sampsons who suffer themselves to be betrayed by white Delilahs.

The whites of Montgomery, Ala., knew J. C. Duke[1] sounded the keynote of the situation — which they would gladly hide from the world, when he said in his paper, "The Herald," five years ago: "Why is it that white women attract negro men now more than in former days? There was a time when such a thing was unheard of. There is a secret to this thing, and we greatly suspect it is the growing appreciation of white Juliets for colored Romeos." Mr. Duke, like the "Free Speech" proprietors, was forced to leave the city for reflecting on the "honah" of white women and his paper suppressed; but the truth remains that Afro-American men do not always rape(?) white women without their consent.

Mr. Duke, before leaving Montgomery, signed a card disclaiming any intention of slandering Southern white women. The editor of the "Free Speech" has no disclaimer to enter, but asserts instead that there are many white women in the South who would marry colored men if such an act would not place them at once beyond the pale of society and within the clutches of the law. The miscegenation laws of the

---

[1] *J. C. Duke:* Both Wells and black Alabama journalist Jesse Chisholm Duke (1853–1916) had earned the ire of the white community by questioning the stereotype of African American male criminality. Duke served as editor of the *Montgomery Herald* and later the *Pine Bluff Weekly Echo.*

South only operate against the legitimate union of the races; they leave the white man free to seduce all the colored girls he can, but it is death to the colored man who yields to the force and advances of a similar attraction in white women. White men lynch the offending Afro-American, not because he is a despoiler of virtue, but because he succumbs to the smiles of white women.

CHAPTER II. THE BLACK AND WHITE OF IT.

The "Cleveland Gazette" of January 16, 1892, publishes a case in point. Mrs. J. S. Underwood, the wife of a minister of Elyria, Ohio, accused an Afro-American of rape. She told her husband that during his absence in 1888, stumping the State for the Prohibition Party, the man came to the kitchen door, forced his way in the house and insulted her. She tried to drive him out with a heavy poker, but he overpowered and chloroformed her, and when she revived her clothing was torn and she was in a horrible condition. She did not know the man but could identify him. She pointed out William Offett, a married man, who was arrested and, being in Ohio, was granted a trial.

The prisoner vehemently denied the charge of rape, but confessed he went to Mrs. Underwood's residence at her invitation and was criminally intimate with her at her request. This availed him nothing against the sworn testimony of a minister's wife, a lady of the highest respectability. He was found guilty, and entered the penitentiary, December 14, 1888, for fifteen years. Some time afterwards the woman's remorse led her to confess to her husband that the man was innocent.

These are her words: "I met Offett at the Post Office. It was raining. He was polite to me, and as I had several bundles in my arms he offered to carry them home for me, which he did. He had a strange fascination for me, and I invited him to call on me. He called, bringing chestnuts and candy for the children. By this means we got them to leave us alone in the room. Then I sat on his lap. He made a proposal to me and I readily consented. Why I did so, I do not know, but that I did is true. He visited me several times after that and each time I was indiscreet. I did not care after the first time. In fact I could not have resisted, and had no desire to resist."

When asked by her husband why she told him she had been outraged,[2] she said: "I had several reasons for telling you. One was the

---

[2] *outraged*: Sexually assaulted.

neighbors saw the fellows here, another was, I was afraid I had contracted a loathsome disease, and still another was that I feared I might
give birth to a Negro baby. I hoped to save my reputation by telling
you a deliberate lie." Her husband horrified by the confession had
Offett, who had already served four years, released and secured a
divorce.

There are thousands of such cases throughout the South, with the
difference that the Southern white men in insatiate fury wreak their
vengeance without intervention of law upon the Afro-Americans who
consort with their women. A few instances to substantiate the assertion that some white women love the company of the Afro-American
will not be out of place. Most of these cases were reported by the daily
papers of the South.

In the winter of 1885–6 the wife of a practicing physician in Memphis, in good social standing whose name has escaped me, left home,
husband and children, and ran away with her black coachman. She
was with him a month before her husband found and brought her
home. The coachman could not be found. The doctor moved his family away from Memphis, and is living in another city under an
assumed name.

In the same city last year a white girl in the dusk of evening
screamed at the approach of some parties that a Negro had assaulted
her on the street. He was captured, tried by a white judge and jury,
that acquitted him of the charge. It is needless to add if there had been
a scrap of evidence on which to convict him of so grave a charge he
would have been convicted.

Sarah Clark of Memphis loved a black man and lived openly with
him. When she was indicted last spring for miscegenation, she swore
in court that she was *not* a white woman. This she did to escape the
penitentiary and continued her illicit relation undisturbed. That she is
of the lower class of whites, does not disturb the fact that she is a white
woman. "The leading citizens" of Memphis are defending the "honor"
of *all* white women, *demi-monde*[3] included.

Since the manager of the "Free Speech" has been run away from
Memphis by the guardians of the honor of Southern white women, a
young girl living on Poplar St., who was discovered in intimate relations with a handsome mulatto young colored man, Will Morgan by
name, stole her father's money to send the young fellow away from
that father's wrath. She has since joined him in Chicago.

---

[3] *demi-monde:* Women of low or questionable reputation.

The Memphis "Ledger" for June 8th has the following; "If Lillie Bailey, a rather pretty white girl seventeen years of age, who is now at the City Hospital, would be somewhat less reserved about her disgrace there would be some very nauseating details in the story of her life. She is the mother of a little coon. The truth might reveal fearful depravity or it might reveal the evidence of a rank outrage. She will not divulge the name of the man who has left such black evidence of her disgrace, and, in fact, says it is a matter in which there can be no interest to the outside world. She came to Memphis nearly three months ago and was taken in at the Women's Refuge in the southern part of the city. She remained there until a few weeks ago, when the child was born. The ladies in charge of the Refuge were horified [sic]. The girl was at once sent to the City Hospital, where she has been since May 30th. She is a country girl. She came to Memphis from her father's farm, a short distance from Hernando, Miss. Just when she left there she would not say. In fact she says she came to Memphis from Arkansas, and says her home is in that State. She is rather good looking, has blue eyes, a low forehead and dark red hair. The ladies at the Woman's Refuge do not know anything about the girl further than what they learned when she was an inmate of the institution; and she would not tell much. When the child was born an attempt was made to get the girl to reveal the name of the Negro who had disgraced her, she obstinately refused and it was impossible to elicit any information from her on the subject."

Note the wording. "The truth might reveal fearful depravity or rank outrage." If it had been a white child or Lillie Bailey had told a pitiful story of Negro outrage, it would have been a case of woman's weakness or assault and she could have remained at the Woman's Refuge. But a Negro child and to withhold its father's name and thus prevent the killing of another Negro "rapist." A case of "fearful depravity."

The very week the "leading citizens" of Memphis were making a spectacle of themselves in defense of all white women of every kind, an Afro-American, M. Stricklin, was found in a white woman's room in that city. Although she made no outcry of rape, he was jailed and would have been lynched, but the woman stated she bought curtains of him (he was a furniture dealer) and his business in her room that night was to put them up. A white woman's word was taken as absolutely in this case as when the cry of rape is made, and he was freed.

What is true of Memphis is true of the entire South. The daily papers last year reported a farmer's wife in Alabama had given birth to a Negro child. When the Negro farm hand who was plowing in the field heard it he took the mule from the plow and fled. The dispatches also told of a woman in South Carolina who gave birth to a Negro child and charged three men with being its father, *every one of whom has since disappeared*. In Tuscumbia, Ala., the colored boy who was lynched there last year for assaulting a white girl told her before his accusers that he had met her there in the woods often before. . . .

In Natchez, Miss., Mrs. Marshall, one of the *creme de la creme* of the city, created a tremendous sensation several years ago. She has a black coachman who was married, and had been in her employ several years. During this time she gave birth to a child whose color was remarked, but traced to some brunette ancestor, and one of the fashionable dames of the city was its godmother. Mrs. Marshall's social position was unquestioned, and wealth showered every dainty on this child which was idolized with its brothers and sisters by its white papa. In course of time another child appeared on the scene, but it was unmistakably dark. All were alarmed, and "rush of blood, strangulation" were the conjectures, but the doctor, when asked the cause, grimly told them it was a Negro child. There was a family conclave, the coachman heard of it and leaving his own family went West, and has never returned. As soon as Mrs. Marshall was able to travel she was sent away in deep disgrace. Her husband died within the year of a broken heart.

Ebenzer Fowler, the wealthiest colored man in Issaquena County, Miss., was shot down on the street in Mayersville, January 30, 1885, just before dark by an armed body of white men who filled his body with bullets. They charged him with writing a note to a white woman of the place, which they intercepted and which proved there was an intimacy existing between them.

Hundreds of such cases might be cited, but enough have been given to prove the assertion that there are white women in the South who love the Afro-American's company even as there are white men notorious for their preference for Afro-American women.

There is hardly a town in the South which has not an instance of the kind which is well-known, and hence the assertion is reiterated that "nobody in the South believes the old thread bare lie that negro men rape white women." Hence there is a growing demand among Afro-Americans that the guilt or innocence of parties accused of rape be fully established. They know the men of the section of the country who refuse this are not so desirous of punishing rapists as they pretend. The utterances of the leading white men show that with them it is not the crime but the *class*. Bishop Fitzgerald[4] has become apologist for lynchers of the rapists of *white* women only. Governor Tillman,[5] of South Carolina, in the month of June, standing under the tree in Barnwell, S. C., on which eight Afro-Americans were hung last year, declared that he would "lead a mob to lynch a *negro* who raped a *white* woman." So say the pulpits, officials and newspapers of the South. But when the victim is a colored woman it is different.

Last winter in Baltimore, Md., three white ruffians assaulted a Miss Camphor, a young Afro-American girl, while out walking with a young man of her own race. They held her escort and outraged the girl. It was a deed dastardly enough to arouse Southern blood, which gives its horror of rape as excuse for lawlessness, but she was an Afro-American. The case went to the courts, an Afro-American lawyer defended the men and they were acquitted.

In Nashville, Tenn., there is a white man, Pat Hanifan, who outraged a little Afro-American girl, and from the physical injuries received, she has been ruined for life. He was jailed for six months, discharged, and is now a detective in that city. In the same city, last May, a white man outraged an Afro-American girl in a drug store. He was arrested, and released on bail at the trial. It was rumored that five hundred Afro-Americans had organized to lynch him. Two hundred and fifty white citizens armed themselves with Winchesters and guarded him. A cannon was placed in front of his home, and the Buchanan Rifles (State Militia) ordered to the scene for his protection. The Afro-American mob did not materialize. Only two weeks before Eph. Grizzard, who had only been *charged* with rape upon a white woman, had been taken from the jail, with Governor Buchanan[6] and the police and militia standing by, dragged through the streets in broad daylight, knives plunged into him at every step, and with every fiendish cruelty a frenzied mob could devise, he was at last swung out on the bridge with hands cut to pieces as he tried to climb up the stanchions. A naked, bloody example of the blood-thirstiness of the nineteenth century civilization of the Athens of the South! No cannon or military was called out in his defense. He dared to visit a white woman.

---

[4] *Bishop Fitzgerald:* Based in Nashville, Tennessee, Methodist clergyman Oscar Penn Fitzgerald (1829–1911) edited the *Christian Advocate* and was a champion of the South.

[5] *Governor Tillman:* Both in his capacity as governor of South Carolina, and later as a U.S. senator, Benjamin "Pitchfork" Tillman (1847–1918) consistently supported lynching and the disenfranchisement of African Americans.

[6] *Governor Buchanan:* Democrat John Price Buchanan (1837–1930) served as governor of Tennessee from 1891 to 1893.

At the very moment these civilized whites were announcing their determination "to protect their wives and daughters," by murdering Grizzard, a white man was in the same jail for raping eight year-old Maggie Reese, an Afro-American girl. He was not harmed. The "honor" of grown women who were glad enough to be supported by the Grizzard boys and Ed Coy, as long as the liaison was not known, needed protection; they were white. The outrage upon helpless childhood needed no avenging in this case; she was black.

A white man in Guthrie, Oklahoma Territory, two months ago inflicted such injuries upon another Afro-American child that she died. He was not punished, but an attempt was made in the same town in the month of June to lynch an Afro-American who visited a white woman.

In Memphis, Tenn., in the month of June, Ellerton L. Dorr, who is the husband of Russell Hancock's widow, was arrested for attempted rape on Mattie Cole, a neighbor's cook; he was only prevented from accomplishing his purpose, by the appearance of Mattie's employer. Dorr's friends say he was drunk and not responsible for his actions. The grand jury refused to indict him and he was discharged.

CHAPTER III. THE NEW CRY.

The appeal of Southern whites to Northern sympathy and sanction, the adroit, insiduous plea made by Bishop Fitzgerald for suspension of judgment because those "who condemn lynching express no sympathy for the *white* woman in the case," falls to the ground in the light of the foregoing.

From this exposition of the race issue in lynch law, the whole matter is explained by the well-known opposition growing out of slavery to the progress of the race. This is crystalized in the oft-repeated slogan: "This is a white man's country and the white man must rule." The South resented giving the Afro-American his freedom, the ballot box and the Civil Rights Law. The raids of the Ku-Klux and White Liners[7] to subvert reconstruction government, the Hamburg and Ellerton, S. C., the Copiah County Miss., and the Layfayette Parish, La., massacres were excused as the natural resentment of intelligence against government by ignorance.

---

[7] *White Liners:* The White Line was a local white supremacist organization operating in Mississippi.

Honest white men practically conceded the necessity of intelligence murdering ignorance to correct the mistake of the general government, and the race was left to the tender mercies of the solid South. Thoughtful Afro-Americans with the strong arm of the government withdrawn and with the hope to stop such wholesale massacres urged the race to sacrifice its political rights for sake of peace. They honestly believed the race should fit itself for government, and when that should be done, the objection to race participation in politics would be removed.

But the sacrifice did not remove the trouble, nor move the South to justice. One by one the Southern States have legally (?) disfranchised the Afro-Americans, and since the repeal of the Civil Rights Bill nearly every Southern State has passed separate car laws with a penalty against their infringement. The race regardless of advancement is penned into filthy, stifling partitions cut off from smoking cars. All this while, although the political cause has been removed, the butcheries of black men at Barnwell, S. C., Carrolton, Miss., Waycross, Ga., and Memphis, Tenn., have gone on; also the flaying alive of a man in Kentucky, the burning of one in Arkansas, the hanging of a fifteen year old girl in Louisiana, a woman in Jackson, Tenn., and one in Hollendale, Miss., until the dark and bloody record of the South shows 728 Afro-Americans lynched during the past 8 years. Not 50 of these were for political causes; the rest were for all manner of accusations from that of rape of white women, to the case of the boy Will Lewis who was hanged at Tullahoma, Tenn., last year for being drunk and "sassy" to white folks.

These statistics compiled by the Chicago "Tribune" were given the first of this year (1892). Since then, not less than one hundred and fifty have been known to have met violent death at the hands of cruel bloodthirsty mobs during the past nine months.

To palliate this record (which grows worse as the Afro-American becomes intelligent) and excuse some of the most heinous crimes that ever stained the history of a country, the South is shielding itself behind the plausible screen of defending the honor of its women. This, too, in the face of the fact that only *one-third* of the 728 victims to mobs have been *charged* with rape, to say nothing of those of that one-third who were innocent of the charge. . . .

Even to the better class of Afro-Americans the crime of rape is so revolting they have too often taken the white man's word and given lynch law neither the investigation nor condemnation it deserved.

They forget that a concession of the right to lynch a man for a certain crime, not only concedes the right to lynch any person for any crime, but (so frequently is the cry of rape now raised) it is in a fair way to stamp us a race of rapists and desperadoes. They have gone on hoping and believing that general education and financial strength would solve the difficulty, and are devoting their energies to the accumulation of both.

The mob spirit has grown with the increasing intelligence of the Afro-American. It has left the out-of-the-way places where ignorance prevails, has thrown off the mask and with this new cry stalks in broad daylight in large cities, the centres of civilization, and is encouraged by the "leading citizens" and the press. . . .

CHAPTER V. THE SOUTH'S POSITION.

. . . The strong arm of the law must be brought to bear upon lynchers in severe punishment, but this cannot and will not be done unless a healthy public sentiment demands and sustains such action.

The men and women in the South who disapprove of lynching and remain silent on the perpetration of such outrages, are particeps criminis, accomplices, accessories before and after the fact, equally guilty with the actual law-breakers who would not persist if they did not know that neither the law nor militia would be employed against them.

CHAPTER VI. SELF HELP.

In the creation of this healthier public sentiment, the Afro-American can do for himself what no one else can do for him. The world looks on with wonder that we have conceded so much and remain law-abiding under such great outrage and provocation.

To Northern capital and Afro-American labor the South owes its rehabilitation. If labor is withdrawn capital will not remain. The Afro-American is thus the backbone of the South. A thorough knowledge and judicious exercise of this power in lynching localities could many times effect a bloodless revolution. The white man's dollar is his god and to stop this will be to stop outrages in many localities.

The Afro-Americans of Memphis denounced the lynching of three of their best citizens, and urged and waited for the authorities to act in the matter and bring the lynchers to justice. No attempt was made to do so, and the black men left the city by thousands, bringing about great stagnation in every branch of business. Those who remained so injured the business of the street car company by staying off the cars, that the superintendent, manager and treasurer called personally on the editor of the "Free Speech," asked them to urge our people to give them their patronage again. Other business men became alarmed over the situation and the "Free Speech" was run away that the colored people might be more easily controlled. A meeting of white citizens in June, three months after the lynching, passed resolutions for the first time, condemning it. *But they did not punish the lynchers.* Every one of them was known by name, because they had been selected to do the dirty work, by some of the very citizens who passed these resolutions. Memphis is fast losing her black population, who proclaim as they go that there is no protection for the life and property of any Afro-American citizen in Memphis who is not a slave. . . .

The appeal to the white man's pocket has ever been more effectual than all the appeals ever made to his conscience. Nothing, absolutely nothing, is to be gained by a further sacrifice of manhood and self-respect. By the right exercise of his power as the industrial factor of the South, the Afro-American can demand and secure his rights, the punishment of lynchers, and a fair trial for accused rapists.

Of the many inhuman outrages of this present year, the only case where the proposed lynching did *not* occur, was where the men armed themselves in Jacksonville, Fla., and Paducah, Ky., and prevented it. The only times an Afro-American who was assaulted got away has been when he had a gun and used it in self-defense.

The lesson this teaches and which every Afro-American should ponder well, is that a Winchester rifle should have a place of honor in every black home, and it should be used for that protection which the law refuses to give. When the white man who is always the aggressor knows he runs as great risk of biting the dust every time his Afro-American victim does, he will have greater respect for Afro-American life. The more the Afro-American yields and cringes and begs, the more he has to do so, the more he is insulted, outraged and lynched.

The assertion has been substantiated throughout these pages that the press contains unreliable and doctored reports of lynchings, and one of the most necessary things for the race to do is to get these facts before the public. The people must know before they can act, and there is no educator to compare with the press.

The Afro-American papers are the only ones which will print the truth, and they lack means to employ agents and detectives to get at the facts. The race must rally a mighty host to the support of their journals, and thus enable them to do much in the way of investigation. . . .

Near Vicksburg, Miss., a murder was committed by a gang of burglars. Of course it must have been done by Negroes, and Negroes were arrested for it. It is believed that 2 men, Smith Tooley and John Adams belonged to a gang controlled by white men and, fearing exposure, on the night of July 4th, they were hanged in the Court House yard by those interested in silencing them. Robberies since committed in the same vicinity have been known to be by white men who had their faces blackened. We strongly believe in the innocence of these murdered men, but we have no proof. No other news goes out to the world save that which stamps us as a race of cut-throats, robbers and lustful wild beasts. So great is Southern hate and prejudice, they legally (?) hung poor little thirteen year old Mildrey Brown at Columbia, S. C., Oct. 7th, on the circumstantial evidence that she poisoned a white infant. If her guilt had been proven unmistakably, had she been white, Mildrey Brown would never have been hung.

The country would have been aroused and South Carolina disgraced forever for such a crime. The Afro-American himself did not know as he should have known as his journals should be in a position to have him know and act.

Nothing is more definitely settled than he must act for himself. I have shown how he may employ the boycott, emigration and the press, and I feel that by a combination of all these agencies can be effectually stamped out lynch law, that last relic of barbarism and slavery. "The gods help those who help themselves."

Turn-of-the-Century Newspaper Reports on Lynching

Among white Americans at the start of the twentieth century, racial violence was certainly not a topic for polite conversation, nor was it addressed in the plantation and local color fiction that graced the pages of popular magazines such as the *Century* and the *Atlantic Monthly*. But nationwide American newspaper audiences were well aware that lynching and race riots were frequent, well-attended occurrences, and white newspaper accounts were particularly noteworthy for their sensationalistic reportage. The following three articles provide some sense of the variety of white reporting on lynching. The brutal 1904 torture of a black Mississippi husband and wife was reprinted in a number of black and white newspapers and periodicals, including the *Vicksburg Evening Post* (February 13, 1904); it was even woven into the plot of the 1905 novel *The Hindered Hand* by the African American minister-novelist Sutton Elbert Griggs (1872–1933). The October 2, 1905, *Atlanta Constitution* front page report of an expected lynching in Texas, complete with information on a date, time, and location, reveal the ways in which objective reporting of facts could serve to promote lynching as a white social event, where participants were so confident of community support that they expected no interference from local police authorities. And finally, the June 8, 1903, report in the *New York Herald* of a lynching in Belleville, Illinois, confirmed that racial violence was by no means solely a southern occurrence. Rather, as lynching and antiblack riots gradually spread North throughout the first decades of the twentieth century, white supremacist violence indeed became a national crisis.

VICKSBURG EVENING POST

Lynched Negro and Wife First Mutilated

Most Horrible

Details of the Burning at the Stake of the Holberts

A citizen from the Doddsville neighborhood, who witnessed the burning of the Holberts, last Sunday was in the city this morning and told of some new horrors connected with the terrible event that have not yet been printed. He said the affair was probably the most terrible one of its kind in history. When the two negroes were captured they were tied to trees and while the funeral pyres were being prepared they were forced to suffer the most fiendish tortures. The blacks were forced to hold out their hands while one finger at a time was chopped

Lynching of Laura Nelson and her son. Courtesy of the Allen/Littlefield Collection of Rare African-Americana, Woodruff Library, Special Collections, Emory University.

off. The fingers were distributed as souvenirs. The ears of the murderers were cut off. Holbert was severely beaten, his skull was fractured, and one of his eyes knocked out with a stick, hung by a shred from the socket. Neither the man nor woman begged for mercy, nor made a groan or plea. When the executioners came forward to lop off fingers Holbert extended his hand without being asked. The most excruciating form of punishment, consisted in the use of a large corkscrew in the hands of some of the mob. This instrument was bored into the flesh of the man and the woman, in the arms, legs and body, and then pulled out, the spirals tearing out big pieces of raw, quivering flesh, every time it was withdrawn. Even this devilish torture did not make the poor brutes cry out. When finally they were thrown on the fire and allowed to be burned to death, this came as a relief to the maimed and suffering victims.

Front of postcard depicting lynching of Jesse Washington, 1916, Waco, Texas. Courtesy of the Allen/Littlefield Collection of Rare African-Americana, Woodruff Library, Special Collections, Emory University.

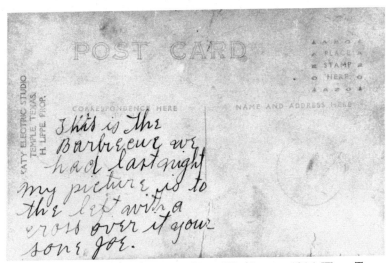

Back of postcard depicting lynching of Jesse Washington, 1916, Waco, Texas. Courtesy of the Allen/Littlefield Collection of Rare African-Americana, Woodruff Library, Special Collections, Emory University.

ATLANTA CONSTITUTION

Victim's Family Begs to See Negro Burned

Mrs. Conditt's Father and Mother Ask that Proposed Lynching Be Delayed

Posse Close on Trail of Supposed Slayer

MONK GIBSON SAID TO BE PRACTICALLY SURROUNDED
AND DETERMINATION SEEMS TO BE TO BURN HIM
AT THE STAKE WHEN CAUGHT.

Edna, Tex. October 1. — A party just arrived in town from the Allen pasture, where the negro Monk Gibson was located this afternoon, reports that the several posses that are in hot pursuit are being augmented every few minutes and capture by midnight is deemed certain. The negro is now known to be on the Navidad bottom between crossings less than two miles apart. The river bottom at this point is from one-half to one mile wide, and the limits are well surrounded.

Two packs of bloodhounds, one from Wharton and the other from Richmond, were taken off at Ganado and at the stock pens two miles above Edna. They were on the ground at 9 o'clock and they will run him down in two hours at the most. The officers will never be allowed to take possession of the negro. He will undoubtedly be brought to Edna as soon as caught and may be held for a very brief period in order to procure evidence from him, but the general opinion is that he will meet death at the stake before daylight Monday morning.

Want to See Execution.

H. H. Beasley, a brother of Mrs. Conditt, the murdered woman, stated that it was the request of his father and mother, made tonight, that the men be pleaded with, in the event that Monk Gibson is captured, not to burn him until morning, as they both desired to be present at the execution and they wanted all the citizens of Edna and Jackson county who desired to see it to be accorded that privilege. They want the burning to occur in a suitable public place in Edna. The desire of the father and mother has been communicated to all of the posses that could be reached, and it is generally agreed that their wishes in the matter will be respected. Should the negro, therefore, be caught tonight, it is very probably that the execution will take place about 10 o'clock Monday morning. Both of these aged people are almost prostrated tonight from grief and the intense strain.

NEW YORK HERALD

Negro Tortured by Illinois Mob

Belleville Citizens Hang, Cut and Burn a Would-Be Murderer.

Batter Down Jail Doors

VICTIM DRAGGED FROM CELL AND TERRIBLY BEATEN
BEFORE RELEASED BY DEATH.

[SPECIAL DESPATCH TO THE HERALD.]

BELLEVILLE, Ill., Sunday. — With the dawn of Sunday the full import of a wild night's work done by a mob of fully two thousand citizens stood revealed to-day.

David Wyatt, a negro, who made an attempt to assassinate Charles Hertel, County Superintendent, in his office last evening, had been taken from a supposedly impregnable jail, hanged to a telegraph pole in the centre of the public square and his body burned.

Two hundred men, armed with sledge hammers, marched up to the jail in the night and attacked the rear doors with vigor. In half an hour the doors gave way to repeated hammer blows. Wyatt was confined in the lower section of a double tier of cells. The chilled steel bars were cut away with chisels, and when the door swung open a mighty shout informed the waiting crowd that the negro was in the hands of his pursuers.

Tried to Defend Himself.

Wyatt was six feet three inches tall and of powerful build. He tried to defend himself, but he was doomed to quick death. His head was mashed almost to a pulp before he was dragged out of the cell.

A rope was placed about his neck and the dying negro was dragged down stairs and into the street. Hundreds of men jumped upon him and literally kicked and tore the bleeding form to shreds.

Two men climbed the telegraph pole. Willing hands tossed up the loose end of a rope and the battered body of the negro quickly swung free in the air. Yelling like mad men, the mob surged around the victim. Knives were drawn and the body was slashed right and left.

Volunteer runners appeared with cans of benzine and gasolene. Signs and pickets from neighboring fences were tossed into a pyre and flames shooting as high as the improvised gallows soon enveloped the negro.

His Victim May Recover.

All this was done while the mob knew that the negro's victim was alive and had a fair chance to recover.

The excuse given is that the lawless element among the negroes has been doing all sorts of deviltry, and that it was determined to teach the negroes a wholesome lesson.

Wyatt's crime was provoked by the refusal of Superintendent Hertel to renew his teaching certificate. The negro demanded favorable action, and on its refusal fired one shot at the superintendent while he was sitting at his desk.

JANE ADDAMS

From *Respect for Law*

Perhaps the foremost white female social worker of her generation, Jane Addams (1860–1935) is rarely associated with debates over violence and racial equality. Indeed, Addams is noted most for cofounding Chicago's Hull House with Ellen Gates Starr in 1887, and as the first American woman to win the Nobel Peace Prize, in 1931. At Hull House she worked to provide language and arts education, medical and legal aid, and general support services to newly established immigrant communities in and around Chicago. However, given that Addams defined social activism broadly enough to include agitation for improved working conditions for the nation's factory workers, the promotion of labor unions, the creation of a juvenile justice system, woman's suffrage, and, when World War I broke out, world peace, it is hardly surprising that she would have given some attention to lynching and "the Negro Problem." Like many of her white contemporaries in the United States, Addams was appalled by lynching, and she saw white mob violence as a community's failure to manage criminality, whether on the part of whites or blacks. Still, though it protests violence, her article "Respect for Law" demonstrates the subtlety and variety in white racist thinking at the turn of the century. The complete article was published in the New York *Independent,* January 3, 1901 (vol. LIII, no. 2718).

We would send this message to our fellow citizens of the South who are once more trying to suppress vice by violence: That the bestial in man, that which leads him to pillage and rape, can never be controlled by public cruelty and dramatic punishment, which too often cover fury and revenge. That violence is the most ineffectual method of dealing with crime, the most preposterous attempt to inculcate lessons of self control. A community has a right to protect itself from the criminal, to restrain him, to segregate him from the rest of society. But when it attempts revenge, when it pursuades [*sic*] itself that exhibitions of cruelty result in reform, it shows itself ignorant of all the teachings of history; it allows itself to be thrown back into the savage state of dealing with criminality.

It further runs a certain risk of brutalizing each spectator, of shaking his belief in law and order, of sowing seed for future violence. It is certainly doubtful whether these scenes could be enacted over and over again, save in a community in which the hardening drama of slavery had once been seen, in which the devastation of war had taken place; and we may be reasonably sure that the next generation of the South cannot escape the result of the lawlessness and violence which are now being indulged in.

Brutality begets brutality; and proceeding on the theory that the negro is undeveloped, and therefore must be treated in this primitive fashion, is to forget that the immature pay little attention to statements, but quickly imitate what they see. The under-developed are never helped by such methods as these, for they learn only by imitation. The child who is managed by a system of bullying and terrorizing is almost sure to be the vicious and stupid child.

And to those Southern citizens who claim that this method has been successful, that in certain localities a lynching has, in point of fact, been followed by a cessation of the crime of which the lynched man was guilty, we would quote the psychologist who tells us that, under the influence of certain strong emotions, such as fear, certain elements of the self can be prevented from coming into action, "inhibited," as they technically call it; but that these elements are thus only stupefied, or drugged, and sooner or later assert themselves with all of their old power, if the fuller self be aroused. All such inhibitive measures must in the end be futile, and, altho they may for a fleeting moment appear successful, they are philosophically and historically unsound.

To those who say that most of these hideous and terrorizing acts have been committed in the name of chivalry, in order to make the lives and honor of women safe, perhaps it is women themselves who can best reply that bloodshed and arson and ungoverned anger have never yet controlled lust. On the contrary, that lust has always been the handmaid of these, and is prone to be found where they exist; that the suppression of the bestial cannot be accomplished by the counter exhibition of the brutal only.

RAY STANNARD BAKER

From *A Race Riot, and After*

A midwesterner by birth, Ray Stannard Baker (1870–1946) became interested in journalism while studying law at the University of Michigan. Leaving law behind he embarked upon a career as a writer, reporter, and investigative journalist that spanned over half a century. Though he originally began writing for the Chicago *News-Record*, he turned to freelance work, periodically anthologizing his essays into books covering themes such as popular science, travel, and economics. By the start of the twentieth century, as with many of his own contemporaries, Baker had turned to "muckraking" journalism, focusing on social reform issues such as political corruption, unfair labor practices, and urban poverty. By 1908, after a lengthy trip through the South, Baker compiled one of his most famous collections of essays, *Following the Color Line: An Account of Negro Citizenship in the American Democracy* (New York: Doubleday, Page and Company, 1908), where he addressed the fraught topic of American race relations. The following excerpt from *Following the Color Line* suggests Baker's attempt at even-handedness as he describes the 1906 Atlanta race riot.

On the twenty-second day of September, 1906, Atlanta had become a veritable "social tinder-box." For months the relation of the races had been growing more strained. The entire South had been sharply annoyed by a shortage of labour accompanied by high wages and, paradoxically, by an increasing number of idle Negroes. In Atlanta the lower class — the "worthless Negro" — had been increasing in numbers: it showed itself too evidently among the swarming saloons, dives, and "clubs" which a complaisant city administration allowed to exist in the very heart of the city. Crime had increased to an alarming extent; an insufficient and ineffective police force seemed unable to cope with it. With a population of 115,000 Atlanta had over 17,000 arrests in 1905; in 1906 the number increased to 21,602. Atlanta had many more arrests than New Orleans with nearly three times the population and twice as many Negroes; and almost four times as many as Milwaukee, Wisconsin, a city nearly three times as large. Race feeling had been sharpened through a long and bitter political campaign, Negro disfranchisement being one of the chief issues under discussion. An inflammatory play called "The Clansman,"[1] though forbidden by public sentiment in many Southern cities, had been given in Atlanta and other places with the effect of increasing the prejudice of both races. Certain newspapers in Atlanta, taking advantage of popular feeling, kept the race issue constantly agitated, emphasising Negro crimes with startling headlines. One newspaper even recommended the formation of organisations of citizens in imitation of the Ku Klux movement of reconstruction days.[2] In the clamour of this growing agitation, the voice of the right-minded white people and industrious, self-respecting Negroes was almost unheard. A few ministers of both races saw the impending storm and sounded a warning — to no effect; and within the week before the riot the citizens, the city administration and the courts all woke up together. There were calls for mass-meetings, the police began to investigate the conditions of the low saloons and dives, the country constabulary was increased in numbers, the grand jury was called to meet in special session on Monday the 24th.

---

[1] *An inflammatory play called "The Clansman":* The year before, white supremacist writer Thomas Dixon Jr. (1864–1946) wrote and produced a stage version of his antiblack novel *The Clansman* (1905).

[2] *in imitation of the Ku Klux movement of reconstruction days:* From its inception in 1866, the Ku Klux Klan used violence, murder, and rape in an attempt to intimidate and control African Americans. Despite federal efforts to suppress the organization during Reconstruction, it survived to enjoy a second flowering into the twentieth century, with chapters expanding to include midwestern states such as Illinois and Indiana.

PROSPERITY AND LAWLESSNESS

But the awakening of moral sentiment in the city, unfortunately, came too late. Crime, made more lurid by agitation, had so kindled the fires of hatred that they could not be extinguished by ordinary methods. The best people of Atlanta were like the citizens of prosperous Northern cities, too busy with money-making to pay attention to public affairs. For Atlanta is growing rapidly. Its bank clearings jumped from ninety millions in 1900 to two hundred and twenty-two millions in 1906, its streets are well paved and well lighted, its street-car service is good, its sky-scrapers are comparable with the best in the North. In other words, it was progressive — few cities I know of more so — but it had forgotten its public duties.

Within a few months before the riot there had been a number of crimes of worthless Negroes against white women. Leading Negroes, while not one of them with whom I talked wished to protect any Negro who was really guilty, asserted that the number of these crimes had been greatly exaggerated and that in special instances the details had been over-emphasised because the criminal was black; that they had been used to further inflame race hatred. I had a personal investigation made of every crime against a white woman committed in the few months before and after the riot. Three, charged to white men, attracted comparatively little attention in the newspapers, although one, the offence of a white man named Turnadge, was shocking in its details. Of twelve such charges against Negroes in the six months preceding the riot two were cases of rape, horrible in their details, three were aggravated attempts at rape, three may have been attempts, three were pure cases of fright on the part of the white woman, and in one the white woman, first asserting that a Negro had assaulted her, finally confessed attempted suicide. . . .

TERROR OF BOTH WHITE AND COLOURED PEOPLE

The effect of a few such crimes as these may be more easily imagined than described. They produced a feeling of alarm which no one who has not lived in such a community can in any wise appreciate. I was astonished in travelling in the South to discover how widely prevalent this dread has become. Many white women in Atlanta dare not leave their homes alone after dark; many white men carry arms to protect themselves and their families. And even these precautions do not always prevent attacks.

But this is not the whole story. Everywhere I went in Atlanta I heard of the fear of the white people, but not much was said of the terror which the Negroes also felt. And yet every Negro I met voiced in some way that fear. It is difficult here in the North for us to understand what such a condition means: a whole community namelessly afraid!

The better-class Negroes have two sources of fear: one of the criminals of their own race — such attacks are rarely given much space in the newspapers — and the other the fear of the white people. My very first impression of what this fear of the Negroes might be came, curiously enough, not from Negroes but from a fine white woman on whom I called shortly after going South. She told this story:

"I had a really terrible experience one evening a few days ago. I was walking along —— Street when I saw a rather good-looking young Negro come out of a hallway to the sidewalk. He was in a great hurry, and, in turning suddenly, as a person sometimes will do, he accidentally brushed my shoulder with his arm. He had not seen me before. When he turned and found it was a white woman he had touched, such a look of abject terror and fear came into his face as I hope never again to see on a human countenance. He knew what it meant if I was frightened, called for help, and accused him of insulting or attacking me. He stood still a moment, then turned and ran down the street, dodging into the first alley he came to. It shows, does n't it, how little it might take to bring punishment upon an innocent man!". . .

Now, I am telling these things just as they look to the Negro; it is quite as important, as a problem in human nature, to know how the Negro feels and what he says, as it is to know how the white man feels.

HOW THE NEWSPAPERS FOMENTED THE RIOT

On the afternoon of the riot the newspapers in flaming headlines chronicled four assaults by Negroes on white women. I had a personal investigation made of each of those cases. Two of them may have been attempts at assaults, but two palpably were nothing more than fright on the part of both the white woman and the Negro. As an instance, in one case an elderly woman, Mrs. Martha Holcombe, going to close her blinds in the evening, saw a Negro on the sidewalk. In a terrible fright she screamed. The news was telephoned to the police station, but before the officials could respond, Mrs. Holcombe telephoned them not to come out. And yet this was one of the "assaults" chronicled in letters five inches high in a newspaper extra.

And finally on this hot Saturday half-holiday, when the country people had come in by hundreds, when everyone was out of doors, when the streets were crowded, when the saloons had been filled since early morning with white men and Negroes, both drinking — certain newspapers in Atlanta began to print extras with big headings announcing new assaults on white women by Negroes. The Atlanta *News* published five such extras, and newsboys cried them through the city:

"Third assault."

"Fourth assault."

The whole city, already deeply agitated, was thrown into a veritable state of panic. The news in the extras was taken as truthful; for the city was not in a mood then for cool investigation. Calls began to come in from every direction for police protection. A loafing Negro in a backyard, who in ordinary times would not have been noticed, became an object of real terror. The police force, too small at best, was thus distracted and separated.

In Atlanta the proportion of men who go armed continually is very large; the pawnshops of Decatur and Peters Streets, with windows like arsenals, furnish the low class of Negroes and whites with cheap revolvers and knives. Every possible element was here, then, for a murderous outbreak. The good citizens, white and black, were far away in their homes; the bad men had been drinking in the dives permitted to exist by the respectable people of Atlanta; and here they were gathered, by night, in the heart of the city.

THE MOB GATHERS

And, finally, a trivial incident fired the tinder. Fear and vengeance generated it: it was marked at first by a sort of rough, half-drunken horseplay, but when once blood was shed, the brute, which is none too well controlled in the best city, came out and gorged itself. Once permit the shackles of law and order to be cast off, and men, white or black, Christian or pagan, revert to primordial savagery. There is no such thing as an orderly mob.

Crime had been committed by Negroes, but this mob made no attempt to find the criminals: it expressed its blind, unreasoning, uncontrolled race hatred by attacking every man, woman, or boy it saw who had a black face. A lame boot-black, an inoffensive, industrious Negro boy, at that moment actually at work shining a man's shoes, was dragged out and cuffed, kicked and beaten to death in the street. Another young Negro was chased and stabbed to death with jack-knives in the most unspeakably horrible manner. The mob entered barber shops where respectable Negro men were at work shaving white customers, pulled them away from their chairs and beat them. Cars were stopped and inoffensive Negroes were thrown through the windows or dragged out and beaten. They did not stop with killing and maiming; they broke into hardware stores and armed themselves, they demolished not only Negro barber shops and restaurants, but they robbed stores kept by white men.

Of course the Mayor came out, and the police force and the fire department, and finally the Governor ordered out the militia — to apply that pound of cure which should have been an ounce of prevention.

It is highly significant of Southern conditions — which the North does not understand — that the first instinct of thousands of Negroes in Atlanta, when the riot broke out, was not to run away from the white people but to run to them. The white man who takes the most radical position in opposition to the Negro race will often be found loaning money to individual Negroes, feeding them and their families from his kitchen, or defending "his Negroes" in court or elsewhere. All of the more prominent white citizens of Atlanta, during the riot, protected and fed many coloured families who ran to them in their terror. Even Hoke Smith,[3] Governor-elect of Georgia, who is more distrusted by the Negroes as a race probably than any other white man in Georgia, protected many Negroes in his house during the disturbance. In many cases white friends armed Negroes and told them to protect themselves. One widow I know of who had a single black servant, placed a shot-gun in his hands and told him to fire on any mob that tried to get him. She trusted him absolutely. Southern people possess a real liking, wholly unknown in the North, for individual Negroes whom they know.

So much for Saturday night. Sunday was quiescent but nervous — the atmosphere full of the electricity of apprehension. Monday night,

---

[3] *Hoke Smith:* Lawyer and former Secretary of the Interior Hoke Smith (1855–1931) served as governor of Georgia from 1906 to 1912, and then as a U.S. senator from 1912 to 1920. As Georgia governor his reform agenda included the disenfranchisement of the state's African Americans.

after a day of alarm and of prowling crowds of men, which might at any moment develop into mobs, the riot broke forth again — in a suburb of Atlanta called Brownsville.

STORY OF THE MOB'S WORK
IN A SOUTHERN NEGRO TOWN

When I went out to Brownsville, knowing of its bloody part in the riot, I expected to find a typical Negro slum. I looked for squalour, ignorance, vice. And I was surprised to find a large settlement of Negroes practically every one of whom owned his own home, some of the houses being as attractive without and as well furnished within as the ordinary homes of middle-class white people. Near at hand, surrounded by beautiful grounds, were two Negro colleges — Clark University and Gammon Theological Seminary.[4] The post-office was kept by a Negro. There were several stores owned by Negroes. The schoolhouse, though supplied with teachers by the county, was built wholly with money personally contributed by the Negroes of the neighbourhood, in order that there might be adequate educational facilities for their children. They had three churches and not a saloon. The residents were all of the industrious, property-owning sort, bearing the best reputation among white people who knew them.

Think, then, of the situation in Brownsville during the riot in Atlanta. All sorts of exaggerated rumours came from the city. *The Negroes of Atlanta were being slaughtered wholesale.* A condition of panic fear developed. Many of the people of the little town sought refuge in Gammon Theological Seminary, where, packed together, they sat up all one night praying. President Bowen[5] did not have his clothes off for days, expecting the mob every moment. He telephoned for police protection on Sunday, but none was provided. Terror also existed among the families which remained in Brownsville; most of the men were armed, and they had decided, should the mob appear, to make a stand in defence of their homes.

[4] *Clark University and Gammon Theological Seminary:* Clark University (later Clark College) was founded in 1869 in Atlanta. While Gammon Theological Seminary was originally established as part of Clark University in 1883, by 1888 it was a separate institution.

[5] *President Bowen:* Methodist minister John Wesley Edward Bowen (1855–1933) was the first African American appointed to a regular professorship at Gammon Theological Seminary, and later served as its president from 1906 to 1910.

At last, on Monday evening, just at dark, a squad of the county police, led by Officer Poole, marched into the settlement at Brownsville. Here, although there had been not the slightest sign of disturbance, they began arresting Negroes for being armed. Several armed white citizens, who were not officers, joined them.

Finally, looking up a little street they saw dimly in the next block a group of Negro men. Part of the officers were left with the prisoners and part went up the street. As they approached the group of Negroes, the officers began firing: the Negroes responded. Officer Heard was shot dead; another officer was wounded, and several Negroes were killed or injured.

The police went back to town with their prisoners. On the way two of the Negroes in their charge were shot. A white man's wife, who saw the outrage, being with child, dropped dead of fright.

The Negroes (all of this is now a matter of court record) declared that they were expecting the mob; that the police — not mounted as usual, not armed as usual, and accompanied by citizens — looked to them in the darkness like a mob. In their fright the firing began.

The wildest reports, of course, were circulated. One sent broadcast was that five hundred students of Clark University, all armed, had decoyed the police in order to shoot them down. As a matter of fact, the university did not open its fall session until October 3d, over a week later — and on this night there were just two students on the grounds. The next morning the police and the troops appeared and arrested a very large proportion of the male inhabitants of the town. Police officers accompanied by white citizens, entered one Negro home, where lay a man named Lewis, badly wounded the night before. He was in bed; they opened his shirt, placed their revolvers at his breast, and in cold blood shot him through the body several times in the presence of his relatives. They left him for dead, but he has since recovered.

President Bowen, of Gammon Theological Seminary, one of the able Negroes in Atlanta, who had nothing whatever to do with the riot, was beaten over the head by one of the police with his rifle-butt. The Negroes were all disarmed, and about sixty of them were finally taken to Atlanta and locked up charged with the murder of Officer Heard. . . .

RESULTS OF THE RIOT

And after the riot in Brownsville, what? Here was a self-respecting community of hard-working Negroes, disturbing no one, getting an honest living. How did the riot affect them? Well, it demoralised them, set them back for years. Not only were four men killed and several wounded, but sixty of their citizens were in jail. Nearly every family had to go to the lawyers, who would not take their cases without money in hand. Hence the little homes had to be sold or mortgaged, or money borrowed in some other way to defend those arrested, doctors' bills were to be paid, the undertaker must be settled with. A riot is not over when the shooting stops! And when the cases finally came up in court and all the evidence was brought out every Negro went free; but two of the county policemen who had taken part in the shooting, were punished. George Muse, one of the foremost merchants of Atlanta, who was foreman of the jury which tried the Brownsville Negroes, said:

"We think the Negroes were gathered just as white people were in other parts of the town, for the purpose of defending their homes. We were shocked by the conduct which the evidence showed some of the county police had been guilty of."

After the riot was over many Negro families, terrified and feeling themselves unprotected, sold out for what they could get — I heard a good many pitiful stories of such sudden and costly sacrifices — and left the country, some going to California, some to Northern cities. The best and most enterprising are those who go: the worst remain. Not only did the Negroes leave Brownsville, but they left the city itself in considerable numbers. Labour was thus still scarcer and wages higher in Atlanta because of the riot. . . .

Besides this effect on the Negroes the riot for a week or more practically paralysed the city of Atlanta. Factories were closed, railroad cars were left unloaded in the yards, the street-car system was crippled, and there was no cab-service (cab-drivers being Negroes), hundreds of servants deserted their places, the bank clearings slumped by hundreds of thousands of dollars, the state fair, then just opening, was a failure. It was, indeed, weeks before confidence was fully restored and the city returned to its normal condition.

WHO MADE UP THE MOB?

One more point I wish to make before taking up the extraordinary reconstructive work which followed the riot. I have not spoken of the men who made up the mob. We know the dangerous Negro class — after all a very small proportion of the entire Negro population. There is a corresponding low class of whites quite as illiterate as the Negroes.

The poor white hates the Negro, and the Negro dislikes the poor white. It is in these lower strata of society, where the races rub together in unclean streets, that the fire is generated. Decatur and Peters streets, with their swarming saloons and dives, furnish the point of contact. I talked with many people who saw the mobs at different times, and the universal testimony was that it was made up largely of boys and young men, and of the low criminal and semi-criminal class. The ignorant Negro and the uneducated white; there lies the trouble!

GEORGE H. WHITE

From *Speech before the U.S. House of Representatives*

One of the few black leaders to survive the antiblack backlash of the post-Reconstruction years was George H. White (1852–1918), a lawyer, businessman, teacher, and member of the U.S. House of Representatives from North Carolina. Born a slave, White was determined to take full advantage of educational opportunities that came his way. After graduating from Howard University he began teaching until he turned to the study of law. By 1880 he was elected to the North Carolina State House of Representatives, where he earned a reputation for supporting black education. Charismatic and well-organized, and with the backing of both the Populists and the politically formidable black Republicans of North Carolina, White was elected to Congress in 1896 and reelected in 1898, the year of the Wilmington race riot. As the only African American elected to Washington by the turn of the century, White fought vigorously but unsuccessfully for the continued enforcement of the Fourteenth Amendment, and for the nation's first antilynching bill. When he left office in 1901, his departure marked the demise of black representation in Congress until Oscar DePriest of Illinois joined the U.S. House of Representatives in 1928. After Washington, White continued work as a lawyer and community activist, and helped establish the all-black settlement of Whitesboro, New Jersey, which by 1906 boasted a hard-working and prosperous population of 800. On February 23, 1900, almost a year before he left Congress, White delivered a stinging address condemning the lynching of blacks and in particular drawing attention to the 1898 Wilmington riot. The full text of the speech reproduced below can be found in the *House Congressional Record,* vol. 33, pt. 3, 2151–54.

Mr. WHITE. Mr. Chairman, perhaps at no time in the history of our nation have there been more questions of moment before us for consideration than we have at this time. Our recent war with Spain[1] and the result in acquisitions of territory by reason of that war, and the necessary legislation for the government of these new possessions in order that they may not work any harm with us, to establish rules, laws, and customs, require the most thoughtful consideration of all of our statesmen. Not only the question that we have before us to-night as to the character of the tariff to be imposed upon Puerto Rico,[2] but the government that shall be established to perpetuate, elevate, and civilize and Christianize the Hawaiian Islands,[3] the Philippine Islands, and, in my opinion at no very distant day, the Cuban Island, also require our very best effort.

The weightiness of the consideration of these questions is increased by the peculiar circumstances surrounding these new possessions. Their relative geographical position, their climate, their distance from our shores, their close proximity to other foreign powers, coupled with a heterogeneous composition of population of these islands, and their want in Christian and civil development, all tend to increase the consideration and make more complex the solution of their future government.

But these responsibilities are ours, taken of our own motion, and our plain duty with reference to these people must not be shirked, but met and disposed of honestly, patriotically, in the spirit of justice between man and man.

As a humble Representative of this House, I would like to feel free to discuss and aid in the disposition of these questions in the same way that my 355 colleagues on this floor do.

Mr. Chairman, it would be a great pleasure to me to know that fairness and justice would be meted out to all the constituent parts of our beloved country alike in such a way as to leave no necessity for a defense of my race in this House against the attacks and unfair charges

[1] *war with Spain:* In reaction both to war-mongering by politicians, and also the belief that the Spanish had sabotaged the U.S. warship the *Maine* while it was moored off Havana, Cuba, the United States declared war on Spain in 1898. The resulting American military success yielded Cuba, Puerto Rico, and the Philippines, and signaled the rise of the United States as a twentieth-century imperial world power.

[2] *the tariff to be imposed upon Puerto Rico:* White delivered his speech during a debate on a bill to impose a tariff on Puerto Rico, newly annexed to the United States as a result of the Spanish-American war.

[3] *Christianize the Hawaiian Islands:* In 1898 the United States staged a military takeover of the independent Pacific island nation of Hawaii.

from any source. The very intimation of this fact with reference to the surroundings of the colored people of this country at this time, naturally causes the inquiry: Should not a nation be just to all of her citizens, protect them alike in all their rights, on every foot of her soil — in a word, show herself capable of governing all within her domain before she undertakes to exercise sovereign authority over those of a foreign land — with foreign notions and habits not at all in harmony with our American system of government? Or, to be more explicit, should not charity first begin at home?

There can be but one candid and fair answer to this inquiry, and that is in the affirmative. But, unfortunately for us, what should have been done has not been done, and to substantiate this assertion we have but to pause for a moment and make a brief survey of the manumitted Afro-American during the last thirty-five years. We have struggled on as best we could with the odds against us at every turn. Our constitutional rights have been trodden under foot; our right of franchise in most every one of the original slave States has been virtually taken away from us, and during the time of our freedom fully 50,000 of my race have been ignominiously murdered by mobs, not 1 per cent of whom have been made to answer for their crimes in the courts of justice, and even here in the nation's Capitol — in the Senate and House — Senators and Representatives have undertaken the unholy task of extenuating and excusing these foul deeds, and in some instances they have gone so far as to justify them. . . .

In order to fasten public sentiment against the negro race and hold them up before the world in their entirety for being responsible for what some are pleased to call "the race crime" — rape — the gentleman from Georgia [Mr. GRIGGS] described in detail the other day the "fiendishness" of Sam Hose,[4] late of his State, and I believe his district, and among other things he said:

> But let me tell you of a case that happened in Georgia last year. A little family a few miles from the town of Newnan were at supper in their modest dining room. The father, the young mother, and the baby were seated at the table. Humble though it was, peace, happiness, and contentment reigned in that modest home. A monster in human form, an

---

[4] *the gentleman from Georgia* [Mr. GRIGGS] . . . *Sam Hose:* Georgia representative James M. Griggs (1861–1910) had earlier raised the specter of the black rapist by recounting the case of Sam Hose. On Sunday, April 23, 1899 the black laborer Hose was lynched in Newnan, Georgia, after being charged with murder and rape. The details of the execution, which included Hose's castration and death by slow burning at the stake, was covered in sensational detail by the white press.

employee on the farm, crept into that happy little home and with an ax knocked out the brains of that father, snatched the child from its mother, threw it across the room out of his way, and then by force accomplished his foul purpose. * * * I do not seek to justify that, but I do say that the man who would condemn those people unqualifiedly under these circumstances has water instead of blood to supply his circulation. Not the limpid water that flows from the mountain streams, Mr. Chairman, but the fetid water found in the cesspools of the cities.

The other side of this horrible story portrays a very different state of affairs. A white man, with no interest in Hose or his victim, declares upon oath that Hose did not commit this atrocious crime charged against him, but was an employee of Cranford, and had importuned him for pay due him for labor. This incensed his employer, who rushed upon Hose with a gun. Hose seized an ax and killed Cranford instantly, in self-defense, and then fled to the woods with the greatest possible speed. I do not vouch for either side of this story, but only refer to it to show the necessity for trying all persons charged with crime, as the law directs.

The gentleman might have gone further and described the butchery in his district of six colored persons arrested upon suspicion of being guilty of arson, and while they were crouching in a warehouse, manacled with irons, and guarded by officers of the law, these poor victims, perhaps guilty of no crime whatever, were horribly shot to death by irresponsibles, no one of whom has ever been brought to justice.

He might have depicted also, if he had been so inclined, the miserable butchery of men, women, and children in Wilmington, N. C., in November, 1898, who had committed no crime, nor were they even charged with crime. He might have taken the minds of his auditors to the horrible scene of the aged and infirm, male and female, women in bed from childbirth, driven from their homes to the woods, with no shelter save the protecting branches of the trees of the forest, where many died from exposure, privation, and disease contracted while exposed to the merciless weather. But this description would not have accomplished the purpose of riveting public sentiment upon every colored man of the South as a rapist from whose brutal assaults every white woman must be protected.

3

The Wilmington Riot

On November 10, 1898, white men with rifles and rapid-fire guns marched into the neighborhoods of Wilmington, North Carolina. After burning the printing press of a black-owned daily newspaper, the insurgents gunned down black residents, caused hundreds of others to flee their homes for outlying swamps, and forced black and white city officials to resign their offices. In the weeks that followed, fourteen hundred African Americans left Wilmington, many at gunpoint. These results exposed the riot for what it was: an act of racial terrorism and political usurpation. But the Wilmington riot also showed how tightly the volatile politics of race were entangled with attitudes and myths about sex. Two days before the riot, a white-owned newspaper, *The Wilmington Messenger,* capped weeks of unsubstantiated reports about black men's sexual assaults on white women by printing the lyrics to a song:

> Rise, ye sons of Carolina!
> Proud Caucasians, one and all;
> Be not deaf to Love's appealing —
> Hear your wives and daughters call,
> See their blanched and anxious faces,
> Note their frail, but lovely forms;
> Rise, defend their spotless virtue
> With your strong and manly arms.
> (*Wilmington Messenger,* November 8, 1898)

In light of the massacre to come, the song's injunction to defend white wives and daughters with "manly arms" carries a striking ambiguity. Does the word "arms" here refer to limbs or to guns? The answer is both. As the arms of proud men who should respond to "Love's appealing," these "strong" and "manly" arms are the virile counterpart to the "lovely forms" of white women's bodies. But as instruments with which white men should "rise" and "defend" those women, the same word cannot but call to mind an image of firearms as well.

Superimposing bodies and weapons, blending sexual defense with white militancy, the poem enacts a drama of symbol making that was also occurring in the culture at large. In white newspapers and magazines, in political speeches and popular novels, the complex realities of southern race relations were often transmuted into a collective fantasy about bodies, a story of the supposed sexual threat that black men posed to white women. By calling up an idealized southern white womanhood whose "spotless virtue" was in imminent danger from black rape, the poem demands the aggression of white men. Notice that the poem's speaker uses the imperative mode: the rise of white men is commanded as an ineluctable duty. As one white man put it in defending the Wilmington coup, "I suppose anything must be justifiable to preserve a woman's virtue, a man's honor, and our Christian Civilization" (qtd. in Gilmore 89).

This sense of threat invited otherwise law-abiding people to see the armed aggression at Wilmington as moral, even honorable, and above all necessary. In point of fact, however, there was no epidemic of rape in the region. Though newspapers created the impression of a marked increase in sexual attacks throughout the state, historian Glenda Gilmore writes that "available crime statistics show no appreciable increase in either rapes or 'assaults with intent to rape' in either 1897 or 1898" (75). What was this rape scare and how did it come to have a role in the events of Wilmington? Only recently have historians paid much attention to the importance of gender roles and sexual taboos for this and other southern conflicts. But Chesnutt, writing in the immediate aftermath of the attack, knew from the start that the riot could not be explained by politics alone, nor even by the force of blunt racism. To understand Wilmington, *Marrow* teaches us, requires that we understand the way the powerful feelings attached to sex and family life could be channeled, through language and symbols, into devastating new forms of racial oppression. The genre of the novel, with its focus on family and the psychology of love, provided Chesnutt with a means for analyzing the complex strands of emotion that fostered a violent antiblack campaign in the name of "protecting" white homes. The documents gathered in this chapter present some of the historical materials associated with the Wilmington riot in order to help readers better understand *Marrow*'s narrative exploration of the forces — emotional and political — that created a new culture of segregation.

Explosive yet calculated, the riot sprang from the confluence of local elections, a statewide white supremacy campaign, and heightened sexual politics. In the months preceding the November 1898 elections, white leaders in the Democratic party had focused obsessively on the intolerable problem, as they saw it, of "Negro domination" in Wilmington. The phrase was hardly an accurate label for the city government: although African American men had come to fill some local posts in recent years, the number of black officeholders in Wilmington was in fact relatively small. But for their white opponents, the mere fact of black men in positions of authority represented an intolerable affront.

In the aftermath of Reconstruction, white Democrats had engineered control of state politics by employing methods of fraud and intimidation that discouraged black voting. But during the 1880s certain segments of the white population began to defect from the Democratic party. Suffering from plunging agricultural prices and other economic conditions, many farmers and other working-class whites grew discontented with the policies of the Democrats, policies they saw as favoring wealthy industrialists and elites. In the later 1890s, the Populist Party broke the Democrats' dominance by forming an alliance with the largely African American members of the Republican Party. The coalition worked. Interracial "fusion" tickets began to win in various state and local elections. The 1894 elections installed a white fusionist, Daniel L. Russell, as North Carolina's governor and gave the new party control of both houses of the state's General Assembly.

But a backlash was already building. As the fusionists proved the effectiveness of interracial coalitions, Wilmington became a flash point for the region's white supremacy movement. An 1898 statewide campaign to "reestablish Anglo-Saxon rule" aimed to create a racial divide so stark that cooperation with African Americans in future elections would become unthinkable for any white voter. Democratic orators, newspaper editors like Josephus Daniels of the *Raleigh News and Observer,* and even supremacists from neighboring states joined forces to represent the modest political gains of black citizens as an unbounded lust for power. African Americans' political participation, supremacists argued, bespoke corruption and a perverse desire for social equality with whites, their natural superiors. The clearest proof, they claimed, was the supposed outbreak of black men's sexual attacks on white women. Editors like Daniels and Thomas W. Clawson of *The Wilmington Messenger* printed daily stories of "atrocities." As elsewhere in the South, an increase in lynching in the area became specious evidence of an epidemic of black-on-white rapes.

Wilmington, with its black majority population and white Republican mayor, became the focus of the growing racial tensions. Behind the scenes, a group of influential white townsmen — later dubbed "the Secret Nine" (in *Marrow* Chesnutt condenses them into his "Big Three" conspirators) — prepared to reclaim power for Democrats, by force if necessary. In public, however, the Democrats emphasized themes of family protection. "Homes have been invaded, and the sanctity of woman endangered," speakers declared, and men must restore security once more to the "white women of the state" (qtd. in Prather 21). Local men organized themselves into militia and began patrolling city streets. As one citizen who joined the nightly patrols explained, "I do not want [my children], and their little friends growing up . . . [among] rapists!" (qtd. in Gilmore 77).

In crafting his novel's plot, Chesnutt found a way to dissect brilliantly the myth of the black predator, as a creation of both fervent outrage and bad faith. When Mrs. Polly Ochiltree is found murdered in her home, a group of white men decide on the spot that she had been raped by a black man. In truth, Ochiltree was never raped and her attacker was white. But the rape is fabricated in an act of collective racial imagining, as insidious as it is reflexive: "The criminal was a negro, the victim a white woman; — it was only reasonable to expect the worst" (p. 156 in this volume). Though feared, the "horror" of black rape is also strangely hoped for. No other crime offered the chance to inflate an isolated fatality into the dimensions of a race war. As one of the white conspirators, Colonel Carteret, phrases it, this "is something more than an ordinary crime, to be dealt with by the ordinary processes of law. It is a murderous and fatal assault upon a woman of our race, — upon our race in the person of its womanhood" (p. 156). In *The Marrow of Tradition,* the collective lie of a black rape — half-believed, half-trumped up — is the occasion for uniting white men in a new race consciousness as aggrieved white defenders. At a huge Democratic rally in October a troop of Red Shirts, the terroristic arm of the Democrats, marched in advance of a float carrying twenty-one young women dressed in white. As important as the physical power displayed here was the power over symbols — whiteness, womanhood, virtue — exercised by the parade's supremacist organizers.

White women, too, learned to wield the force of these symbolic constructs of race and sex. Perhaps the most famous instance — certainly the most far-reaching — occurred when Rebecca Latimer Felton, the wife of a former Georgia congressman, made a widely reported speech at a Georgia agricultural fair. A newspaper account of the speech is reprinted in this chapter. If there is not "enough manhood in the country to put a sheltering arm about innocence and virtue," Felton declared, then the path is clear: "if it takes lynching to protect woman's dearest possession from drunken, ravening human beasts — then I say lynch a thousand a week if it becomes necessary" (p. 411). When Alexander Manly, a black journalist, published an editorial protesting Felton's race baiting, however, he learned that whites' control over these sexually charged symbols could be challenged only at tremendous risk.

Manly was the editor of the Wilmington *Daily Record,* a black-owned daily newspaper. When in August 1898 the *Wilmington Messenger* recycled the year-old speech by Felton, Manly's response in the *Record,* also reprinted here, boldly called the rape scare a tissue of lies. His countercharge was the assertion — then almost unspeakable — that white women in such cases frequently chose to have sexual liaisons with black men, men "sufficiently attractive for white girls of culture and refinement to fall in love with them, as is well known to all" (p. 408). As word spread of Manly's column, white editors and politicians across the South reacted with fury. The headlines from white newspapers that reprinted Manly's editorial — headlines such as "Negro Defamer of White Women," and "Infamous Attack on White Women" — were telling in their imagery: merely by daring to question openly the sexualized myths of the white South, Manly himself became a version of the black sexual "brute," a black man with vicious designs on white women. There were even calls for his lynching.

But Manly's editorial, however much resented, also provided Democrats with a target they were eager to exploit. The *Wilmington Messenger* reprinted Manly's August editorial every day until the election, holding it up as further evidence of the dangerous "insolence" and sexual disorder fostered by black participation in public life. But Manly's own family history — like Chesnutt's — was proof of the fact that sexual and family relations had long cut across the color line, or rather had made the color line itself a dubious biological boundary in the first place. Manly was the grandson of North Carolina's former governor, Charles Manly. A white man with a wife and children, Charles had also fathered and eventually freed a second family with a slave woman who became Alexander's paternal grandmother. Alex Manly's white ancestry was widely known, and it must have been particularly galling for Wilmington's white supremacists to have him publicly give the lie to what Chesnutt's narrator calls "a fanciful purity of race" (p. 97).

But Manly's attempt to unveil the racial politics of the rape scare only intensified the campaign against black citizens. Alfred M. Waddell, a former congressman, stirred white crowds with visions of a coming race war, famously vowing "we will never surrender to a ragged raffle of negroes even if we have to choke Cape Fear River with carcasses" (*Wilmington Morning Post,* October 25, 1898). In the weeks before the election, Wilmington saw almost daily acts of public intimidation: white supremacy meetings, street marches, and nighttime rallies. The night before the elections, Waddell spoke plainly: "Go to the polls tomorrow, and if you find the negro out voting, tell him to leave the polls, and if he refuses, kill him" (*Wilmington Morning Post,* October 25, 1898).

It was a relief to many, then, when election day passed without incident. The barrage of threats kept black Republicans away from the polls, and the majority of voters — including, presumably, former white fusionist voters — supported Democrats. Jane Murphy Cronly, a white woman whose account of the riot is included in this chapter, reported that "I awoke that morning with thankful heart that the election had passed without the shedding of the blood of either the innocent or the guilty" (p. 418). But in the end, Democrats' success at the polls may have actually encouraged the violent coup. Most municipal offices in Wilmington were not up for contest in 1898 and a number of elected fusionists had one or two years left on their terms. The Democratic victories in other races seems to have made the leading conspirators even more determined to eliminate any African Americans or white fusionists from their elected positions.

The morning after the election, hundreds responded to the Democrats' announcement in the *Wilmington Messenger* ("Attention White Men") and gathered in the town courthouse. The crowd clamored for Waddell, who went to the podium and read aloud a document drawn up by the Secret Nine. "The White Man's Declaration of Independence," included in this chapter, begins by invoking the U.S. Constitution as the foundation for principles of white supremacy, proclaims an end to interracial governance, and calls for Manly's banishment from the city.

Manly himself had long since left Wilmington, but that morning a crowd of 500 armed men broke down the door of the black-owned hall where Manly's press was housed and eventually burned the building to the ground. As the mob swelled to over 2,000, some black citizens began to flee, though a few gathered in the street with arms. As gunfire broke out, white insurgents began chasing and shooting down black men on the street. Soon a group of Red Shirts, awaiting the signal, joined the battle. The Wilmington Light Infantry also marched into the fray, accompanied by cannons and a mounted Gatling gun; Jane Murphy Cronly reported that the militia men began cutting down African Americans "right and left . . . killing one man who was simply standing at a corner waiting to get back to his work" (p. 419). Black women were strip-searched on the streets. Several male leaders were hunted down and either shot or run out of town.

The number of dead has never been reliably fixed. Newspapers reported a death toll that ranged from eleven to sixteen. Waddell later put the number at about twenty, while other conspirators proclaimed that ninety African Americans had been killed. A black coroner arranged for examinations of fourteen bodies while reporting that other black victims had been secretly buried. Oral tradition sometimes put the number of dead in the hundreds. Whatever the actual number, the indiscriminate killing terrorized black Wilmington. Over five hundred residents streamed into the woods outside of town and hid overnight. Meanwhile, the mob leaders regrouped for a political takeover. Waddell's men demanded the resignation of the mayor, chief of police, and other officials and replaced them with Democrats from their own ranks, whereupon the city aldermen unanimously appointed Alfred Waddell mayor of Wilmington. The coup was complete.

The responses of private African American citizens have been largely lost to history. A letter to President McKinley from an anonymous African American woman, however, voiced the anguished question that was no doubt asked by many: "Why do you forsake the Negro?" The letter, included in full in this chapter, predicted all too accurately that the truth of the events in Wilmington would likely be distorted. "There was not any rioting," she wrote, "simply the strong slaying the weak" (p. 416).

Like the anonymous author of the letter to McKinley, Chesnutt is at pains to point out in *Marrow* that the violence in Wilmington was actually not a riot in the usual sense. For all the spontaneous chaos in the streets, the acts of violence in Wilmington were carefully intended to serve as symbols with the power to enforce a hierarchical social order. As Chesnutt's protagonist, the black physician Miller, hurries through the streets on the day of the riot, he realizes that the killing of black men has turned human bodies into signs or texts that are to be "read." Seeing the "dead body of a negro" lying in the street, Miller knows that the corpse was intended to make a black body into a symbol of its own racial abjection and a trophy for white power. What Miller "shuddered at was not so much the thought of death, to the sight of which his profession had accustomed him, as the suggestion of what it signified" (p. 220). As with the display of lynched bodies, the corpses of black people have been turned into a public spectacle whose meaning is directed at all surviving African Americans. "The negroes seemed to have been killed, as the band plays in circus parades, at the street intersections, where the example would be most effective" (p. 221). With this detail Chesnutt conveys the crucial insight that the riot, a thing of fury and confusion, was still a carefully designed display of racial meaning, as deliberate as the placid "black" and "white" signs in the segregated railway cars whose purpose was to impose a "great gulf" between two groups of American citizens (p. 79).

ALEXANDER MANLY

Editorial

Alexander Manly, the son of African American parents, was an illegitimate grandson of Charles Manly, North Carolina's white governor from 1849 to 1851. Alex Manly was born in Wake County, North Carolina, on May 13, 1866. After attending the Hampton Institute, he moved to Wilmington and started a painting business. Manly also worked as register of deeds before taking over as publisher of the Wilmington *Daily Record,* advertised as "the only Negro daily in the world."

Manly drew the ire of Wilmington's white residents in 1898 for his contentious editorial written in response to reports of Rebecca Latimer Felton's widely publicized "lynch 1,000 a day" speech. In the editorial, reprinted here, Manly argues against the notion that all sexual relations between white women and black men constitute rape, writing "colored men" are "sufficiently attractive for white girls of culture and refinement

Alexander Manly. UNC Southern Historical Collection.

to fall in love with." He also contends that many illicit affairs happen between white men and "colored women," calling on Felton to "[t]each your men purity" (p. 408).

White residents of Wilmington made Manly a key target in the white supremacy campaign that ignited the November massacre. With the help of an affluent white citizen, the light-skinned Manly was able to pass for white and successfully flee the city, eventually settling in Philadelphia, where he died in 1944. The editorial is reprinted from *The Literary Digest*, November 26, 1898.

"A Mrs. Felton,[1] from Georgia, makes a speech before the Agricultural Society at Tybee, Ga., in which she advocates lynching as an extreme measure. This woman makes a strong plea for womanhood, and if the alleged crimes of race were half so frequent as is ofttimes reported, her plea would be worthy of consideration.

"Mrs. Felton, like many other so-called Christians, loses sight of the basic principle of the religion of Christ in her plea for one class of people as against another. If a missionary spirit is essential for the uplifting of the poor white girls, why is it? The morals of the poor white people are on a par with their colored neighbors of like conditions, and if any one doubts the statement let him visit among them. The whole lump needs to be leavened by those who profess so much religion and showing them that the preservation of virtue is an essential for the life of any people.

"Mrs. Felton begins well, for she admits that education will better protect girls on the farm from the assaulter. This we admit, and it should not be confined to the white any more than to the colored girls. The papers are filled often with reports of rapes of white women, and the subsequent lynching of the alleged rapists. The editors pour forth volleys of aspersions against all negroes because of the few who may be guilty. If the papers and speakers of the other race would condemn the commission of crime because it is crime and not try to make it appear that the negroes were the only criminals, they would find their strongest allies in the intelligent negroes themselves, and together the whites and blacks would root the evil out of both races.

"We suggest that the whites guard their women more closely, as Mrs. Felton says, thus giving no opportunity for the human fiend, be he white or black. You leave your goods out of doors and then complain because they are taken away. Poor white men are careless in the matter of protecting their women, especially on farms. They are careless of their conduct toward them, and our experience among poor

---

[1] Rebecca Latimer Felton (1835–1930) was a public speaker and political activist who delivered a widely disseminated speech in which she condoned the lynching of black men when necessary to protect white women.

Building that housed Manly's newspaper, with top floor in ruins. The University of Michigan Library.

white people in the country teaches us that the women of that race are not any more particular in the matter of clandestine meetings with colored men than are the white men with colored women. Meetings of this kind go on for some time, until the woman's infatuation or the man's boldness bring attention to them and the man is lynched for rape. Every negro lynched is called a 'big, burly, black brute,' when in fact many of those who have thus been dealt with had white men for their fathers, and were not only not 'black' and 'burly,' but were sufficiently attractive for white girls of culture and refinement to fall in love with them, as is well known to all.

"Mrs. Felton must begin at the fountain-head, if she wishes to purify the stream.

"Teach your men purity. Let virtue be something more than an excuse for them to intimidate and torture a helpless people. Tell your men that it is no worse for a black man to be intimate with a white woman than for a white man to be intimate with a colored woman.

"You set yourselves down as a lot of carping hypocrites; in fact, you cry aloud for the virtue of your women, while you seek to destroy the morality of ours. Don't think ever that your women will remain pure while you are debauching ours. You sow the seed — the harvest will come in due time."

REBECCA LATIMER FELTON

Letter to the Atlanta Constitution

Rebecca Latimer Felton was born on June 10, 1835, in Decatur, Georgia, to a locally prominent planter. In 1852, she graduated first in her class from Georgia's Madison Female College and married William Herrel Felton, a Methodist minister with political aspirations, the following year. Following the Civil War, Rebecca Felton managed her husband's successful campaigns for the U.S. Congress, where he served as Georgia's Seventh District Representative from 1875 to 1881. She remained active in his political career and regularly submitted pseudonymous opinion pieces to Georgia newspapers defending her husband's record.

In the 1890s, Felton began her own career in politics. Working as a well-recognized public speaker and journalist, she advanced such issues as woman's enfranchisement, prison reform, labor laws, and racial segregation. Indeed, a central tenet of her belief in a woman's right to vote was her argument that white women's votes would help keep African Americans and immigrants disenfranchised.

In the report republished here from the December 19, 1898, Atlanta *Constitution* (clipping in Scrapbook 24, pp. 76–77. Felton Collection, Hargrett Rare Book and Manuscript Library, University of Georgia, Athens), Felton recounts a speech she delivered to a meeting of the Georgia State Agricultural Society in 1897. The article records Felton's most infamous and inflammatory claim: "[I]f it takes lynching to protect woman's dearest possession from drunken, ravening human beasts — then I say lynch a thousand a week," she told the crowd in Tybee, Georgia (p. 411). Felton's rhetoric provoked Alexander Manly, the editor and publisher of Wilmington's black newspaper, to write the editorial response published in this volume.

In 1922, Felton received a symbolic one-day appointment to the U.S. Senate. Felton died in Atlanta on January 24, 1930.

In the month of August, 1897, I delivered an address to the State Agricultural Society at Tybee, upon the invitation and solicitation of the society, expressed by its president. My subject was "The Needs of Farmers' Wives." I spoke to a large audience of representative men, the bone and sinew of Georgia's prosperity and patriotism. I told of the necessity for better buildings, better food, recreation in their lives,

Rebecca Latimer Felton. Courtesy of the Library of Congress.

appreciation of their work and security in their homes for their young daughters. I warned these representative men of the terrible effects that were already seen in the corruption of the negro vote, their venality, the use of whisky, the debasement of the ignorant and the incitement of evil passion in the vicious. That week there were seven lynchings published in Georgia from the fearful crime of rape. I told them that these crimes had grown and increased by reason of the corruption and debasement of the right of suffrage; that it would grow and increase with every election where white men equalized themselves at the polls with an inferior race and controlled their votes by bribery and whiskey. A crime nearly unknown before and during the war had become an almost daily occurrence and mob law had also become omnipotent — in the face of such intolerable outrages on helpless womankind — but said I, "When there is not enough religion in the pulpit to organize a crusade against this sin, nor enough justice in the courhouse [*sic*] to promptly punish the crime and not enough manhood in the country to put a sheltering arm about innocence and virtue, then I say to you that if anything else will or can happen — if it takes lynching to protect woman's dearest possession from drunken, ravening human beasts — then I say lynch a thousand a week if it becomes necessary."

There were hundreds of good, true men who listened to me. They cheered me to the echo; they understood my rebuke to the politics which has made the purchase and bribery of negro voters a disgrace of the south; they knew I was sounding a note of entreaty and warning . . .

I spoke the truth, for when all other remedies fail, when churches fail to rouse their members to the dangers, when courts fail to convict the criminal, when the authorities pardon rapists and women are [raped on] public highways and in their homes by drunken, lust filled fiends in human shape, then husbands and fathers will rise in their wrath and desperation and rebuke the crime with a short shrift and a strong rope! That's Georgia law gentlemen — and that assemblage of farmers at Tybee said, "Amen!"

APPLETON'S ANNUAL ENCYCLOPEDIA

From *White Man's Declaration of Independence*

On Election Day in 1898, the conspirators behind the white supremacy campaign published a notice calling for the "White Men" of Wilmington to assemble the next day at the town courthouse. At ten the following morning, Alfred Waddell, a former U.S. representative, read aloud before the assembled crowd a document drawn up by the Secret Nine conspirators entitled "White Man's Declaration of Independence." The document is sometimes referred to as the "Wilmington Declaration of Independence."

Claiming that the framers of the U.S. Constitution never intended descendants of Africans to enjoy legal enfranchisement, the Declaration demanded an end to any black participation in politics. It also announced that jobs held by black people would be given to white men and ordered the shutdown of the black-owned Wilmington *Record,* along with the banishment of its editor, Alexander Manly. When Waddell read the resolution that black men would never again share political power in Wilmington, he received a standing ovation.

That evening, a committee headed by Waddell summoned a group of thirty-two African American men to the courthouse. Waddell read the Declaration aloud and delivered an ultimatum: black people would never again share in any governance of Wilmington, and the editor Manly must leave town immediately. The African American citizens, fully aware of the white men's desire for a showdown, drafted a reply designed to appease the leaders of the coup. But the black attorney chosen to bring the reply to Waddell's residence mistakenly put the letter in a mailbox, and the next morning white leaders seized the chance to gather a mob and march on the building that housed Manly's press. The mob burned to the ground the black-owned building and the newspaper press within it. The Declaration is reprinted from *Appleton's Annual Encyclopedia and Register of Important Events of the Year 1898,* 3rd series, vol. 3 (New York: D. Appleton and Company, 1899).

On the day after the election, Nov. 9, a mass meeting, attended by about 1,000 persons, was held in Wilmington, which unanimously expressed itself as follows:

"Believing that the Constitution of the United States contemplated a government to be carried on by an enlightened people; believing that its framers did not anticipate the enfranchisement of an ignorant population of African origin, and believing that the men of the State of North Carolina who joined in forming the Union did not contemplate for their descendants a subjection to an inferior race;

"We, the undersigned, citizens of the city of Wilmington and county of New Hanover, do hereby declare that we will no longer be ruled, and will never again be ruled, by men of African origin. This condition we have in part endured because we felt that the consequences of the war of secession were such as to deprive us of the fair consideration of many of our countrymen.

"We believe that, after more than thirty years, this is no longer the case.

"The stand we now pledge ourselves to is forced upon us suddenly by a crisis, and our eyes are open to the fact that we must act now or leave our descendants to a fate too gloomy to be borne.

"While we recognize the authority of the United States, and will yield to it if exerted, we would not for a moment believe that it is the purpose of more than 60,000,000 of our own race to subject us permanently to a fate to which no Anglo-Saxon has ever been forced to submit.

"We, therefore, believing that we represent unequivocally the sentiment of the white people of this county and city, hereby for ourselves, and representing them, proclaim:

"1. That the time has passed for the intelligent citizens of this community, owning 95 per cent. of the property and paying taxes in like proportion, to be ruled by negroes.

"2. That we will not tolerate the action of unscrupulous white men in affiliating with the negroes so that by means of their votes they can dominate the intelligent and thrifty element in the community, thus causing business to stagnate and progress to be out of the question.

"3. That the negro has demonstrated, by antagonizing our interest in every way, and especially by his ballot, that he is incapable of realizing that his interests are and should be identical with those of the community.

"4. That the progressive element in any community is the white population, and that the giving of nearly all of the employment to negro laborers has been against the best interests of this county and city, and is a sufficient reason why the city of Wilmington, with its natural advantages, has not become a city of at least 50,000 inhabitants.

"5. That we propose in future to give to white men a large part of the employment heretofore given to negroes, because we realize that white families can not thrive here unless there are more opportunities for employment for the different members of said families.

"6. That the white men expect to live in this community peaceably, to have and provide absolute protection for their families, who shall be safe from insult from all persons whomsoever. We are prepared to treat the negroes with justice and consideration in all matters which do not involve sacrifices of the interest of the intelligent and progressive portion of the community. But we are equally prepared now and immediately to enforce what we know to be our rights.

"7. That we have been, in our desire for harmony and peace, blinded both to our best interests and our rights. A climax was reached when the negro paper of this city published an article so vile and slanderous that it would in most communities have resulted in the lynching of the editor. We deprecate lynching, and yet there is no punishment provided by the laws adequate for this offense. We therefore owe it to the people of this community and of this city, as a protection against such license in future, that the paper known as the "Record" cease to be published, and that its editor be banished from this community.

"We demand that he leave this city within twenty-four hours after the issuance of this proclamation; second, that the printing press from which the "Record" has been issued be packed and shipped from the city without delay; that we be notified within twelve hours of the acceptance or rejection of this demand. If the demand is agreed to within twelve hours, we counsel forbearance on the part of all white men. If the demand is refused, or if no answer is given within the time mentioned, then the editor, Manly,[1] will be expelled by force."

---

[1] *Manly:* Alexander Manly was the African American editor and publisher of the Wilmington *Daily Record.*

Letter to William McKinley

The November events in Wilmington received national attention, sparking wide consternation. But as white editors and observers began to present the riot as a symbol of the doomed fate of southern race relations, readers came to see the massacre as an inevitable conflict, if an unfortunate one. Though some northern newspapers condemned the supremacists' takeover of elected municipal offices, most national publications printed uncontested the accounts offered by spokesmen for the coup. *Collier's* magazine ran Alfred Waddell's own narrative, in which he claimed the white insurgents had taken action out of dire necessity.

African American leaders such as W. E. B. Du Bois and George White protested vigorously to the Republican U.S. president, William McKinley, and held mass meetings throughout the country. Manly himself was a speaker at a number of these rallies. But McKinley and federal officials largely ignored the petitions and let stand the violent overthrow of democratically elected officials. No perpetrators were every brought to trial for murder or any other offense.

The inaction of the federal government was predicted by an African American woman even as she pleaded with McKinley to "please send relief as soon as possible or we perish."[1] Writing from Wilmington on November 13, 1898, in the aftermath of the riot, the woman sent the anonymous letter ("I cannot sign my name and live") printed below. Her lament that "there is no paper to tell the truth about the Negro here in this or any other Southern state" proved true, though the rueful eloquence of her own account has been preserved in the National Archives.

WILMINGTON, N.C. Nov. 13, 1898

William McKinley:— President of the United States of America
Hon. Sir,

I, a Negro woman of this city, appeal to you from the depths of my heart, to do something in the Negro's behalf. The outside world only knows one side of the trouble here, there is no paper to tell the truth about the Negro here in this or any other Southern state. The Negro in this town had no arms, (except pistols perhaps in some instances) with which to defend themselves from the attack of lawless whites. On the 10th Thursday morning between eight and nine o'clock, when all Negro men had gone to their places of work, the white men led by Col. A.M. Waddell, D. Bellamy, & S.H. Fishblate marched from the Light Infantry armory on Market St. up to seventh down seventh to Love & Charity Hall (which was owned by a society of Negroes. And where the Negro daily press was.) and set it afire & burnt it up. And firing guns Winchesters, they also had a Hotchkiss gun & two Colt rapid fire guns. We the negro expected nothing of this [illeg.] kind as they (the whites) had frightened them from the polls [illeg.] saying they would be there with their shot guns, so the few that did vote did so quietly. And we thought after giving up to them and they carried the state it was settled. But they or [John] D. Bellamy told them — in addition to the guns they already had they could keep back federal interference, And he could have the Soldiers at Ft. Caswell to take up arms against the United States. After destroying the building they went over in Brooklyn another Negro settlement mostly, and began searching every one and if you did not submit, would be shot down on the spot. They

---

[1] This sentence appears in the top margin of the first page of the letter.

searched all the Negro churches. And to day (Sunday) we dare not go to our places of worship. They found no guns or amunition [*sic*] in any of the places, for there was none, And to satisfy their Blood thirsty appetites would kill unoffending Negro men to or on their way from dinner, Some of our most worthy Negro men have been made to leave the city. Also some Whites, G.J. French, Deputy sheriff, Chief of police [John] R. Melton, Dr. S.P. Wright Mayor and R.H. Bunting United States Comissioner [*sic*]. We don't know where Mr. Chadbourn the Post Master is, and two or three others white. I call on you the head of the American Nation to help these humble subjects. We are loyal we go when duty calls us, And are we to die like rats in a trap? With no place to seek redress or to go with our grievances? Can we call on any other nation for help? Why do you forsake the Negro? Who is not to blame for being here. This Grand and noble nation who flies to the help of suffering humanity of another nation? And leave the Secessionists and born Rioters to slay us. Oh, that we had never seen the light of the work, When our parents belonged to them, why the Negro was all right now, when they work and accumalate [*sic*] property they are all wrong. The Negroes that have been banished are all property owners to considerable extent, had they been worthless negros, we would not care.

Will you for God sake in your next message to Congress give us some relief. If you send us all to Africa [illeg.] we will be willing or a number of us will gladly go. Is this the land of the free and the home of the brave? How can the Negro sing My Country tis of thee? For Humanity sake help us. For Christ sake do. We the Negro can do nothing but pray. There seem to be no help for us. No paper will tell the truth about the Negro. The men of the 1st North Carolina were home on a furlough and they took a high hand in the nefarious work. Also, the companies from every little town came in to kill the negro. There was not any rioting simply the strong slaying the weak. They speak of special police every white man and boy from 12 years up had a gun or pistol, and the negro had nothing, his soul he could not say was his own. Oh, [illeg.] see how we are slaughtered, when our husbands go to work we do not look for their return. The man who promises the Negro protection now as Mayor is the one who in his speech at the Opera house said the Cape Fear should be strewn with carcasses. Some papers I see, say it was right to eject the Negro editor, that is all right but why should a whole city full of negroes suffer for Manly when he was hundred of miles away? And the paper had ceased publication. We were glad it was so for our own safety. But they tried to slay us all. To day we are mourners in a strange land with no protection near. God help us. Do something to alleviate our sorrows, if you please. I cannot sign my name and live. But every word of this is true. The laws of our state is not good for the Negro anyhow. Yours in much distress

Wilmington, N.C.

JANE MURPHY CRONLY

From *An Account of the Race Riot in Wilmington, N.C.*

Jane Murphy Cronly was one of nine children born to Michael Cronly Sr. and Margaret McLaurin Cronly. The Cronly Family Papers housed at Duke University contain the letters and writings of this prominent Wilmington family. The senior Michael Cronly was president of the Wilmington, Charlotte, and Rutherford Railroad Company. His son, Michael Cronly Jr., was involved in some of the political affairs of the Democratic Party in Wilmington. Among the estate papers in the collection are receipts for the sale of slaves. Union soldiers plundered the Cronly home in 1865.

Jane Murphy Cronly was an avid writer, though it appears she never published any of her works. Among her papers are a novel entitled "Reclaimed XYZ" and several short stories. Fragments of Jane Cronly's diaries are in the collection, as are her memoirs about life during the Civil War and the Reconstruction era. Her recollection of the day of the 1898 riot, published here, is a graphic account of the violence in Wilmington streets and homes. Especially striking is Cronly's description of the obvious terror suffered by black citizens. She calls "entirely false" the claim that the violent coup was necessary for white protection. Inflicting terror, Cronly argues, was the real aim of the massacre: "the object of the whole persecution," she writes, was "to make Nov. 10th a day to be remembered by the whole race for all time" (p. 419). Jane Cronly died in 1935.

For the first time in my life I have been ashamed of my state and of the Democratic party in North Carolina, and I hope I utter the sentiment of many other women when I lift up my voice in solemn protest against the proceedings in Wilmington, North Carolina on last Thursday, November 10th.

It will ever be a day to be remembered in my heart with indignation and sorrow. At first indignation overwhelmed me; now sorrow has taken its place. I waited hoping a stronger voice than mine would be lifted up in defense of a helpless and much injured race, but such has not been the case. There was not a shadow of excuse for what occurred after the election had been carried in favor of the Democratic party, and our colored people had quietly accepted the fact.

The oft repeated cry it was necessary either is false; utterly, entirely false. ———[?] property has ever been in danger from the colored race here. They have been as good a set of people as could be found any-where, as witness the way the very people who have been villifying and abusing them have entrusted to them the care of their little children on the street and walked the streets them-selves.

I awoke that morning with thankful heart that the election had passed without the shedding of the blood of either the innocent or the guilty. I heard the colored people going by to their work talking cheer-fully to-gether as had not been the case for many days. Three hours later how changed was all this. Men with guns were standing on our side-walk, yells and cheers were heard in the distance, and a little later the fire bell began to ring. We learned afterward that the press of the Record had been destroyed by 1000 white men. The men of the col-ored race were in a distant part of the city at their work. The women fled in terror before the press destroyers, and upon seeing the flames thought their homes, many of them situated very near, were to be burned. Some of them managed to evade the white citizens situated upon every block to keep back colored citizens, who might wish to at-tack the press destroyers, and told them what they believed to be true.

This unarmed body of men rushing from their work to defend their wives and children from they knew not what manner of violence was pent up, ordered back, and kept at bay by the white citizens stationed on the blocks who were soon reinforced by the salient press destroy-ers, who began shooting off guns and pistols, having avowed as they went along toward the scene that they were "going gunning for nig-gers." Some blood was drawn by a colored man it is claimed, for I sup-pose a few armed colored men hearing the uproar, had appeared on the scene, and then the carnage began. It is pitiful to hear the accounts of reliable eye-witnesses to the harrowing scenes. "We are just shoot-ing to see the niggers run," they cried as the black men began to fall in every direction.

A few true-hearted and disinterested men besides also the owners of the compress who had steamers waiting to be loaded with cotton went hither and thither at the risk of being shot among the poor laborers trying to soothe and persuade them to go back and assuring them that their families were in no danger, but it was of no use and when all even possible danger was over for these press destroyers they were conducted to their homes. Some Naval Reserves and a small squad of the Home Guard Light Infantry (the real Cos. being still in the N. — Service) had finally appeared on the scene, but if they did any good besides killing a few "niggers" themselves, I haven't heard it, except in one instance. Mr. Buck Buckheimer rode up and down among the rioters (I suppose I can call that class now on the scene), calling out, "Shame, men; stop this. Stop this. Don't you see these dead men?" They kept snapping their pistols at him, but I suppose that he did have some influence. These rioters also shot at Mr. Sprunt's driver and buggy, saying they cared no more for Mr. S's tale[?] than for a birds. The Light Infantry squad has much to answer for. It shot down right and left in a most unlawful way, killing one man who was simply standing at a corner waiting to get back to his work. Another, Mr. Josh Halsey, had gone home, went to bed sick with fright I suppose. A little later a poor colored boy in the neighborhood, goaded by desperation, shot at the L.I.[1] whom I expect he thought were pressing him (and no doubt they were). They then searched every house in the neighborhood. When they reached Halsey's, his poor little child ran in and begged her father to get up and run for the soldiers were coming after him. The poor creature jumped up and ran out of the back door in frantic terror to be shot down like a dog by armed soldiers ostensibly sent to preserve the peace. Two soldiers were seen to have a mail carrier on his knees and one of them was advocating shooting him. The other warned him that it would not do, so after a little ————[?] threatening, he was allowed to go. The man wore the uniform of the ———— ————[?]. I do not think either was so idiotic as not to beware of doing this. The whole thing was with the object of striking terror to the man's heart, so that he would never vote again. For this was the object of the whole persecution; to make Nov. 10th a day to be remembered by the whole race for all time. "An object lesson" yes, and one that may perhaps be remembered by both races in the reactionary consequences which it might bring in its wake. The negroes here are an excellent race, and under all the abuse which has been vented upon

---

[1] *L.I.*: The Wilmington Light Infantry.

them for months they have gone quietly on and have been almost obsequiously polite as if to ward off the persecution they seemed involuntarily [to have] felt to be in the air.

In spite of all the goading and persecuting that has been done all summer the negroes have doing [done] nothing that could call down vengeance on their heads. The whole or nearly the whole Democratic party has broken faith again and again with the race and yet it has patiently submitted; first they were told that if they registered they were to be dismissed from their situations. In most cases they did regis-ter, for the average negro has a most exalted opinion of the value of his vote. He imagines the whole constitution will fall to pieces if his vote fails it. So, after registering, they were discharged and that measure having failed, they were threatened with dire things if they dared to vote. The secret committee of twenty-five now began pointing shot guns at helpless Republican heads and requiring them to write letters announcing their intention to vote the Democratic ticket in this elec-tion from their own honest convictions of course (the pistol point was not mentioned in public, of course). They then absolutely forbade any Republican speakers to come here. They sent a committee to Raleigh. No ticket to be nominated. They rode the mares[?] so successfully that they kept up the enjoyment even to planning and having carried into execution the killing of negroes, the driving them out of town into the woods and cemeteries, the arresting of the leaders — that is, all men who had property (who might be presumed[?] to be leaders, for really they had no leaders) whose lynching was only prevented by the deter-mined efforts of a few men. Then when the negroes had been informed by a circular the day before written by Gov. Russell[2] and quoting Dr. Hoge to the effect that they would be allowed to vote for state senator, the only Republican candidate running, they growled angrily, and about three o'clock on Nov. 8th, election day, the negroes, having been practically disarmed, they started down with the ———[?] and Hotchkiss guns to mow them down at the poles [sic], but Mr. Eliott and some other sharp lawyers scurried down and told them it would be the worse possible policy, that the Republican leaders would plead intimidation at the polls and so have the whole vote thrown out, and we would loose [sic] our congressman. Well, the day passed off with-out much racket, though that night the Capt. of block N. ———[?] Rankin rushed in — it was about ten o'clock — and in a very excited

---

[2] North Carolina Governor Daniel L. Russell was a white Republican elected in 1894 by an interracial coalition of Populists and Republicans.

manner called M. out to patrol the sidewalk, for fear the negroes, disappointed in having been cheated out of the election, might set fire to somebody's property. This fear was probably the outcome of anxiety on the part of those people, who having abused and maltreated the negroes were fearful of their just vengeance.

M.[3] took his gun and went out in spite of our protestations. After being out in the cold and damp for three hours, he came in a moment, and four women took hold of him so vigorously that they made him promise to come in before very long, threatening to go out with him if he did not. He knew what a perfect farce it was to be out there in the damp and cold, watching for poor cowed disarmed negroes frightened to death by the threats that had been made against them and too glad to huddle in their homes and keep quiet. So after a time he came home and went to bed.

The next day Nov. 9th was passed I suppose in counting the vote.

[3] M.: Probably a reference to Michael Cronly Jr., Jane Cronly's brother.

4

Segregation as Culture: Etiquette, Spectacle, and Fiction

Segregation in the South was not simply imposed by laws and acts of violence. It was also created and enforced by everyday practices, collective habits, local beliefs, and public entertainment. Unspoken societal rules were as important as court-issued laws. Under segregation, the most casual social encounter — making eye contact, passing on a sidewalk, removing a hat — became part of a system of racial regulation. The special brilliance of *The Marrow of Tradition* is its ability to dissect southern segregation as a way of life. Chesnutt asks his readers to recognize the links, subtle but pervasive, joining informal matters of etiquette and entertainment with new legal restrictions and even eruptions of violence, all working in concert to ensure black people's subordination to whites.

Chesnutt's novel, then, makes it clear that southern segregation was not designed to separate racial groups but rather to fix them in a close and ongoing relation, a hierarchy of white over black. Just as there were no slaves after abolition, there were also no longer any masters. As a result, many white Southerners sought to impose a social order that could reinvent the superior value — Chesnutt's white characters often call it the "prestige" or "dignity" — that white people had formerly commanded during slavery. Chesnutt's Colonel Carteret makes it clear that the prestige of the white man after slavery was still measured in relation to a subordinate black population. Carteret is determined to secure for his son a social value "commensurate with the dignity of his ancestors, one of whom . . . had owned an estate of ninety thousand acres of land and six thousand slaves" (p. 62 in this volume). Just as the plantation had relied upon the labor of slaves, so did segregation require a black population near at hand against which to define the contrasting value of whiteness.

The culture of segregation was designed to control and indeed encourage racial interactions that would provide thousands of daily affirmations of white supremacy. Everyday manners and social conventions were the foundation of Jim Crow culture. These unspoken rules of racial etiquette were often clearest when transgressed. Chesnutt's Olivia Carteret, for instance, blames her child's near-fall from a window on the "brazen glances" of Janet Miller, a biracial woman who, though she is Olivia's own half-sister, is not permitted to acknowledge in any fashion their cross-racial kinship. Even some African Americans, Chesnutt shows, felt compelled to censure any violation of racial manners, as when Mammy Jane declares that it "don't look right" for Janet Miller to ride around town in her private horse-drawn carriage. When Major Carteret, traveling in a carriage with other whites, notices the failure of black workers to "salute the party respectfully," his anger also carries a profound distress. "The negroes around this town are becoming absolutely insufferable," he announces. "They are sadly in need of a lesson in manners" (p. 132).

Chesnutt's attention to the minutia of manners reflects the charged importance of racial etiquette in the weeks preceding the Wilmington riot. As political tensions increased, white newspapers reported daily the "outrageous" violations of the courtesies expected of black people. According to one report, when an African American woman in Wilmington refused to yield the sidewalk to a group of white women, the breach of racial decorum so infuriated one of the white women that she seized the black woman and pushed her bodily out of the way. In retaliation, the woman began striking her white assailant with an umbrella (*Raleigh News* 4). As this example might suggest, manners could also serve as a means of protest against segregationist culture. Transgressions of even the smallest customs of racial deference carried far-reaching significance. If black people refused to perform their roles as racial subordinates, the psychic rewards for being white would become hollow. Every public gesture, large or small, was a potential racial contest. As the number of segregation laws mounted, it became criminal for black people to violate racial etiquette. Jim Crow culture was designed to prevent the unsettling sight of African Americans behaving as independent agents and social equals, what George Cable called "the apparition of the colored man or woman as his or her own master" (415).

To counter the unnerving "apparition" of black self-sovereignty, the white South also produced a visual culture designed to produce the "look" of an unassailable white superiority, not only in public streets and stores but in advertisements, cartoons, monuments, commercial amusements, and public spectacles. At the same time that the civil rights of African Americans were being restricted, there was a remarkable expansion in the number and kinds of public reproductions of the black image. Everywhere in print and public performance one could see the grotesque smiling features of the minstrel buffoon, the face of the genial mammy and the solicitous male servant, the frolicking of the cute black child — all visual icons that projected a friendly but subordinate relation to a viewer presumed white. The explosion of images at this time was partly due to technological innovations that made visual images markedly cheaper to reproduce in mass quantities. Black caricatures appeared on trade cards, in magazine ads, as mechanical toys and dolls, and on lithographic posters. Ironically, these technological advances and mass-produced commodities helped invent the southern fantasy of an idyllic rural past, an antebellum world W. E. B. Du Bois called the "fairy tale of a beautiful Southern slave civilization" (*Black Reconstruction* 715). Expansive mass markets then helped create a national audience of white Americans who began to see the Old South as a collective national heritage. By 1893, when the smiling face of Aunt Jemima debuted as a pancake mix trademark at the Chicago World's Fair, national markets had merged the South's peculiar brand of nostalgia with the conventions of minstrel entertainment and mass consumption to produce the "Old Negro" figure as a national icon.

Two years later, at the 1895 Cotton States and International Exhibition, Atlanta formally presented southern segregationist culture to the world. The event marked a debut of sorts for the Jim Crow era as the fair organizers harnessed the power of modern spectacle to segregationist goals. They permitted African Americans to display their industrial goods and handiwork at the fair but housed their exhibits in a distinct "Negro Building" apart from the displays by white Americans. Even more telling, however, was the popular site on the midway called the "Old Plantation." Boasting "real negroes as the actors," the recreated plantation offered white fairgoers the chance to revisit a vanished slave society as modern entertainment. The banner announcing "The Old Plantation," visible in a photograph reproduced in this chapter (p. 435), advertises black life of an antebellum past for a white viewer's pleasure. Like the Ferris wheel and scenic railway — two other midway features — the imitation slave plantation offered visitors an absorbing experience unavailable in everyday life. Through this spectacle the fundamental coercion of the plantation system underwent a visual transformation and the forced labor of slaves became the paid performance of black entertainers — slavery as show business.

It would be a mistake, though, to assume that fair visitors enjoyed the site simply because it recreated a slaveholding past absolved of white guilt or coercion. The Old Plantation won popularity in large part because it promised historical authenticity, "real" antebellum slave life. The late nineteenth century saw an awakened interest in black folk life, both in the United States and abroad. Even as racist minstrelsy expanded in this era there grew alongside it a new fascination with forms of African American dance, belief, and ritual. The official program for the Cotton States exhibition demonstrates the new interest for middle-class Americans in racially unfamiliar or exotic cultures, especially insofar as they were purported to be "genuine." In the program section describing the midway attractions (p. 432), the Old Plantation is clearly conceived as an exotic world akin to the other foreign attractions on the midway, a collection of "strange nationalities forming a unique anthropological exhibit." Appearing alongside the Sioux, Mexican, Chinese, and Japanese Villages, the Old South had become an ethnological attraction valued for the "genuineness of the production" (p. 434).

Yet the fair program also reveals just how closely the anthropological interest in unfamiliar cultures could coexist with an exploitative desire for novelty or sheer sensation. After all, fairgoers visiting the plantation were also attending bullfights in the Mexican Village and glimpsing "sensual Oriental dances" in a theater on Cairo Street. Authenticity had become an entertainment value. In a telling sentence, the fair program observes of the Plantation exhibit that the performance of "real negroes" was "as much superior to negro minstrelsy by white men as real life is to acting" (p. 434). The fact that the black performers at the exhibit (like any white performer in blackface) were only pretending to be slaves is all but forgotten as their "genuine" blackness becomes a sign of "real life" on the plantation.

The tendency for "exotic" cultures to be consumed as spectacle, then, presented a complex set of issues for African American performers. Performing traditional arts in public could be gratifying and sometimes well paying but it opened African American culture to exploitation by the dominant white culture. The "cakewalk" advertised and performed at the Atlanta fair Plantation is an instructive example of this difficulty. In its early plantation origins, the stylized dancing and strutting that came to be called the cakewalk was a vital part of the community life of enslaved Africans. The celebratory dancing probably drew upon rites that originated in African homelands, but descendants introduced innovations that included moves — exaggerated or grotesque stepping — enacting a disguised mockery of white owners. As novelist Ralph Ellison described it, the cakewalk grew from slaves "burlesqueing the white folks and then going on to force the steps into a choreography uniquely their own" (223). Even with its coded criticisms, however, the cakewalk was seized upon by white performers in blackface and turned into the centerpiece of countless racist minstrel shows during this period (Stuckey, Sundquist, Toll, Wittke).

In the memoir excerpted for this chapter (p. 435), black performer Tom Fletcher chronicles the international fascination with the cakewalk and describes the opportunity it helped create for African American artists to enjoy careers as respected performers. Developing their own distinctive styles, men and women like Fletcher reclaimed a black expressive form from white performers and producers. But Fletcher's account also reveals how the range of public productions, from the Old South recreation at the Philadelphia Centennial exhibition in 1876 to the shows before huge crowds in Madison Square Garden, converted black life into commercial spectacles that African American performers could not consistently direct or control. As Chesnutt cannily suggests in *Marrow,* the pleasures of the cakewalk could easily become a snare that trapped black performers while feeding the complacency of white observers. At the same time, however, the sheer number and the enormity of these Old South productions attest to the fact that white interest in black folk life was, quite literally, *excessive,* beyond bounds, and therefore not always predictably in the service of white control. One panoramic production that toured American cities the same year as the Wilmington riot, for instance, aspired to represent the whole history of the black South. Billed as "Darkest America" and boasting an all-black cast and management, the gigantic production featured a cotton gin, a sugar plantation, a prize fight, and a black ballroom scene, to name only a few of the elaborate sets (Wittke 153–54). Such spectacles were a telling if unpredictable feature of segregationist culture: they represented a way of imposing racial distance even as they fed new kinds of cross-racial attraction and interest. As

Fletcher tells it, wealthy industrialists in New York and the nobility in Europe not only wanted to see the cakewalk but to learn for themselves its stylized movements and rhythms. The white elite now wished to imitate the black dances that had once imitated white pomposity.

The most glaring — and potentially most destructive — aspect of the racial spectacles in this era, however, was their tendency to visually remove African Americans from the present and transport them to a mythic southern past. The effect was a subtle segregation in time rather than space: black people, such spectacles suggested, "belonged" to the past. Aware of its pernicious effect, African Americans and their white supporters were concerned to counter this tendency. At the 1900 World's Fair in Paris, for instance, W. E. B. Du Bois helped curate a photo exhibition that featured dozens of pictures of African Americans of all hues posed individually before the camera. In counterpoint to the vast number of Old South icons and shows, these modern photographs and all they evoked — technology, prosperity, individual achievement — exhibited visual proof that African Americans were diverse, modern citizens (Smith 157–86).

A white photographer, Frances Benjamin Johnston, made the same point more explicitly — if more problematically — in a series of photographs of life at Hampton College, a black institution in Atlanta. Like Du Bois, Johnston displayed her photographs at the 1900 Paris Exhibition. Johnston's *Hampton Album* features pairs of photos that juxtaposed re-created Old South scenes with contrasting pictures of successful "New Negroes." An artificially posed picture of "slaves" standing before a crude cabin, for instance, is countered by a photo of the fine modern home of a "Hampton graduate." In the pair of photos reproduced in this chapter (pp. 441–42), a scene featuring an old man and woman eating a meal in a slave hut is contrasted with a photo in which well-dressed parents sit with two children for a meal in their finely appointed Victorian dining room. The series of matched photographs can be seen as directly answering the segregationist iconography that favored placing black people in nostalgic recreations of antebellum life.

At the same time, however, Johnston's photographs risk affirming a future for black Americans only in the narrow terms of middle-class advancement. The "New Negro" in her photographs is depicted as college-bred, a homeowner, a professional, or his middle-class wife; the vast majority of modern African Americans at the time, poorly paid laborers, are nowhere visible. To an extent, Chesnutt's *Marrow of Tradition* shares Johnston's technique of using middle-class professionals as ideal representatives of the race. Yet Chesnutt's novel also shows what Johnston's photographs leave out. Even if the prosperous Millers are the novel's best hope for African Americans' future, their property and professional success make them no less vulnerable to racist violence — indeed, their class status may actually provoke fury in an era of segregation for the challenge it poses to black subordination.

The tension between stereotypes of "Old" and "New Negroes" was also central to the field of southern fiction in this era. Chesnutt recognized the complex pull of white nostalgia for a plantation past that never was. Nostalgia's ability to erase hard truths through memory no doubt fed the popularity that plantation fiction enjoyed in the 1880s and 1890s. Authors such as Thomas Nelson Page, Joel Chandler Harris, and James Lane Allen found there was a large audience for colorful and idealizing tales of the Old South under slavery. Chesnutt's first successful publications made a bid for the same audience. His collection of short stories entitled *The Conjure Woman* repeats many of the narrative conventions of plantation fiction. Yet Chesnutt's Uncle Julius, the "Old Negro" figure who recounts the tales of vanished plantation life, also manipulates the readiness of his white northern listeners to be charmed by nostalgic stories. Though his criticisms were largely disguised, Chesnutt used the tradition of plantation fiction to undercut the genre's own tendency to foster readers' wishful thinking.

In *The Marrow of Tradition*, Chesnutt openly dissects the plantation novel by drawing upon some of the genre's standard material: the Mammy figure, the minstrel-like black fool, the loyal ex-slave and his protective former master. But in *Marrow* these types are revealed to be ineffective as individuals and outmoded as literary characters. As Chesnutt's narrative unfolds, Mammy Jane and the obsequious Jerry Letlow die, the devoted Sandy Cambell is nearly lynched, and Sandy's former master, the paternalistic Mr. Delamere, turns out to be powerless to stop the momentum of racial violence. *Marrow* aspires to serve as an epitaph for the plantation romance. Its distortions, Chesnutt believed, blinded white readers to African Americans' aspirations and frustrations alike and hid the real sources of white aggression. Chesnutt saw in the drama of the Wilmington riot the origins of a counternarrative, a story able to expose the myths perpetuated by these popular novels and stories.

Just as the violence of Wilmington was the culmination of civil and political struggles, however, the same November event became the site of a literary battle of sorts. The riot was incorporated into at least two other novels besides Chesnutt's. Thomas Dixon's novel *The Leopard's Spots* (1902) transformed the myths of plantation fiction into a fiercely antiblack vision of the postwar South. Whereas authors like Page and Harris had tended to portray freedmen as loyal subordinates, Dixon presented a picture of ungovernable black criminals, rapists, and grasping politicians. In *The Leopard's Spots* the Wilmington coup is a necessary triumph for the defenders of Anglo-Saxon liberty, a second "Revolution of Independence." An African American journalist, David Bryant Fulton, also wrote a novel about the riot, *Hanover: Or the Persecution of the Lowly, A Story of the Wilmington Massacre,* which he published under the pen name "Jack Thorne." Like Dixon, Fulton applauds his most militant characters, though of course the men with valor in *Hanover* are African Americans. Fulton also extends heroic agency to black women, who urge resistance to white terror. *Hanover* is dedicated to the antilynching activist Ida B. Wells, a tribute that matches the novel's concern with championing forceful opposition to the violence at the heart of segregation. Whereas Chesnutt in *Marrow* offered a more "sociological" study of southern psychology and culture, Fulton brought a journalist's talent for imparting a sense of immediacy to historic events.

Dixon's novel proved far more popular than either Fulton's or Chesnutt's. A national bestseller, *The Leopard's Spots* glamorized the idea that a noble "revolution" required warlike tactics against African Americans in the South. In Dixon's narrative (which was later incorporated into D. W. Griffith's early epic film *Birth of a Nation*), black people themselves incite violent retribution by otherwise peaceful white communities. Segregation is a necessary defense of white culture. But even as Jim Crow laws became entrenched in state and federal courts, writers such as Chesnutt, David Bryant Fulton, W. E. B. Du Bois, George White, and the anonymous woman who wrote to President McKinley used novels, speeches, and letters to try to make readers understand the multiple forms of coercion within the culture of segregation.

RALEIGH NEWS AND OBSERVER

Is a Race Clash Unavoidable?

In the months preceding the Wilmington riot, white newspapers in the South published numerous articles about the "impudent" public conduct of African American residents, especially that of black women. A report from Winston, North Carolina, reprinted below, alleged that black women were not yielding the sidewalk when white women on bicycles assumed the right of way.

It is impossible to determine how accurate these reports of violations of racial etiquette really were. The published accounts, unreliable though they are, might suggest that these kinds of public confrontations expressed the anger of black women at the intensifying white supremacy campaign.

What is clear, however, is the fact that white people perceived these affronts as proof of the harmful effects of black participation in public governance. In the article included below, published on September 22, 1898, in the Raleigh *News and Observer,* the editor Josephus Daniels blamed the incivility on the Republican Party. "Such exasperating occurrences would not happen but for the fact that the negro party is in power in North Carolina" (p. 430). By this theory, the increased enfranchisement of black men had somehow emboldened black women to express hostility against white residents. In Wilmington a group of self-organized "Minute Men" vowed to crack down on "negro women parad[ing] the streets and insult[ing] men and ladies" (qtd. in Gilmore 83).

A Number of Instances of Negro Impudence and Meanness.

The White People Must Stand Together.
Can a Clash Between the Races be Avoided.

(Winston Free Press.)

Mrs. J. F. Taylor and Mrs. H. E. Mosley were out riding on their wheels one evening last week. They turned into a narrow side path to avoid meeting a lot of negroes who were going home from the tobacco stemmery. There were several negro woman [sic] in the path. The negro wenches seemed determined not to step aside to allow the ladies to pass. Mrs. Taylor was in front and determined that she would ride ahead anyway, so she brushed past the negroes. One of the wenches then got right in the middle of the path and Mrs. Mosley had to dismount from her wheel and roll it around the impudent negro wench, and all the impudent wenches laughed loudly and clapped their hands at making her dismount. Such exasperating occurrences would not happen but for the fact that the negro party is in power in North Carolina, and that there are negro magistrates and other negro officials in office, which emboldens bad negroes to display their evil, impudent and mean natures.

Negro men on wheels do not turn out at all for ladies but would ride right over white women if they did not get out of the way. Their brazen impudence is a result of the negro party being in power.

A negro woman whipped one of Dr. Faulkner's little boys one day last week with a buggy whip. It was done without the slightest provocation that we can learn. Dr. Faulkner is awfully mad, as he has just cause to be, and is trying his best to learn the name of the nasty, mean negro wench.

The negro Congressman White, said in his speech here Saturday that the Populists were in honor bound to vote for him. He slandered the Populists. Hereafter there should be no Populists. The place for all white men, with white principles, is in the Democratic party. All true white men must work together and vote together to restore white government in North Carolina.

Saturday evening Chief of Police J. H. Rouse arrested John Bright, a negro, for being drunk and disorderly. The negro resisted arrest. When Rouse took hold of him the negro tried to stamp the policeman's feet, and the latter hit the negro over the head with his billy.

Amos Grainger, another negro, said to the negroes: "Will you all stand around here and let the — — white man arrest one of your race?"

The negro Bright was finally arrested and lodged in jail and then Chief Rouse arrested Amos Grainger for counselling resistance to an officer. Both negroes gave bail for their appearance for trial Tuesday.

A negro woman was also cursing and snorting around advising resistance to an officer, but Chief Rouse could not find her after he made the other arrests.

The Free Press has only given a few facts. There are many others of a similar nature constantly occurring. The condition is becoming unbearable. We have proper regard for good negroes who know and keep their places, but for mean, impudent and unruly negroes we have the utmost contempt. The rule of the fusionists has served to develop in the bad negroes all their mean traits. It is rapidly approaching the point where the patience of all true white men will be exhausted — when such men will take the law in their own hands and by organized force make the negroes behave themselves. Unless white government is restored at the next election this point will certainly be reached and there is strong probability that it will be reached before the election.

There are many good negroes, who are disposed to be, and are, polite and respectful. If this class has any influence over the unruly ones of their race, it is high time they were exerting it. Unless they do, a clash is surely coming between the races, and in such clashes the white race is always victorious.

From *The Cotton States and International Exposition Program*

In the late summer and fall of 1895, over a million people descended on Atlanta, Georgia, for the Cotton States and International Exposition. Following successful international exhibitions in northern cities such as Philadelphia (1876) and Chicago (1893), the South attempted to present itself to the world as a region in racial harmony and ripe for economic development. Between 1885 and 1897, the major urban centers of Atlanta, Nashville, and New Orleans each staged its own world's fair.

The fair's careful orchestration of racial issues was apparent from the opening of the Cotton States Exposition. In one of the opening addresses, Booker T. Washington delivered his famous speech, later called "The Atlanta Compromise," which is included in this volume (p. 274). In his address, Washington controversially promoted segregation as a means of self-reliance for African Americans. In that spirit, while the fair was unique in allowing African Americans to produce and manage their own exhibitions, these exhibitions were housed in a separate hall, the "Negro Building."

The Cotton States and International Exposition and South Illustrated, by Walter G. Cooper (Atlanta, GA: The Illustrator Company, 1896), excerpted here, describes the fair's midway attractions. Visitors to Atlanta's "Midway Heights" could expect to find mirror mazes, popular games such as "Shoot the Chute," beauty shows, and racy dances, but also exhibits of re-created foreign villages like those described in the program. Along with these villages, fairgoers could also see the Old Plantation, a live reenactment of a working antebellum plantation. With an acknowledged likeness to both the museum and the circus, the Midway's villages and plantation capture the vexed implications of offering recreations of "authentic" cultures as mass entertainment.

MIDWAY HEIGHTS.

. . . The Midway possessed the features of the circus, the menagerie, the museum and the vaudeville, with an odd collection of strange nationalities forming a unique anthropological exhibit. The visitor who had examined the series of figures from the Smithsonian Institution, representing the various types of man, could see many of them in very live flesh and blood by taking a turn through the Midway. Mexicans, Chinese, Japanese, Arabs, Turks, Syrians, East Indians, Dahomeyans,[1] Eskimo and Sioux Indians were there in force, while almost every nationality of the Caucasian and the African races was to be seen in the crowd which streamed through. Mechanical devices for amusement were not wanting. Chief among these were the Phœnix Wheel, the Scenic Railway, and that most exhilarating of all amusements, "Shooting the Chutes." There was a Shakespearean variety of human nature of high and low degree, and the range from horse-play to high comedy was daily presented. . . .

There were certain attractions called villages. The Mexican Village included many of the characteristic types of that country, with much of the local color for which Mexico is famous. This village was the most ambitious enterprise of the Midway group, and one of the best. Mexican musicians, families of peons, and representatives of the higher classes were all occupants of the place. There were also Mexican toreadors and matadors, and only the action of the authorities prevented the production of bloodless bull-fights. The intention to do so was widely discussed, and drew from the press of the United States a tremendous and angry chorus of condemnation. It was never intended to allow the shedding of blood, and it was finally concluded that the terror of the horses would be cruelty in its worst form. For this reason, and in deference to public opinion, the bull-fight was prohibited. The concessionaires had already been to some expense, and the Exposition Company found it necessary to make an allowance for this in the final settlement.

The Chinese Village was populated by 200 men, women and boys, imported directly from the Celestial Empire by way of Vancouver. A Chinese theatre was erected, and the grotesque performances of the Chinese stage were given with a very good setting and a liberal supply of accessories and elaborate costumes.

The Japanese Village, though located in another part of the park, may be considered a part of the anthropological display of the Midway group. The elaborate display of articles of Japanese handicraft was accompanied by a series of remarkable performances by Japanese acrobats. One of the most popular and pleasing features was

---

[1] *Dahomeyans:* Dahomey is the former name of the West African nation of Benin, a country that borders Nigeria to the west.

the Japanese tea-house, where the beverage was served in Oriental style.

Cairo Street, with its booths and bazaars, was reproduced with picturesque realism, and the camels, with Arabs as drivers, were ever-present witnesses of the genuineness of the production. The enclosure also included the theatre in which the sensuous Oriental dances were given.

The Indian Village was an exhibit of historic as well as ethnological interest. The Sioux Indians included several chiefs prominent in the war which resulted in the Custer massacre. The famous "Two Strikes," hardly less of a warrior than "Sitting Bull," was here, and the old chief, "Stand-and-Look-Back," who held General Reno at bay while the Custer massacre was in progress, remained to the last. Many of the men were participants in the "ghost dances" of 1890 and the fights which followed. The lodges of the Indian village on which the United States troops turned their Gatling guns were there, occupied by the same Indians. One of the women, "Yellow Dogface," had been wounded by a bullet from one of the Gatling guns, and her papoose, now grown to be a boy of seven or eight years, had received two bullets in his little body. This boy, known as "Little Wound," seems to be no worse physically for his early taste of war, and during the Exposition showed all the lively and mischievous tendencies of a robust urchin. . . .

The Old Plantation was one of the popular features of the Midway and the only one which President Cleveland honored with his presence. It was what its name signifies, with real negroes as the actors, and was as much superior to negro minstrelsy by white men as real life is to acting.

The Hagenbeck menagerie[2] contained trained animals of rare intelligence, but the name fully explains the character of the attraction. Such attractions as the Mystic Maze, the Palace of Illusion, and the Camera Obscura[3] occupied the remainder of the street. The " '49 Mining Camp" was a curious feature of the fair which, though located elsewhere, may be classed with the Midway group.

---

[2] *Hagenbeck menagerie:* Karl Hagenbeck (1844–1913) was a German entrepreneur credited with the invention of the modern zoological garden. He traveled around the world exhibiting his menageries, displaying animals in natural surroundings rather than cages.

[3] *Camera Obscura:* From the Latin for "dark chamber," a darkened room in which a lens projects a real image of an object in natural color onto a separate surface.

Photograph of "Old Plantation" Midway Booth at the 1896 Cotton States Exposition in Atlanta, Georgia. Courtesy of the Library of Congress.

TOM FLETCHER

From *100 Years of the Negro in Show Business*

Tom Fletcher's *100 Years of the Negro in Show Business*, first published in 1954 (rpt. New York: Da Capo Press, 1984), remains as one of the few sources that records the early history of the post–Civil War black entertainment industry. On May 16, 1873, Fletcher was born in Portsmouth, Ohio, a town that frequently served as a stop for many touring minstrel shows. He began his career at age fifteen, traveling with Howard's Novelty Colored Minstrels as a vocalist. He would go on to perform with some of the best-known minstrel groups in the country. Before the turn of the century, Fletcher also performed as a vocalist, bass drummer, and dancer in Prof. J. H. Bruster's Georgia Minstrels. As a sometime stage manager and booking agent, Fletcher learned about the economics of the changing black entertainment field.

Fletcher continued drumming and dancing in shows designed by the successful black producer Percy G. Williams, and made films in the early part of the twentieth century. He went on to teach dance and music and work on the Keith vaudeville circuit, appeared with the New York Syncopated Orchestra, and made his Broadway debut in 1944.

100 Years of the Negro in Show Business is a rare account of the people and events that shaped the day-to-day life of a traveling black entertainer at the turn of the century. Fletcher offers insight to performance traditions such as the cakewalk as it emerged as a form of mass entertainment in the United States and Europe. With a career that began in nineteenth-century minstrel shows and ended in collaborations with such prestigious black performers as jazz clarinetist Sidney Bechet and choreographer Katherine Dunham, Fletcher witnessed the complex and dynamic emergence of African American theatrical performance. Fletcher died in New York City in 1954.

CHAPTER 12. BILLY McCLAIN

ONE OF the outstanding old time minstrel men, musicians and actors of the early years in show business was Billy McClain.[1] A big feature in many of the big shows of that period, even though he seldom got top billing, McClain was always looking for ways to put more and more people in show business. Free-born and possessing a formal education, he was a smooth talker and had plenty of nerve and through the years his activities were directly responsible for the employment of thousands of colored people in show business. . . .

. . . McClain's idea was to put on a big novelty extravaganza, a cavalcade of colored people, in some large outdoor arena. When he mentioned the idea to his friends most of them gave him the laugh, pointing out that he had no place to present such a show and furthermore, the cost of the scenery and salaries for the number of people he wanted — even though salaries in those times weren't very large — put the idea way beyond his reach.

. . . Billy promptly set about collecting the cast of over 500 people he needed. Since the spectacle was to be put on in the summer time he

---

[1] *Billy McClain:* African American entertainer and impresario who performed in and directed minstrel shows across America and overseas (he took a troupe of performers to Australia in 1898). Fletcher calls him "an unsung pioneer" of show business.

Promotion poster for white minstrel performer Carroll Johnson, one portrait of himself, one in blackface, 1899. Courtesy of the Library of Congress.

had a chance at all of the top show people of the period; names like Madam Flowers, Fred Piper, Charley Johnson, May Bohee, Madam Cordelia McClain, Jube Johnson, Ed Harris, Billy Farrell, Doc Sayles. He was also able to get the most beautiful girls, singers and dancers. He procured 63 quartets from all parts of the country, and a group of men who had served with the U. S. Ninth Cavalry were brought together to form a squadron performing their regular army maneuvers.

The cast was finally assembled and rehearsals started. Billy served as talent scout and stage manager, a sort of prototype of the modern technical director. The site chosen for the production was *Ambrose Park* in Brooklyn, N. Y. The park was transformed into the likeness of a southern plantation. Cotton bushes, with buds blossoming, were transplanted. Bales of cotton were brought in and a cotton gin in working order set up. Poultry and live stock were brought in and real cabins built, a large part of the company using these cabins as living quarters for the season. This entire layout provided atmosphere through which the audiences would roam at random before the show itself started. Fifteen minutes before show time a signal would be given and the crowds would find their seats in the huge outdoor amphitheater which was covered by canvas.

This was the *"Black America"* company and it was another huge success, marking a milestone in the development of show business. . . .

CHAPTER 13. THE CAKE WALK

Just about 10 years after the end of slavery, at the Centennial of American Independence at Philadelphia in 1876, one of the features was a large plantation scene with a great many ex-slaves, and free-born Colored people singing Spirituals, work songs, and other original songs. The added attraction was the *"cake walk";* done in the original fashion, known to some as the *"chalkline-walk"* and to some as the *"walk-around."* The prize was an enormous cake to the winning couple.

The *Cake Walk* was developed from a *"Prize Walk"* done in the days of slavery, generally at get-togethers on the plantation. It was done in the minstrel shows by all men, some of them putting on dresses and makeup and wigs to act as walking partners for the others, because minstrel show companies were all men in the beginning. In fact, up to the period of 1890, *"Uncle Tom's Cabin"*[2] companies were about the only shows to carry women, and they did so because there were certain parts in the cast for women.

It was in the period of 1890 that the Sam T. Jack's *"Creole Company"* started the ball rolling as far as including women in the cake walk was concerned. This company had a minstrel, first part, with all women in the circle and a woman for the interlocutor. Men were used on the ends to tell the jokes and use the bones and tambos.[3] In the finale of that show they did the Cake Walk.

From then on, nearly every colored show, minstrels and all, put women in the cast. This made possible all sorts of improvisations in

---

[2] *Uncle Tom's Cabin:* Harriet Beecher Stowe's famous antislavery novel, first published in serial from 1851 to 1852 and then as a book in 1852 to wide popular reception. The story follows Uncle Tom through his tribulations as a slave in the South and Eliza, also a slave, in her escape to the North.

[3] *the bones and tambos:* "Mistah Bones" and "Mistah Tambo" were standard comic characters in minstrel shows. They derived their names from the instruments they played: castanets (a palm-sized shell-like instrument) made of bone or hard wood and the tambourine.

1896 minstrel poster. Courtesy of the Library of Congress.

the Walk, and the original was soon changed into a grotesque dance. Furthermore, with women travelling with the companies, each couple began to work out its own original routines. A number of the men married their partners while travelling in the same companies.

The *Cake Walk* dance became very popular all over the country. When playing in the large cities, the big colored companies would set a night aside and, as an added attraction, offer a prize to the best local couple among those entering the competition. As a result the Cake Walk craze spread like wildfire.

Every town that could would put on a Cake Walk contest. Soon great big prizes of cash as well as cakes were given as awards. The old *Madison Square Garden* in New York City became the place where the national championship contests were held, very much like the *Harvest Moon Dance* Contests of today, although the latter are local with contestants coming almost exclusively from the metropolitan New York area. The contestants in the Cake Walk contests came from all over the country. They were the winners and the semi-finalists in their home town contests.

The *Madison Square Garden* competition was always a sell-out. Before the contest there would be a big plantation scene with the cast of about 150 singers and dancers and some great vocal soloist of the period. After this show was over, the judges, including many of New York's prominent brokers, sportsmen and athletes, especially prize fighters, would take their places on the stage. Walter F. Craig and his orchestra of fifty pieces would be seated on the stage to provide the music.

The inside of *Madison Square Garden* on such occasions was arranged like a race track. The space for the Cake Walkers ran alongside the boxes and loges. Chairs were placed on the floor to mark off the space for the contestants. When the contest music started, first would appear a drum major who would go through a routine with his baton then return to his place as leader. Then the curtain would part and 50 or 60 couples would come from behind the stage on to the floor, prancing and dancing to the tempo of the music. It was very reminiscent of the grand entry at a circus. . . .

Cake Walk winners were judged by time, style and execution. Mr. and Mrs. Luke Blackburn, who did the original walk ran out of the competition. They became a big feature and would appear only to show the way the *Cake Walk* started. The younger people went for the new style. The couples that emerged winners or runners-up usually formed Variety or Vaudeville acts. All of the couples that took part in the contests were good singers and dancers, and the winning of the championship at Madison Square Garden was a great help to them in getting bookings from all over the world because this American dance which originated among the colored people during slavery was a sensation all over the globe.

Of all the dances from that time until now the *Cake Walk* has topped all in its popularity. From the plantation it moved to be taught to and danced by everyone in the mansions of the Four Hundred[4] and the palaces of the royal families. When I was a child my grandparents told me about it, but when I asked them when it started they didn't have the answer.

. . . Resort hotels that used colored help would put on special *Cake Walks*. The *Royal Ponciana* at Palm Beach, Florida, which used the greatest number of colored help, would give men and women Cake Walkers easy work during the season in order to have them on hand for the *Cake Walk* contest.

---

[4] *mansions of the Four Hundred:* The Astor Four Hundred was a list of New York City's social elites compiled by famous New York socialite Caroline Schermerhorn Astor (1830–1908). In the nineteenth century, "the Four Hundred" was used more generally to describe the wealthy and socially powerful in America.

FRANCES BENJAMIN JOHNSTON

From *The Hampton Album*

One of the most noted photographers of the late nineteenth century, Frances Benjamin Johnston was born in Rochester, New York, on January 15, 1864. After moving to Washington, D.C., as a child, Johnston received a liberal arts education at the Notre Dame Academy of Govanston, Massachusetts, before enrolling in the leading foreign language arts academy of Paris, Académie Julian, where she studied for three years, from 1883 to 1885. Upon returning to the United States, Johnston settled in Washington, D.C., where she opened a successful portrait studio. Her subjects included U.S. presidents and their families, Mark Twain, and Susan B. Anthony.

Johnston was commissioned in 1899 to take photographs of the famous Hampton Normal and Agricultural Institute in Hampton, Virginia, for exhibition at the Paris Exposition of 1900. Johnston would also

"Old Negro" photograph from *The Hampton Album* by Frances Benjamin Johnston. Courtesy of the Library of Congress.

"New Negro" photograph from *The Hampton Album* by Frances Benjamin Johnston. Courtesy of the Library of Congress.

photograph Booker T. Washington's Tuskegee Institute in 1902 and spent the rest of her life lecturing and working as a photographer. She died in New Orleans on March 16, 1952.

At the Paris Exposition, Johnston's work was part of the Contemporary American Negro Lives exhibition, along with the photographs arranged by noted sociologist and intellectual W. E. B. Du Bois. Johnston's photographs attempt to document for a skeptical white public African Americans' potential for advancement. At the same time, her technique of pairing scenes of middle-class life with corresponding "antebellum" plantation scenes, re-created by contemporary African Americans, perpetuated the troubling division between representations of "Old" and "New Negroes" that appeared in a good deal of popular culture.

CHARLES CHESNUTT

Literary Memoranda

The success of Chesnutt's first novel, *The House Behind the Cedars,* encouraged him to begin planning a second work about race relations in the South. In September 1900, he jotted down notes for a story involving the 1898 race riot in Wilmington, North Carolina. A physician from Wilmington had visited Chesnutt in Cleveland and recounted for him his firsthand recollections of the events, including the physician's carriage ride through the streets during the height of the riot.

Having decided to write a full-length novel about Wilmington, Chesnutt traveled South in February 1901 to study the institutions of the cotton states and to learn as much as he could about the riot. In March Chesnutt returned to Cleveland and began the five months of concentrated writing that produced *The Marrow of Tradition.*

The handwritten notes from September 1900 are part of the Charles Chesnutt Papers housed at Fisk University (box 13, folder 5). The two sketches show Chesnutt's changing ideas about the climactic resolution of the novel. In the second memoranda, for instance, the word "Forgiveness" is written and then crossed out, hinting at Chesnutt's divided feelings about the question of racial reconciliation in the novel.

"PLOT FOR SHORT STORY: RACE RIOT

Young colored man, educated, decides to settle in a Southern city, where he can be of more direct use to his people, personally as well as by example. He must be of some pursuit or profession, preferably medicine, and must have distinguished himself in some specialty. A race riot breaks out, in which he suffers terribly, his house and his drugstore being destroyed, and his child and mother being killed or dying of fright. There is no redress and no hope of redress. The doctor prepares to leave the town. The child or wife of one of the chief promoters of the riot is taken suddenly and violently ill. There is only one white physician in the town who is capable of treating the case, which requires immediate attention, and this physician is called. He refused; is persuaded, wavers, argues, yields, and saves the child's life. Is begged to remain in town and is offered the white man's protection. Declines — does not want protection but wants rights and opportunities of a man.

His new found friend would not be able to stop or turn aside the forces he has set into motion."

"RACE RIOT STORY

Doctor. Settled South among his people. Ruined by a riot in which his child or wife is killed. He prepares to leave town. Child of leading agitator against Negro is taken ill and requires very delicate operation. Only one other physician in town who knows how to perform it. (Or perhaps have it simple and all other doctors out of town. Father is forced to call on Colored doctor. Swallows pride, and makes the appeal. Fight it out [Forgiveness]. Dr. is waiting on his own sick wife who is prostrated from the loss of her child, and find this a reason to give his conscience for refusing to go. One feature of this the story is that the white man did not know of the colored man's loss (of child), and is dramatically shown the body when he calls at the house. (He has first sent a servant, who is told to send the master himself.) The white man is a man of iron nerve and recognizes the justness of the negro's attitude. He goes away hoping that the disease may take a turn for the better. Child gets worse. The mother goes to the doctor's wife. The appeal is successful. The child is saved. Nevertheless, the doctor moves away, in spite of many nice things said, and moves away in a Jim Crow car."

CHARLES CHESNUTT

Po' Sandy

The 1880s and 1890s saw a vogue for nostalgic fiction about the Old South. Joel Chandler Harris's Uncle Remus tales, for instance, created a recognizable name and visual image for the figure of the loyal ex-slave. By recalling plantation life through the storytelling of Uncle Remus or of Marse Chan (the character invented by writer Thomas Nelson Page), this popular body of white-authored plantation fiction romanticized the slave-holding past as a "green and gracious" world remembered fondly even by former slaves themselves. Despite the distortions from white nostalgia, however, plantation fiction was also capable of including darker under-currents. In his rendering of Remus's Brer Rabbit stories and other animal tales, for instance, Harris published African American folklore that often included a subtle yet incisive allegory of the ongoing power struggles within slavery, as Brer Rabbit uses his wiles to survive the designs of stronger fellow creatures.

Chesnutt learned Harris's lesson about subtext and improved upon it. His first successful publications, stories he published in 1899 in a collection called *The Conjure Woman*, introd. Robert M. Farnsworth (Ann Arbor: University of Michigan Press, 1969), followed fairly closely the structure of Harris's Uncle Remus fiction. Chesnutt's narrator, the elderly Uncle Julius, tells tales of plantation "conjuring" — magical spells that transform people into objects like trees or animals — to a northern husband and wife who have moved to North Carolina after the war. As with plantation fiction, Chesnutt's conjure stories use black dialect to signify an insider's appreciation of black vernacular culture. But at the same time, Chesnutt's stories subtly commented on their own genre. His choice of two educated Northerners as the designated audience for Julius's stories is a clue to Chesnutt's canny understanding of the existing market for this fiction.

Chesnutt knew that contemporary readers — much like his naive Northerners John and Annie — were drawn to quaint and exotic southern lore as an escape from the more routine existence of industrialized urban centers. Just as Julius subtly cons John and Annie, Chesnutt performs a literary trick of his own by making conventions of plantation fiction serve as an indictment of the violence and humiliations at the heart of southern slavery. Chesnutt's most powerful plantation stories — "Po' Sandy" and "Dave's Neckliss," for instance — use the device of magical transformation to expose the sadistic denial of the slave's humanity.

On the northeast corner of my vineyard in central North Carolina, and fronting on the Lumberton plank-road, there stood a small frame house, of the simplest construction. It was built of pine lumber, and contained but one room, to which one window gave light and one door admission. Its weather-beaten sides revealed a virgin innocence of paint. Against one end of the house, and occupying half its width, there stood a huge brick chimney: the crumbling mortar had left large cracks between the bricks; the bricks themselves had begun to scale off in large flakes, leaving the chimney sprinkled with unsightly blotches. These evidences of decay were but partially concealed by a creeping vine, which extended its slender branches hither and thither in an ambitious but futile attempt to cover the whole chimney. The wooden shutter, which had once protected the unglazed window, had fallen from its hinges, and lay rotting in the rank grass and jimson-weeds beneath. This building, I learned when I bought the place, had been used as a schoolhouse for several years prior to the breaking out of the war, since which time it had remained unoccupied, save when some stray cow or vagrant hog had sought shelter within its walls from the chill rains and nipping winds of winter.

One day my wife requested me to build her a new kitchen. The house erected by us, when we first came to live upon the vineyard, contained a very conveniently arranged kitchen; but for some occult reason my wife wanted a kitchen in the back yard, apart from the dwelling-house, after the usual Southern fashion. Of course I had to build it.

To save expense, I decided to tear down the old schoolhouse, and use the lumber, which was in a good state of preservation, in the construction of the new kitchen. Before demolishing the old house, however, I made an estimate of the amount of material contained in it, and found that I would have to buy several hundred feet of lumber additional, in order to build the new kitchen according to my wife's plan.

One morning old Julius McAdoo, our colored coachman, harnessed the gray mare to the rockaway, and drove my wife and me over to the sawmill from which I meant to order the new lumber. We drove down the long lane which led from our house to the plank-road; following the plank-road for about a mile, we turned into a road running through the forest and across the swamp to the sawmill beyond. Our carriage jolted over the half-rotted corduroy road which traversed the swamp, and then climbed the long hill leading to the sawmill. When we reached the mill, the foreman had gone over to a neighboring farmhouse, probably to smoke or gossip, and we were compelled to await his return before we could transact our business. We remained seated in the carriage, a few rods from the mill, and watched the leisurely movements of the mill-hands. We had not waited long before a huge pine log was placed in position, the machinery of the mill was set in motion, and the circular saw began to eat its way through the log, with a loud whir which resounded throughout the vicinity of the mill. The sound rose and fell in a sort of rhythmic cadence, which, heard from where we sat, was not unpleasing, and not loud enough to prevent conversation. When the saw started on its second journey through the log, Julius observed, in a lugubrious tone, and with a perceptible shudder: —

"Ugh! but dat des do cuddle my blood!"

"What's the matter, Uncle Julius?" inquired my wife, who is of a very sympathetic turn of mind. "Does the noise affect your nerves?"

"No, Mis' Annie," replied the old man, with emotion, "I ain' narvous; but dat saw, a-cuttin' en grindin' thoo dat stick er timber, en moanin', en groanin,' en sweekin', kyars my 'memb'ance back ter ole times, en 'min's me er po' Sandy." The pathetic intonation with which he lengthened out the "po' Sandy" touched a responsive chord in our own hearts.

"And who was poor Sandy?" asked my wife, who takes a deep interest in the stories of plantation life which she hears from the lips of the older colored people. Some of these stories are quaintly humorous; others wildly extravagant, revealing the Oriental cast of the negro's imagination; while others, poured freely into the sympathetic ear of a Northern-bred woman, disclose many a tragic incident of the darker side of slavery.

"Sandy," said Julius, in reply to my wife's question, "was a nigger w'at useter b'long ter ole Mars Marrabo McSwayne. Mars Marrabo's place wuz on de yuther side'n de swamp, right nex' ter yo' place. Sandy wuz a monst'us good nigger, en could do so many things erbout a plantation, en alluz 'ten' ter his wuk so well, dat w'en Mars Marrabo's chilluns growed up en married off, dey all un 'em wanted dey daddy fer ter gin 'em Sandy fer a weddin' present. But Mars Marrabo knowed de res' would n' be satisfied ef he gin Sandy ter a'er one un 'em; so w'en dey wuz all done married, he fix it by 'lowin' one er his chilluns ter take Sandy fer a mont' er so, en den ernudder for a mont' er so, en so on dat erway tel dey had all had 'im de same lenk er time; en den dey would all take him roun' ag'in, 'cep'n' oncet in a w'ile w'en Mars Marrabo would len' 'im ter some er his yuther kinfolks 'roun' de country, w'en dey wuz short er han's; tel bimeby it go so Sandy did n' hardly knowed whar he wuz gwine ter stay fum one week's een' ter de yuther.

"One time w'en Sandy wuz lent out ez yushal, a spekilater come erlong wid a lot er niggers, en Mars Marrabo swap' Sandy's wife off fer a noo 'oman. W'en Sandy come back, Mars Marrabo gin 'im a dollar, en 'lowed he wuz monst'us sorry fer ter break up de fambly, but de spekilater had gin 'im big boot, en times wuz hard en money skase, en so he wuz bleedst ter make de trade. Sandy tuk on some 'bout losin' his wife, but he soon seed dey want no use cryin' ober spilt merlasses; en bein' ez he lacked de looks er de noo 'oman, he tuk up wid her atter she 'd be'n on de plantation a mont' er so.

"Sandy en his noo wife got on mighty well tergedder, en de niggers all 'mence' ter talk about how lovin' dey wuz. W'en Tenie wuz tuk sick oncet, Sandy useter set up all night wid 'er, en den go ter wuk in de mawnin' des lack he had his reg'lar sleep; en Tenie would 'a' done anythin' in de worl' for her Sandy.

"Sandy en Tenie had n' be'n libbin' tergedder fer mo' d'n two mont's befo' Mars Marrabo's old uncle, w'at libbed down in Robeson County, sent up ter fin' out ef Mars Marrabo could n' len' 'im er hire 'im a good han' fer a mont' er so. Sandy's marster wuz one er dese yer easy-gwine folks w'at wanter please eve'ybody, en he says yas, he could len' 'im Sandy. En Mars Marrabo tol' Sandy fer ter git ready ter go down ter Robeson nex' day, fer ter stay a mont' er so.

"It wuz monst'us hard on Sandy fer ter take 'im 'way fum Tenie. It wuz so fur down ter Robeson dat he did n' hab no chance er comin' back ter see her tel de time wuz up; he would n' 'a' mine comin' ten er fifteen mile at night ter see Tenie, but Mars Marrabo's uncle's plantation wuz mo' d'n forty mile off. Sandy wuz mighty sad en cas' down atter w'at Mars Marrabo tol' 'im, en he says ter Tenie, sezee: —

"'I'm gittin' monst'us ti'ed er dish yer gwine roun' so much. Here I is lent ter Mars Jeems dis mont', en I got ter do so-en-so; en ter Mars Archie de nex' mont', en I got ter do so-en-so; den I got ter go ter Miss Jinnie's: en hit 's Sandy dis en Sandy dat, en Sandy yer en Sandy dere, tel it 'pears ter me I ain' got no home, ner no marster, ner no mistiss, ner no nuffin. I can't eben keep a wife: my yuther ole 'oman wuz sol' away widout my gittin' a chance fer ter tell her good-by; en now I got ter go off en leab you, Tenie, en I dunno whe'r I 'm eber gwine ter see you ag'in er no. I wisht I wuz a tree, er a stump, er a rock, er sump'n w'at could stay on de plantation fer a w'ile.'

"Atter Sandy got thoo talkin', Tenie did n' say naer word, but des sot dere by de fier, studyin' en studyin'. Bimeby she up'n' says: —

"'Sandy, is I eber tol' you I wuz a cunjuh 'oman?'

"Co'se Sandy had n' nebber dremp' er nuffin lack dat, en he made a great 'miration w'en he hear w'at Tenie say. Bimeby Tenie went on: —

"'I ain' goophered nobody, ner done no cunjuh wuk, fer fifteen year er mo'; en w'en I got religion I made up my mine I wouldn' wuk no mo' goopher. But dey is some things I doan b'lieve it 's no sin fer ter do; en ef you doan wanter be sent roun' fum pillar ter pos', en ef you doan wanter go down ter Robeson, I kin fix things so you won't haf ter. Ef you'll des say de word, I kin turn you ter w'ateber you wanter be, en you kin stay right whar you wanter, ez long ez you mineter.'

"Sandy say he doan keer; he 's willin' fer ter do anythin' fer ter stay close ter Tenie. Den Tenie ax 'im ef he doan wanter be turnt inter a rabbit.

"Sandy say, 'No, de dogs mought git atter me.'

"'Shill I turn you ter a wolf?' sez Tenie.

"'No, eve'ybody 's skeered er a wolf, en I doan want nobody ter be skeered er me.'

"'Shill I turn you ter a mawkin'-bird?'

"'No, a hawk mought ketch me. I wanter be turnt inter sump'n w'at'll stay in one place.'

"'I kin turn you ter a tree,' sez Tenie. 'You won't hab no mouf ner years, but I kin turn you back oncet in a w'ile, so you kin git sump'n ter eat, en hear w'at 's gwine on.'

"Well, Sandy say dat 'll do. En so Tenie tuk 'im down by de aidge er de swamp, not fur fum de quarters, en turnt 'im inter a big pine-tree, en sot 'im out 'mongs' some yuther trees. En de nex' mawnin', ez some er de fiel' han's wuz gwine long dere, dey seed a tree w'at dey did n' 'member er habbin' seed befo'; it wuz monst'us quare, en dey wuz bleedst ter 'low dat dey had n' 'membered right, er e'se one er de saplin's had be'n growin' monst'us fas'.

"W'en Mars Marrabo 'skiver' dat Sandy wuz gone, he 'lowed Sandy had runned away. He got de dogs out, but de las' place dey could track Sandy ter wuz de foot er dat pine-tree. En dere de dogs stood en barked, en bayed, en pawed at de tree, en tried ter climb up on it; en w'en dey wuz tuk roun' thoo de swamp ter look fer de scent, dey broke loose en made fer dat tree ag'in. It wuz de beatenis' thing de w'ite folks eber hearn of, en Mars Marrabo 'lowed dat Sandy must 'a' clim' up on de tree en jump' off on a mule er sump'n, en rid fur ernuff fer ter spile de scent. Mars Marrabo wanted ter 'cuse some er de yuther niggers er heppin' Sandy off, but dey all 'nied it ter de las'; en eve'ybody knowed Tenie sot too much sto' by Sandy fer ter he'p 'im run away whar she could n' nebber see 'im no mo'.

"W'en Sandy had be'n gone long ernuff fer folks ter think he done got clean away, Tenie useter go down ter de woods at night en turn 'im back, en den dey 'd slip up ter de cabin en set by de fire en talk. But dey ha' ter be monst'us keerful, er e'se somebody would 'a' seed 'em, en dat would 'a' spile' de whole thing; so Tenie alluz turnt Sandy back in de mawnin' early, befo' anybody wuz a-stirrin'.

"But Sandy did n' git erlong widout his trials en tribberlations. One day a woodpecker come erlong en 'mence' ter peck at de tree'; en de nex' time Sandy wuz turnt back he had a little roun' hole in his arm, des lack a sharp stick be'n stuck in it. Atter dat Tenie sot a sparrer-hawk fer ter watch de tree; en w'en de woodpecker come erlong nex' mawnin' fer ter finish his nes', he got gobble' up mos' 'fo' he stuck his bill in de bark.

"Nudder time, Mars Marrabo sent a nigger out in de woods fer ter chop tuppentime boxes. De man chop a box in dish yer tree, en hack' de bark up two er th'ee feet, fer ter let de tuppentime run. De nex' time Sandy wuz turnt back he had a big skyar on his lef' leg, des lack it be'n skunt; en it tuk Tenie nigh 'bout all night fer ter fix a mixtry ter kyo it up. Atter dat, Tenie sot a hawnet fer ter watch de tree; en w'en de nig-ger come back ag'in fer ter cut ernudder box on de yuther side'n de tree, de hawnet stung 'im so hard dat de ax slip en cut his foot nigh 'bout off.

"W'en Tenie see so many things happenin' ter de tree, she 'cluded she'd ha' ter turn Sandy ter sump'n e'se; en atter studyin' de matter ober, en talkin' wid Sandy one ebenin', she made up her mine fer ter fix up a goopher mixtry w'at would turn herse'f en Sandy ter foxes, er sump'n, so dey could run away en go some'rs whar dey could be free en lib lack w'ite folks.

"But dey ain' no tellin' w'at 's gwine ter happen in dis worl'. Tenie had got de night sot fer her en Sandy ter run away, w'en dat ve'y day one er Mars Marrabo's sons rid up ter de big house in his buggy, en say his wife wuz monst'us sick, en he want his mammy ter len' 'im a 'oman fer ter nuss his wife. Tenie's mistiss say sen' Tenie; she wuz a good nuss. Young mars wuz in a tarrible hurry fer ter git back home. Tenie wuz washin' at de big house dat day, en her mistiss say she should go right 'long wid her young marster. Tenie tried ter make some 'scuse fer ter git away en hide 'tel night, w'en she would have eve'ything fix' up fer her en Sandy; she say she wanter go ter her cabin fer ter git her bon-net. Her mistiss say it doan matter 'bout de bonnet; her head-hankcher wuz good ernuff. Den Tenie say she wanter git her bes' frock; her mis-tiss say no, she doan need no mo' frock, en w'en dat one got dirty she could git a clean one whar she wuz gwine. So Tenie had ter git in de buggy en go 'long wid young Mars Dunkin ter his plantation, w'ich wuz mo' d'n twenty mile away; en dey wa'n't no chance er her seein' Sandy no mo' 'tel she come back home. De po' gal felt monst'us bad 'bout de way things wuz gwine on, en she knowed Sandy mus' be a wond'rin' why she didn' come en turn 'im back no mo'.

"W'iles Tenie wuz away nussin' young Mars Dunkin's wife, Mars Marrabo tuk a notion fer ter buil' 'im a noo kitchen; en bein' ez he had lots er timber on his place, he begun ter look 'roun' fer a tree ter hab de lumber sawed out'n. En I dunno how it come to be so, but he happen fer ter hit on de ve'y tree w'at Sandy wuz turnt inter. Tenie wuz gone, en dey wa'n't nobody ner nuffin fer ter watch de tree.

"De two men w'at cut de tree down say dey nebber had sech a time wid a tree befo': dey axes would glansh off, en did n' 'pear ter make no prōgress thoo de wood; en of all de creakin', en shakin', en wobblin' you eber see, dat tree done it w'en it commence' ter fall. It wuz de beat-enis' thing!

"W'en dey got de tree all trim' up, dey chain it up ter a timber wag-gin, en start fer de sawmill. But dey had a hard time gittin' de log dere: fus' dey got stuck in de mud w'en dey wuz gwine crosst de swamp, en it wuz two er th'ee hours befo' dey could git out. W'en dey start' on ag'in, de chain kep' a-comin' loose, en dey had ter keep a-stoppin' en a-stoppin' fer ter hitch de log up ag'in. W'en dey commence' ter climb de hill ter de sawmill, de log broke loose, en roll down de hill en in 'mongs' de trees, en hit tuk nigh 'bout half a day mo' ter git it haul' up ter de sawmill.

"De nex' mawnin' atter de day de tree wuz haul' ter de sawmill, Tenie come home. W'en she got back ter her cabin, de fus' thing she done wuz ter run down ter de woods en see how Sandy wuz gittin' on. W'en she seed de stump standin' dere, wid de sap runnin' out'n it, en de limbs layin' scattered roun', she nigh 'bout went out'n her min'. She run ter her cabin, en got her goopher mixtry, en den follered de track er de timber waggin ter de sawmill. She knowed Sandy could n' lib mo' d'n a minute er so ef she turnt him back, fer he wuz all chop' up so he 'd 'a' be'n bleedst ter die. But she wanted ter turn 'im back long ernuff fer ter 'splain ter 'im dat she had n' went off a-purpose, en lef' 'im ter be chop' down en sawed up. She did n' want Sandy ter die wid no hard feelin's to'ds her.

"De han's at de sawmill had des got de big log on de kerridge, en wuz startin' up de saw, w'en dey seed a 'oman runnin' up de hill, all out er bref, cryin' en gwine on des lack she wuz plumb 'stracted. It wuz Tenie; she come right inter de mill, en th'owed herse'f on de log, right in front er de saw, a-hollerin' en cryin' ter her Sandy ter fergib her, en not ter think hard er her, fer it wa'n't no fault er hern. Den Tenie 'membered de tree did n' hab no years, en she wuz gittin' ready fer ter wuk her goopher mixtry so ez ter turn Sandy back, w'en de mill-hands kotch holt er her en tied her arms wid a rope, en fasten' her to one er de posts in de sawmill; en den dey started de saw up ag'in, en cut de log up inter bo'ds en scantlin's right befo' her eyes. But it wuz mighty hard wuk; fer of all de sweekin', en moanin', en groanin', dat log done it w'iles de saw wuz a-cuttin' thoo it. De saw wuz one er dese yer ole-timey, up-en-down saws, en hit tuk longer dem days ter saw a log 'en it do now. Dey greased de saw, but dat did n' stop de fuss; hit kep' right on, tel fin'ly dey got de log all sawed up.

"W'en de oberseah w'at run de sawmill come fum breakfas', de han's up en tell him 'bout de crazy 'oman — ez dey s'posed she wuz — w'at had come runnin' in de sawmill, a-hollerin' en gwine on, en tried ter th'ow herse'f befo' de saw. En de oberseah sent two er th'ee er de han's fer ter take Tenie back ter her marster's plantation.

"Tenie 'peared ter be out'n her min' fer a long time, en her marster ha' ter lock her up in de smoke-'ouse 'tel she got ober her spells. Mars Marrabo wuz monst'us mad, en hit would 'a' made yo' flesh crawl fer ter hear him cuss, 'caze he say de spekilater w'at he got Tenie fum had fooled 'im by wukkin' a crazy 'oman off on him. W'iles Tenie wuz lock up in de smoke-'ouse, Mars Marrabo tuk 'n' haul de lumber fum de sawmill, en put up his noo kitchen.

"W'en Tenie got quiet' down, so she could be 'lowed ter go 'roun' de plantation, she up'n' tole her marster all erbout Sandy en de pine-tree; en w'en Mars Marrabo hearn it, he 'lowed she wuz de wuss 'stracted nigger he eber hearn of. He did n' know w'at ter do wid Tenie: fus' he thought he'd put her in de po'-house; but fin'ly, seein' ez she did n' do no harm ter nobody ner nuffin, but des went 'roun' moanin', en groanin', en shakin' her head, he 'cluded ter let her stay on de plantation en nuss de little nigger chilluns w'en dey mammies wuz ter wuk in de cotton-fiel'.

"De noo kitchen Mars Marrabo buil' wuz n' much use, fer it had n' be'n put up long befo' de niggers 'mence' ter notice quare things erbout it. Dey could hear sump'n moanin' en groanin' 'bout de kitchen in de night-time, en w'en de win' would blow dey could hear sump'n a-hollerin' en sweekin' lack it wuz in great pain en sufferin'. En it got so atter a w'ile dat it wuz all Mars Marrabo's wife could do ter git a 'oman ter stay in de kitchen in de daytime long ernuff ter do de cookin'; en dey wa'n't naer nigger on de plantation w'at would n' rudder take forty dan ter go 'bout dat kitchen atter dark, — dat is, 'cep'n' Tenie; she did n' 'pear ter min' de ha'nts. She useter slip 'roun' at night, en set on de kitchen steps, en lean up agin de do'-jamb, en run on ter herse'f wid some kine er foolishness w'at nobody could n' make out; fer Mars Marrabo had th'eaten' ter sen' her off'n de plantation ef she say anything ter any er de yuther niggers 'bout de pine-tree. But some-how er 'nudder de niggers foun' out all erbout it, en dey all knowed de kitchen wuz ha'nted by Sandy's sperrit. En bimeby hit got so Mars Marrabo's wife herse'f wuz skeered ter go out in de yard atter dark.

"W'en it come ter dat, Mars Marrabo tuk en to' de kitchen down, en use' de lumber fer ter buil' dat ole school'ouse w'at you er talkin' 'bout pullin' down. De school'ouse wuz n' use' 'cep'n' in de daytime, en on dark nights folks gwine 'long de road would hear quare soun's en see quare things. Po' ole Tenie useter go down dere at night, en wander 'roun' de school'ouse; en de niggers all 'lowed she went fer ter talk wid Sandy's sperrit. En one winter mawnin', w'en one er de boys went ter school early fer ter start de fire, w'at should he fin' but po' ole Tenie, layin' on de flo', stiff, en col', en dead. Dere did n' 'pear ter be nuffin pertickler de matter wid her, — she had des grieve' herse'f ter def fer her Sandy. Mars Marrabo did n' shed no tears. He thought Tenie wuz crazy, en dey wa'n't no tellin' w'at she mought do nex'; en dey ain' much room in dis worl' fer crazy w'ite folks, let 'lone a crazy nigger.

"Hit wa'n't long atter dat befo' Mars Marrabo sol' a piece er his track er lan' ter Mars Dugal' McAdoo, — *my* ole marster, — en dat's how de ole school'ouse happen to be on yo' place. W'en de wah broke out, de school stop', en de ole school'ouse be'n stannin' empty ever sence, — dat is, 'cep'n' fer de ha'nts. En folks sez dat de ole school'ouse, er any yuther house w'at got any er dat lumber in it w'at wuz sawed out'n de tree w'at Sandy wuz turnt inter, is gwine ter be ha'nted tel de las' piece er plank is rotted en crumble' inter dus'."

Annie had listened to this gruesome narrative with strained attention.

"What a system it was," she exclaimed, when Julius had finished, "under which such things were possible!"

"What things?" I asked, in amazement. "Are you seriously considering the possibility of a man's being turned into a tree?"

"Oh, no," she replied quickly, "not that;" and then she murmured absently, and with a dim look in her fine eyes, "Poor Tenie!"

We ordered the lumber, and returned home. That night, after we had gone to bed, and my wife had to all appearances been sound asleep for half an hour, she startled me out of an incipient doze by exclaiming suddenly, —

"John, I don't believe I want my new kitchen built out of the lumber in that old schoolhouse."

"You would n't for a moment allow yourself," I replied, with some asperity, "to be influenced by that absurdly impossible yarn which Julius was spinning to-day?"

"I know the story is absurd," she replied dreamily, "and I am not so silly as to believe it. But I don't think I should ever be able to take any pleasure in that kitchen if it were built out of that lumber. Besides, I think the kitchen would look better and last longer if the lumber were all new."

Of course she had her way. I bought the new lumber, though not without grumbling. A week or two later I was called away from home on business. On my return, after an absence of several days, my wife remarked to me, —

"John, there has been a split in the Sandy Run Colored Baptist Church, on the temperance question. About half the members have come out from the main body, and set up for themselves. Uncle Julius is one of the seceders, and he came to me yesterday and asked if they might not hold their meetings in the old schoolhouse for the present."

"I hope you did n't let the old rascal have it," I returned, with some warmth. I had just received a bill for the new lumber I had bought.

"Well," she replied, "I could n't refuse him the use of the house for so good a purpose."

"And I 'll venture to say," I continued, "that you subscribed something toward the support of the new church?"

She did not attempt to deny it.

"What are they going to do about the ghost?" I asked, somewhat curious to know how Julius would get around this obstacle.

"Oh," replied Annie, "Uncle Julius says that ghosts never disturb religious worship, but that if Sandy's spirit *should* happen to stray into meeting by mistake, no doubt the preaching would do it good."

WILLIAM DEAN HOWELLS

From *A Psychological Counter-Current in Recent Fiction*

William Dean Howells, the leading critic of American literature at the turn of the century, was an early mentor of Chesnutt. Howells published one of Chesnutt's first short stories in the prestigious *Atlantic* magazine, and wrote an admiring review of the young author's 1899 collection, *The Conjure Woman*. Howells originally encouraged Chesnutt to write the book that would become *The Marrow of Tradition,* soliciting from him a novel "about the color-line, and of as actual and immediate an interest as possible" (Andrews 124). The review Howells wrote after *Marrow*'s publication, however, demonstrates that the editor had notable qualms about the picture of "the color-line" that Chesnutt eventually painted in his Wilmington novel.

The review, reprinted below, first appeared in the *North American Review* in December 1901. Howells begins by lamenting that realism, the literary movement he championed, had been eclipsed by a "counter-current" in American fiction. He discusses *Marrow* along with five other novels whose elements of "psychologism" Howells finds partly hopeful and partly worrisome. In his discussion of *The Marrow of Tradition*, Howells's assessment of the "great power" of Chesnutt's novel is qualified by his unease at what he deems the novelist's "bitter, bitter" sentiments about the events in Wilmington. The "psychologism" he finds in *Marrow*, then, locates a fault line in Howells's views about fiction. Howells concedes the justice in Chesnutt's portrait of race relations. But the very accuracy of that portrait calls into doubt what Howells elsewhere in the essay calls the "higher function" of fiction "to teach that men are somehow masters of their fate" (Howells 873).

It is consoling as often as dismaying to find in what seems a cataclysmal tide of a certain direction a strong drift to the opposite quarter. It is so divinable, if not so perceptible, that its presence may usually be recognized as a beginning of the turn in every tide which is sure, sooner or later, to come. In reform, it is the menace of reaction; in reaction, it is the promise of reform; we may take heart as we must lose heart from it. A few years ago, when a movement which carried fiction to the highest place in literature was apparently of such onward and upward sweep that there could be no return or descent, there was a counter-current in it which stayed it at last, and pulled it back to that lamentable level where fiction is now sunk, and the word "novel" is again the synonym of all that is morally false and mentally despicable. Yet that this, too, is partly apparent, I think can be shown from some phases of actual fiction which happen to be its very latest phases, and which are of a significance as hopeful as it is interesting.[1] Quite as surely as romanticism

[1] Howells reviewed the following books in the full-length version of this article: "The Right of Way." A Novel. By Gilbert Parker. Harper & Brothers; "The Ruling Passion. Tales of nature and human nature." By Henry Van Dyke. Charles Scribner's Sons; "Spoils and Stratagems. Stories of love and politics." By Wm. Allen White. Charles Scribner's Sons; "Fomá Gordyéeff." By Maxim Gorky. Translated from the Russian by Isabel F. Hapgood. Charles Scribner's Sons; "Circumstances." By S. Weir Mitchell, M. D. The Century Company; "A Japanese Nightingale." By Onoto Watana. Harper & Brothers; "The Marrow of Tradition." By Charles W. Chesnutt. Houghton, Mifflin & Co.; "Lay Down Your Arms. The autobiography of Martha von Tilling." By Bertha von Süttner. Authorized Translation. By T. Holmes. Longmans, Green & Co.; "Let Not Man Put Asunder." By Basil King. Harper & Brothers.

lurked at the heart of realism, something that we may call "psychologism" has been present in the romanticism of the last four or five years, and has now begun to evolve itself in examples which it is the pleasure as well as the duty of criticism to deal with. . . .

I wish that I could at all times praise as much the literature of an author who speaks for another colored race, not so far from us as the Japenese [sic], but of as much claim upon our conscience, if not our interest. Mr. Chesnutt, it seems to me, has lost literary quality in acquiring literary quantity, and though his book, "The Marrow of Tradition," is of the same strong material as his earlier books, it is less simple throughout, and therefore less excellent in manner. At his worst, he is no worse than the higher average of the ordinary novelist, but he ought always to be very much better, for he began better, and he is of that race which has, first of all, to get rid of the cakewalk, if it will not suffer from a smile far more blighting than any frown. He is fighting a battle, and it is not for him to pick up the cheap graces and poses of the jouster. He does, indeed, cast them all from him when he gets down to his work, and in the dramatic climaxes and closes of his story he shortens his weapons and deals his blows so absolutely without flourish that I have nothing but admiration for him. "The Marrow of Tradition," like everything else he has written, has to do with the relations of the blacks and whites, and in that republic of letters where all men are free and equal he stands up for his own people with a courage which has more justice than mercy in it. The book is, in fact, bitter, bitter. There is no reason in history why it should not be so, if wrong is to be repaid with hate, and yet it would be better if it was not so bitter. I am not saying that he is so inartistic as to play the advocate; whatever his minor foibles may be, he is an artist whom his stepbrother Americans may well be proud of; but while he recognizes pretty well all the facts in the case, he is too clearly of a judgment that is made up. One cannot blame him for that; what would one be one's self? If the tables could once be turned, and it could be that it was the black race which violently and lastingly triumphed in the bloody revolution at Wilmington, North Carolina, a few years ago, what would not we excuse to the white man who made the atrocity the argument of his fiction?

Mr. Chesnutt goes far back of the historic event in his novel, and shows us the sources of the cataclysm which swept away a legal government and perpetuated an insurrection, but he does not paint the blacks all good, or the whites all bad. He paints them as slavery made them on both sides, and if in the very end he gives the moral victory to the blacks — if he suffers the daughter of the black wife to have pity on her father's daughter by his white wife, and while her own child lies dead from a shot fired in the revolt, gives her husband's skill to save the life of her sister's child — it cannot be said that either his æsthetics or ethics are false. Those who would question either must allow, at least, that the negroes have had the greater practice in forgiveness, and that there are many probabilities to favor his interpretation of the fact. No one who reads the book can deny that the case is presented with great power, or fail to recognize in the writer a portent of the sort of negro equality against which no series of hangings and burnings will finally avail.

Selected Bibliography

The Bibliography is divided into two parts, "Works Cited" and "Suggestions for Further Reading." The "Works Cited" section contains all books and articles quoted or discussed in the introductions and headnotes for this volume. "Suggestions for Further Reading" lists selected primary and secondary materials that may be useful for the further study of Chesnutt and his times. This portion of the bibliography consists of four subdivisions; "Works by Chesnutt," "Biographies," "Critical Studies on Chesnutt" (most titles are studies of *The Marrow of Tradition*), and "Literary and Historical Studies." A number of works in this final subdivision include chapters devoted to Chesnutt, though most are broader studies of literary and cultural history. Some, though not all, titles in the "Works Cited" list are also included in "Suggestions for Further Reading."

WORKS CITED

Andrews, William L. *The Literary Career of Charles W. Chesnutt.* Baton Rouge: Louisiana State UP, 1980.

Anonymous. Letter to President William McKinley. November 13, 1898. File 17743-1898. Record Group RG60, Department of Justice. National Archives, Washington, D.C.

Bruce, John Edward. "The Application of Force." 1889. *The Selected Writings of John Edward Bruce: Militant Black Journalist.* Ed. Peter Gilbert. New York: Arno, 1971. 29–32.

———. "Color Prejudice Among Negroes." *The Selected Writings of John Edward Bruce: Militant Black Journalist.* Ed. Peter Gilbert. New York: Arno, 1971. 125–28.

Cable, George Washington. "The Freedman's Case in Equity." *The Negro Question: A Selection of Writings on Civil Rights in the South.* Ed. Arlin Turner. New York: Doubleday, 1958. 49–74.

———. *The Grandissimes.* New York: Scribner's, 1880.

———. *The Negro Question.* New York: Scribner's, 1890.

———. *Old Creole Days.* New York: Scribner's, 1879.

———. "The Silent South." 1885. *The Silent South.* Ed. Arlin Turner. Montclair, NJ: Patterson Smith, 1969. 43–112.

Chesnutt, Charles W. "Charles W. Chesnutt's Own View of His New Story, *The Marrow of Tradition.*" Cleveland *World* October 20, 1901. Rpt. in *Charles W. Chesnutt: Essays and Speeches.* Ed. Joseph R. McElrath Jr., Robert C. Leitz III, and Jesse S. Crisler. Stanford, CA: Stanford UP, 1999. 169–70.

———. *The Journals of Charles W. Chesnutt.* Ed. Richard Brodhead. Durham, NC: Duke UP, 1993.

———. *"To Be an Author": Letters of Charles W. Chesnutt, 1889–1905.* Ed. Joseph R. McElrath Jr. and Robert C. Leitz III. Princeton, NJ: Princeton UP, 1997.

Chesnutt, Helen M. *Charles Waddell Chesnutt: Pioneer of the Color Line.* Chapel Hill: U of North Carolina P, 1952.

Cooper, Walter G. *The Cotton States and International Exposition South Illustrated.* Atlanta, GA: The Illustrator Company, 1896.

Cronly, Jane Murphy. "An Account of the Race Riot in Wilmington, N.C., in 1898." Cronly Family Papers. Duke University Rare Book, Manuscript, and Special Collections Library.

Du Bois, W. E. B. *Black Reconstruction in America.* 1935. New York: Atheneum, 1962.

———. *The Souls of Black Folk.* 1903. Rpt. in *Three Negro Classics.* Intro. John Hope Franklin. New York: Avon, 1965.

Ellison, Ralph. *Going to the Territory.* New York: Random, 1986.

Felton, Rebecca Latimer. "Mrs. Felton's Reply." Felton to the *Atlanta Constitution.* Scrapbook 24, 76–77. Felton Collection, Hargrett Rare Book and Manuscript Library, University of Georgia.

Fletcher, Tom. *100 Years of the Negro in Show Business.* 1954. New York: Da Capo, 1984.

Foner, Eric. *A Short History of Reconstruction, 1863–1877.* New York: Harper, 1990.

Fulton, David Bryant [Jake Thorne]. *Hanover; Or, the Persecution of the Lowly: A Story of the Wilmington Massacre.* 1901. New York: Arno, 1969.

Gatewood, Willard B. *Aristocrats of Color: The Black Elite, 1880–1920.* Bloomington: U of Indiana P, 1990.

Gilmore, Glenda E. "Murder, Memory, and the Flight of the
    Incubus." *Democracy Betrayed: The Wilmington Riot of 1898
    and Its Legacy*. Ed. David S. Cecelski and Timothy B. Tyson.
    Chapel Hill: U of North Carolina P, 1998. 73–93.
Hale, Grace Elizabeth. *Making Whiteness: The Culture of Segregation
    in the South, 1890–1940*. New York: Pantheon, 1998.
Harlan, Louis R. *Booker T. Washington: The Making of a Race
    Leader, 1856–1901*. New York: Oxford UP, 1972.
Honey, Michael. "Class, Race, and Power in the New South: Racial
    Violence and the Delusions of White Supremacy." *Democracy
    Betrayed: The Wilmington Race Riot of 1898 and Its Legacy*. Ed.
    David S. Cecelski and Timothy B. Tyson. Chapel Hill: U of North
    Carolina P, 1998. 161–84.
Howells, William Dean. "Mr. Charles Chesnutt's Short Stories."
    Atlantic Monthly 85 (1900): 699–701.
———. "A Psychological Counter-Current in Recent Fiction." *North
    American Review* 173 (1901): 872–88.
Johnston, Frances Benjamin. *The Hampton Album*. Ed. Lincoln
    Kirstein. New York: Museum of Modern Art, 1966.
Manly, Alexander. Editorial, *Wilmington Daily Record* August 18,
    1898. Rpt. in *The Literary Digest* 17. 22 (November 26, 1898):
    623–24.
Oggel, Terry. "Late-19th-Century Literature." *American Literary
    Scholarship: An Annual 1999*. Ed. David J. Nordloh. Durham,
    NC: Duke UP, 2001.
Page, Thomas Nelson. *In Ole Virginia*. 1887. Chapel Hill, NC: U of
    North Carolina P, 1969.
Prather Sr., H. Leon. "We Have Taken a City: A Centennial Essay."
    *Democracy Betrayed: The Wilmington Riot of 1898 and Its
    Legacy*. Ed. David S. Cecelski and Timothy B. Tyson. Chapel Hill:
    U of North Carolina P, 1998. 15–41.
Roediger, David. "Whiteness and Ethnicity in the History of 'White
    Ethnics' in the United States." *Towards the Abolition of White-
    ness: Essays on Race, Politics and Working Class History*. Lon-
    don: Verso, 1994. 1811–98.
Smith, Shawn Michelle. *American Archives: Gender, Race, and Class
    in Visual Culture*. Princeton, NJ: Princeton UP, 1999.
Stuckey, Sterling. *Slave Culture: Nationalist Theory and the Founda-
    tion of Black America*. New York: Oxford UP, 1987.
Sundquist, Eric. *To Wake the Nations: Race in the Making of Ameri-
    can Literature*. Cambridge, MA: Harvard UP, 1993.
Terrell, Mary Church. "Lynching from a Negro's Point of View."
    North American Review 178 (June 1904): 854–68.
Toll, Robert C. *Blacking Up: The Minstrel Show in Nineteenth-Cen-
    tury America*. New York: Oxford UP, 1974.

U.S. Supreme Court Reports. Rochester, NY: Lawyer's Cooperative Publishing Company, 1901.

Washington, Booker T. *Up From Slavery: An Autobiography.* New York: A. L. Burt, 1900.

Wells, Ida B. *Crusader for Justice: The Autobiography of Ida B. Wells.* Ed. Alfreda Duster. Chicago: U of Chicago P, 1970.

Wideman, John Edgar. "Charles W. Chesnutt: *The Marrow of Tradition.*" *American Scholar* 42 (1972): 128–34.

Williamson, Joel. *The Crucible of Race: Black-White Relations in the American South Since Emancipation.* New York: Oxford UP, 1984.

Wittke, Carl. *Tambo and Bones: A History of the American Minstrel Stage.* Durham: Duke UP, 1930.

Yarborough, Richard. "Race, Violence, and Manhood: The Masculine Ideal in Frederick Douglass's 'The Heroic Slave.'" *Frederick Douglass: New Literary and Historical Essays.* Ed. Eric J. Sundquist. New York: Cambridge UP, 1990.

———. "Violence, Manhood, and Black Heroism: The Wilmington Riot in Two Turn-of-the-Century African American Novels." *Democracy Betrayed: The Wilmington Riot of 1898 and Its Legacy.* Ed. David S. Cecelski and Timothy B. Tyson. Chapel Hill: U of North Carolina P, 1998. 225–251.

SUGGESTIONS FOR FURTHER READING

Works by Chesnutt

Charles W. Chesnutt: Essays and Speeches. Ed. Joseph R. McElrath, Robert C. Leitz III, and Jesse S. Crisler. Standford: Stanford UP, 1999.

The Colonel's Dream. New York: Doubleday, 1905.

The Conjure Woman. Boston: Houghton, 1899.

Frederick Douglass. Boston: Small, Maynard & Company, 1899.

The House Behind the Cedars. Boston: Houghton, 1900.

The Journals of Charles W. Chesnutt. Ed. Richard H. Brodhead. Durham, NC: Duke UP, 1993.

Mandy Oxendine. Ed. Charles Hackenberry. Urbana: U of Illinois P, 1997.

The Marrow of Tradition. Boston: Houghton, 1901.

Paul Marchand, F.M.C. Ed. Dean McWilliams. Princeton: Princeton UP, 1998.

The Quarry. Ed. Dean McWilliams. Princeton: Princeton UP, 1999.

The Short Fiction of Charles W. Chesnutt. 1974. Rev. ed. Ed. Sylvia Lyons Render. Washington, DC: Howard UP, 1981.

"To Be an Author": Letters of Charles W. Chesnutt, 1889–1905. Ed.
Joseph R. McElrath Jr. and Robert C. Leitz III. Princeton: Princeton UP, 1997.
The Wife of His Youth and Other Stories of the Color Line.
Houghton, 1899.

Biographies

Chesnutt, Helen. *Charles Waddell Chesnutt: Pioneer of the Color Line.* Chapel Hill: U of North Carolina P, 1952.
Heermance, J. Noel. *Charles W. Chesnutt: America's First Great Black Novelist.* Hamden, CT: Archon Books, 1974.
Keller, Frances Richardson. *An American Crusade: The Life of Charles Waddell Chesnutt.* Provo, UT: Brigham Young UP, 1978.
Render, Sylvia Lyons. *Charles W. Chesnutt.* Boston: Twayne, 1980.

Critical Studies on Chesnutt

Andrews, William L. *The Literary Career of Charles W. Chesnutt.* Baton Rouge: Louisiana State UP, 1980.
Duncan, Charles. *The Absent Man: The Narrative Craft of Charles W. Chesnutt.* Athens: Ohio UP, 1998.
Elder, Arlene. " 'The Future American Race': Charles W. Chesnutt's Utopian Illusion." *MELUS* 15 (1988): 121–29.
Ferguson, Sally Ann H. "Chesnutt's Genuine Blacks and Future Americans." *MELUS* 15 (1988): 109–19.
Finseth, Ian. "How Shall the Truth Be Told? Language and Race in *The Marrow of Tradition.*" *American Literary Realism* 31 (1999): 1–20.
Gillman, Susan. "Micheaux's Chesnutt." *PMLA* 114 (1999): 1080–88.
Gleason, William. "Voices at the Nadir: Charles Chesnutt and David Bryant Fulton." *American Literary Realism* 24 (1992): 22–41.
Knadler, Stephen P. "Untragic Mulatto: Charles Chesnutt and the Discourse of Whiteness." *American Literary History* 8 (1996): 426–48.
McElrath, Joseph R. Jr., ed. *Critical Essays on Charles W. Chesnutt.* New York: G. K. Hall, 1999.
Moddelmog, William W. "Lawful Entitlements: Chesnutt's Fictions of Ownership." *Texas Studies in Literature and Language* 41 (1999): 47–69.
Najmi, Samina. "Janet, Polly, and Olivia: Constructs of Blackness and White Femininity in Charles Chesnutt's *The Marrow of Tradition.*" *Southern Literary Journal* 32 (1999): 1–19.

Pettis, Joyce. "The Literary Imagination and the Historic Event: Chesnutt's Use of History in *The Marrow of Tradition*." *South Atlantic Review* 55 (1990): 37–48.

Price, Kenneth M. "Charles Chesnutt, the Atlantic Monthly, and the Intersection of African-American Fiction and Elite Culture." *Periodical Literature in Nineteenth-Century America*. Ed. Kenneth M. Price and Susan Belasco Smith. Charlottesville: U of Virginia P, 1995. 257–74.

Roe, Jae. "Keeping an 'Old Wound' Alive: *The Marrow of Tradition* and the Legacy of Wilmington." *African American Review* 33 (1999): 231–43.

Wagner, Bryan. "Charles Chesnutt and the Epistemology of Racial Violence." *American Literature* 73 (2001): 311–37.

Wegener, Frederick. "Charles W. Chesnutt and the Anti-Imperialist Matrix of African-American Writing, 1898–1905." *Criticism* 41 (1999): 465–93.

Werner, Craig. "The Framing of Charles W. Chesnutt: Practical Deconstruction in the Afro-American Tradition." *Southern Literature and Literary Theory*. Ed. Humphries Jefferson. Athens: U of Georgia P, 1990. 465–93.

Williamson, Joel. *New People: Miscegenation and Mulattoes in the United States*. New York: Free, 1980.

Wonham, Henry B. " 'The Curious Psychological Spectacle of a Mind Enslaved': Charles W. Chesnutt and Dialect Fiction." *Mississippi Quarterly* 51 (1998): 55–69.

Yarborough, Richard. "Violence, Manhood, and Black Heroism: The Wilmington Riot in Two Turn-of-the-Century African American Novels." *Democracy Betrayed: The Wilmington Riot of 1898 and Its Legacy*. Ed. David S. Cecelski and Timothy B. Tyson. Chapel Hill: U of North Carolina P, 1998. 225–51.

Historical and Cultural Studies

Ayers, Edward L. *Vengeance and Justice: Crime and Punishment in the Nineteenth Century American South*. New York: Oxford UP, 1984.

Baker, Houston. *Modernism and the Harlem Renaissance*. Chicago: U of Chicago P, 1987.

Bederman, Gail. *Manliness and Civilization: A Cultural History of Gender and Race in the United States, 1880–1917*. Chicago: U of Chicago P, 1995.

Bell, Bernard W. *The Afro-American Novel and Its Tradition*. Amherst: U of Massachusetts P, 1987.

Blaustein, Albert P., and Robert L. Zangrando. *Civil Rights and the Black American: A Documentary History*. New York: Washington Square, 1968.

Carby, Hazel. *Reconstructing Womanhood: The Emergence of the Afro-American Woman Novelist*. New York: Oxford UP, 1981.

Cecelski, David S., and Timothy B. Tyson, eds. *Democracy Betrayed: The Wilmington Riot of 1898 and Its Legacy*. Chapel Hill: U of North Carolina P, 1998.

Doyle, Bertram Wilbur. *The Etiquette of Race Relations in the South: A Study in Social Control*. 1937. New York: Schocken, 1971.

Edmonds, Helen G. *The Negro and Fusion Politics in North Carolina, 1894–1901*. Chapel Hill: U of North Carolina P, 1951.

Foner, Eric. *Reconstruction: America's Unfinished Revolution, 1863–1877*. New York: Harper, 1988.

Franklin, John Hope. *From Slavery to Freedom: A History of Negro Americans*. 5th ed. New York: Knopf, 1980.

Gaines, Kevin K. *Uplifting the Race: Black Leadership, Politics, and Culture in the Twentieth-Century*. Chapel Hill: U of North Carolina P, 1996.

Gilman, Charlotte Perkins. *Herland*. New York: Pantheon, 1979.

———. *The Home: Its Work and Influence*. New York: McLure, Phillips, 1903.

———. *The Man-Made World; or, Our Androcentric Culture*. New York: Charlton, 1911.

———. "A Suggestion on the Negro Problem." *American Journal of Sociology* 14 (July 1908): 78–85.

———. *The Yellow Wallpaper: A Novella*. Boston: Small, Maynard, 1900.

Gillman, Susan. "The Mulatto, Tragic or Triumphant? The Nineteenth-Century American Race Melodrama." *The Culture of Sentiment: Race, Gender and Sentimentality in Nineteenth-Century America*. Durham, NC: Duke UP, 1990. 221–43.

Gilmore, Glenda Elizabeth. *Gender and Jim Crow: Women and the Politics of White Supremacy in North Carolina, 1896–1920*. Chapel Hill: U of North Carolina P, 1996.

Gunning, Sandra. *Race, Rape, and Lynching: The Red Record of American Literature, 1890–1912*. New York: Oxford UP, 1996.

Hale, Grace Elizabeth. *Making Whiteness: The Culture of Segregation in the South, 1890–1940*. New York: Pantheon, 1998.

Hunter, Tera W. *To 'Joy My Freedom': Southern Black Women's Lives and Labor After the Civil War*. Cambridge: Harvard UP, 1997.

Justesen, Benjamin R. *George Henry White: An Even Chance in the Race of Life*. Baton Rouge: Louisiana State UP, 2001.

Kawash, Samira. *Dislocating the Color Line: Identity, Hybridity, and Singularity in African-American Narrative*. Stanford: Stanford UP, 1997.

Litwack, Leon. *Been in the Storm So Long: The Aftermath of Slavery.* New York: Vintage, 1980.

Lott, Eric. *Love and Theft: Blackface Minstrelsy and the American Working Class.* New York: Oxford UP, 1993.

McMurry, Linda O. *To Keep the Waters Troubled: The Life of Ida B. Wells.* New York: Oxford UP, 1998.

Moses, Wilson Jeremiah. *The Golden Age of Black Nationalism, 1850–1925.* New York: Oxford UP, 1978.

Newman, Louise Michele. *White Women's Rights: The Racial Origins of Feminism in the United States.* New York: Oxford UP, 1999.

Prather, Leon H. *We Have Taken a City: The Wilmington Racial Massacre and Coup of 1898.* Rutherford, NJ: Farleigh Dickinson UP, 1984.

Reeves, William M. *"Strength Through Struggle": The Chronological and Historical Record of the African-American Community in Wilmington, North Carolina 1865–1950.* Wilmington, NC: New Hanover Public Library, 1998.

Shapiro, Herbert. *White Violence and Black Response: From Reconstruction to Montgomery.* Amherst: U of Massachusetts P, 1988.

Sollors, Werner. *Neither Black Nor White Yet Both: Thematic Explorations of Interracial Literature.* New York: Oxford UP, 1997.

Spillers, Hortense J. "Notes on an Alternative Model — Neither/Nor." *The Difference Within: Feminism and Critical Theory.* Ed. Elizabeth Meese and Alice Parker. Philadelphia: J. Benjamins, 1989. 165–85.

Sundquist, Eric. *To Wake the Nations: Race in the Making of American Literature.* Cambridge, MA: Harvard UP, 1993.

Tate, Claudia. *The Coupling Convention: Sex, Text, and Tradition in Black Women's Fiction.* New York: Oxford UP, 1993.

Thomas, Brook. *American Literary Realism and the Failed Promise of Contract.* Berkeley: U of California P, 1997.